WORLD TRADE ORGANIZATION

Dispute Settlement Reports

1997
Volume I

Pages 1-587

 CAMBRIDGE
UNIVERSITY PRESS

PUBLISHED BY THE PRESS SYNDICATE OF THE UNIVERSITY OF CAMBRIDGE
The Pitt Building, Trumpington Street, Cambridge, United Kingdom

CAMBRIDGE UNIVERSITY PRESS
The Edinburgh Building, Cambridge CB2 2RU, UK   http://www.cup.cam.ac.uk
40 West 20th Street, New York, NY 10011–4211, USA   http://www.cup.org
10 Stamford Road, Oakleigh, Melbourne 3166, Australia
Ruiz de Alarcón 13, 28014 Madrid, Spain

Printed in the United Kingdom at the University Press, Cambridge

French edition and Spanish edition paperbacks of this title are both available directly from WTO Publications, World Trade Organization, Centre William Rappard, 154 rue de Lausanne, CH-1211 Geneva 21, Switzerland   http://www.wto.org

ISBN 0 521 78096 9 hardback
ISBN 0 521 78582 0 paperback

THE WTO DISPUTE SETTLEMENT REPORTS

The *Dispute Settlement Reports* of the World Trade Organization (the "WTO") include panel and Appellate Body reports, as well as arbitration awards, in disputes concerning the rights and obligations of WTO Members under the provisions of the *Marrakesh Agreement Establishing the World Trade Organization.* The *Dispute Settlement Reports* are available in English, French and Spanish.

This volume may be cited as DSR 1997:I

TABLE OF CONTENTS

JAPAN - TAXES ON ALCOHOLIC BEVERAGES

Arbitration
under Article 21(3)(c) of the
Understanding on Rules and Procedures
Governing the Settlement of Disputes

Award of the Arbitrator
Julio Lacarte-Muró
WT/DS8/15, WT/DS10/15, WT/DS11/13

Circulated to Members on 14 February 1997

I. INTRODUCTION

1.   On 1 November 1996, the Dispute Settlement Body (the "DSB") adopted
(WT/DSB/M/25) the Appellate Body Report and the Panel Report, as modified
by the Appellate Body Report, in *Japan - Taxes on Alcoholic Beverages*
(WT/DS8/11, WT/DS10/11 and WT/DS11/8). As required by Article 21(3) of
the *Understanding on Rules and Procedures Governing the Settlement of Disputes* (the *"DSU"*), Japan informed the DSB on 20 November 1996 of its inten-
tions in respect of the implementation of the DSB's recommendations and rulings
(WT/DSB/M/26). Japan indicated that it would not be able to implement immediately but only within a "reasonable period of time". Japan did not propose to
the DSB a "reasonable period of time" for the latter's approval as provided for
under Article 21(3)(a) of the *DSU*. It indicated that it would initiate negotiations
with the European Communities, the United States and Canada, the other parties
to the dispute, on what constitutes "a reasonable period of time". These negotiations did not succeed, and no mutual agreement within the meaning of Article
21(3)(b) of the *DSU* was reached. The negotiations with the European Communities did, however, lead to an agreement on an accelerated reduction of the tariff
rates on whisky and brandy as compensation for delayed implementation, but this
agreement does not prejudice their position on the issue of a "reasonable period of
time".

2.   In the absence of an agreement under Article 21(3)(b) of the *DSU*, the
United States requested on 24 December 1996, that the "reasonable period of
time" should be determined through binding arbitration as is provided for by Article 21(3)(c). After Japan and the United States failed to agree on the appoint-
ment of an arbitrator within the ten days envisaged by the note to Article
21(3)(c), the United States requested on 7 January 1997 that the Director-General
appoint an arbitrator. Following consultations with the United States and Japan,
the Director-General appointed me as arbitrator on 17 January 1997.

3.   At an organizational meeting on 20 January 1997, it was agreed that all the original parties to the dispute could participate in the arbitration process, notwithstanding that only the United States had requested binding arbitration. It was further agreed that, in the circumstances of this case, the 90-day period provided for by Article 21(3)(c) of the *DSU*, which started on 1 November 1996, would not provide sufficient time for a full review of the matter. Accordingly, the parties agreed to extend the deadline for the arbitrator's award by two weeks, to expire on 14 February 1997. The parties gave written assurances that the arbitrator's award would nevertheless be accepted by them as "binding arbitration" within the meaning of Article 21(3)(c).

4.   Written submissions were received from Japan and the United States on 27 January 1997. I requested certain additional information from Japan on 28 January 1997. Japan replied to this request promptly, on 30 January 1997.

5.   Having reached a political consensus on the necessary liquor tax amendments in mid-December 1996 after consultations with the government party (the Liberal Democratic Party) and with the interest groups concerned, the Government of Japan formally adopted its proposal for a Law to Amend a Portion of the Liquor Tax Law (Law No. 6, 1953) and submitted it to the Diet for approval on 31 January 1997, i.e. the deadline for proposals for new tax legislation. Throughout these arbitration proceedings, the Government of Japan has insisted that it would ordinarily be almost impossible to amend the draft legislation now before the Diet.

6.   An oral hearing was held on 3 February 1997, and was attended by all four parties to the dispute.

II.   THE PROPOSED IMPLEMENTING LEGISLATION

7.   In the proposal currently before the Diet, the Government of Japan proposes to implement the recommendations and rulings of the DSB in *Japan - Taxes on Alcoholic Beverages* in three steps. In the first step, on 1 October 1997, Japan would reduce the tax rates on brown spirits (whisky, etc.), and increase the tax rates on Shochu A and Shochu B. The applicable rates would remain respectively greater and less than those levied on white spirits (vodka, etc.), i.e. the rate towards which all other rates are to converge. Liqueurs would be taxed at the same rates as white spirits. In the second step, on 1 October 1998, the rate of tax imposed on Shochu A would become equal to that levied on white spirits and liqueurs. The tax on brown spirits (whisky, etc.) would be further reduced, but would remain greater than that imposed on white spirits and liqueurs (i.e. 3% higher). The tax on Shochu B would be further increased, remaining less than that imposed on white spirits and liqueurs. In the third step, on 1 October 2001, Japan would increase the tax rate on Shochu B to the level imposed on white spirits and liqueurs.

8.   The proposed amendments to the Liquor Tax Law would implement the recommendations and rulings of the DSB within 23 months of 1 November 1996,

except insofar as they apply to Shochu B. With regard to Shochu B, the increase of the tax would be implemented in three stages[1] and full compliance with the DSB's recommendations and rulings would be attained by 1 October 2001, i.e. within five years.

III. THE LEGAL FRAMEWORK

9.   As a general and fundamental obligation imposed on all WTO Members, Article XVI:4 of the *Marrakesh Agreement Establishing the World Trade Organization* (the *"WTO Agreement"*) requires that each Member shall ensure the conformity of its laws, regulations and administrative procedures with its obligations as provided in the *WTO Agreement*. To preserve the rights and obligations of Members under the *WTO Agreement*, the WTO provides for a dispute settlement system that is set out in the *DSU*.

10.   As basic principles of WTO dispute settlement, Article 3(3) of the *DSU* stipulates that:

> The prompt settlement of situations in which a Member considers that any benefits accruing to it directly or indirectly under the covered agreements are being impaired by measures taken by another Member is essential to the effective functioning of the WTO and the maintenance of a proper balance between the rights and obligations of Members.

and Article 3(7) of the *DSU* states that:

> In the absence of a mutually agreed solution, the first objective of the dispute settlement mechanism is usually to secure the withdrawal of the measures concerned if these are found to be inconsistent with the provisions of the covered agreements.

11.   Article 21(1) of the *DSU* stipulates that "*prompt compliance* with recommendations and rulings of the DSB is essential in order to ensure effective resolution of disputes to the benefit of all Members" (emphasis added). This obligation is further elaborated in Article 21(3) of the *DSU*, where it is stipulated that "if it is impracticable to comply *immediately* with the recommendations and rulings, the Member concerned shall have a reasonable period of time in which to do so" (emphasis added). When this "reasonable period of time" is determined through binding arbitration as provided for under Article 21(3)(c) of the *DSU*, this provision states that a "guideline" for the arbitrator should be that the "rea-

---

[1]   On 1 October 1997, the tax on Shochu B would be increased from 102,100 Yen/kilolitre of alcohol to 150,700 Yen/kilolitre, on 1 October 1998 to 199,400 Yen/kilolitre and finally on 1 October 2001 to 248,100 Yen/kilolitre.

sonable period of time" should not exceed 15 months from the date of the adoption of a panel or Appellate Body Report. Article 21(3)(c) of the *DSU* also stipulates, however, that the "reasonable period of time" may be shorter or longer than 15 months, depending upon the "particular circumstances". The term, "particular circumstances", is not defined in the *DSU*.

IV.   ARGUMENTS OF THE PARTIES

United States

12.   With regard to what constitutes the "particular circumstances" which need to be taken into account when determining the "reasonable period of time" for the purpose of Article 21(3)(c) of the *DSU*, the United States argues that only the following are relevant:

    (a)   the type (legislation, regulation, decree, etc.) and technical complexity (e.g. making a simple change in a tariff rate, as compared to making more complex changes like the development of a new scientific standard) of the measures that the Member must draft, adopt and implement; and

    (b)   the minimum period of time in which the Member can achieve implementation, assuming that the Member acts in good faith.

13.   According to the United States, the question of "particular circumstances" does not, therefore, imply a policy judgement, but rather a technical inquiry into the domestic legislative or regulatory system in the Member country concerned. Domestic political, economic and social considerations should not be taken into account. The United States asserts that hardship of an economic and/or social nature and political tension are inevitable whenever a government proposes to end its protection of a domestic industry. The United States argues that if such considerations are taken into account, this would threaten the integrity of the WTO dispute settlement system. The question for the arbitrator is what is the shortest period of time in which implementation can practicably take place, not whether a longer period of time would make implementation less burdensome and painful for the implementing Member.

14.   Applying these general considerations in this particular case, the United States argues that it would be reasonable to determine that Japan can implement the necessary tax changes in April 1997, i.e. five months from the adoption of the DSB's recommendations and rulings. The United States suggests this period because:

    (a)   it falls within the one to six-month period that Japan allegedly claimed it generally needed to change indirect taxes;

    (b)   it is more than adequate to achieve the simple amendment to the Liquor Tax Law needed to change tax rates on alcoholic beverages;

(c)   the Diet normally enacts fiscal measures in March each year; and

(d)   it is the beginning of Japan's fiscal year when tax changes are routinely implemented.

15.   The United States also points out that Japan has demonstrated in the past that it is capable of implementing changes to its Liquor Tax Law in a short period of time. The amendment to the Liquor Tax Law passed on 10 April 1984 came into effect 20 days later, and the legislation which was adopted in implementation of the 1987 GATT panel on *Japan - Customs Duties, Taxes and Labelling Practices on Imported Wines and Alcoholic Beverages*[2] and which involved more sweeping reforms, was implemented in just over three months following the passage of the bill.

16.   More generally, the United States asserts that WTO Members have a strong interest in establishing an example of prompt compliance with, and full implementation of, the DSB's recommendations and rulings. Although it would be hypothetically possible to reach an immediate settlement that would partially offset some of the commercial losses associated with the deficiencies in Japan's proposed implementation, the United States maintains that such a settlement would not address the competitive harm produced by a continuing national treatment violation. The United States also suggests that the failure of Japan, as one of the world's leading trading nations, to comply fully and in a timely manner with the DSB's recommendations and rulings would be damaging to the credibility of the WTO dispute settlement system. The United States believes that allowing for a 5-year "reasonable period of time" would have a devastating impact on the dispute settlement system.

Japan

17.   Japan agrees that, in general, the "reasonable period of time" should be determined in light of the *DSU*'s general objective of prompt compliance, but it notes that the *DSU* is also very clear in allowing for flexibility. Japan stresses that although Article 21(3)(c) of the *DSU* indicates that 15 months is a guideline for the arbitrator to award for implementation, this period of time can be extended if "particular circumstances" exist. Japan considers that nowhere in the *DSU* are there any provisions which prescribe the scope of the "particular circumstances" to be considered and argues that each and every circumstance relevant to each individual case should be carefully examined. Japan considers that in the present case, a 23-month period for implementation is a "reasonable period of time" because there are a number of "particular circumstances" justifying such a period.

18.   First, Japan invokes, as a relevant "particular circumstance", the limited powers of the executive branch over taxation and the need for formal legislation

---

[2]   BISD 34S/83, adopted on 10 November 1987.

adopted by the Diet in order to implement the recommendations and rulings of the DSB. Since the proposed amendments involve drastic increases in the taxes on shochu and are, therefore, very unpopular and have met with considerable political opposition, the procedure for preparing and adopting these amendments has been and will be difficult and complex. Adding to the difficulty and complexity of the legislative process is the fact that the current government does not have a majority in either Chamber of the Diet.

19.   Secondly, Japan invokes, as a relevant "particular circumstance", the adverse effects of the tax increases on Japanese consumers and shochu producers. Under the proposed tax reform, the tax on Shochu A will be increased by 1.6 times and on Shochu B by 2.4 times. Japan contends that a 2.4 times increase, without staging, would be unprecedented in the history of any developed country. Japan argues that in order to mitigate the adverse impact of the liquor tax increases on consumers and producers, it is only normal to spread these increases over time. Japan recognizes that this was not done for the 1989 liquor tax increases, but submits that the situation was different then. The tax increases were less drastic and also affected the competing saké. In addition, shochu producers received more financial support in the context of the implementation of the 1987 Panel Report.

20.   Furthermore, Japan points out that in April 1997, there will already be a very substantive increase in the consumption tax, which was decided in November 1994, and that it would be unacceptable for the liquor tax increases and the consumption tax increase to be carried out simultaneously. Japan also points out that large-scale increases in taxes normally take place in one-year intervals to mitigate the impact on consumers. Thus, as the consumption tax will take effect on 1 April 1997, the liquor tax increases should normally become effective one year later, on 1 April 1998. Since this would, however, have brought the first stage of the liquor tax amendments beyond the 15-month "reasonable period of time", Japan has proposed to bring forward the first stage of the implementation to 1 October 1997 (i.e. 11 months after the DSB decision). According to Japan, this represents a major effort on its part, and an indication that Japan takes the Article 21(3)(c) guideline of 15 months very seriously. In this context, Japan also argues that by bringing forward the first stage of implementation (from 1 February 1998, i.e. 15 months after the DSB decision, to 1 October 1997, i.e. 11 months after the DSB decision), an advantage is created for importers that is equivalent to the disadvantages arising from the fact that the implementation is not fully realized within 15 months.

21.   Finally, Japan invokes, as a relevant "particular circumstance", the administrative constraints on the execution of taxation. The proposed changes in the tax system will have to be notified and explained to 180,000 wholesalers and retailers in advance and this notification alone will take a considerable amount of time. Furthermore, Japan argues that liquor distributors will need time to adjust their computer programmes and advertising material.

22.   As an important factor underlying the arguments set out above, Japan invokes the rigidity of the domestic process for the adoption of the annual budget. Under this process, the government decides, after intensive consultations with the government party, on the contents of any tax reform in mid-December in order to be able to submit to the Diet the draft budget and all proposals for tax legislation by the end of January. During the oral hearing, Japan indicated that if this timing is missed, the tax legislation concerned can ordinarily no longer be amended for the following fiscal year. The Diet is unwilling to consider draft tax legislation outside of this time schedule.

23.   As mentioned above, with regard to Shochu B, full compliance with the DSB's recommendations and rulings would, under the current Japanese proposal for tax reform, only be attained in October 2001, i.e. after five years. Japan does not argue that this 5-year period constitutes a "reasonable period of time" within the meaning of Article 21(3)(c) of the *DSU*. To compensate for the delayed implementation, Japan has, therefore, offered the European Communities, the United States and Canada an accelerated reduction of the tariff rates on alcoholic beverages as negotiated in the context of the Uruguay Round. The European Communities have accepted this offer but the United States and Canada have not. Furthermore, Japan argues with regard to Shochu B that the tax differential remaining in the period between October 1998 and October 2001 will not have adverse effects on imported whisky or brandy in practice, because this tax differential will already have been significantly reduced from its current level. Japan suggests that any negative impact on imported whisky or brandy will be further minimized by the fact that the majority of Shochu B is consumed in a limited region in the south of Kyushu Island. This argument is strongly contested by the United States which submits that all the information it has received from its producers of alcoholic beverages points to the contrary.

24.   Japan argues that the reasonable period of time for implementation of the DSB's recommendations and rulings should not be influenced by circumstances surrounding the earlier dispute concerning the Liquor Tax Law that resulted in the 1987 Panel Report. According to Japan, therefore, the present matter should be examined in its own context, and in the light of the "particular circumstances" described above. The United States, on the other hand, does refer to the 1987 Panel Report to demonstrate that it is possible for Japan to implement changes to its Liquor Tax Law within a considerably shorter period than proposed by Japan in this case.

European Communities and Canada

25.   Without taking a position on the question whether or not 23 months is, in the present case, a "reasonable period of time", the European Communities state that in general the "reasonable period of time" should be 15 months.

26.   Canada, on the contrary, takes the position that 23 months and certainly 5 years are not "reasonable periods of time". It does not consider the "particular circumstances" advanced by Japan to be relevant. Canada notes furthermore that

"particular circumstances" are always unique and should not be construed as having precedential value for future cases. Finally, Canada notes that Japan appears to be suggesting that a longer period of time (five years) is required with respect to Shochu B because the tax differential that needs to be eliminated is so much greater than with respect to Shochu A. This is tantamount to arguing, Canada observes, that the greater the degree of inconsistency with WTO obligations, the greater the period of time a Member should be granted to bring that measure into conformity with the *WTO Agreement*.

V.   AWARD

27.   As stated in Article 3(2) of the *DSU*, the dispute settlement system of the WTO is a central element in providing security and predictability to the multilateral trading system. Therefore, all WTO Members have a strong interest in prompt compliance with and full implementation of the recommendations and rulings of the DSB. This interest is clearly reflected in the provisions of the *DSU*, and in particular in Article 21(3)(c), which stipulates that a "reasonable period of time" for implementation should not exceed 15 months unless there are "particular circumstances" justifying a longer or shorter period. In this case, I am not persuaded that the "particular circumstances" advanced by Japan and the United States justify a departure from the 15-month "guideline" either way. I conclude, therefore, that a "reasonable period of time" within the meaning of Article 21(3)(c) of the *DSU* for Japan to implement the recommendations and rulings of the DSB of 1 November 1996 in *Japan - Taxes on Alcoholic Beverages* is 15 months.

UNITED STATES - RESTRICTIONS ON IMPORTS OF COTTON AND MAN-MADE FIBRE UNDERWEAR

Report of the Appellate Body
WT/DS24/AB/R

Adopted by the Dispute Settlement Body on 25 February 1997

Costa Rica, Appellant	Present:
United States, Appellee	Ehlermann, Presiding Member
India, Third Participant	Feliciano, Member
	Matsushita, Member

I.   INTRODUCTION: FACTUAL BACKGROUND AND STATEMENT OF THE APPEAL

This is an appeal by Costa Rica from certain issues of law and legal interpretations set out in the Panel Report, *United States - Restrictions on Imports of Cotton and Man-made Fibre Underwear*[1] (the "Panel Report"). That Panel (the "Panel") had been established to consider a complaint by Costa Rica relating to a transitional safeguard measure imposed by the United States on imports of cotton and man-made fibre underwear from Costa Rica under Article 6 of the *Agreement on Textiles and Clothing ("ATC")*.[2]

The factual background essential to understanding this appeal, may be sketched quickly.

On 27 March 1995, the United States requested consultations with Costa Rica on trade in cotton and man-made underwear under Article 6.7 of the *ATC* . At the same time, the United States provided Costa Rica with a "Statement of Serious Damage", dated March 1995 (the "March Statement"), on the basis of which the United States proposed the introduction of a restraint on imports of underwear from Costa Rica. Notice of the request for consultations, the proposed restraint and the proposed restraint level was published in the United States Federal Register on 21 April 1995. The consultations were held but the United States and Costa Rica failed to negotiate a mutually acceptable settlement during these consultations. The United States then invoked Article 6.10 of the *ATC*, and intro-

---

[1]   WT/DS24/R.
[2]   Establishment of an Import Limit for Certain Cotton and Man-Made Fibre Textile Products Produced or Manufactured in Costa Rica, 60 Federal Register 32653, 23 June 1995.

duced a transitional safeguard measure in respect of cotton and man-made fibre underwear imports from Costa Rica on 23 June 1995. The measure was, by its terms, to be valid for a period of 12 months, effective as of 27 March 1995 (*i.e.*, the date of the request for consultations).

At the same time, the United States referred the matter to the Textiles Monitoring Body (the "TMB"). The TMB found that the United States had failed to demonstrate serious damage to the United States domestic industry. However, the TMB did not reach a consensus on the existence of an actual threat of serious damage. The TMB similarly failed to make any findings on the effective date of application of the United States restraint. Accordingly, the TMB recommended that the United States and Costa Rica hold further consultations with a view to resolving the matter. In the absence of any settlement, the parties reverted to the TMB, which confirmed its earlier findings and considered its review of the matter completed. Although further consultations took place between the United States and Costa Rica in November 1995, no agreement was reached. In December 1995, therefore, Costa Rica invoked the dispute settlement provisions of the *Understanding on Rules and Procedures Governing the Settlement of Disputes* (the "*DSU*").

A panel was established to examine this matter on 5 March 1996. On 27 March 1996, the United States renewed the transitional safeguard measure for a second period of 12 months. In due time, after the full course of written submissions and hearings and the Interim Review, the Panel rendered its Report.

The Panel Report was circulated to Members of the World Trade Organization (the "WTO") on 8 November 1996. It contains the following conclusions:

    (i)   the United States violated its obligations under Article 6.2 and 6.4 of the *ATC* by imposing a restriction on Costa Rican exports without having demonstrated that serious damage or actual threat thereof was caused by such imports to the United States' domestic industry;[3]

    (ii)   the United States violated its obligations under Article 6.6(d) of the *ATC* by not granting the more favourable treatment to Costa Rican re-imports contemplated by that sub-paragraph;[4]

    (iii)   the United States violated its obligations under Article 2.4 of the *ATC* by imposing a restriction in a manner inconsistent with its obligations under Article 6 of the *ATC*;[5] and

---

[3]   Panel Report, paras. 7.52 and 7.55.
[4]   Panel Report, para. 7.59.
[5]   Panel Report, para. 7.71.

(iv) the United States violated its obligations under Article X:2 of the *General Agreement on Tariffs and Trade 1994* (the *"General Agreement"*) and Article 6.10 of the *ATC* by setting the start of the restraint period on the date of the request for consultations, rather than the subsequent date of publication of information about the restraint.[6]

The Panel recommended that the Dispute Settlement Body request the United States to bring the measure challenged by Costa Rica into compliance with the United States' obligations under the *ATC*. The Panel stated that such compliance can best be achieved, and further nullification and impairment of benefits accruing to Costa Rica under the *ATC* best avoided, by "prompt removal of the measure inconsistent with the obligations of the United States". The Panel further suggested that the United States bring the measure challenged by Costa Rica into compliance with United States' obligations under the *ATC* by "immediately withdrawing the restriction imposed by the measure".[7]

On 11 November 1996, Costa Rica notified the Dispute Settlement Body[8] of the WTO of its decision to appeal certain issues of law covered in the Panel Report and legal interpretations developed by the Panel, pursuant to paragraph 4 of Article 16 of the *DSU*. On the same day, Costa Rica filed a Notice of Appeal with the Appellate Body, pursuant to Rule 20 of the *Working Procedures for Appellate Review* (the *"Working Procedures"*).[9] Costa Rica filed its appellant's submission on 21 November 1996.[10] On 6 December 1996, the United States filed an appellee's submission.[11] That same day, India submitted a third participant's submission.[12] No other submissions by either the United States or Costa Rica, whether *qua* appellant or *qua* appellee, were made. The complete record of the Panel proceedings was duly transmitted to the Appellate Body.[13]

The oral hearing contemplated by Rule 27 of the *Working Procedures* was held on 16 December 1996. At the hearing, oral arguments were made respectively by the participants and the third participant. Questions were put to them by the Division. All of these questions were answered orally. The participants and third participant did not take advantage of an invitation by the Division to submit post-hearing memoranda. On 18 December 1996, the United States submitted a written clarification and amplification of its oral response to one of the Division's

---

[6] Panel Report, para. 7.69.
[7] Panel Report, para. 8.3.
[8] WT/DS/24/5.
[9] WT/AB/WP/1, 15 February 1996.
[10] Pursuant to Rule 21(1) of the *Working Procedures*.
[11] Pursuant to Rule 23(3) of the *Working Procedures*.
[12] Pursuant to Rule 24 of the *Working Procedures*.
[13] Pursuant to Rule 25 of the *Working Procedures*.

questions. The next day, Costa Rica responded in writing to the United States' clarification.

II. THE BASIC CONTENTIONS OF THE PARTICIPANTS AND THE THIRD PARTICIPANT

1.   The Claims of Error by Appellant Costa Rica

Costa Rica appeals only from the Panel's conclusions relating to the permissible effective date of application of the United States' transitional safeguard measure.

It is claimed by Costa Rica that the Panel erred in finding that the United States' restraint measure could have legal effect between the date of publication of the notice of consultations (between the United States and several countries, including Costa Rica) in the Federal Register (i.e., 21 April 1995) and the date of the application of that measure (i.e. 23 June 1995). The restriction was "introduced" on 23 June 1995 for a period of 12 months starting on 27 March 1995, i.e., starting on the day the United States requested the several Members concerned for consultations under Article 6.7 of the *ATC*. Invoking Article 2.4 of the *ATC*, Costa Rica argues that new restrictions may be imposed in the textiles sector only under either (i) the *ATC* or (ii) the "relevant" provisions of the *General Agreement*. More specifically, a transitional safeguard measure may be imposed only if it meets the requirements of (i) Articles XI[14] and XIII of the *General Agreement*, or of (ii) Article 6 of the *ATC*. Since, Costa Rica argues, Article XIII:3(b) of the *General Agreement* generally prohibits the backdating of import quotas, a backdated transitional safeguard measure restricting imports would be permissible only if it is expressly authorized by Article 6 of the *ATC*, and this, Article 6 does not. Costa Rica accordingly concludes that such a safeguard measure cannot impose a backdated quota.

(a)   Concerning Article XIII of the General Agreement

Costa Rica contends that Article XIII:3(b) of the *General Agreement* sets out a general prohibition against the retroactive application of import quotas and allows backdating of such quotas only in the   circumstances expressly provided for, i.e., in respect of goods *en route* to the importing country at the time public notice of the restraint is given. To Costa Rica, the reasoning of the panel in the 1989 *Chilean Apples* case[15] applies as well in the present case, because there, as

---

[14]   Costa Rica, however, did not submit any arguments in respect of Article XI, *General Agreement*.

[15]   *European Economic Community - Restrictions on Imports of Dessert Apples: Complaint by Chile*, BISD 36S/93, adopted 22 June 1989, p. 132. See also *European Economic Community - Restrictions on Imports of Apples: Complaint by the United States*, BISD 36S/135, adopted 22 June 1989, p. 166.

here, the import quota became effective before the publication of the restraint. Article XIII:3(b) requires "public notice of the total quantity - of the product or products which will be permitted to be imported during a specific future period". It is urged by Costa Rica that the notice published in the Federal Register on 21 April 1995 does not satisfy the requirements of Article XIII:3(b), since the publication of a contingent notice, which provides merely for the possibility of a restraint rather than the actual establishment or adoption of a safeguard measure, fails to bring about the legal certainty and predictability sought by Article XIII:3(b). The Panel erred, Costa Rica concludes, in finding in effect that the United States' backdated restraint substantially complies with the requisites of Article XIII:3(b).

(b)   Concerning Article X of the General Agreement

It is further in effect claimed by Costa Rica that even the limited backdating of the United States' restraint measure approved as permissible by the Panel, i.e,. to 21 April 1995 (the date when the request for consultations was published in the Federal Register) rather than to 27 March 1995, (the date when consultations were in fact requested and initiated), cannot be justified by Article X of the *General Agreement*. In Costa Rica's view, any backdating that could result from application of Article X would be precluded by the "conflict clause" of the *General Interpretative Note to Annex IA* of the *Marrakesh Agreement Establishing the World Trade Organization* (the "*WTO Agreement*"):[16]   the provisions of Article 6 of the *ATC* which do not provide for backdating must prevail over Article X of the General Agreement. A procedural argument is also made by Costa Rica in noting that the parties to the present dispute had not raised the application of Article X before the Panel. Costa Rica thus concludes that the Panel had erred in applying Article X of the General Agreement.

(c)   Concerning Article 6 of the ATC

Costa Rica states that Article 6 of the *ATC* is "silent" on the question of backdated transitional safeguard measures, and that certain considerations concerning Article 6 prevent an interpretation of the provisions thereof which would permit any backdating. To permit, Costa Rica argues firstly, WTO Members to impose restraints within the 30-day post-consultation "window" which become effective at some point outside (whether before or after) that 30-day period, could

---

[16]   The text of the *General interpretative note for Annex 1A* reads:

> In the event of conflict between a provision of the General Agreement on Tariffs and Trade 1994 and a provision of another agreement in Annex 1A to the Agreement Establishing the World Trade Organization (referred to in the agreements in Annex 1A as the "WTO Agreement"), the provision of the other agreement shall prevail to the extent of the conflict.

lead to circumvention of an important requirement or objective of Article 6.10 of the *ATC*: that an importing country must take a definitive or final decision during the 30-day period on whether or not to impose a proposed restraint at all.

Next, Costa Rica underscores the absence in Article 6.10 of the *ATC* of a clause equivalent to that found in Article 3:5(i) of the *Arrangement Regarding International Trade in Textiles* which became effective on 1 January 1974 and which is widely known as the *Multifibre Arrangement* (the "*MFA*"). Article 3:5(i) of the *MFA* expressly permitted the importing country imposing a restraint measure to backdate the effectivity of such measure "beginning on the day when the request [for consultations] was received by the participating exporting country or countries", where no agreement is reached after a period of 60 days from receipt of the request for consultations. It is urged by Costa Rica that the absence of equivalent wording in Article 6.10 of the *ATC* was deliberate and should not be remedied by the expansive interpretation of Article 6.10 adopted by the Panel. Along the same vein, Costa Rica notes the absence in Article 6.10 of the *ATC* of wording similar or comparable to the provisions expressly allowing retroactive application of provisional restraint measures under Article 10 of the *Agreement on Implementation of Article VI of the GATT 1994* (the "*Anti-Dumping Agreement*") and under Article 20 of the *Agreement on Subsidies and Countervailing Measures* (the "*SCM Agreement*"). According to Costa Rica, had the drafters of the *ATC* wanted to provide for retroactive safeguard restraints, they would have done so expressly.

Costa Rica also rejects the Panel's statements concerning the possibility of speculative trade being caused by the request of the importing country for consultations required in Article 6.7 of the *ATC*. Since no evidence had been presented to the Panel on the matter, appellant Costa Rica denies that the Panel made a factual finding establishing the general prevalence of speculative trade. While acknowledging that a speculative "flood of imports" could arise in unusual and critical circumstances, appellant denies that such speculative trade could or had arisen in the present case and contends that, in any event, the appropriate remedy for such speculation is to be found in Article 6.11 of the *ATC*, not in Article 6.10.

Finally, Costa Rica contends, the "highly exceptional nature" of an Article 6 transitional safeguard mechanism should be taken into account in interpreting that Article of the *ATC*. No other WTO provision allows the imposition of "selective" (i.e. discriminatory, country-specific), Member-by-Member, restrictive measures against fair trade upon the ground that such trade is causing or threatens to cause serious damage to the importing Member's domestic industry. Accordingly, Costa Rica notes, Article 6.1 of the *ATC* directs that a transitional safeguard should be applied "as sparingly as possible". In the appellant's view, the Panel had failed to consider the exceptional nature of the *ATC* transitional safeguard mechanism.

2. The Arguments of Appellee United States

The Appellee contends that the Panel correctly found that the United States would have acted consistently with Article 6.10 of the *ATC* in applying a transitional safeguard measure against Costa Rican underwear on 21 April 1995, the date of publication in the Federal Register of the request for consultations. A basic contention of the United States is that no provisions of the *ATC* or of the *General Agreement* prohibits the setting as the "initial date" of a transitional safeguard measure (i.e. the date from which imports may be "counted" against the quota imposed), of the date of the public notice announcing the request for consultations. The second principal argument of the Appellee is that the Panel correctly distinguished *Chilean Apples* by stressing that the 21 April 1995 notice was published before the measure was imposed on 23 June 1995.

(a) Concerning Article 6.10 of the ATC

The United States claims that the text of Article 6.10 of the *ATC* is "silent" on the initial date of a transitional safeguard measure and that, accordingly, the ordinary meaning of Article 6.10 does not prevent a Member from setting the date of the public notice announcing the request for consultations as the "initial date" of a safeguard measure. In its view, the term "apply" contained in Article 6.10 refers to the date on which goods counted under the restraint may be "embargoed", and does not bear upon the "initial date" of the restraint.

The United States argues that, in the absence of guidance from the language of Article 6.10 of the *ATC*, the Panel had appropriate recourse to the provisions of Articles X:2 of the *General Agreement*. That recourse is sustained by the principle of effectiveness in treaty interpretation, in view of the "important factual finding" of the Panel that "there would be a flood of imports" after publication of the request for consultations if a transitional safeguard measure could become effective only as of its date of application. In the view of the Appellee, the Panel's interpretation renders Article 6.10 of the *ATC* an " 'effective' component of the transitional safeguard mechanism of Article 6 of the *ATC*", in line with the requirement of Article 6.1 that transitional safeguard measures should be applied "consistently - with the effective implementation of the integration process" under the *ATC*. The United States further suggests that Article 6.11 of the *ATC* pointed to by Costa Rica is an "extraordinary remedy" not intended to address the "flood of imports" that typically follows publication of the request for consultations. To the United States, the Appellant's effort to dispute the "factual finding" of the Panel falls outside the proper scope of this appeal, in view of the provisions of Article 17.6 of the *DSU*.

Clearly regarding them as part of the context of Article 6.10, the United States refers to Articles 6.2, 6.3 and 6.4 of the *ATC* the requisites of which must be complied with by an importing country making the determination of serious damage on the basis of which consultations with particular exporting countries are requested under Article 6.7. The United States contends that, considering the "rigorous analysis" to which such a determination is subjected, for purposes of

WTO dispute settlement, that determination is "in the nature of a final determination". Therefore, the United States submits, it is "appropriate" for a Member making such a "final determination" to be able to count imports as within a restraint from the date of public announcement of that determination of serious damage.

Upon the other hand, the Appellee dismisses Appellant's suggestion that the *Anti-Dumping Agreement* and the *SCM Agreement* form part of the context of Article 6.10 of the *ATC*, upon the ground that those two Agreements are different from the *ATC*. The Appellee also rejects the inference which the Appellant would draw from the absence in Article 6.10 of the *ATC* of language equivalent to the express permission for backdating a restraint measure under Article 3.5(i) of the *MFA*. The United States states that there was no debate on this point during the negotiations of the *ATC*.

(b)   Concerning Article XIII:3(b) of the General Agreement

The United States, turning to Costa Rica's arguments relating to Article XIII:3(b), supports the Panel's decision to distinguish *Chilean Apples*[17] on its facts. It also traverses Costa Rica's claim that Article XIII:3(b) was infringed because the United States gave public notice merely of the initiation of a procedure which could possibly lead to the imposition of a restraint measure, rather than of the imposition of the restraint measure itself. The principal contention of the Appellee here is that the wording of Article XIII:3(b) recognizes the possibility that the quota announced in the original public notice may change, and does not prohibit notice of future quotas that may be subject to a contingency, such as the contingency that consultations may not be successful and the proposed restraint may in fact be adopted.

3.   The Arguments of the Third Participant India

The Third Participant endorses all of the arguments submitted by Costa Rica, providing additional statements on a number of particular points. For example, India argues that a plain reading of Article 6.10 of the *ATC* precludes the imposition of transitional safeguard measures either before or after the 30-day post-consultation period. According to India, the absence of a provision permitting retroactive transitional safeguard measures, of the sort envisaged by Article 3:5(i) of the *MFA*, is deliberate. In addition, the argument is submitted that Article XIII of the *General Agreement* and Article 6.10 of the *ATC* should be interpreted consistently with each other, such that Members should not be allowed to announce the possibility of trade action *ex ante* and actually apply any resultant measure *ex post*. The Third Participant also recalls the right of WTO Members to apply provisional safeguard measures under Article 6.11 of the *ATC*, noting that

---

[17]   *Supra*, footnote 15.

the United States chose not to invoke that provision in the present case. Finally, India emphasizes the exceptional nature of the *ATC* transitional safeguard mechanism recognized in Article 6.1 of the *ATC* itself, noting that Article 6 of the *ATC* allows Members to impose quantitative restrictions in a manner inconsistent with Article XI of the *General Agreement* and on a selective, "Member-by-Member" basis.

III.   THE ISSUES RAISED IN THIS APPEAL

We must note at the outset the narrowness of the present appeal. Costa Rica appeals from only one finding of the Panel: the finding allowing the back-dating of the transitional safeguard measure here involved to the date of publication in the Federal Register of the request for consultations with, *inter alia*, Costa Rica. At the same time, Costa Rica questions certain legal interpretations adopted by the Panel in the course of reaching that finding.

The United States has not appealed from any of the findings of the Panel, either by filing an Appellant's submission under Rule 23(1) of the *Working Procedures* or by bringing a separate appeal under Rule 23(4) of the same *Procedures*. In its submissions, written and oral, as Appellee, the United States endorses the Panel's finding from which Costa Rica appeals, as well as the legal interpretations adopted by the Panel in the process of making that finding. Thus, Costa Rica is the only Appellant in AB-1996-3.

On the basis of the written submissions and oral statements made by the participants and the third participant, this appeal may be said to raise the following issues:

1.   Whether or not backdating of the effectivity of a transitional safeguard measure is permitted by Article 6.10 of the *ATC* ;

2.   Whether or not Article XIII:3(b), *General Agreement*, is applicable to a transitional safeguard measure taken under Article 6, *ATC*; and

3.   Whether or not Article X:2, *General Agreement*, is applicable to a transitional safeguard measure taken under Article 6, *ATC*.

IV.   THE ISSUE OF BACKDATING THE EFFECTIVITY OF A TRANSITIONAL SAFEGUARD MEASURE TAKEN UNDER ARTICLE 6.10 OF THE *ATC*

The *Agreement on Textiles and Clothing*, one of the Multilateral Trade Agreements in Annex 1A of the *WTO Agreement*, sets out provisions to be applied by WTO Members during a 10-year transition period leading to the integration of the textiles and clothing sector into the regime of the *General Agreement*. The Members have recognized that, during this transition period, it may become necessary "to apply a specific transitional safeguard mechanism" to textile and clothing products not yet integrated into the *General Agreement*. A transitional safeguard mechanism is in essence a measure establishing, for a certain period of time, a quantitative restraint on the importation of specified categories of goods from an identified Member or Members. Many legal and operating aspects of this mechanism are defined and regulated in varying degrees of detail by Article 6 of the *ATC*.

In its Report, the Panel formulated the particular issue we are here addressing in the following manner:

> Costa Rica argues that the United States retroactively applied the restriction in violation of Article 6.10 of the ATC. The restriction was introduced on 23 June 1995 for a period of 12 months starting on 27 March 1995, which was the date of the request for consultations under Article 6.7 of the ATC. Although Article 6.10 of the ATC allows the importing country to "apply the restraint, ... within 30 days following the 60-day period for consultations", it is silent about the initial date from which the restraint period should be calculated. In contrast, Article 3.5(i) of the Multifibre Arrangement (MFA) stated that the restraint could be instituted "for the twelve-month period beginning on the day when the request was received by the participating exporting country or countries". Thus, the question before the Panel is whether the silence of the ATC in this regard should be interpreted as prohibition of a practice which was explicitly recognized under the MFA, and if so, what should be the appropriate date from which the restraint period is to be calculated under the ATC.[18] (Emphases added)

Apparently taking its assumed premise literally - i.e. that Article 6.10 "is *silent* about the initial date from which the restraint period should be conducted ..." and describing the issue as "a technical question regarding the opening date of a quota period",[19] the Panel went outside the four corners of the *ATC*. Proceeding to the provisions of the *General Agreement*, the Panel then took Article X:2 thereof as its applicable and controlling text. The Panel held that the United States' safeguard restraint measure was "a measure of general application" within the meaning of Article X:2,[20] and concluded;

> ... that the prevalent practice under the MFA of setting the initial date of a restraint period as the date of request for consultations cannot be maintained under the ATC. However, we note that *if the importing country publishes the proposed restraint period and restraint level after the re-*

---

[18] Panel Report, para. 7.62.
[19] *Id.*, para. 7.63.
[20] *Id.*, para. 7.65.

quest for consultations, it can later set the initial date of the restraint period as the date of the publication of the proposed restraint. In the present case, *the United States violated its obligations under Article X:2 of GATT 1994* and consequently under Article 6.10 of the ATC *by setting the restraint period for 12 months starting on 27 March 1995.* However, *had it set the restraint period starting on 21 April 1995, which was the date of the publication of the information about the request for consultations, it would not have acted inconsistently with GATT 1994 or the ATC in respect of the restraint period.* The United States argues that it did not "enforce" the restraint until 23 June 1995. We note the US argument. However, *in so far as the restraint was applied to exports from Costa Rica which had taken place prior to the publication, it was implemented and therefore enforced within the meaning of Article X:2 of GATT 1994.*[21] (Emphases added)

While we agree with the Panel, as pointed out below,[22] that the United States' restraint measure here involved is appropriately regarded as "a measure of general application" for purposes of Article X:2 of the *General Agreement*, we are unable to share and affirm the above conclusion of the Panel.

1. *Interpreting Article 6.10 of the ATC: Textual and Contextual Considerations and the Principle of Effectiveness*

We must focus upon Article 6.10 of the *ATC* which needs to be quoted in full:

Article 6

x x x

10.   If, however, after the expiry of the period of 60 days from the date on which the request for consultations was received, there has been no agreement between the Members, the Member which proposed to take safeguard action may apply the restraint by date of import or date of export, in accordance with the provisions of this Article, within 30 days following the 60-day period for consultations, and at the same time refer the matter to the TMB. It shall be open to either Member to refer the matter to the TMB before the expiry of the period of 60 days. In either case, the TMB

---

[21]   Panel Report, para. 7.69.
[22]   *Infra*, 29.

> shall promptly conduct an examination of the matter, in-
> cluding the determination of serious damage, or actual
> threat thereof, and its causes, and make appropriate recom-
> mendations to the Members concerned within 30 days. In
> order to conduct such examination, the TMB shall have
> available to it the factual data provided to the Chairman of
> the TMB, referred to in paragraph 7, as well as any other
> relevant information provided by the Members concerned.
>
> x x x

The first thing which must be noted about Article 6.10 of the *ATC* is that its terms make no express reference to backdating the effectivity of a safeguard restraint measure to some date prior to the promulgation or imposition of such measure. To this extent, we agree with the Panel that Article 6.10 *ATC* is silent on the question of backdating a safeguard restraint measure. We do *not*, however, believe that Article 6.10 does not substantively address that issue. To the con-trary, we believe it does and that the answer to this question is to be found within Article 6.10 itself - its text and context - considered in the light of the objective and purpose of Article 6 and the *ATC*.

Under the express terms of Article 6.10, the importing Member which "propose[s] to take safeguard action" may, "*after the expiry of the period of 60 days*" from the date of receipt of the request for consultations without agreement having been reached, "*apply the restraint (measure)*" "within 30 days following the 60-day period for consultations ...". As we understand it, "apply" when used as here in respect of a governmental measure - whether a statute or an adminis-trative regulation - means, in ordinary acceptation, putting such measure into operation. To apply a measure is to make it effective with respect to things or events or acts falling within its scope. Put in a slightly different way, a govern-ment functionary who evaluates and characterizes things, events or acts in terms of the requirements set out in a restraint measure, is "applying" or "implement-ing" or "enforcing" that measure.

It is essential to note that, under the express terms of Article 6.10, *ATC*, the restraint measure may be "applied" only "after the expiry of the period of 60 days" for consultations, without success, and only within the "window" of 30 days immediately following the 60-day period.[23] Accordingly, we believe that, in the absence of an express authorization in Article 6.10, *ATC*, to backdate the ef-fectivity of a safeguard restraint measure, a presumption arises from the very text of Article 6.10 that such a measure may be applied only prospectively. This pre-

---

[23] Under Article 6.5, *ATC*, the maximum period of validity of a determination of "serious damage or actual threat thereof", for purposes of application of an *ATC*-consistent restraint measure, is 90 days after the date of initial notification of such damage. After the 90-day period, a new determina-tion of "serious damage or actual threat thereof" will have to be made if no restraint measure had been imposed.

sumption appears to us entirely appropriate in respect of measures which are limitative or deprivational in character or tenor and impact upon Member countries and their rights or privileges and upon private persons and their acts.

We turn to the context of Article 6.10 of the *ATC*. That context includes, of course, the whole of Article 6.

Article 6.1, *ATC* offers some reflected light on the question of backdating a restraint. Article 6.1 reads, in pertinent part:

> Members recognize that during the transition period *it may be necessary to apply a specific transitional safeguard mechanism* (referred to in this Agreement as "transitional safeguard"). The transitional safeguard may be applied by any Member to products covered by the Annex, except those integrated into GATT 1994 under the provisions of Article 2. ... The transitional safeguard *should be applied as sparingly as possible, consistently with the provisions of this Article* and *the effective implementation of the integration process under this Agreement.* (Emphases added)

Article 6.1 directs that transitional safeguard measures be applied "*as sparingly as possible*" on the one hand and, on the other, applied "*consistently with the provisions of [Article 6] and the effective implementation of the integration process under [the ATC]*". It appears to the Appellate Body that to inject into Article 6.10 an authorization for backdating the effectivity of a restraint measure will encourage return to the practice of backdating restraint measures which appears to have been widespread under the regime of the *MFA*, a regime which has now ended, as discussed below, with the advent of the *ATC*. Such an introjection would moreover loosen up the carefully negotiated language of Article 6.10, which reflects an equally carefully drawn balance of rights and obligations of Members, by allowing the importing Member an enhanced ability to restrict the entry into its territory of goods in the exportation of which no unfair trade practice such as dumping or fraud or deception as to origin, is alleged or proven. For retroactive application of a restraint measure effectively enables the importing Member to exclude more goods by enforcing the quota measure earlier rather than later.

It further appears to us that to read Article 6.10 as somehow authorizing the backdating, as a matter of course, of the effectivity or operation of a restraint measure, will tend to diminish the utility and significance of prior consultations with the identified exporting Member or Members. Article 6.7 of the *ATC* provides for those consultations in very substantial detail. Thus, Article 6.7 requires that the request for consultations be accompanied by specific, relevant and up-to-date information on the factors which led the importing Member to make a determination of "serious damage" (listed in Article 6.3) and the factors which led to the unilateral attribution of such damage to an identified exporting Member or Members (referred to in Article 6.4). One clear objective of requiring a 60-day period for consultations is to give such Member or Members a real and fair, not merely *pro forma*, opportunity to rebut or moderate those factors. The requirement of consultations is thus grounded on, among other things, due process considerations; that requirement should be protected from erosion or attenuation by a treaty interpreter. It is, again, noteworthy that Article 6.7 refers *repeatedly* to the Member "*proposing* to take safeguard action", or who "*proposes* to invoke the safeguard action" and to the level at which imports of the goods specified "are *proposed* to be restrained". The common, day-to-day, implication which arises from this language is clear to us: the restraint is to be applied *in the future, after* the consultations, should these prove fruitless and the proposed measure not withdrawn. The principle of effectiveness in treaty interpretation[24] sustains this implication.

We turn to another element of the context of Article 6.10 of the *ATC*: the prior existence and demise, as it were, of the *MFA*. Article 3(5)(i) of the *MFA* provided as follows:

> If, however, after a period of sixty days from the date on which the request has been received by the participating exporting country or countries, there has been no agreement either on the request for export restraint or on any alternative solution, the requesting participating country may decline to accept imports for retention from the participating country or countries referred to in paragraph 3 above of the textiles and textile products causing market disruption (as defined in Annex A) at a level *for the twelve-month period beginning on the day when the request was received by the participating exporting country or countries* not less than the level provided for in Annex B. Such level may be adjusted upwards to avoid undue hardship to the commercial participants in the trade involved to the extent possible consistent with the purposes of this Article. At the same time the matter shall be brought for immediate attention to the Textile Surveillance Body. (Emphases added)

It is recognized by Appellant and Appellee and the Third Participant, and the Panel as well, that Article 3(5)(i) of the *MFA* expressly permitted backdating of the effectivity of a restraint measure to the date of the importing Member's call for consultations.[25] The above underscored clause of Article 3(5)(i), *MFA*, how-

---

[24] See Report of the Appellate Body, "*United States - Standards for Reformulated and Conventional Gasoline*", AB-1996-1 (adopted 20 May 1996), DSR 1996:I, 3, at 21; and Report of the Appellate Body, "*Japan - Taxes on Alcoholic Beverages*", AB-1996-2 (adopted 1 November 1996), DSR 1996:I, 97, at 106.

[25] Simply as a matter of comparative texts, it may be noted that like Article 6.10 of the *ATC*, Article XIX of the *General Agreement* and the *Agreement on Safeguards* do *not* contain any language expressly permitting backdating of the effectivity of a safeguard restraint measure taken thereunder with respect to categories of goods already integrated into the *General Agreement*. In contrast, it may

ever, disappeared with the supersession of the *MFA* by the new *ATC*; no comparable clause was carried over into Article 6.10 of the *ATC*.[26] The Panel did not draw any operable inference from the disappearance of the *MFA* clause.[27] Appellant Costa Rica urges that the absence of an equivalent clause in Article 6.10 of the *ATC* means that backdating of a restraint measure may no longer be resorted to under Article 6.10, *ATC*. Appellee United States, in contrast, insists that such backdating is nevertheless available under the regime of the *ATC*.

We believe the disappearance in the *ATC* of the earlier *MFA* express provision for backdating the operative effect of a restraint measure, strongly reinforces the presumption that such retroactive application is no longer permissable. This is the commonplace inference that is properly drawn from such disappearance. We are not entitled to assume that that disappearance was merely accidental or an inadvertent oversight on the part of either harassed negotiators or inattentive draftsmen. That no official record may exist of discussions or statements of delegations on this particular point is, of course, no basis for making such an assumption. At the oral hearing, the United States stated that since 1974, for over 20 years, all importing countries had "counted" imports in the textile area against quotas imposed by restraints from the date of the request for consultations. While that may well have been the practice of many importing countries, it was, of course, the practice *under the MFA*. Two considerations bear upon this matter. Firstly, assuming, *arguendo* only, that the WTO Members had wanted to keep that practice, it is very difficult to understand why the treaty basis for such practice was not maintained but was instead wiped out. Secondly, it has not been suggested that such a widely followed practice has arisen *under Article 6.10 of the ATC* notwithstanding the absence of the *MFA* backdating clause. At any rate, it is much too early for practice to have arisen under the *ATC* regime which commenced only on 1 January 1995.

---

also be noted that both Article 10(2) of the *Anti-dumping Agreement* and Article 20(2) of the *SCM Agreement expressly authorize, under certain conditions*, the *retroactive levying* of anti-dumping and countervailing duties for the period when provisional measures were in force.

[26] With the demise of the *MFA*, its place has been taken with respect to WTO Members, firstly, in respect of textile and clothing items not yet integrated into the *General Agreement*, by the *ATC*. Secondly, in respect of items already integrated into the *General Agreement*, the *MFA* safeguard measure is displaced by Article XIX of the *General Agreement* and the *Agreement on Safeguards*.

[27] We have noted in page 12 that the Panel "conclude[d] that *the prevalent practice under the MFA* of setting the initial date of a restraint period as the date of request for consultations *cannot be maintained under the ATC*". Immediately thereafter, however, the Panel held that backdating could be resorted to (in 1995, under the *ATC*) provided that the date of initial effectivity is not earlier than the date of publication of the call for consultations (Panel Report, para. 7.69). This ruling appears at odds with the Panel's own immediately preceding conclusion.

2. *The Problem of a Speculative "Flood of Imports" upon Notice of a Call for Consultations*

The United States claims that the Panel made an "important factual finding" that there would always or "typically" be a "flood of imports" after an announcement of a call for consultations between the importing Member proposing to impose a safeguard restraint measure and the identified exporting Member or Members. It is emphasized that the announcement of a possible restraint measure generates a powerful incentive to maximize exports before the restraint can go into effect. The thrust of the United States' argument is that authority to backdate a restraint measure is essential if the importing Member is effectively to protect itself from such speculative surges of imports. Article 6.10 of the *ATC*, in the United States' view, must be considered as impliedly granting such authority if that paragraph is to be an "effective component" of the transitional safeguard mechanism of the *ATC*.

We have been unable to locate such a broad-ranging "factual finding" in the Panel's Report.

At the same time, we must recognize that in the world of international trade and commerce as we know it, a speculative "flood of imports" *could* in fact *materialize*, in a particular case, upon public announcement of consultations. We cannot exclude *a priori* the possibility of such a situation arising. Whether or not, in a specific given case, a "flood of imports" would actually follow publication of a call for consultations relating to a proposed restraint measure will, in our view, depend upon any number of variable factors. Such factors would include, for instance, the particular kind of textile or clothing item involved, the "high fashion", high-value or alternatively the fungible, low-value nature of the goods subjected to a quota, the seasonality of demand for such items, the length of production time, the presence or absence of abnormally high inventories of such goods in the exporting country, and so forth. Another kind of factor which may bear upon the possibility of a "flood of imports", is the level of the minimum or floor quota guaranteed to the exporting Member[s] by Articles 6.7 and 6.8, *ATC*, and public awareness of such guaranteed quota level within the importing and exporting countries.

It appears to us that the above is basically all that the Panel sought to convey in its brief statement on the matter:

> Finally, we note the US *argument* that if the safeguard measure could only be applied starting at some time later than the date of the request for consultations, *there would be a flood of imports in anticipation of the eventual restriction*, which *might* defeat the whole purpose of the transitional safeguard measure. We find *this argument to be persuasive from a practical point of view.* In order to avoid

such a consequence, in our view, all that is needed on the part of the importing country is to publish the content of the request for consultations immediately.[28] (Emphases added)

Turning to the legal contention made by the United States concerning the necessity for authority to backdate a restraint measure to prevent or deal with "a flood of imports", that contention may be seen to assume that no other recourse is available to the importing country should speculative "flooding" of imports pose a clear and imminent threat or actually come about in a particular situation.

We do not believe it is necessary to make such an assumption.

When and to the extent that a speculative "flood of imports" turns out, in a particular situation, to be a real and serious problem engaging the legitimate interests of the Member proposing a safeguard measure, we consider that recourse may be had to Article 6.11 of the *ATC*. Article 6.11 authorizes the importing Member, "in highly unusual and critical circumstances, where delay would cause damage which would be difficult to repair", to impose and apply *immediately*, albeit provisionally, the restraint measure authorized under Article 6.10. The request for consultations and the notification to the Textile Monitoring Board must, however, be issued within five working days after the taking of provisional action. In other words, the requirements of Article 6.10 must nevertheless be observed. Action under Article 6.11 of the *ATC* is not in lieu of, and does not supersede, action taken or begun under Article 6.10, *ATC*. Provisional action under Article 6.11 is folded into action under Article 6.10. Considering that Article 6.11 permits the provisional imposition of a restraint measure even *before* consultations, *a fortiori* it would permit such imposition *after* consultations have in fact begun, so long as the requisites of both Articles 6.10 and 6.11 are met or continue to be met.

The standards established in Article 6.11 - "highly unusual and critical circumstances, where delay would cause damage which would be difficult to repair" - are obviously not susceptible of specific quantitative description. The appreciation of when such circumstances may reasonably be regarded as having arisen, can only be done in concrete cases and on a case-to-case basis. Such appreciation would have to take into account that the standards and requisites of Articles 6.10 and 6.11 are to be read together against the background consideration that the *ATC* constitutes a temporary and transitional regime with complete integration of the textile and clothing sector into the *General Agreement* as the final goal.[29]

---

[28] Panel Report, para. 7.68.

[29] The standard found in Article 6.11, *ATC*, may be compared textually with the counterpart language in Article XIX:2, *General Agreement*, and Article 6 of the *Agreement on Safeguards*: "in critical circumstances, where delay would cause damage which it would be difficult to repair ...". This language presently applies to all goods already integrated into the *General Agreement* and will apply, at the end of the transitional period, to goods currently not yet so integrated.

The conclusion we have arrived at, in respect of the issue of permissibility of backdating, is that the giving of retroactive effect to a safeguard restraint measure is no longer permissible under the regime of Article 6 of the *ATC* and is in fact prohibited under Article 6.10 of that *Agreement*. The presumption of prospective effect only, has not been overturned; it is a proposition not simply presumptively correct but one requiring our assent. We believe, accordingly, and so hold, that the Panel erred in ruling that Article 6.10 of the *ATC* had nothing to say on the issue of backdating and that such backdating to 21 April 1995, the date of publication of the call for consultations, was permissible under Article X:2 of the *General Agreement*. The importing Member is, however, not defenceless against a speculative "flood of imports" where it is confronted with the circumstances contemplated in Article 6.11. Its appropriate recourse is, in other words, to action under Article 6.11 of the *ATC*, complying in the process with the requirements of Article 6.10 and Article 6.11.

V.   THE ISSUE OF APPLICABILITY OF ARTICLE XIII:3(B), *GENERAL AGREEMENT*, TO A TRANSITIONAL SAFEGUARD MEASURE TAKEN UNDER ARTICLE 6.10, *ATC*

In the written and oral submissions before the Appellate Body, the issue of applicability of Article XIII:3(b) of the *General Agreement* to the restraint measure here at stake, was much discussed by Appellant Costa Rica. The Appellee United States also dealt with this issue, though with less enthusiasm.

Considering the conclusion we have above reached in respect of the first issue, there is no necessity for dealing with this second issue at any length. Had we concluded that under Article 6.10, *ATC*, backdating the effectivity of a restraint measure remained permissible, it would have been necessary to determine whether a different result would be compelled by Article XIII(3)(b) of the *General Agreement* and, in particular, the meaning and applicability of the words "the Contracting Party applying the restrictions shall give public notice of the total quantity or value of the product or products which will be permitted to be imported during a specified future period ...". In any case, there is nothing in this provision which runs counter to our conclusion that backdating is prohibited under Article 6.10 of the *ATC*.

VI.   THE ISSUE OF APPLICABILITY OF ARTICLE X:2 OF THE *GENERAL AGREEMENT*, TO A TRANSITIONAL SAFEGUARD MEASURE TAKEN UNDER ARTICLE 6.10, *ATC*

Article X, *General Agreement*, provides in part:

Article X

Publication and Administration of Trade Regulations

x x x

2. No *measure of general application* taken by any contracting party effecting an advance in a rate of duty or other charge on imports under an established and uniform practice, or *imposing a new or more burdensome requirement, restriction* or prohibition *on imports*, or on the transfer of payments therefor, shall be enforced before such measure has been officially published. (Emphases added)

x x x

The Panel found that the safeguard restraint measure imposed by the United States is "a measure of general application" within the contemplation of Article X:2. We agree with this finding. While the restraint measure was addressed to particular, i.e. named, exporting Members, including Appellant Costa Rica, as contemplated by Article 6.4, *ATC*, we note that the measure did not try to become specific as to the individual persons or entities engaged in exporting the specified textile or clothing items to the importing Member and hence affected by the proposed restraint.

Article X:2, *General Agreement*, may be seen to embody a principle of fundamental importance - that of promoting full disclosure of governmental acts affecting Members and private persons and enterprises, whether of domestic or foreign nationality. The relevant policy principle is widely known as the principle of transparency and has obviously due process dimensions. The essential implication is that Members and other persons affected, or likely to be affected, by governmental measures imposing restraints, requirements and other burdens, should have a reasonable opportunity to acquire authentic information about such measures and accordingly to protect and adjust their activities or alternatively to seek modification of such measures. We believe that the Panel here gave to Article X:2, *General Agreement*, an interpretation that is appropriately protective of the basic principle there projected.

At the same time, we are bound to observe that Article X:2 of the *General Agreement*, does not speak to, and hence does not resolve, the issue of permissibility of giving retroactive effect to a safeguard restraint measure. The presumption of prospective effect only does, of course, relate to the basic principles of transparency and due process, being grounded on, among other things, these principles. But prior publication is required for all measures falling within the scope of Article X:2, not just *ATC* safeguard restraint measures sought to be applied retrospectively. Prior publication may be an autonomous condition for giving effect at all to a restraint measure. Where no authority exists to give retroactive effect to a restrictive governmental measure, that deficiency is not cured by publishing the measure sometime before its actual application. The necessary authorization is not supplied by Article X:2 of the *General Agreement*.

Our finding, therefore, that the safeguard restraint measure here involved is properly regarded as "a measure of general application" under Article X:2 does not conflict with, and does not affect our conclusion under the first issue above that backdating the effectivity of a restraint measure is prohibited by Article 6.10 of the *ATC*.

VII. FINDINGS AND CONCLUSIONS

For the reasons set out in the preceding sections of this Report, the Appellate Body has reached the following conclusion:

the Panel erred in law in concluding that under Article 6.10 *ATC* "if the importing country publishes the proposed restraint period and restraint level after the request for consultations, it can later set the initial date of the restraint period as the date of the publication of the proposed restraint", and that "had it set the restraint period starting on 21 April 1995, which was the date of the publication of the information about the request for consultations, it would not have acted inconsistently with GATT 1994 or the ATC in respect of the restraint period".

The foregoing legal conclusion modifies the conclusions of the Panel as set out in paragraph 7.69 of its Report. The Appellate Body's conclusion leaves intact the conclusions of the Panel that were not the subject of appeal.

The Appellate Body *recommends* that the Dispute Settlement Body request the United States to bring its measure restricting Costa Rican exports of cotton and man-made fibre underwear, category 352/652, 60 Federal Register 32653, into conformity with its obligations under the *ATC*.

UNITED STATES - RESTRICTIONS ON IMPORTS OF COTTON AND MAN-MADE FIBRE UNDERWEAR

Report of the Panel
WT/DS24/R

*Adopted by the Dispute Settlement Body on 25 February 1997
as modified by the Appellate Body Report*

TABLE OF CONTENTS

I.   INTRODUCTION

1.1   On 22 December 1995, Costa Rica requested consultations with the United States under Article 4 and other relevant provisions of the Understanding on Rules and   Procedures Governing the Settlement of Disputes (DSU), Article XXIII of the General Agreement on Tariffs and Trade 1994 (GATT 1994) and the corresponding provisions of the Agreement on Textiles and Clothing (ATC)   (WT/DS24/1).   Consultations   were   held   on   18 January   and 1 February 1996, however, no mutually satisfactory solution was reached. On 22 February 1996,   Costa   Rica   requested   the   establishment   of   a   panel (WT/DS24/2) which was considered by the DSB at its meeting on 5 March 1996 (WT/DSB/M/12). The Dispute Settlement Body (DSB) accordingly agreed to establish a panel with standard terms of reference in accordance with Article 6 of the DSU.

1.2   On 19 April 1996, the DSB was informed that the terms of reference and the composition of the Panel (WT/DS24/3) were as follows:

Terms of Reference

> "To examine, in the light of the relevant provisions of the covered   agreements   cited   by   Costa Rica   in   document WT/DS24/2, the matter referred to the DSB by Costa Rica in that document and to make such findings as will assist the DSB in making the recommendations or in giving the rulings provided for in those agreements".

Composition

Chairman: Mr. Thomas Cottier

Panelists: Mr. Martin Harvey

Mr. Johannes Human

1.3   The Panel heard the parties to the dispute on 24-25 June 1996   and 29 July 1996. The Panel also met with the parties on 15 October 1996 to review aspects of the interim report, at the request of the parties. The Panel submitted its complete   findings   and   conclusions   to   the   parties   to   the   dispute   on 25 October 1996.

* * * * *

II.   FACTUAL ASPECTS

Outward Processing Regime: "807 Trade" and "Guaranteed Access Levels"

2.1   In the course of the last six years, there has been a significant change in the US cotton and man-made fibre underwear manufacturing industry which has significantly switched from producing and assembling underwear domestically to producing components in the United States for assembly in other countries and subsequent return to the same enterprises in the United States for marketing. This pattern of co-production has enabled the companies in this industry to maintain their share of the US market by making use of the labour force available outside the country while at the same time controlling the source of raw materials, the production timetable, the types and amounts of underwear to be produced and the marketing of the final product. Moreover, these co-production operations were consistent with the policies of the United States, which was encouraging investment and production in Mexico and the Caribbean Basin.

2.2   Item 9802.00.80 of the Harmonized Tariff Schedule of the United States (HTSUS)[1] provides for re-importation into the US of goods that have been assembled abroad from US-made components; it provides the basis for a type of outward processing regime which enables US manufacturers of relatively labour-intensive products to export US parts for assembly abroad and return of the assembled products to the United States with partial exemption from US duties. This programme is not limited to apparel, although it is widely used in apparel trade because of the high labour content and the substantial US duties on apparel imports. To qualify for partial duty exemption under item 9802.00.80, articles must be assembled abroad in whole or in part of fabricated components, the product of the United States, which has been exported in condition ready for assembly without further fabrication; has not lost its physical identity in such articles by change in form, shape or otherwise; and has not been advanced in value or improved in condition abroad except by being assembled and except by operations incidental to the assembly process such as cleaning, lubricating and painting.

2.3   The exported articles used in the imported goods must be "fabricated US components," i.e., manufactured articles ready for assembly in their exported condition, except for operations incidental to the assembly process. Integrated circuits, compressors, zippers, buttons and precut or preformed sections of a garment are examples of fabricated components in this sense. To be considered "US components," the exported articles do not necessarily need to be fabricated from materials or components wholly made in the United States. If a foreign product undergoes processing in the United States sufficient to confer US origin for customs purposes, then the resulting processed goods may be exported, assembled abroad and re-imported and still qualify for partial duty exemption under item 9802.00.80. Thus, in an 807 operation, the cloth can come from any country in the world: what is important is to have it cut in the United States. There is no obligation to re-import the articles assembled abroad into the United States; producers of underwear assembled from US components could sell the underwear to any market in the world.

---

[1]   This provision is frequently referred to as "807 trade" as it was covered by that chapter in the former US tariff schedules.

2.4　An article imported under item 9802.00.80 is treated as a foreign article for customs purposes and recorded as a foreign article in US import statistics. Chapter 98, Subchapter II, Note 2 of the HTSUS, provides that any product of the US which is returned after having been advanced in value or improved in condition abroad, or assembled abroad, shall be a "foreign article" for the purposes of the Tariff Act of 1930, as amended. It is not legally of US origin even if the pieces of a garment re-imported are cut in the United States. This rule has been provided as an explicit exception to the US rule of origin for textiles and apparel, in force up to 30 June 1996, which normally deems such products to originate from the place where garment pieces are cut. This exception remains even in the revised rules of origin for textiles which took effect on 1 July 1996. HTSUS Note 2 also provided that textile or apparel articles are to be treated as foreign articles even if they are assembled or processed in whole of fabricated components that are a product of the United States or are processed in whole of ingredients (other than water) that are a product of the United States, in beneficiary countries of the Caribbean Basin Initiative.

2.5　An article imported under item 9802.00.80 is dutiable under the rate otherwise applicable to the assembled product, but the dutiable value is reduced by deducting the cost or value of the exported fabricated components from the value of the imported assembled product. For instance, the underwear re-imports in the present case are subject to customs duties at the rate applicable to underwear, but their customs value is reduced by deducting the cost or value of the exported garment sections, elastic, zippers, buttons, thread, etc. used in assembling the underwear in Costa Rica. The duty reduction (which is not regulated by the ATC) is a key factor in making the offshore assembly operations in Costa Rica economically viable. The "807" programme is not mandated by tax, social or industrial requirements. However, the underlying intent encompasses a variety of broader social and economic objectives, such as aiding structural adjustment, assisting the economic development of foreign countries, maintaining the competitiveness of US industry, lowering prices for consumers, and reducing the tax burden on US companies.

Guaranteed Access Levels

2.6　Guaranteed Access Levels, or GALs, are provided for textile re-imports under the US Special Access Programme, a programme designed to develop and expand manufacturing in the Caribbean Basin, Andean Trade Preference countries and Mexico (under the North American Free Trade Agreement (NAFTA)) by allowing guaranteed access to the US market for re-imports of apparel made with fabric formed and cut in the United States. The United States employs this programme as a form of "more favourable treatment" for certain re-imports - those using US formed and cut fabric - as provided for in Article 6.6(d) of the ATC. Under this programme, guaranteed quota access ("GALs") for particular apparel products are specified by agreement with the relevant exporting country. Garment pieces cut in the United States from US-formed fabric (e.g. woven or knitted in the United States) are exported to that country, where they are assembled; the apparel assembled from them is guaranteed access to the United States at the negotiated level, and is entered under HTSUS subparagraph 9802.00.8015, which corresponds to the former Item 807A in the pre-HTSUS tariff nomenclature. Entries must be accompanied by an ITA 370-P form, which certifies the facts necessary for eligibility of the goods under this subparagraph. The Special Access Programme only affects access to the US market for textiles and apparel articles, and does not affect the effective duty rate for imports.

Specific Limits

2.7   A specific limit (SL) refers to the level of restraint (quota) on the exports or imports of the product in question during a set period of time. The ATC provision setting out the method for calculating the applicable restraint level is found in Article 6.8.

Chronology of Events

2.8   In early 1995 the United States Committee for the Implementation of Textiles Agreements (CITA) reviewed data on total imports of cotton and man-made fibre underwear (category 352/652) and examined the state of the domestic industry producing such goods. Based on the factors examined, the CITA determined that there was a situation of serious damage or actual threat thereof to the US underwear industry. The United States attributed the serious damage or actual threat thereof, to imports from seven countries, Colombia, Costa Rica, Dominican Republic, El Salvador, Honduras, Thailand and Turkey. (See Section V.A.)

2.9   Based on its findings, the United States requested consultations on 27 March 1995 with, *inter alia*, Costa Rica on trade in cotton and man-made fibre underwear (US textile category 352/652), with a view to initiating the transitional safeguard procedure for establishing a quantitative restriction on that product in accordance with Article 6 of the ATC and provided a statement of serious damage setting out the factual information in the matter (Annex). The United States proposed a level of restraint for underwear imports from Costa Rica pursuant to Article 6.8 of the ATC. On 21 April 1995, the United States published the contents of the request for consultations, including the restraint level and period, in the Federal Register.

2.10   Consultations were held on 1-2 June 1995 at which the United States proposed a two-part measure comprising a specific limit (SL) of 1.25 million dozen and a guaranteed access level (GAL) of 20 million dozen. Costa Rica did not consider that the United States had substantiated its case under the provisions of the ATC and the consultations did not result in a mutually acceptable solution.

2.11   On 22 June 1995, the United States made a new proposal for the establishment of a quantitative restriction at a level of 1.325 million dozen specific level (SL) with annual growth of 6 per cent and 20 million dozen GAL for 1996.

2.12   Because no mutual agreement had been reached between the United States and Costa Rica by the end of 30 days after the 60-day consultation period provided for in Article 6.7 of the ATC, the United States implemented a restraint on imports from Costa Rica effective 23 June 1995 for a 12-month quota period starting 27 March 1995 and referred the matter to the Textiles Monitoring Body (TMB), pursuant to Article 6.10 of the ATC.

2.13   On 10 July 1995, the United States sent Costa Rica a further proposal for a specific limit for 1996 of 3 million dozen with 6 per cent annual growth and a guaranteed access level of 30 million dozen. This proposal included a provision to reduce the specific limit to 1.5 million dozen in the event the US Congress passed a law providing for quota-free treatment for goods from the Caribbean Basin that prescribed certain rules of origin (the "ratchet-down" clause). Costa Rica continued to question the basis for the request for a restriction and did not respond to this proposal.

2.14   On 12 July 1995 the US made a proposal to Costa Rica with the same levels as on 10 July but which did not specify the reduction in the specific limit in the event of the above-mentioned law being passed and subjected reduction in SL to subsequent negotiations.

Review by the TMB

2.15   The TMB reviewed this case, and others, in accordance with Article 6.10 of the ATC and heard presentations from the United States, Costa Rica, Honduras, Thailand and Turkey from 13-21 July 1995. During the proceedings, the United States provided updated data and other relevant information (July 1995 Market Statement, see paragraphs 5.135-5.138). These data were used to update the data presented in March so that all of the data would be consistent with the reference period of the call, the year ending in December 1994. The United States also supplied the TMB with additional information requested by Members subject to the call and by the TMB members concerning the industry, re-imports and exports.

2.16   During its review of this safeguard action by the United States against imports of category 352/652 from *inter alia* Costa Rica, the TMB found that serious damage had not been demonstrated. The TMB could not, however, reach consensus on the existence of actual threat of serious damage. The TMB recommended that further consultations be held between the United States and Costa Rica,

> "with a view to arriving at a mutual understanding, bearing in mind the above, and with due consideration to the particular features of this case, as well as equity considerations" (G/TMB/R/2).

2.17   A new round of consultations was held on 16-17 August 1995 at which a number of issues were raised by Costa Rica with respect to the justification of US actions. The consultations did not produce an agreement and both parties reported the situation to the TMB.

2.18   At its meeting on 16-20 October 1995, the TMB received reports from Costa Rica and the United States on the bilateral consultations they had had following the TMB recommendation. It took note of the reports and of the fact that the two parties had not reached a mutual understanding during the consultations. The TMB's discussions confirmed the Body's previous findings in this matter; there being no further requests by the parties involved, the TMB considered its review of the matter completed (G/TMB/R/5).

Further Consultations

2.19   On 22 November 1995, a further consultation was held at which the United States made a new restraint proposal for a specific limit of 7 million dozen (sub-limit of 4 million dozen for knit products) and a GAL of 40 million dozen for the period 1 April 1996 to 31 March 1997 and also including the previously mentioned "ratchet-down" clause and 6 per cent growth. Costa Rica submitted a proposal for a specific limit of 21 million dozen for 1996 followed by a second proposal fixing SL and GAL access for the period corresponding to 1996-1997 at 15.4 and 40 million dozen respectively. These were not accepted by the United States. Thereafter, Costa Rica requested consultations under Article 4 of the DSU.

2.20   The restriction, augmented by the application of a growth rate of 6 per cent was renewed for a second 12-month period on 27 March 1996.

* * * * *

Action Under the Dispute Settlement Understanding

2.21   On 22 December 1995, Costa Rica requested the US Government to hold consultations under Article 4 of the ATC and the other relevant provisions of the DSU, Article XXIII of GATT 1994 and the corresponding provisions of the ATC. The two countries met on two occasions, on 18 January and 1 February 1996.

2.22   At the first of these meetings, Costa Rica raised a number of questions, which it subsequently submitted in writing, requesting the earliest possible written reply. Moreover, reiterating its view that the call for consultations was not justified under the ATC, Costa Rica again requested that it be withdrawn. On 18 January 1996, Costa Rica proposed establishing, instead of a restriction, a mechanism for monitoring the composition and patterns of trade between the two countries in the category in question. However, this suggestion was not accepted by the United States.

2.23   At a meeting held on 1 February 1996 the United States made a new proposal to Costa Rica offering access for 57 million dozen during the period 27 March 1995 to 30 September 1996. In addition, access for the 18-month period from 1 October 1996 to 26 March 1998 would be fixed at 12 million dozen SL, with a sub-limit of 6.8 million dozen for knitwear, and 30 million GAL. This restraint proposal included a "ratchet-down" clause, in accordance with which SL access would be reduced to 1.5 and 1.6 million dozen for each of the periods covered by the restriction. Once again, Costa Rica rejected this proposal as inconsistent with the corresponding provisions of the ATC.

2.24   The period of 60 days for consultations provided for in the DSU ended without any satisfactory agreement having been reached between the parties, and the United States continued to maintain its unilateral restrictions on the products in question. Consequently, on 5 March 1996, Costa Rica made a request to the DSB, which was granted, for the establishment of a Panel.

* * * * *

III.   FINDINGS REQUESTED

3.1   *Costa Rica* requested the Panel to find specifically, *inter alia*, on the following aspects:

1. That as a result of having imposed a new restriction on the trade in cotton and man-made fibre underwear in violation of the provisions of the ATC, the United States was in breach of Article 2 of that Agreement;

2. That the increase in "807 trade" could not be considered to constitute increased imports, within the meaning of Article 6.2 of the ATC;

3. That if, the above notwithstanding, it was considered that these increased imports did fall within the provisions of Article 6.2 of the ATC, the fact was that this showed the US industry manufacturing underwear cut pieces to be in excellent condition and not to be in need of any protection;

4. That serious damage and actual threat of serious damage were two different concepts which, to be demonstrated, required the submission of separate information and a different analysis;

5. That the finding of the TMB to the effect that the United States had not demonstrated serious damage to its underwear-manufacturing industry should be upheld;

6. That, given the unreliable, erroneous, contradictory and incomplete nature of the information submitted by the United States in an attempt to justify its account of the situation of its industry, that country had failed to fulfil its obligation to demonstrate serious damage;

7. That the United States, having changed the ostensible basis for its measure, had nonetheless never submitted the information required

or provided the analysis necessary to demonstrate the existence of actual threat of serious damage to its underwear-manufacturing industry;

8.   That, even assuming the existence of increased imports and serious damage or actual threat of serious damage, the United States had not demonstrated the existence of a causal link between the two, and indeed that the agreements which it had reached with the other countries called to consultations in this category confirmed the non-existence of such a causal link;

9.   That, even supposing that the United States had met the three basic requirements for entitlement to resort to the special transitional safeguard mechanism, it had never submitted the information necessary nor carried out the analysis required to attribute the alleged damage or threat to imports from Costa Rica;

10.   That the various factors present in this case and, in particular, the proposals for restraint made by the United States to Costa Rica and the quota levels which it had negotiated with the other countries called to consultations in this category, indicated that what the United States was really seeking was to protect not the underwear-manufacturing industry but rather the branch of the domestic industry which manufactured the cloth used in underwear production;

11.   That the ATC did not permit the imposition of a safeguard measure on an imported clothing product in order to protect the cloth used to produce it;

12.   That the United States had imposed and renewed the restriction on the basis of the existence of an actual threat of serious damage, despite never having held consultations on the subject;

13.   That in June 1995 the United States had imposed a unilateral restriction on Costa Rica, making it retroactive to March of that year, despite the fact that under the ATC it had no authority to do so; and

14.   That the United States violated the spirit and the letter of Article 8 of the ATC by refusing, without any justification, to follow the recommendations made by the TMB, in particular, that it should hold consultations with Costa Rica bearing in mind that serious damage had not been demonstrated, that no consensus could be reached on the existence of actual threat of serious damage, that the trade concerned had particular features and that there were equity considerations which should be taken into account, and by failing to submit a report explaining its inability to conform with those recommendations.

3.2   *Costa Rica* further requested the Panel, on the basis of the above considerations and in view of the fact that the United States had proceeded in violation of the ATC, to find in its report that the Government of the United States should ensure that the unilateral restriction adopted against Costa Rica should comply with the ATC and that in this particular case compliance should be through the immediate withdrawal of the measure. Costa Rica based its request on Article 19.1 of the DSU, which authorized the Panel to specify the appropriate way of applying its recommendations.

3.3   The *United States* requested the Panel to find that:

-    the United States application and maintenance of a safeguard restriction on imports of cotton and man-made fibre underwear from Costa Rica was consistent with Article 6 of the ATC;

-    the restriction was not inconsistent with Articles 2 and 8 of the ATC; and

-    the above measure did not nullify and impair benefits accruing to Costa Rica under the ATC or GATT 1994.

3.4   With respect to Costa Rica's request that the Panel find

"in accordance with the terms of reference assigned to it by the DSB, that the United States should withdraw the unilateral restriction imposed on Costa Rica forthwith",

and also to find in its report

"that the United States should proceed to bring its measure into conformity with the ATC, which implies immediately withdrawing it";

the *United States* considered that the heterogeneity of phrasing left Costa Rica's objective in doubt, but argued that if the request was for a Panel recommendation that specific actions should be taken, or for findings that would amount in effect to such a recommendation, the request was inconsistent with Article 19.1 of the DSU.

3.5   In the view of the *United States*, the DSU gave WTO panels explicit instructions with respect to the one and only recommendation that properly may be offered if the measures of a Member were found to be inconsistent with its obligations: to bring the measures into conformity with its obligations. The avoidance of granting specific remedies, such as the withdrawal or modification of a measure, was a well-established practice under the GATT, and had been codified in Article 19.1 of the DSU, which provided:

"Where a panel or the Appellate Body concludes that a measure is inconsistent with a covered agreement, it shall recommend that the Member concerned bring the measure into conformity with that agreement."

The Panel need to make no recommendations at all, as the measures at issue were fully consistent with US obligations under the ATC; however, if any recommendation was made, in their view, the Panel was not authorized to make any recommendation other than that provided for in Article 19.1 of the DSU.

3.6   *Costa Rica* replied that, Article 19.1 of the DSU, contrary to the statement made by the United States, authorized the Panel to specify the appropriate way of applying its recommendations by providing that:

> "Where a panel or the Appellate Body concludes that a measure is inconsistent with a covered agreement, it shall recommend that the Member concerned bring the measure into conformity with that agreement. In addition to its recommendations, the panel or Appellate Body may suggest ways in which the Member concerned could implement the recommendations."

* * * * *

Other Issues

3.7   On 21 June 1996, the *United States* requested the Panel's attention to breaches in confidentiality by Costa Rica concerning proposals made by the United States in consultations, and Costa Rica's use of that information in this proceeding to prejudice the United States case. On 24 June 1996, Costa Rica had responded in the first substantive meeting of the Panel with information concerning disclosures made by the US embassy in San Jose, Costa Rica, concerning US proposals in consultations with Costa Rica. Subsequently, the US had investigated those disclosures and discovered that they were made in response to the numerous press statements in San Jose by journalists and members of the Costa Rican Government. US embassy statements had been made solely in response to this press offensive by Costa Rica.

3.8   *Costa Rica* emphasized that publication of any article prior to the initiation of the dispute settlement procedure under the DSU, which in any case was at the initiative of the United States as part of their strategy to exert pressure on the Government of Costa Rica, was irrelevant from the point of view of the confidentiality prescribed by Article 4.6 of the DSU because this applied to consultations initiated under the dispute settlement mechanism of the DSU and not to any event that occurred prior to that time. Accordingly, one of the documents referred to by the United States was irrelevant as it was published prior to the initiation of the consultation procedure under the DSU. The other two articles were replies to public declarations by representatives of the United States Government or by the enterprise which the United States was seeking to protect. Moreover, Costa Rica indicated that the fact that Article 4.6 stated that consultations were confidential could not be interpreted as a limitation on the rights of parties at the Panel stage. On the contrary, confidentiality must be understood as referring to parties not involved in the dispute and to the public, but not in any way to the Panel itself. It was not the intention of Article 4.6 to limit the possibilities available to the Panel to be apprised of information on the dispute before it because this would be to the detriment of the procedure itself.

3.9   The *United States* accepted that since the US embassy was responsible for some of the disclosures, they withdrew the request. This withdrawal was made without prejudice to the other points made concerning Costa Rica's misuse and distortion of information on consultations in this case.

* * * * *

IV. THIRD PARTY SUBMISSION: INDIA

4.1   *India* had indicated their interest in the matter and their desire to participate in the Panel process as an interested third party pursuant to Article 10 of the DSU. Accordingly, India was invited to present their views to the Panel at its first meeting on 25 June 1996. In their submission India reviewed the measure taken by the United States and provided views on various aspects. In particular, India requested the Panel to include in its findings:

(a)   that the United States did not have the option of claiming a situation of actual threat of serious damage in July 1995 after having determined in March 1995 that there was a situation of serious damage and having issued the consultation call to Costa Rica on that basis;

(b)   that all the data necessary to be provided to Costa Rica in terms of the provisions of Article 6 of ATC had not been provided by the United States and some of the data provided was not compiled objectively and therefore lacked reliability;

(c)   that the data available had not indicated that there had been either a situation of serious damage or one of actual threat of serious damage to the domestic industry of the United States, attributable to imports;

(d)   that imports from Costa Rica which had been almost entirely from US components supplied by the US industry producing underwear and mostly produced in Costa Rica by units established by US underwear manufacturers could not have contributed to serious damage of actual threat thereof to the same US industry which engaged voluntarily in such co-production activities;

(e)   that the US action actually sought to protect the US industry producing fabrics for underwear and not the industry producing underwear and this was inconsistent with the provisions of the Article 6 of the ATC;

(f)   that a temporary safeguard action under Article 6 of the ATC had to be pursued by the importing country and reviewed by the TMB entirely on the basis of data that had been available to the importing country at the time they made a determination that there was a situation of serious damage or actual threat thereof;

(g)   that the importing country had to choose between the grounds of serious damage and of actual threat of serious damage at the time of determination of the market situation before initiating the safe-guard action and the data requirements for these two grounds was different in nature and not in degree;

(h)   that there was no provision in the ATC for retroactive restraints; and

(i)   that if not endorsed by the TMB after the mandatory review, a safeguard action would not survive.

4.2   With reference to the submission by India, the *United States* expressed the view that the ATC did not require the importing country to choose between serious damage and actual threat when making its determination and so the United States had relied upon both, and referred to both, in their request for consultations. Also, Article 6.3 of the ATC did not provide any separate criteria for evaluating serious damage on the one hand, and actual threat thereof on the other. The ATC also had no provisions specifically addressing actual threat (unlike the WTO legal provisions concerning anti-dumping duties, countervailing duties, or GATT Article XIX safeguards). India had also referred to "sharp and substantial" and "imminent" increases in their submission. However, in the view of the *United States*, those standards applied to a determination of attribution under Article 6.4 of the ATC, and were irrelevant to a determination under Article 6.2 of the ATC.

4.3   *Costa Rica* endorsed and formally incorporated in its submission the arguments and observations contained in the submission made by India and took the view that the Panel should make reference in its written report to the points it had developed and to rule on each of them.

* * * * *

V.   MAIN ARGUMENTS BY THE PARTIES

A.   The Safeguard Action Taken by the United States

Statement of Serious Damage: Category 352/652 (March 1995 Market Statement)

5.1   *Costa Rica* noted that the March Market Statement of the United States (annexed to this report) had said nothing about the percentage of "807 trade" in the production and import data and made no attempt to analyze the impact of this factor on the trade in this category. Accordingly, there was no way of determining whether domestic production really grew or not; what the actual market share of the United States industry was; and the true ratio of imports to domestic production.

5.2   The *United States* explained by way of background that their Office of Textiles and Apparel (OTEXA) at the Department of Commerce was responsible for collecting data and producing statements of serious damage or actual threat thereof for consideration by the CITA. In early 1995, the CITA had reviewed the data on total imports of cotton and man-made fibre underwear (category 352/652) into the United States in accordance with Article 6.2 of the ATC. Following the criteria in that Article, the United States had looked at total imports of category 352/652. In so doing, they had found that such imports had surged from 65,507,000 dozen in 1992 to 79,962,000 dozen in 1993. The CITA had found that total imports continued to surge in 1994, reaching 97,375,000 dozen, 22 per cent above the 1993 level and 49 per cent above the 1992 level. These data included re-imports.

5.3   The CITA had estimated that approximately 395 establishments in the United States manufacturing underwear employed about 6 per cent of total US apparel workers, and had annual shipments of $3.2 billion, accounting for approximately 5 per cent of total annual apparel shipments. The concentration of firms in this industry was higher in the men's underwear segment than in the women's segment. In the men's segment, four firms had accounted for over 60 per cent of the shipments. The production of women's underwear was more subject to fashion changes. As a result, production was less standardized, requiring different types of knitting machines and a greater number of workers being employed. There was, however, a large number of smaller producers which generally did not have integrated operations but usually purchased fabrics and then cut and sewed them.

5.4   The CITA had then examined factors listed in Article 6.3 of the ATC, such as US production, market share loss, employment, domestic prices, profits and investment, production capacity and sales. The CITA had found that US production in category 352/652 had declined from 175,542,000 dozen in 1992 to 168,802,000 dozen in 1993, representing a 4 per cent decline. Production had continued to decline in 1994 falling to 126,962,000 dozen during the first 9 months of 1994, four per cent below the January-September 1993 production level. US manufacturers' domestic market share had dropped from 73 per cent in 1992 to 68 per cent in 1993, a decline of 5 percentage points. During the first 9 months of 1994 that share had dropped to 65 percent. As a per cent of US production, imports had increased from 37 per cent in 1992 to 47 per cent in 1993, and had grown by 54 per cent in the first nine months of 1994.

5.5   *Costa Rica* questioned if the data on employment and man-hours were a special situation linked to increased imports or if they reflected a continuing trend within the industry. It was also observed that no numbers were given for layoffs; there was no causal link made between imports and job losses; and no basis was given for the statements about postponed investment or disinvestment, nor was consideration given to the possibility that these might represent economically rational decisions on the part of the companies concerned and might have no causal relationship at all with the trend or level of imports. The comment was also made that shifting production capacity to other product lines should be regarded as a positive trend, favouring the interests of the United States companies themselves.

5.6   *Costa Rica* affirmed that the United States had not satisfactorily established the existence of problems affecting employment, sales and profits, investment or capacity in its industry inasmuch as it was not possible to establish clearly the state of the industry on the basis of evidence from one or two enterprises. The United States had not properly established either the facts related to imports, domestic production and market size, especially because of the total absence of any analysis of the question of 807 trade in its March statement.

5.7   The *United States* also pointed out that the CITA had found that the number of production workers in the US underwear industry had dropped from 46,377 in 1992 to 44,056 in 1994, declining by 5 per cent, resulting in the loss of 2,321 workers. Average annual man-hours worked had dropped from 86.2 million in 1992 to 81.5 million in 1994. Based on a survey of individual firms producing cotton and man-made fibre underwear, the following conditions were reported: individual firms had reported layoffs, import-related plant closings and slowed sales; one firm had reported a decline in sales of 17 per cent in 1994 and a decline in profits by 18 per cent and there was pressure on the bottom line throughout the industry due to rising costs and stiff import competition. The uncertainty due to the increasing imports had caused US companies to postpone investment in this industry. Some companies had also closed plants permanently or shifted production capacity offshore, and additional disinvestment of this nature was contemplated by underwear manufacturing firms. Import prices were very low and placed considerable pressure on domestic producers.

5.8   *Costa Rica* did not accept that an increase in raw cotton prices had affected the producers of cotton fabric or yarn or the producers of cotton or man-made fibre underwear. As to the price-edge which imports enjoyed over domestically produced goods, there was no indication whether this meant all imports or some imports were produced with lower priced fabric and no justification was given for these assertions. Also, these statements did not take into consideration the fact that most of the growth in "imports" of the products in question was concentrated in those assembled outside the United States from US components. This meant that the domestic industry used the same raw material as the "imports" of products assembled from US components, so that the cotton price increases mentioned should have had no effect at all on import levels.

5.9   The *United States*, however, argued that competing imports had enjoyed a price edge over domestically produced goods because the imports were produced with lower-priced foreign fabric. As a result of the increased market share in underwear held by imports, average retail prices of underwear in the United States had generally declined during the past two years, at a time when US manufacturers' costs, particularly for raw cotton, had increased substantially. This development had seriously eroded the profitability of US underwear manufacturers. Based on the above factors and in accordance with Articles 6.2 and 6.3 of the ATC, the CITA had determined that there was serious damage, or actual threat thereof, to the US underwear industry. The United States then proceeded to identify Member countries to whom this damage could be attributed, as required by Article 6.4 of the ATC.

Attribution to Exporting Countries

5.10   *Costa Rica* noted that data on their exports to the US made no reference to the process of production sharing between the two countries, even though all the increase in imports could be attributed precisely to such co-production.

5.11   The *United States* explained that in applying the criteria in Article 6.4 of the ATC, the CITA had attributed the serious damage, or actual threat thereof, to imports from five WTO member countries - Costa Rica, the Dominican Republic, Honduras, Thailand, and Turkey - and to two countries that had not yet become WTO Members - Colombia and El Salvador. Total imports from the five WTO countries had increased from 22,675,508 dozen in 1992 to 40,293,259 dozen in 1994. This increase had represented a collective sharp and substantial increase of 78 per cent. Together, imports from these countries had increased 32 per cent in 1994 over their 1993 level. Imports in 1992 for these countries were 35 per cent of total US imports in cotton and man-made fibre underwear. In 1994, their share had increased to 41 per cent.

5.12   In the case of Costa Rica, the CITA had found that the increase in imports from Costa Rica alone was higher than the level of imports of category 352/652 from at least 85 other countries and had exceeded the levels of six other suppliers whose imports were under quota. Costa Rica was the second largest supplier to the United States. Consistent with the criteria in Article 6.4 of the ATC, the CITA had found that there was a sharp and substantial increase of low-priced imports from Costa Rica, as imports of cotton and man made fibre underwear had reached 14,423,178 dozen in 1994, a 22 per cent increase above the 1993 level of 11,844,331 dozen and 61 per cent above the 1992 level. Such imports had entered the United States from Costa Rica at an average landed duty-paid value of $9.39 per dozen, 69 per cent below the US producers' average price for the product. The CITA had also found that imports from Costa Rica were equivalent to 8.8 per cent of US production of category 352/652 in the year ending September 1994.

Consultations with Costa Rica

5.13   The *United States* advised that, based on their findings, the CITA had requested consultations with Costa Rica. In accordance with Article 6.7 of the ATC, the request was accompanied by a statement (the March Market Statement) complying with Articles 6.2, 6.3 and 6.4 of the ATC. Further, as required by Article 6.7 of the ATC, the United States had proposed a level of restraint for underwear imports from Costa Rica which would be at a level not less than the level existing at 12 of the 14 months preceding the month of the request for consultations.

5.14   During the first round of consultations, on 1-2 June 1995, the United States had discussed the basis for its request for consultations and the high level of estimated re-imports in Costa Rican trade, approximately 94 per cent of their total trade of 14,423,178 dozen at the time of the call. Taking its estimates of re-imports from Costa Rica into account, the United States had proposed a specific limit (SL) of 1.25 million dozen to cover the portion of imports not qualifying for more favourable treatment that would have grown to 1,488,770 dozen in the final year of the three-year restraint period specified in the ATC. Re-imports had represented a significant portion of Costa Rica's total underwear exports to the United States. Accordingly, consistent with US policy and its obligation under Article 6.6(d) of the ATC to provide more favourable treatment to such re-imports, the United States had proposed a guaranteed access level (0GAL) of 20,000,000 dozen. Costa Rica did not make a counterproposal, but maintained that the request for consultations was unsubstantiated.

5.15   With respect to the first bilateral consultations, *Costa Rica* said that they had drawn attention to a series of inconsistencies, defects and omissions in the March Market Statement, raising numerous points with a view to questioning the compatibility of the Statement with the parameters established by Article 6 of the ATC and hence showing that the Statement could not serve as a basis for the imposition of a restriction.

5.16   *Costa Rica* also observed that the remedy being proposed by the United States (21.25 million dozen) consisted of an extra dose (30 per cent or more) of the level they claimed to be attacking (14.4 million dozen). Although 14.4 million dozen was supposed to be causing serious damage, the United States had proposed that trade be restricted to 21.52 million dozen. From that point on, a serious question had arisen as to the objective being pursued by the United States in their attempt to establish new restrictions: was it to protect the underwear manufacturers - by guaranteeing them a further increase in imports, or was it to benefit the US makers of the cloth used for manufacturing the product? Without having replied to any of the questions raised by Costa Rica in connection with the March Market Statement, on 22 June 1995 the United States had made a new proposal for the establishment of a quantitative restriction, this time offering 1.3 million dozen SL and 20 million GAL for the period from 1 January 1996 to 31 December 1996, with an increase of 6 per cent on the quota for subsequent periods. Again, Costa Rica rejected this proposal as the United States was still not complying with the requirements of the ATC for the application of a transitional safeguard.

B.   Review by the Textiles Monitoring Body

Determining Domestic Market Data

5.17   In its review (see paragraphs 2.15 to 2.18), the TMB members had inquired concerning double-counting in the data presented by the United States because in official US data, re-imports had appeared in both imports and production. Such double-counting had resulted in an overstatement of the size of the domestic market. The *United States* pointed out that the US Census Bureau counted domestic apparel production by collecting data on unassembled garment parts cut in the United States before they were assembled domestically or shipped offshore for assembly. As a result, Census statistics reflected re-imports as apparel which was cut in the US, sent outside the country to be sewn, and then returned under the tariff provision for re-imports as a finished garment. Re-imports were included as domestic output (cut parts), exports (unassembled cut parts), and imports (finished garments).

5.18   Since export quantity data were generally less reliable than import data, the domestic market for textile and apparel categories as derived by the United States for quota purposes, was: production + imports. As the TMB had requested export data, the United States was now defining the domestic market as: production + imports - exports. Consequently, the domestic market was overstated by the amount of the re-imported products, since re-imported products were counted as production (before assembled) and imports (when finished). In an attempt to remove the double-counting from the US market, the United States had subtracted the re-imports from domestic production. Costa Rica had claimed during the TMB proceeding that such overstatement should be resolved by deducting re-imports from import data instead of production data. However, as an exception the general rule, the Harmonized Tariff Schedule identified re-imported textile and apparel articles as foreign goods. Therefore, the re-imports were properly counted in import data. After adjusting for the overstatement of the size of the market, the US producers' share of the domestic market had fallen from 69 per cent in 1992 to 62 per cent in 1993 and to 55 per cent in 1994, a 14 percentage point drop in two years.

5.19   *Costa Rica* highlighted that in the case of imports of cut pieces for assembly in the United States, the United States Government had been treating the product as originating in the country in which the pieces were cut. Thus, for example, fabric cut in China and then assembled in Costa Rica had been treated as a product of China on entering the United States market. At the same time, the US Census Bureau considered that fabric cut, for example in Alabama for assembly in Costa Rica was United States domestic production. That was why "re-imports" were considered to be domestic production by that US statistical office and why the United States included them as such in its March Statement. However, it was also clear that the United States treated the same garments as "imports" when entered under heading 9802 of its tariff, for the purpose of collecting duty on the value added abroad and preventing the use of the "Made in the United States" label.

5.20   The *United States* also said that when the TMB had suggested later in the proceeding that the overstatement in the US domestic market should be adjusted by introducing US export data, they had pointed out to the TMB that the data derived from this formula would still be flawed because export data were generally less reliable than import data. Despite its concerns about the validity of the available export data, the United States had supplied the TMB with the requested export data. The introduction of export data had left the import/production ratio unchanged from the ratio in the March Market Statement, demonstrating the same picture of declining domestic production and surging imports. Data showing the value of exports had been first presented because of their greater reliability. Data in quantity terms had also been presented in a revised market calculation. The US producers' share of the domestic market had shown a drop from 70 per cent in 1992 to 63 per cent in 1993 and to 57 per cent in 1994, a 13 percentage point drop in two years.

5.21   *Costa Rica* recalled that they had asserted on numerous occasions that the requirements of "actual threat of serious damage" had not been evaluated in the March Statement, nor was it included in the publications in the Federal Register nor alleged by the United States in the first four proposals of restriction it presented to Costa Rica.

The July 1995 Market Statement

5.22   *Costa Rica* considered that the updated data presented by the US was not relevant information intended to develop the information contained in the March Market Statement but was information which openly and expressly contradicted it. The United States was endeavouring to submit completely revised and adjusted information in an attempt to justify the adoption of a restriction which it had already adopted. The introduction of a new statement at that point was unacceptable to Costa Rica inasmuch as the data and determinations contained in the March Market Statement had been those which had served to initiate the consultations, impose a unilateral restriction and provide the grounds for the review by the TMB.

5.23   The *United States* noted that they had supplied updated data and new relevant information at the July 1995 TMB proceeding. Although not required, these submissions had been provided to the TMB consistent with Article 6.10 of the ATC and as part of the practice of the CITA to bring the data up-to-date, to make them as consistent as possible with the reference period for the March 1995 Market Statement, and to provide further information demonstrating that the finding of serious damage, or actual threat thereof remained justified in light of the additional information continually becoming available. The CITA had based its determinations of serious damage, or actual threat thereof on publicly available information from official US Government sources. There was no need to independently verify this information. The production, import, and market share data on which cases were based were published quarterly by the OTEXA and available to all interested parties. The collection and analysis of this data were part of a longstanding process that had been in place for as long as there had been a comprehensive international textile trade agreement, i.e., since the MFA began in 1974.

5.24   The additional relevant information supplied at the time had concerned trade adjustment assistance for US companies adversely impacted by imports and import prices. All of the information provided at the time of the July TMB session had supported and was consistent with the March 1995 Market Statement and the basic justification for the United States safeguard action with respect to underwear imports from Costa Rica remained fully warranted.

5.25 *Costa Rica* pointed out that, in the July Market Statement there were 302 establishments in the United States that manufactured garments classified in category 352/652, whereas according to the March Market Statement the number of establishments was 395. The March and July Statements indicated that annual shipments had amounted to $3.2 billion, although the data on which it was based (domestic production and the US producers' average price) were not the same in the two Statements. According to the July Statement, in 1992 employment in the sector was 35,191, falling in 1994 to 33,309. According to the March Statement, employment in the sector was 46,377 in 1992, dropping to 44,056 in 1994. The July Statement did not explain why there should be this difference of about 10,000 between the figures given in the two Statements. Nor did the data for annual man-hours coincide, inasmuch as the July Statement gave a figure of 65.4 million in 1992 falling to 61.6 million in 1994, whereas the corresponding figures in the March Statement were 86.2 million and 81.5 million respectively.

5.26 *Costa Rica* also noted that the July Market Statement included a section on trade adjustment assistance for United States companies adversely impacted by imports, giving data on the current US federal programmes for assisting industries and workers that had been unfavourably impacted by imports. It was questioned how these programmes could be put forward as additional justification for imposing a quantitative restriction when their purpose was precisely to provide alternatives to the imposition of a restriction on imports. The fourth section of the July Statement which concerned the countries contributing to serious damage described the price difference between US underwear production and underwear production in other countries. It was noted that this section contained a discrepancy between the July and March Statements, namely whereas in March the average United States producers' price was said to be $30 per dozen, the July Statement indicated that that price varied between $16 and $20 per dozen, depending on where the product was assembled. No information had been given to explain the reason for such a substantial error in the March Statement.

5.27 The *United States* commented that Costa Rica was incorrect in its characterization of the Trade Adjustment Assistance programme as an "alternative" to safeguard action under the ATC. The United States had not created the programme to replace US rights and obligations under the ATC, Section 204, or similar actions under US law and the WTO. As regards the differences in price and other figures between the March and July Statements, the United States noted that even though there were differences in the updated data, the CITA's determination of serious damage or actual threat thereof was still sustainable.

Outcome of the TMB Review

5.28 At the conclusion of its examination, the TMB had decided that the United States had not demonstrated serious damage, but it could not reach consensus on the existence of actual threat of serious damage (G/TMB/R/2). As a result, the TMB had not reached the issue of attribution. The TMB had, however, recommended that the United States, Costa Rica and Honduras consult further,

> "with a view to arriving at a mutual understanding, bearing in mind the above, with due consideration to the particular features of this case, as well as equity considerations". (G/TMB/R/2)

5.29   According to *Costa Rica*, at the new round of consultations as recommended by the TMB, held on 17-18 August 1995, they had asked the United States to clarify the difference between serious damage and actual threat of serious damage and for relevant factual information in support of the latter. They had also urged the United States to explain why, having a market supposedly threatened by the importation of 14.4 million dozen garments from Costa Rica, they had proposed to establish a quantitative restriction which would allow imports of Costa Rican underwear to rise to 33 million dozen. The United States had not offered any explanation, at least at that meeting, which ended without a satisfactory solution having been reached. The two parties then submitted their reports to the TMB for review purposes.

5.30   *Costa Rica* also pointed out that in October 1995, the OTEXA had published new statistics for the category in question which showed the production situation to be different from that indicated in the March and July Statements. Whereas according to the March Statement production had declined by 4 per cent between 1992 and 1993 and by 4 per cent between 1993 and 1994, the July data indicated that the decline was 4 per cent for the first period and almost non-existent in the second, while according to the October information the percentage decreases were of the order of 1.5 per cent and 2.6 per cent respectively.

5.31   At its meeting on 16-20 October 1995, the TMB received reports from Costa Rica and the United States on the bilateral consultations they had held following the TMB recommendation. It took note of the reports and of the fact that the two parties had not reached a mutual understanding during the consultations. The TMB's discussions confirmed the Body's previous findings in this matter; there being no further requests by the parties involved, the TMB considered its review of the matter completed (G/TMB/R/5).

C.   The Standard of Review and Burden of Proof

Standard of Review - The "Fur Felt Hat" Case[2]

5.32   The *United States* considered that the appropriate standard to apply to the importing country's determination was a standard of reasonableness. Article 6 of the ATC referred to "a determination by a Member," based on weighing of evidence on certain factors. The standard for panel evaluation of such determinations should follow established GATT practice, which was based on the

---

[2]   Report on the Withdrawal by the United States of a Tariff Concession under Article XIX of the General Agreement on Tariffs and Trade Concerning Women's Fur Felt Hats and Hat Bodies, 27 March 1951 - CP/106.

GATT 1947 case concerning the withdrawal by the United States under Article XIX of a tariff concession on women's fur felt hats and hat bodies. In the Fur Felt Hat case, the Czechoslovak Government had sought a determination that the US invocation of Article XIX had been improper, and asserted that the United States had not met certain conditions under Article XIX to take the action, seeking revocation of the measure. The Working Party rejected the Czechoslovak argument and stated:

> "...it may be observed that the Working Party naturally could not have the facilities available to the United States authorities for examining interested parties and independent witnesses from the United States hat-making areas, and for forming judgements on the basis of such examination. Further, it is perhaps inevitable that governments should on occasion lend greater weight to the difficulties or fears of their domestic producers than would any international body, and that they may feel it necessary on social grounds, e.g. because of lack of alternative employment in the localities concerned, to afford a high degree of protection to individual industries which in terms of cost of production are not economic. Moreover, the United States is not called upon to prove conclusively that the degree of injury caused or threatened in this case must be regarded as serious; since the question under consideration is whether or not they are in breach of Article XIX, they are entitled to the benefit of any reasonable doubt" ("Fur Felt Hat" case, paragraph 30).

5.33   The *United States* recalled that the US action involved in the 1951 GATT working party Report had been taken under GATT Article XIX:1, which referred to the factual existence of increased imports under conditions

> "such ... as to cause or threaten serious injury to domestic producers ... of like or directly competitive products".

The legal standard, and the facts required to be found, were similar to those involved in the case of transitional safeguards under Article 6.2 of the ATC.

5.34   In October 1950, just before the Fifth Session of the CONTRACTING PARTIES, the United States had announced its intention to withdraw the concession in question under Article XIX. The US Government had entered into consultation with the contracting party with which the concessions had been negotiated and with several contracting parties having a substantial supplying interest. The following month, Czechoslovakia brought a complaint claiming that the action taken did not meet the criteria of Article XIX:1, and sought a determination by the CONTRACTING PARTIES that this action was inconsistent with Article XIX. The complaint was referred to a working party for study. The working party had examined separately each of the conditions for invocation of Article XIX, and presented a report in March 1951 which embodied the findings of the members other than the two parties to the dispute. This report was then adopted at the Sixth Session in 1951. The report had found that the United States had satisfied these conditions.

5.35   The *United States* suggested that the information used by the "Fur Felt Hat" working party as a basis for its conclusions should be noted, that is GATT notifications, summary records of discussions at the Fifth Session, some additional data submitted at the working party's request, and the report made by the US Tariff Commission in connection with its determination of serious injury. However, in examining whether serious injury and the other conditions in Article XIX:1 existed, the working party chose to rely mainly on the data in the Tariff Commission report. These data were not perfect; for instance, they failed to separate figures on production of men's and women's hat bodies. However, they were the data available at the point in time determined by the working party to be legally relevant in evaluating compliance with Article XIX. As the report stated:

> "Since the Working Party was required to consider whether the action taken by the United States in autumn 1950 fulfilled the requirements of Article XIX, the question here to be considered is whether serious injury or a threat thereof to the United States women's hat body industry could be considered to have existed at the time of the United States Tariff Commission investigation on which the United States action was based ...".

5.36   The working party then examined the data and found them inconclusive. It stated that:

> "... the United States is not called upon to prove conclusively that the degree of injury caused or threatened in this case must be regarded as serious; since the question under consideration is whether or not they are in breach of Article XIX, they are entitled to the benefit of any reasonable doubt. No facts have been advanced which provide any convincing evidence that it would be unreasonable to regard the adverse effects on the domestic industry concerned as a result of increased imports as amounting to serious injury of a threat thereof; and the facts as a whole certainly tend to show that some degree of adverse effect has been caused or threatened. It must be concluded, therefore, that the Czechoslovak Government has failed to establish that no serious injury has been sustained or threatened."

5.37   The working party members, excluding the two disputants, concluded that they were satisfied that the US authorities had investigated the matter thoroughly on the basis of the data available to them at the time of their inquiry, and had reached in good faith the conclusion that the proposed action fell within the terms of Article XIX. If the working party in its appraisal of the facts naturally gave weight to international factors, and the US authorities would normally give more weight to domestic factors, "it must be recognized that any view on such a matter must be to a certain extent a matter of economic judgment and that it is natural that governments should on occasion be greatly influenced by social factors, such as local employment problems. It would not be proper to regard the consequent withdrawal of a tariff concession as *ipso facto* contrary to Article XIX unless the weight attached by the government concerned to such factors was clearly unreasonably great".

Thus, the working party concluded that there was no conclusive evidence that the safeguard measure in question constituted a breach of obligations under the GATT.

Applying the "Fur Felt Hat" Case to the Present Case

5.38   The *United States* argued that the reasoning of the "Fur Felt Hat" case applied equally to the present case. Both the working party in that case and the present Panel have been charged with determining whether a safeguard action was properly taken at the time that the decision was made. In the case of Article XIX, the working party had examined the information collected by the Tariff Commission in the investigation which was the basis for the decision, and whether the Commission's evaluation of that information had been unreasonable. In the present case, the Panel had been asked to evaluate the consistency of the CITA determination under Article 6.2 of the ATC with the requirements of Articles 6.2 and 6.3 of the ATC. Article 6.2 of the ATC referred to certain facts to be demonstrated "on the basis of a determination by a Member" and Article 6.3 of the ATC required that certain analyses be carried out in making such a determination. Thus, in the view of the *United States* the focus of the Panel's examination should be not the question of whether serious damage or threat of serious damage exists now, but whether the CITA could reasonably determine that it existed at the time of the CITA determination in March 1995 and whether, after giving the CITA the benefit of any reasonable doubt, Costa Rica had established that no serious damage or threat thereof existed at that time.

5.39   The CITA determination could therefore only be evaluated on the basis of data existing at the time of its original determination. The data presented later to the TMB in fact corroborated the analysis done in March 1995, but they were not legally relevant in evaluating US conformity with Articles 6.2 and 6.3 of the ATC. Article 6.10 of the ATC provided for later refinement of data and for response to TMB requests for additional information, consistent with the TMB spirit of conciliation, compromise and negotiation. However, it was the March data that were legally relevant for evaluating the determination, not the later data. The data recorded in the March Market Statement formed the entire basis of the CITA's determination.

5.40   The data available in March need not have been perfect, as seen in the "Fur Felt Hat" case. Article 6 of the ATC was a safeguard provision invoked in cases of serious damage or threat to an industry, and could not be interpreted to require that the importing Member wait until its industry had succumbed because a complete census of the industry had not yet been conducted. Article 6.7 of the ATC recognized this fact by requiring only that the data submitted with the request for consultations must be "as up-to-date as possible".

5.41   In the present case the burden was on Costa Rica to bring forward evidence and arguments demonstrating a *prima facie* case that the United States had acted inconsistently with Articles 6.2 and 6.3 of the ATC. When evaluating the CITA's analysis of the data available to it in March 1995, the Panel should take into account that domestic authorities were uniquely well-placed to scrutinize and evaluate the situation in a domestic industry, and that the facts in the March Statement clearly indicated that there were adverse effects on the US underwear industry resulting from increased imports of underwear. The Panel should examine whether Costa Rica had advanced facts which provided convincing evidence that it was unreasonable for the CITA to determine that the adverse effects of increased underwear imports on the US domestic underwear industry amounted to serious damage, or actual threat thereof. A similar examination should be applied with respect to determinations under Article 6.4 of the ATC.

5.42   The *United States* considered that the "Fur Felt Hat" case was still relevant for purposes of the present dispute, even after the incorporation of the Agreement on Safeguards in the WTO Agreement. The Agreement on Safeguards provided for a package of rights and obligations differing from those under Article XIX of the GATT 1994. This package included new procedural and transparency requirements; additional obligations regarding the duration and review of safeguards measures; an explicit ban on grey area measures; and on the other hand, a ban on compensatory withdrawals under Article XIX:3 if the safeguard measure satisfied certain conditions. The standards for action provided in the Agreement also reflected a shift in focus incorporating the jurisprudence of the "Fur Felt Hat" case. While Article XIX itself referred to the existence of serious injury or threat, in the "Fur Felt Hat" case the working party had focused instead on the evidence found by the authorities in the importing country before their determination and the extent to which it had been shown that the authorities' evaluation of that evidence was unreasonable. The Agreement on Safeguards adopted this approach. Its standards were not phrased in terms of facts that the importing Member must prove (if necessary to a panel). Rather, they were phrased explicitly in terms of the investigation to be undertaken by the competent authorities in the importing country. For instance, Article 2.1 of the Agreement on Safeguards provided that:

> "A Member may apply a safeguard measure to a product only if that Member has determined, pursuant to the provisions set out below, that such product is being imported into its territory in such increased quantities, absolute or relative to domestic production, and under such conditions as to cause or threaten to cause serious injury to the domestic industry that produces like or directly competitive products."

Thus, the *United States* argued, a panel's evaluation of measures taken pursuant to the Agreement on Safeguards should follow the approach taken in the "Fur Felt Hat" case.

5.43   It was noted by the *United States* that the approach adopted in the "Fur Felt Hat" working party report had also been adopted in the Agreement on Safeguards because it had come to be widely accepted. In 1951 the "Fur Felt Hat" report was viewed as an important precedent, and it was agreed that, because of its value in relation to the interpretation of Article XIX of the General Agreement, the text of the report should be published. This working party report had become the accepted benchmark for panel evaluation of safeguards actions. No assertion was made that the approach adopted by that working party had been legally incorrect. Indeed, the general acquiescence to this standard, in spite of the many invocations of Article XIX:1 recorded in over 45 years of later GATT history, indicated that this approach had become customary law, or at the least,

> "subsequent practice in the application of the treaty which establishes the agreement of the parties regarding its interpretation",

in the sense of Article 31.3(b) of the Vienna Convention on the Law of Treaties.

5.44   The *United States* stated that they had not argued, and would not argue, that the regime now governing textile trade in the WTO was a *sui generis* regime. It was a safeguards regime just as the regime under Article XIX and the Agreement on Safeguards were safeguard regimes. Both regimes permitted a Member to restrict trade in fairly traded goods on the basis of a determination made by that Member, subject to certain limitations. The textile regime diverged from Article XIX but many of its basic concepts depended on the fundamental concepts behind Article XIX; like English and American law, the two were originally one, have diverged over time, but still shared fundamental concepts and structure. Where the negotiators had indicated their desire that the two regimes differ (for instance, concerning the selectivity of actions taken or the duration of safeguards once imposed), the difference in rights and obligations provided in the negotiated text must be respected. However, the "Fur Felt Hat" case, an accepted precedent which predated the divergence between the two regimes, was relevant and persuasive in interpreting the provisions in both, or either, of these regimes concerning the initial decision to take safeguards action.

5.45   The *United States* confirmed its argument that the standard of review appropriate for this case was the one enunciated in the "Fur Felt Hat" case. That is, the Panel should look to see whether the authority's determinations were reasonable in light of the requirements of the relevant agreement, in this case the ATC, and considering the data available at the time. The United States did not advocate *de novo* review. In response to the Panel's question, the United States said that if "adequately motivated" meant that the Panel was to explore the possible motives underlying the CITA's decision making process, the United States disagreed with such a standard of review. If "adequately motivated" meant that the Panel was to examine whether the domestic authorities had based their determination on an examination of factors required in the ATC, and whether the basis for the determination had been adequately explained, the United States would agree with this formulation as it was compatible with the standard of review in the "Fur Felt Hat" case, and the United States did not advocate a position on how the TMB's finding by consensus on serious damage should be treated by the Panel. It was only stated that the United States did not agree with the TMB's finding and the ATC, Article 8, did not require them to inform the TMB concerning their view on their finding. Instead, the ATC required that Members endeavour to comply with recommendations and inform the TMB if recommendations could not be accepted. In this case the TMB recommendation did not include a recommendation that they expressed a particular view on the TMB's consensus finding or the lack of consensus on threat.

Views of Costa Rica on Standard of Review

5.46   As regards the standard of review, *Costa Rica* recalled that the United States had proposed that the Panel should restrict itself, solely and exclusively, to verifying whether the United States had followed the procedures laid down in Article 6 of the ATC and to ruling that its determination was reasonable considering the information available at the time the determination was made. *Costa Rica* argued and requested the Panel to rule accordingly, that on this point the United States was wrong, since the standard of review which the Panel should apply was a very different one

5.47   In the view of *Costa Rica*, the standard of review applicable to this case, which must be based on the general principles of GATT law and the provisions of the DSU, required the Panel to undertake an analysis and monitor the following five aspects: compliance with the procedural rules; proper establishment of the facts; objective and impartial evaluation of the facts in the light of the rules of the ATC; proper exercise of discretion in interpretation of the rules; and compliance with the rules.

5.48   Although novel in the textile field, the standard of review to be applied by a panel, was not new in the context of the GATT dispute settlement mechanism nor in the context of many legal systems. Nor was it a question foreign to the WTO itself, since it had arisen in various WTO Agreements. Neither was it unknown to the jurisprudence which, although not very abundant, nevertheless threw useful light on the matter.

5.49   Firstly, *Costa Rica* noted that this subject had been dealt with on numerous occasions in the reports of various panels set up to review the consistency of a particular measure with the GATT rules, especially in the anti-dumping field. For example, in the case of the New Zealand transformers,[3] the Panel did not share the view expressed by New Zealand to the effect that the determination of

---

[3]   "New Zealand - Imports of Electrical Transformers from Finland", BISD 32S/67, paragraph 4.4.

"material injury" could not be challenged or scrutinized by other contracting parties nor indeed by the CONTRACTING PARTIES themselves. In support of its ruling, the Panel pointed out that:

> "To conclude otherwise would give governments complete freedom and unrestricted discretion in deciding anti-dumping cases without any possibility to review the action taken in the GATT. This would lead to an unacceptable situation under the aspect of law and order in international trade relations as governed by the GATT."

5.50   Thus, the first thing that *Costa Rica* noted was that the GATT jurisprudence on this particular point had not been uniform over the course of time and in relation to different subjects. It followed that the above-mentioned "Fur Felt Hat" case could not be regarded as a leading case in this field which ought necessarily to be followed by subsequent panels. The second argument was based on a general principle of GATT law according to which, in the absence of an express rule to the contrary, it was not possible to assume any limitation on the standard of review. This principle was clearly expressed in Article 11 of the DSU, according to which:

> "The function of panels is to assist the DSB in discharging its responsibilities under this Understanding and the covered agreements. Accordingly, a panel should make an objective assessment of the matter before it, including an ob jective assessment of the facts of the case and the applicability of and conformity with the relevant covered agreements, and make such other findings as will assist the DSB in making the recommendations or in giving the rulings provided for in the covered agreements...".

5.51   At the same time, according to Article 3.2 of the DSU, the essential functions of the WTO's dispute settlement system - and, consequently, of the DSB - were:

> "... to preserve the rights and obligations of Members under the covered agreements, and ... to clarify the existing provisions of those agreements in accordance with customary rules of interpretation of public international law ...".

5.52   On the basis of these provisions, in *Costa Rica*'s view, in order properly to perform its task of preserving the rights and obligations of Members and clarifying the existing provisions of the WTO Agreements, the DSB must require that the work of panels not be subjected to *a priori* limitations, based on a putative restriction on its powers of review in a particular case.

5.53   With reference to Costa Rica's argument that the reference to objective assessment in Article 11 of the DSU required that panels' scope of review not be limited, the *United States* pointed out that they had not argued that panels could not review Article 6 determinations by domestic authorities; they had simply argued that these determinations should be accorded the proper weight. It should also be noted that this reference to "objective assessment" and to making findings in DSU Article 11 did not represent a policy-making initiative in the Uruguay Round, but it was the wholesale incorporation of paragraph 16 of the 1979 GATT Understanding Regarding Notification, Consultation, Dispute Settlement and Surveillance. As the drafters of the DSU had sought to make the review a comprehensive text incorporating all prior codification efforts on dispute settlement, the GATT Contracting Parties had intended the 1979 Understanding and its annex to reflect customary practice and improvements in that practice, which included the standard of review in the "Fur Felt Hat" case.

5.54   *Costa Rica* pointed out that in the case of the Agreement on Safeguards and the ATC there was no explicit (or implicit) provision establishing limitations on a panel's freedom of review, which was why the above-mentioned general principle should be applied. Where anti-dumping was concerned, the situation was different. Given the actual existence of Article 17.6 of the Agreement on Implementation of Article VI of the GATT 1994 (hereinafter the "Anti-Dumping Agreement"), according to which, in examining the matter submitted to it, the Panel:

> "(i)   in its assessment of the facts of the matter, shall determine whether the authorities' establishment of the facts was proper and whether their evaluation of those facts was unbiased and objective. If the establishment of the facts was proper and the evaluation was unbiased and objective, even though the Panel might have reached a different conclusion, the evaluation shall not be overturned;
>
> (ii)   shall interpret the relevant provisions of the Agreement in accordance with customary rules of interpretation of public international law. Where the Panel finds that a relevant provision of the Agreement admits of more than one permissible interpretation, the Panel shall find the authorities' measure to be in conformity with the Agreement if its rests upon one of those permissible interpretations."

Views of Authors Relating to Standard of Review

5.55   *Costa Rica* referred to this provision and the history of its negotiation, and noted that the authors Croley and Jackson had pointed out that the aim of those behind the drafting of this Article had been to establish limits on the standard of review which could be applied by a WTO panel, for which purpose they had based themselves on the jurisprudence of United States administrative law.[4] The idea was to establish an express rule mainly for the purpose of introducing limitations, in the specific case of anti-dumping matters, on the general principle mentioned above.

5.56   The *United States* considered the above-cited article by Croley and Jackson to be largely irrelevant to the work of this Panel as it focused almost entirely on specific provisions of a different agreement outside the Panel's terms of reference, the Anti-Dumping Agreement. They nevertheless noted in examining this article that it too recognized the importance of the "Fur Felt Hat" case in GATT law,[5] and referred to other GATT cases recognizing a restrained standard of review.[6] They had also noted that the authors, in their conclusions, overall had recommended caution on the part of WTO panels, arguing that:

> "... panels should also recognize that national governments often have legitimate reasons for the decisions they take. At times for example such governments can justifiably argue that an appropriate allocation of power should tilt in favour of the national governments that are closest to the constituencies most affected by a given decision."[7]

Relationship to Other GATT Provisions

5.57   In the view of *Costa Rica*, these authors had clearly explained how it followed unequivocally from the Decision on Review of Article 17.6 of the Anti-Dumping Agreement and the Declaration on Dispute Settlement Pursuant to the Agreement on Implementation of Article VI of the GATT 1994 or Part V of the Agreement on Subsidies and Countervailing Measures that this limited standard of review was applicable solely to the review of anti-dumping measures. It was important to make this clear as it provided a useful guide to defining what should be the standard of review in a case in which what was being scrutinized was the consistency of a clothing trade restriction with the requirements of Article VI. As already pointed out, the limitation on the standard of review in anti-dumping matters operated solely and exclusively in that field and, in that respect, must be regarded as an exception to the general rule outlined above.

5.58   *Costa Rica* argued that, in view of the above, it was not possible to accept a standard of review which would be just as restricted or even more restricted

---

[4]   Steven P. Croley and John H. Jackson, "WTO Dispute Procedures, Standard of Review, and Deference to National Governments", in *American Journal of International Law*, Vol. 90, No. 2, April 1996, page 199.

[5]   Croley and Jackson, *op. cit.* page 196.

[6]   Citations include "United States - Restrictions on Imports of Tuna", DS29/R, paragraph 3.73; "United States -Imposition of Anti-Dumping Duties on Imports of Fresh and Chilled Atlantic Salmon from Norway", ADP/87, paragraph 232; "United States - Imposition of Countervailing Duties on Imports of Fresh and Chilled Atlantic Salmon from Norway", SCM/153, paragraphs 209-212.

[7]   Croley and Jackson, pages 212-213.

than that established in Article 17.6 of the Anti-Dumping Agreement when a panel scrutinized matters other than those covered by that Agreement, as the United States insisted. In fact, in the present case the United States wanted the standard of review to consist in verifying that the procedures established in Article 6 of the ATC were followed and ruling that the determination by the United States was reasonable, which was even more limited than the obligation imposed upon any panel under the above-mentioned Article 17.6 of the Anti-Dumping Agreement. This interpretation was not acceptable. The standard of review of this Panel was and must be much broader than that proposed by the United States and that which Article 17.6 of the Anti-Dumping Agreement established for the review of anti-dumping measures.

5.59   The *United States* noted the various GATT cases concerning anti-dumping determinations, which Costa Rica had cited. In the US view, however, this was not an anti-dumping case. An interpretation of the GATT or the Agreement on the Implementation of Article VI was clearly outside of the scope of the terms of reference of the Panel. In any event, the US had never argued that an importing Member was not required to carry out an investigation and carefully examine the facts before making its Article 6.2 of the ATC determinations under Articles 6.2 and 6.4 of the ATC. The US had also never argued that the determinations were exempt from Panel review. The US authorities had carried out a careful investigation, the results of which appeared in the March Market Statement annexed to their first submission. In that submission, they had established the facts of the case by going through the March Statement and pointing out systematically how the CITA had met the requirements of Article 6 of the ATC. They had simply argued that the expertise of US authorities and the findings in the investigation should be accorded an appropriate weight or margin of appreciation. This would also be consistent with the transitional nature of the ATC and the role of the TMB in monitoring measures taken while textile and apparel trade was integrated into the GATT 1994 and other Annex 1A Agreements.

5.60   Furthermore, according to the   *United States*, Costa Rica's reference to anti-dumping cases was also irrelevant because in an anti-dumping case before a WTO panel, Article 17.6 of the Anti-Dumping Agreement superseded panel reports under GATT Article VI. Even in the "Transformers" case cited by Costa Rica, the Panel had recognized the appropriateness in the context of deferring to factual expertise of domestic investigating authorities:

> "The Panel ... considered the evidence put forward by both sides as to the appropriateness of the cost elements used by the New Zealand authorities in arriving at their decision that dumping had occurred. The Panel noted that this evidence was of a highly technical nature, especially because it related to complicated custom-built products. It also noted that Article VI did not contain any specific guidelines for the calculation of cost-of-production and considered that the method used in this particular case appeared to be a reasonable one. In view of this and having noted the arguments of

> both sides ... the Panel considered that there was no basis on which to disagree with the New Zealand authorities' finding of dumping ...".[8]

5.61   *Costa Rica* argued that in order to define this standard of review for the specific case in question, it was important to bear in mind various considerations. Firstly, effective compliance with the substantive requirements of the ATC for the adoption of a transitional safeguard could not be achieved without the certainty that the full extent of the determinations of the importing Member was open to review. Without such a guarantee there was very little incentive for an importing Member to comply with the basic rules of the Agreement which, in practice, meant a return to the situation that existed in the textiles and clothing trade before the Uruguay Round. It was important to note the increasing legalization of the dispute settlement system, firstly of the GATT and now of the WTO, with the aim of raising legal standards. It was not for nothing that Article 8 and Article 14 of the Agreement on Safeguards subjected the measures adopted to their review procedures, in accordance with the rules of the above-mentioned dispute settlement mechanism.

Deference to National Authorities

5.62   *Costa Rica* recognized that although the national authorities could usually count on having access to most of the factual information needed to carry out an effective investigation, for example for the purpose of determining whether a domestic industry had suffered serious damage, it was also clear that those same national authorities could become a hostage to the local forces of protectionism so that they were prevented from carrying out the investigation properly or interpreting and applying the rules of the agreement in question to the best effect. In this connection, for example, Meier wrote that for deference to be paid to the decisions of a national body:

> "... there should be agreement that the national body be independent of government, that all interests be given due consideration, and that the national procedure of enquiry be similar to that followed by the United States International Trade Commission".[9]

Pursuing this question further, Meier expresses the opinion that Article XIX of the GATT should be revised in order to incorporate two key principles:

> "(i) that the determination of conditions on which the executive is called to take action be entrusted to a statutory

---

[8]   L/5814, adopted on 18 July 1985, BISD 32S/55, 67, paragraph 4.3.

[9]   Gerald M. Meier, "Externality Law and Market Safeguards: Applications in the GATT Multilateral Trade Negotiations", in *Harvard International Law Journal*, Volume 18, Number 3, Summer 1977, footnote 10, page 510.

> body whose term of office should not be coextensive with
> that of the executive, and (ii) that, after a preliminary inves-
> tigation by its own specialized personnel, this body should
> hold public hearings in which all interested parties, includ-
> ing the foreign firms, could be represented and not only pre-
> sent their views but also cross-examine each other within an
> adversary procedure".[10]

5.63   *Costa Rica* considered that the national body entrusted with applying the
transitional safeguard in the United States, CITA in no way resembled that described by Meier and neither did the procedure it used to arrive at its determination bear any resemblance to that recommended for enabling the decisions of the
national body to be held in greater respect. Accordingly, at least in connection
with the review of a determination to apply a transitional safeguard, this argument should not carry much weight with the Panel. Finally, the reasons for
adopting a restrictive standard of review in the domestic administrative law of
some countries, for example the United States, not only could not be transposed
to the context of the WTO but, in many cases, if so transposed, would produce
the opposite effect.

5.64   In the view of the *United States*, the points Costa Rica had cited from the
article by Meier were wrong or peculiar. The Uruguay Round negotiators appeared in practice to have overruled Meier as they negotiated an original Agreement on Safeguards which facilitates access to Article XIX while barring grey-
area measures. Moreover Costa Rica had urged that the Panel adopt proposals by
Meier in 1977 for revision of Article XIX, which amounted to requiring that all
governments install an imitation of the US international trade commission. The
Uruguay Round negotiators had rejected this point as well. The WTO Agreements do not regulate the separation of powers or delegation of authority by governments to domestic institutions of any WTO Member. US law happens to separate the authority for the implementation of safeguards taken on textiles and
clothing purposes and that for safeguards under Article XIX. It would be inappropriate, and legally unsupported to impose a model on any government as a
matter of its WTO obligations or to accord that model a legally privileged position as argued by Costa Rica. The notifications made to the WTO concerning
national safeguard systems clearly showed great diversity in trade policy making
and implementation, a diversity which the WTO has not only tolerated but welcomed. In any event, the determination of serious damage or actual threat thereof
made by the US authorities in this case must be evaluated not against one academic proposal, but against the law and practice of the ATC.

---

[10]   Gerald M. Meier, "Externality Law and Market Safeguards: Applications in the GATT Multilateral Trade Negotiations", in *Harvard International Law Journal*, Volume 18, Number 3, Summer 1977, page 515.

5.65   On the basis of the above, even if a high degree of deference was paid to the decision taken by the national authorities, *Costa Rica* was of the opinion that the standard of review applicable in this case required the Panel to scrutinize and verify the following aspects:

(i)   Compliance with the procedural rules: this meant formally confirming not only that all the steps in the process of applying the transitional safeguard followed each other chronologically - as the United States would have it - but also that each of these procedural rules was actually complied with. In this connection, the utmost importance attached to the obligation upon the importing Member to bring evidence, as already indicated, and, above all, the effective fulfilment of that obligation through the submission of specific and relevant information, as required by the ATC, and the proper scrutiny of that information in relation to the parameters of the Agreement, as Costa Rica had previously pointed out. This same aspect also included the obligation upon the importing Member to establish, at the time of making the determination, whether the test of serious damage or actual threat of serious damage had been applied, as well as the obligation to hold consultations with the exporting Member on the basis of the premises on which the case was founded.

(ii)   The proper establishment of the facts: from this aspect, the Panel should confirm that, on the basis of the specific and relevant information submitted, a detailed examination had been carried out, thereby enabling the facts to be properly established. From this it followed that there must be a reliable and logical correlation between the information in question and its examination, on the one hand, and between the latter and the establishment of the facts, on the other. This meant, *inter alia*, properly justifying each of the facts established and, conversely, that it was not possible to establish facts which had not been duly justified. With this in mind, for example, it was not possible in the view of *Costa Rica* to accept that the United States had demonstrated the existence of problems affecting employment, sales and profits, investment or capacity in its industry, inasmuch as these facts had not been properly substantiated, having been established on the basis of the evidence of only one or two enterprises. Nor was it possible to accept that the data on imports, domestic production and market size resulted in the establishment of the facts adduced by the United States, considering the problem created in this particular case by the fact that "807 trade" was counted twice, not to mention the total absence of analysis of this question within the underwear trade.

(iii)   The objective and impartial evaluation of the facts in the light of the rules of the ATC: the Panel must determine whether the facts had been objectively and impartially evaluated by the national body within the framework of the rules of the ATC. Accordingly, the Panel must verify that the process of subsumption of the facts in the legal arguments provided for by the rules had proceeded logically and naturally, without distorting the evaluation of the facts or involving errors of judgement or abuse of power which might have led to a result different from that which could have been anticipated under conditions of objectivity and impartiality. Thus, for example, it was impossible to conclude that the establishment of an SL quota below the call level could constitute the more favourable treatment for re-imports envisaged in Article 6.6(d) of the ATC.

(iv)   The proper exercise of discretion in the interpretation of the rules: when it became necessary to interpret a rule of the ATC, the national body may not assume unlimited powers of discretion, inasmuch as the ATC itself imposed limits which must be respected. Thus, as *Costa Rica* had already pointed, the principles underlying the adoption of a transitional safeguard were clearly established in Article 6.1 of the ATC, according to which the safeguard should be applied,

"as sparingly as possible, consistently with the provisions of this Article and the effective implementaltion of the integration process under this Agreement".

Given these limits, the rules could not be understood, for example, to mean that the ATC authorized the retroactive imposition of a safeguard measure.

(v)   Compliance with the rules: finally, the Panel must make sure that, despite having complied with the requirements mentioned above, the importing Member had not infringed the ATC in some other way.

5.66   Only a case which survived the scrutiny of a Panel on the basis of the above standard of review could be considered consistent with the ATC. In the case in question, it had already been amply shown that the restriction adopted by the United States on this occasion could not survive scrutiny of this kind, which was why Costa Rica had requested the Panel to rule that it be withdrawn.

Burden of Proof

5.67   Recalling that the measures at issue were taken as an invocation of the multilaterally-agreed safeguard provisions set forth in Article 6 of the ATC, the *United States* argued that, consistent with accepted GATT dispute settlement practice that had been carried over in the WTO, the burden was on Costa Rica in the first instance to demonstrate that United States actions were inconsistent with the ATC. The burden was not on the United States to re-demonstrate that its actions were justified. It was considered that the United States had presented ample material in the TMB justifying the safeguard measure, and they were prepared to refute the claims that Costa Rica had made; however, the Panel should first determine whether Costa Rica had indeed brought forward factual information and legal arguments substantiating its case, which, in their view, Costa Rica had not done.

5.68   *Costa Rica* argued that this particular conclusion by the United States was wrong, since the burden of proof in a dispute settlement proceeding under the DSU for the purpose of determining the consistency of a clothing trade restriction with Article 6 of the ATC fell upon the importing Member which had adopted the restriction. This followed from the ATC, since Article 6.2 of the ATC expressly stated that the importing Member must demonstrate the fulfilment of the basic requirements which must be satisfied before a transitional safeguard can be adopted. Accordingly, the importing Member must show or prove that the actual situation against which it would protect itself fully satisfied the basic requirements. The importing Member had two obligations to fulfil: firstly, they must submit specific and relevant factual information in support of their claim and, secondly, review the factors listed in Article 6 and show how their case fitted within the substantive criteria established by the ATC as prerequisites for the adoption of a special transitional safeguard.

5.69   In the view of *Costa Rica*, the importing Member had an obligation to demonstrate the satisfaction of these requirements not only to the exporting Member during the consultations but also to the TMB and, where appropriate, to the Panel. In accordance with Articles 6.7, 6.9 and 6.10 of the ATC, it was clear that the importing Member must demonstrate its compliance with the basic requirements of the ATC to the TMB. In the case in question the TMB had ruled that "the existence of serious damage had not been demonstrated" and "did not reach consensus on the existence of actual threat of serious damage". From this it clearly followed that the burden of proof *vis-à-vis* the TMB fell upon the importing Member, who must demonstrate the existence of the conditions laid down by the ATC. The importing Member was also obliged to demonstrate the existence of damage in a dispute settlement proceeding under the DSU, since logic forbid that, in this stage, suddenly and for no reason, the burden of proof should be reversed, requiring the exporting Member to demonstrate that the basic requirements of the ATC had not been fulfilled by the importing Member. To proceed in this way would be to establish a presumption in favour of the latter, in the sense that any restriction on the textile and clothing trade adopted by a Member would have to be assumed to be consistent with Article 6 of the ATC unless the exporting Member could prove otherwise. It was clear that such a rule would make completely pointless the existence of the substantive requirements established by the ATC to ensure that the special transitional safeguard remained an emergency measure and did not become the general rule. There was no reason to "reward" a Member which was unable to demonstrate its case to the TMB by relieving this burden of proof. Moreover, establishing a presumption in favour of the importing Member even against the ruling of the TMB did not make sense, since that would imply depriving the TMB of any role in the supervision of the operation of the ATC.

5.70   *Costa Rica* pointed out that the United States was justifying its position on the basis of a single case, whose findings should not be taken into consideration by the Panel since, in their view, they were wrong. They stressed that no other panel, from 1951 up to today, had based its findings on that case. It was also important to note that panels set up in other cases, in particular where anti-dumping measures were concerned, had treated the question of the burden of proof very differently. For example, when Finland requested a review of its dispute with New Zealand over an anti-dumping proceeding initiated against shipments of electrical transformers from a Finnish company to a local power company in New Zealand (see also paragraph 5.49), the panel had shared the view expressed by the panel on complaints set up to examine a complaint against anti-dumping duties applied by Sweden (BISD, 3S/81) to the effect that:

> "it was clear from the wording of Article VI (of the GATT) that no anti-dumping duties should be levied until certain facts had been established. As this represented an obligation on the part of the contracting party imposing such duties, it would be reasonable to expect that that contracting party should establish the existence of these facts when its action is challenged."

The report of that Panel did no more than recognize what was a general principle of GATT law, according to which the burden of proof fell upon the Member which invoked Article VI or Article XIX of the General Agreement. In this respect, the principle was clearly laid down in Articles 3 and 11 of the Agreement on Safeguards, according to which it was the importing Member which, in accordance with a series of pre-established procedures, must demonstrate compliance with the basic requirements in order to be able to proceed with the adoption of a safeguard measure. As the principle was of general application, it should also govern the adoption of a special transitional safeguard under the ATC, especially as Article 6.2 of the ATC itself was clearly based on the same principle.

5.71   The *United States* failed to see the relevance of the Costa Rican arguments that legal duties under the ATC flowed from a general principle of GATT law; that the burden of proof fell on the member which invoked GATT Articles VI or XIX; or that since a Member invoking safeguard action under Article XIX must establish certain facts under Articles 3 and 11 of the Agreement on Safeguards, that principle should govern transitional safeguards under the ATC. Interpretation of the GATT or the Safeguard Agreement was beyond the Panel's terms of reference. Moreover since the US had not yet integrated the apparel categories in question, neither the GATT nor the Safeguards Agreement applied in this case. Even if Articles 3 and 11 of the Safeguards Agreement applied here, their provisions only required that the importing country conduct an investigation, provide due process to interested parties and publish a report. In particular there was nothing in either of these articles that shifted the burden of proof in WTO Dispute Settlement to the importing Member.

5.72   *Costa Rica* noted that various authors had very sharply criticised the report on the "Fur Felt Hat" case. Thus, for example, Meier wrote:

> "In the United States withdrawal case (Hatters' Fur case), for example, the working party held that the invoking party (United States) was 'entitled to the benefit of any reasonable doubt' and that the complainant (Czechoslovakia) 'has failed to establish that no serious injury has been sustained or threatened'. This has made it difficult to maintain the substantive requirements with respect to causation of 'injury', and it has made access to Article XIX freer than it should be. This procedural rule should be revised to require the invoking party to go forward with the burden of proof of 'serious injury'."[11]

5.73   Commenting on the same case, Dam pointed out that:

> "Whatever distinctions may be made between the burden of coming forward with evidence and the burden of convincing the working party, it is clear that the effect of this procedural rule is to permit much freer access to Article XIX relief than might appear possible from the language of that article ...".[12]

5.74   *Costa Rica* suggested that the Panel should take this opportunity to correct the approach taken in the case cited by the United States and proceed on the basis of the considerations previously advanced to establish clearly that the burden of proof in this case rests upon the United States, which must demonstrate to the satisfaction of the Panel that it has complied with the requirements laid down by the ATC for the adoption of a transitional safeguard.

5.75   The *United States* noted that Article 3.1 of the DSU affirmed Members' adherence to the principle in Article XVI:1 of the Agreement Establishing the WTO that Members must be guided by the decisions, procedures and customary practices of the GATT 1947 and that such practice included findings and recommendations of the "Fur Felt Hat" working party. Therefore, the United States suggested that the Panel refrain from intervening, as requested by Costa Rica, to alter the established practice.

---

[11]   Meier, *op. cit.*, page 516.
[12]   Kenneth W. Dam, *The GATT Law and International Economic Organization*, The University of Chicago Press, Chicago and London, 1970, page 103.

D.   Article 6 of the ATC: General Views on its Application

5.76   *Costa Rica* argued that the United States had failed to comply with the principles applicable to the adoption of a safeguard measure under Article 6 of the ATC. Article 6.1 of the ATC established two principles that must guide the application of any safeguard to be adopted under the said provision. Firstly, "The transitional safeguard should be applied as sparingly as possible ...". This principle of sparing application of the measure carried an obligation of tempering or adjusting safeguard action prudently or sensitively, avoiding excess. It imposed an obligation to be as scrupulous as possible when seeking to establish new restrictions. Failure to comply with this principle would hinder or might even altogether prevent attainment of the objective of further liberalization of trade in textiles and clothing. Secondly, Article 6.1 of the ATC went on to say that the transitional safeguard should be applied. "... consistently with the provisions of this Article and the effective implementation of the integration process under this Agreement".

5.77   *Costa Rica* further argued that in accordance with this second principle, it was clear, firstly, that any Member wishing to use this mechanism had an obligation to comply with the provisions established by the Article for this purpose, and secondly, that the application of the measure must be guided by the final objective of the ATC which was the full integration of textiles and clothing into the GATT rules. When considering these two principles together, it was clear that Article 6 of the ATC sought to prevent the arbitrary and/or unjustified use of the transitional safeguard, by imposing on all Members a reference framework to which the application of any safeguard measure was subject and against which the adoption of every safeguard must be measured. The imposition of the unilateral restriction by the United States on trade from Costa Rica in the category under consideration had infringed Article 6.1 of the ATC because it was an arbitrary and unjustified action that did not comply with the provisions of this Article.

5.78   The *United States* commented that Costa Rica's argument consistently depended on the assumption that the ATC integration process must be read into Article 6 so as to accelerate the pace of integration. This was not the case. It was clear in the ATC that integration was an independently determined process, and that Article 6 applied only to products not yet integrated.

5.79   The *United States* noted that both parties to the dispute had agreed that the ATC was the only relevant agreement in this case. In its view, it was clear from the structure of the ATC, Article 6 in particular, and the express direction of Article 3.2 of the DSU, that the Panel's report,

> "cannot add to or diminish the rights and obligations provided in the covered agreements".

Accordingly, where the negotiators of the ATC had failed to agree on certain provisions or otherwise had chosen not to address them in the ATC, the Panel must refrain from appearing to create such obligations. Article 6 of the ATC emphasized that it was the importing Member that made the determination based on the "relevant factual information, as up-to-date as possible" and "information ... related, as closely as possible, to identifiable segments of production and to the reference period set out in paragraph 8" of Article 6 of the ATC.

5.80   Accordingly, when examining conformity with the relevant procedures of Article 6 of the ATC, the *United States* argued that the Panel should seek only to determine whether the investigating authority had followed the procedures in Article 6 of the ATC and whether based on data available, the investigating authority had acted reasonably (see Standard of Review in Section C). The substantive standard for making safeguard determinations for textiles and clothing not yet integrated into GATT 1994 was provided for in the ATC and was substantially, as Costa Rica admitted in its submission, the same as that existing under Article 3 of the Multifibre Arrangement (MFA).

5.81   The *United States* further argued that Article 6 of the ATC was not the same as other trade remedy provisions with respect to substantive standards. The above-mentioned articles were the relevant provisions to be considered by the Panel in its review. These provisions contained the universe of factors and procedures to be followed by Members taking safeguard action. Article 6 of the ATC did not include more detailed procedures for investigation, nor did it provide more specific definitions to interpret the standard of law to be applied. This omission was a deliberate choice by the Uruguay Round negotiators who in other contexts, such as the Agreement on Safeguards or the Agreement on Subsidies and Countervailing Measures, were capable of providing detailed standards and procedures.

5.82   In the *United States'* view, the appropriate standard to apply to the importing country's determination was a standard of reasonableness. Article 6 of the ATC referred to "a determination by a Member," based on weighing of evidence on certain factors. The standard for panel evaluation of such determinations should follow established GATT practice, which was based on the 1951 "Fur Felt Hat" case (see Section C).

5.83   The *United States* argued that although the quantum of injury required to be demonstrated under Article XIX was greater than that under the ATC Article 6, the fundamental process for weighing information was the same. The Panel must determine whether based on the information available, the US determination was made in good faith application of and, was therefore, consistent with Article 6 of the ATC.

E.   Requirements for the Application of a Safeguard Measure

5.84   *Costa Rica* argued that the United States had not fulfilled the specific requirements for the adoption of a transitional safeguard measure. Such action required a demonstration of the existence of a number of substantive elements laid down by Article 6 of the ATC itself. Thus, in accordance with paragraphs 2 and 4 of that Article, two stages may be distinguished, with their corresponding substantive requirements, that must be strictly fulfilled in order to be able to impose such a measure. In a first stage, it was necessary to demonstrate the existence of the substantive prerequisites for the importing Member to be entitled to have recourse to a transitional safeguard. Thus, Article 6.2 of the ATC provided:

> "Safeguard action may be taken under this Article when, on the basis of a determination by a Member, it is demonstrated that a particular product is being imported into its territory in such increased quantities as to cause serious damage, or actual threat thereof, to the domestic industry producing like and/or directly competitive products ...".

5.85   The *United States* argued that the CITA had followed all of the procedures required under Article 6 of the ATC in making its serious damage, or actual threat thereof, determination.

Determination of Serious Damage or Actual Threat Thereof

5.86   In the view of *Costa Rica*, Article 6.2 of the ATC established three requirements that must be fulfilled and were the prerequisites for being able to impose a specific safeguard, namely: (a) an increase in total imports of a particular product, regardless of their origin; (b) serious damage or actual threat thereof to the domestic industry producing like and/or directly competitive products; and (c) a causal relationship between the increase in total imports and the existence of the serious damage or actual threat of serious damage.

5.87   The establishment of these three requirements, which were developed in detail in paragraphs 2 and 3 of Article 6 of the ATC, was not new in foreign trade law, as in one way or another they were the conditions laid down by Article XIX of GATT 1994 and by the WTO Agreement on Safeguards for the imposition of a safeguard measure. Broadly speaking, the idea was that these measures were by definition an exception to the rule of free trade. Furthermore, since what they were intended to restrict was fair trade and not unfair trade, such measures must comply with a number of strict requirements so as to be able to "justify" departing from the principles of free trade. The fact that the ATC had established a specific safeguard mechanism for use during the transition period did not deprive it of the intrinsic nature or philosophy of any safeguard mechanism, and in particular its character of being a temporary exception to free trade based on strict fulfilment of a number of requirements. Indeed, in so far as the transitional safeguard provided for by the ATC did not require compensation, its application must be strictly subject to the substantive criteria laid down by the ATC, and this must be judged very rigorously.

5.88   The *United States* noted that the ATC transitional safeguard departed from the GATT Article XIX requirement that the safeguard be applied on a non-discriminatory basis and that compensation must be provided. The safeguard standard was serious damage, or actual threat thereof. Under the ATC, Members must first determine that a product such as, in this case, underwear, was being imported in such increased quantities as to cause serious damage or actual threat thereof to their domestic industry producing like or directly competitive products. Article 6.2 of the ATC provided that:

> "safeguard action may be taken under this Article when, on the basis of a determination by a Member,[footnote omitted] it is demonstrated that a particular product is being imported into its territory in such increased quantities as to cause serious damage, or actual threat thereof, to the domestic industry producing like and/or directly competitive products. Serious damage or actual threat thereof must demonstrably be caused by such increased quantities in total imports of that product and not by such other factors as technological changes or changes in consumer preferences."

5.89   *Costa Rica* submitted that to have the right to take safeguard action, the importing Member must fulfil the requirements established for this purpose in Article 6.2 of the ATC as developed in detail in that Article and in Article 6.3 of the ATC. Article 6.2 of the ATC obliged an importing Member to demonstrate that the substantive requirements had been met before imposing a transitional safeguard. This demonstration procedure required the Member to submit specific and relevant information on the facts giving rise to its claim and to make the required examination of this information in relation to the parameters of the Agreement. This information, together with the corresponding analysis, must be submitted at the correct time, namely the time the importing Member determines the state of the market, so that the exporting Member can exercise their right of defence. Any failure to observe the provisions could not be remedied by the subsequent submission of information (the July or October Statements) since, the information that was legally relevant for the purpose of analysing conformity of the measure with the ATC was that contained in the March Statement. The exhaustion of this first stage, with the fulfilment of each and every one of its requirements, was a *sine qua non* condition for acquiring what might be called a "generic" entitlement to the use of a specific safeguard measure, which may only be particularized or materialized against a specific Member when the second stage of the process had also been fulfilled. The United States had not fulfilled its obligation to demonstrate the existence of the substantive factors that were part of this first stage, and thus had failed to fulfil the requirements laid down in Articles 6.2 and 6.3 of the ATC.

5.90   The *United States* pointed out that Article 6.3 of the ATC required that in making a determination of serious damage, or actual threat thereof, a Member

> "shall examine the effect of those imports on the state of the particular industry, as reflected in changes in such relevant economic variables as output, productivity, utilization of capacity, inventories, market share, exports, wages, employment, domestic prices, profits and investment; none of which, either alone or combined with other factors, can necessarily give decisive guidance."

This text required that a Member seriously examine the effects of imports on the industry as reflected in changes in economic data on that industry. However, it did not require that the importing Member examine only the listed variables, or all the listed variables. It only required that the importing Member examine variables such as those listed. CITA had in fact examined many variables including those listed as relevant in Article 6.3 of the ATC. The March Market Statement noted that CITA had examined production, market share, imports, employment, profits, investment, sales, capacity, prices and manhours. All of the information provided in the March Market Statement contained all the substantive economic information on which CITA's decision had been based. While Costa Rica had pointed in particular to exports, exports were only one variable of a long list in Article 6.3 of the ATC and as that Article stipulated, any one variable alone could not necessarily give decisive guidance.

5.91   The *United States* noted that while export data were generally not as reliable as import data, at the request of the TMB, the US had supplied an export table. Even after using export data to adjust for the overstatement in the market, the figures before the TMB had confirmed the determination made by CITA. After examining the import data, CITA examined output, market share, employment, domestic price and profits and investment information. That information had led CITA to the conclusion that there was a case of serious damage, or actual threat thereof to the US domestic industry. While the United States did not supply data on productivity, inventory, wages and exports, it was not required to do so under Article 6.3 of the ATC. The variables in Article 6.3 of the ATC not directly included in the March Market Statement (productivity, inventories and wages) had been discussed during the TMB examination in oral responses by the United States to questions from TMB members. Costa Rica had omitted any recognition of the express proviso in Article 6.3 of the ATC that:

> "none of [these factors] either alone or combined with other factors, can necessarily give decisive guidance."

A similar proviso was also found concerning the additional factors for consideration in Article 6.4 of the ATC. Nevertheless, the United States had provided verbal responses to questions concerning productivity, wages, and inventory to the TMB.

Increase in Imports into the United States
(see also The Counting of Re-imports, paragraphs 5.142-5.149)

5.92   *Costa Rica* further argued that, in accordance with its obligation to demonstrate the existence of an increase in imports, the United States should have presented specific and relevant factual information on the subject, and then have analyzed it. In this regard, however, the March Market Statement only indicated that imports in this category had increased from 65.5 million dozen in 1992 to 79.9 million dozen in 1993 and 97.3 million dozen in 1994, reflecting increases of 22 per cent in each year with respect to the previous year. The United States had not made any distinction concerning the nature of this trade, nor any analysis thereof, an omission which was particularly serious in this case given the increasing importance of "807 trade" in this category. In fact, over the last six years there had been a substantial change in the United States industry producing cotton and man-made fibre underwear. There had been a shift from producing and assembling the product locally to producing the product components locally, which were then assembled abroad and returned to the same companies in the United States for marketing. This co-production process (see Section II) had enabled the United States industries to retain their market share in the United States.

5.93 *Costa Rica* questioned whether, in the case of clothing produced on the basis of the co-production process, one was dealing with "imports" or rather with a case of domestic production which, despite assembly in another country, did not for that reason alone cease to be domestic production. In fact, the United States itself had considered imports of cut parts for assembly in the United States as products of the country where the parts were cut. United States exports of cut parts should be considered United States products. Furthermore, when this case was reviewed by the TMB in July 1995, the United States itself had submitted a loose sheet giving alleged export data in this category, in which cut parts subsequently assembled abroad were included as exports, which logically showed that for this industry these were part of domestic production.

5.94 *Costa Rica* noted that the "807 trade" had risen from 31.8 million dozen in 1992 to 42 million dozen in 1993 and 57 million dozen in 1994, accounting for an ever larger part of trade in category 352/652. This reflected a pattern which, by all indications, would continue and become more pronounced in the future, driven by the investment policies and incentives that the United States maintained in relation to the Caribbean Basin and Mexico.

5.95 In the view of *Costa Rica*, much of the cited increase in imports did not in fact exist, and therefore the United States did not have the right to use the transitional safeguard. By nevertheless having done so, it violated Article 6.2 of the ATC. However, if it were to be considered that there was in fact an increase in imports of underwear, it was quite clear that if such imports were increasing it was because United States production of the cut pieces, that were subsequently assembled, was increasing in the same proportions. In other words, if ever more underwear was being assembled in other countries it was because in the United States ever more cut pieces for underwear were being produced that need to be assembled, from which it necessarily followed that any industry producing cut pieces for underwear was thriving and therefore did not need to be protected from something that was rather of benefit to it.

5.96 The *United States* considered that the ATC did not prohibit inclusion of re-imports in imports; on the contrary, Article 6.2 of the ATC directed importing Members to examine increases in "total" imports. The ATC also did not require Members to separate re-imports from total imports. In fact, all textile and apparel re-imports were defined under United States law as foreign articles. The US Bureau of the Census' statistics reflected HTSUS 9802 re-imports as apparel which were cut in the US, exported to be assembled, and then re-imported under HTSUS 9802 as finished garments. HTSUS 9802 re-imports were included in domestic production (cut parts), exports (cut parts), and imports (finished garments). Re-imports must clear customs like any other imported good. Costa Rica had admitted to the TMB that companies producing goods for re-import into the United States were subject to the same laws, fees and taxes as other domestic Costa Rican manufacturers. HTSUS 9802 apparel re-imports into the US received duty reductions to the extent that they incorporated US content.

Application of Safeguard to Individual Member(s)

5.97   *Costa Rica* argued that in the case of the ATC, since the Agreement allowed the selective and discriminatory application of a safeguard measure, it was necessary to fulfil this second stage which was not normally present in other existing safeguard mechanisms in the multilateral system, precisely in order to be able to identify the Member or Members to which the measure would be applied. Thus, Article 6.4 of the ATC stated that:

> "Any measure invoked pursuant to the provisions of this Article shall be applied on a Member-by-Member basis. The Member or Members to whom serious damage, or actual threat thereof, referred to in paragraphs 2 and 3, is attributed, shall be determined on the basis of a sharp and substantial increase in imports, actual or imminent, from such a Member or Members individually, and on the basis of the level of imports as compared with imports from other sources, market share, and import and domestic prices at a comparable stage of commercial transaction: none of these factors, either alone or combined with other factors, can necessarily give decisive guidance ... ".

5.98   In the view of *Costa Rica*, in the second, attribution stage, the importing Member must demonstrate the fulfilment of two substantive requirements: a sharp and substantial increase in imports, actual or imminent, from such a Member or Members individually; and the causal relationship between this increase and the serious damage or actual threat thereof created by total imports. In accordance with the above provisions, the fulfilment of the three requirements set out in the first stage was an essential pre-condition to be able to go on to the second stage of the demonstration process. Only when, after having fulfilled the requirements of the first stage, and it had also fulfilled the two requirements of the second stage, may the importing Member apply a transitional safeguard to an exporting Member.

Obligation of Demonstration - Fulfilment of Substantive Requirements

5.99   *Costa Rica* argued that, in order to be able to fulfil the above-mentioned requirements, the ATC imposed on the importing Member an obligation of demonstration. Under Article 6.2 of the ATC, the Member wishing to apply a transitional safeguard was obliged to make a determination prior to adopting the measure. In the determination, the Member had the obligation to demonstrate fulfilment of the substantive requirements laid down in order to be able to establish such a measure. It was noted that while it was the Member's obligation to make the determination, the actual content of the determination was clearly established by Article 6 of the ATC itself: it consisted in demonstrating the existence of the substantive requirements that must be fulfilled in order to adopt a transitional safeguard. It was not a question of stating, alleging or repeating opinions without any grounds, but rather of showing or proving that the factual situation on which the Member wished to take protective action fully met the specified conditions. The burden of proof rested with the Member intending to restrict trade. If the Member took safeguard action without having demonstrated the existence of all the substantive requirements in the two stages as described above - as the United States had done in this case, it was violating the ATC (see also Burden of Proof in Section C).

5.100 This demonstration process which the Member wishing to impose the safeguard must carry out may in turn be divided into two: firstly, the Member must present the specific and relevant information on the facts giving rise to its claim in accordance with Article 6.7 of the ATC; and secondly, it must make an examination of the factors listed in Articles 6.2, 6.3 and 6.4 and of how the conditions it was presenting fell within the substantive criteria laid down by the ATC as necessary requirements to justify the adoption of a safeguard measure. If the information was not presented, the necessary analysis could not be carried out, and consequently there would be a breach of the ATC. In the case under consideration, the United States had failed to demonstrate the existence of the substantive elements of the first stage of the demonstration process, and still less those of the second stage, thereby violating Articles 6.2, 6.3, 6.4 and 6.7.

5.101 The *United States* stated that it had met all of the substantive requirements of Article 6 of the ATC and that after doing so, met its burden of proof and the transitional safeguard action was justified. It was now up to Costa Rica to show that the United States determination was unreasonable and inconsistent with the requirements of the ATC, in particular Article 6.2, 6.3, 6.4, 6.7 and 6.6(d).

Consultations on Safeguard

5.102 The *United States* noted that, once the determination had been made, the importing Member must request consultations with the relevant exporting Members. Article 6.7 of the ATC also provided that requests for consultations on proposed safeguard action must be accompanied by "specific and relevant factual information, as up-to-date as possible," particularly factors referenced in Articles 6.3 and 6.4 of the ATC.

5.103 As under the Multifibre Arrangement (MFA) system, during consultations on the application of the safeguard, importing Members must take into account four areas of more favourable treatment as appropriate. One area of more favourable treatment relevant in this matter was that accorded to re-imports included in the determination of serious damage, or actual threat thereof that constituted a significant proportion of an exporting Member's trade. It was not until the consultation stage that the United States was required to give more favourable treatment in accordance with Article 6.6(d) of the ATC. The ATC left the definition of re-imports and the manner of applying more favourable treatment to the importing Member. If the consultations provided for in Article 6.7 of the ATC did not result in a mutual solution, the importing Member must exercise its option to take action to limit the relevant imports within 30 days. Once that action was taken, Article 6 of the ATC required automatic review by the TMB.

Data Required for Consultations and Other Relevant Information

5.104 *Costa Rica* considered that the "other relevant information" should be understood as information relevant or related to the information specified in the earlier paragraph, which was taken into consideration by the importing Member at the time of making its determination about the market situation and which was available to the exporting Member. The main task of the TMB in this respect was, in accordance with Article 6.10 of the ATC, to examine whether the determination made by the importing Member fit the requirements of the ATC. Thus, the examination was restricted to those elements which the importing Member had taken into consideration in making its determination and of which the exporting Member was duly cognizant at the time. These may be different from the factual elements mentioned in Article 6.7 of the ATC, but they must be related to them. It could not be argued that the TMB could conduct its examination on the basis of information which the importing Member had not taken into consideration at the time of making its determination - because it did not exist, because it was not available or for any other reason - and which the exporting Member did not have an opportunity to examine and refute before the imposition of the restraint. To do otherwise would jeopardize the rights of the exporting Member and would be contrary to the provisions of the ATC.

5.105 *Costa Rica* recognized that paragraphs 2, 3 and 4 of Article 6 of the ATC did not distinguish between "re-imports" and imports, but used only the latter term. However, they did not consider that this by itself should be taken to mean that "807 trade" should necessarily be regarded as imports. On the contrary, the word "imports" should be analysed in the context of the case in question and the economic rationale of "807 trade", in order to determine whether, in this particular case, "807 trade" could or could not be regarded as imports for the purposes of Articles 6.2, 6.3 and 6.4.

5.106 The *United States* pointed out that Article 6.7 of the ATC required that the call for consultations must be "accompanied by specific and relevant data, as up-to-date as possible" relating to the factors referred to in Articles 6.3 and 6.4 of the ATC. Like the working party in the "Fur Felt Hat" case, Article 6.7 of the ATC did not require perfect data. The data relied upon by the CITA at the time of its determination in March were in fact as up-to-date as possible, and provided information as close as possible to the reference period. The United States had presented revised and updated data to the TMB in July which only confirmed the correctness of the CITA's analysis in March that transitional safeguard action was appropriate.

5.107 The data to be used in examining whether a determination was consistent with Article 6 of the ATC must be those data actually used by the authorities of the importing Member at the time it made the determination. The relevant data in this case were those required by Article 6.7 of the ATC. Nevertheless, all later updated or supplementary data only corroborated the data in the March Market Statement.

5.108 The *United States* pointed out that the TMB must review the case, determine whether the safeguard action was justified and make appropriate recommendations to the Members concerned. In addition to the data supplied in accordance with Articles 6.7 and 6.10 of the ATC also allowed the TMB to consider "any other relevant information provided by the Members concerned." Importing Members must notify the Chairman of the TMB, providing relevant factual data at the same time the request for consultations was made. When a restriction was in place, the ATC placed a three-year cap on the duration of safeguard measures applied by Members, unless the product concerned was integrated earlier.

F.   Serious Damage or Actual Threat Thereof

5.109 *Costa Rica* submitted that the second substantive requirement that any Member wishing to acquire the right to take safeguard action must demonstrate was serious damage or actual threat thereof to the domestic industry producing like and/or directly competitive products, as stated in Article 6.2 of the ATC. It was noted that Article 6.2 of the ATC referred to the fulfilment of a requirement that may take one of two forms: it may be that what existed was serious damage to the domestic industry, or it may be that what existed was the actual threat of serious damage to the domestic industry. However, it was also noted that while the requirement was fulfilled by the existence of either of the two conditions, they were precisely two different hypotheses, owing to the time factor. In the case of serious damage, the injury to the domestic industry had already occurred, whereas in the case of actual threat of serious damage the injury to the industry had not yet occurred but there was an imminent and hence actual possibility that it would occur. It was not possible to use the same information and the same type of analysis to prove both that a supposed fact had occurred or that it was about to occur.

5.110 *Costa Rica* claimed that it was the understanding of the TMB itself that serious damage and actual threat of serious damage were not the same thing, since in this particular case it had concluded that the existence of serious damage had not been found, but it could not reach a consensus on the existence of actual threat of serious damage. If the two conditions were a single hypothesis, the conclusion that one did not exist would necessarily lead to the conclusion that the other did not exist. However, the TMB had not taken this view. The most important consequence of this difference was that the nature of the information submitted and of the analysis made to demonstrate each hypothetical condition was necessarily different, as it was not the same thing to demonstrate that damage had already occurred as to demonstrate that damage might occur. That was why the logical corollary of this difference was that an importing Member could not submit the same information in this connection and carry out the same type of analysis in order to argue indiscriminately that what had existed was damage or threat of damage. At a given point in time - the moment when the call for consultations was made - either one condition existed or the other condition existed. To make an appropriate demonstration thereof the importing Member must at that point in time define what the supposed situation of its industry actually was and make the call, submitting the corresponding information and, if appropriate, adopting the restriction on the basis of the condition it selected.

5.111 *Costa Rica* stated that correct identification by the importing Member of the supposed claim made in relation to the state of its domestic production was essential in order to comply properly with its demonstration obligation. In the view of Costa Rica, it was only when the TMB had determined that the existence of serious damage had not been proven that the United States changed tack and appeared to assume that it could maintain its restriction on the basis of the purported threat, which had not been alleged or proved previously. The United States affirmed that as the ATC was not worded in the same terms as other WTO Agreements, it was not possible to require the presentation of different information in order to prove serious damage or actual threat of serious damage. However, Costa Rica argued that even though something may not be specifically stated in an agreement, common understanding required it, because it was not possible to use the same information and the same type of analysis to prove both that a supposed fact has occurred or that it is about to occur.

5.112 *Costa Rica* argued that, in some measure, that was what the United States had done in this process. The great majority of the communications initially sent by the United States in connection with the case, the Statement submitted in March and the adoption of the unilateral restriction in June were all based on the purported existence of serious damage to the United States industry. The United States had begun this case and had adopted this restriction on the basis of the existence of serious damage, and had not considered that a threat existed. That was why the element of actual threat had not even been taken into account. Hence, at the moment when the TMB determined that serious damage did not exist, the United States should have withdrawn the unilateral restriction it had imposed.

5.113 However, the United States had not withdrawn the restriction, but had maintained and even renewed it. Although the United States had not explicitly argued this at any time, it appeared to have assumed that it was authorized to maintain the measure on the basis that the TMB could not reach a consensus on the existence of actual threat of serious damage. In the view of *Costa Rica*, this reasoning was incorrect and violated Articles 6.2 and 6.3 of the ATC, which specifically required the demonstration that this was the condition, with the presentation and analysis of specific and relevant information concerning the existence of actual threat of serious damage. The fact was that there existed neither serious damage to the United States industry, nor actual threat of serious damage to that industry, which was why, by adopting a restriction without this second requirement being fulfilled, the United States had violated Articles 6.2 and 6.3 of the ATC.

5.114 The *United States* argued that Article 6.2 of the ATC required that a Member determine that a particular product was being imported into its territory in such increased quantities as to cause "serious damage, or actual threat thereof" to the domestic industry producing like or directly competitive products. Unlike other agreements such as the Agreement on Implementation of Article VI, the ATC did not provide separate requirements for determinations of threat of injury. "Serious damage" or "actual threat" never appeared separately in the text of Article 6 of the ATC; each reference to one of these two different legal concepts was coupled with a reference to the other. Thus, Article 6 of the ATC provided only one standard, with one set of criteria, for determinations of serious damage or actual threat thereof. This standard and these criteria had been employed in the CITA determination of March 1995. Thus, this determination of "serious damage, or actual threat thereof" was fully consistent with Articles 6.2 and 6.3 of the ATC.

5.115 The *United States* noted that their 27 March 1995 diplomatic note to Costa Rica making the actual call for consultations had referred to "serious damage, or actual threat thereof" to the industry producing underwear in the United States, even if the March Market Statement which accompanied it abbreviated this reference to "serious damage". Furthermore, during consultations with Costa Rica the United States had consistently taken the position that underwear imports from Costa Rica were causing both serious damage and actual threat of serious damage. During TMB deliberations, in July 1995, it was clarified that the reference in the March Statement had included both serious damage and actual threat of serious damage, and the United States had corrected the statement accordingly.

5.116 *Costa Rica* was of the view that the US diplomatic note of 27 March 1995 was merely a standard form used by the United States for its calls. Even though the note alleged a threat of serious damage, the fact was that the statement attached to it in order to justify the restriction - the March Market Statement - did not contain any information or analysis relating to this allegation. Moreover, during the consultations held between the two governments under Article 6 of the ATC, no evidence or analysis of any kind was submitted that might have demonstrated the existence of such a threat. Similarly, there was no mention of the existence of a threat of serious damage as justification for the adoption of a safeguard in the notes which the United States had attached to the various restraint proposals it submitted to the Government of Costa Rica.

5.117 With respect to the status of the TMB finding that serious damage had not been demonstrated, the *United States* pointed out that they did not agree with the TMB finding and did not at the time it was made; nothing in the ATC made TMB findings or recommendations binding on the parties concerned. As a practical matter in light of the TMB's initial finding the United States had been compelled to shift the focus of its argument to "actual threat" after July 1995, but as a matter of law the ATC did not confer upon the TMB the power to make findings of fact that legally bound Members. Moreover, as noted in relation to the standard of review, the burden of proof was on Costa Rica to produce a *prima facie* case that the US determination was inconsistent with Articles 6.2 and 6.3 of the ATC; the United States did not have the burden here of proving that its actions had been consistent with the ATC (see also Section V:C). Furthermore, the question to be addressed was not the existence of "serious damage" as such, but whether facts had been advanced which provided convincing evidence that it was unreasonable for CITA to determine that the adverse effects of increased underwear imports on the US domestic underwear industry had amounted to serious damage, or actual threat thereof.

5.118 *Costa Rica* observed that, in its first review of this case, the TMB had reached the clear conclusion that "serious damage ... had not been demonstrated", as required by Articles 6.2 and 6.3 of the ATC. It was clear that the restriction imposed by the United States infringed the above-mentioned provision because the United States had failed to demonstrate the existence of serious damage to its industry. As the TMB decision in this regard had not been challenged, it had to be understood that both parties had accepted it. Consequently, the discussion as to the supposed existence of serious damage should not be reopened, since it was clear that this was not demonstrated at the time when it should have been demonstrated.

5.119 *Costa Rica* argued that the United States had also failed to demonstrate the purported actual threat of serious damage. The industry producing clothing classified in category 352/652 was not only not suffering any serious damage but also not suffering any actual threat of serious damage, as required under Article 6 of the ATC. Firstly, the United States itself did not consider that actual threat of serious damage existed in this case. It never argued that this was the case in order to justify the unilateral restriction imposed on Costa Rica. This was shown by the unreliable, erroneous, contradictory and incomplete information it had included in the March Market Statement, which did not serve for making an analysis of whether serious damage existed, and was not even designed to be used as a basis for an alleged actual threat of serious damage. When the United States made the call for consultations, the condition it had in view was that of serious damage and not of actual threat of serious damage. That was why the March Statement did not make any specific reference to the issue of threat, except indirectly in a single sentence of the text. That is also why, when the United States published in the Federal Register the request for public comments concerning these negotiations, it referred only to serious damage, and not to actual threat of serious damage.

5.120 The supposition of actual threat of serious damage became important when the TMB, after having reached the conclusion that the existence of serious damage had not been demonstrated, did not reach a consensus as to the existence of actual threat of serious damage - a strange decision, considering that the hypothetical condition of actual threat was not in itself under consideration - and recommended that the parties hold further consultations bearing this in mind, *inter alia.* It may be thought that, following the TMB's decision, the only option open to the United States was to try to justify *a posteriori* the restriction adopted, by now invoking a supposed threat to its underwear-producing industry. However, the fact was that it also failed to establish this justification, even in subsequent months.

5.121 *Costa Rica* argued that neither the March Market Statement, nor the July Statement, nor any other information furnished by the United States, not even following the imposition of the unilateral restriction, provided evidence or furnished an analysis of the kind required to demonstrate the existence of actual threat. The obligation to demonstrate the actual threat of serious damage had two dimensions. Firstly, it was necessary to demonstrate that an imminent increase in imports existed, on the basis of objective criteria, such as the goods having already been exported and en route; or that they were in port waiting to be shipped; or that they were covered by a contract and would be shipped once production had been completed. A second dimension, closely linked to the first, referred to volume, in the sense that not every possible increase in imports was capable of creating a threat. It followed from the foregoing that it was necessary that the goods should be able to be counted, which in turn was linked with the need for objective criteria to determine the imminence of the imports.

5.122 The *United States* argued that they were not required by the ATC to choose between serious damage and actual threat in making their determination. The ATC standard allowed Members to assert, at the same time, both serious damage or actual threat. The plain meaning of the standard invoked merely the notion that there could be a determination on the basis of serious damage or actual threat. Neither was exclusive of the other. There was no obligation in other safeguard proceedings that one standard must be alleged instead of the other. The ATC treats them equally, that is, without any special factors to establish a case for one or the other. The simple fact was that Members could allege both based on the same factors. In addition, contrary to the assertion of Costa Rica, it did not follow that if the TMB found that there was no serious damage, and reached no consensus on threat, there was no threat. No consensus on threat was just that. No consensus on that finding, therefore, no finding or decision on threat.

5.123 Upon request of the Panel, the *United States* argued that they did not take the view that a finding of actual threat of serious damage implied some sort of prospective analysis because there was no provision of this kind in the ATC that would have guided the United States in making its determination. The United States did not split the phrase "serious damage, or actual threat thereof" and was not asking the Panel to do so. The ATC did not provide separate criteria for threat. They maintained that whatever analysis was chosen by the Panel must not add to or diminish the rights and obligations of the parties. They believed that the ATC must be observed and that any interpretation that would re-write the ATC would probably require the re-opening of the Marrakesh Agreement Establishing the WTO.

The March 1995 Market Statement

5.124 *Costa Rica* considered that the United States could base its restriction only on the March Market Statement which was the statement the United States had notified within the terms of Article 6 of the ATC and on the basis of which consultations had been held. It also provided the basis for the United States' adoption of a unilateral restraint. Thus, it was clear that the March Market Statement alone ought to be examined by the Panel in order to determine whether the restriction applied by the United States complied with Article 6 of the ATC.

5.125 Conversely, *Costa Rica* was of the view that a finding of actual threat of serious damage implied a prospective analysis. Since the ATC required that the threat be "actual", this implied that the Member wishing to impose this ground could not do so on the basis of conjecture of speculation, but must effectively demonstrate that there was an imminent damaging impact on the industry which was about to occur in the future. Once this specific and relevant information had been presented, the importing Member must carry out a prospective, forward-looking analysis of what could happen to its industry, bearing in mind that what was under examination was the imminence of a situation that had not yet occurred. In the case under consideration, the United States had submitted absolutely no information aimed at seeking to demonstrate the existence of actual threat of serious damage, still less to carry out any kind of analysis to that end. Hence, it was impossible to consider that the unilateral restriction imposed could have been based on the existence of a supposed actual threat.

5.126 *Costa Rica* contrasted the requirements of Article 6.3 of the ATC with the information included in the March Market Statement. According to Article 6.3 of the ATC, in making a determination of serious damage,

> "The Member shall examine the effect of those imports on the state of the particular industry, as reflected in changes in such relevant economic variables as output, productivity, utilization of capacity, inventories, market share, exports, wages, employment, domestic prices, profits and investment; none of which, either alone or combined with other factors, can necessarily give decisive guidance."

5.127 *Costa Rica* argued that, pursuant to this provision, the United States had to demonstrate the effect of imports from Costa Rica on the state of its underwear producing industry, as reflected in changes in the relevant economic variables. The first stage of this process of demonstration consisted of the presentation of the necessary information to be able subsequently to make an analysis of the information. In this connection, Article 6.7 of the ATC provided that:

> "The request for consultations shall be accompanied by specific and relevant factual information, as up-to-date as possible, particularly in regard to: (a) the factors referred to in paragraph 3, on which the Member invoking the action has based its determination of the existence of serious damage or actual threat thereof; ...".

5.128 Given the characteristics of the information in the March Market Statement - summarized by *Costa Rica* in the following table - it was impossible in their view for the United States to fulfil their obligation to demonstrate the existence of serious damage.

Information Required Under the ATC and Information
Presented by the United States

ATC	Information included in the March Statement (MS) submitted by the United States
Output	The MS mentioned that production had declined by 4% in 1992 and 1993 and a further 4% between 1993 and 1994; in July the United States indicated that the percentage of decline of the first period remains the same but that in the second there was no decline; in October the United States believed that for the first period there was a decline of 1.5%, whereas in the second the supposed decline was 2.6%.
Productivity	No information was included on this variable.
Utilization of capacity	No specific information was included on this variable, apart from a sentence stating that because of the import competition, firms reported shifting production capacity to other product lines. The source of this information was the survey which the United States says that it had carried out, but the slightest details of which were unknown.
Inventories	No information was included on this variable.
Market share	The MS states that the domestic industry's share of the market fell from 73% to 68%. The problem of how to treat "807 trade" was not taken into consideration, and therefore it was not determined for certain that the domestic industry's market share did not rather increase.
Exports	The MS did not include any information of this variable. In July the United States had submitted a loose sheet stating that exports had increased from $284 million in 1992 to $406 million in 1993 and to $458 million in 1994. This loose sheet did not indicate the source of the information.
Wages	No information was included on this variable.
Employment	The MS stated that employment declined from 46,377 workers in 1992 to 44,056 workers in 1994. In July, however, the United States said that the number of workers in 1992 was 35,191 and that the number had declined to 33,309.
Domestic prices	The MS stated that the producers' average price is $30 per dozen in 1994, without giving the source of the information. In July the United States "corrected" this information and indicated that it believes that this price is between $16 and $20 per dozen.
Profits	The MS stated that profits were down 18% at one firm - of the 395 which supposedly existed - and there was pressure on the bottom line throughout the industry due to rising costs and stiff import competition. The MS also stated that sales declined and that one company had reported that their sales were down about 17% in 1994. No statistics were given in this respect. The source of this information was the survey that the United States said it carried out, but the details of which were unknown.

ATC	Information included in the March Statement (MS) submitted by the United States
Investment	The MS stated that companies "generally" had been postponing investment in this industry, that some companies had closed plants permanently or shifted production offshore, and additional disinvestment of this nature "was being contemplated". No statistics were given in this respect. The source of this information was the survey that the United States said it carried out, but the details of which were unknown.

5.129 *Costa Rica* noted that of the 11 factors listed in Article 6.3 of the ATC, the March Market Statement had not included any information concerning four of them; it had included information which the United States itself subsequently considered wrong in the case of three of them (two of which were output and prices); and included information for three factors based on a survey whose coverage, methodology, representativeness, dates etc. were not mentioned - and indeed, on another occasion the United States itself declared that it could not use this type of instrument to collect information in these cases. In these circumstances, the only possible conclusion was that the information submitted by the United States was unreliable, erroneous, contradictory and lacking, and therefore any measure based on it was in breach of Articles 6.2, 6.3 and 6.7 of the ATC.

5.130 *Costa Rica* argued that the information submitted was unreliable for three reasons: firstly, much of it did not give the source from which it is taken; secondly, where a source was specified, it turned out not to be very serious; and lastly, the best evidence that the information of the March Market Statement was unreliable was that in July the United States itself submitted fresh information that substantially contradicted all the major indicators covered in the March Statement. Then, a few months later the United States again published information that was at variance both with the information produced in July and with the information included in the March Statement.

5.131 *Costa Rica* recalled that Section III of the March Market Statement was divided into two sections, the first headed "serious damage to the domestic industry" and the second "industry statements". The first of these sections included data on domestic production, market share loss and import penetration, for which the source was given. In the case of the information on employment and man hours it stated that the data were derived from various sources, which were not identified with any degree of precision. It was noted that the industry statements had a questionable source, being

> "Based on a survey of individual firms producing cotton and man-made fibre underwear ... the observations are concentrated in the men's underwear sector but also include the even more heavily import-impacted ladies underwear sector."

5.132 In effect, the data on employment, sales, profits, investment, capacity and prices included in the March Market Statement were based on an alleged survey whose coverage, methodology, representativeness, date, etc., were unknown since the Statement was completely silent in this respect. This explained the opinions included in the Statement for which there was so little basis or justification. Clearly, it was impossible to make generalizations of any kind or determine the state of the industry on the basis of a number of opinions from one or two firms - it was recalled that the Statement itself stated that there were 395 establishments producing in this category - for which no grounds or explanations were given and included in a survey whose details were unknown. It was also obvious that this could not constitute any kind of demonstration of the impact of imports on the industry in question, since it did not shed any light on the effect of the increased imports on the variables mentioned.

5.133 *Costa Rica* did not consider the data based on the alleged survey of individual firms, of which nothing was known, to be serious. The survey referred to the opinions of one or two firms as to capacity utilization, inventories, exports, wages, profits and investment. The submission of information was so important that the United States should have included in its Statement data on at least all the factors set out in Article 6.3 of the ATC and perhaps even on some others; however, it had failed to do so.

5.134 The problem of the March Market Statement was not confined to the lack of information but also to the total absence of any analysis of that information. The United States did not make any kind of analysis of the information, although given the incoherencies of that information, it would have been difficult to do so. This led *Costa Rica* to the conclusion that with the information submitted, the United States had failed to fulfil its obligation to demonstrate the existence of serious damage to its industry, as required under Articles 6.2 and 6.3 of the ATC, and as the TMB itself had found.

The July 1995 Market Statement

5.135 *Costa Rica* considered that the reliability of the information was also brought into question by the United States, which published further data in July and again in October 1995, altering the March data substantially. Thus, in July data that differed from the March data were given in essential fields including: (a) number of establishments producing underwear in category 352/652: in March there were 395, but in July there were 302; (b) supposed decline in output: whereas in March output was believed to have declined by 4 per cent between 1992 and 1993 and by a further 4 per cent between 1993 and 1994, in July it was indicated that the first percentage remained the same but that in the second period there was no decline; (c) market size: whereas in March, "807" production was wrongly counted twice, both as domestic production and as imports, in July this market size was "adjusted", introducing significant alterations compared with the March Statement; (d) number of workers employed in the sector: whereas the March Statement stated that 46,377 people worked in the sector in 1992, in July it was stated that that was not the number, but rather 35,191 persons, in other words the March Statement was wrong by 11,000 workers; (e) average price of United States underwear production: whereas in March it was stated that this was

$30 per dozen, in July it was "clarified" that this figure had a margin of error of nearly 100 per cent, the price being between $16 and $20 per dozen.

5.136 *Costa Rica* emphasized that the March Market Statement, on which the consultations had been held and the unilateral restriction imposed in June 1995, had so many errors that all its main parameters were modified in July. Virtually the only section of the March Statement that was not modified was that based on the survey. Furthermore, in October 1995 the Textile and Apparel Office of the United States Department of Commerce had published updated statistics to June 1995 for category 352/652 in which some of the data given in July were "revised" once again, having already been "revised" with respect to the March Statement, and the results obtained were at variance with those submitted earlier. It thus turned out once again that the data for output and market size were different. This lack of reliability of the information submitted by the United States was enough to maintain beyond all doubt that the United States had failed in its primary duty of presenting the necessary information to proceed to carry out an analysis of whether the serious damage it alleged actually existed.

5.137 The July Statement had been used by the United States from July 1995 and up to the establishment of the Panel as an "ex post facto" justification for the restriction applied to Costa Rican trade in this category in June 1995. Nevertheless, Costa Rica had always maintained that the July Statement could not be regarded as the basis for the call, since it was not. The information contained in the July Statement was not that which should be analysed for the purpose of determining whether the restriction adopted by the United States complied with Article 6 of the ATC. In this respect, it was correct to say that this statement had no legal relevance. The July Statement was useful for confirming how erroneous was the information included in the March Statement which formed the basis of the unilateral restriction adopted in June 1995. This Statement - which for the most part was based on the same information that was available in March - was useful as evidence, inasmuch as it showed that the information which served as basis for the adoption of the restriction in question was seriously flawed.

5.138 The *United States* pointed out that it had a general practice of monitoring and updating textile and apparel production and trade data. The data provided in July only confirmed the correctness of the CITA's analysis in March that transitional safeguard action was appropriate. As regards the updated information provided in October 1995, these were equally irrelevant. The United States pointed out, however, that the October 1995 data still showed a 5.5 per cent decline in underwear production during the January-June 1995 period. Furthermore, more recent published updates in March 1996 showed that underwear production actually declined by 2.8 per cent for the period from 1 October 1994 to 30 September 1995. This and other updated information demonstrated that the situation for US underwear manufacturers progressively deteriorated during 1995.

Analysis of March and July Market Statements

5.139 According to *Costa Rica*, both the March Market Statement and the July Market Statement, annual shipments amounted to $3.2 billion. However, analysing the data on the basis of which this information had been obtained it found that this figure was not correct. Thus, considering that the amount of annual shipments was obtained by multiplying the volume of clothing produced by the average producer price of the clothing, and making this calculation for 1994, the ensuing result would be $5.06 billion according to the data in the March Statement, while according to the information in the July Statement this figure could be $3.37 billion or $3.03 billion, according to which United States producer price was used. In any case, what was important to stress was that while one section of each of the Statements gave a figure, if the data in the Statement itself were multiplied in order to obtain the same figure a different result was obtained. Clearly, there was an error in the figure of the annual shipments, production data or in the price, which then also significantly affected other data included in the Statement.

5.140 The *United States* considered that the information provided in the March and July Statements was not contradictory and was consistent with the requirements of Article 6 of the ATC. Costa Rica had asserted that the data available in March 1995 contradicted the updated data the United States had provided to the TMB in July 1995. The March Statement presented by the United States contained data from a variety of official sources, current at that time. Article 6.7 of the ATC provided that when requesting consultations the requesting Member must supply "factual information as up-to-date as possible". The March data had satisfied that requirement, even though some of the information had been preliminary. During consultations and the TMB proceeding, the United States had been asked to provide other and updated information. The TMB had put many questions to the United States for response during the proceeding as well. In the context of the Article 6.10 of the ATC reference that the TMB must consider the earlier statement and "any other relevant information", the United States had provided a revised statement during the July proceeding which was accepted by the TMB.

5.141 The information in the July Statement had not, in the view of the *United States* contradicted the March Statement, but had only supported it. Since Article 6.7 of the ATC stated that

> "the request for consultation shall be accompanied by specific and relevant factual information, as up-to-date as possible, ..." and that "... the information shall be related, as closely as possible, to identifiable segments of production and to the reference period ..."

of the call action, there was no credibility issue with respect to the data presented in March or July. Article 6.7 of the ATC clearly recognized that the data upon which the initial request for consultations was based, would necessarily be imperfect. Article 6.10 of the ATC similarly acknowledged that data would not be as accurate as desired at the time of the call, requiring that the TMB

> "have available to it the factual data provided to the Chairman of the TMB, referred to in paragraph 7, as well as any other relevant information provided by the Members concerned".

The latter was clearly designed to include further updated information that was available at the time of TMB review.

The Counting of Re-imports
(see also Increase in Imports, paragraphs 5.92-5.96)

5.142 According to *Costa Rica*, one of the most serious mistakes in the March Market Statement, was the double counting of "807" production and the problem of the alteration of market size. In its statistics, the United States had rightly included as domestic production the production of pieces that were part of a garment subsequently assembled in another country and then reimported into the United States under tariff heading 9802.00.80. However, it had also included as imports the same pieces once they had been assembled, even though they had already been counted as domestic production. This resulted in an alteration in the size of the market, because the same product was included twice.

5.143 Having been made aware of this problem by the comments addressed to it by Costa Rica, the United States had tried to correct the situation in its July Market Statement, but, according to *Costa Rica*, in the wrong way. Thus, in July the United States counted "807" production once; but it chose to include "807" production as imports and not as domestic output, which appeared inconsistent as "807" production was domestic production in the sense of manufacture and/or cutting of cloth. Assembly, which was the only part of the process carried out abroad, had a much smaller weight in the final cost of production of underwear, and therefore this "807" production should not have been counted as imports.

5.144 In support of this same approach, although in contradiction with what it had done in the July Statement, when the case was being reviewed by the TMB in July the United States submitted a loose sheet giving the supposed export data in this category, in which it included cut pieces as exports. In other words, whereas in the July Statement the United States counted "807" production as imports, in the export data it provided in the same month it counted it as domestic production. Then, in the data published in October they returned to the March situation, disregarding the entire problem of double counting of "807" production which the July Statement had tried to take into consideration.

5.145 The *United States* explained that under Article 6.2 of the ATC, before taking safeguard action an importing Member's authorities must make a determination that a particular product was being imported in such increased quantities as to cause serious damage or actual threat thereof; this serious damage or actual threat thereof must be caused by increased quantities of "total imports" of the product concerned. The reference to "total" imports included re-imports. No distinction was made between re-imports and other imports in Articles 6.2, 6.3 or 6.4 of the ATC. The drafters of the ATC were quite aware of the existence of re-imports and outward processing trade, which were significant commercial factors in world textile and clothing trade and which were explicitly referred to in Article 6.6 of the MFA. The drafters had chosen to refer specifically to re-imports in Article 6.6(d) of the ATC, in relation to the application of a transitional safeguard, after the determinations necessary for a safeguard action have been made. Thus, if the drafters had meant to exclude re-imports from the scope of "total imports", thus barring transitional safeguard action against re-imports, they certainly could have done so. However, they did not, and it must be assumed that this omission was intentional. It therefore could not be assumed that re-imports are incapable of causing or threatening damage to the industry of an importing Member. Thus, the increase in "total imports" referred to in Article 6.2 of the ATC included increases in re-imports as well.

5.146 The *United States* referred to the allegation of Costa Rica that the March Statement had overstated the level of imports through its treatment of re-imports. It was explained that during the process of negotiations and the TMB examination of this case, it was recognized that there was double-counting of re-imports, and the United States had made appropriate corrections. However, the effect of this double-counting was not an overstatement of the level of imports but an overstatement of the size of the US underwear market. CITA practice, long accepted by the TSB in their examination of calls by the United States, had consistently been to treat the total market for a textile or apparel category as production plus imports. In response to questions during bilateral consultations with Costa Rica, the United States had deducted re-imports from production, because re-imports are of foreign origin under the relevant US rule of origin. Costa Rica has repeatedly asserted that the origin of apparel re-imports was determined by the place where the pieces were cut, but, as discussed below, this is a factual error.

5.147 Costa Rica had then claimed during the TMB proceeding that re-imports should be deducted from imports. The TMB had suggested that the overstatement in the US domestic market should be adjusted by using US export data. The United States had pointed out to the TMB that export data were generally less reliable than import data, but they supplied the TMB with the requested export data in a table adjusting for the overstatement in the US underwear market. The changes in the data did not contradict the March Statement. In fact, the data corroborated the original determination of serious damage or actual threat thereof. The change in the data was minimal; even as adjusted, the data still showed a large increase in imports. The adjustment in market size also had no impact in the data on important factors listed in Article 6.3 of the ATC, such as production, output, capacity, employment, domestic prices, profits and investment. Even taking the adjustments into account, the data as a whole still showed a picture of a seriously damaged industry threatened with further damage.

5.148 The *United States* also noted that the updated data and other relevant information presented to the TMB only supported the basis for the determination of the United States. At the time when the data were initially presented in the March 1995 statement, they were the latest available and most correct. The updated data presented in the July 1995 statement to the TMB also provided import data through April 1995, indicating that imports continued to increase, supporting the determination. Contrary to the statement of Costa Rica in its submission, the *United States* considered that the TMB had not excluded or disregarded the updated data provided in July. In fact, the TMB referred mostly to the revised data throughout its examination. The TMB considered the updated and other relevant data in the July Statement, with full regard to the relevant provisions in Articles 6.7 and 6.10 of the ATC, despite attempts of Costa Rica and others to characterize the data in both statements as inaccurate and contradictory. In fact, during the TMB proceeding the United States had adjusted data to reflect concerns about double counting of re-imports. The United States had initially properly deducted re-imports from production. The United States had then responded to TMB comments and requests by further adjusting the data, using US export data. After these adjustments, the data still showed declines in production and increases in imports.

5.149 In the view of *Costa Rica*, by failing to treat this aspect correctly in its March Market Statement or in July or October, the United States was not only making a mistake from the standpoint of the counting of data; this error also proved to be very important in this particular case, given the nature of the trade between Costa Rica and the United States in this category. If the United States had not differentiated this "807" production, it should not have continued with this case. Accordingly, *Costa Rica* argued that the information submitted by the United States to demonstrate the supposed serious damage was not only unreliable, erroneous and contradictory, but above all it was also incomplete.

G.   Existence of a Causal Link

5.150 *Costa Rica* claimed that the third requirement whose existence the United States should have demonstrated in order to be able to invoke a transitional safeguard measure was the existence of a causal link between the supposed increase in imports and the supposed serious damage or actual threat of serious damage to the domestic industry producing a like and/or directly competing product. The United States did not do so, and consequently violated Article 6.2 of the ATC. This Article provided that a measure of the kind described may be applied when an importing Member demonstrated that:

> "... a particular product is being imported into its territory in such increased quantities as to cause serious damage, or actual threat thereof, to the domestic industry producing like and/or directly competitive products. Serious damage or actual threat thereof must demonstrably be caused by such increased quantities in total imports of that product and not by such other factors as technological changes or changes in consumer preference" .

5.151 It followed that, prior to demonstrating the existence of a causal link, the United States should have demonstrated the existence of the two conditions which it would be trying to link in this exercise, namely, the increase in imports and the serious damage or actual threat thereof. Since the United States had failed to fulfil that part of the exercise, it was impossible to analyze whether or not a causal link existed. Even assuming for the sake of argument that there had existed an increase in imports and serious damage or actual threat thereof to the United States industry producing cotton and man-made fibre underwear - which, as repeatedly stated by *Costa Rica*, did not exist - it would not be possible to conclude that this supposed damage or threat was being caused by imports.

Restraint Agreements with Other Countries

5.152 In *Costa Rica's* view, the best proof of the non-existence of this causal relationship lay in the levels of restraint which the United States had obtained with the other countries that had been called for consultations in category 352/652 - Colombia, El Salvador, Honduras, the Dominican Republic and Turkey. It was pointed out that the access which the United States had granted to the five countries with which it had reached an understanding in this category was about 170 million dozen for 1996, equivalent to an increase of 478 per cent with respect to imports from the same five countries in 1994, which amounted to 29 million dozen. If 29 million dozen were causing or threatening to cause serious damage, how could the United States have negotiated an increase in this quantity by a percentage of 478 per cent?

5.153 *Costa Rica* argued that the foregoing provided grounds for categorically maintaining that if the United States underwear industry was suffering any serious damage or actual threat thereof - which, it claimed, it was not - it was impossible to believe that imports were the cause of it, as in that case it would be most strange for the United States itself to seek to increase the source of its supposed problems in such a significant way as to cause its ruin. The only reasonable conclusion was that imports were neither causing nor threatening to cause serious damage to the United States industry and that by nevertheless taking safeguard action the United States had violated Article 6.2 of the ATC.

5.154 The *United States* noted that Costa Rica had made extensive use of information on negotiated settlements with countries not party to this dispute in its first submission and at the first substantive Panel meeting. This information, in the US view, was inappropriate to the Panel's task and the Panel should not allow it to be used to prejudice US rights in this case. Article 6.9 of the ATC provided a mechanism for collective review of negotiated settlements in the form of TMB review. Costa Rica's argument undercut and attacked those settlements in a manner which also undercut the TMB. These settlements and Article 6.9 of the ATC were not within the Panel's terms of reference. However, since the Panel's questions had focused in part on these settlements, the United States responded to the question while reserving their rights in this matter.

5.155 Upon request of the Panel, the *United States* commented that the Panel should consider the situation which required them to impose the restraint on Costa Rican underwear in a broader context. When a finding of serious damage or threat thereof was made, and in the resulting imposition of a restraint and formulation of a negotiating strategy, various considerations needed to be taken into account, some of which may be in conflict as measures were devised to achieve the greatest degree of fairness to all concerned. These included: special attributes of the individual major suppliers, which affected equity considerations towards other countries under restriction; the US obligation to comply with Article 6.6(d) of the ATC; and the diverse nature of the US industry and the differing impact of the increased quantities of underwear imports on the individual segments of the industry. After making a finding of serious damage, or actual threat thereof, affecting the industry producing a particular product, the United States must then consider attribution to the particular countries whose imports were causing the serious damage, or actual threat thereof. It was at this stage of the process that a range of factors must be integrated into the decision such as the nature of the imports, the various levels of imports accounted for by the supplying countries (both controlled and uncontrolled), and the specific impact on the US firms and their employees (including those that participate in outward processing and those that do not). When the underwear calls were made, there were many divergent interests involved.

5.156 In establishing attribution to individual countries, the basic situation facing the CITA was that in the 352/652 category, half of the import total was accounted for by imports under outward processing arrangements (cut parts assembled offshore), and 30 per cent of the imports were from the two largest suppliers, Dominican Republic and Costa Rica, both uncontrolled. The United States had to establish a balance when implementing policies affecting its own outward processing programmes with no one consideration taking precedence over another. The underwear restraint on Costa Rica was an example.

5.157 The *United States* explained that many countries supplying underwear to the United States that were under restriction, did not utilize the "807" programme and were not eligible for the "807A" programme. Many of the specific limits to which these countries were subject had been substantially exceeded by the import level attained by Costa Rica at the time its restraint was imposed. Costa Rica's higher level was attained because of its participation in outward processing, yet it evidently was not interested in participating in the programme designed to give more favourable treatment to the trade. The US policy allowing liberal import access for Caribbean-assembled clothing thus had resulted in a situation whereby competing imports from non-CBI countries in category 352/652 had been placed at a disadvantage. The proposed levels were intended as a partial redress to this situation. In a safeguard action, a number of factors such as equity towards other suppliers, welfare of US firms, and broader trade policy considerations were also reflected in the overall position taken in negotiations. In conjunction with the offer of substantial GAL made to Costa Rica, the United States had proposed to set a Specific Limit to cover the imports of underwear made from fabric not formed and cut in the United States that, while lower than the call level, was more than enough to allow for the estimated existing level of this trade. This offer was consistent with the offers accepted by other major suppliers, the Dominican Republic, for example, which agreed to an SL well below the level of trade.

5.158 The limits established covering the 1995 underwear calls were heavily weighted in favour of "807A trade". The US policy to allow more liberal treatment for the CBI products that contain US-made fabric obviously maximised the benefit to US economic welfare. In evaluating the damaging impact of imports, absolute levels were only one of many elements taken into consideration, along with rates of growth, the ability of the domestic producers to adjust, employment patterns, industry structure, etc. Goods imported under the "807A" provision were not regarded as less damaging than non-GAL 807 and other imports, but it was recognized that the nature of their effect on the domestic industry could be significantly different. Unlike GALs, non-GAL imports were not eligible for increased quota access. One significant distinction among US companies was between those that had moved their finished garment assembly facilities to the Caribbean to take advantage of the 807 duty provision and CBI liberal access, and those that continued to produce finished garments domestically. The former were the companies which had moved the bulk of their underwear production offshore and were reaping enormous benefit from the trade concessions affecting the CBI. At the same time, the restrictions were also intended to furnish a degree of temporary protection for the US producers which had not yet begun to or were in the early stages of making the adjustment to increased international competition in this product category.

5.159 In the view of the *United States*, the GAL programme recognized the economic realities of apparel manufacturing and was intended to furnish a competitive option to US firms operating in this industry and, from a policy perspective, provides some important benefits: (i) the comparatively high levels offered allowed sufficient flexibility and latitude for US companies and their CBI partners to efficiently serve the market, while providing some certainty and a reference level for those domestic producers that were unable or unwilling to participate in outward processing arrangements; (ii) prior to eventual CBI parity with the NAFTA, the GAL programme provided a means of identifying the goods that would qualify for parity while allowing a lower Specific Limit to exercise a degree of control over the non-GAL component of trade which could conceivably be filled by goods with non US content; and (iii) the high GAL levels offered in 352/652 were intended as a guarantee of ample access to the US market during the three-year term of the restraint and in anticipation of the CBI countries' future inclusion in a wider Free Trade Area of the Americas. They were not expected to be fully filled immediately.

5.160 *Costa Rica* pointed out that none of these considerations were included in the ATC: Therefore, they could not be used as justifications to deviate from the ATC provisions. Although these considerations could be useful at the domestic level, they did not authorize the United States to breach its obligations under the ATC.

5.161 *Costa Rica* emphasized that GAL trade and "807 trade" were not the same thing. The "807 trade" referred to products assembled using US components which could represent all or part of the components used to assemble the product and must be cut in the US, although the fabric could be sourced from anywhere. Thus, within "807 trade", there might be garments that qualify for GAL, which would be those made from fabric formed and cut in the US, and others that require SL, which would be those made with any amount of non-US formed and cut fabric. In sum, for US restraints, "807" trade included both SL and GAL to the extent that both of them shared the characteristic of being made from at least some fabric cut in the US.

5.162 The United States, commenting on the above, agreed that it was impossible to distinguish, from the data available, between Category 352/652 products that would qualify for a GAL quota and those that would not. This had been their position throughout the proceeding. This consideration was, in fact, a major element in the US offers of a GAL quota in negotiations with Costa Rica, since such a determination could not be made without an agreement in place containing a GAL provision.

5.163 *Costa Rica* also drew particular reference to the US statement in the penultimate sentence of paragraph 5.149. With reference to this, Costa Rica pointed out two aspects, first, it was only after finding that the imposition of a restraint was justified that the importing Member could implement it, bearing in mind its obligation to grant the minimum SL level mandated by Article 6.8 of the ATC, which in the present case would be equal to 14,423,178 dozen. Moreover, according to the language of Article 6.6(d), a "more favourable treatment" to re-imports, which would necessarily represent an improvement in the conditions to which the Member whose trade had been restricted would have been entitled, must also be granted. Any other interpretation of this provision was considered to be incorrect. Costa Rica further argued that by pretending to impose on Costa Rica an SL quota lower than the call level and attempting to justify its action under Article 6.6(d) of the ATC by granting a GAL quota of 40 million, the United States was violating Article 6.8 of the ATC as well as Article 6.6(d). Article 6.8 mandated that the minimum SL level should be the quota level. On top of that level, the importing Member was obliged to offer a more favourable treatment to re-imports from the exporting Member. In any case, an unconditioned access could not be substituted by a conditioned access, even if the latter were larger in quantitative terms than the former.

5.164 *Costa Rica* reiterated that in the absence of GAL procedures, it was impossible for the US to identify and monitor imports that might be entitled to the GAL programme and therefore to determine that the SL quota offered, although lower than the call level, was "more than enough" since there was no data to determine that amount. The standard provided in the ATC was not an SL level that was more than enough, but an SL level that equalled the call level as a minimum. The United States was justifying its offers on estimates that had no basis, being only arbitrary estimates made by the US Government.

5.165 In response to the above point, the *United States* agreed that it was only after the importing Member had determined that a safeguard restriction was necessary and justified that the Member could implement the restriction. The United States had always maintained that this was the case here. They disagreed that their proposals during consultations were inconsistent with Article 6.8 of the ATC. It was clear that all proposals to Costa Rica involved levels above the reference period mandated in Article 6.8. The proposals made concerning the guaranteed access level (GAL) component of the restriction were consistent with Article 6.8 and the requirements of Article 6.6(d) of the ATC. The GAL proposals were offered with the understanding that the programme was improved access for Costa Rica. The improved access was evidenced in earlier agreements with Costa Rica, and other Caribbean Basin countries, as well as the fact that companies established in Costa Rica participating in the GAL programme had resulted in more employment for Costa Rican nationals and investment in Costa Rica and that products exported to the United States under the GAL programme were treated even in Costa Rican statistics as Costa Rican products when exported to the United States (and as imports when entering Costa Rica as cut parts).

5.166 The *United States* had met its obligation under the ATC to provide more favourable treatment to re-imports. That obligation had been met after the United States satisfied the requirements of Articles 6.2, 6.3 and 6.4. Article 6.6(d) gave the importing Member wide discretion on how more favourable treatment to re-imports was to be provided. That is the way the text was negotiated. The United States has established a GAL programme which requires, for proper monitoring and certification, the agreement of the exporting Member. The United States could not be faulted if Costa Rica chose not to accept its offer of more favourable treatment. All outward processing programmes in other countries typically were preferential programmes which allowed the importing country the latitude to establish the criteria for participation in the programme - including the conditioning of the use of fabric manufactured in the importing country. The United States was not alone concerning that condition; other WTO Members maintained quotas, which limited outward processing traffic. The policy basis for the various conditions for participation in an importing country's outward processing programme may inherently represent the balancing of various domestic interests. In the case of the United States, the balancing of interests reached beyond the industry provided relief when safeguard action was taken on imports that includes re-imports. The safeguard action taken in this case was not action to provide adjustment to an "upstream" product.

5.167 *Costa Rica* pointed out that the US had mentioned that equity was one of the factors taken into account when establishing a safeguard. However, the United States, besides having no justification, never achieved half of the minimum SL level to which Costa Rica was entitled, nor was this level comparable in either relative or absolute terms to the levels agreed with the other countries called under this same category. Other countries received an SL quota higher than their call levels, in some instances obtaining increases that went up from 54 to 99 per cent in SL access. In the view of Costa Rica, the Dominican Republic had accepted an SL quota lower than its call level as a result of findings reached by the US after a number of investigations that determined the existence of transshipment in this category.

5.168 The *United States* responded to the above point, stating that the equity considerations taken by the United States were discussed thoroughly with Costa Rica and other countries during consultations. Costa Rica insisted on access that was beyond what was equitable in the case of access to the US market for Costa Rica and compared to other countries. It was incorrect that all of the other countries received SL's higher than the call level. Most egregious of Costa Rica's assertions on that point was the false statement that the lower SL portion for the Dominican Republic was to account for transshipments. The alleged transshipments referred to by Costa Rica were already covered before the agreement with the Dominican Republic, and the transshipment cases took place before the time frame of the safeguard action. Further, in the view of the US, even the Dominican Republic did not agree with the assertion of Costa Rica.

5.169 *Costa Rica* also noted that the US had stated (paragraph 5.158) that "unlike GALs, non-GAL imports are not eligible for increased quota access"; however, the US had notified both SL and GALs under Article 2 of the ATC. Therefore, both quotas were subject to the increased percentages mandated by Article 2.1 of the ATC. Also, the US considerations intended to justify the GAL levels offered and agreed in this category (NAFTA Parity Programme or the Free Trade Area of the Americas) could not be used as justifications to deviate from the ATC provisions.

5.170 The *United States* argued that Costa Rica was incorrect in its interpretation of Article 2.1 of the ATC concerning growth for quotas, and in particular growth for GALs notified by the United States under Article 2. First, Costa Rica did not understand what the United States meant concerning eligibility for increased quota access. Eligibility for increased quota access referred to the requirements of the GAL programme which was a US domestic programme, not established under the ATC. Second, the United States could not discern any increased percentages of quotas mandated by Article 2.1 of the ATC as claimed by Costa Rica. Even if Costa Rica meant to refer to another provision of Article 2, the provision would only apply to those levels that were specifically allocated growth before notification under Article 2. The GALs notified under Article 2 specifically did not include growth percentages since GAL quotas already provide preferential access. US policy considerations when providing more favourable treatment or negotiating any settlement with Costa Rica, especially when those policy considerations included benefits for both the United States and Costa Rica, were not breaches of the ATC. There was no issue here concerning whether the ATC contained or required any policy considerations. The United States noted in this proceeding, however, that the very discretion provided in Article 6.6(d) for more favourable treatment did account for such policy considerations - including taking into account NAFTA parity for textile and apparel products - which the United States thought was of general interest to Costa Rica.

The United States Policies in Applying the Safeguard

5.171 In the *United States*' view, the CITA determination had been entirely reasonable, based on the situation of serious damage or actual threat, and Costa Rica had not demonstrated otherwise. If the United States had shown generosity in the context of its bilateral negotiating strategy, this still did not change the fact that the original determination had been made on the basis of serious damage or actual threat thereof. In bilateral textile negotiations, the United States formulated its overall position by integrating a number of policies, such as the need for time for structural adjustment in the US industry, equity toward other suppliers, the requirements of ATC Article 6.6 of the ATC, and broader trade policy and foreign policy considerations. The ATC did not limit the policies that could be taken into account in this context; indeed, to do so would be contrary to the interests of textile and apparel exporters. Should the ATC be interpreted in accordance with Costa Rica's arguments, so as to require an importing Member to offer in negotiations only the most restricted access to its market?

5.172 In the context of Article 6.6(d) of the ATC, the *United States* had proposed to Costa Rica a restraint of 7 million dozen on a specific limit (SL) basis and an additional 40 million dozen guaranteed access level for future GAL-qualifying trade. CITA had determined that imports in Category 352/652 were causing serious damage or actual threat thereof to the US underwear industry, and that this serious damage was attributable to the 14.4 million dozen imports from Costa Rica. The access levels proposed to Costa Rica were designed to provide security of access for Costa Rican exports during the restraint period. In return, the agreement would have provided for an orderly flow of imports from Costa Rica, allowing the US industry time to adjust to the increased import competition in the US underwear market.

5.173 The *United States* argued that, in evaluating the GAL programme, the Panel should not lose sight of the overall goals of the ATC. The Agreement will accomplish the long-sought integration of the textile and clothing sector into the GATT, over its ten-year lifetime. Accomplishment of that goal will require substantial and difficult structural adjustment by the textile and apparel industries of importing Members during that period. The GAL programme served as an adjustment mechanism. Safeguards under Article 6 of the ATC were only transitory matters, lasting a maximum of three years. However, the Agreement had recognized the need for such safeguards in order to allow industry to adjust and prepare for the post-integration environment that was now less than ten years away. The Agreement provided procedural provisions that required that such safeguards not be taken without consultation and discussion with the exporting country and maximized the possibility that safeguards would be implemented consensually in a manner that took the interests of the exporting country into account. The GAL programme was fully consistent with those policies.

H.   Attribution to Individual Exporting Country(ies)

5.174 *Costa Rica* noted that the application of a transitional safeguard measure to the trade of a particular Member required the fulfilment of two successive stages, each of which had its own substantive requirements. In the case under consideration, the United States had failed to demonstrate the prerequisites for having the right to resort to the safeguard mechanism in accordance with Articles 6.2 and 6.3 of the ATC. Consequently, an analysis of whether or not it had fulfilled the substantive requirements laid down for the attribution stage provided for in Article 6.4 of the ATC was not required. Nevertheless, for illustration, an analysis of how the United States had also failed to fulfil this second stage of the process, thus once again demonstrating the unjustified nature of the restriction adopted against Costa Rican trade in category 352/652, was provided.

5.175 The first requirement which the importing Member must demonstrate in this second stage of the process was, under Article 6.4 of the ATC, the following:

> " ... The Member or Members to whom serious damage, or actual threat thereof, referred to in paragraphs 2 and 3, is attributed, shall be determined on the basis of a sharp and substantial increase in the imports, actual or imminent, from such a Member or Members individually ...".

For these purposes, Article 6.7 of the ATC provided that

> "... The request for consultations should be accompanied by specific and relevant factual information, as up-to-date as possible, particularly in regard to: ... (b) the factors, referred to in paragraph 4, on the basis of which it proposes to invoke the safeguard action with respect to the Member or Members concerned".

Obligation to Submit Specific and Relevant Information

5.176 *Costa Rica* argued that in accordance with the above, the United States had the obligation to submit specific and relevant information and to carry out an examination, on an individual basis, of the specific case of Costa Rican trade. In the March Market Statement, the basis of the unilateral restriction, the United States had claimed to show in four lines that there was a sharp and substantial, real or imminent increase, in imports from Costa Rica. To this end, the United States had provided a few statistics, without any kind of analysis. This omission of any analysis, which was part of its demonstration obligation for this requirement, was extremely serious, all the more serious in this case since, as the impact of "807 trade" on Costa Rican trade in products classified in category 352/652 was all-important.

5.177 The possibility of attributing a particular condition of serious damage or actual threat thereof to another Member obviously depended on the existence of the serious damage or actual threat thereof. In the case under consideration, firstly it was highly questionable whether an increase in Costa Rican imports of this product existed, except if such imports were considered purely and simply as such, without regard for their special features, and secondly, no such serious damage or actual threat thereof existed.

5.178 It could be demonstrated that if such damage or threat had existed, it could not be attributed to imports from Costa Rica, by referring to the proposals made by the United States to Costa Rica in seeking to reach an agreement on the volume of the quantitative restriction. How could it be argued that 14.4 million dozen of underwear, which was what Costa Rica exported in 1994, was causing serious damage or actual threat thereof to the United States underwear industry if the United States had proposed to Costa Rica that the restriction for this category should be in the order of 47 million dozen? The only possible conclusion was that the United States had also failed to demonstrate this substantive requirement, thus infringing Article 6.4 of the ATC.

The Nature of Costa Rica's Exports

5.179 It was recalled by *Costa Rica* that 99.5 per cent of their exports in category 352/652 in 1993, and 99.76 per cent of their exports in 1994, had entered the United States under tariff subheading 9802.00.80, in order to benefit from the tariff exemption provided for that subheading. This meant that trade in the category under consideration between Costa Rica and the United States concerned almost exclusively a process of co-production or shared production. In this condition, it was questionable whether one was dealing with "imports" or rather with domestic production, which, while assembled in Costa Rica, did not cease to be domestic production simply for that reason. It was recalled that the United States itself considered imports of cut parts for assembly in the United States as products of the country in which the parts were cut. In these circumstances, United States exports of cut pieces should logically have been considered United States products. Accordingly, one could not speak of an increase in "imports", since they were not really imports.

5.180 The *United States* noted that Article 6.6(d) of the ATC stated that re-imports were "... defined by the laws and practices of the importing Member." All apparel re-imports, qualifying for special quota access or not, were defined under United States law and practice as "foreign articles" and were accorded duty reductions to the extent of their US content. Under US law, quota benefits accrued if an agreement with the exporting country had been concluded for apparel assembled with US formed and cut fabric. However, a high percentage of US content did not automatically confer US origin or make a re-import a US good under US law.

5.181 The *United States* considered that Costa Rica had been given incorrect information with respect to the re-imports of textile and apparel articles. Costa Rica had asserted in its submission that the rule of origin in the United States for products entering under tariff heading 9802.00.80 was the place where the pieces were cut. Thus, Costa Rica was asserting that because underwear exported by Costa Rica to the United States had been cut in the United States, it was US origin under US law. Cutting did not confer origin for these products under US law. Neither the rule of origin for textiles and apparel which was in effect at that time nor the revised rule of origin, which became effective on 1 July 1996, had any applicability to apparel re-imports because the US headnote to HTSUS 9802 clearly stated that such goods were "foreign articles" and not US goods. Therefore, underwear re-imported from Costa Rica to the United States was treated by US law as Costa Rican goods.

5.182 *Costa Rica* argued that, if it were decided to consider that there had been an increase in imports of Costa Rican underwear, it was quite clear that if such imports were increasing it was because United States production of cut pieces that were subsequently assembled in Costa Rica was increasing in the same proportion. If ever more underwear was being assembled in Costa Rica it was because in the United States ever more cut pieces for underwear were being produced that needed to be assembled. It therefore followed that any industry producing cut pieces for underwear was in a thriving condition and so did not need to be protected from something that was rather of benefit to the underwear producing industry. Consequently, under either hypothesis, the fact was that the measure imposed by the United States against Costa Rica's trade in products included in category 352/652 had no grounds in Article 6.4 of the ATC.

I.   More Favourable Treatment for Re-Imports

5.183 With respect to the provision of preferential treatment under Article 6.6(d) of the ATC, *Costa Rica* considered that there were three aspects to be taken into account: (i) before establishing a restriction it had to be justified under the terms of Articles 6.2 and 6.3 of the ATC; (ii) only after that stage had been fulfilled, the importing Member could implement such a restriction, bearing in mind its obligation to grant the minimum SL level mandated by Article 6.8 of the ATC (i.e. in the present case 14,426,178 SL quota) and only over that minimum extend the more favourable treatment established in Article 6.6(d) of the ATC; and (iii) according to the language of Article 6.6(d) of the ATC this more favourable treatment was mandatory and shall represent an improvement on conditions to which the Member whose trade has been restricted would have been entitled to if it had not had the right to such more favourable treatment. Upon request of the Panel, *Costa Rica* clarified that it had never rejected a more preferential treatment because such treatment had never been offered by the United States. The best SL quota offered to Costa Rica had not even reached half of the minimum SL level to which it was entitled under Article 6.8 of the ATC. Furthermore, the SL had been more restrictive to the extent that it was subject to a sub-limit and to the "ratchet down" provision.

5.184 The *United States* noted that the sole reference to re-imports in the ATC appeared after the stage when the importing Member had made its determination of serious damage, or actual threat thereof, and attribution, in the context of consultations on the application of the transitional safeguard. The United States had sought to provide preferential treatment to re-imports from Costa Rica consistent with the requirements of Article 6.6(d) of the ATC which provided, in part, that,

> "[i]n the application of the transitional safeguard, particular account shall be taken of the interests of exporting Members as set out below: (d) more favourable treatment shall be accorded to re-imports by a Member of textile and clothing products which that Member has exported to another Member for processing and subsequent reimportation, as defined by the laws and practices of the importing Member, and subject to satisfactory control and certification procedures, when these products are imported from a Member for which this type of trade represents a significant proportion of its total exports of textiles and clothing."

5.185 The *United States* argued that, in accordance with customary rules of international law concerning treaty interpretation, as reflected in the Vienna Convention on the Law of Treaties, the United States had looked to the plain meaning of the terms in their context and object and purpose. The plain meaning of "more favourable treatment" did not mean that re-imports must be excluded from safeguard action. If that were the intent, the agreement would have so stated. Concerning the context of Article 6.6(d) of the ATC, they saw that this and the other provisions for favourable treatment in Article 6.6 of the ATC appeared in the text of Article 6 of the ATC after and separate from the provisions on the requirements for making determinations of the serious damage, or actual threat thereof, and attribution. Also, the "chapeau" of Article 6.6 of the ATC plainly stated "in the application of the transitional safeguard... ." To the extent that the meaning of the plain text of Article 6.6 of the ATC may be considered ambiguous, Article 32 of the Vienna Convention on the Law of Treaties permitted recourse to supplementary means of interpretation "in order to confirm the meaning resulting from the application of Article 31" of the Convention. They could find supplementary assistance in a similar provision in the MFA.

5.186 Article 6.6(d) of the ATC was derived from Article 6.6 of the MFA and paragraph 15 of the 1986 Protocol to the MFA concerning more favourable treatment to re-imports. These provisions for more favourable treatment for re-imports were largely demanded by exporting countries benefitting from outward processing programmes. MFA Article 6.6 provided that

> "[c]onsideration shall be given to special and differential treatment to re-imports into a participating country of textile products which that country has exported to another participating country for processing and subsequent re-importation, in the light of the special nature of such trade without prejudice to the provisions of Article 3 [MFA safeguard]." Paragraph 15 of 1986 Protocol added that: "in conformity with the provisions of Article 6.6 of the Arrangement for consideration to be given to special differen-

tial and more favourable treatment, in the light of the special nature of the trade referred to therein, participants agreed that, in negotiating bilateral restraints account shall be taken of the relative degree to which these exports contribute to situations of market disruption or real risk thereof."

5.187 It was noted that one commentator in the United States[13] had observed concerning the interpretation of paragraph 15:

> "To the extent it could be argued that paragraph 15 does go beyond Article 6 [of the MFA] by defining 'special and differential treatment' to include an accounting of the extent to which such merchandise contributes to market disruption, it appears to be applicable only in the negotiation of bilateral restraints. In any event, neither the [MFA] nor the Protocol creates a presumption that re-imports cannot cause or contribute to market disruption."

Both of these provisions clearly indicated that the preferential consideration for re-imports arose only after the determination of market disruption had been made; that is, in the application of the safeguard and in proposals for restraints to be applied by mutual agreement. The *United States* considered that they had followed the requirements in Article 6.6(d) of the ATC in consultations with Costa Rica.

5.188 The *United States* also argued that the form of "more favourable treatment" was left to the importing Member. Whereas other provisions for favourable treatment in the ATC provided for specific types of favourable treatment to be given, Article 6.6(d) of the ATC indicated that it was the importing Member which accorded the more favourable treatment, and the negotiators had left it up to the importing Member to assign the type of treatment to be given to re-imports. It followed that even the definition of what kind of more favourable treatment was to be given to re-imports was left to the law and practice, or otherwise discretion, of the importing Member. The relevant laws and practices included customs laws, which affected the applied duty rate on re-imports, as well as the laws and regulations governing textile and apparel trade quota programme, which affected the treatment accorded re-imports in this context.

5.189 The ATC did not define how an importing country must give more favourable treatment. Nothing in the text or negotiating history of Article 6.6(d) of the ATC provided otherwise. Importing countries had different ways of according more favourable treatment to re-imports. No one country defined its outward processing programmes the same way. Article 6.6(d) of the ATC, and the MFA provisions from which it was derived, allowed for that fact. In this case, the

---

[13] Jacob, B. "Renewal and Expansion of the Multifibre Arrangement" 19 Law and Policy in International Business 7, 33 (Georgetown University Law Center, 1987).

United States had made use of the GAL programme as its means of providing preferential quantitative treatment for apparel re-imports from the Caribbean Basin. The United States could mitigate the effects of serious damage and actual threat thereof to its domestic producers by offering more favourable treatment to some re-imports than it provided to other re-imports.

5.190 *Costa Rica* considered that the restraint proposals made by the United States could not lead to the conclusion that these could be situated within the concept of more favourable treatment provided for in Article 6.6(d) of the ATC. The specific restraint level (SL) offered to Costa Rica was not even close to the minimum SL level to which Costa Rica would have had the right pursuant to Article 6.8 of the ATC which obliged the United States to offer as a minimum an SL quota of 14,423,178 dozen whereas the US' most generous proposal did not even reach half the level at the time of the request for consultations and was even more restrictive due to the fixing of a sub-limit and the "ratchet-down" provision. Since the United States had not granted the minimum level to which Costa Rica had a right, it was not possible to consider that they had granted the more favoured treatment prescribed in Article 6.6(d) of the ATC. On the contrary, the United States had granted Costa Rica less favourable treatment than the treatment it was obliged to grant to any Member of the WTO under Article 6.8 of the ATC.

5.191 The establishment of an SL quota below the level provided for in Article 6.8 of the ATC, together with the establishment of a GAL quota to cover the difference and if necessary exceed this level, was contrary to the spirit and letter of Article 6.6(d) of the ATC and would place an exporting Member that did not participate in co-production in a better situation than a Member that does participate because the former would enjoy the minimal unconditional level of access provided for in Article 6.8 of the ATC, while the second would see their market access subject to rigid conditions.

5.192 In the *United States'* view, Costa Rica's arguments treated the process of making determinations under Article 6 of the ATC as a one-dimensional process in which the sole factors that governed action by importing Members were those listed in Articles 6.3 and 6.4 of the ATC. In Article 6.6(d), the ATC fully permitted Members to be flexible "in the application of the transitional safeguard" for special needs of the exporting country and the importing country. Article 6.6(d) of the ATC permitted the importing country to provide more favourable treatment by taking advantage of special access policies, such as the 807A (GAL) outward processing programme. It did not require that such programmes reflect solely the needs of the exporting country. In fact, the access levels offered in the context of the GAL programme do not legally correspond to the determinations required under Articles 6.2, 6.3 and 6.4 of the ATC. These factors were distinct from the factors that the authorities should take into account when making the determinations required in Articles 6.2, 6.3 and 6.4 of the ATC. GALs were arranged through negotiation and agreement in order to verify and certify that such goods met the requirements of the programme. Article 6.6(d) of the ATC even made reference to satisfactory control and certification procedures. A country may opt, as did Costa Rica, not to accept the type of more favourable treatment offered.

5.193 The purpose of the safeguard was to provide relief from import surges, not to prevent growth of imports. Therefore, if re-imports were surging, they would contribute to serious damage and actual threat thereof. Unlike the other provisions for special treatment, Article 6.6(d) of the ATC allowed importing countries the most flexibility to decide how to provide favourable treatment for re-imports, taking into account the special nature of the trade, but it did not mandate any particular form or manner of providing favourable treatment. The other subparagraphs in Article 6.6 of the ATC provided more specific guidance on how the special treatment should be given in those cases. The United States at one point had offered 7 million dozen specific limit and 40 million dozen GAL to Costa Rica. This offer was made to provide security of access for Costa Rica exports throughout the three-year term of the restriction. It also would have provided for orderly access of imports from Costa Rica allowing the US industry to adjust to increased import competition in the US underwear market. The offers made concerning a combination of SL and GAL access were consistent with the ATC and overall US policy interests and were consistent with US policy under the MFA.

5.194 The *United States* referred to the assertion of Costa Rica that since some of the provisions for special treatment in Article 6.6 of the ATC specified the form such treatment was to take, and Article 6.6(d) of the ATC did not, then an importing Member must accord favourable treatment to re-imports at some earlier point: while making its determination of serious damage, or actual threat thereof; while making its attribution determination; and/or before consultations. This argument was without basis in Articles 6.2, 6.3 or 6.4 of the ATC, which did not even mention re-imports, let alone provide for special treatment. The only provision for special treatment was Article 6.6 of the ATC, which only addressed special treatment to be given "[i]n the application of the transitional safeguard". DSU Article 3.2 stated the fundamental principle that DSB recommendations could not "add to ... the rights and obligations provided in the covered agreements." To read obligations into the purposeful blanks left in Article 6.6(d) of the ATC would contradict this principle, which was central to the stability of the dispute settlement system. The notion that favourable treatment under Article 6.6(d) of the ATC *must* be accorded in a particular form was inconsistent with the plain text of Article 6.6(d) of the ATC, which provided no such limitation on treatment.

5.195 The *United States* estimated that 94 per cent of Costa Rica's exports were re-imports made from fabric cut in the United States. The remaining 6 per cent, made from fabric not cut in the United States, amounted to 889,101 dozen. This meant that the portion made from fabric not cut in the United States would not qualify for the guaranteed access level. The 889,101 dozen alone would still have led the United States to attribute serious damage, or actual threat thereof to Costa Rica's imports. Therefore, Costa Rica's assertion that the remaining 6 per cent could not damage or threaten damage to the US domestic industry was false. Finally, the re-imports had posed a threat to the US domestic industry that did not participate in outward processing (approximately 60 per cent of the US firms producing underwear in the United States). The United States had taken this into account during negotiations when balancing the effect of re-imports on the domestic industry and formulating proposals for more favourable treatment under Article 6.6(d) of the ATC.

5.196 *Costa Rica* was concerned that there could be some confusion about the levels of trade in "807" and those in GALs. In their view, the United States could not know prior to the implementation of a GAL programmes which clothing was "eligible" or not under the programme because it was only when the customs inspections under the programme were carried out that it was possible to know which clothing had been manufactured using cloth formed and cut in the United States. The figure of 94 per cent which the United States had referred to was not necessarily all eligible for GAL. In fact, according to the statistics published by the United States Department of Trade, the percentage of Costa Rican trade in the 352/652 category within the framework of "807 trade" exceeded 99 per cent. However, even if 99 per cent of a country's trade was under the "807 trade" framework, this would bear no relation to the percentage of its trade which utilized fabric formed in the United States.

5.197 The *United States* pointed out that it had always stated in this proceeding that it could not identify GAL eligible products until a country entered into an agreement with the US for GALs and the proper certification was in place that would verify that US "formed" fabric was used, not just that it was fabric "cut" in the US. Before a GAL agreement was established, the US only had data on fabric "cut" in the US, not "formed" in the US as well. For GAL eligibility, US "formed" and "cut" fabric must be used. As the United States had stated in its submissions, the 94 per cent figure only indicated "cut" parts not whether the fabric was also "formed" in the United States. The United States had verified that 94 per cent of Costa Rica's trade was made from parts "cut" in the United States.

The United States Fabric Industry

5.198 *Costa Rica* claimed that, from its analysis the question arose: what was the domestic industry which the United States was really trying to protect by imposing the safeguard on Costa Rica in this category? In accordance with Article 6.2 of the ATC it was clear that a safeguard measure as provided for therein had the purpose of providing temporary protection for the domestic industry producing "like and/or directly competitive products" with respect to the specific products that were being imported. That was why the proper action to provide such protection, once the due justification had been provided, was the restriction of imports.

5.199 *Costa Rica* argued that, as the product being imported was cotton and man-made fibre underwear, the only domestic industry which it could be sought to protect through Article 6 of the ATC was the United States industry that produced cotton and man-made fibre underwear, and not any other industry. Although the United States had formally stated that the industry it was seeking to protect was the cotton and man-made fibre underwear industry, the fact of the matter was that in view of the proposals made by the United States to Costa Rica and the agreements it had reached with other countries called for consultations over this category, the clear conclusion was that the United States was not seeking to protect the domestic industry producing such products. It was impossible to consider that that was its objective when in the negotiations it had agreed to a substantial increase in market access for imports of such products. On the other hand, neither did it appear reasonable to consider that the United States had no motives for its decision to apply a specific safeguard measure to Costa Rica in category 352/652. The United States certainly did have a motive, but, in the view of *Costa Rica*, that motive was not covered by the ATC.

5.200   *Costa Rica* considered that the reply to this question was to be found both in the proposals made by the United States to Costa Rica and in the agreements reached with the other countries called for consultations in this category, and it was the following: what the United States was seeking to do was to protect the domestic industry that produced the fabric used in the production of underwear. For this purpose, the United States had followed two routes: firstly, it had sought to restrict access to its market for underwear made from fabric not produced in the United States, and secondly, it had guaranteed wider and substantial access to its market for underwear made from fabric formed and cut in the United States. As the same time as imports of underwear produced from non-US fabric were restricted, a guaranteed broad level of access was provided for imports using fabric formed and cut in the United States. That was why the various proposals made by the United States to Costa Rica to try to reach an agreement on the level of restriction were two-fold in nature: a lower access level for non-conditional or specific level (SL) trade - in the order of 1.5 to 4.5 million dozen versus the 14.4 million dozen which was the minimum guaranteed for Costa Rica by the ATC - and a "generous" level for conditional or GAL trade, amounting to as much as 40 million dozen depending on the specific proposal. That was also why among the agreements reached with the other countries called for consultation in this category, more than 80 per cent of the negotiated restraint volumes - or access volumes - required the use of United States formed fabric, while only the remaining 20 per cent may use non-United States formed fabric.

5.201   *Costa Rica* stated that the United States may wish to promote the use of fabric produced in that country; however, the problem lay in the mechanism it had decided to use for this purpose. Imposing a restriction on imports of underwear from a country in order to oblige that country to use United States cloth for the production of the underwear as a requirement for it to be able to enter the United States market was not a condition provided for in Article 6 of the ATC. The ATC did not allow imposition of a safeguard measure on a clothing product in order to protect the fabric used to produce it. The ATC only envisaged the safeguard governed by Article 6 of the Agreement to protect the domestic industry producing "like and/or directly competitive products". Underwear was not a like or directly competing product with respect to the fabric used to produce it, since these were products which had different characteristics from the standpoint of any objective or subjective criterion. The fact that underwear and fabric were not like or directly competitive products was recognized by the United States itself. This was shown by the fact that the United States had not even attempted to argue this openly, since in its reports it had always argued that the domestic industry allegedly affected was the underwear industry and did not mention the fabric industry explicitly. However, the reason why the case was confusing was that basically the United States was trying to justify an action whose true objective was very different from its apparent objective in order to try to bring it within the terms of a provision which did not authorize action to attain the objective which the United States was actually pursuing. By proceeding in this way, the United States had affected not only Costa Rica but also all the producers of this type of fabric, whose rights would be impaired in so far as the action restricted and possibly hindered their ability to become suppliers of this raw material.

5.202 The *United States* argued that they had properly based their determination on damage or threat to the domestic industry producing like or directly competitive products. The United States had satisfied the Article 6 requirement that the serious damage, or actual threat thereof, must be to the domestic industry producing like or directly competitive products, as could be seen from the March 1995 Statement and further confirmed by the US statements. Unlike agreements that permit other safeguard actions, the ATC did not provide a definition of domestic industry nor did it require that the importing member apply a transitional safeguard that corresponded exactly to the scope of the industry seriously damaged or actually threatened by serious damage. While the US fabric industry may incidentally benefit from the more favourable treatment provided for re-imports incorporating US formed and cut fabric, it had been made clear in the March 1995 Statement that the serious damage, or actual threat thereof determination was made solely on the basis of the situation in the US underwear industry, which included both vertically integrated firms which manufactured their own fabric and domestic firms that did not use offshore operations. There were approximately 220 underwear manufacturers in the United States, 85 of which used outward processing operations and the remaining 60 per cent, or 135 firms, which did not use offshore operations. In making its determination under Article 6.2 of the ATC, the CITA had examined the situation of the broad array of US underwear producers, including the integrated firms which spun their own yarn, knit fabric, and cut and assembled the finished product; the large number of small "cut and sew" operators who obtained their fabric and trim from a variety of independent sources, and did not have offshore operations; and those operators who knit fabric and cut pieces in the United States for final assembly overseas. The fact that the underwear industry in the United States was a diverse industry, and that some producers also made their own fabric, did not change the fact that the CITA's determination was based on the economic conditions in the *underwear* industry, not the industry producing only fabric.

5.203 The *United States* noted that many countries with outward processing programmes condition participation in that programme on use of fabric manufactured in their countries. They also maintain quantitative limits on how much of that trade can be re-imported.

5.204 In the view of the *United States*, the facts before the CITA and the record before the Panel demonstrated that US underwear producers (including both those which did and those which did not manufacture offshore) had been seriously damaged or actually threatened with such damage from a surge in re-imports. It was the responsibility of the United States to balance the damage to and interests of many different types of domestic underwear producers. The ATC permitted Members to impose a transitional safeguard even if the damage did not extend to 100 per cent of the industry. Any requirement that the damage must be sustained by a percentage or majority of the industry or a certain size or type of firm, was conspicuously omitted from the ATC. In other WTO safeguard procedures, there were express requirements with respect to the proportion of the affected industry represented. Clearly, the negotiators of the ATC had been aware of those procedures, but had chosen to continue the safeguard mechanism used under the MFA system.

J.   The Requirement to Hold Consultations

5.205 *Costa Rica* argued that even if, for illustration, it was considered that the United States had fulfilled the substantive requirements needed to have the right to apply a transitional safeguard measure to Costa Rican trade in category 352/652, which, as they had already shown, the United States had not done, the fact was that the unilateral restriction imposed was fraught with its own problems and in itself also violated the ATC. The adoption, maintenance and renewal by the United States of this unilateral restriction suffered from two serious flaws of different kinds. First, the United States had adopted, maintained and renewed a measure unilaterally, without having held consultations on the basis of the substantive requirement on which the measure was supposedly based, thus violating Articles 6.7 and 6.10 of the ATC. And second, it had applied the measure retroactively to the date of the call for consultations, thus violating Article 6.10 of the Agreement.

5.206 The request for consultations made by the United States, the information presented in the Statement on which the action taken was based, the consultations held with Members and the unilateral restriction adopted in this case all referred to the condition of the existence of serious damage to the United States industry. In other words, the United States made the call for consultations and proceeded thereafter until it adopted the transitional safeguard in June 1995 on the basis of the purported existence of serious damage to its industry.

5.207 *Costa Rica* noted that, at its July meeting the TMB had determined that serious damage did not exist. The United States should then have immediately withdrawn the measure. Nevertheless, it did not do so, but rather appeared to have interpreted that, as the TMB had not reached a conclusion as to the existence or not of actual threat of serious damage, it could continue maintaining the measure on that basis. By proceeding in this way, the United States had violated Articles 6.7 and 6.10 of the ATC, in so far as they contained an obligation to hold consultations during a 60-day period before a unilateral restriction may be adopted. In other words, it was impossible to adopt a unilateral restriction without having held consultations with the Member affected, as provided for by the various paragraphs of Article 6 of the ATC.

5.208 This meant that, in order to have been able to adopt a measure on the basis of the existence of actual threat of serious damage, the United States should have made the call, presented the information and held consultations on that basis. It could not be admitted that a unilateral restriction may be imposed without specifically having had the opportunity to rebut the alleged existence of a substantive requirement on which the measure was allegedly based. To maintain the contrary would imply leaving the exporting Member completely defenceless, because there would not be a point in the proceedings at which it could try to defend itself. In the case under consideration, if the United States had considered that the basis for its call was the existence of actual threat of serious damage, it should have said so in its call for consultations, and should have presented the factors and information required to demonstrate its existence, and then should have imposed the unilateral restriction on that basis.

5.209 The *United States* pointed out that Article 6.10 of the ATC regulated the date when, if consultations had failed to reach agreement, an importing Member may move ahead unilaterally with implementation of the textile restriction in question. Provision of such deadlines was fully consistent with the scheme of Article 6 of the ATC, which attempted to maximize the possibility that transitional safeguards would be applied on a consensual basis; any negotiator could appreciate that a lack of deadlines would mean lack of any incentive for negotiation and agreement. However, Article 6.10 of the ATC did *not* regulate the effective date for a unilateral transitional safeguard. The United States had applied its transitional safeguard with respect to imports of underwear from Costa Rica effective on 23 June 1995. This date fell within 30 days following the 60-day period for consultations after the initial call made on 27 March 1995. The reference year for imports within the levels specified in this transitional safeguard began on March 27. This reference year was fully consistent with US obligations under Article 6.10 of the ATC.

5.210 *Costa Rica* argued that, when the TMB determined that serious damage to the United States industry did not exist in this case, what the United States should properly have done was to withdraw the measure adopted on that basis and, if there really were grounds justifying the existence of actual threat of serious damage, begin the procedure anew on that ground, to comply with Articles 6.7 and 6.10 of the ATC, and give Costa Rica a chance to defend itself. By failing to do so, the United States violated the above-mentioned provisions.

5.211 The *United States* argued that they were not required by the ATC to choose between serious damage and actual threat in making their determination.

The ATC standard allowed Members to assert, at the same time, both serious damage or actual threat. The plain meaning of the standard invoked merely the notion that there could be a determination on the basis of serious damage, or actual threat. Neither was exclusive of the other. There was no obligation in other safeguard proceedings that one standard must be alleged instead of the other. The ATC treated them equally, that is, without any special factors to establish a case for one or the other. The simple fact was that Members could allege both based on the same factors. In addition, contrary to the assertion of Costa Rica, it did not follow that if the TMB had found that there was no serious damage, and reached no consensus on threat, there was no threat. No consensus on threat was just that. No consensus on that finding, therefore, no finding or decision on threat.

5.212 The *United States* also stated that it held consultations with Costa Rica in accordance with Article 6.7 of the ATC before placing a restriction. It then applied the restraint, and referred the matter to the TMB, pursuant to Article 6.10. Article 6.12 therefore permitted the United States to maintain the restraint for up to three years, without extension. Article 6.10 expressly allowed for the placement of a unilateral restraint before TMB review. Nothing in the text indicated that the restraint must be withdrawn in the absence of any recommendation to do so. A lack of consensus in the TMB, or even a finding without a recommendation to withdraw, did not obligate an importing Member to withdraw a restraint. Even if there was a recommendation to withdraw a restraint, Members must only "endeavour" to comply, and provide reasons to the TMB if they could not comply with the recommendation. In this case, the United States had complied with the TMB recommendation.

K. *Effective Date of the Restriction*

5.213 *Costa Rica* also argued that the United States had applied retroactively the unilateral restriction imposed on trade with Costa Rica in category 352/652, thereby violating Article 6.10 of the ATC. This Article provided that:

> "If, however, after the expiry of the period of 60 days from the date on which the request for consultations was received, there has been no agreement between the Members, the Member which proposed to take safeguard action may apply the restraint by date of import or date of export, in accordance with the provisions of this Article, within 30 days following the 60-day period for consultations ...".

5.214 In accordance with the above, if the Members failed to reach agreement on the application of the safeguard once the 60-day period fixed for holding consultations had expired, the Member which proposed to take safeguard action may do so unilaterally within the following 30 days. Thus, the provision under consideration granted the importing Member the power during a specified period to impose a unilateral restriction on the imports after a certain number of days had passed. Nowhere, in *Costa Rica's* view, did Article 6.10 of the ATC authorize the imposition of a unilateral restriction retroactive to the date of the call for consultations. The fact was that retroactivity could not be assumed, but must be explicitly authorized, as it was under the MFA. Article 3.5(i) of the MFA explicitly stated that:

> "... If, however, after a period of sixty days from the date on which the request has been received by the participating exporting country or countries, there has been no agreement either on the request for export restraint or on any alternative solution, the requesting participating country may decline to accept imports for retention from the participating country or countries referred to in paragraph 3 above of the textiles and textile products causing market disruption (as defined in Annex A) at a level for the twelve-month period beginning on the day when the request was received by the participating exporting country or countries not less than the level provided for in Annex B ...".

5.215 *Costa Rica* further argued that, if retroactivity was not explicitly provided for, as in the case of Article 6.10 of the ATC, the measure in question must be applied "forwards". This was particularly clear in the case of this provision of the ATC which, when establishing a procedure similar to that provided for in the MFA for the imposition of a unilateral restriction, differed from the latter in respect of retroactivity, by eliminating the explicit provision the MFA contained in this regard. This interpretation was bolstered by the principles established in Article 6.1 of the ATC, according to which:

> "... The transitional safeguard should be applied as sparingly as possible, consistently with the provisions of this article and the effective implementation of the integration process under this Agreement".

5.216 Since any gaps or doubts arising in the legal text governing the imposition of a transitional safeguard must be interpreted on the basis of the principles and spirit guiding the ATC, it was not possible to conclude that a restriction adopted under the Agreement may be applied retroactively in the absence of any explicit provision to that effect. This interpretation was supported by other agreements that were an integral part of the WTO Agreement and which therefore must also serve as interpretative sources for the ATC in the absence of any express provision in the latter. Thus, for example, Article XIII:3(b) of GATT 1994, referring to import restrictions involving the fixing of quotas, expressly authorized retroactive application of a restriction only for products that were en route at the time at which public notice was given of the restriction.

5.217 Accordingly, in the view of *Costa Rica*, the only possible conclusion was that, where Members had not reached agreement, the importing Member may, within the following 30 days, adopt a unilateral restriction which would begin to be applied as from the time when it was adopted, and not before. This meant that the imposition of the restriction by the United States should have begun as from

16 June 1995, the date when the restriction was established, and could not be made retroactive to 27 March 1995, the date of the request for consultations, as the United States in fact had done. By proceeding in this way, and by continuing to do so, the United States had disregarded the very significant revisions of the information presented as a basis for its action, disregarded all the aspects discussed in the consultations, and the conclusions of the TMB and had violated Article 6.10 of the ATC.

5.218 The *United States* argued that the ATC was silent concerning the effective date of safeguard measures, and did not prevent a Member from providing that the effective date would be the date of the request for consultations. The United States had held consultations with Costa Rica in accordance with Article 6.7 of the ATC before placing a restriction; had then applied the restraint at issue in this case; and had referred the matter to the TMB, pursuant to Article 6.10 of the ATC. Article 6.12 of the ATC therefore, permitted the United States to maintain the restraint for up to three years, without extension. When asked by exporting countries including Costa Rica to address this question, the TMB had responded recognizing this fact. The TMB had noted that

> "with respect to the introduction of a safeguard measure, the [ATC] does not provide any indication with respect to the effective date of implementation of that measure" (G/TMB/R/2).

The MFA explicitly recognized the customary practice of counting imports during the consultation period against restraint levels, and the ATC did not change this practice. The universal application of textile restraints on this basis and the recognition accorded to this practice generally in the TSB and TMB, demonstrated that it was in fact a matter of accepted custom which constitutes "subsequent practice in the application of the treaty which establishes the agreement of the parties regarding its interpretation" in the sense of Article 31.3(b) of the Vienna Convention on the Law of Treaties (1969).

5.219 In this regard the *United States* (and Costa Rica) were of the view that the reference in Article XVI:1 of the WTO Agreement to "decisions, procedures and customary practices followed by the CONTRACTING PARTIES to GATT 1947 and the bodies established in the framework of GATT 1947" did not include the MFA. Costa Rica noted that GATT 1947 and the MFA were two independent, self-standing agreements while the United States pointed out that to some extent, the MFA was an agreement relevant to the history of the ATC, as even though the MFA had expired, many of the provisions of the ATC were drawn from the MFA.

5.220 The *United States* emphasized that the omission of an explicit reference to the effective date of the restriction in the ATC could not be construed as an attempt to prevent it. It was essential to the effective application of transitional safeguard as an adjustment mechanism. Textile restrictions would not work without the flexibility to set the effective date. Without it, a flood of imports would vitiate their adjustment function. Under Article XIX an importing country could simply act when it had made its determination of serious injury, but under the MFA and the ATC importing countries had been required to wait for consultations before acting. It was argued that the principle of effective treaty interpretation requires that transitional safeguards under Article 6 of the ATC must be permitted to have an effective date as of the date of the request of consultations as any contrary position would make the ATC-consistent transitional safeguards ineffective.

5.221 Along these same lines, it was observed that restraints were normally applied effective on the date of the call as a call would trigger speculative trade. If traders believed that imports before completion of the consultation process would not be counted, speculative imports would aggravate injury or bankrupt the remaining industry. A transitional safeguard was an adjustment measure which facilitated the ultimate accomplishment of the ten-year programme of the ATC. A sudden flood of speculative imports for stockpiling in warehouses could not be permitted to frustrate this adjustment process. The widespread recognition of application of textile restrictions as from the date of the request reflected a common-sense appreciation of the practical aspects of this larger policy imperative. As a matter of treaty law, the principle of effective application of treaties (*ut res magis valeat quam pereat*) argues that restrictions must be permitted to have an effective date as of the date of the request for consultations, as any contrary position would make ATC-consistent transitional safeguards ineffective.

5.222 Article 6.10 of the ATC expressly allowed for the placement of a unilateral restraint before TMB review. Nothing in the text indicated that the restraint must be withdrawn in the absence of any TMB recommendation to do so. A lack of consensus in the TMB, or even a finding without a recommendation to withdraw, did not obligate an importing Member to withdraw a restraint. Even if there was a recommendation to withdraw a restraint, Members must only "endeavour" to comply, and provide reasons to the TMB if they could not comply with the recommendation.

5.223 The *United States* noted that the ATC provided for an absolute sunset of three years for an Article 6 safeguard measure. Furthermore, it was recalled that such safeguards were transitional and could only be invoked until the ATC expired, eight and a half years from now. The United States had continuously reviewed data on products subject to restraint and monitored production and trade data on a voluntary basis, even though the ATC did not so require. When new data warranted review of a safeguard measure, the United States considered whether it was necessary to maintain the restraint.

5.224 With respect to the Panel's question to the *United States* concerning "retroactive application of treaty obligations"; this could be read to refer to Article 28 of the 1969 Vienna Convention. However, this was not a case of retroactive application of a treaty to events which took place before the treaty entered into force; Article 28 was not relevant at all. All events which had led to this dispute took place *after* entry into force of the WTO Agreement, and in particular took place within the time frame provided for under ATC Article 6, including

Articles 6.7 and 6.8. It could not be argued that Costa Rica was unaware of the applicable treaty rules at the time these events took place.

L.   *Article 2 of the ATC*

5.225 *Costa Rica* argued that the United States had introduced a new restriction on its trade in the clothing products classified in category 352/652, without basing itself on the provisions of the ATC, and thereby violated Article 2.4, of the said Agreement. As recalled in the Preamble of the ATC, the terms of reference of the Uruguay Round Negotiating Group on Textiles and Clothing had established that:

> "Negotiations in the area of textiles and clothing shall aim to formulate modalities that would permit the eventual integration of this sector into GATT on the basis of strengthened GATT rules and disciplines, thereby also contributing to the objective of further liberalization of trade."

In order to carry out this mandate, Article 1.1 of the ATC, provided that:

> "This Agreement sets out provisions to be applied by Members during a transition period for the integration of the textiles and clothing sector into GATT 1994."

Costa Rica further argued that for the purpose of attaining this objective, the ATC strictly defined, *inter alia*, what type of restrictions may be applied to trade in textiles and clothing under cover of the safeguard clause. These restrictions must necessarily fall within one of the following three categories:

(a)   Quantitative restrictions within bilateral agreements maintained under the MFA in force on the day before the entry into force of the WTO Agreement and notified in accordance with Article 2.1 of the ATC, which would continue to be governed by the provisions of the ATC in this respect:

(b)   restrictions established under the specific transitional safeguard mechanism governed by Article 6 of the ATC, which may be applied, in accordance with paragraph 1 of that Article, to all textile and clothing products that had not yet been integrated into GATT 1994; or

(c)   restrictions established in accordance with Article XIX of GATT 1994, in the case of products already integrated into GATT 1994.

5.226 Thus, Article 2.4 of the ATC, provided very clearly that:

> "No new restrictions in terms of products or Members shall be introduced except under the provision of this Agreement or relevant GATT 1994 provisions."

Conversely, it followed from this provision that the introduction of new restriction in terms of products or Members that had not been introduced in accordance with the rules of the ATC or GATT 1994 infringed Article 2.4 of the ATC.

5.227 In the case in point, imports into the United States from Costa Rica in category 352/652 were not subject to any quantitative restriction based on the Multifibre Arrangement prior to the entry into force of the WTO Agreement, and therefore the first option was ruled out. Furthermore, cotton and man-made fibre underwear was not a product that the United States had already incorporated into GATT 1994 and therefore Article XIX was likewise not applicable. Hence, the only possibility open to the United States to restrict the imports under consideration was to apply the specific transitional safeguard mechanism in accordance with the criteria established in Article 6 of the ATC. However, the United States had failed to demonstrate the existence of the requirements laid down in Article 6 of the ATC as an essential condition for being able to apply a transitional safeguard. Consequently, the United States had violated Article 2.4 of the ATC, as it had applied to Costa Rica a new restriction on trade in products classified in category 352/652 without complying with the provisions of Article 6 of the ATC.

5.228 The *United States* argued that because the safeguard action taken on imports of underwear in category 352/652 from Costa Rica was fully consistent with Article 6 of the ATC, there was no violation of Article 2 of the ATC.

M. A Member Must Endeavour to Accept Recommendations of the TMB

5.229 *Costa Rica* argued that the United States had violated Article 8 of the ATC, which in its paragraphs 9 and 10, defined the nature of the recommendations made by the TMB. Thus, the first of these paragraphs provided that: "The Members shall endeavour to accept in full the recommendations of the TMB ...". Paragraph 10 provided that:

> "If a Member considers itself unable to conform with the recommendations of the TMB; it shall provide the TMB with the reasons therefor not later than one month after the receipt of such recommendations ...".

5.230 In the view of *Costa Rica*, it was clear from an analysis of these two provisions that the TMB's recommendations were not binding. However, it was also clear that the formulation of such recommendations must have some purpose, because it was meaningless for the ATC to provide for the TMB to carry out an exercise without any purpose. This aspect became clear from the reading of paragraphs 9 and 10 of Article 8 of the ATC, from which it may be concluded that although Article 8 does not impose the obligation to abide by the recommendations of the TMB, it does impose other obligations on Members. Article 8 of the ATC laid down two obligations on Members: firstly, in paragraph 9 it imposed an obligation for Members to endeavour to accept in full the recommendations of the TMB. This was a "best-endeavours" obligation, in the sense that while the

TMB recommendations were not binding, there was an obligation for Members to do their best to accept them. If, given the TMB's recommendations, a Member did not even try to accept them, it would be violating the best-endeavours obligation of Article 6.9 of the ATC.

5.231 Secondly, Article 8.10 of the ATC imposed on Members another obligation that complemented the first, namely, that where a Member, having endeavoured to accept the recommendations of the TMB, found itself unable to conform with them, it shall provide the TMB with the reasons therefor. The imperative character of the verb used in this Article clearly indicated that, while the TMB recommendations may not be binding, this provision did impose on a Member the obligation to justify, "not later than one month after receipt of such recommendations", the reasons why it was unable to conform with them.

5.232 *Costa Rica* argued that in the case under consideration, the United States not only had not tried to accept the TMB recommendations, but furthermore did not submit to that body any document explaining the reasons why it considered itself unable to conform with the recommendations, and therefore it was in breach of Articles 8.9 and 8.10 of the ATC.

5.233 The *United States* argued that Costa Rica's allegation that the US had violated Article 6.9 of the ATC was without legal or factual foundation. They had proceeded in good faith to reach mutual understanding in consultations recommended by the TMB, consistent with obligations inherent in Article 8 of the ATC. They also noted that the TMB recommendation had been directed to both the United States and Costa Rica. Contrary to the assertion of Costa Rica, the United States had followed the TMB recommendation to consult and to take into account the considerations it had cited. Therefore, there was no need to invoke Article 8.10 of the ATC and provide reasons to the TMB for not accepting its recommendation in this case. As evidenced by the initiation of these Panel proceedings, it was Costa Rica that could not ultimately comply with the TMB recommendation. The TMB's response in October 1995 to the reports of the United States and Costa Rica did not characterize the United States as having failed to follow the TMB's recommendation. The TMB stated that:

> "[i]t took note of the reports and of the fact that the two parties did not reach a mutual understanding during the consultations. The TMB's discussions confirmed the Body's previous findings in this matter (G/TMB/R/2, first two sentences of paragraph 16). There being no further requests by the parties involved, the TMB considered its review of the matter completed" (G/TMB/R/5).

5.234 *Costa Rica* argued that the violation by the United States of the best-endeavours obligation imposed by Article 8.9 of the ATC was clearly demonstrated by the following facts. In July 1995, the TMB, pursuant to Article 6.10 of the ATC, had proceeded to examine the unilateral restriction applied by the United States to Costa Rica in category 352/652. On that occasion, the TMB had found that "serious damage", as envisaged in Articles 6.2 and 6.3 of the ATC, "had not been demonstrated", but "could not, however, reach consensus on the existence of actual threat of serious damage". Therefore, the TMB recommended:

> " ... that further consultations be held between the United States and the parties concerned, with a view to arriving at a mutual understanding, bearing in mind the above, and with due consideration to the particular features of this case, as well as equity considerations".

Thus, the recommendation of the TMB had been that Costa Rica and the United States should hold new consultations, but also that these consultations should be conducted on the basis of three considerations: (a) that it was clear that the United States had not demonstrated the existence of serious damage, but that a consensus had not been reached in the TMB as to the existence of actual threat of serious damage; (b) that trade in this category between the United States and Costa Rica had some particular features, which should be borne in mind; and (c) that equity considerations should be borne in mind, with respect to the levels of restriction agreed by the United States with other countries called for consultations on this same category.

5.235 In the view of the *United States*, the TMB recommendation went no further than a recommendation to consult further and report back to the TMB. The TMB did not recommend that the parties actually reach agreement, nor did it recommend that the United States withdraw the safeguard measure, nor did it recommend that the parties even discuss dropping the restriction. Also, a lack of consensus in the TMB did not translate into a recommendation to drop a restriction. In accordance with the TMB's recommendation, the United States had duly consulted, and duly reported back; thus, the United States had complied fully with the TMB recommendation. In its note of October 1995, the TMB had stated that the parties had reported no solution and that it considered its review completed.

5.236 In *Costa Rica*'s view, what subsequently had occurred, however, showed that the United States had not fulfilled the obligation imposed by Article 8.9 of the ATC in the sense of at least endeavouring to proceed in accordance with the recommendations of the TMB. Firstly, the United States did not even attempt to justify the adoption of the safeguard measure on the basis of the alleged actual threat of serious damage. Once the TMB had determined that serious damage did not exist and that there was no consensus as to the existence of actual threat of serious damage, the United States - as a minimum at that stage of the proceedings - should have demonstrated the existence of this latter hypothetical condition brought to light by the TMB. However, the fact was that they did not even attempt to do so, nor did it take into account the special characteristics or trade between the two countries in this category - feigning to ignore the overriding importance of so-called 807 trade - nor did it take into account any considerations of equity because, even if there were grounds for imposing the safeguard in question, the levels of restriction proposed to Costa Rica were very different to those offered and granted to other countries involved in consultations.

5.237 The *United States* argued that Costa Rica had misinterpreted the TMB recommendation to mean that the TMB had asked the United States to reconsider, in consultations, its determination that there was serious damage, or actual threat thereof to the domestic underwear producing industry which had been attributed to imports from Costa Rica. Further, Costa Rica had misinterpreted the TMB recommendation to take into account equity considerations in light of the specific case to mean that the United States was to deem the re-import content in Costa Rica's trade not to cause or actually threaten serious damage to US industry. Based on these misinterpretations, Costa Rica had asserted that the United States was required in consultations to withdraw the restraint.

5.238 *Costa Rica* held that if the United States genuinely had accepted to consider the recommendations of the TMB, when taking into account that the TMB had not reached a consensus as to the existence of actual threat of serious damage it should have lifted the quota unilaterally imposed on Costa Rica in category 352/652. This was because the letter and spirit of the ATC were very clear: the ATC was conceived as a transitional system whose essential function was to integrate trade in textiles and clothing into the rules and the disciplines of GATT 1994. From this statement, the transitional safeguard provided for in Article 6 of the ATC was extraordinary by nature and should be applied only in cases where it had been possible to demonstrate the existence of the requirements laid down by paragraphs 2 and 3 of that Article, and where consequently the TMB had arrived at a consensus that the existence of the threat had been demonstrated. Conversely, if the TMB had not arrived at a consensus to that effect, a restriction that had been imposed could not be maintained, because it would mean that the TMB had not found the necessary justification for taking such action. There was nothing in the ATC to establish a presumption that, in the absence of consensus in the TMB, it should be presumed that the importing Member had the necessary justification to impose the measure. In the absence of any explicit provision to that effect, following Article 6.1 of the ATC and the spirit of the ATC it was necessary to proceed in the least restrictive manner, that is to say, the imposed restriction should have been lifted as there was no justification for adopting it.

5.239 In this respect, the *United States* considered that Costa Rica had construed the TMB recommendation to mean that the United States was to rescind the restraint on Costa Rican exports by including an analysis of Article 6.1 of the ATC. Reference to integration and the taking of transitional safeguard action and the re-import content of Costa Rican exports supported the notion that the United States was required to rescind the restraint when it consulted with Costa Rica. Costa Rica's argument consistently depended on the assumption that the ATC integration process must be read into Article 6 so as to accelerate the pace of the integration. This was not the case. It was clear in the ATC that integration was an independently determined process, and that Article 6 applied only to products not yet integrated. Article 2 of the ATC specifically allowed Members to designate what products would be integrated and when, as long as they were chosen from the Annex to the ATC, from certain product groups and comprised the appropriate proportion of trade indicated for each stage of the transition. Nothing in the

ATC required the United States or other Members to schedule sensitive products at certain stages for integration. The negotiators had specifically left that decision to the importing Members. Thus, Costa Rica could not use this Panel proceeding to compel integration of this category.

5.240   *Costa Rica* also argued that, in accordance with the TMB's recommendations, the United States was obliged to take into consideration the particular features of the trade in this category between the two countries. This meant that the United States should have borne in mind that, given that virtually all exports from Costa Rica in category 352/652 were "807 trade" , the possibility that they should have been causing serious damage or actual threat thereof was really non-existent. If the United States had endeavoured to accept the recommendation of the TMB to consider the particular features of trade with Costa Rica in this category, it would clearly have appreciated how absurd it was to impose a quota in such circumstances. However, the United States had not made any effort to accept the recommendation of the TMB.

5.241   The *United States* further argued that the TMB recommendation did not say what Costa Rica claimed it did. Again, the TMB had not, in its 25 October 1995 note, responded to Costa Rica's same assertions in their report back to the TMB dated 24 August 1995. (G/TMB/SPEC/107)   The lack of TMB consensus on actual threat of serious damage did not translate into a "recommendation" that a restraint be withdrawn. Accordingly, there was no obligation on the United States, in consultations, to assume such a proposition.

5.242   In the view of *Costa Rica*, if the United States had insisted on adopting a safeguard measure in these circumstances - when in fact it should have withdrawn the measure - it should at least have borne in mind the obligation to grant more favourable treatment to re-imports from Costa Rica, as provided for in Article 6.6(d) of the ATC. In this regard, however, the position of the United States appeared to have been somewhat self-contradictory. On the one hand, it started from the position that the rise in imports of these products was causing serious damage to its industry, but on the other, the level of these imports was of no importance whatsoever provided the product in question was produced using fabric formed and cut in the United States. The ATC established this obligation to grant more favourable treatment to re-imports - which the United States had never tried to fulfil in any of its proposals - but what it certainly did not provide for was the establishment of new restrictions in order to ensure that future trade consists solely of re-imports.

5.243   *Costa Rica* noted that the TMB had also indicated that equity considerations should be borne in mind, by which it was referring to the fact that the same treatment should be accorded to those who were in the same position. In this connection, apart from Costa Rica, the United States had called for consultations six other countries concerning this category, had withdrawn the call addressed to one of them and had reached an agreement with the remaining five. In the case of each of the latter, the United States had agreed on specific level (SL) restraints that were much higher than the respective "call" levels. Thus - and assuming that the United States had the right to adopt a safeguard, which, in the view of Costa Rica, was not the case - in order to comply with the TMB's recommendation it should have made restraint proposals to Costa Rica that reflected SL restraint levels which provided for increases in relation to the call level, in the same way as it had granted to the other countries. In none of the proposals formulated by the United States to Costa Rica was this equity factor taken into consideration, because not even in its last proposal did the United States propose a SL restraint level approaching the call level, still less exceeding it. In fact, the highest level that the United States had offered at any time for the establishment of the SL restraint was about 40 per cent below what should have been the level for Costa Rica in accordance with the ATC itself - assuming that the necessary requirements for imposing it had been demonstrated, which was not the case.

5.244 *Costa Rica* argued that, on the basis of the above explanation, it was clearly demonstrated that the United States had completely disregarded the recommendations adopted by the TMB in July 1995, without even endeavouring to accept them as provided for in Article 8.9 of the ATC. Furthermore, the United States had violated Article 8.10 of the ATC, which imposed on Members another obligation that complemented the obligation established in Article 8.9 of the ATC. That is to say, the United States had not fulfilled the obligation of presenting to the TMB its reasons explaining why it considered itself unable to conform with the TMB's recommendations. Suffice it to say that the United States had never at any time presented to the TMB any document to that effect. Failure to comply with this requirement imposed under Article 8.10 of the ATC may be due to the fact that, since the United States had not even attempted to follow the TMB's recommendations, it would be difficult, if not impossible, for it to justify a hypothetical failure in its attempt to accept those recommendations, since it had made no such attempt.

5.245 *Costa Rica* also noted that the United States had declared that they did not agree with the finding of the TMB that the existence of serious damage had not been demonstrated. Moreover, as in the US view there was no provision in the ATC that made the TMB's findings binding, the Panel was obliged to consider the question of serious damage. In this connection, *Costa Rica* emphasized that the United States had not contested at the appropriate moment in the procedure the TMB's finding that the existence of serious damage had not been demonstrated, as required by Articles 6.2 and 6.3 of the ATC. Costa Rica was, therefore, concerned that contesting the action of the TMB at this stage of the procedure and calling into question its decisions would mean divesting the Body of any function related to monitoring the implementation of the ATC.

5.246 The *United States* argued that they had made efforts to reach a mutual understanding with Costa Rica. As recommended by the TMB, the United States had taken into account that the TMB could not reach consensus on actual threat of serious damage (though they maintained that they had demonstrated the existence of serious damage); had examined the nature of trade from Costa Rica; and, in the interest of equity, had again compared Costa Rica's trade with trade from other countries to which the serious damage and actual threat had been attributed.

The record showed that Costa Rica had refused to respond. In so doing, the United States had made a proposal to Costa Rica that, in its view, took these factors into account in an effort towards mutual understanding. The United States stated that the record showed that Costa Rica had refused to respond. The United States stated that there was no requirement in the ATC that the United States respond to "findings" but must "endeavour to comply" with TMB "recommendations". The United States did comply with the TMB recommendation.

N. Nullification or Impairment of Benefits

5.247 *Costa Rica argued* that the unilateral restriction imposed by the United States on trade in clothing classified in category 352/652 from Costa Rica was a blatant violation of the obligations laid down in the ATC, in particular Articles 2, 6 and 8. On this basis, and given that the ATC was a "covered agreement" within the meaning of Article 1 of the DSU, the provisions of Article 3.8 of the DSU applied. That Article stated:

> "In cases where there is an infringement of the obligations assumed under a covered agreement, the action is considered prima facie to constitute a case of nullification or impairment ...".

It clearly followed from the above provision that in the case under consideration, given the infringement of Articles 2, 6 and 8 by the United States, benefits accruing to Costa Rica under the WTO Agreement, and in particular under the ATC, had been nullified or impaired.

5.248 Considering that Article 3.1 of the DSU stipulated that

> "Members affirm their adherence to the principles for the management of disputes heretofore applied under Articles XXII and XXIII of GATT 1947 ...",

it was important to note that these Articles had established that the benefits accruing under the GATT Rules - and consequently the WTO Rules - did not comprise exclusively those derived from the Agreement at the time when a concession came into effect, but also the future trading opportunities that would result from that concession. Thus, and by virtue of the *prima facie* case of nullification or impairment of benefits that existed in cases of infringement of the obligations assumed under a covered agreement, such as the ATC, the claims presented by one or more Members relating to the imposition of infringing unilateral measures must be accepted even where statistical evidence of commercial damage cannot exist.

5.249 It was also necessary to emphasize that nullification or impairment should be considered not only in relation to the effect which the violation in question may have had on the volume of trade but also in relation to possible increases in transaction costs and the creation of uncertainty liable to affect investment plans.

5.250 As a result of all the foregoing, *Costa Rica* considered that the Panel should find that the unilateral restriction imposed by the United States on the trade of Costa Rica in category 352/652 infringed Articles 2, 6 and 8 of the ATC and that, consequently, these infringements entailed the nullification or impairment of benefits accruing to Costa Rica under the WTO Agreement. Accordingly, Costa Rica urged the Panel to find in its report that the United States should proceed to bring its measure into conformity with the ATC, which implied immediately withdrawing it.

5.251 The *United States* argued that Costa Rica's rights and benefits under the ATC had not been nullified and impaired. The United States had demonstrated that they had not violated Articles 2, 6 or 8 of the ATC. Thus, nullification and impairment of any benefits and rights accruing to Costa Rica in this case could not be presumed.

* * * * *

VI.   INTERIM REVIEW

6.1   On 4 October 1996, the United States and Costa Rica requested the Panel to review, in accordance with Article 15.2 of the DSU, precise aspects of the interim report that had been issued to the parties on 20 September 1996. Both Costa Rica and the United States requested the Panel to hold a meeting for that purpose. The Panel met with the parties on 15 October 1996 to hear their arguments concerning the interim report. The Panel carefully reviewed the arguments presented by the parties.

6.2   In approaching the interim review stage, the Panel drew guidance from Article 15.2 of the DSU, which states that "a party may submit a written request for the panel to review precise aspects of the interim report prior to circulation of the final report to Members". While the Panel was willing to approach the interim review stage with the broadest possible interpretation of Article 15.2 of the DSU, it was of the view that the purpose of the review meeting was not to provide the parties with an opportunity to introduce new legal issues and evidence, or to enter into a debate with the Panel. The purpose of the interim review, in the Panel's view, was to consider specific and particular aspects of the interim report. Consequently, the Panel addressed the entire range of such arguments presented by the parties which it considered to be sufficiently specific and detailed.

6.3   The United States submitted to the Panel at the review meeting copies of press reports relating to the interim report. At the meeting, the Panel expressed its disappointment about the apparent breach of confidentiality and reiterated the utmost importance of maintaining confidentiality so as to preserve the credibility and integrity of the dispute settlement process, particularly at the interim review stage.

6.4   Regarding the timing of settlements with other exporters, the United States argued that the Panel had erroneously stated that the United States requested consultations with Costa Rica while at the same time it settled with other countries. In order to clarify its findings, the Panel introduced some drafting modifications in the final report at paragraphs 7.50 and 7.51.

6.5   The United States disagreed with the interim report that use of the ATC safeguard should be exceptional. It based its argument on the fact that Article 6.1 of the ATC couples the term "sparingly" with "as possible", suggesting that the standard was relative. The Panel was not persuaded by this argument, which in effect would result in reading the text of the Article as meaning that the transitional safeguard "should be applied sparingly *if* possible".

6.6   Regarding the causation analysis required under Article 6.2 of the ATC, the United States argued that the Panel's finding in paragraph 7.46 of the final report was a mischaracterization of the CITA's conclusions. The Panel slightly modified the language of this paragraph so as to avoid any misunderstanding of its findings.

6.7   In respect of the relationship between Articles 6.2 and 6.4 of the ATC, the United States argued that the Panel incorrectly merged the analyses under these two paragraphs. This was not the intention of the Panel. To clarify its findings, the Panel introduced certain drafting changes in paragraphs 7.23, 7.24, 7.47 and 7.48.

6.8   The United States argued that in its review of the March Market Statement, the Panel had erred by relying on the July Market Statement. It specifically argued that if Members were penalized in the dispute settlement process for supplying updated data to the TMB, there would be a disincentive to providing it at the TMB level. The Panel consequently examined the issue, as spelled out in paragraphs 7.29 and 7.45 of its final report.

6.9   Regarding the Panel's interpretation of Article 6.6(d) of the ATC, the United States argued that finding the United States in violation of this provision based on the requirements under Article 6.8 was erroneous because the US action was taken based on Article 6.10. The Panel's additional discussion on this point is reflected in paragraph 7.59.

6.10   Both the United States and Costa Rica disagreed with the Panel's interpretation of Article 6.10 of the ATC regarding the effective date of application of the restriction. The United States argued that the restraint was not a measure "of general application" within the meaning of Article X:2 of GATT 1994. It further argued that the restraint was not "enforced" until 23 June 1995, which was after the date of the publication. The Panel's finding on these points can be found in paragraphs 7.65 and 7.69 of the final report. Costa Rica questioned the compatibility of the Panel's general approach that Article 6 of the ATC should be interpreted narrowly and its interpretation of Article X:2 of GATT 1994. The Panel failed to see any incompatibility or contradiction between the two approaches. Costa Rica further questioned the Panel's consideration of practical aspects of this issue. The Panel carefully examined Costa Rica's argument, and decided to maintain paragraph 7.68 of the final report.

6.11   Costa Rica and the United States differed with respect to acceptable figures for the percentage of 807 or 807A trade in Costa Rican underwear exports to the United States. In the absence of clear verification by the importing country (i.e., the United States), the Panel decided to use the most conservative figure of 94 per cent, coupled with the expression "at least" in paragraph 7.46 of the final report.

6.12   Costa Rica and the United States made some other suggestions concerning language changes, which the Panel accepted and introduced in its final report.

VII.   FINDINGS

A.   Claims of the Parties

Introduction

7.1   We note that the issues in dispute arise essentially from the following facts: On 27 March 1995, the United States requested consultations with Costa Rica on trade in cotton and man-made fibre underwear (US category 352/652) under Article 6.7 of the ATC. As consultations between the two countries did not result in a mutually acceptable solution, on 23 June 1995 the United States implemented a restriction on underwear imports from Costa Rica for a period of 12 months starting from 27 March 1995. At the same time, the United States referred the matter to the TMB in accordance with Article 6.10 of the ATC. The TMB found that serious damage had not been demonstrated by the United States, but it could not reach consensus on the existence of actual threat of serious damage. The TMB recommended further consultations between the two parties. A series of further consultations was held in which the United States put forward several new proposals as far as the level of the restriction was concerned. However, the parties failed to reach a mutually agreed solution. The restriction, augmented by the application of a growth rate of 6 per cent, was renewed for a 12-month period on 27 March 1996.

Main Substantive Claims

7.2   Costa Rica essentially claims before the Panel that the United States, by imposing a unilateral quantitative restriction on cotton and man-made fibre underwear classified in category 352/652, has acted in violation of Articles 2, 6 and 8 of the ATC. Costa Rica requests the Panel to recommend that the United States withdraw the measure in question.

7.3   The United States essentially claims that it respected its obligations under the ATC when imposing the restriction on cotton and man-made fibre underwear classified in category 352/652. Consequently, the United States requests the Panel to dismiss Costa Rica's claim.

7.4   There is no disagreement between the parties to the dispute that the restriction applied by the United States is a "transitional safeguard" and that transitional safeguards are to be applied in accordance with Article 6 of the ATC. In this respect, Costa Rica claims that the United States has violated a number of provisions of this Article. In particular, Costa Rica claims that the United States violated its obligations under Article 6 of the ATC by:

(a)   imposing a restriction on imports from Costa Rica without having satisfied the conditions laid down in Article 6.2 and 6.4 of the ATC, namely by not having shown that serious damage or actual threat thereof resulted from those imports;

(b)   not granting, when applying the restriction, more favourable treatment to re-imports from Costa Rica in contravention of Article 6.6(d) of the ATC;

(c)   not consulting with Costa Rica on the issue of actual threat of serious damage contrary to its obligations under Article 6.7 and 6.10 of the ATC; and

(d)   applying the restriction retroactively in contravention of Article 6.10 of the ATC.

Costa Rica also claims that the United States violated Articles 2 and 8 of the ATC. In this respect, Costa Rica claims that the United States violated Article 2.4 of the ATC which stipulates that: " [n]o new restrictions in terms of products or Members shall be introduced except under the provisions of this Agreement or relevant GATT 1994 provisions". With respect to the alleged violation of Article 8 of the ATC, Costa Rica essentially claims that the United States has not respected the recommendations made by the TMB in this case.

7.5   We will deal first with what we view as Costa Rica's basic claim under Article 6 of the ATC: that the United States imposed restrictions on imports into the United States of underwear without having demonstrated, as required by Article 6.2 and 6.4 of the ATC, that the US underwear industry had suffered serious damage from Costa Rican imports or that there was an actual threat of such damage. In considering this claim, we examine the issues in the following order: First we consider general interpretative issues. Second, we consider Costa Rica's basic claim by reviewing the findings by the US investigating authorities on serious damage attributed to Costa Rica. Third, we consider the question of actual threat of serious damage - a matter relating to the scope of Costa Rica's basic claim. Finally, we consider Costa Rica's other claims, namely, its claims with respect to Article 6.6(d) of the ATC, with respect to the alleged failure of the United States to consult, with respect to the alleged retroactive application of the US restriction, with respect to the alleged violation of Article 2.4 of the ATC and with respect to the alleged violation of Article 8 of the ATC.

B.   General Interpretative Issues

7.6   Before turning to the examination of the specific import restriction, we deal with four interpretative issues relating to the application of the ATC, namely:

(a)   the standard of review that should be applied in this case;

(b)   the burden of proof;

(c)   the interpretation of the ATC; and

(d)   the structure of Article 6 of the ATC.

Standard of Review

7.7   We note that the two parties to the dispute present diverging views with respect to the standard of review to be applied by the Panel in this case. The United States advocates a standard of review similar to that applied in the "Fur Felt Hat" case,[14] in which the neutral members of the Working Party, examining a US escape clause measure in light of the requirements of Article XIX of the General Agreement on Tariffs and Trade (GATT) 1947, afforded to the US authorities considerable discretion by concluding that the United States was not called upon to prove conclusively that the degree of injury caused or threatened in that case should be regarded as serious. Costa Rica argues in favour of a five-step procedure whereby the Panel would certify whether the administrative authority of the importing country, when imposing the restriction had: (i) complied with the ATC's procedural rules; (ii) properly established the facts; (iii) made an objective and impartial evaluation of the facts in the light of the rules of the ATC; (iv) properly exercised its discretion in the interpretation of the rules; and (v) complied with the rules in general, while also having complied with the other four requirements mentioned above.

7.8   We note that the ATC does not establish a standard of review for panels, contrary, for example, to the WTO Agreement on Implementation of Article VI of the General Agreement on Tariffs and Trade 1994, where Article 17.6 defines the standard of review that panels have to apply when reviewing cases arising under that Agreement. We further note that the DSU does not contain a provision mandating a specific standard of review.

7.9   In our view, the main relevant provision of the DSU in this respect is Article 11, which reads as follows:

> "The function of panels is to assist the DSB in discharging its responsibilities under this Understanding and the covered agreements. Accordingly, a panel should make an objective assessment of the matter before it, including an objective assessment of the facts of the case and the applicability of and conformity with the relevant covered agreements, and make such other findings as will assist the DSB

---

[14]   See "Report on the Withdrawal by the United States of a Tariff Concession Under Article XIX of the General Agreement on Tariffs and Trade", GATT document CP/106, adopted on 22 October 1951 (CP.6/SR.19), version published by the Secretariat in November 1951, preface by E. Wyndham White.

in making the recommendations or in giving the rulings provided for in the covered agreements".

7.10   In our opinion, a policy of total deference to the findings of the national authorities could not ensure an "objective assessment" as foreseen by Article 11 of the DSU. This conclusion is supported, in our view, by previous panel reports that have dealt with this issue, and most notably in the panel report on the "Transformers" case.[15]

7.11   The panel in the "Transformers" case was confronted with the argument of New Zealand that the determination of "material injury" by the competent New Zealand investigating authority could not be scrutinized by the panel. The "Transformers" panel responded to this argument as follows:

> "The Panel agreed that the responsibility to make a determination of material injury caused by dumped imports rested in the first place with the authorities of the importing contracting party concerned. However, the Panel could not share the view that such a determination could not be scrutinized if it were challenged by another contracting party. On the contrary, the Panel believed that if a contracting party affected by the determination could make a case that the importation could not in itself have the effect of causing material injury to the industry in question, that contracting party was entitled, under the relevant GATT provisions and in particular Article XXIII, that its representations be given sympathetic consideration and that eventually, if no satisfactory adjustment was effected, it might refer the matter to the CONTRACTING PARTIES, as had been done by Finland in the present case. To conclude otherwise would give governments complete freedom and unrestricted discretion in deciding anti-dumping cases without any possibility to review the action taken in the GATT. This would lead to an unacceptable situation under the aspect of law and order in international trade relations as governed by the GATT".

7.12   We see great force in this argument. We do not, however, see our review as a substitute for the proceedings conducted by national investigating authorities or by the TMB. Rather, in our view, the Panel's function should be to assess objectively the review conducted by the national investigating authority, in this case the CITA. We draw particular attention to the fact that a series of panel reports in the anti-dumping and subsidies/countervailing duties context have made it clear

---

[15]   "New Zealand - Imports of Electrical Transformers from Finland", adopted on 18 July 1985, BISD 32S/55.

that it is not the role of panels to engage in a *de novo* review.[16] In our view, the same is true for panels operating in the context of the ATC, since they would be called upon, as in the context of cases dealing with anti-dumping and/or subsidies/countervailing duties, to review the consistency of a determination by a national investigating authority imposing a restriction under the relevant provisions of the relevant WTO legal instruments, in this case the ATC. In our view, the task of the Panel is to examine the consistency of the US action with the international obligations of the United States, and not the consistency of the US action with the US domestic statute implementing the international obligations of the United States. Consequently, the ATC constitutes, in our view, the relevant legal framework in this matter.

7.13   We have therefore decided, in accordance with Article 11 of the DSU, to make an objective assessment of the Statement issued by the US authorities on 23 March 1995 (the "March Statement) which, as the parties to the dispute agreed, constitutes the scope of the matter properly before the Panel without, however, engaging in a *de novo* review.[17] In our view, an objective assessment would entail an examination of whether the CITA had examined all relevant facts before it (including facts which might detract from an affirmative determination in accordance with the second sentence of Article 6.2 of the ATC), whether adequate explanation had been provided of how the facts as a whole supported the determination made, and, consequently, whether the determination made was consistent with the international obligations of the United States.[18] We note in this respect, that in response to a question by the Panel, the United States argued that the Panel had to examine whether the domestic authorities *had* based their determination on an examination of factors required by the ATC and whether the basis for the determination was adequately explained. In the US view, such an approach was compatible with the standard of review adopted in the "Fur Felt Hat" case.[19]

---

[16]   See the panel reports on "Korea - Anti-Dumping Duties on Imports of Polyacetal Resins from the United States", adopted on 27 April 1993, BISD 40S/205; "United States - Imposition of Anti-Dumping Duties on Imports of Fresh and Chilled Atlantic Salmon from Norway", adopted on 27 April 1994; "United States -Initiation of a Countervailing Duty Investigation into Softwood Lumber Products from Canada", adopted on 3 June 1987, BISD 34S/194.

[17]   A *de novo* review, if at all, is to be conducted by the TMB. Article 8.3 of the ATC reads as follows: "The TMB...shall rely on notifications and information supplied by the Members under the relevant Articles of the Agreement, supplemented by any additional information or necessary details they may submit or it may decide to seek from them". Article 8.5 of the ATC calls for a "thorough and prompt" review of the matter by the TMB.

[18]   This approach is largely consistent with the approach adopted by the panel reports cited in footnote 16, although it should be pointed out that the standard of review was expressed in slightly different terms in each of the aforementioned panel reports.

[19]   See paragraph 5.45 above.

Burden of Proof

7.14   The parties to the dispute have divergent views on the question of burden of proof. The United States essentially argues that it is not its duty to re-establish the consistency of the restriction with the relevant rules of the ATC, since it has already established that in the March Statement. Costa Rica, on the other hand, insists that in accordance with Article 6.2 and 6.4 of the ATC, it is incumbent upon the United States to establish to the Panel's satisfaction that the conditions required before imposing a restriction have in fact been met.

7.15   We recall in this context that one of the central elements of the ATC is the prohibition, in principle, for Members to have recourse to any new restrictions beyond those notified under Article 2.1 of the ATC. Article 2.4 of the ATC reads as follows:

> "... No new restrictions in terms of products or Members shall be introduced *except* under the provisions of this Agreement or relevant GATT 1994 provisions" (emphasis added).

We further note that Article 6.2 of the ATC reads as follows:

> "Safeguard action may be taken under this Article when, on the basis of a determination by a Member, it is *demonstrated* that..." (emphasis added).

7.16   In our view, Article 6 of the ATC is an exception to the rule of Article 2.4 of the ATC. It is a general principle of law, well-established by panels in prior GATT practice, that the party which invokes an exception in order to justify its action carries the burden of proof that it has fulfilled the conditions for invoking the exception. Consequently, in our view, it is up to the United States to demonstrate that it had fulfilled the requirements contained in Article 6.2 and 6.4 of the ATC in the March Statement which, as the parties to the dispute agreed, constitutes the scope of the matter properly before the Panel.

The Interpretation of the ATC

7.17   Article 3.2 of the DSU requires panels to interpret the covered agreements "in accordance with customary rules of interpretation of public international law". The customary rules of interpretation of public international law are embodied in the text of the Vienna Convention on the Law of Treaties (VCLT).[20]

> Article 31.1 of the VCLT reads:

> > "A treaty shall be interpreted in good faith in accordance with the ordinary meaning to be given to the terms of the

---

[20]   See the Appellate Body Decision on "United States - Standards for Reformulated and Conventional Gasoline", WT/DS2/AB/R, DSR 1996:I, 3, at 15.

treaty in their context and in the light of its object and purpose".

7.18   First, we pay attention to the phrase "ordinary meaning to be given to the
terms of the treaty in their context". The reason why, in our view, particular attention is paid to the context is simply that the terms of a treaty should not be
interpreted in isolation, but in their particular context in the entire agreement. We
recall that Article 31.2 of the VCLT expressly defines the context of the treaty to
include the text. Thus, it is clear that the entire text of the ATC is relevant in order to interpret Article 6.2 to 6.4 of the ATC.

7.19   Second, the overall purpose of the ATC is to integrate the textiles and
clothing sector into GATT 1994. Article 1 of the ATC makes this point clear. To
this effect, the ATC requires notification of all existing quantitative restrictions
(Article 2 of the ATC) and provides that they will have to be terminated by the
year 2004 (Article 9 of the ATC). The ATC allows adoption of new restrictions
in addition to those notified under Article 2 of the ATC for products not yet integrated into GATT 1994 pursuant to Article 2.6 to 2.8 of the ATC only excep-
tionally and in accordance with the relevant provisions of the ATC or in accordance with the relevant provisions of GATT 1994. Article 2.4 of the ATC reads:

> "...No new restrictions in terms of products or Members
> shall be introduced *except* under the provisions of this
> Agreement or relevant GATT 1994 provisions" (emphasis
> added).[21]

The exceptional nature of these restrictions is confirmed by the wording of Article 6.1 of the ATC which reads as follows:

> "...The transitional safeguard should be applied as *sparingly*
> as possible, consistently with the provisions of this Article
> and the effective implementation of the integration process
> under this Agreement" (emphasis added).

7.20   Finally, we recall that the relevant provisions have to be interpreted in
good faith. Based upon the wording, the context and the overall purpose of the
Agreement, exporting Members can legitimately expect that transitional safeguards, adopted under Article 6 of the ATC, would only be applied sparingly in
order to serve the narrow purpose of protecting domestic producers of like and/or
directly competitive products. Exporting Members can, in other words, legitimately expect that market access and investments made would not be frustrated
by importing Members taking improper recourse to such action.

7.21   We conclude from the interpretation of these provisions in the light of
Article 31 of the VCLT that recourse to transitional safeguards should be taken

---

[21]   We note that a footnote to Article 2.4 of the ATC reads as follows: "The relevant GATT 1994
provisions shall not include Article XIX in respect of products not yet integrated into GATT 1994,
except as specifically provided in paragraph 3 of the Annex".

on an exceptional basis only. Consequently, in our view, Article 6 of the ATC should be interpreted narrowly. This conclusion is consistent with the past practice of GATT panels.[22]

The Structure of Article 6 of the ATC

7.22   Article 6.2 of the ATC conditions the application of a transitional safeguard on a finding that a product is being imported in such increased quantities so as to cause serious damage, or actual threat thereof, to the domestic industry producing like and/or directly competitive products. Article 6.2 of the ATC reads as follows:

> "Safeguard action may be taken under this Article when, on the basis of a determination by a Member, it is demonstrated that a particular product is being imported into its territory in such increased quantities as to cause serious damage, or actual threat thereof, to the domestic industry producing like and/or directly competitive products. Serious damage or actual threat thereof must demonstrably be caused by such increased quantities in total imports of that product and not by such other facts as technological changes or changes in consumer preference".

Article 6.3 of the ATC contains an indicative list of economic variables that can be taken into account in order to assess the serious damage or actual threat thereof. After having satisfied the conditions of Article 6.2 of the ATC, Members must attribute the serious damage or actual threat thereof to a particular Member or Members, since, in accordance with Article 6.4 of the ATC, transitional safeguards "shall be applied on a Member-by-Member basis". Article 6.4 of the ATC reads as follows:

> "Any measure invoked pursuant to the provisions of this Article shall be applied on a Member-by-Member basis. The Member or Members to whom serious damage, or actual threat thereof, referred to in paragraphs 2 and 3, is attributed, shall be determined on the basis of a sharp and

---

[22]   See the panel reports on "Canada - Administration of the Foreign Investment Review Act (FIRA)", adopted on 7 February 1984, BISD 30S/140; "United States - Customs User Fee", adopted on 2 February 1988, BISD 35S/245; "Japan - Restrictions on Imports of Certain Agricultural Products", adopted on 22 March 1988, BISD 35S/163; "European Economic Community - Restrictions on Imports of Dessert Apples", Complaint by Chile, adopted on 22 June 1989, BISD 36S/93; "Canada - Import Restrictions on Ice Cream and Yogurt", adopted on 5 December 1989, BISD 36S/68; "European Economic Community - Regulation on Imports of Parts and Components", adopted on 16 May 1990, BISD 37S/132; "United States - Countervailing Duties on Fresh, Chilled and Frozen Pork from Canada", adopted on 11 July 1991, BISD 38S/30; "United States - Definition of Industry Concerning Wine and Grape Products", adopted on 28 April 1992, BISD 39S/436; "United States - Measures Affecting Alcoholic and Malt Beverages", adopted on 19 June 1992, BISD 39S/206.

substantial increase in imports, actual or imminent,[23] from such a Member or Members individually, and on the basis of the level of imports as compared with imports from other sources, market share, and import and domestic prices at a comparable stage of commercial transaction; none of these factors, either alone or combined with other factors, can necessarily give decisive guidance. Such safeguard measure shall not be applied to the exports of any Member whose exports of the particular product are already under restraint under this Agreement."

7.23   The overall purpose of Article 6 of the ATC is to give Members the possibility to adopt new restrictions on products not already integrated into GATT 1994 pursuant to Article 2.6 to 2.8 of the ATC and not under existing restrictions, i.e., not notified under Article 2.1 of the ATC. Article 6 of the ATC, in our view, establishes a three-step approach which has to be followed for a new restriction to be imposed. Articles 6.2 and 6.4 of the ATC constitute the first two steps which, taken together, amount to a determination that serious damage has occurred or is actually threatening to occur and that it may be attributed to a sharp and substantial increase in imports from a particular Member or Members: No action can be taken on the basis of Article 6.2 alone.

7.24   A determination under Article 6.2 of the ATC is, therefore, a necessary but not sufficient condition to have recourse to bilateral consultations under Article 6.7 of the ATC. Only when serious damage or actual threat thereof has been demonstrated under Article 6.2 and has been attributed to a particular Member or Members under Article 6.4 of the ATC, can recourse to Article 6.7 of the ATC be made in a way consistent with the provisions of the ATC.

C.   *Review of the Findings by the US Investigating Authorities on Serious Damage Attributable to Costa Rican Imports*

7.25   We now turn to an examination of Costa Rica's basic claim: that the United States imposed restrictions on imports of underwear into the United States without having demonstrated, as required by Article 6.2 and 6.4 of the ATC, that the US underwear industry suffered serious damage from Costa Rican imports. We first discuss the scope of the matter before us, i.e., the information that we will consider in our examination of Costa Rica's claim. We then undertake an objective assessment of the US action and its conformity with the ATC in accordance with the standard of review set out above. In this respect, we will examine the determination by the United States in respect of (i) whether the US industry

---

[23]   Footnote 6 accompanying this text reads: "Such an imminent increase shall be a measurable one and shall not be determined to exist on the basis of allegation, conjecture or mere possibility arising, for example, from the existence of production capacity in the exporting Members".

suffered serious damage, (ii) the cause of the serious damage and (iii) the attribution of serious damage to Costa Rican imports.

The Scope of the Matter

7.26   We agree with the parties to the dispute that we should restrict our review to an examination of the March Statement. We believe that statements subsequent to the March Statement should not be viewed as a legally independent basis for establishing serious damage or actual threat thereof in the present case. A restriction may be imposed, in a manner consistent with Article 6 of the ATC, when based on a determination made in accordance with the procedure embodied in Article 6.2 and 6.4 of the ATC. This is precisely the role that the March Statement is called upon to play. Consequently, to review the alleged inconsistency of the US action with the ATC, we must focus our legal analysis on the March Statement as the relevant legal basis for the safeguard action taken by the United States.

7.27   Costa Rica submitted to the Panel information concerning the bilateral negotiations that took place between Costa Rica and the United States before and after the imposition of the restriction. More specifically, Costa Rica submitted information relating to settlement offers made by the United States concerning the level of the restriction to be imposed. In this respect, we note that Article 4.6 of the DSU reads as follows:

> "Consultations shall be confidential, and without prejudice
> to the rights of any Member in any further proceedings."

In our view, the wording of Article 4.6 of the DSU makes it clear that offers made in the context of consultations are, in case a mutually agreed solution is not reached, of no legal consequence to the later stages of dispute settlement, as far as the rights of the parties to the dispute are concerned. Consequently, we will not base our findings on such information.

Serious Damage

7.28   Article 6.2 of the ATC authorizes safeguard action following a demonstration that a particular product is being imported in such increased quantities as to cause serious damage, or actual threat thereof, to the domestic industry. The factors that should be taken into account in order to establish serious damage are listed in Article 6.3 of the ATC, which reads as follows:

> "In making a determination of serious damage, or actual
> threat thereof, as referred to in paragraph 2, the Member
> shall examine the effect of those imports on the state of the
> particular industry, as reflected in changes in such relevant
> economic variables as output, productivity, utilization of
> capacity, inventories, market share, exports, wages, em-
> ployment, domestic prices, profits and investment; *none of*

> *which, either alone or combined with other factors, can*
> *necessarily give decisive guidance"* (emphasis added).

The United States determination in this regard is contained in the March Statement.

7.29   The March Statement included under the heading "Market Situation" one sub-heading entitled "Serious Damage to the Domestic Industry" (sub-heading A), which contained general information about the effect of underwear imports in Category 352/652, and a second sub-heading "Industry Statements" (sub-heading B), which summarized statements to the US authorities by individual US companies. To some extent, there was an overlap between the information contained under the two sub-headings. The same categories of information were equally discussed in a statement submitted to the TMB by the United States in July 1995 (the" July Statement"). While we have concluded that the July Statement should not be viewed as a legally independent basis for establishing serious damage or actual threat thereof, we feel that we can legitimately take the July Statement into account as evidence submitted by the United States in our assessment of the overall accuracy of the March Statement. Consequently, we will use the July Statement for this limited purpose only. By doing so, we do not share the concerns expressed by the United States that such use of the July Statement would impair proceedings in the TMB in the future. We consider that a reluctance to submit updated information would normally adversely affect Members concerned. The interest to cooperate as required by Articles 6.7 and 6.9 of the ATC would prevail.

7.30   In the following paragraphs, we evaluate the information in the March Statement in light of the economic variables listed in Article 6.3 of the ATC, to the extent and in the order that they were raised in the March Statement.

Overview

7.31   The March Statement under the heading "Industry Profile" refers to 395 establishments that manufacture cotton and man-made fibre underwear, while the July Statement under the same heading refers to "approximately 302 establishments". In our view, this basic and substantial inconsistency concerning the scope of the domestic industry raises serious questions about the accuracy of the information contained in the March Statement and the conclusion that serious damage exists.

Output (US Production)

7.32   The March Statement contains general information on the evolution of US production of underwear. In this connection, however, Costa Rica argues that the US restriction was introduced to protect the US fabric-producing industry and not the US underwear industry. We see two aspects to this argument. First, this argument may be viewed as a claim that the United States had not demonstrated the existence of serious damage to the US domestic industry producing products that were like and/or directly competitive with products imported from Costa Rica (i.e., underwear). In this connection, we do not see anywhere in the March Statement where fabric producers were treated as the domestic industry. Rather, the Statement consistently refers to the industry that manufactures "cotton and man-made fibre underwear", which is the subject of the restriction in question. The statistics all purport to relate to that industry. Thus, the claim by Costa Rica would seem to lack a factual basis.

7.33   There is, however, a second aspect to Costa Rica's argument. The parties agree that the industry situation within the United Sates is different between those manufacturers that produce underwear in a totally domestic process and those that utilize the outward processing regime ("807 or 807A trade"). The manufacturers in the latter category are engaged in the cutting process, while assembly of the cut pieces is contracted out to overseas manufacturers and then the finished products are re-imported by the US manufacturers for sale in the US market. It is quite possible that in the case of increased imports damage could occur to manufacturers in the former category, while those in the latter category could see their position improve. The March Statement contains no breakdown of the effect of imports on these two components of the US industry. That such an analysis would have been appropriate is indirectly confirmed by statements of the United States, which recognize that the nature of the effect of 807 or 807A trade on the domestic industry could be significantly different than non 807/807A trade (paragraph 5.158).

7.34   Finally, we would note that the general statistics on declining production of underwear only weakly support a demonstration of serious damage. For example, if those firms with declining underwear production shifted their capacity to other products (see below under "Utilization of Capacity", where this is reported as occurring), then it is quite possible that neither the firms nor their workers would be seriously damaged. This uncertainty about the relation of production declines to serious damage arises because of the limited statistics and cursory analysis contained in the March Statement.

Market Share (Market Share Loss/Import Penetration)

7.35   The March Statement contains general information on the market share of US underwear producers and on import penetration levels. As noted in the preceding paragraph, however, the failure of the March Statement to analyze the extent of 807 or 807A trade detracts from its conclusion that serious damage was caused by the increase in imports.

7.36   With respect to the US analysis of imports, Costa Rica argues the volume of importation is overstated because 807/807A trade should not be counted as imports by the United States. We disagree with this assertion. Article 6.6(d) of the ATC clearly acknowledges the possibility that Members might impose restrictions on re-imports "as defined by the laws and practices of the importing Member". According to the United States, 807/807A trade is considered as re-imports. Consequently, the United States could consider 807 and 807A trade originating in Costa Rica in its analysis of whether the US underwear industry had suffered serious damage and could impose a restraint on such trade, provided that the rest of the conditions of Article 6 of the ATC were met.

Employment

7.37   With respect to "Employment", the March Statement reads as follows:

> "Employment in the US cotton and man-made fibre underwear industry dropped from 46,377 production workers in 1992 to 44,056 workers in 1994, a five percent decline and a loss of 2,321 employees".

The same heading in the July Statement reads as follows:

> "Employment in the US cotton and man-made fibre underwear industry dropped from 35,191 production workers in 1992 to 33,309 workers in 1994, a five percent decline and a loss of 1,882 employees".

As we noted in respect of the general industry description discussed above, the extent of the discrepancy between the statistics in the March and July Statements, which purported to cover the same time period, raises questions about the accuracy of the information contained in the March Statement. This concern was not alleviated by the industry statement in sub-heading B since information as to employment was obtained from only two companies out of the more than 300 establishments in the industry, of which only one was apparently suffering damage. The March Statement reads in this respect as follows:

> "... one company reported that employees were also being transferred to production of other types of garments. Employment losses have also occurred because of import-related plant closing. A company that has already closed two plants employing 165 workers is anticipating two additional closures in 1995 representing total employment of about 400".

Man-Hours

7.38   Under the heading "Man-Hours", the March Statement reads as follows:

> "Average annual man-hours dropped from 86.2 million in 1992 to 81.5 million in 1994, a five per cent decline."

The same heading in the July Statement reads as follows:

> "Average annual man-hours worked dropped from 65.4 million in 1992 to 61.6 million in 1994, a six per cent decline."

In our view, as expressed above, the extent of the discrepancy in the information included in the two statements casts doubts as to the sufficient accuracy of the data included in the March Statement.

Sales

7.39   The March Statement reads as follows:

> "Sales have slowed, and one company reported that their sales were down about 17 per cent in 1994".

The information on only one company, however, does not suffice, in our view, to support the general statement that sales have slowed.

Profits

7.40   The March Statement reads as follows:

> "Profits were down 18 per cent at one firm, and there is pressure on the bottom line throughout the industry due to rising costs and stiff import competition".

Again, information on only one company does not suffice, in our view, to support the general statement that profits were under "pressure" (whatever that may mean) generally.

Investment

7.41   The March Statement reads as follows:

> "Because of the impact of imports and the uncertainty they have caused in the market, US companies generally have been postponing investment in this industry. Some companies have closed plants permanently or shifted production off-shore, and additional disinvestment of this nature is being contemplated by underwear manufacturing firms".

In our view, the information contained in this statement is not sufficiently conclusive. We fail to see, for reasons discussed above (paragraph 7.34), a sufficient causal link between imports and "postponing investment" in the US industry. Moreover, the second sentence of this statement is indefinite ("some companies") and merely speculative ("is being contemplated") and cannot support any definite conclusion on the reasons why investment were slowing down in the United States. Finally, we note the absence of any statistics on, or analysis of, the evolution of investment in the US industry.

Utilization of Capacity

7.42   The March Statement reads as follows:

> "Because of the import competition, firms report shifting production capacity to other product lines including outerwear".

Again, the statement is vague as no quantification is given. Moreover, it is not clear that a shift of production, as opposed to a decline, would support the determination of serious damage in any event.

Prices

7.43   The March Statement indicates that the US producers' average price was $30.00 per dozen in 1994, while the July Statement indicates that the average US price was $20.00 per dozen. The extent of this discrepancy between the March and July Statements raises serious questions about the accuracy of the information contained in the March Statement.

7.44   In addition, in respect of "Prices", the March Statement reads as follows:

> "Import prices in these sectors have been very low which has placed considerable pressure on domestic producers:
>
> (a)   Raw cotton costs in the United States have increased substantially, seriously eroding US underwear producers' margins. These cost increases have not been recouped because prices cannot be raised without becoming uncompetitive with imports.
>
> (b)   Competing imports enjoy a price edge over domestically produced goods because the imports are produced with lower priced foreign fabric which often reflects a subsidized cotton price. As a result of the increased import market share in underwear, average retail prices of underwear in the United States have generally declined during the past two years at a time when US manufacturers' costs, particularly for raw cotton, have increased substantially. This development has seriously eroded the profitability of US underwear manufacturing".

It could be argued that points (a) and (b) show that the damage to the US industry was not due only to imports, but also to increases in the US price for raw cotton. The relative importance of these two causes is not analyzed. There is, for example, no discussion of why US cotton prices increased and, more to the point, whether the price increases are expected to continue in effect. Moreover, to the extent that imports are 807A trade, the increase in cotton prices would be reflected in their prices as well, but here again there was no consideration of 807A trade in respect of this item. Finally, we find that the conclusion that profitability has been "seriously eroded" is not sufficiently precise to serve as a basis for establishing serious damage.

7.45   In conclusion, in our view, the information submitted in the March Statement under the heading "Market Situation" suffers from two important weaknesses: the information in some cases is inconsistent with other information later submitted by the United States to the TMB and in other cases is inadequate to demonstrate serious damage to the US industry. This latter problem is generally true in respect of the information supplied by specific companies in sub-heading B, where the March Statement typically refers to only one or two companies of indeterminate size or market share out of an industry consisting of 395 establishments. Moreover, while there are general statistics on declines in production and market share, there is no information at all on the general state and performance of the US underwear industry. For example, the discussion of profits in the industry refers to only one company. In this connection generally, we note that the TMB, in its more fact-intensive review in accordance with Article 8.3 of the ATC, has by consensus concluded in this case that there was absence of serious damage caused to the US industry. The weaknesses in the March Statement that are discussed above raise considerable doubts as to whether serious damage has been demonstrated. However, we refrain from making a finding on this point of law. The factors listed in Article 6.3 of the ATC do not provide sufficient and exclusive guidance in this case. We are, therefore, not in a position to conclude that the United States has failed to demonstrate serious damage or actual threat thereof.

Causality

7.46   In addition to establishing serious damage or actual threat thereof, the United States was required to demonstrate that such damage or threat was caused by imports. Article 6.2 of the ATC, second sentence, reads as follows:

> "Serious damage or actual threat thereof must *demonstrably* be caused by such increased quantities in total imports of that product and not by such other factors as technological changes or changes in consumer preference" (emphasis added).

Nowhere in the March Statement could we find a discussion or demonstration of causality as required under this provision, beyond the mere statement that the imports were responsible for the damage. This assertion is inadequate, in our view, because of special factors affecting trade in underwear between the United States and a number of exporting Members including Costa Rica. (As noted above, most of this trade with Costa Rica - at least 94 per cent - is apparently 807 or 807A trade.) While such trade may certainly cause damage to the domestic industry, the nature of the trade is such that it may benefit the domestic firms that participate in it (see paragraph 7.44). Thus, in a discussion of whether such trade has caused serious damage, it is necessary to look at this trade to determine its effects on the industry. Because of the nature of the trade it is not possible in these circumstances to conclude from the simple fact that there has been a fall in production that there has also been serious damage. The March Statement undertakes no such discussion. Moreover, the March Statement suggests other possible causes of serious damage, such as rising cotton prices (see paragraph 7.44), but does not consider their role as a cause of such damage. Thus, it cannot be said that the March Statement "demonstrably" shows that serious damage was caused by increased levels of imports. We find, therefore, that an objective assessment of the March Statement leads to the conclusion that the United States failed to comply with its obligations under Article 6.2 of the ATC by imposing a restriction on imports of Costa Rican underwear without adequately demonstrating that increased imports had caused serious damage.

Attribution of Serious Damage to Costa Rica

7.47   We now turn to the issue of whether the March Statement adequately attributed serious damage to Costa Rica. Article 6.4 of the ATC requires the attribution of serious damage, or actual threat thereof, to a Member or Members before their imports may be restricted. This also raises an issue of causality since attribution results in a direct linkage being drawn between exports from a particular Member or Members and serious damage to the domestic industry of the importing Member. The question facing the CITA in the present case was whether Costa Rican exports contributed to serious damage in the US domestic industry. Since the US authorities have attributed serious damage in the present case to imports from Costa Rica, all of the deficiencies with respect to the analysis of serious damage and causality that are detailed in the preceding sections are relevant to the analysis under Article 6.4 of the ATC.

7.48   With respect to serious damage attributed to imports from Costa Rica, the March Statement reads as follows:

> "The sharp and substantial increase of low priced imports from Costa Rica is causing serious damage to the US domestic industry producing cotton and man-made fibre underwear.

> "US imports of cotton and man-made fibre underwear, Category 352/652, from Costa Rica reached 14,423,178 dozen in 1994, 22 per cent above the 11,844,331 dozen imported in 1993 and 61 per cent above its 1992 level.

> "US imports of cotton and man-made fibre underwear, from Costa Rica in Category 352/652, entered the US at an average landed duty-paid value of $9.39 per dozen, 69 per cent below U.S. producers' average price for cotton and man-made fibre underwear.

> "Costa Rica is the number two supplier of Category 352/652 imports with 15 per cent of total US imports of Category 352/652 in 1994. Category 352/652 imports from Costa Rica were equivalent to 8.8 per cent of US production of Category 352/652 in the year ending September 1994."

7.49 Article 6.4 of the ATC requires that the attribution of serious damage to individual Members be made on the basis of "a sharp and substantial increase in imports" and on the basis of "the level of imports compared with imports from other sources, market share and import and domestic prices ... ". While there has been a significant increase in imports of underwear from Costa Rica, we would note in overview that the position of Costa Rica in respect of each of these factors is not significantly different from that of the other five exporting Members considered in the March Statement and that the March Statement undertakes no comparative assessment of imports from Costa Rica and those five exporting Members.

7.50 In our analysis of whether the US authorities appropriately attributed serious damage to Costa Rican imports, we pay particular attention to the fact that imports into the United States from Costa Rica had reached 14,423,178 dozen in 1994, an increase of 22 per cent during the period of investigation. However, we also note the following facts: The restraint was imposed on Costa Rica on 23 June 1995; Bilateral agreements were concluded with Colombia on 27 June 1995, with the Dominican Republic on 25 June 1995 and with El Salvador on 6 July 1995; Later, agreements were concluded with Honduras on 15 September 1995 and with Turkey on 19 July 1995. The United States imposed the restraint on underwear imports from Costa Rica while, during the period that immediately ensued, it reached agreement with five other exporters on quotas of 170,305,774 dozen, an increase of 478 per cent compared to the actual exports from these countries during the period of investigation.

7.51 Thus, taking into account the US agreements with its other suppliers and the statement by the United States that goods imported under 807A are not regarded as less damaging than non-GAL 807 and other imports (paragraph 5.159), we cannot reconcile the US restriction on imports from Costa Rica with the requirements of attribution under Article 6.4 of the ATC. More specifically, in light of the purpose of Article 6, we find that the United States cannot enter into agreements permitting imports of 170,305,774 dozen units of a product (an increase of 478 per cent over then current import levels) and at the same time claim that imports of 14,423,178 dozen units (an increase of 22 per cent over then current import levels) are contributing to serious damage. In this regard, we recall the TMB's consensus conclusion that the United States had not demonstrated that imports were causing serious damage to the US underwear industry. We find therefore that an objective assessment of the March Statement leads to the conclusion that the United States failed to comply with its obligations under Article 6.4 of the ATC by imposing a restriction on imports of Costa Rican underwear without making an adequate attribution of serious damage to such imports.[24]

---

[24] We note that by the same reasoning we could have concluded that the United States failed to demonstrate the existence of serious damage in the March Statement as required by Article 6.2 of the ATC. The fact that the US underwear industry was able to accept and withstand such a huge inroad of products from the five other exporting Members suggests that there was no serious damage to the

7.52   In light of (i) the fact that restrictions under Article 6 of the ATC are to be applied only sparingly, (ii) the fact that the United States has the burden of proving that it has complied with the requirements of Article 6 of the ATC, (iii) the deficiencies detailed above in respect of the evidence on the existence of serious damage, which raise serious questions in our view as to whether there was serious damage shown under Article 6.2 at all, (iv) the fact that the United States failed to demonstrate adequately that the cause of serious damage was imports, and (v) the fact that the United States voluntarily agreed to accept import limits from other countries exporting underwear to the United States that permitted increases over their current export levels that were far in excess of Costa Rica's export levels to the United States, we conclude that the United States failed to demonstrate adequately in the March Statement that its domestic industry suffered serious damage that could be attributed to Costa Rican imports and thus, by imposing import restrictions on imports of Costa Rican underwear, the United States failed to comply with its obligations under Article 6.2 and 6.4 of the ATC.

D.   Actual Threat of Serious Damage

7.53   We next turn to a question related to the scope of Costa Rica's basic claim: Whether the March Statement contained a finding on actual threat of serious damage.

7.54   The United States argued before the Panel that the March Statement supports a finding on actual threat. We note that the March Statement contains no reference to actual threat; the findings included related exclusively to serious damage. We recall, however, that the parties to the dispute agreed that the Diplomatic Note that was handed to Costa Rica along with the March Statement made reference to actual threat of serious damage.

7.55   Article 6.2 and 6.4 of the ATC make reference to "serious damage, or actual threat thereof". The word "thereof", in our view, clearly refers to "serious damage". The word "or" distinguishes between "serious damage" and "actual threat thereof". In our view, "serious damage" refers to a situation that has already occurred, whereas "actual threat of serious damage" refers to a situation existing at present which might lead to serious damage in the future. Consequently, in our view, a finding on "serious damage" requires the party that takes action to demonstrate that damage has already occurred, whereas a finding on "actual threat of serious damage" requires the same party to demonstrate that, unless action is taken, damage will most likely occur in the near future.[25] The

---

industry in the first place. However, we felt that the inadequacy of the US measure was more acutely represented in the attribution under Article 6.4, which requires a source-specific or Member-by-Member analysis, as opposed to the analysis of total imports under Article 6.2. See also our discussion in paragraph 7.45 above.

[25]   See the panel reports on "United States - Measures Affecting Imports of Softwood Lumber from Canada", adopted on 27 October 1993, BISD 40S/358, paras. 402, 408; "New Zealand - Imports of

March Statement contains no elements of such a prospective analysis.[26] In our view, even if the mention of "actual threat" in the Diplomatic Note accompanying the March Statement were to be considered, the fact that the March Statement made no reference to actual threat and contained no elements of such a prospective analysis was dispositive *per se*. Consequently, we do not agree with the US argument that the March Statement supports a finding on actual threat of serious damage.

E.   Other Claims

Article 6.6(d) of the ATC

7.56   Costa Rica claims that the United States violated Article 6.6(d) of the ATC by not granting a more favourable treatment to Costa Rican imports under "807 trade". Article 6.6(d) of the ATC reads as follows:

> "In the application of the transitional safeguard, particular account shall be taken of the interests of exporting Members as set out below:
>
> (d)   more favourable treatment shall be accorded to re-imports by a Member of textile and clothing products which that Member has exported to another Member for processing and subsequent reimportation, as defined by the laws and practices of the importing Member, and subject to satisfactory control and certification procedures, when these products are imported from a Member for which this type of trade represents a significant proportion of its total exports of textiles and clothing".

7.57   The United States accepted before the Panel that "807 trade" should be considered a re-import according to US laws. In our view, the legal issue before us is the interpretation of the term "more favourable treatment". The "chapeau" to Article 6.6(d) of the ATC makes it clear that the more favourable treatment must be granted "in the *application* of the transitional safeguard" (emphasis added). This means, in our view, that Members availing themselves of the Article 6 transitional safeguard are obliged to grant more favourable treatment to re-imports,

---

Electrical Transformers from Finland", *op. cit.*, para. 4.8; and "Korea - Antidumping Duties on Imports of Polyacetal Resins from the United States", *op. cit.*, paras. 253, 272, 278.

[26]   We note that the only elements that could be used in a prospective analysis were the following: in sub-heading B ("Industry Statements") under "Employment", the March Statement reads: "A company ... is anticipating two additional closures in 1995 representing total employment of about 400". In the same sub-heading, under "Investment", the March Statement reads: "... additional disinvestment of this nature is being contemplated by underwear manufacturing firms". We note that both elements were used in the March Statement to support a finding on serious damage. Even if, however, these elements were used to support a finding on actual threat, they could hardly constitute adequate evidence of actual threat of serious damage.

independently of whether such treatment has been previously rejected by the affected Member during the bilateral consultations or whether other privileges were envisaged to be accorded to such a Member in negotiations based upon the implemented safeguard measure. The term "more favourable treatment" is not further qualified in the ATC. We, therefore, reject the United States argument (paragraph 5.157) that they had complied with Article 6.6(d) of the ATC by offering Costa Rica enhanced access under GAL programmes during the course of the consultations.

7.58   Costa Rica specifically argues in this respect that the United States was obliged to grant to Costa Rican imports a quantitatively more favourable treatment. Costa Rica argues that the United States was obliged to grant Costa Rica a quota larger than that under Article 6.8 of the ATC, which provides that a quota cannot be fixed at a level:

> "lower than the actual level of exports or imports from the Member concerned during the 12-month period terminating two months preceding that month in which the request for consultation was made".

We cannot fully share the approach advocated by Costa Rica. We agree with Costa Rica that quantitatively more favourable treatment for the full three-year period is one of the options available to Members in order to comply with the requirements of Article 6.6(d) of the ATC. We do not consider it, however, to be the only option. In our view, a Member could, for example, comply with the requirements under Article 6.6(d) of the ATC by imposing a restriction for a period shorter than three years.

7.59   However, in our view, under Article 6.10 of the ATC, the level of Costa Rican imports required to be admitted to the United States under an Article 6 of the ATC restraint was 14,423,178 dozen, which equals the minimum level under Article 6.8. We reach this conclusion because of the following two reasons: First, in the absence of a mutual agreement under Article 6.8, Article 6.10 authorizes the application of "the" restraint. In our view, this reference points to Article 6.8. Second, the absence of a minimum restraint level under Article 6.10, set at the level specified in Article 6.8, would fundamentally undermine the balance of rights and obligations between exporting and importing Members and any interest they might have to enter into negotiations. The restriction imposed on Costa Rican imports under the implementing order of the March Statement was 14,423,178 dozen, i.e., identical to the level required under Article 6.8 of the ATC, and did not make allowance for re-imports in a quantitative way.[27] Nor does the implementing order make allowance for re-imports in any other way. We, consequently, conclude that the United States has violated its obligations under Article 6.6(d) of the ATC.

---

[27]   See the Implementing Order published in 60 Federal Register 32653, No. 121, 23 June 1995.

Obligation to Consult

7.60 We next examine Costa Rica's claim that the United States violated Article 6.7 of the ATC by failing to hold consultations on the basis of actual threat of serious damage following the TMB's conclusion that the existence of serious damage was not demonstrated, since all the bilateral consultations were based on the March Statement which explicitly based its findings on the existence of serious damage. We note that the United States maintains that the reference to "serious damage" in the March statement was an abbreviated expression for "serious damage, or actual threat thereof" and the Diplomatic Note to Costa Rica making the actual request for consultations in fact referred to "serious damage, or actual threat thereof".

7.61 Since consultations under Article 6.7 are essentially a bilateral process and no official records are kept, a panel generally is not in a position to know exactly what has been discussed during the consultations. However, in our view, it is unnecessary to decide whether the basis of the consultations in the present case was "serious damage" or "actual threat thereof", because we have already found that the issue of actual threat did not dispose of this particular dispute. Both Costa Rica and the United States agree that the March Statement should be the sole basis for the Panel to examine the legality of the US action, and as noted above, in our view, the March Statement was not predicated on and did not demonstrate the existence of actual threat.

Date of Application of the Restriction

7.62 Costa Rica argues that the United States retroactively applied the restriction in violation of Article 6.10 of the ATC. The restriction was introduced on 23 June 1995 for a period of 12 months starting on 27 March 1995, which was the date of the request for consultations under Article 6.7 of the ATC. Although Article 6.10 of the ATC allows the importing country to "apply the restraint, ... within 30 days following the 60-day period for consultations", it is silent about the initial date from which the restraint period should be calculated. In contrast, Article 3.5(i) of the Multifibre Arrangement (MFA) stated that the restraint could be instituted "for the twelve-month period beginning on the day when the request was received by the participating exporting country or countries". Thus, the question before the Panel is whether the silence of the ATC in this regard should be interpreted as prohibition of a practice which was explicitly recognized under the MFA, and if so, what should be the appropriate date from which the restraint period is to be calculated under the ATC.

7.63 In our view, this is not a question of retroactive application of a treaty to events that took place before the entry into force of the treaty, as envisaged in Article 28 of the Vienna Convention on the Law of Treaties (VCLT). Rather, it is a technical question regarding the opening date of a quota period.

7.64 Since the ATC is silent on this question, we will first examine how the matter is treated under the provisions of the GATT 1994, which is an integral part of the WTO Agreement along with the ATC. Article 1.6 of the ATC states that "[u]nless otherwise provided in this Agreement, its provisions shall not affect the rights and obligations of Members under the provisions of the WTO Agreement and the Multilateral Trade Agreements". Members assume under the WTO certain transparency obligations when they implement trade-restrictive measures. Article X:2 of GATT 1994 is the relevant provision, which reads:

> "No measure of general application taken by any [Member] effecting an advance in a rate of duty or other charge on imports under an established and uniform practice, or imposing a new or more burdensome requirement, restriction or prohibition of imports, or on the transfer of payments therefor, shall be enforced before such measure has been officially published".

7.65   We note that Article X:1 of GATT 1994, which also uses the language "of general application", includes "administrative rulings" in its scope. The mere fact that the restraint at issue was an administrative order does not prevent us from concluding that the restraint was a measure of general application. Nor does the fact that it was a country-specific measure exclude the possibility of it being a measure of general application. If, for instance, the restraint was addressed to a specific company or applied to a specific shipment, it would not have qualified as a measure of general application. However, to the extent that the restraint affects an unidentified number of economic operators, including domestic and foreign producers, we find it to be a measure of general application.

7.66   In the absence of a provision comparable to Article 3.5(i) of the MFA in the ATC, a Member's obligation under this provision applies in the application of transitional safeguard measures for textiles. If a Member sets the initial date of a restraint period as the date of the request for consultations, without having officially published the content of the request for consultations, the Member is acting in violation of Article X:2 of GATT 1994. Conversely, if the Member has published that information, specifying the proposed restraint level and restraint period, it can, when implementing the restraint at a later time, set the initial date as the date of the publication of the information, which could be the date of the request for consultation if the information were published on the same day.

7.67   In this context, we note that the Panel report on the "Chilean Apples" case stated that "the allocation of back-dated quotas, that is, quotas declared to have been filled at the time of their announcement, did not conform to the requirements of Article XIII:3(b) and Article XIII:3 (c)" of the GATT.[28] While we agree with this conclusion, we note that the facts are different in the present case. After having made the request for consultations on 27 March 1995, the United States published the proposed restraint period and the restraint level in the Federal

---

[28]   "European Economic Community - Restrictions on Imports of Dessert Apples", Complaint by Chile, *op. cit.*, at para. 12.26.

Register on 21 April 1995. The United States therefore did not "back-date" the restraint period in the way which was found to be inconsistent in the report on "Chilean Apples" since here it was made public well before the measure was imposed on 23 June 1995.

7.68   Finally, we note the US argument that if the safeguard measure could only be applied starting at some time later than the date of the request for consultations, there would be a flood of imports in anticipation of the eventual restriction, which might defeat the whole purpose of the transitional safeguard measure. We find this argument to be persuasive from a practical point of view. In order to avoid such a consequence, in our view, all that is needed on the part of the importing country is to publish the content of the request for consultations immediately.

7.69   In light of the foregoing, we conclude that the prevalent practice under the MFA of setting the initial date of a restraint period as the date of request for consultations cannot be maintained under the ATC. However, we note that if the importing country publishes the proposed restraint period and restraint level after the request for consultations, it can later set the initial date of the restraint period as the date of the publication of the proposed restraint. In the present case, the United States violated its obligations under Article X:2 of GATT 1994 and consequently under Article 6.10 of the ATC by setting the restraint period for 12 months starting on 27 March 1995. However, had it set the restraint period starting on 21 April 1995, which was the date of the publication of the information about the request for consultations, it would not have acted inconsistently with GATT 1994 or the ATC in respect of the restraint period. The United States argues that it did not "enforce" the restraint until 23 June 1995. We note the US argument. However, in so far as the restraint was applied to exports from Costa Rica which had taken place prior to the publication, it was implemented and therefore enforced within the meaning of Article X:2 of GATT 1994.[29]

Article 2.4 of the ATC

7.70   In our view, a finding that the United States violated Article 2.4 of the ATC would depend on a previous finding that the United States violated Article 6 of the ATC; conversely, a finding by the Panel that the United States acted consistently with its obligations under Article 6 of the ATC would automatically mean that Article 2.4 of the ATC was not violated.

7.71   We note our previous conclusion that the United States imposed the restriction in a manner inconsistent with its obligations under Articles 6.2, 6.4 and 6.6(d) of the ATC. In our view, the United States by violating its obligations un-

---

[29]   A similar conclusion was reached by the panel on "European Economic Community - Restrictions on Imports of Apples", Complaint by the United States, adopted on 22 June 1989, BISD 36S/135, at para. 5.23.

der Article 6 of the ATC has *ipso facto* violated its obligations under Article 2.4 of the ATC as well.

Article 8 of the ATC

7.72   Finally, we turn to Costa Rica's claim that the United States violated Article 8 of the ATC by refusing to follow the recommendations made by the TMB and by failing to submit a report explaining its inability to conform with the recommendations.

7.73   We have examined the contents of recommendations made by the TMB in the present case. In the relevant part of its report, the TMB made the following recommendations after the review conducted between 13 and 21 July 1995:

> "During its review under paragraphs 2 and 3 of Article 6 of the safeguard action taken by the United States against imports of category 352/652 from Costa Rica and Honduras, the TMB found that serious damage, as envisaged in these provisions, had not been demonstrated. The TMB could not, however, reach consensus on the existence of actual threat of serious damage. The TMB recommended that further consultations be held between the United States and the parties concerned, with a view to arriving at a mutual understanding, bearing in mind the above, and with due consideration to the particular features of this case, as well as equity considerations.
>
> "These consultations shall be held consistent with the Agreement on Textiles and Clothing, in particular with Articles 6 and 4, and be concluded within 30 days. Parties shall report to the TMB on the outcome of such consultations no later than at the end of that period."[30]

7.74   We note that the only obligation the United States assumed under these recommendations was to hold consultations with Costa Rica regarding the safeguard action in question. The United States and Costa Rica in fact held consultations on 16-17 August 1995. Therefore, we conclude that the United States did not act inconsistently with its obligations under Article 8 of the ATC.

* * * * *

---

[30]   Textiles Monitoring Body, Report of the Second Meeting (G/TMB/R/2), paras. 16 and 17.

VIII. RECOMMENDATION

8.1   Costa Rica requests the Panel to recommend if it reached the conclusion that the US restriction was imposed in a manner inconsistent with the obligations of the United States under the ATC that the United States withdraw the illegal act. The United States essentially argues that Article 19.1 of the DSU prohibits panels from recommending such a remedy.

Article 19.1 of the DSU reads as follows:

> "Where a panel or the Appellate Body concludes that a measure is inconsistent with a covered agreement, it shall recommend that the member concerned bring the measure into conformity with that agreement. In addition to its recommendations, the panel or Appellate Body may suggest ways in which the member concerned could implement the recommendations".

8.2   Under the second sentence of Article 19.1 of the DSU, panels can, in addition to their recommendations, "suggest ways in which the Member concerned could implement the recommendations".

8.3   We recall our conclusions that the United States violated its obligations under Article 6.2 and 6.4 of the ATC by imposing a restriction on Costa Rican exports without having demonstrated that serious damage or actual threat thereof was caused by such imports to the US domestic industry and under Article 6.6(d) of the ATC by not granting treatment more favourable to Costa Rican re-imports. We further recall our conclusion that the United States violated its obligations under Article 2.4 of the ATC by imposing a restriction in a manner inconsistent with its obligations under Article 6 of the ATC. We also recall our conclusion that the United States violated its obligations under Article 6.10 of the ATC by setting the restraint period starting on the date of the request for consultations, rather than the date of publication of that information. We, consequently, recommend that the Dispute Settlement Body request the United States to bring the measure challenged by Costa Rica into compliance with US obligations under the ATC. We find that such compliance can best be achieved and further nullification and impairment of benefits accruing to Costa Rica under the ATC best be avoided by prompt removal of the measure inconsistent with the obligations of the United States. We further suggest that the United States bring the measure challenged by Costa Rica into compliance with US obligations under the ATC by immediately withdrawing the restriction imposed by the measure.

STATEMENT OF SERIOUS DAMAGE: CATEGORY 352/652
Cotton and Man-made Fibre Underwear
Category 352/652
TABLE OF CONTENTS

---

[1]   Called under domestic legal authority. Not a WTO Member.

STATEMENT OF SERIOUS DAMAGE: CATEGORY 352/652

Cotton and Man-made Fibre Underwear
Category 352/652

I. PRODUCT DESCRIPTION

Category 352/652 covers men's and boys', and women's and girls' underwear. The term "underwear" refers to garments which are worn under other garments and are not exposed to view when the wearer is conventionally dressed. Men's and boys' and women's and girls' knit underwear is provided for in Harmonized Tariff Schedule (HTS) headings 6107, 6108 and 6109. Woven underwear is provided for in HTS headings 6207 and 6208.

II. INDUSTRY PROFILE

There are approximately 395 establishments in the US that manufacture cotton and man-made fibre underwear, Category 352/652. The establishments are located mainly in the Atlantic seaboard states, especially New York, Pennsylvania, North Carolina, and Georgia. This industry employs close to 6 per cent of the total apparel workers in the US, and the annual shipments from these establishments at $3.2 billion account for approximately 5 per cent of the total annual apparel industry shipments.

The concentration of firms in this industry is higher in the men's and boys' underwear than in the women's and girls'. In the men's and boys' segment, four firms account for over 60 per cent of the shipments. The production of women's and girls' underwear is more diversified, largely because women's underwear is subject to more fashion changes. As a result production is less standardized, requiring different types of knitting machines and a greater number of workers employed. There is, however, a large number of smaller producers which generally do not have integrated operations but usually purchase fabric and then cut and sew it.

III. MARKET SITUATION

A. Serious Damage to the Domestic Industry

The sharp and substantial increase in imports of cotton and man-made fibre underwear, Category 352/652, is causing serious damage to the US industry producing cotton and man-made fibre underwear.

Category 352/652 imports surged from 65,507,000 dozen in 1992 to 79,962,000 dozen in 1993, a 22 per cent increase. Cotton and man-made fibre underwear, Category 352/652, imports continued to increase in 1994, reaching 97,375,000 dozen, 22 per cent above the 1993 level and 49 per cent above the level imported in 1992 (see Table I).

Serious damage to the domestic industry resulting from the sharp and substantial increase in imports of cotton and man-made fibre underwear is attributed to imports from the Dominican Republic, Costa Rica, Honduras, Thailand and Turkey.[2] The combination of high import levels, surging imports, and low-priced goods from these countries have resulted in loss of domestic output, market share, investment, employment and man-hours worked.

1. US Production

US production of cotton and man-made fibre underwear, Category 352/652, declined from 175,542,000 dozen in 1992 to 168,802,000 dozen in 1993, a decline of 4 per cent. Production continued to decline in 1994, falling to 126,962,000 dozen during the first nine months of 1994, 4 per cent below January-September 1993 production level (Table II).

2. Market Share Loss

The share of this market held by domestic manufacturers fell from 73 per cent in 1992 to 68 per cent in 1993, a decline of five percentage points. The domestic market share dropped to 65 per cent during the first nine months of 1994 (Table II).

3. Import Penetration

The ratio of imports to domestic production increased from 37 per cent in 1992 to 47 per cent in 1993, and reached 54 per cent during January-September 1994 (Table II).

---

[2] El Salvador and Colombia called under domestic legal authority not WTO.

4.   Employment

Employment in the US cotton and man-made fibre under-wear industry dropped from 46,377 production workers in 1992 to 44,056 workers in 1994, a 5 per cent decline and a loss of 2,321 employees (Table III).

5.   Man-hours

Average annual man-hours worked dropped from 86.2 million in 1992 to 81.5 million in 1994, a 5 per cent decline (Table III).

B.   Industry Statements

Based on a survey of individual firms producing cotton and man-made fibre underwear the following conditions were reported. The observations are concentrated in the mens' underwear sector but also include the even more heavily import-impacted ladies underwear sector.

1.   Employment

There have been layoffs in the sector and one company reported that employees were also being transferred to production of other types of garments. Employment losses have also occurred because of import-related plant closings. A company that has already closed two plants employing 165 workers is anticipating two additional closures in 1995 representing total employment of about 400.

2.   Sales

Sales have slowed, and one company reported that their sales were down about 17 per cent in 1994.

3.   Profits

Profits were down 18 per cent at one firm, and there is pressure on the bottom line throughout the industry due to rising costs and stiff import competition.

4.   Investment

Because of the impact of imports and the uncertainty they have caused in the market, US companies generally have been postponing investment in this industry. Some companies have closed plants permanently or shifted production offshore, and additional disinvestment of this nature is being contemplated by underwear manufacturing firms.

5. *Capacity*

Because of the import competition, firms report shifting production capacity to other product lines including outerwear.

6. *Prices*

Import prices in these sectors have been very low which has placed considerable pressure on domestic producers:

(a)   Raw cotton costs in the US have increased substantially, seriously eroding US underwear producers' margins. These cost increases have not been recouped because prices cannot be raised without becoming uncompetitive with imports.

(b)   Competing imports enjoy a price edge over domestically produced goods because the imports are produced with lower priced foreign fabric which often reflects a subsidized cotton price. As a result of the increased import market share in underwear, average retail prices of underwear in the United States have generally declined during the past two years at a time when US manufacturers' costs, particularly for raw cotton, have increased substantially. This development has seriously eroded the profitability of US underwear manufacturing.

IV.   COUNTRIES CONTRIBUTING TO SERIOUS DAMAGE: CATEGORY 352/652 (TABLE I, IV AND V)

Serious damage, or actual threat thereof, to US producers of cotton and man-made fibre underwear, Category 352/652, is attributed to the sharp and substantial increase in imports from the Dominican Republic, Costa Rica, Honduras, Thailand and Turkey.[3]

Total imports from the five countries listed above increased from 22,675,508 dozen in 1992 to 40,293,259 dozen in 1994, a sharp and substantial increase of 78 per cent. As a group their imports were up 32 per cent in 1994 over their 1993 level. Together their 1992 imports were 35 per cent of total Category 352/652 imports. Their share of total category imports increased to 41 per cent in 1994.

---

[3]   El Salvador and Colombia called under domestic legal authority not WTO.

A. Dominican Republic

The sharp and substantial increase of low-priced imports from the Dominican Republic is causing serious damage to the US domestic industry producing cotton and man-made fibre underwear.

US imports of cotton and man-made fibre underwear, Category 352/652, from the Dominican Republic reached 16,442,148 dozen in 1994, 20 per cent above the 13,691,280 dozen imported in 1993 and 60 per cent above its 1992 level.

US imports of cotton and man-made fibre underwear, from the Dominican Republic in Category 352/652, entered the US at an average landed duty-paid value of $10.10 per dozen, 66 per cent below US producers' average price for cotton and man-made fibre underwear.

The Dominican Republic is the number one supplier of Category 352/652 imports with 17 per cent of total US imports of Category 352/652 in 1994. Category 352/652 imports from the Dominican Republic in 1994 were equivalent to 10 per cent of US production of Category 352/652 in the year ending September 1994.

B. Costa Rica

The sharp and substantial increase of low-priced imports from Costa Rica is causing serious damage to the US domestic industry producing cotton and man-made fibre underwear.

US imports of cotton and man-made fibre underwear, Category 352/652, from Costa Rica reached 14,423,178 dozen in 1994, 22 per cent above the 11,844,331 dozen imported in 1993 and 61 per cent above its 1992 level.

US imports of cotton and man-made fibre underwear, from Costa Rica in Category 352/652, entered the US at an average landed duty-paid value of $9.39 per dozen, 69 per cent below US producers' average price for cotton and man-made fibre underwear.

Costa Rica is the number two supplier of Category 352/652 imports with 15 per cent of total US imports of Category 352/652 in 1994. Category 352/652 imports from Costa Rica were equivalent to 8.8 per cent of US production of Category 352/652 in the year ending September 1994.

C. Honduras

The sharp and substantial increase of low-priced imports from Honduras is causing serious damage to the US domestic industry producing cotton and man-made fibre underwear.

US imports of cotton and man-made fibre underwear, Category 352/652, from Honduras reached 6,550,810 dozen in 1994,

108 per cent above the 3,153,608 dozen imported in 1993 and 182 per cent above its 1992 level.

US imports of cotton and man-made fibre underwear, from Honduras in Category 352/652, entered the US at an average landed duty-paid value of $11.39 per dozen, 62 per cent below US producers' average price for cotton and man-made fibre underwear.

Imports from Honduras were 6.7 per cent of total US imports of Category 352/652 in 1994, and were equivalent to 4 per cent of US production of Category 352/652 in the year ending September 1994.

D. Thailand

The sharp and substantial increase of low-priced imports from Thailand is causing serious damage to the US domestic industry producing cotton and man-made fibre underwear.

US imports of cotton and man-made fibre underwear, Category 352/652, from Thailand reached 1,586,005 dozen in 1994, 20 per cent above the 1,323,116 dozen imported in 1993 and nearly double its 1992 level.

US imports of cotton and man-made fibre underwear, from Thailand in Category 352/652, entered the US at an average landed duty-paid value of $18.58 per dozen, 38 per cent below US producers' average price for cotton and man-made fibre underwear.

Imports from Thailand were 1.6 per cent of total US imports of Category 352/652 in 1994, and were equivalent to nearly 1 per cent of US production of Category 352/652 in the year ending September 1994.

E. Turkey

The sharp and substantial increase of low-priced imports from Turkey is causing serious damage to the US domestic industry producing cotton and man-made fibre underwear.

US imports of cotton and man-made fibre underwear, Category 352/652, from Turkey reached 1,291,118 dozen in 1994, 133 per cent above the 553,442 dozen imported in 1993 and two and a half times its 1992 level.

US imports of cotton and man-made fibre underwear, from Turkey in Category 352/652, entered the US at an average landed duty-paid value of $10.43 per dozen, 65 per cent below US producers' average price for cotton and man-made fibre underwear.

Imports from Turkey were 1.3 per cent of total US imports of Category 352/652 in 1994, and were equivalent to 0.8 per cent of US production of Category 352/652 in the year ending September 1994.

MARCH 1995

STATEMENT OF SERIOUS DAMAGE: CATEGORY 352/652

Table I
US Imports from Selected Suppliers
Cotton and Man-made Fibre Underwear
Category 352/652
(Dozen)

	1992	1993	1994	94/92 % Change	94/93 % Change
World	**65,507,078**	**79,961,555**	**97,375,350**	**48.65**	**21.78**
Dominican Republic	10,264,139	13,691,280	16,442,148	60.19	20.09
Costa Rica	8,935,565	11,844,331	14,423,178	61.41	21.77
Honduras	2,318,683	3,153,608	6,550,810	182.52	107.72
Thailand	796,235	1,323,116	1,586,005	99.19	19.87
Turkey	360,886	553,442	1,291,118	257.76	133.29
TOTAL	**22,675,508**	**30,565,777**	**40,293,259**	**77.7**	**31.8**

Table II
Category 352/652
Cotton and Man-made Fibre Underwear
US Production, Imports, Market, Import/
Production Ratio and Domestic Market Share

Period	Production[1]	Imports	Market[2]	I/P	Domestic Market Share
	1,000 dozen			**Per cent**	
1992	175,542	65,507	241,049	37	73
1993	168,802	79,962	248,764	47	68
Year Ending September					
1993	175,392	77,368	252,760	44	69
1994	164,252	88,961	253,213	54	65
January-September					
1993	131,512	59,388	190,900	45	69
1994	126,962	68,387	195,349	54	65

---

[1]   A new benchmark was established with the 1992 Census of Manufacturers Survey, therefore, US apparel production data for 1992 forward is not comparable to previous years' data.
[2]   US market for domestically produced and imported cotton and man-made fibre underwear.

MARCH 1995
STATEMENT OF SERIOUS DAMAGE: CATEGORY 352/652

Table III
Employment Data for Industry[3] Producing Cotton and Man-made
Fibre Underwea
Category 352/652

Employment Data	1992	1993	1994
Number of Production Workers	46,377	44,379	44,056
Average Weekly Hours	35.8	37.1	35.6
Average Annual Manhours (million)	86.2	82.5	81.5

Table IV
Average Landed Duty-Paid Value of Imports of Cotton and Man-made
Fibre Underwear
Category 352/652

	1994 Unit Value ($ per Doz)	% Above or Below US Producers' Price
US Producers' Average Price	**30.00**	
World	**12.11**	**-60**
Thailand	18.58	-38
Honduras	11.39	-62
Turkey	10.43	-65
Dominican Republic	10.10	-66
Costa Rica	9.39	-69

Table V
Selected Suppliers' Share of Imports and Production
Cotton and Man-made Fibre Underwear
Category 352/652
(Dozen)

	1992 % of Imports	1994 % of Imports	1992 % of Production	Y/E 9/1994 % of Production
World	**100.0**	**100.0**	**37.3**	**59.3**
Dominican Republic	15.7	16.9	5.8	10.0
Costa Rica	13.6	14.8	5.1	8.8
Honduras	3.5	6.7	1.3	4.0
Thailand	1.2	1.6	0.5	1.0
Turkey	0.6	1.3	0.2	0.8
Total	**34.6**	**41.4**	**12.9**	**24.5**

---

[3]   Data derived from 1992 US Census of manufacturers, Apparel Current Industrial Reports, and data from the Bureau of Labor Statistics.

MARCH 1995

STATEMENT OF SERIOUS DAMAGE: CATEGORY 352/652

Table VI

Suppliers Report

Cotton and Man-made Fibre Underwear

Category 352/652

(Data in Dozens)

Country	1992	1993	12/93	12/94	% Change	12/93	10/94	11/94	12/94	% Change	% Share
World	65,507,078	79,961,555	79,961,555	97,375,350	21.78	79,961,555	91,625,866	94,555,451	97,375,350	21.78	100.00
Dom Rep	10,264,139	13,691,280	13,691,280	16,442,148	20.09	13,691,280	15,676,793	15,902,873	16,442,148	20.09	16.89
C Rica	8,935,565	11,844,331	11,844,331	14,423,178	21.77	11,844,331	13,846,643	14,196,660	14,423,178	21.77	14.81
SL Jamaica	6,596,435	8,106,198	8,106,198	9,978,577	23.10	8,106,198	9,169,675	9,665,903	9,978,577	23.10	10.25
FTAs[1]	5,490,979	6,464,009	6,464,009	9,860,275	52.54	6,464,009	8,743,600	9,344,737	9,860,275	52.54	10.13
SL Hg Kong	9,169,333	9,085,459	9,085,459	9,541,766	5.02	9,085,459	10,401,446	9,995,260	9,541,766	5.02	9.80
Bangladesh	5,164,020	6,819,003	6,819,003	7,830,510	14.83	6,819,003	7,127,727	7,527,240	7,830,510	14.83	8.04
Honduras	2,318,683	3,153,608	3,153,608	6,550,810	107.72	3,153,608	5,421,420	5,983,533	6,550,810	107.72	6.73
El Salvador	765,769	2,053,364	2,053,364	3,687,034	79.56	2,053,364	3,243,942	3,478,203	3,687,034	79.56	3.79
SL China P	4,437,640	3,484,724	3,484,724	3,562,255	2.22	3,484,724	3,302,675	3,373,159	3,562,255	2.22	3.66
SL China T	2,409,266	2,685,501	2,685,501	2,063,022	-23.18	2,685,501	2,254,257	2,176,921	2,063,022	-23.18	2.12
Thailand	796,235	1,323,116	1,323,116	1,586,005	19.87	1,323,116	1,463,139	1,512,123	1,586,005	19.87	1.63
Colombia	578,279	1,032,210	1,032,210	1,509,880	46.28	1,032,210	1,328,882	1,430,758	1,509,880	46.28	1.55

[1] Free Trade Arrangements: Canada, Mexico, Israel.

Country	1992	1993	12/93	12/94	% Change	12/93	10/94	11/94	12/94	% Change	% Share
World	65,507,078	79,961,555	79,961,555	97,375,350	21.78	79,961,555	91,625,866	94,555,451	97,375,350	21.78	100.00
SL Phil R	2,048,570	1,727,028	1,727,028	1,478,666	-14.38	1,727,028	1,420,086	1,463,627	1,478,666	-14.38	1.52
Turkey	360,886	553,442	553,442	1,291,118	133.29	553,442	1,115,084	1,177,758	1,291,118	133.29	1.33
SL Sri Lanka	798,776	989,448	989,448	1,137,616	14.97	989,448	1,120,226	1,099,663	1,137,616	14.97	1.17
Guatemala	326,737	828,515	828,515	959,160	15.77	828,515	950,353	941,687	959,160	15.77	0.99
Bahrain	137,417	716,778	716,778	691,230	-3.56	716,778	704,461	671,224	691,230	-3.56	0.71
Parama	145,468	393,336	393,336	502,240	27.69	393,336	543,352	520,857	502,240	27.69	0.52
SL Mauritius	609,979	862,584	862,584	494,726	-42.65	862,584	487,706	526,852	494,726	-42.65	0.51
Indonesia	443,659	383,209	383,209	459,638	19.94	383,209	382,965	437,614	459,638	19.94	0.47
Macau	163,885	81,710	81,710	404,474	395.01	81,710	149,441	296,165	404,474	395.01	0.42
SL Pakistan	376,607	430,932	430,932	391,567	-9.13	430,932	373,324	384,040	391,567	-9.13	0.40
Malaysia	303,221	355,939	355,939	375,266	5.43	355,939	317,227	330,718	375,266	5.43	0.39
EC[2]	473,808	414,549	414,549	352,212	-15.04	414,549	364,664	362,983	352,212	-15.04	0.36
Haiti	923,951	872,826	872,826	228,920	-73.77	872,826	302,108	261,023	228,920	-73.77	0.24
Kor Rep	184,097	174,729	174,729	167,517	-4.13	174,729	149,556	150,762	167,517	-4.13	0.17
Guyana	124,382	83,955	83,955	160,373	91.02	83,955	127,108	145,311	160,373	91.02	0.16
Swaziland	64,290	148,958	148,958	147,389	-1.05	148,958	119,311	148,291	147,389	-1.05	0.15
Chile	11,990	84,730	84,730	128,507	51.67	84,730	147,957	135,107	128,507	51.67	0.13
Myanmar	0	0	0	125,705	*	0	48,125	71,126	125,705	*	0.13
Nicaragua	0	24,651	24,651	125,625	409.61	24,651	134,632	133,028	125,625	409.61	0.13

2 European Union.

Country	1992	1993	12/93	12/94	% Change	12/93	10/94	11/94	12/94	% Change	% Share
World	65,507,078	79,961,555	79,961,555	97,375,350	21.78	79,961,555	91,625,866	94,555,451	97,375,350	21.78	100.00
Bulgaria	0	123,367	123,367	119,775	-2.91	123,367	110,211	119,775	119,775	-2.91	0.12
Brazil	80,027	64,349	64,349	93,206	44.84	64,349	80,935	88,630	93,206	44.84	0.10
Egypt	203,163	29,528	29,528	82,926	180.84	29,528	75,854	81,133	82,926	180.84	0.09
SL Arab Em	1,000	50,388	50,388	55,598	10.34	50,388	50,302	50,552	55,598	10.34	0.06
Peru	74,285	85,630	85,630	51,302	-40.09	85,630	34,173	47,298	51,302	-40.09	0.05
Syria	49,458	64,088	64,088	42,752	-33.29	64,088	47,680	46,832	42,752	-33.29	0.04
Mongolia	0	0	0	35,664	*	0	25,104	25,104	35,664	*	0.04
Ecuador	21,150	53,566	53,566	34,512	-35.57	53,566	45,523	41,821	34,512	-35.57	0.04
Australia	7,774	16,875	16,875	24,613	45.85	16,875	24,562	24,307	24,613	45.85	0.03
Barbados	23,778	31,977	31,977	24,490	-23.41	31,977	22,965	23,191	24,490	-23.41	0.03
Lesotho	375	11,748	11,748	21,248	80.86	11,748	26,848	21,248	21,248	80.86	0.02
S Lucia	14,939	21,324	21,324	20,457	-4.07	21,324	20,548	20,344	20,457	-4.07	0.02
India	851	4,832	4,832	14,885	208.05	4,832	7,650	11,689	14,885	208.05	0.02
Palau	0	0	0	13,044	*	0	13,044	13,044	13,044	*	0.01
Singapore	36,474	51,590	51,590	11,286	-78.12	51,590	17,010	13,111	11,286	-78.12	0.01
Switzerland	11,738	8,977	8,977	10,557	17.60	8,977	9,588	9,727	10,557	17.60	0.01
Japan	12,353	6,602	6,602	9,344	41.53	6,602	7,611	8,045	9,344	41.53	0.01
Qatar	6,950	0	0	8,890	*	0	5,408	8,890	8,890	*	0.01
Dominica	0	0	0	6,397	*	0	0	0	6,397	*	0.01
Maldives	153,021	177,739	177,739	5,174	-97.09	177,739	12,247	5,570	5,174	-97.09	0.01
Russia	*	4,836	4,836	4,913	1.59	4,836	3,345	4,913	4,913	1.59	0.01
Nepal	0	0	0	3,465	*	0	0	3,264	3,465	*	0.00
Ukraine	*	10,418	10,418	3,342	-67.92	10,418	9,142	9,142	3,342	-67.92	0.00
Jordan	0	139	139	3,150	2,166.19	139	3,289	3,289	3,150	2,166.19	0.00
St Kitts N	133,297	119,810	119,810	2,891	-97.59	119,810	22,382	15,119	2,891	-97.59	0.00

Country	1992	1993	12/93	12/94	% Change	12/93	10/94	11/94	12/94	% Change	% Share
World	65,507,078	79,961,555	79,961,555	97,375,350	21.78	79,961,555	91,625,866	94,555,451	97,375,350	21.78	100.00
Venezuela	141,555	2,363	2,363	2,387	1.02	2,363	3,221	2,721	2,387	1.02	0.00
Poland	0	2	2	2,030	101,400.00	2	0	1,870	2,030	101,400.00	0.00
Lebanon	419	63,702	63,702	1,607	-97.48	63,702	1,448	1,607	1,607	-97.48	0.00
Rep S Af	0	538	538	1,365	153.72	538	1,365	1,365	1,365	153.72	0.00
Cyprus	7,512	10,144	10,144	1,334	-86.85	10,144	1,334	1,334	1,334	-86.85	0.00
Trinidad	0	808	808	1,165	44.18	808	1,165	1,165	1,165	44.18	0.00
Fiji	89,754	0	0	990	*	0	990	990	990	*	0.00
Tokelau	0	6	6	790	13,066.67	6	790	790	790	13,066.67	0.00
N Zealand	37	68	68	687	910.29	68	731	731	687	910.29	0.00
Oman	0	464	464	655	41.16	464	655	655	655	41.16	0.00
Cocos Is.	0	0	0	442		0	442	442	442	*	0.00
St. Vincent	0	0	0	124	*	0	124	124	124	*	0.00
N Antilles	0	0	0	77	*	0	77	77	77	*	0.00
Vietnam	0	0	0	73	*	0	73	73	73	*	0.00
Turisia	0	52	52	71	36.34	52	18	24	71	36.54	0.00
Brunei	0	0	0	60	*	0	60	60	60	*	0.00
Morocco	546	61	61	44	-27.87	61	11	11	44	-27.87	0.00
Monsrat	0	0	0	42	*	0	42	42	42	*	0.00
Romania	0	0	0	40	*	0	0	40	40	*	0.00
Hungary	4,452	0	0	30	*	0	30	30	30	*	0.00
Malta	0	0	0	21	*	0	21	21	21	*	0.00
Slovenia	*	0	0	13	*	0	0	13	13	*	0.00
Zimbabwe	0	0	0	7	*	0	7	7	7	*	0.00
Norway	441	23	23	6	-73.91	23	9	15	6	-73.91	0.00

BRAZIL - MEASURES AFFECTING DESICCATED COCONUT

Report of the Appellate Body
WT/DS22/AB/R

Adopted by the Dispute Settlement Body on 20 March 1997

Philippines, Appellant/Appellee	Present:
Brazil, Appellant/Appellee	El-Naggar, Presiding Member
European Communities, United	Ehlermann, Member
States, Third Participants	Lacarte-Muró, Member

I.   INTRODUCTION

The Philippines and Brazil appeal from certain issues of law and legal interpretations in the Panel Report, *Brazil - Measures Affecting Desiccated Coconut*[1] (the "Panel Report"). That Panel was established to consider a complaint by the Philippines against Brazil relating to the countervailing duties imposed by Brazil on imports of desiccated coconut from the Philippines pursuant to Inter-ministerial Ordinance No. 11 (the "Ordinance") on 18 August 1995.

The application for initiation of the countervailing duty investigation was filed with the Brazilian authorities on 17 January 1994. The investigation was initiated on 21 June 1994, provisional countervailing duties were imposed on 23 March 1995, and definitive countervailing duties were imposed on 18 August 1995. The *Marrakesh Agreement Establishing the World Trade Organization*[2] (the "*WTO Agreement*") entered into force for both parties to this dispute, Brazil and the Philippines, on 1 January 1995, that is, after the application for, and the initiation of, the investigation and prior to the imposition of the provisional and definitive countervailing duties.

The Panel Report was circulated to Members of the World Trade Organization (the "WTO") on 17 October 1996. It contains the following conclusions:

a.   Article VI of GATT 1994 does not constitute applicable law for the purposes of this dispute. As a result, the substance of the Phil-

---

[1]   WT/DS22/R, 17 October 1996.
[2]   Done at Marrakesh, Morocco, 15 April 1994.

ippines' claims under that Article, and of its claims under Articles I and II of GATT 1994 which derive from their claims of inconsistency with Article VI of GATT 1994, cannot be considered by this Panel.

b.   The Agreement on Agriculture does not constitute applicable law for the purposes of this dispute. As a result, the substance of the Philippines' claims under that Agreement cannot be considered by this Panel.

c.   The Philippines' claim regarding Brazil's failure to consult is not within the terms of reference of this Panel and therefore its substance cannot be considered.[3]

The Panel made the following recommendation:

The Panel, having concluded that the substance of the Philippines' claims are not properly before it, recommends that the Dispute Settlement Body make such a ruling.[4]

On 16 December 1996, the Philippines notified the Dispute Settlement Body[5] (the "DSB") of its intention to appeal certain issues of law covered in the Panel Report and legal interpretations developed by the Panel, pursuant to paragraph 4 of Article 16 of the *Understanding on Rules and Procedures Governing the Settlement of Disputes* (the *"DSU"*) and filed a Notice of Appeal with the Appellate Body, pursuant to Rule 20 of the *Working Procedures for Appellate Review* (the *"Working Procedures"*).

On 9 January 1997, the Philippines filed an appellant's submission.[6] On 14 January 1997, Brazil filed an appellant's submission pursuant to Rule 23(1) of the *Working Procedures*. On 24 January 1997, Brazil filed an appellee's submission pursuant to Rule 22 of the *Working Procedures* and the Philippines filed an appellee's submission pursuant to Rule 23(3) of the *Working Procedures*. That same day, the European Communities and the United States submitted third participants' submissions pursuant to Rule 24 of the *Working Procedures*.

The oral hearing provided for in Rule 27 of the *Working Procedures* was held on 30 January 1997. The participants and third participants presented their arguments and answered questions from the Division of the Appellate Body hearing the appeal.

---

[3]   Panel Report, para. 294.
[4]   Panel Report, para. 295.
[5]   WT/DS22/8, 18 December 1996.
[6]   Pursuant to Rule 21(1) of the *Working Procedures*.

II.   ARGUMENTS OF PARTICIPANTS AND THIRD PARTICIPANTS

A.   The Philippines

The Philippines appeals from certain of the Panel's legal findings and conclusions, as well as from certain legal interpretations developed by the Panel. The
Philippines submits that the Panel erred in concluding that Article VI of the *General Agreement on Tariffs and Trade 1994* (the "GATT 1994") cannot be independently applied in transitional situations where the *Agreement on Subsidies
and Countervailing Measures* (the "*SCM Agreement*") is not applicable pursuant
to Article 32.3 of the *SCM Agreement,* and that the inapplicability of Article VI
of the GATT 1994 renders Articles I and II of the GATT 1994 inapplicable. In
the Philippines' view, the Panel erroneously treated the Philippines' reliance on
Articles I and II of the GATT 1994 as one that "derive[s] from" the Philippines'
invocation of Article VI of the GATT 1994.

According to the Philippines, the Panel's analysis is flawed by its failure
to address this dispute in accordance with the proper relationship between Articles I, II and VI of the GATT 1994 and Article 32.3 of the *SCM Agreement*. The
Panel erred in starting and focusing its analysis on Article 32.3 of the *SCM
Agreement*, which the Philippines did not invoke. The Panel should have first
evaluated whether the disputed measure is inconsistent with Articles I and II of
the GATT 1994, and if it was found to be inconsistent, then the Panel should
have examined whether the measure could be justified under Article VI of the
GATT 1994. Moreover, because Brazil's defence is predicated on an exception
(Article 32.3 of the *SCM Agreement*) to yet another exception (Article VI of the
GATT 1994) to the general rule (Articles I and II of the GATT 1994), the Panel
should have interpreted Article 32.3 of the *SCM Agreement* narrowly.

The Philippines argues that, when the *WTO Agreement* entered into force
for both Brazil and the Philippines on 1 January 1995, the Philippines became
entitled to invoke its rights under Articles I and II of the GATT 1994, and its
rights arising under Article VI of the GATT 1994, in regard to any countervailing
measure imposed against the Philippines by any WTO Member, including Brazil,
after the *WTO Agreement*'s entry into force. Article 32.3 of the *SCM Agreement*,
at most, precludes the application of the *SCM Agreement* to WTO-era measures
applied for before the entry into force of the *WTO Agreement* due to the differences between the *SCM Agreement* and the *Agreement on Interpretation and
Application of Articles VI, XVI and XXIII of the General Agreement on Tariffs
and Trade* (the *"Tokyo Round SCM Code"*), but such a transitional rule does not
affect the applicability of Articles I, II and VI of the GATT 1994, whose texts are
exactly identical to their counterpart provisions in the *General Agreement on
Tariffs and Trade 1947* (the "GATT 1947").

The Philippines asserts that international law principles as codified in the *Vienna Convention on the Law of Treaties* (the *"Vienna Convention"*)[7] ensure the non-retroactive application of treaties. Article 28 of the *Vienna Convention* insulates an act that took place before the new treaty's entry into force from the obligations of that treaty. As the substance and conclusion of the investigation leading to the imposition by Brazil of the countervailing measure at issue in this dispute occurred after the entry into force of the *WTO Agreement*, Articles I, II and VI of the GATT 1994 constitute the law applicable to the measure in dispute, and such applicability does not involve retroactivity. The Philippines challenges the Panel's finding that the application of Article VI of the GATT 1994 to the countervailing duty measure in dispute leads to a "manifestly absurd or unreasonable" result. In the Philippines' view, application of Article VI of the GATT 1994 to a definitive countervailing duty is no less fair than applying WTO norms to other pre-WTO measures, such as occurred in *United States - Standards for Reformulated and Conventional Gasoline*[8] (*"United States - Gasoline"*).

In the Philippines' view, the Panel improperly disregarded the Philippines' argument that the transitional decisions[9] recognize the right of WTO Members to invoke WTO norms even in situations involving elements that occurred prior to the entry into force of the *WTO Agreement*. The Decision on Transitional Co-Existence of the Tokyo Round SCM Code and the WTO Agreement expressly recognizes the availability of WTO dispute resolution not only as an option, but as an immediate pre-emptive choice in matters also covered by the *Tokyo Round SCM Code*. The Decision on Consequences of Withdrawal from or Termination of the Tokyo Round SCM Code is permissive, expressly recognizing the right of a signatory to the *Tokyo Round SCM Code*, that is also a WTO Member, to choose under which regime it will vindicate its rights. The Philippines contends that it has the procedural right to resort to the *DSU* to enforce its substantive WTO rights.

While Article 28 of the *Vienna Convention* recognizes that its limitations on non-retroactivity may be qualified where "a different intention appears from the treaty or is otherwise established", the Philippines argues that no such intention is indisputably established by Article 32.3 of the *SCM Agreement* and the other provisions upon which the Panel relied. It was wrong for the Panel Report

---

[7]   23 May 1969, 1155 U.N.T.S. 331; 8 *International Legal Materials* 679.

[8]   WT/DS2/9, adopted 20 May 1996.

[9]   By "transitional decisions", we refer to the Decision on Transitional Co-Existence of the GATT 1947 and the WTO Agreement, PC/12-L/7583, 13 December 1994; the Decision on Transitional Co-Existence of the Agreement on Interpretation and Application of Articles VI, XVI and XXIII of the General Agreement on Tariffs and Trade and the Marrakesh Agreement Establishing the World Trade Organization (the "Decision on Transitional Co-existence of the Tokyo Round SCM Code and the WTO Agreement"), SCM/186, 16 December 1994; and the Decision on Consequences of Withdrawal from or Termination of the Agreement on Interpretation and Application of Articles VI, XVI and XXIII of the General Agreement on Tariffs and Trade (the "Decision on Consequences of Withdrawal from or Termination of the Tokyo Round SCM Code"), SCM/187, 16 December 1994.

to vary the plain meaning of the term, "this Agreement", in Article 32.3 of the *SCM Agreement* so as to refer also to the GATT 1994.

In the Philippines' view, the context of Article 32.3 of the *SCM Agreement* does not warrant inferring a reference to Article VI of the GATT 1994. Article 32.1 of the *SCM Agreement* confirms that the reference in Article 32.3 of the *SCM Agreement* to "this Agreement" means only the *SCM Agreement*. The omission in the *SCM Agreement* of note 2 to the preamble of the *Tokyo Round SCM Code* does not support, and in fact undercuts, the Panel's non-separability finding. The presence of cross-references from Articles 10 and 32.1 of the *SCM Agreement* to Article VI of the GATT 1994 does not make Article VI of the GATT 1994 so inseparable from the *SCM Agreement* as to negate the rights of WTO Members to invoke Article VI of the GATT 1994 independently. Such a right to choose existed under the pre-WTO regime despite similar cross-references in the *Tokyo Round SCM Code* to Article VI of the GATT 1947. Furthermore, it was improper for the Panel to support its non-separability finding with the broad argument that Article 7.1 of the *DSU* fosters an "integrated" dispute settlement framework that "allows a panel to interpret provisions of covered agreements in the light of the WTO Agreement as a whole".[10]

According to the Philippines, the object and purpose of Article 32.3 of the *SCM Agreement* and the *WTO Agreement* also do not warrant interpreting the phrase "this Agreement" in Article 32.3 of the *SCM Agreement* to include Article VI of the GATT 1994.

In the Philippines' view, the panel report in *United States - Countervailing Duties on Fresh, Chilled and Frozen Pork from Canada*[11] ("*United States - Pork*") offers persuasive guidance on the separate applicability of Article VI of the GATT 1994. The panel in *European Economic Community - Payments and Subsidies Paid to Processors and Producers of Oilseeds and Related Animal-Feed Proteins*[12] ("*EEC - Oilseeds*") in effect addressed the separability issue and resolved it in favour of applying GATT 1947 separately from the *Tokyo Round SCM Code*. In addition, the Panel Report failed to give due weight to the *United States - Gasoline* case as evidence that a complaining WTO Member is not required to invoke all agreements that are potentially relevant to a dispute.

In the view of the Philippines, the unavailability of the *SCM Agreement's* definitions, or the possibility of interpretations inconsistent therewith, when Article VI of the GATT 1994 is interpreted independently, do not negate the right of WTO Members to invoke Article VI of the GATT 1994 independently in transitional situations where the *SCM Agreement* is inapplicable. In addition, when independently applied, Article VI of the GATT 1994 can be properly interpreted

---

[10]   Panel Report, para. 242.
[11]   BISD 38S/30, adopted 11 July 1991.
[12]   BISD 37S/86, adopted 25 January 1990.

in light of practice under Article VI of the GATT 1947 that antedated, and/or was not dependent on, the *Tokyo Round SCM Code*.

The Philippines further argues that it was not the intent of the original WTO Members to allow prospective new WTO Members to use applications for investigations filed prior to their accession to the *WTO Agreement* as a basis for insulating from the GATT 1994 any countervailing measures that such prospective WTO Members may impose after their admission into the WTO. In addition, the Panel's ruling could leave some WTO Members without any remedy for at least five years, until such time as the "sunset" review provision in Article 21.3 of the *SCM Agreement* becomes effective.

If the Appellate Body reverses the Panel's conclusions that Articles I, II and VI of the GATT 1994 are inapplicable to this dispute, the Philippines requests that the Appellate Body adopt a procedure for this appeal under Rule 16(1) of the *Working Procedures* for the resolution of the substantive merits of the Philippines' claims. The Philippines incorporates its arguments made before the Panel and submits that the subsidy and injury determinations of the Ordinance, and the countervailing measure based thereon, are inconsistent with Articles I and II of the GATT 1994, and not justified by Articles VI:3 and VI:6(a) of the GATT 1994.

With respect to the point of appeal raised in Brazil's appellant's submission, the Philippines argues that Brazil did not ask the Panel to refrain from considering whether or not Articles I and II of the GATT 1994 are applicable to this dispute. On the contrary, Brazil requested the Panel to consider the issue of the applicability or inapplicability of the GATT 1994. In any event, Articles I and II of the GATT 1994 are covered by the terms of reference because they are "relevant provisions" within the agreement "cited" by the Philippines.

B.   Brazil

Brazil generally agrees with the Panel's findings and conclusions concerning the law applicable to this dispute, but nevertheless appeals on one issue. Brazil claims that the issue of the applicability of Articles I and II of the GATT 1994 was not within the terms of reference of the Panel in this dispute and should not have been addressed by the Panel.

With respect to the points of appeal raised in the Philippines' appellant's submission, Brazil considers it appropriate, and in accordance with principles of international law, that the Panel first determined whether it had jurisdiction to consider the dispute before considering the substantive merits of the Philippines' claims. The question of whether the *WTO Agreement* applies to the substance of the dispute is not merely a "defence" as claimed by the Philippines, but a fundamental jurisdictional issue. While Brazil does not contest that the Philippines has the procedural right to resort to the *DSU* to enforce its substantive WTO rights, Brazil asserts that the Panel properly found that this dispute did not involve any substantive WTO rights. The Panel's conclusion that it did not have jurisdiction is correct, and the *Tokyo Round SCM Code* constitutes the law applicable to this dispute.

In Brazil's view, the Panel properly applied the customary rules of interpretation of public international law as set out in Articles 31 and 32 of the *Vienna Convention* to conclude that the *WTO Agreement* did not apply to this dispute. The plain language of Article 32.3 of the *SCM Agreement* prohibits the application of at least the *SCM Agreement* to this dispute, and the context of the *WTO Agreement* indicates that Article 32.3 of the *SCM Agreement* prevents the application of any portion of the *WTO Agreement* to this dispute. There are numerous indicia that the *WTO Agreement* and its Multilateral Trade Agreements were intended to apply as a whole. Article II:2 of the *WTO Agreement* states that the agreements and associated legal instruments included in Annexes 1, 2 and 3 - encompassing both the GATT 1994 and the *SCM Agreement* - are "integral parts" of the Agreement. There is a unified dispute settlement mechanism that applies to disputes raised under the *WTO Agreement*, the GATT 1994 and the other covered agreements. The general interpretative note to Annex 1A of the *WTO Agreement* indicates that the GATT 1994 and the other agreements are to be considered together. Article 10 of the *SCM Agreement* indicates that countervailing duties may only be imposed in accordance with the provisions of Article VI of the GATT 1994 and the terms of the *SCM Agreement*. As the Panel noted, several of the provisions of the *SCM Agreement* seek to interpret or provide guidance on terms used in Article VI. As the Panel further observed, applying Article VI of the GATT 1994 separately from Article VI of the GATT 1994 *and* the *SCM Agreement* could lead to differing interpretations of the benefits and obligations conferred by Article VI of the GATT 1994 as between the same Members.

In Brazil's view, *United States - Gasoline* does not support the application of Article VI of the GATT 1994 without reference to the *SCM Agreement*. The *Agreement on Technical Barriers to Trade*, invoked in *United States - Gasoline*, does not purport to interpret any articles of GATT 1994, nor does it contain any language similar to that of Article 10 of the *SCM Agreement* linking it to specific articles of the GATT 1994.

Brazil asserts that the Panel's consideration of the Decision on Consequences of Withdrawal from or Termination of the Tokyo Round SCM Code was consistent with the reference to a "subsequent agreement" within the meaning of Article 31(3)(a) of the *Vienna Convention*. To the extent that "subsequent practice" within the meaning of Article 31(3)(b) of the *Vienna Convention* has developed, it supports the Panel's conclusion that Article VI of the GATT 1994 does not apply to this dispute. Brazil further asserts that Article 28 of the *Vienna Convention*, as a "relevant rule of international law applicable in the relations between the parties" referred to in Article 31(3)(c) of the *Vienna Convention*, supports the Panel's conclusions on the law applicable to this dispute.

Brazil contends that the panel reports in *United States - Pork* and *EEC - Oilseeds*, invoked by the Philippines, provide no guidance for this dispute. As the issue of applicable law was never raised in *United States - Pork*, it therefore gives no indication of past practice on this issue. Moreover, because the structure of the various agreements in this case differs from the structure of the agreements in *EEC - Oilseeds*, that panel report provides no guidance on the interpretation of the *WTO Agreement*.

Should the Appellate Body find that the *WTO Agreement* applies, Brazil argues that it is not appropriate for the Appellate Body to rule on the substantive issues in this dispute. The Appellate Body's authority is limited by paragraphs 6 and 13 of Article 17 of the *DSU*. Brazil further argues that *United States - Gasoline* does not support the examination by the Appellate Body of these issues. If, however, the Appellate Body considers it appropriate to address the substantive issues, Brazil incorporates by reference all its submissions, both oral and written, to the Panel concerning those issues. If the Appellate Body decides that Article VI of the GATT 1994 applies, it must be interpreted on its own without reference to the *Tokyo Round SCM Code* or the *SCM Agreement*.

C. European Communities

The European Communities supports the legal findings and conclusions of the Panel. The European Communities asserts that the Panel correctly concluded that Article VI of the GATT 1994 is inapplicable to the measure in dispute and that the inapplicability of Article VI of the GATT 1994 also renders Articles I and II of the GATT 1994 inapplicable.

In the European Communities' view, the Panel's findings are in conformity with the principles of customary international law regarding the temporal application of treaty obligations, contained in Article 28 of the *Vienna Convention*, which apply "[u]nless a different intention appears from the treaty or is otherwise established". The Panel correctly considered the text of the relevant provisions in the light of their context, and of the object and purpose of the *WTO Agreement*, to reach its legal conclusion that Article VI of the GATT 1994 cannot be applied independently. It was, therefore, no longer necessary for the Panel to resort to the subsidiary rule contained in Article 28 of the *Vienna Convention*. In any case, the application of this subsidiary rule would also lead to the conclusion that Article VI of the GATT 1994 does not apply in the present dispute.

According to the European Communities, the *United States - Pork* and *EEC - Oilseeds* panel reports invoked by the Philippines are not relevant to this dispute, as the relationship of the GATT 1947 to the *Tokyo Round SCM Code* is different from the relationship of the *SCM Agreement* to the GATT 1994. The transitional decisions do not support the independent application of Article VI of the GATT 1994. Moreover, the independent application of Article III:4 of the GATT 1994 in *United States - Gasoline* does not support the independent application of Article VI of the GATT 1994, as the relationship between Article III of the GATT 1994 and the *Agreement on Technical Barriers to Trade* is different from the relationship between Article VI of the GATT 1994 and the *SCM Agreement*.

D. United States

The United States disagrees with certain of the legal findings and conclusions of the Panel, and requests that the Appellate Body take into consideration its arguments before the Panel as described in paragraphs 211-224 of the Panel Report. The United States asserts that Article VI of the GATT 1994 is applicable to Brazil's countervailing duty measure and that, as of 1 January 1995, Brazil was bound to levy countervailing duties consistently with the provisions of the GATT 1994. If the Appellate Body considers the substantive merits of this dispute, it must do so under Article VI of the GATT 1994 alone, without reference to the *Tokyo Round SCM Code*. The United States submits that the panel report in *EEC - Oilseeds* is instructive in this regard.

III. ISSUES RAISED IN THIS APPEAL

The Philippines appeals from two legal findings and conclusions of the Panel. First, the Philippines submits that the Panel erred in concluding that Article VI of the GATT 1994 cannot be applied independently in transitional situations where the *SCM Agreement* is not applicable pursuant to Article 32.3 of the *SCM Agreement*. Second, the Philippines claims that the Panel erred in finding that the inapplicability of Article VI of the GATT 1994 also renders Articles I and II of the GATT 1994 inapplicable. Brazil appeals from the Panel's legal findings and conclusions concerning Articles I and II of the GATT 1994. Brazil argues that the issue of the consistency of Brazil's countervailing duty measure with its obligations under Articles I and II of the GATT 1994 was not within the terms of reference of the Panel.

On the basis of the written submissions and oral statements made by the participants and third participants, this appeal raises the following issues:

1. Whether Article VI of the GATT 1994 applies, independently of the *SCM Agreement*, to a countervailing duty measure imposed as a result of an investigation initiated pursuant to an application made before the entry into force of the *WTO Agreement*;

2. Whether a finding with respect to the applicability of Article VI of the GATT 1994 determines the applicability of Articles I and II of the GATT 1994; and

3. Whether the Philippines' claims under Articles I and II of the GATT 1994 were within the terms of reference of the Panel.

IV. APPLICABILITY OF ARTICLE VI OF THE GATT 1994

A. Background

This appeal deals with a countervailing duty investigation which was initiated pursuant to an application filed with the Brazilian authorities on 17 January 1994. The investigation was initiated on 21 June 1994, provisional countervailing duties were imposed on 23 March 1995, and definitive countervailing duties were imposed on imports of desiccated coconut from the Philippines on 18 August 1995. The *WTO Agreement* entered into force for both parties to this dispute, Brazil and the Philippines, on 1 January 1995.

With respect to the measure at issue in this appeal, we see a decision to impose a definitive countervailing duty as the culminating act of a domestic legal process which starts with the filing of an application by the domestic industry, includes the initiation and conduct of an investigation by an investigating authority, and normally leads to a preliminary determination and a final determination. A positive final determination that subsidized imports are causing injury to a domestic industry authorizes the domestic authorities to impose a definitive countervailing duty on subsidized imports.

B. WTO Agreement: An Integrated System

The *WTO Agreement* is fundamentally different from the GATT system which preceded it. The previous system was made up of several agreements, understandings and legal instruments, the most significant of which were the GATT 1947 and the nine Tokyo Round Agreements, including the *Tokyo Round SCM Code*. Each of these major agreements was a treaty with different membership, an independent governing body and a separate dispute settlement mechanism.[13] The GATT 1947 was administered by the CONTRACTING PARTIES, whereas the *Tokyo Round SCM Code* was administered by the Tokyo Round Committee on Subsidies and Countervailing Duty Measures comprised of the signatories to that *Code*.[14] With respect to disputes brought under Article XXIII of the GATT 1947, the CONTRACTING PARTIES were responsible for dispute settlement, including establishment of panels, adoption of panel reports, surveillance of implementation of rulings and recommendations, and authorization of suspension of concessions or other obligations. The Tokyo Round Committee on Subsidies and Countervailing Measures was responsible for administering and monitoring dispute settlement under Articles 12, 13, 17 and 18 of the *Tokyo Round SCM Code*.

---

[13] *Agreement on Technical Barriers to Trade*, BISD 26S/8; *Agreement on Implementation of Article VII of the GATT - Protocol to the Agreement on Implementation of Article VII of the GATT*, BISD 26S/116, 151; *Agreement on Implementation of Article VI of the GATT* (the *"Tokyo Round Anti-dumping Code"*), BISD 26S/171; *Agreement on Interpretation and Application of Articles VI, XVI and XXIII of the General Agreement on Tariffs and Trade* (the *"Tokyo Round SCM Code"*), BISD 26S/56; *Agreement on Import Licensing Procedures*, BISD 26S/154; *Agreement on Government Procurement*, BISD 26S/33; *Agreement on Trade in Civil Aircraft*, BISD 26S/162; *Arrangement Regarding Bovine Meat*, BISD 26S/84; and *International Dairy Arrangement*, BISD 26S/91. The *Agreement on Import Licensing Procedures and the Agreement on Trade in Civil Aircraft* made reference to Articles XXII and XXIII of the GATT 1947 for dispute settlement. The *Arrangement Regarding Bovine Meat and the International Dairy Arrangement* did not explicitly provide for dispute settlement.

[14] By the end of 1994, the GATT 1947 had 128 contracting parties, whereas the *Tokyo Round SCM Code* had 24 signatories.

As a result of the separate legal identity of the GATT 1947 and the *Tokyo Round SCM Code*, a complaining party either had to bring a dispute under Article VI of the GATT 1947, in which case it would invoke the dispute settlement provisions of Article XXIII of the GATT 1947, or alternatively, under the provisions of the *Tokyo Round SCM Code*, in which case it would commence consultations under that *Code*. Most disputes involving countervailing duty measures between 1979 and 1994 were brought under the *Tokyo Round SCM Code*.[15] In the *United States - Pork* case, notwithstanding that both Canada and the United States were signatories to the *Tokyo Round SCM Code*, Canada chose to bring the matter under the dispute settlement provisions of Article XXIII of the GATT 1947, relying solely on its claims under Article VI of the GATT 1947.

Unlike the previous GATT system, the *WTO Agreement* is a single treaty instrument which was accepted by the WTO Members as a "single undertaking". Article II:2 of the *WTO Agreement* provides that the Multilateral Trade Agreements in Annexes 1, 2 and 3 are "integral parts" of the *WTO Agreement*, binding on all Members. Annex 1A contains thirteen multilateral agreements relating to trade in goods, including the GATT 1994 which was incorporated by reference into that Annex. A general interpretative note was included in Annex 1A in order to clarify the legal relationship of the GATT 1994 with the other agreements in Annex 1A. It provides that in the event of a conflict between a provision of the GATT 1994 and a provision of another agreement in Annex 1A, the latter shall prevail to the extent of the conflict. Article II:4 of the *WTO Agreement* provides that the GATT 1994 "as specified in Annex 1A ... is legally distinct from the General Agreement on Tariffs and Trade, dated 30 October 1947 ...".

The single undertaking is further reflected in the provisions of the *WTO Agreement* dealing with original membership, accession, non-application of the Multilateral Trade Agreements between particular Members, acceptance of the *WTO Agreement*, and withdrawal from it.[16] Within this framework, all WTO

---

[15] *Canadian Countervailing Duties on Grain Corn from the United States*, BISD 39S/411, adopted 26 March 1992; *United States - Definition of Industry Concerning Wine and Grape Products*, BISD 39S/436, adopted 28 April 1992; *United States - Measures Affecting Imports of Softwood Lumber from Canada*, SCM/162, adopted 27 October 1993; *Brazil - Imposition of Provisional and Definitive Countervailing Duties on Milk Powder and Certain Types of Milk from the European Economic Community*, SCM/179, adopted 28 April 1994; *United States - Imposition of Countervailing Duties on Imports of Fresh and Chilled Atlantic Salmon From Norway*, SCM/153, adopted 28 April 1994; *United States - Countervailing Duties on Non-Rubber Footwear from Brazil*, SCM/94, adopted 13 June 1995; *EEC - Subsidies on Exports of Wheat Flour*, SCM/42, 21 March 1983, unadopted; *EEC - Subsidies on Exports of Pasta Products*, SCM/43, 19 May 1983, unadopted; *Canada - Imposition of Countervailing Duties on Imports of Boneless Manufacturing Beef from the EEC*, SCM/85, 13 October 1987, unadopted; *German Exchange Rate Scheme for Deutsche Airbus*, SCM/142, 4 March 1992, unadopted; *United States - Imposition of Countervailing Duties on Certain Hot-Rolled Lead and Bismuth Carbon Steel Products Originating in France, Germany and the United Kingdom*, SCM/185, 15 November 1994, unadopted.
[16] *WTO Agreement*, Articles XI, XII, XIII, XIV and XV, respectively.

Members are bound by all the rights and obligations in the *WTO Agreement* and its Annexes 1, 2 and 3.

The *DSU* provides an integrated dispute settlement mechanism applicable to disputes arising under any of the "covered agreements". Article 2 of the *DSU* provides that the DSB has the "authority to establish panels, adopt panel and Appellate Body Reports, maintain surveillance and implementation of rulings and recommendations, and authorize suspension of concessions and other obligations under the covered agreements". The "covered agreements" include the *WTO Agreement*, the Agreements in Annexes 1 and 2, as well as any Plurilateral Trade Agreement in Annex 4 where its Committee of signatories has taken a decision to apply the *DSU*.[17] In a dispute brought to the DSB, a panel may deal with all the relevant provisions of the covered agreements cited by the parties to the dispute in one proceeding.[18]

C.   GATT 1994 within the WTO Agreement

The *WTO Agreement* is a successor treaty to the GATT 1947, the *Tokyo Round* SCM Code and the other agreements and understandings which formed the previous GATT system. Although it is a new treaty which the WTO Members accepted definitively, Article XVI:1 of the *WTO Agreement* provides as follows:

> Except as otherwise provided under this Agreement or the Multilateral Trade Agreements, the WTO shall be guided by the decisions, procedures and customary practices followed by the CONTRACTING PARTIES to GATT 1947 and the bodies established in the framework of GATT 1947.

The GATT 1994 was incorporated by reference into Annex 1A of the *WTO Agreement*. The reference language includes the provisions of the GATT 1947, as rectified, amended or modified before the entry into force of the *WTO Agreement*; the provisions of legal instruments that entered into force under the GATT 1947 prior to the entry into force of the *WTO Agreement*, such as protocols and certifications relating to tariff concessions, protocols of accession (excluding the provisions concerning provisional application and "grandfather rights"), decisions on waivers granted under Article XXV of the GATT 1947 and other decisions of the CONTRACTING PARTIES to the GATT 1947; as well as the Understandings which amended specific articles of the GATT 1947 as a result of the Uruguay Round Multilateral Trade Negotiations. In many ways, therefore, the provisions of the GATT 1994 differ from the provisions of the GATT 1947.

The relationship between the GATT 1994 and the other goods agreements in Annex 1A is complex and must be examined on a case-by-case basis. Although

---

[17]   *DSU*, Article 1 and Appendix 1.
[18]   *DSU*, Article 7.

the provisions of the GATT 1947 were incorporated into, and became a part of the GATT 1994, they are not the sum total of the rights and obligations of WTO Members concerning a particular matter. For example, with respect to subsidies on agricultural products, Articles II, VI and XVI of the GATT 1994 alone do not represent the total rights and obligations of WTO Members. The *Agreement on Agriculture* and the *SCM Agreement* reflect the latest statement of WTO Members as to their rights and obligations concerning agricultural subsidies. The general interpretative note to Annex 1A was added to reflect that the other goods agreements in Annex 1A, in many ways, represent a substantial elaboration of the provisions of the GATT 1994, and to the extent that the provisions of the other goods agreements conflict with the provisions of the GATT 1994, the provisions of the other goods agreements prevail. This does not mean, however, that the other goods agreements in Annex 1A, such as the *SCM Agreement*, supersede the GATT 1994. As the Panel has said:

> ... the question for consideration is not whether the SCM Agreement supersedes Article VI of GATT 1994. Rather, it is whether Article VI creates rules which are separate and distinct from those of the SCM Agreement, and which can be applied without reference to that Agreement, or whether Article VI of GATT 1994 and the SCM Agreement represent an inseparable package of rights and disciplines that must be considered in conjunction.[19]

D. Principle of Non-Retroactivity of Treaties

The fundamental question in this case is one of the temporal application of one set of international legal norms, or the successor set of norms, to a particular measure taken during the period of co-existence of the GATT 1947 and the *Tokyo Round SCM Code* with the *WTO Agreement*. Article 28 of the *Vienna Convention* contains a general principle of international law concerning the non-retroactivity of treaties. It provides as follows:

> Unless a different intention appears from the treaty or is otherwise established, its provisions do not bind a party in relation to any act or fact which took place or any situation which ceased to exist before the date of the entry into force of the treaty with respect to that party.

Article 28 states the general principle that a treaty shall not be applied retroactively "unless a different intention appears from the treaty or is otherwise established". Absent a contrary intention, a treaty cannot apply to acts or facts which took place, or situations which ceased to exist, before the date of its entry

---

[19] Panel Report, para. 227.

into force. Article 32.3 of the *SCM Agreement* is an express statement of intention which we will now examine.

E. Interpretation of Article 32.3 of the SCM Agreement

1. Text

Article 32.3 of the *SCM Agreement* reads as follows:

> ... the provisions of this Agreement shall apply to investigations, and reviews of existing measures, initiated pursuant to applications which have been made on or after the date of entry into force for a Member of the WTO Agreement.

Examination of the ordinary meaning of this provision alone could lead us to the conclusion that the term, "this Agreement", in Article 32.3 means the *SCM Agreement*. However, it is necessary also to consider this provision in its context and in light of the object and purpose of the *WTO Agreement*.

2. Context

The relationship between the *SCM Agreement* and Article VI of the GATT 1994 is set out in Articles 10 and 32.1 of the *SCM Agreement*. Article 10 reads as follows:

> #### Application of Article VI of GATT 1994
>
> Members shall take all necessary steps to ensure that the imposition of a countervailing duty[36] on any product of the territory of any Member imported into the territory of another Member is in accordance with the provisions of Article VI of GATT 1994 and the terms of this Agreement. Countervailing duties may only be imposed pursuant to investigations initiated and conducted in accordance with the provisions of this Agreement and the Agreement on Agriculture.

> ---
> [36] The term "countervailing duty" shall be understood to mean a special duty levied for the purpose of offsetting any subsidy bestowed directly or indirectly upon the manufacture, production or export of any merchandise, as provided for in paragraph 3 of Article VI of GATT 1994.

Article 32.1 reads as follows:

> No specific action against a subsidy of another Member can be taken except in accordance with the provisions of GATT 1994, as interpreted by this Agreement.[56]

> ---
> [56] This paragraph is not intended to preclude action under other relevant provisions of GATT 1994, where appropriate.

From reading Article 10, it is clear that countervailing duties may only be imposed in accordance with Article VI of the GATT 1994 *and* the *SCM Agreement*. A countervailing duty being a specific action against a subsidy of another WTO Member, pursuant to Article 32.1, it can only be imposed "in accordance with the provisions of GATT 1994, as interpreted by this Agreement". The ordinary meaning of these provisions taken in their context leads us to the conclusion that the negotiators of the *SCM Agreement* clearly intended that, under the integrated *WTO Agreement*, countervailing duties may only be imposed in accordance with the provisions of Part V of the *SCM Agreement and* Article VI of the GATT 1994, taken together. If there is a conflict between the provisions of the *SCM Agreement* and Article VI of the GATT 1994, furthermore, the provisions of the *SCM Agreement* would prevail as a result of the general interpretative note to Annex 1A.

We turn to the omission of note 2 to the preamble of the *Tokyo Round SCM Code* from the *SCM Agreement*. That note reads:

> Wherever in this Agreement there is reference to "the terms of this Agreement" or the "articles" or "provisions of this Agreement" it shall be taken to mean, as the context requires, the provisions of the General Agreement as interpreted and applied by this Agreement.

This note related to a provision in the preamble to the *Tokyo Round SCM Code* which demonstrated the Tokyo Round signatories' desire "to apply fully and to interpret the provisions of Articles VI, XVI and XXIII" of the GATT 1947. The preamble was not retained in the new text of the *SCM Agreement*. Consequently, the note also disappeared. The *SCM Agreement* contains a set of rights and obligations that go well beyond merely applying and interpreting Articles VI, XVI and XXIII of the GATT 1947. The title to the *SCM Agreement* was also modified in this respect. Like the Panel, "we do not consider that the exclusion of this provision from the SCM Agreement sheds much light on the question before us".[20]

If Article 32.3 is read in conjunction with Articles 10 and 32.1 of the *SCM Agreement*, it becomes clear that the term "this Agreement" in Article 32.3 means "this Agreement *and* Article VI of the GATT 1994". We agree with the Panel that:

> Article VI of GATT 1947 and the Tokyo Round SCM Code represent, as among Code signatories, a package of rights and obligations regarding the use of countervailing measures, and Article VI of GATT 1994 and the SCM Agreement represent a new and different package of rights and obligations, as among WTO Members, regarding the use of

---

[20] Panel Report, para. 236, note 62.

countervailing duties. Thus, Article VI and the respective SCM Agreements impose obligations on a potential user of countervailing duties, in the form of conditions that have to be fulfilled in order to impose a duty, but they also confer the right to impose a countervailing duty when those conditions are satisfied. The SCM Agreements do not merely impose *additional* substantive and procedural *obligations* on a potential user of countervailing measures. Rather, the SCM Agreements and Article VI together define, clarify and in some cases modify the whole package of *rights* and obligations of a potential user of countervailing measures.[21]

3. Object and Purpose of the WTO Agreement

The fact that Article VI of the GATT 1947 could be invoked independently of the *Tokyo Round SCM Code* under the previous GATT system[22] does not mean that Article VI of GATT 1994 can be applied independently of the *SCM Agreement* in the context of the WTO. The authors of the new WTO regime intended to put an end to the fragmentation that had characterized the previous system. This can be seen from the preamble to the *WTO Agreement* which states, in pertinent part:

> *Resolved*, therefore, to develop an integrated, more viable and durable multilateral trading system encompassing the General Agreement on Tariffs and Trade, the results of past trade liberalization efforts, and all of the results of the Uruguay Round of Multilateral Trade Negotiations.

Article II:2 of the *WTO Agreement* also provides that the Multilateral Trade Agreements are "integral parts" of the *WTO Agreement*, "binding on all Members". The single undertaking is further reflected in the articles of the *WTO Agreement* on original membership, accession, non-application, acceptance and withdrawal. Furthermore, the *DSU* establishes an integrated dispute settlement system which applies to all the "covered agreements", allowing all the provisions of the *WTO Agreement* relevant to a particular dispute to be examined in one proceeding.

The Appellate Body sees Article 32.3 of the *SCM Agreement* as a clear statement that for countervailing duty investigations or reviews, the dividing line between the application of the GATT 1947 system of agreements and the *WTO Agreement* is to be determined by the date on which the application was made for the countervailing duty investigation or review. Article 32.3 has limited applica-

---

[21] Panel Report, para. 246; we understand the Panel's reference to "*SCM Agreements*" in this paragraph to mean the *SCM Agreement* and the *Tokyo Round SCM Code*.

[22] As demonstrated by the *United States - Pork* panel.

tion only in specific circumstances where a countervailing duty proceeding, either an investigation or a review, was underway at the time of entry into force of the *WTO Agreement*. This does not mean that the *WTO Agreement* does not apply as of 1 January 1995 to all other acts, facts and situations which come within the provisions of the *SCM Agreement* and Article VI of the GATT 1994. However, the Uruguay Round negotiators expressed an explicit intention to draw the line of application of the new *WTO Agreement* to countervailing duty investigations and reviews[23] at a different point in time from that for other general measures.[24] Because a countervailing duty is imposed only as a result of a sequence of acts, a line had to be drawn, and drawn sharply, to avoid uncertainty, unpredictability and unfairness concerning the rights of states and private parties under the domestic laws in force when the *WTO Agreement* came into effect.

We agree with the Philippines that the transitional decisions approved by the Tokyo Round Subsidies and Countervailing Measures Committee and the CONTRACTING PARTIES[25] do not modify the scope of rights and obligations under the *WTO Agreement*. We believe, however, that they contribute to understanding the significance of Article 32.3 of the *SCM Agreement* as a transitional rule. The Decision on Transitional Co-Existence of the GATT 1947 and the WTO Agreement and the Decision on Transitional Co-Existence of the Tokyo Round SCM Code and the WTO Agreement provide for the legal termination of the GATT 1947 and the *Tokyo Round SCM Code* one year after the date of entry into force of the *WTO Agreement*, i.e. by 31 December 1995. They also permit

---

[23] There is an identical provision to Article 32.3 of the *SCM Agreement* contained in Article 18.3 of the *Agreement on Implementation of Article VI of the General Agreement on Tariffs and Trade 1994* (the *"Anti-dumping Agreement"*). Similarly, there are mirror transitional decisions approved by the Tokyo Round Committee on Anti-dumping Measures, in the Decision on Transitional Co-Existence of the Agreement on Implementation of Article VI of the General Agreement on Tariffs and Trade and the Marrakesh Agreement Establishing the World Trade Organization, ADP/131, 16 December 1994; and the Decision on Consequences of Withdrawal from or Termination of the Agreement on Implementation of Article VI of the General Agreement on Tariffs and Trade, ADP/132, 16 December 1994.

[24] In its appellant's submission dated 9 January 1997, at p. 37, para. 59, the Philippines argues that in *United States - Gasoline*, both the panel and the Appellate Body assessed the pre-WTO domestic regulatory process that led to the imposition of the United States' environmental measure at issue in that dispute. We note that, in that case, there was no issue with respect to the temporal application of the measure in dispute, nor did the panel or the Appellate Body examine the applicability of the *Agreement on Technical Barriers to Trade*.

[25] The Decision on Transitional Co-Existence of the GATT 1947 and the WTO Agreement (PC/12-L/7583, 13 December 1994) was adopted by the CONTRACTING PARTIES to the GATT 1947 (6SS/SR/1); the Decision on Transitional Co-Existence of the Tokyo Round SCM Code and the WTO Agreement (SCM/186, 16 December 1994) was adopted by the Tokyo Round Committee on Subsidies and Countervailing Measures and noted by the CONTRACTING PARTIES (6SS/SR/1) and the WTO Committee on Subsidies and Countervailing Measures (G/SCM/M/1). The Decision on Consequences of Withdrawal from or Termination of the Tokyo Round SCM Code (SCM/187, 16 December 1994) was adopted by the Tokyo Round Committee on Subsidies and Countervailing Measures and noted by the CONTRACTING PARTIES (6SS/SR/1) and the WTO Committee on Subsidies and Countervailing Measures (G/SCM/M/1).

WTO Members, during the period of co-existence of the GATT 1947 and the *Tokyo Round SCM Code* with the *WTO Agreement*, to bring their disputes under the *DSU* where the measure in issue is one to which the *WTO Agreement* applies.

The Decision on Consequences of Withdrawal from or Termination of the Tokyo Round SCM Code, adopted by the Tokyo Round Subsidies and Countervailing Measures Committee, extended dispute settlement under the *Tokyo Round SCM Code* for two years, one year beyond the legal termination of the *Tokyo Round SCM Code*. The Tokyo Round Committee on Subsidies and Countervailing Measures was to remain in operation by agreement of the signatories to the *Tokyo Round SCM Code* until 31 December 1996, to deal with disputes arising out of countervailing duty investigations or reviews initiated pursuant to applications made prior to 1 January 1995. Signatories to the *Tokyo Round SCM Code* agreed to make their best efforts to expedite domestic investigations and dispute settlement procedures to permit the Tokyo Round Subsidies and Countervailing Measures Committee to consider covered disputes within this two-year period. This Decision avoided the application of Article 70 of the *Vienna Convention*, which provides that the termination of a treaty releases the parties from any obligation further to perform the treaty.

Like the Panel, "we are hesitant, in interpreting the WTO Agreement, to give great weight to the effect of decisions that had not yet been taken at the time the WTO Agreement was signed".[26] We agree with the Panel's statement that:

> The availability of Article VI of GATT 1994 as applicable law in this dispute is a matter to be determined on the basis of the WTO Agreement, rather than on the basis of a subsequent decision by the signatories of the Tokyo Round SCM Code taken at the invitation of the Preparatory Committee.[27]

While we agree with the Panel that these transitional decisions are of limited relevance in determining whether Article VI of the GATT 1994 can be applied independently of the *SCM Agreement*, they reflect the intention of the *Tokyo Round SCM Code* signatories to provide a forum for dispute settlement arising out of disputes under the *Tokyo Round SCM Code* for one year after its legal termination date. At the time the *Tokyo Round SCM Code* signatories agreed to these decisions, they were fully cognizant of the implications of the operation of Article 32.3 of the *SCM Agreement*.

We agree with the Panel that the complaining party in this dispute, the Philippines, had legal options available to it, and, therefore, was not left without a right of action as a result of the operation of Article 32.3 of the *SCM Agreement*. Until 31 December 1995, the GATT 1947 continued to co-exist with the *WTO Agreement*, and dispute settlement was available to the Philippines pursuant to Articles VI and XXIII of the GATT 1947. Until 31 December 1996, as a result

---

[26] Panel Report, para. 270.
[27] Panel Report, para. 272.

of the Decision on Consequences of Withdrawal from or Termination of the Tokyo Round SCM Code approved by the signatories to the *Tokyo Round SCM Code*, dispute settlement was available under the provisions of the *Tokyo Round SCM Code*. Within a reasonable period of time after the definitive countervailing duty was imposed, the Philippines had the right to request a review pursuant to Article 21.2 of the *SCM Agreement* - a right which remains available to the Philippines today.

Any WTO Member, which was not a signatory to the *Tokyo Round SCM Code*, had a right of action under Articles VI and XXIII of the GATT 1947 until 31 December 1995, and, like the Philippines, has a continuing right to request a review under Article 21.2 of the *SCM Agreement*.

We believe that the situation of a prospective Member of the WTO, which accedes under the provisions of Article XII of the *WTO Agreement*, is different from that of former contracting parties to the GATT 1947 or signatories to the *Tokyo Round SCM Code* because those agreements did not apply previously to its trading relations with other states. Article XII:1 of the *WTO Agreement* provides, furthermore, that a state may accede "on terms to be agreed between it and the WTO".

In light of the above, we believe that it is not necessary to determine whether applying Article VI of the GATT 1994 independently of the *SCM Agreement* would be more onerous than applying them together.

V.   APPLICABILITY OF ARTICLES I AND II OF THE GATT 1994

We have concluded that, as a result of the integrated nature of the *WTO Agreement* and the specific language in Articles 10 and 32.1 of the *SCM Agreement*, the provisions of the *SCM Agreement* relating to countervailing duty investigations are not separable from the rights and obligations of the GATT 1994 or the *WTO Agreement* taken as a whole. We find, therefore, that the Panel did not err in concluding at paragraphs 280 and 281 of the Panel Report that the applicability of Article VI of the GATT 1994 to the countervailing duty investigation which is the subject of this dispute, also determines the applicability of Articles I and II of the GATT 1994 to that investigation. In the same manner as the Panel found that "the measures are neither-consistent′ nor-inconsistent′ with Article VI of GATT 1994; rather, they are simply not subject to that Article",[28] we believe that the measures here are neither "consistent" nor "inconsistent" with Articles I and II of the GATT 1994, because those Articles are also not applicable law for the purposes of this dispute.

---

[28]   Panel Report, para. 280, note 71.

VI.   TERMS OF REFERENCE

Brazil argues in its appellant's submission that the issue of consistency of its countervailing duty measures with Articles I and II of the GATT 1994 is not within the terms of reference of the Panel, and, therefore, should not have been addressed by the Panel.[29] In this appeal, the parties to the dispute, the Philippines and Brazil, agreed on the following special terms of reference pursuant to Article 7.3 of the *DSU*:

> To examine, in the light of the relevant provisions in GATT 1994 and the Agreement on Agriculture, the matter referred to the DSB by the Philippines in document WT/DS22/5, taking into account the submission made by Brazil in document WT/DS22/3 and the record of discussions at the meeting of the DSB on 21 February 1996, and to make such findings as will assist the DSB in making the recommendations or in giving the rulings provided for in those agreements.[30]

A panel's terms of reference are important for two reasons. First, terms of reference fulfil an important due process objective - they give the parties and third parties sufficient information concerning the claims at issue in the dispute in order to allow them an opportunity to respond to the complainant's case. Second, they establish the jurisdiction of the panel by defining the precise claims at issue in the dispute.

We agree, furthermore, with the conclusions expressed by previous panels under the GATT 1947, as well as under the *Tokyo Round SCM Code* and the *Tokyo Round Anti-dumping Code*, that the "matter" referred to a panel for consideration consists of the specific claims stated by the parties to the dispute in the relevant documents specified in the terms of reference.[31] We agree with the approach taken in previous adopted panel reports that a matter, which includes the claims composing that matter, does not fall within a panel's terms of reference unless the claims are identified in the documents referred to or contained in the terms of reference.

In the present case, because we agree with the conclusions of the Panel concerning applicable law, we believe it is not necessary to determine whether

---

[29] Brazil's appellant's submission, dated 14 January 1997, p. 1, para. 2.

[30] WT/DS22/6, 18 April 1996.

[31] *United States - Denial of Most-Favoured-Nation Treatment as to Non-Rubber Footwear from Brazil*, BISD 39S/128, adopted 19 June 1992, para. 6.2; *EC - Imposition of Anti-dumping Duties on Imports of Cotton Yarn from Brazil*, ADP/137, adopted 30 October 1995, para. 456; *United States - Imposition of Countervailing Duties on Imports of Fresh and Chilled Atlantic Salmon from Norway*, SCM/153, adopted 28 April 1994, para. 212; *United States - Imposition of Anti-Dumping Duties on Imports of Fresh and Chilled Atlantic Salmon from Norway*, ADP/87, adopted 26-27 April 1994, para. 336.

the Philippines' claims under Articles I and II of the GATT 1994 were within the Panel's terms of reference.

VII.   FINDINGS AND CONCLUSIONS

For the reasons set out in this Report, the Appellate Body upholds the legal findings and conclusions of the Panel.

The Appellate Body *recommends* that the Dispute Settlement Body make a ruling consistent with the legal findings and conclusions in the Panel Report and this Report.

BRAZIL - MEASURES AFFECTING DESICCATED COCONUT

Report of the Panel
WT/DS22/R

Adopted by the Dispute Settlement Body on 20 March 1997
as upheld by the Appellate Body Report

TABLE OF CONTENTS

I.   INTRODUCTION

1.   On 27 November 1995, the Philippines requested consultations with Brazil under Article XXIII:1 of the General Agreement on Tariffs and Trade 1994 ("GATT 1994") concerning the countervailing duty imposed by Brazil on imports of desiccated coconut from the Philippines. (WT/DS22/1/Rev.1).

2.   On 8 December 1995, Brazil replied that it was prepared to enter into consultations with the Philippines as long as it was mutually understood that those consultations would be undertaken exclusively under the 1979 Agreement on Interpretation and Application of Articles VI, XVI and XXIII of the General Agreement on Tariffs and Trade ("Tokyo Round SCM Code"), under the auspices of which Brazil conducted the coconut subsidies investigations and imposed the countervailing duties.

3.   On 13 December 1995, the Philippines replied that Brazil's response constituted a refusal of the request for consultations under Article XXIII:1.

4.   Taking the view that Brazil had failed to enter into consultations within the period provided for in the Understanding on Rules and Procedures Governing the Settlement of Disputes ("DSU"), the Philippines, on 17 January 1996, requested the establishment of a Panel with standard terms of reference, pursuant to Article XXIII:2 of GATT 1994 and Articles 4.3 and 6 of the DSU. (WT/DS22/2).

5.   At Brazil's request, a copy of document SCM/193, on the issue of the countervailing duties in question, was circulated to the Dispute Settlement Body ("DSB"). In that document, Brazil stated its view that the Tokyo Round SCM Code was the only legal framework applicable to the dispute. Brazil also indicated its understanding that the DSB was not the appropriate forum for the discussion on the dispute with the Philippines, and that document SCM/193 was circulated for information purposes only and without prejudice to its rights under

the Tokyo Round SCM Code and to its position on the applicable law. (WT/DS22/3, attached as Annex 1).

6.   At the 31 January 1996 meeting of the DSB, the Philippines stated that, for reasons mutually agreed to, the Philippines had not objected to postponing consideration of its request for establishment of a panel, but would make a statement at the next meeting of the DSB when this request would be considered. Brazil noted that its arguments concerning the dispute were explained in document WT/DS22/3, and that it invited the Philippines for consultations on the question of the applicable law before any further steps were taken toward establishment of a panel. The DSB agreed to revert to the matter at its next meeting. (WT/DSB/M/10).

7.   Continuing to take the view that Brazil had failed to enter into consultations within the period provided for in the DSU, the Philippines, on 5 February 1996, again requested the establishment of a Panel with standard terms of reference, pursuant to Article XXIII:2 of GATT 1994 and Articles 4.3 and 6 of the DSU. (WT/DS22/5, attached as Annex 2).

8.   At its meeting of 21 February 1996, the DSB considered the Philippines' request for establishment of a panel. Both the Philippines and Brazil stated their views on the matter of the countervailing duties imposed by Brazil on imports of desiccated coconut from the Philippines, and the question of the law applicable to the dispute. The representatives of Indonesia, speaking on behalf of ASEAN countries, and Sri Lanka, supported the Philippines' request for establishment of a panel. Brazil considered it premature to establish a panel at that meeting, and the DSB agreed to revert to the matter at its next meeting. (WT/DSB/M/11, attached as Annex 3).

9.   At its meeting of 5 March 1996, pursuant to the Philippines' request and with Brazil's acceptance, the DSB established a Panel to examine the matter. The Philippines requested that the Panel be established with standard terms of reference. Brazil requested consultations on the terms of reference. The DSB authorized the Chairman to draw up terms of reference in consultation with the parties, in accordance with Article 7.3 of the DSU.

10.   On 22 March 1996 the parties agreed that the Panel would have the following terms of reference:

> "To examine, in the light of the relevant provisions in GATT 1994 and the Agreement on Agriculture, the matter referred to the DSB by the Philippines in document WT/DS22/5, taking into account the submission made by Brazil in document WT/DS22/3 and the record of discussions at the meeting of the DSB on 21 February 1996, and to make such findings as will assist the DSB in making the recommendations or in giving the rulings provided for in those agreements". (WT/DS22/6).

11.   On 16 April 1996, the Panel was constituted with the following composition:

Chairman: Mr. Maamoun Abdel-Fattah

Members: Mr. Zdenek Jung

Mr. Joseph Weiler

12.   Canada, the European Community, Indonesia, Malaysia, Sri Lanka and the United States reserved their rights as third parties to the dispute. Malaysia later withdrew as a third party.

II.   FACTUAL ASPECTS

13.   This dispute concerns countervailing duties imposed by Brazil on imports of desiccated coconut from the Philippines. On 21 June 1994, based on a request for an investigation by the domestic industry filed on 17 January 1994, Brazil initiated an investigation regarding allegedly subsidized imports of desiccated coconut and coconut milk from the Philippines, Côte d'Ivoire, Indonesia, Malaysia, and Sri Lanka. On 23 March 1995, Brazil imposed provisional duties on imports of desiccated coconut from the Philippines, Côte d'Ivoire, Indonesia, and Sri Lanka, and on imports of coconut milk from Sri Lanka.[1] On 18 August 1995, Brazil issued Interministerial Ordinance No. 11 (the "Ordinance"), pursuant to which it imposed a countervailing duty in the amount of 121.5 per cent on imports of desiccated coconut from the Philippines.[2]

14.   Brazil investigated eight Philippine programmes which allegedly conferred subsidies on coconut fruit.[3] However, Brazil considered that it was unable, based on the information obtained from the Philippines, to determine the amount of the subsidy conferred on coconut fruit by each programme. Brazil also concluded that desiccated coconut indirectly benefitted from the subsidy provided to coconut fruit. Brazil determined the amount of the subsidy conferred on desiccated coconut by comparing the price of subsidized desiccated coconut, based on the price actually paid for coconut fruit, and a constructed unsubsidized price, based on what it considered to be the constructed unsubsidized price for coconut

---

[1]   Interministerial Decree No. 113 (23 March 1995).

[2]   Interministerial Ordinance No. 11 (18 August 1995). Imports of desiccated coconut from the other countries under investigation were also found to be subsidized, as well as imports of coconut milk from Sri Lanka. Those aspects of the determination are not before the Panel.

[3]   The eight programmes investigated were:
   1)   the Programme under Presidential Decree No. 582/74,
   2)   the National Coconut Productivity Programme, and its successors, the Expanded National Coconut Intercropping Programme and the Farm Assistance and Livelihood project,
   3)   the Small Coconut Farm Development Project,
   4)   the Agrarian Reform Programme,
   5)   the Country Economic Development Programme,
   6)   the Small Coconut Farmer Organizations,
   7)   Income Tax Exemptions and Credits, Deductions, and other Tax Benefits, and
   8)   The Coconut Replanting Programme and Programme of Additional Incentives to Accelerate the Coconut Production Programme.

fruit. Brazil considered that the difference between the prices equalled the subsidy amount that affected the price of desiccated coconut.

15.   Brazil further found that the subsidized imports, on a cumulated basis, caused material injury to the Brazilian industry.

III.   FINDINGS AND RECOMMENDATIONS REQUESTED BY THE PARTIES

16.   The Philippines requests the Panel to make the following rulings, findings, and recommendations:

> "(a)   That the Panel find that the Ordinance imposing a countervailing duty of 121.5 per cent on desiccated coconut from the Philippines for a period of five years from 18 August 1995 is inconsistent with Brazil's obligations under Articles I and II, and is not justified by Article VI:3 and VI:6(a) of GATT 1994.

> "(b)   That the Panel find that Brazil's failure to revoke the Ordinance and to reimburse any duties paid under it, notwithstanding the representations of the Philippines, was inconsistent with its obligations under Article VI:3 and 6(a) of GATT 1994.

> "(c)   That the Panel recommend that Brazil bring the above measure into conformity with its obligations under GATT 1994.

> "(d)   That Brazil's refusal to hold consultations under Article XXIII:1 of GATT 1994 on its measures affecting desiccated coconuts was inconsistent with Brazil's obligation under that Article and Article 4:1, 2 and 3 of the Understanding on Rules and Procedures Governing the Settlement of Disputes.

> "(e)   In the event the Panel were to find that the countervailing duty imposed by Brazil was consistent with Articles I and II of GATT 1994 or justified by Article VI of GATT 1994, the Philippines requests that the Panel find that the imposition of the countervailing duty and its subsequent non-revocation were inconsistent with Article 13 of the Agreement on Agriculture, and recommend that Brazil bring the measure referred to above into conformity with its obligations under the Agreement on Agriculture".

17.   Brazil asks the Panel to make the following findings:

> (a)   That the only obligations applicable to this dispute are those in the Tokyo Round SCM Code, and that potential violations of that Code cannot be addressed by this Panel.

> (b)   That Brazil's injury finding, its obligations under Articles I and II of GATT 1994, its obligations under the Agreement on Agriculture, and its alleged failure to consult are not within the terms of reference of the Panel, and arguments concerning those matters should be excluded from the proceeding.

(c)   That the Philippines failed to demonstrate that the requirements for the exemption it claims under the Agreement on Agriculture were met.

(d)   In the event the Panel reaches the substance of Brazil's determination, that Brazil's actions were fully consistent with its obligations under Article VI of GATT 1994.

IV.   MAIN ARGUMENTS OF THE PARTIES

A.   *Preliminary Arguments*

18.   Brazil requested that, as an initial matter, the Panel make a preliminary ruling on the questions of applicable law and the scope of the terms of reference. Brazil argued that both issues are procedural in nature, not substantive, and that a speedy resolution would greatly promote the efficiency of the panel process by permitting the Panel and the parties to focus on the substantive issues. Brazil asserted that there was precedent under GATT 1947 for such early rulings on procedural issues, referring, *inter alia*, to *EC - Imposition of Anti-Dumping Duties on Imports of Cotton Yarn from Brazil*, ADP/137 (adopted 30 October 1995) ("*Cotton Yarn"*), para. 4, in which the Panel issued an early ruling concerning which claims were covered by the terms of reference.[4]

19.   Brazil viewed the first question as fundamental: what obligations to consider in determining whether Brazil's actions were consistent with its multilateral obligations. Brazil had maintained from the start of the consultation process that since the subsidy investigation was conducted under the auspices of the Tokyo Round SCM Code, it should be judged in relation to Brazil's obligations under that Code, by a panel established under that Code. In Brazil's view, because the answer to the question affected both which issues would be briefed and whether the Panel should consider the dispute, this issue merited immediate decision.

20.   The second issue also concerned a procedural matter - whether certain claims raised by the Philippines in its first submission to the Panel were properly within the terms of reference of this Panel. Brazil alleged that the Philippines' claims concerning Brazil's injury finding, Articles I and II of GATT 1994, the WTO Agreement on Agriculture, and Brazil's alleged refusal to consult, as well as most of the requested findings and recommendations, were not within the terms of reference of this Panel and urged the Panel to issue an immediate ruling to that effect in order to avoid the necessity of arguing irrelevant points.

---

[4]   In this regard, Brazil also referred to the Panel decisions in *United States - Measures Affecting Alcoholic and Malt Beverages*, DS23/R (adopted 19 June 1992) BISD 39S/206, *United States - Denial of Most-Favoured-Nation Treatment as to Non-Rubber Footwear from Brazil*, DS18/R (adopted 19 June 1992) BISD 39S/129, ("*Non-Rubber Footwear MFN*"), and *Report of Korea - Restrictions on Imports of Beef*, L/6503, L/6504, L/6505 (adopted 7 November 1989) BISD 36S/268, 202, 234, respectively.

1. Applicable Law

21.   The Philippines invoked the provisions of Articles I, II, and VI of GATT 1994 and Article 13 of the Agreement on Agriculture. The Philippines did not invoke the provisions of the Tokyo Round SCM Code or the Agreement on Subsidies and Countervailing Measures (the "SCM Agreement").

22.   Brazil argued that the Philippines may not invoke any provisions of GATT 1994 or the Agreement on Agriculture in this dispute. Brazil contended that only the provisions of the Tokyo Round SCM Code are applicable to this matter, and that the Philippines is entitled only to dispute settlement under the provisions of that Code. Brazil further argued that the Tokyo Round SCM Code is not a covered agreement under Article 1.1 of the DSU, and that the Panel may therefore not apply that Code in this dispute.

(a)   Principles of International Law

(i)   Article 28 of the Vienna Convention

23.   Brazil argued that customary rules of public international law do not permit the retroactive application of treaty obligations. Brazil pointed out that the investigation at issue in this dispute was initiated in 1994, at which time the Tokyo Round SCM Code, and Brazilian law which incorporated the requirements of that Code, were in effect. Brazil had no obligations under GATT 1994 or the WTO Agreement at that time, because those agreements did not enter into force until 1 January 1995. Article 28 of the Vienna Convention on the Law of Treaties ("Vienna Convention") states that a treaty does not "bind a party in relation to any action or fact which took place or any situation which ceased to exist before the date of entry into force of that treaty with respect to that party". Brazil took the position that the relevant act at issue in this dispute was the initiation and subsequent conduct of a countervailing duty investigation, which began on 21 June 1994, before the date of entry into force of the WTO Agreement and GATT 1994 on 1 January 1995. Therefore, GATT 1994 could not bind Brazil with respect to this investigation.

24.   Brazil argued that in the context of the current dispute, an act could mean the investigation which must be considered to have taken place at the time of initiation. Brazil proposed several reasons for such an interpretation. First, the right to challenge a countervailing duty investigation arises at the time of the initiation.[5] Second, the investigation must review facts that already exist. In this dispute, Brazil looked at subsidies to Philippine coconut growers in the period May 1993 through April 1994 to determine whether imports from the Philippines were subsidized. Third, in Brazil's view, the conduct of the investigation, what information was considered and the basis for the determination, were at issue in

---

[5]   In this regard, Brazil referred to the decision of the Panel in *United States - Measures Affecting Imports of Softwood Lumber from Canada*, SCM/162 (adopted 27-28 October 1993) BISD 40S/358.

this dispute. Such procedural rules could not change during the course of the investigation. Had the Members intended to change the rules for investigations initiated prior to 1 January 1995, they would not have included Article 32:3 in the SCM Agreement.

25.   The Philippines argued that Brazil's reliance on Article 28 of the Vienna Convention was misguided because the act in question in this dispute was the imposition of the countervailing measure on 18 August 1995, after the WTO Agreement was in force between the parties. It was at this point that the Philippines suffered nullification of its rights under the WTO Agreements, specifically GATT 1994. According to the Philippines, the only act that Brazil undertook and completed prior to the entry into force of the WTO Agreements was the initiation of the investigation. All other significant acts, e.g. the imposition of provisional measures, the conclusion of the investigation, the order imposing the final countervailing duty, and the levying of the final countervailing duties, occurred after the WTO Agreements came into force. Of these four acts, the Philippines was contesting only the imposition and levying of the countervailing duty. The Philippines emphasized that the countervailing duty did not merely continue after the effective date of the WTO Agreements, but was in fact imposed after that date. In the Philippines' view, relating the imposition of the duty to the date of the application for countervailing duty was a chronological fiction. The Philippines argued that Brazil, in effect, sought to convert the pre-WTO initiation of the investigation into a protective umbrella, similar to a grandfather clause, that would shield measures imposed after the entry into force of the WTO from the application of WTO norms. In the Philippines' view, there was a wide gap between the initiation of Brazil's investigation before the entry into force of the WTO and the imposition of the final countervailing measure. Article 28 of the Vienna Convention does not provide an umbrella to shield this kind of gap - any shield against retroactive application applied only until the entry into force of the new treaty.

26.   The Philippines argued that general principles of international law, as codified in the Vienna Convention, require that even pre-existing measures must be reviewed in light of new obligations imposed by a new agreement. Therefore, in the Philippines' view, even if Brazil's investigation had been concluded and the countervailing measure had been imposed before the entry into force of the WTO Agreement, Brazil's continued implementation of such a pre-existing measure would have to be reviewed and examined in light of its obligations under GATT 1994. Because in fact Brazil's investigation ended and the countervailing duty was imposed after the entry into force of the WTO Agreement, the Philippines maintained that GATT 1994 and the Agreement on Agriculture are applicable.

27.   Moreover, the Philippines noted that Brazil, in response to a question from the Philippines, had admitted that the WTO Agreements presumably apply to the actual collection of duties after 18 August 1995. In the Philippines' view, the practical effect of applying the WTO Agreements to continued collection of the duties was the application of the WTO Agreements to the imposition of the measures. In this regard, the Philippines referred to the decision of the Appellate Body in *United States - Standards for Reformulated and Conventional Gaso-*

line.[6] The Philippines considered that the Appellate Body had examined the United States' rule-making process, which took place prior to the effective date of the WTO Agreements, in assessing the validity of the United States' standards for reformulated and conventional gasoline at issue in that dispute, which standards were themselves imposed prior to the effective date of the WTO Agreements. In the Philippines' view, this demonstrated that the Panel could consider events prior to the entry into force of the WTO Agreements in evaluating the consistency of a measure with those Agreements. Moreover, the Philippines noted that, in response to a question from the Philippines, Brazil denied neither the fact nor the propriety of the Appellate Body's consideration of the rule making process in *Reformulated Gasoline*.

28.   Brazil, on the other hand, maintained that the decision in *Reformulated Gasoline* did not support the Philippine position. In Brazil's view, in that case Venezuela and Brazil had challenged the continued maintenance of discriminatory standards by the United States after the entry into force of the WTO, but not the rule-making process that had led to the imposition of those standards. Thus, in terms of the current case, the analogous challenge would be to the continued imposition of duties, not the investigation and decision to impose duties. Moreover, Brazil noted that unlike the current case, there was no mechanism for a review of the United States' standards under domestic law in the *Reformulated Gasoline* situation, whereas in this case, the Philippines had the ability under the SCM Agreement and Brazilian law to request a review of the continued imposition of countervailing measures, under the standards of the SCM Agreement.

29.   The Philippines argued that the Panel's decision in *U.S. - Countervailing Duties on Non-Rubber Footwear from Brazil* (adopted 13 June 1995), SCM/94, paras. 4.5 and 4.10 (*"Non-Rubber Footwear"*), recognized that general principles of international law required that pre-existing measures must be reviewed in light of new obligations imposed by a new agreement. The Philippines argued that in *Non-Rubber Footwear* the Panel concluded that the continued imposition of countervailing measures first imposed by the United States prior to the entry into force of the Tokyo Round SCM Code was subject to the Code's requirement of an injury test. The Philippines maintained that applying the logic of that decision to this case required that Brazil's countervailing measures be subject to the requirements of GATT 1994.

30.   Brazil contended that the Panel decision in *Non-Rubber Footwear* did not support the Philippines' argument. Even assuming *arguendo* that the report had precedential or interpretive value, in Brazil's view, the Panel had concluded that any obligation under the Tokyo Round SCM Code would be met by conducting a review in conformity with the new obligations at the request of an interested

---

[6]   WT/DS2/R (29 January 1996), WT/DS2/AB/R (22 April 1996) (both adopted 20 May 1996) (*"Reformulated Gasoline"*).

party.[7] *Non-Rubber Footwear*, paras. 4.4 and 4.6. Brazil pointed out that Brazilian law and Article 21 of the SCM Agreement permit reviews upon request. Under Brazilian law, such a review would be conducted in accordance with Brazil's obligations under the SCM Agreement. Brazil noted that the Philippines had not requested such a review.[8]

31.   In addition, Brazil contended that *Non-Rubber Footwear* states that Article 28 of the Vienna Convention prevents applying the new treaty to the preexisting act, i.e., the actual investigation, and only permits its application to the continuing implementation.[9] Brazil distinguished between the investigation and findings made that led to imposition of final countervailing duties, and the continued collection of duties. According to Brazil, the findings made in the investigation could only be challenged under the rules then applicable - the Tokyo Round SCM Code. Moreover, Brazil noted that it did not argue that the WTO and its covered agreements do not apply to the continued collection of the duties, only that those obligations do not apply to the conduct of the investigation and the determinations made as part of that investigation. The continued collection of the duty constitutes a "situation" within the meaning of Article 28. Thus, since that situation has continued after entry into force of the WTO, the collection of duties is subject to the WTO Agreements, and the Philippines can seek a review to ensure that the continued collection is consistent with the WTO rules.

32.   Brazil referred to the decision of the Permanent Court of International Justice in *Phosphates in Morocco* ("*Phosphates*") as providing guidance on the meaning of the concept of retroactive application addressed in Article 28. In that case, there is a lengthy discussion of whether the "situation" was subject to the Agreement at issue or whether it occurred prior to that Agreement. The majority opinion notes:

> "The situations and facts which form the subject of the limitation *ratione temporis* have to be considered from the point of view both of their date in relation to the date of ratification and of their connection with the birth of the dispute. Situations or facts subsequent to the ratification could serve to found the Court's compulsory jurisdiction only if it

---

[7]   Brazil observed that the Panel report also indicates that the obligation at issue in that case, an injury finding, was not a new obligation, but rather a pre-existing obligation under Article VI of GATT 1947. *Non-Rubber Footwear*, para. 4.10

[8]   Brazil argued that the Panel report in *Non-Rubber Footwear* indicates that until a request for review is made, there can be no violation, referring to the following language:

"If, however, the signatory subject to the pre-existing countervailing duty were to choose not to invoke its right as of that date but made its request at a later date, again there was nothing in Article VI or in its subsequent interpretation in the Code to imply that any earlier date than the date of the request would be relevant for an injury determination and possible revocation of countervailing duties".

Non-Rubber Footwear, para. 4.6.

[9]   *Non-Rubber Footwear*, para. 4.5.

was with regard to them that the dispute arose. ... it is necessary always to bear in mind the will of the State which only accepted the compulsory jurisdiction within specified limits, and consequently only intended to submit to that jurisdiction disputes having actually arisen from situations or facts subsequent to its acceptance. But it would be impossible to admit the existence of such a relationship between a dispute and subsequent factors which either presume the existence or are merely the confirmation or development of earlier situations or facts constituting the real cause of the dispute".[10]

In that dispute the Italian government had raised a complaint against the French government over the "monopolization" of the phosphate trade as a result of a regime created in 1920, prior to the ratification in 1931 of the Agreement under which the complaint was brought. The Court found that the act underlying the dispute was the regime creating the cartel that led to monopolization. Therefore, even though this monopolization continued after 1931, it was because of an act initiated prior to that date, and therefore could not be brought under the Agreement. In Brazil's view, this decision established the international law principle reflected in Article 28 of the Vienna Convention. Similar to the situation in the *Phosphates* case, the WTO Members only intended to be subject to WTO obligations after the date of entry into force, as evidenced by the creation of a date of entry into force for the WTO Agreement, rather than having it enter into force as soon as a sufficient number of countries had ratified them.

33.   The Philippines argued that the decision in *Phosphates* did not support Brazil's definition of retroactive application. In the Philippines' view, the Court in that case had simply held that it had no jurisdiction over disputes involving alleged international law violations that originated in definitive acts that occurred before the parties ratified the instruments through which they submitted to the Court's compulsory jurisdiction. In that case, the acts were a 1920 law and a 1925 administrative decision issued prior to ratification of the Court's compulsory jurisdiction agreement. However, the Court ruled that "situations or facts subsequent to the ratification could serve to found the Court's compulsory jurisdiction. ... if it was with regard to them that the dispute arose". *Phosphates* at 18. Moreover, the date of the act underlying a dispute was determined with reference to the "definitive act" that resulted in the alleged violation. In the Philippines' view, in this case, the relevant act was the imposition of the final countervailing duty, which occurred after the WTO Agreements came into effect.

34.   The Philippines, moreover, viewed the right to a review under Brazilian law as limited, and thus not an effective remedy. The Philippines noted that under Brazilian law, a review would not take place for at least one year after imposition

---

[10]   *Phosphates in Morocco*, Permanent Court of International Justice (14 June 1938) at 18.

of the measures, and even then, a change in circumstances or a new fact was required for initiation of a review. Moreover, such a review would only address the continued imposition of the measures, not the original imposition.

35.   Brazil asserted that Decree No. 93,962 (22 January 1987) permitted reviews upon request beginning one year after the imposition of countervailing duties. The current law, Decree No. 1751 (19 December 1995), permits reviews upon request beginning one year after imposition of duties. In exceptional cases a review may be initiated sooner upon the request of the exporting government or on Brazil's own initiative. Brazil also noted that this was consistent with the practice of other Members, for example the United States and the European Union.

36.   The Philippines asserted that, while Article 32.3 of the SCM provides a party the option to seek a review of the continuation of a measure (but not the original imposition), the initiation of such review is not mandatory, and in any event would only address the continued imposition of the measure, not its original imposition. Moreover, referring to the report of the Panel in *United States - Imposition of Countervailing Duties on Imports of Fresh and Chilled Atlantic Salmon from Norway* (*"Salmon"*), SCM/153 (adopted 24 April 1994), paras. 218-220, the Philippines argued that there was no requirement in any WTO Agreement that a party first seek a review from the country imposing a measure before resorting to multilateral dispute resolution. If the Philippines were limited to seeking a review during this transitional period, instead of being able to resort immediately to the dispute settlement mechanism of the WTO, it would be subjected to delay and continued trade losses, effectively nullifying its rights of free trade under the WTO. The Philippines, in its view, was entitled to resort to WTO dispute resolution proceedings in order to invoke WTO norms against Brazil's countervailing measures.

(ii)   Other Provisions of the Vienna Convention

37.   The Philippines also referred to Article 30:3 of the Vienna Convention, which provides that where there are successive treaties relating to the same subject-matter among the same parties, "the earlier treaty applies only to the extent that its provisions are compatible with those of the later treaty", and argued that, between the Philippines and Brazil, the WTO Agreement and GATT 1994, as the subsequent treaty, override the Tokyo Round SCM Code.

38.   Brazil argued that Article 30.3 of the Vienna Convention did not require that the applicable law in this dispute be GATT 1994. Even assuming the WTO Agreement applied in this case as the successive treaty, the portion of that treaty relating to the same subject matter as the Tokyo Round SCM Code is the SCM Agreement. Article 32.3 of the SCM Agreement provides that "the provisions of this Agreement shall apply to investigations, and reviews of existing measures, initiated pursuant to applications made on or after the date of entry into force for a Member of the WTO Agreement". Thus, in Brazil's view, since the investiga-

tion at issue here was initiated pursuant to an application made before the date of entry into force of the WTO Agreement, the SCM Agreement does not apply.

39.   The Philippines referred to Articles 18, 26, and 31 of the Vienna Convention as indicating the fundamental principle in international law that parties to a treaty must act consistent with the treaty's objectives. Signatories bind themselves fully to all substantive obligations of the treaty and must refrain from acts which defeat the object and purpose of the treaty. In the Philippines' view, this requirement existed before the new treaty entered into force, and applied even more strongly after the new treaty entered into force. Therefore, the WTO Agreement must be interpreted in accordance with the ordinary meaning to be given to the terms of the treaty in their proper context and in light of its object and purpose. In the Philippines' view, it was not reasonable to infer that the negotiators of the WTO Agreements intended an interpretation of the Agreements that would suspend the rights of WTO Members for two years (while the transitional decisions regarding the Tokyo Round SCM Code were in effect), preventing them from seeking dispute settlement under the WTO Agreements, by limiting them to either dispute settlement under the Tokyo Round SCM Code or a review under the domestic law of the Member imposing the measure, of a measure imposed eight months after the WTO Agreements entered into force.

40.   Brazil contested the Philippines' argument that Brazil's interpretation suspends WTO Members' rights for two years. Brazil maintained that the Philippines misstated the purpose of Article 18 of the Vienna Convention in arguing that it creates a duty to ensure that all actions prior to entry into force of the WTO Agreements were consistent with Brazil's obligations under those Agreements. In Brazil's view, Article 18 reflects an obligation to act in good faith and not to act in such a way as to make it more difficult or impossible for any party to the treaty to meet its obligations. The imposition of countervailing duties based on pre-existing obligations does not make it impossible for any party to the WTO Agreement to meet its obligations. Moreover, in Brazil's view, the interpretation of Article 18 proposed by the Philippines would conflict with the requirement of Article 28 of the Vienna Convention that a treaty not be applied retroactively unless the parties agreed to such retroactive application. For the Panel to accept the Philippine interpretation would mean that the conduct of all investigations begun prior to 1 January 1995 is subject to WTO review under Article VI of GATT 1994. Brazil considered it unlikely that such a major step would have been contemplated by the negotiators without an express provision in the text.

41.   Brazil noted that under Article 32.3 of the SCM Agreement, WTO Members have immediate rights with respect to any countervailing duty investigation or review initiated based on an application filed on or after 1 January 1995. In addition, Members have the right to challenge the conduct of a countervailing duty investigation at any time in the investigation proceeding; they do not have to wait until the investigation is completed. WTO Members also have the right to request the national authorities to review any pre-1995 investigation, which review would be subject to WTO obligations and could be challenged under the DSU. Further, the transition decisions of the Tokyo Round SCM Committee give

the signatories to the Tokyo Round SCM Code, including the Philippines, the right through 31 December 1996 to challenge an investigation initiated prior to 1 January 1995, under the procedures of the Tokyo Round SCM Code.

(b) Article 32.3 of the SCM Agreement

42.   Brazil argued that Article VI of GATT 1994 must be considered in conjunction with the SCM Agreement. Article II:2 of the Marrakesh Agreement Establishing the World Trade Organization (the "Marrakesh Agreement") states that the "agreements and associated legal instruments", including the SCM Agreement and GATT 1994, are integral parts of the Marrakesh Agreement. Moreover, Article 10 of the SCM Agreement states that "Members shall take all necessary steps to ensure that the imposition of a countervailing duty ... is in accordance with the provisions of Article VI of GATT 1994 *and* the terms of this Agreement ... " (emphasis added). Thus, in Brazil's view, Article II:2 of the Marrakesh Agreement and Article 10 of the SCM Agreement contemplate that Article VI of GATT 1994 and the SCM Agreement must be considered together. Brazil asserted that, considered together, Article 32.3 states explicitly that they do not apply to investigations begun before 1 January 1995. In Brazil's view, this was a necessary corollary of the integrated nature of the WTO. Otherwise, a Panel could interpret an article of GATT 1994 in a manner different than the detailed WTO Agreement on the same subject matter.

43.   The Philippines disputed Brazil's position that Article VI of GATT 1994 and the SCM Agreement must be invoked together. The Philippines noted that language virtually identical to Article 10 of the SCM Agreement was found in the Tokyo Round SCM Code. Yet, this had not precluded signatories to that Code from invoking only Article VI of GATT 1947 in dispute resolution. In this regard, the Philippines also noted that, in the *Reformulated Gasoline* dispute, both the Panel and the Appellate Body resolved the dispute with reference only to GATT 1994, and did not address the requirements of the Agreement on Technical Barriers to Trade, which had also been invoked by the complaining parties as applicable to the disputed U.S. measures.

44.   The Philippines contended that Brazil's position regarding Article 32.3 misrepresented the scope and functions of that provision. The Philippines took the position that Article 32.3 clearly applies only to procedural obligations under the SCM Agreement - not GATT 1994 or the Agreement on Agriculture - and only to the obligations relating to investigations. In the Philippines' view, Article 32.3 could not be used to bar a claim premised on a substantive right clearly provided for in Article VI of GATT 1994. The purpose of this provision was to prevent WTO Members from having to redo investigations which were started before they were bound by the SCM Agreement in order to apply the new and more detailed procedural requirements governing the conduct of investigations set out in that Agreement. In addition, Article 32.3 was needed to clarify at which stage in ongoing investigations the switch to the new procedural requirements of the SCM Agreement would have to take place. In the Philippines' view, these

rationales underlying Article 32.3 did not apply to the requirements of Article VI of GATT 1994 because the standards under that provision are not textually different from those of Article VI of GATT 1947, which already existed for WTO Members who were also Contracting Parties of GATT 1947 at the time of the entry into force of the WTO Agreement.

45. Brazil agreed with the Philippines that the purpose of Article 32.3 was to prevent WTO Members from having to redo investigations which were started before they were bound by the SCM Agreement. Brazil maintained that this was precisely the situation at issue here. The Philippines was attempting to use the WTO to object to an investigation begun before Brazil was bound by the WTO Agreements. Brazil did not believe it should have to redo an investigation to conform to obligations that did not exist when the investigation was started.

46. The Philippines also maintained that Brazil's interpretation of Article 32.3 obscured the rights and obligations of WTO Members who were not signatories to the Tokyo Round SCM Code. In the Philippines' view, if Article VI of GATT 1994 were deemed inapplicable to investigations conducted prior to the entry into force of the WTO Agreement, such Members would be denied any remedy against countervailing measures imposed on them after the entry into force of the WTO Agreement. The Philippines maintained that this result could not have been contemplated by the WTO Agreement.

47. The Philippines argued that Article 32.3 of the SCM Agreement does not automatically preclude the application of the SCM Agreement to measures imposed after the date of entry into force of the WTO Agreement pursuant to investigations initiated prior to the entry into force of the WTO Agreement. Indeed, Article 32.3 provides that a review of an existing measure, i.e. one in existence on the date of entry into force of the WTO Agreement, initiated pursuant to an application filed after the entry into force of the WTO Agreement, is subject to the requirements of the SCM Agreement. Obviously, the investigation that preceded such an existing measure would have been initiated prior to the entry into force of the WTO Agreement. Thus, in the Philippines' view the fact that an investigation was initiated prior to the effective date of the WTO does not, as such, preclude application of the SCM Agreement if that investigation leads to a measure imposed after the effective date of the WTO which then becomes the subject of review under the WTO. Moreover, the Philippines noted that the measure in question here was not imposed prior to the effective date of the WTO Agreement, and thus was not an existing measure as of that date. Thus, in the Philippines' view, Article 32.3 did not resolve the question of what law was applicable to the measure.

48. The Philippines argued that Brazil could not be surprised at the substance of the standards under GATT 1994, and thus there was no inequity in subjecting the measures imposed after the effective date of that agreement to its requirements. The provisions of Articles I, II and VI of GATT 1994 were identical to those of Articles I, II and VI of GATT 1947, which applied to both Brazil and the Philippines. The text of the provisions of GATT 1947 applied when the in-

vestigation was initiated, and the provisions of GATT 1994 were in effect in 1995 when Brazil imposed the countervailing duties. The Philippines therefore was not asking the Panel to apply to the measures rules whose content did not already exist when the procedures that led to their imposition were initiated, and when the countervailing duties were imposed.

49.   In Brazil's view, the fact that the language of Article VI of GATT 1994 is the same as the language of Article VI of GATT 1947 did not permit retroactive application of the provisions of GATT 1994 to the measures in question. Brazil noted that, according to Article II:4 of the Marrakesh Agreement, GATT 1994 and GATT 1947 are legally distinct documents. Thus, the obligations of GATT 1947 are not legally binding once it terminated on 31 December 1995, and because of their legally distinct status, application of GATT 1994 would be retroactive application which is contrary to customary rules of public international law.

50.   The Philippines asserted that the legal distinction between GATT 1947 and GATT 1994 was not intended to preclude WTO Members from invoking GATT 1994 as against identical provisions in GATT 1947, but rather to avoid the "free-rider" problem posed by the prospect of GATT 1947 Contracting Parties demanding and obtaining WTO benefits on the basis of the most-favoured-nation clause in GATT 1947. Thus, in the Philippines' view, the legal distinction between GATT 1947 and GATT 1994 did not support Brazil's position on retroactivity. The Philippines also referred to the decision of the Appellate Body in *Reformulated Gasoline*, which noted that the relevant provisions in that case had not changed as a result of the Uruguay Round negotiations. The Philippines argued that the legal distinction between GATT 1947 and GATT 1994 did not bar the interpretation of the latter in light of the former.

(c)   Transition Decisions of the Tokyo Round SCM Committee

51.   The Philippines argued that the Tokyo Round SCM Committee's Decision on Transitional Co-Existence of the Agreement on Interpretation and Application of Articles VI, XVI and XXIII of the General Agreement on Tariffs and Trade and the Marrakesh Agreement Establishing the World Trade Organization ("Decision on Transitional Co-Existence")[11] accorded a temporary and limited right to look to the Tokyo Round SCM Code even after its termination, but was not intended to curtail the right of a WTO Member to resort to the dispute settlement procedures of the WTO. The Philippines noted that the Decision on Transitional Co-Existence provided that the Tokyo Round SCM Code would "continue to apply with respect to any countervailing duty investigation or review which is not subject to application of the WTO [Subsidies] Agreement pursuant to the terms

---

[11]   SCM/186 (adopted 8 December 1994).

of Article 32.3 of that Agreement". The Philippines referred to sub-paragraph (d) of the Decision on Transitional Co-Existence, which provides in pertinent part that:

> "With respect to such disputes for which consultations are requested after the date of this Decision, signatories and panels will be guided by Article 19 of the Understanding on Rules and Procedures Governing the Settlement of Disputes in Annex 2 of the WTO Agreement".

In turn, Article 19 of the DSU (as well as Article 3.2 to which it refers) cautions that a WTO Panel "cannot add to or diminish the rights and obligations provided in the [WTO] covered agreements". Thus, in the Philippines' view, the Decision on Transitional Co-Existence is not in derogation of a WTO Member's right to invoke the WTO Agreement.

52.   In the Philippines' view, the Decision on Transitional Co-Existence recognized that invocation of the WTO Agreement was not constrained by any Tokyo Round SCM Code obligations. Indeed, the Decision indicates that a Member's invocation of the WTO Agreement precluded another Member from objecting based on any purported inconsistency with the Tokyo Round SCM Code.

53.   Brazil took a different view of the effect of the transition decisions of the Tokyo Round SCM Committee. Brazil argued that the Decision on Transitional Co-Existence and the Decision on Consequences of Withdrawal from or Termination of the Agreement on Interpretation and Application of Articles VI, XVI and XXIII of the General Agreement on Tariffs and Trade ("Decision on Consequences of Termination")[12] reflected the intent that there would be no retroactive application of the new Agreements. In Brazil's view, the Decision on Transitional Co-Existence, by permitting, but not requiring, the adoption during the transition period of any measure consistent with the SCM Agreement, regardless of whether it was consistent with Tokyo Round SCM Code obligations, gives some guidance on the applicable law. Because it does not require parties to adopt immediately measures consistent with the WTO, it contemplates the continuing application of Tokyo Round SCM Code obligations, at least to the measures initiated under the Tokyo Round SCM Code. Paragraph 2(a), referred to by the Philippines in its requests for dispute settlement proceedings, permits disputes to be brought in accordance with the DSU but does not address what law is applicable in considering the dispute. Finally, the Decision on Transitional Co-Existence provides that for its purposes the Tokyo Round SCM Code terminated one year after entry into force of the WTO, i.e. on 31 December 1995. Thus, in accordance with this Decision, the Tokyo Round SCM Code is terminated and was terminated before this Panel was requested. Therefore, the Philippines' reliance on this Decision as a basis for this Panel was unfounded.

---

[12]   SCM/187 (adopted 8 December 1994).

54.   Brazil also argued that the Decision on Consequences of Termination addresses disputes arising once the Tokyo Round SCM Code was terminated, as is the case here. It provides, *inter alia*, that for dispute settlement purposes, the Tokyo Round SCM Committee shall continue in force for two years after the entry into force of the WTO, i.e. through 31 December 1996. Thus, in Brazil's view, during 1996 the Decision on Consequences of Termination controls disputes originating out of a countervailing duty investigation begun before 1 January 1995, as is the case here. Paragraph (a) provides that the Tokyo Round SCM Code shall continue to apply with respect to any investigation or review begun prior to the entry into force of the WTO. Brazil maintained that this was consistent with Article 32.3 of the SCM Agreement, allowing for coverage of all subsidies disputes. Brazil contended that, in accordance with the Decision on Consequences of Termination, the applicable law for the current dispute is the Tokyo Round SCM Code. The Decision on Consequences of Termination also provides, in paragraph (d), for disputes to be raised in accordance with "rules and procedures for the settlement of disputes arising under the Agreement applicable immediately prior to the date of entry into force of the WTO Agreement" for any disputes arising out of an investigation or review begun prior to entry into force of the WTO.

55.   In Brazil's view, the Philippines' reliance on one provision of paragraph (d) of the Decision on Consequences of Termination in support of its claim that GATT 1994 applies reads that provision out of context. Paragraph (d) states that the dispute rules in effect immediately prior to entry into force of the WTO apply, but that if consultations are requested after entry into force of the WTO Agreement, Article 19 of the DSU shall guide panels. Article 19 of the DSU says only that, where a violation is found, the Panel shall recommend that the violating Member bring its measure into conformity with the violated agreement and may suggest ways the recommendations could be implemented. This does not, in Brazil's view, mean either that the complaint can be brought under the DSU or that GATT 1994 or its covered agreements constitute the applicable law. Brazil noted that the Decision on Consequences of Termination will remain in effect through 31 December 1996, and therefore, the Philippines has had and will continue to have recourse to dispute settlement under the Tokyo Round SCM Code until 1 January 1997.[13]

---

[13]   In this regard, Brazil noted that, in the anti-dumping area, where there are similar transition agreements, Canada had recently requested conciliation under the 1979 Tokyo Round Anti-Dumping Code against Mexico, (ADP/142), the United States had recently held consultations (under the auspices of the 1979 Tokyo Round Anti-Dumping Code) with Brazil on the Brazilian imposition of anti-dumping duties on blood collection tubes from the United States, and the United States had been considering requesting consultations on the EU anti-dumping duties on soda ash from the United States. These proceedings indicated that, under facts similar to those at issue here, Canada and the United States continued to have recourse to, and Canada, Mexico, and the United States consider the appropriate rules and forum for resolving disputes involving an investigation initiated under a Tokyo Round Code, to be the Tokyo Round Code, not Article VI of GATT 1994. Brazil

56.   The Philippines argued that whatever the effect of the Tokyo Round SCM Committee's transition   decisions, a decision of the signatories to the Tokyo Round SCM Code did not bind the Members of the WTO, the majority of which were not signatories to that Code. While the signatories to the Tokyo Round SCM Code may have decided to adjust their rights and obligations under that Code to take into account the existence of the WTO Agreement, the WTO adopted no corresponding decision on the coexistence of the Tokyo Round SCM Code and the WTO Agreement. Nor did WTO Members adopt any other decision that could be interpreted as an understanding that Members' rights under the WTO Agreement are in any way diminished by the existence or continued application of the Tokyo Round SCM Code. Hence, the Philippines argued that as a WTO Member, it was free to enforce its rights under the WTO Agreement.

(d)   Right to Choose Legal Basis for Claims

57.   The Philippines considered it well established that where a party has alternative legal grounds upon which to base its claim, the party has the right to choose the legal basis for its claim, and suggested that to question that right would be to deny the complaining party its rights under any agreements that the other party argues should not be applied. In this regard, the Philippines referred to the Panel decisions in *United States - Countervailing Duties on Fresh, Chilled and Frozen Pork from Canada* (adopted 11 July 1991), BISD 38S/30 ("*Pork*") and *EEC - Payments and Subsidies Paid to Processors and Producers of Oilseeds and Related Animal-Feed Proteins* (adopted 25 January 1990), BISD 37S/116, para. 110 ("*Oilseeds*"). In those cases, the decision of GATT Contracting Parties who were also signatories to the Tokyo Round SCM Code to proceed under provisions of the GATT 1947, rather than the Tokyo Round SCM Code, was not questioned by the respective Panels.

58.   In the Philippines' view, there were important legal and policy or institutional reasons why panels have consistently respected the right of the participants to choose the legal basis of their claims. This right permits the participants in the multilateral trading system to choose the instrument that contains the most favourable substantive provisions and that is most effectively enforced. It thereby strengthens the multilateral trading order.

59.   The Philippines noted in particular that in *Pork*, Canada chose to invoke its rights under GATT 1947 rather than the Tokyo Round SCM Code apparently because the dispute settlement procedures of the Tokyo Round Agreements had broken down. The fact that Canada had the choice of invoking its GATT rights furthered the objectives of the system, which might otherwise have been wholly frustrated. Similarly, the Philippines in this case considered the dispute settlement procedures and covered agreements of the WTO to be more effective than

---

argued that subsequent practice of the parties to a treaty is one of the primary sources for interpretation of that treaty, referring to Article 31.3(b) of the Vienna Convention.

those of the now-terminated Tokyo Round SCM Code. The Philippines believed that, by choosing to exercise its rights under the WTO Agreement, it furthered its trade interests as well as the interests of all participants in the multilateral trading system by invoking the most effective instrument currently available governing the application of countervailing duties.

60.   Brazil argued that the Philippines' position that it could resort to dispute settlement under the WTO, invoking GATT 1994, because WTO dispute settlement was more effective did not affect the central issue of determining what set of obligations were in force during the investigation in order to determine the appropriate procedures for dispute settlement. In Brazil's view, there was no support for the choice of dispute settlement procedures on the basis of what is considered "most effective" independent of the alleged violation. There are specific dispute settlement procedures for each case and GATT 1994 obligations cannot be invoked for past acts merely because one Member considers its dispute settlement procedures "more effective" than those of the applicable law. Brazil argued that there should be a clear separation between the dispute settlement procedures a Member may invoke and the obligations concerning the investigation process. Under the Philippines's view, Brazil argued, it would be possible to invoke GATT 1994 dispute settlement procedures at any time and, as a consequence, it would be possible to invoke the WTO DSU with regard to obligations under any prior agreement whatsoever.

61.   The Philippines clarified that it had identified the greater effectiveness of dispute settlement under the DSU as one of its reasons for exercising the right to proceed under the WTO and not the Tokyo Round SCM Code, not as the basis of that right. In the Philippines's view, that right existed independently of the complaining party's reasons for invoking it. For example, the Philippines argued that the Panels in *Pork* and *Oilseeds* had not conditioned the exercise of parties' rights to choose dispute settlement under GATT 1947 rather than under the applicable Tokyo Round SCM Code on the reasons, motives or purposes of the complaining party for exercising that right. The Philippines stated that its principal reason for considering the WTO dispute settlement mechanism more effective was that, under the WTO system, Brazil would not have the ability to block the report of this Panel on the merits that it would have had under the old GATT system. The Philippines asserted that Brazil had, in the past, blocked adoption of a panel report, referring to *Non-Rubber Footwear* (report issued 4 October 1989, adopted 13 June 1995).

62.   Brazil took issue with the suggestion that it would block a panel report under the Tokyo Round SCM Code, thus rendering dispute settlement ineffective. Brazil asserted that every panel report in a dispute involving Brazil had been adopted.

(e)   Interpretation of Article VI of GATT 1994

63.   Brazil also argued that if the Panel decided that Article VI of GATT 1994 applies to this dispute, it must be interpreted without reference to the substantive

provisions of the Tokyo Round SCM Code or the SCM Agreement. The Tokyo Round SCM Code interpreted Articles VI, XVI and XXIII of GATT 1947, not GATT 1994. Article II:4 of the Marrakesh Agreement specifically states that the two GATTs are legally distinct. Moreover, except for the extension of dispute resolution under the Decision on Consequences of Termination, the Tokyo Round SCM Code terminated on 31 December 1995 by agreement of the signatories to the Code. Therefore, it cannot be applied to interpret Article VI of GATT 1994. Moreover, Brazil argued that to apply the rights and obligations contained in the Tokyo Round SCM Code would either add to or diminish the rights and obligations provided for in Article VI of GATT 1994 - an action prohibited by Articles 3:2 and 19:2 of the DSU.

64.   Brazil argued that, if the Panel decided that Article VI of GATT 1994 could be applied to this dispute despite the fact that the SCM Agreement did not apply, the Panel should nonetheless reject all arguments raised by the Philippines that rely on concepts, rights, and obligations found in the Tokyo Round SCM Code or the SCM Agreement, but not found within the plain language of Article VI of GATT 1994. In this regard, Brazil noted certain arguments raised by the Philippines that, in Brazil's view, arose from concepts set forth in and requirements of the Tokyo Round SCM Code or the SCM Agreement that were not found in Article VI of GATT 1994. Brazil referred specifically to the argument that the Agrarian Land Reform programme is not a subsidy because it is of general application to all poor Philippine farmers, the argument that Brazil was required to consider whether there was a significant increase in imports, a price effect from the imports, and price depression or suppression in making an injury determination, and the argument that Brazil did not adequately examine other factors that adversely affected production of desiccated coconut. Brazil maintained that Article VI of GATT 1994 did not contain a requirement for a finding of specificity in determining the existence of a subsidy, and did not contain any requirements on the analysis of injury.

65.   The Philippines noted out that Article XVI:1 of the Marrakesh Agreement permits WTO dispute settlement panels to seek guidance from "decisions, procedures and customary practices followed by the CONTRACTING PARTIES to GATT 1947 and the bodies established in the framework of GATT 1947". The Philippines also observed that in *Reformulated Gasoline*, both the Panel and the Appellate Body sought guidance from old GATT decisions. In addition, the Philippines asserted that the Panel in *Non-Rubber Footwear* had acknowledged that certain interpretations of Article VI of GATT 1947 antedated, and were merely reflected by, the Tokyo Round SCM Code.[14]

---

[14]   *Non-Rubber Footwear*, para. 4.10.

(f)   Application of the Agreement on Agriculture

66.   Brazil also argued that application of the Agreement on Agriculture to this dispute would constitute retroactive application and that there was no agreement among the parties to such retroactive application. In addition, Brazil maintained that Article 13 of the Agreement on Agriculture cannot apply if the SCM Agreement does not apply. Since the SCM Agreement - by the terms of Article 32.3 - does not apply to this dispute, Article 13 of the Agreement on Agriculture also cannot apply.

67.   Brazil noted that the chapeau of Article 13 is based specifically on the provisions of GATT 1994 *and* the SCM Agreement. Article 13 acts as a constraint upon actions taken under the combined auspices of GATT 1994 and the SCM Agreement. Because this dispute is not under the auspices of the SCM Agreement, because of the wording of Article 32.3 of that Agreement, Article 13 cannot apply to this dispute. In addition, Article 13 constrains countervailing duties as defined in footnote 4 to Article 13. That footnote states that the countervailing duties so constrained "are those covered by Article VI of GATT 1994 and Part V of the Agreement on Subsidies and Countervailing Measures". Therefore, for Article 13 to be applicable, the duties at issue must be covered by Part V of the SCM Agreement as well as by Article VI of GATT 1994. Because the SCM Agreement does not apply to this investigation or the resulting duties, by reason of Article 32.3, the countervailing duties at issue in this dispute cannot be subject to Article 13 of the Agreement on Agriculture.

68.   The Philippines argued that Brazil's reading of Article 13 of the Agreement on Agriculture was strained and stilted. In the Philippines' view, the word "and" in Article 13 of the Agriculture Agreement must be understood in the disjunctive sense and thus did not limit the applicability of the Agreement on Agriculture only to situations where both Article VI of GATT 1994 and the SCM Agreement must be invoked. Rather, that provision means that the Agreement on Agriculture applies to situations covered by either Article VI of GATT 1994 or the SCM Agreement, or both.

2.   Terms of Reference

69.   Brazil argued that, in its first submission to the Panel, the Philippines had sought to broaden the scope of the terms of reference beyond the matters set forth in its request for establishment of a panel, which request defines the substantive mandate of the Panel. Brazil identified the following as being beyond the proper scope of the Panel's terms of reference:

(a)   Articles I and II of GATT 1994.

(b)   Brazil's failure to revoke the Ordinance and reimburse duties collected based on representations by the Philippines as a violation of Article VI of GATT 1994.

(c)   Brazil's refusal to consult under GATT 1994 as inconsistent with its obligations.

(d)   Article 13 of the Agreement on Agriculture.

(e)   Brazil's injury determination.

70.   Brazil referred to Article 6.2 of the DSU, which provides in part that "The request for the establishment of a panel shall be made in writing. It shall indicate whether consultations were held, identify the specific measures at issue and provide a brief summary of the legal basis of the complaint sufficient to present the problem clearly". Brazil asserted that Article 6.2 of the DSU reflects substantial past panel practice that each claim in a dispute must be specified with some particularity within the documents included in the terms of reference. In this regard, Brazil referred to the report of the Panel in *Cotton Yarn*, where the Panel stated that "the fundamental purpose" of the terms of reference is to give advance notice to the defendant and third parties of the claim at issue and therefore, the claim had to be "expressly referred to" in the request for establishment of a panel in order to be within the terms of reference.[15] Brazil also referred to the report of the Panel in *Salmon*, which noted that the term "matter" identified in the terms of reference "consisted of the specific claims stated by Norway in these documents [the Panel Request and addendum] with respect to the imposition of these duties by the United States".[16] The Panel further addressed the importance of the notice function of the terms of reference:

> "The notice function of terms of reference was particularly important in providing the basis for each Party to determine how its interests might be affected and whether it would wish to exercise its right to participate in a dispute as an interested third party. The Panel observed that terms of reference often were standard terms of reference, as in the present dispute, in which the definition of the matter had been supplied by a written statement prepared entirely by the complaining Party. In the light of these considerations, the Panel concluded that a matter, including each claim composing that matter, could not be examined by a panel under the Agreement unless that same matter was within the scope of, and had been identified in, the written statement or statements referred to or contained in the terms of reference".[17]

Brazil also noted that in *Non-Rubber Footwear MFN*,[18] the Panel had found that the terms of reference were limited to matters raised by Brazil in its request for establishment of a panel. Thus, Brazil argued that the requirement that the claims

---

[15]   *Cotton Yarn*, para. 463.

[16]   *Salmon*, para. 212.

[17]   *Salmon*, para. 208. Brazil noted that this point was reiterated in the companion anti-dumping Panel report. *United States - Imposition of Anti-Dumping Duties on Imports of Fresh and Chilled Atlantic Salmon from Norway*, ADP/187 (adopted 24 April 1994) ("*Salmon ADP*"), para. 336.

[18]   *Non-Rubber Footwear MFN*, para. 6.2.

be stated with some particularity in the request for establishment of a panel (or other documents included within the terms of reference) is a long-standing practice that was explicitly recognized by Article 6.2 of the DSU.

71.   The Philippines asserted that its requests for relief did not broaden the terms of reference. The Philippines contended that Article 6.2 of the DSU requires only that the statement of a claim be specific enough "to present the problem clearly", which it contended was the case here. The Philippines also noted that the standard terms of reference under the old GATT system ("examine in the light of the relevant GATT provisions") differed from the standard terms of reference under Articles 7.1 and 7.2 of the DSU ("address the relevant provisions in any covered agreement cited by the parties"). In the Philippines' view, the latter more sharply defines the Panel's mandate to address the "relevant" provisions in the cited agreements, not only "cited" provisions. Moreover, the Philippines asserted that, unlike Part F(a) of the Montreal *Improvements to the GATT Dispute Settlement Rules and Procedures*, L/6489 (13 April 1989), Article 6.2 of the DSU omits any reference to a complaint's "factual" basis and simply requires a summary of the complaint's "legal" basis. The Philippines argued that some of Brazil's criticisms confused the notion of "claims" with the concepts of "relevant provisions" and the relief requested.

(a)   Articles I and II of GATT 1994

72.   Brazil argued that Articles I and II of GATT 1994 were not even mentioned in any of the documents referred to in the terms of reference. Thus, any claims under those Articles were beyond the scope of the Panel's mandate. Brazil further maintained that the Philippines' claim that Brazil had violated Article VI of GATT 1994 was not a sufficient basis from which to infer a claim of violation of Articles I and II of GATT 1994. A claim under Articles I and II must be specifically identified. In this regard, Brazil referred to the Panel decision in *Non-Rubber Footwear MFN*.[19] In that case, the Panel disallowed claims under Articles X and XXIII:1(b) and (c) of GATT 1947 because it found that although the question of discrimination had been raised, it had not been raised in such a way in the request for establishment of a panel as to implicate Article X. With respect to Article XXIII:1(b) and (c), the Panel found that Brazil had argued the United States had acted inconsistently with its obligations but had not claimed that benefits accruing to it under the General Agreement were nullified or impaired. Therefore, the Panel found that matters raised by Brazil with respect to Article XXIII:1(b) and (c) were not within the terms of reference of the Panel.[20] Brazil maintained that this case was similar, in that the Philippine request for establishment of a panel argued that Brazil's actions were inconsistent with Article VI of

---

[19]   *Non-Rubber Footwear MFN*, para. 6.2.
[20]   *Non-Rubber Footwear MFN*.

GATT 1994, but did not claim that they were inconsistent with its obligations under Articles I and II of GATT 1994.

73.   The Philippines argued that Articles I and II of GATT 1994 are covered by the terms of reference because they are relevant provisions of the agreement, GATT 1994, cited by the Philippines. The Philippines asserted that Articles I and II lay down the general rule of non-discrimination, to which Article VI is an exception, citing the *Pork* Panel, para. 4.4. In the Philippines' view, Articles 7:1 and 2 of the DSU indicate that, while a panel's mandate is limited to the agreement cited by the parties in the terms of reference, a panel is authorized to examine and base its ruling on all relevant provisions of the cited agreement, in this case, GATT 1994. The Philippines considered Articles I and II relevant because they lay down the most-favoured-nation principle and the commitment to tariff bindings to which Article VI allows a limited exception for the imposition of countervailing duties.

(b)   Failure to Revoke and Reimburse

74.   Brazil noted that the request for establishment of a panel sought a finding that the imposition of the duties was a violation of Article VI of GATT 1994, and a recommendation that the duties be revoked and reimbursed. However, in Brazil's view, this did not constitute a claim that a failure to revoke the measure and reimburse duties prior to the completion of the dispute settlement process was itself a violation of GATT 1994. Brazil argued that it was incomprehensible how a failure to revoke the measure and reimburse duties could possibly constitute a violation of GATT 1994 in the absence of a finding that the imposition of the measure was inconsistent with its obligations.

75.   The Philippines argued that its request for relief concerning Brazil's failure to revoke the measure and reimburse the collected duties simply addressed Brazil's continued implementation of its countervailing measure despite Philippine representations on the impropriety of that measure. The Philippines clarified that it was simply requesting the Panel to include reimbursement of duties paid under the disputed measure among the reliefs to be granted to the Philippines, referring to WT/DS22/5, page 2, penultimate paragraph, sub-paragraph 2.

(c)   Failure to Consult

76.   Brazil recognized that the request for establishment of a panel described the Philippines' view of the consultation history, but denied that this in itself stated a claim before the Panel. Brazil noted that the consultation history is usually included in a request for establishment of a panel, but argued that it does not constitute the basis of a claim in its own right unless a specific claim was identified in the request for establishment of a panel, which Brazil maintained was not the case here.

77.   The Philippines contended that Brazil's argument that the description of the consultation history cannot form the basis of a claim merely begs the question

whether a refusal to consult, which would of course be part of the consultation history, could be the subject matter of a claim. The Philippines maintained that its request for establishment of a panel accused Brazil of refusing a request for consultations under Article XXIII:1 and alleged a failure to enter into consultations with the Philippines in accordance with XXIII:1 of GATT 1994, thereby violating its obligations under Article XXIII:1 of GATT 1994 and Article 4 of the DSU.

(d)   Injury and the Agreement on Agriculture

78.   Brazil argued that the Philippines' claims regarding injury and the Agreement on Agriculture did not meet the requirement of Article 6.2 of the DSU that a request for establishment of a panel "identify the specific measures at issue and provide a brief summary of the legal basis of the complaint sufficient to present the problem clearly". In Brazil's view, none of the points set forth in the Philippines' request for establishment of a panel stated the legal basis of any claim with respect to injury or the Agreement on Agriculture. Brazil noted that document WT/DS22/3 and statements made by Brazil and the Philippines at the DSB meeting where the request for establishment of a panel was first discussed addressed only the question of applicable law. Thus, in Brazil's view, the only basis for raising claims concerning the injury determination or the Agreement on Agriculture would be the request for establishment of a panel itself. Brazil recognized that WT/DS22/5 contained a citation to paragraph 6(a) of Article VI of GATT 1994, implicitly referencing injury, and a citation to Article 13 of the WTO Agreement on Agriculture. However, Brazil noted that the term injury was not even used in the request for establishment of a panel, although it did refer to like product. That reference was in the context of the subsidy calculation, not injury. Thus, in Brazil's view, no claim was raised with respect to like product in the context of Brazil's determination of injury. Moreover, Brazil contended that there was no explanation of how the Philippines considered Brazil to have violated either the injury requirement of Article VI, or Article 13 of the Agreement on Agriculture. Thus, in Brazil's view, the request for establishment of a panel did not state a claim with respect to either provision.

79.   In this regard, Brazil cited the Panel report in *Cotton Yarn* as providing a description of what constitutes a claim. According to that report, "a claim [is] the specification of the particular legal and factual basis upon which it was alleged that a provision of this Agreement had been breached".[21] The Panel also noted that since there may be more than one legal basis for alleging the breach of the same provision of the Agreement a claim for one would not constitute a claim for the other.[22] Finally, the Panel indicated that the legal basis for the claim must be

---

[21]   *Cotton Yarn*, para. 444.
[22]   *Cotton Yarn*, para. 444.

described in the documents within the terms of reference.[23] Since, in Brazil's view, none of the documents within the terms of reference of this Panel provided any description of the legal or factual basis for the Philippines' claims regarding injury and the Agreement on Agriculture, such claims were not within the terms of reference of this Panel.

80.   The Philippines maintained that its request for establishment of a panel adequately set forth a claim pertaining to Brazil's injury determination, and that Brazil had had notice that the Philippines considered that determination deficient. The Philippines noted that Brazil recognized that the request for establishment of a panel implicitly referred to the issue of injury by citing Article VI:6(a) of GATT 1994. Moreover, the Philippines' request also discussed like product in the context of criticizing Brazil's calculation of the countervailing duty, in addition to the calculation of the subsidy. In this connection, the Philippines' request noted that Brazil was a producer of coconuts and desiccated coconut, both of which are available in the domestic market of Brazil. Thus, in the Philippines' view, Brazil was duly apprised that the Philippines was contesting Brazil's injury findings.

81.   The Philippines referred to the report of the Panel in *Cotton Yarn* as having recognized that a general criticism of an anti-dumping methodology can encompass more specific aspects of that methodology. *Cotton Yarn*, para. 463. The Philippines' criticism of Brazil's injury and causation findings simply related to the basic requirement of Article VI.6(a) of GATT 1994 that such determinations be based on adequate facts and reasons. The thrust of that criticism was that Brazil had relied on indeterminate and inconsistent facts, some of which undercut Brazil's own conclusions, and advanced reasons that could not be supported by such indeterminate facts. In the Philippines' view, these asserted deficiencies were sufficiently encompassed by the basic criticism that the injury findings were inconsistent with Article VI:6(a) of GATT 1994. Moreover, the Philippines pointed out that following an informal meeting between the parties on 27 October 1995 the Philippines had sent Brazil a letter requesting additional information about Brazil's injury determination, which showed that Brazil was fully aware of the Philippines' questions about Brazil's injury determination.

82.   Finally, the Philippines asserted that its request for a ruling on the measure's inconsistency with the Agreement on Agriculture was a sufficient statement of a claim of violation of that Agreement. The Philippines' request for establishment of a panel clearly alleged that the disputed measure was inconsistent with Article 13 of the Agreement on Agriculture, and asserted that the investigated programmes, as implemented by a developing country like the Philippines, should not have been considered as subsidies *per se*. In the Philippine's view, Brazil was put sufficiently on notice concerning the Philippines' claims under the Agreement on Agriculture.

---

[23]   *Cotton Yarn*, para. 456.

83.   In Brazil's view, the Philippines' argument invited the Panel to ignore the requirement set forth in Article 6:2 of the DSU that the request for establishment of a panel must "provide a brief summary of the legal basis of the complaint sufficient to present the problem clearly". Brazil asserted that, in arguing that Brazil was on notice concerning the Philippines' claims regarding injury, despite the fact that the request for establishment of a panel does not even mention the term "injury," merely because Brazil had received questions from the Philippines raising concerns about the injury finding during the course of the informal bilateral consultations, the Philippines failed to recognize the importance of the notice function of the panel request. Brazil further noted that the questions referred to by the Philippines concerned Brazil's injury determination in light of Brazil's obligations under the Tokyo Round SCM Code. Thus, in Brazil's view, these questions did not provide any notice of concern under GATT 1994.

84.   Brazil argued that whether issues are raised in the process leading up to a request for establishment of a panel is a separate question from whether they are properly within the terms of reference of the Panel by being set forth in the documents cited in the terms of reference. Brazil argued that previous Panels have recognized the importance of the notice function, not just for the party against whom the complaint is made, but, equally importantly, for third parties in order to enable them to determine whether their interests are affected by the dispute. In this regard, Brazil referred to the Panel decision in *Salmon*, where the Panel stated:

> "The Panel considered that the terms of reference served two purposes: definition of the scope of a panel proceeding, and provision of notice to the defending signatory and other signatories that could be affected by the panel decision and the outcome of the dispute. The notice function in the terms of reference was particularly important in providing the basis for each signatory to determine how its interests might be affected and whether it would wish to exercise its right to participate in a dispute as an interested third party".[24]

More recently the *Cotton Yarn* Panel stated:

> "The Panel considered that it was not sufficient that a contention simply "can reasonably be interpreted" as amounting to a claim, as that implied there could be indeterminacy or ambiguity regarding the ambit of the claim. This would in the view of the Panel, run counter to the fundamental purpose of the terms of reference, which was to give advance notice to the defendant and to third parties of the claim at issue".[25]

---

[24]   *Salmon*, para. 208.
[25]   *Cotton Yarn*, para. 456.

Thus, in Brazil's view, the fact that the Philippines may have indicated concerns at prior stages of this dispute was an insufficient basis for the conclusion that they constituted claims within the terms of reference of the Panel, unless they were specifically stated in the request for establishment of a panel. Indeed, Brazil noted that issues could well have been discussed in the consultation process and then not raised before the Panel, as the clarification and resolution of issues if possible was one function of the consultations.

3. Burden of Proof

85. The Philippines took the position that the allowance of countervailing duties under Article VI:3 of GATT 1947 is an exception to the basic free trade principles of Article I:1 of GATT 1947. Accordingly, in the Philippines' view, Article VI:3 has been interpreted narrowly, and any party invoking it has the burden of proving compliance with its requirements.[26] These principles also apply to the identical provisions of GATT 1994. Thus, the Philippines argued that Brazil bore the burden of identifying positive evidence that its imposition of a countervailing measure against Philippine desiccated coconut met all requirements for the application of a countervailing measure under the exception provided for in Article VI. The Philippines asserted that, consistent with GATT 1947 precedents and practice, Article VI of GATT 1994 prohibits the imposition of a countervailing duty unless the following three elements are established: (a) a subsidy of the relevant product by the government of the exporting country; (b) material injury to the domestic industry producing the same or a like product in the importing country; and, (c) a causal relationship between the allegedly subsidized imports and the alleged injury to the pertinent domestic industry. The Philippines asserted that Brazil had failed to prove any of the necessary elements for the imposition of a countervailing duty.

86. Brazil took the position that longstanding panel practice required that the party that invokes the dispute settlement provisions substantiate its claims,[27] and that this burden was not shifted for disputes under Article VI. Brazil referred to several disputes in which, it asserted, Panels had chosen not to rule on the question of whether Article VI constituted an exception and had proceeded to accord the burden to the complaining party, just as with other GATT dispute settle-

---

[26] In support of this position, the Philippines referred to the Panel reports in *Pork*, para. 4.4, and *New Zealand - Imports of Electrical Transformers from Finland*, (adopted 18 July 1985), BISD 32S/55, para. 4:4.

[27] In this regard, Brazil cited the Panel reports in *Uruguayan Recourse to Article XXIII*, L/1923 (adopted 16 November 1962), BISD 11S/95, paras. 15-16 and *Canada - Import, Distribution and Sale of Certain Alcoholic Drinks by Provincial Marketing Agencies*, DS17/R (adopted 18 February 1992) ("*Alcoholic Drinks*"), BISD 39S/27, para. 5.3.

ments.[28] Thus, in Brazil's view, the burden in this case was on the Philippines to establish that Brazil's actions were inconsistent with its obligations.

87.   The Philippines argued that Brazil's reliance on the report of the Panel in *Uruguayan Recourse to Article XXIII* was mistaken and misleading. The Philippines argued that the Panel had concluded in that case that the complaining party has the burden of proof only in a *non-violation* complaint under Article XXIII:1(b).[29] However, in the Philippines' view, the Panel had recognized that in a violation complaint, the offending "action would *prima facie*, constitute a case of nullification or impairment".[30] As the Philippines' request for establishment of a panel made clear, this dispute involved a violation complaint under Article XXIII:1(a), in which the burden of proof was on Brazil as the party that imposed the countervailing duty. The Philippines also argued that Brazil's reliance on *Alcoholic Drinks* was misplaced and misleading. In the Philippines's view, the issue in that case involved whether the complaining party was required to prove the existence of the practices complained against where there was a factual dispute between the parties as to the existence of some of those practices.[31] The Panel concluded that it was necessary for the complaining party to prove the existence of the practices complained against before the Panel could evaluate those practices in light of GATT obligations. In this case, by contrast, there was no question that Brazil had imposed the countervailing measure at issue. Thus, the Philippines considered that it had satisfied the preliminary need to identify the existence of the disputed measure, which Brazil then had the burden of justifying.

88.   Brazil took the position that although it agreed with the Philippines' contention that in the case of a *prima facie* nullification or impairment of benefits, there was a presumption of adverse impact on the complaining party and the responding party bore the burden of rebutting that presumption, that was not the situation before this Panel. A case of *prima facie* nullification and impairment can be found only if an infringement of obligations is first found. In Brazil's view, the question before this Panel was whether there had been an infringement of Brazil's obligations in the first place. In that situation, Brazil considered that past practice indicated that the burden of proof was on the complaining party.

---

[28]   *Cotton Yarn*, para. 516, *EC - Anti-Dumping Duties on Audio Tapes in Cassettes Originating in Japan*, ADP/136 (unadopted, 28 April 1995) ("*Audiocassettes*") paras. 358-359, *Salmon ADP*, para. 483.
[29]   The Philippines also considered that Article 26:1(a) of the DSU recognizes that it is only with respect to non-violation complaints under Article XXIII:1(b) that the complainant bears the burden of "present[ing] a detailed justification in support of any complaint relating to a measure which does not conflict with the relevant covered agreement".
[30]   *Uruguayan Recourse to Article XXIII*, para. 15.
[31]   *Alcoholic Drinks*, para. 5.3.

4. Scope of the Panel's Examination of Brazil's Decision

89.   The Philippines asserted that, in examining whether Brazil's findings satisfied the prerequisites of Article VI of GATT 1994 for imposition of a countervailing measure, the Panel must examine the factual and legal reasons set forth in the Ordinance containing Brazil's final determination, but must disregard any alleged evidence and reasons not covered in the Ordinance itself, because to take into account considerations beyond the Ordinance would be tantamount to allowing a party to modify and rationalize its determination *ex post facto*.[32] In the Philippines' view, the Ordinance fell short of the requirements for the imposition of countervailing duties, in that Brazil did not identify adequate evidence and reasons to support its findings, and ignored evidence that favoured the Philippines.

90.   Brazil asserted that the Panel should examine not only the factual and legal reasoning set forth in the final Ordinance but also that set forth in DTIC Opinion 006/95. Brazil stated that, under Brazilian law, the Ordinance, published in the *Diario Official*, is a summary of the reasons and bases for its decision, which are reflected more fully in DTIC Opinion 006/95. Brazil noted that, in its first submission, the Philippines had repeatedly referred to another document, DTIC Opinion 004/95. Brazil asserted that the Philippines erred in referring to DTIC Opinion 004/95, because the final determination was based on DTIC Opinion 006/95.[33]

91.   Brazil stated that, while not published in the *Diario Official*, DTIC Opinion 006/95, which was signed by the individuals responsible for the investigation and preceded the published final Ordinance, was available to all interested parties upon request. Brazil maintained that consideration of DTIC Opinion 006/95 would not constitute an *ex post facto* modification or rationalization of Brazil's decision. Rather, Brazil contended, consideration of DTIC Opinion 006/95 would be consistent with prior panel practice, referring to the Panel reports in *Korea - Anti-Dumping Duties on Imports of Polyacetal Resins from the United States*, ADP/92 (adopted 27 April 1993) ("*Polyacetal Resins*"), BISD 40S/205, para. 211, and *Brazil - Imposition of Provisional and Definitive Countervailing Duties on Milk Powder and Certain Types of Milk from the European Economic Community*, SCM/179 (adopted 28 April 1994) ("*Milk Powder*"), para. 291. Brazil asserted that, unlike the transcript of deliberations the Panel declined to consider in *Polyacetal Resins*, DTIC Opinion 006/95 is a formal statement of the issues of fact and law considered material and the reasons and bases therefore,

---

[32]   However, the Philippines argued that the administrative record can be considered in connection with any relevant evidence that the Ordinance improperly ignored.

[33]   In this regard, Brazil noted that the Ordinance itself indicates that DTIC Opinion 004/95 is not the basis of the final determination. In its discussion of the case history, the Ordinance notes that after the 21 July 1995 meeting with the Conselho Tecnico Consultivo (Technical Consultative Counsel) at which DTIC Opinion 004/95 was considered, that opinion was discussed and the investigation was continued until additional information had been gathered.

signed by the investigating authorities responsible, and made publicly available to the interested parties. Moreover, following the Panel report in *Milk Powder*, where the Panel looked only at the explanation provided in the published notice of Brazil's determination, stating that "it could not have regard to factual reasons presented by Brazil to the Panel but not stated in the public notice of the findings or otherwise contained in a public statement of reasons issued by the Brazilian authorities at the time of that finding," the Brazilian authorities had revised their procedures. Consequently, in this investigation, DTIC Opinion 006/95 was issued by the Brazilian authorities at the time of the final finding and was publicly available to the interested parties upon request. Brazil noted that DTIC Opinion 006/95 was, in fact, requested and provided to one Philippine exporter. The co-petitioners had also requested and received a copy. Brazil maintained that the Philippine government was offered the opportunity to review the record and receive a copy of DTIC Opinion 006/95 but did not avail itself of the opportunity.[34] Thus, in Brazil's view, DTIC Opinion 006/95 is part of the public statement of reasons accompanying the final determination, along with the Ordinance published in the *Diario Official*, and must be considered in the Panel's review of Brazil's determination.

92.   The Philippines challenged Brazil's reliance on DTIC Opinion 006/95. The Philippines noted that this opinion was not mentioned in the Ordinance, although DTIC Opinion 004/95, dated 18 July 1995, was. Moreover, the Philippines asserted that it was unaware of the existence of DTIC Opinion 006/95 until it received Brazil's first submission, despite having requested that Brazil provide it with a copy of any internal memorandum relied upon in the determination. In the Philippines' view, DTIC Opinion 006/95 was at most a portion of the administrative record that could not be considered as a basis for the Ordinance's findings unless duly identified in the Ordinance itself. In this regard, the Philippines referred to the Panel report in *Milk Powder*, paras. 286-87, 291, 312:

> "The administrative record of an investigation did not constitute a statement of reasons but was simply a collection of documents containing facts and arguments. ... It was incumbent upon the investigating authorities to provide a reasoned opinion explaining how such facts and arguments had led to their finding. ... [T]o take into account ... considerations [beyond the Order imposing measures] would be tantamount to allowing a Party to modify and rationalize its determination *ex post facto*".

93.   The Philippines also referred to the report of the Panel in *Polyacetal Resins*, paras. 251-54 and 284, where the Panel did not consider data in a "staff re-

---

[34]   Brazil acknowledged that the Philippine government did request any memorandum that formed the basis of the final determination in a letter submitted a few days before the final decision was made. Under Brazilian practice DTIC Opinions are not final and part of the record until the final determination is made, so Brazil did not supply it at that time.

port" because it was not mentioned or discussed in, and thus was deemed not relied on by, the public statement of reasons for the determination. In the Philippines' view, DTIC Opinion 006/95 merely contained recommendations, and was not mentioned or discussed in the Ordinance, which should identify and explain any adopted recommendations.

94.   The Philippines considered Brazil's argument that DTIC Opinion 006/95 was part of the public statement of reasons, because it was a formal statement that was available to the interested parties, to be without merit. In this regard, the Philippines referred to the report of the Panel in *Milk Powder*, which stated "That [the investigated country] might have had access to the record containing the facts considered by the Brazilian authorities was irrelevant in ... respect" to the "lack of explanation of the reasons" for Brazil's findings. *Milk Powder*, para. 294. Moreover, the Philippines alleged that Brazil had precluded the Philippines' access to DTIC Opinion 006/95 by not mentioning it in the Ordinance, and had failed to provide the Philippines with a copy despite the fact that the Philippines had requested a copy of any internal memorandum that formed the basis of the determination in the Ordinance. The Philippines acknowledged that its request was made before the issuance of the Ordinance, but considered that this did not justify Brazil's failure to provide it with a copy after the Ordinance had been issued. The Philippines noted that the request from the Philippine exporter who did receive a copy of DTIC Opinion 006/95 was also received by Brazil before the issuance of the Ordinance. Moreover, the Philippines had continued to seek clarification from Brazil concerning the Ordinance, including a letter dated 27 October 1995, more than two months after issuance of the Ordinance, containing questions concerning Brazil's determination. However, Brazil had not taken that opportunity to provide the Philippines with a copy of DTIC Opinion 006/95, and had not even responded to the Philippines' questions. Thus, in the Philippines' view, Brazil itself had obstructed both the publicity and the accessibility of DTIC Opinion 006/95, and therefore could not rely on it in support of its determination as set forth in the Ordinance.

95.   Brazil responded that the cited previous panels' analyses regarding what documents to consider were based on procedural requirements of the Tokyo Round Codes, not of Article VI. Article VI of GATT 1994 did not require any public notice of the reasons or bases for the decision. In the view of Brazil, therefore, it was irrelevant under Article VI whether the documents were publicly available. As long as those documents were official, contemporaneous statements of the reason and bases of the decision, they should be considered by this Panel.

5.   Translation of DTIC Opinion 006/95

96.   On 12 June 1996, the second day of the Panel's first meeting with the parties, Brazil provided the Panel with a two-page document setting forth corrections to its translations of Interministerial Ordinance No. 11 and DTIC Opinion 006/95. Brazil indicated that the initial translation did not properly reflect the original Portuguese-language determinations.

97.   The Philippines objected to the consideration by the Panel of the corrected translations of the two texts. The Philippines considered that there were
substantive differences between the initial and corrected translations. The Philippines argued that it lacked the resources to check the corrected translation, that to
do so would delay the dispute settlement process, and that to accept the corrected
translations at this late date would be unfair to the Philippines.

98.   At the meeting, the Panel took note of the corrected translations submitted
by Brazil. It informed the Philippines that if it believed the corrected translation
inaccurately reflected the original determination it should so inform the Panel,
and the Panel would make any such ruling as might be required. The Panel indicated that if the Philippines considered that it needed more time as a result of the
submission of the corrected translations, the Panel would grant such additional
time.

99.   The Philippines subsequently submitted a letter objecting to the "acceptance" by the Panel of the corrected translations. The Philippines objected to
Brazil's failure to provide advance warning of the pending corrections, and inferred that the corrections were submitted in response to arguments made during
the oral presentation of the Philippines and third parties and/or to address some
of the concerns expressed by the Panel in its questions to Brazil. The Philippines
indicated that it lacked the resources to engage a professional translator, but
pointed out three instances in which it considered that Brazil had gone beyond
translation corrections to change the substance of the documents in question.

B.   Failure to Consult

100.   The Philippines observed that the duty to accord sympathetic consideration to and afford adequate opportunity for consultations regarding any representations made by another Member concerning measures affecting the operation
of any of the WTO Agreements was one of the most important procedural obligations of the Members of the WTO, citing Article 4:1 of the DSU.

101.   The Philippines maintained that the reasons cited by Brazil for its refusal
to consult, that the Philippines did not invoke the applicable law, and should invoke its rights under the Tokyo Round SCM Code instead, were arguments which
Brazil could have advanced in the consultations, but did not justify a refusal to
consult. The obligation to consult would be meaningless if WTO Members could
refuse to consult when they did not consider the legal claims of the WTO Member requesting consultations to be justified. Moreover, agreeing to consult under
the GATT 1994 would in no way have prejudged Brazil's position on the applicable law in the present Panel proceedings since Article 4:6 of the DSU makes
explicit that "consultations shall be ... without prejudice to the rights of any
Member in any further proceeding". The Philippines asserted that, under international law and in GATT practice, it is recognized that a legal finding may be
sought for the purpose of obtaining satisfaction or a guarantee of non-repetition.
Therefore the Philippines submitted that a finding on this issue was necessary to
strengthen the consultative process in general and, in particular, to reduce the

likelihood of Brazil's resort to similar arguments to avoid consultations in the future.

102.   Brazil disputed the Philippines' contention that it "refused" to consult. Brazil noted that it had offered to consult under the Tokyo Round SCM Code three times. In addition, Brazil submitted a list of the informal consultations that were held, noting that these consultations were considered "informal" at the request of the Philippines.

C.   Subsidy Issues

1.   Reliance on Best Information Available

103.   Brazil argued that the Philippines consistently failed to meet its obligation to supply necessary information within the applicable time periods, despite numerous extensions, and Brazil therefore properly based its subsidy decision on the best information available. Moreover, Brazil asserted that in making its determination it in fact relied mainly on information the Philippines did submit. Brazil maintained that Article VI of GATT 1994 does not contain any administrative provision specifically addressing information gathering. Logically, however, it must contemplate an investigation into the existence and nature of the subsidies prior to imposition of a countervailing duty, since it requires a finding of subsidization and injury. Any such investigation presumes the cooperation of the party being investigated in providing the necessary information to enable the investigating authorities to make those determinations. Brazil argued that this interpretation is supported by past practice with respect to Article VI of GATT 1947, which contained identical language. Brazil referred to the Second Report of the Group of Experts, which addressed this issue:

> "Paragraph 3 of Article VI stipulated that no countervailing duty could be collected beyond the 'estimated' amount of the bounty or of the subsidy granted. In order to arrive at this estimate, the majority of the Group considered it normal, and at least desirable, that the country which became aware of the existence of a subsidy and which ascertained the injury which the subsidy caused, should enter into direct contact with the government of the exporting country. It was also desirable that the latter country should give information requested without delay. This would after all be in its own interest in that it would avoid the imposition of a countervailing duty on its exports at a rate which, failing this information might be fixed at too high a level".[35]

---

[35]   L/1141 (adopted 27 May 1960), BISD 9S/194, para. 35. Brazil did not concede that any precedent from GATT 1947 was binding on the WTO. Nor, in Brazil's view, does such precedent fall within the scope of any source of material for treaty interpretation recognized by the Vienna Con-

In Brazil's view, the last sentence of this section contemplates the use of the best information available. Brazil also noted that Article 2:9 of the Tokyo Round SCM Code specifically permits the use of best information available:

> "In cases in which any interested party or signatory refuses access to, or otherwise does not provide necessary information within a reasonable period or significantly impedes the investigation, preliminary and final findings, affirmative or negative, may be made on the basis of the facts available".

Brazil noted that it discussed the Tokyo Round SCM Code because the obligations of that Code were the obligations in force on Brazil during the investigation.

104.   Brazil argued that the Philippines failed to submit requested information that would have enabled Brazil to determine, on a programme-specific basis, the per unit level of subsidization. Among the information not provided was information as to the annual disbursements of the programmes (including how many growers benefitted), the actual costs of administering the programmes, any specific eligibility criteria, and other requested information.

105.   The Philippines asserted that it was the only country that fully cooperated with Brazil during the investigation, making good faith efforts to submit extensive information in meetings and documentation. The Philippines observed that, because it had always believed there were no subsidies on Philippine coconut fruit, it had simply responded to Brazil's questions without unduly trying to discern Brazil's possible purposes for asking those questions or to facilitate purported subsidy calculations.

106.   The Philippines considered that Brazil's reliance on best information available in fact reflected that Brazil had not fully considered the Philippines' responses, and had only selectively relied on those responses. In this regard, the Philippines noted that Brazil had relied on the "Cost Worksheet" provided by the Philippines to construct the per hectare production cost of hybrid coconut trees, but ignored the per hectare fruit yield reflected in that same worksheet in calculating the per fruit production cost. In the Philippines' view, there were several clear instances when Brazil simply disregarded relevant Philippine responses. The Philippines also argued that Brazil had improperly treated some of the information provided by the Philippines as unsupported assertions. For example, Brazil considered as evidence of levy allocations a list that showed how records of the Marcos regime accounted for the levy funds, but deemed unsupported assertions the contents of the book written by a knowledgeable coconut industry official discussing the unreliability of that list.[36] Indeed, the Philippines asserted

---

vention. Nevertheless, Brazil argued that in facing a new issue, past practice or interpretation of similar language might help guide considerations.

[36]   In this regard, the Philippines noted Brazil's current legislation, Decree No. 1751 (19 December 1995), which, although not in effect during the investigation, recognizes the admissibility of secon-

that Brazil neither mentioned nor evaluated the book, *20 Million Farmers are Victims of Levy Racket*, and did not even acknowledge that the Philippines submitted material assailing the reliability of the list. In the Philippines' view, this represented an improper one-sided treatment of the Philippines' submissions.

107.   Moreover, the Philippines argued, referring to the report of the Panel in *Salmon*, that, before an investigating country can resort to the use of best information available, "the first question to be asked [is] whether the information requested ... was of the type that would make it possible to calculate the amount of a subsidy ... if this information had been requested, and had not been provided, then subsidy findings could be made `on the basis of the facts available'".[37] In the Philippines view, Brazil never asked the types of questions required for, *inter alia*, the downstream subsidy analysis called for by the Panel report in *Pork*. The questionnaire issued by Brazil sought information pertaining to programmes for the upstream product, coconut fruit. Thus, in the Philippines' view, Brazil had no basis for using best information available in regard to the consideration of subsidies to the downstream product, desiccated coconut.

108.   Brazil noted that, with respect to the various programmes investigated, the following information was requested and not provided: the official reports of the officials responsible for administering the programme, "administrative norms and regulations, duly-updated, documents that prove the actual coverage of the programmes covered by legislation, commercial conditions of the benefits conceded, and businesses in questions and our cultivators of coconuts benefitted in the period of investigation," supporting documentation to confirm the information provided in response to the first questionnaire, the actual expenditures for the programme during the period of investigation, detailed information requested about each component of the programme, for example the number of farmers benefitted by the "intercropping," the number of hectares occupied by nurseries, and the actual costs of the nurseries. In response to a question from the Panel, Brazil specified that it had requested copies of official reports relative to each of the programmes; the source for any data provided; the official annual reports of the government entities in charge of the programmes cited; for each identified programme, the commercial conditions of the benefits conceded, businesses covered by the programmes, and cultivators of coconuts that benefitted in the period of investigation; information needed to quantify subsidies received during the period of investigation, for example, with respect to the Presidential Decree No. 582/74 programme, the amount received by each farmer, how many farmers benefitted from loans under the programme, the interest rates at which the loans were granted, percentages of borrowers for each interest rate, loan amortization conditions, whether the farmers get (or could get) private loans in the absence of the programme, and if so, at what interest rate and amortization conditions. Bra-

---

dary evidence, which is subject to Brazil's verification but can be disregarded only if found to be false or misleading.

[37]   *Salmon*, para. 250.

zil recognized that the Philippines provided information during the investigation, but maintained that the Philippines did not provide sufficient information to enable Brazil to make its determination without reliance on best information available. Brazil reiterated that it had relied where possible on the information provided by the Philippines.

2. *Existence of Subsidies*

109. The Philippines maintained that, of the seven Philippine programmes Brazil assertedly concluded involved subsidies, five involve the redistribution to the coconut farmers of a levy previously collected from them, one comprised a land reform programme that generally applied to landless Philippine citizens; and the last consisted of investment incentives for which traditional coconut products were not eligible, but which the Ordinance speculated might be available to such products in the future. In the Philippines' view, these programmes cannot be characterized as subsidies.

110. The Philippines took the position that industry programmes funded by direct collections from their beneficiaries are not subsidies, referring to the Interpretative Notes to Article XVI:3 of both GATT 1947 and GATT 1994, which state in part that price stabilization schemes can be characterized as subsidies only if "wholly or partly financed out of government funds in addition to funds collected from producers in respect of the product concerned". Accordingly, the five groups of replanting and livelihood programmes involving redistribution to farmers of a levy collected from them from 1973 to 1982 were not subsidies. The Philippines argued that Brazil did not deny that levy-funded programmes are not subsidies, but instead had surmised that programmes after 1984 must have been funded by the Philippine Government because a list of allocations of those funds purported to show that the funds had already been completely redistributed as of 1984. However, the Philippines maintained that Brazil had ignored evidence showing that only a small portion of the levy funds were actually redistributed to the farmers.[38] Moreover, the Philippines argued that the prior misuse of the levy funds had both factual and legal implications for purposes of determining whether the Philippine replanting and livelihood programmes were levy-funded. As a factual matter, any levy funds that were diverted from the coconut industry cannot, in the Philippines' view, be deemed to have subsidized those programmes. As a legal matter, the Philippines was of the view that any coconut industry programmes after February 1986, the departure of former Philippine President Ferdinand E. Marcos, could be pursued in conjunction with the Philip-

---

[38] The Philippines argued that Brazil neither mentioned nor addressed the book submitted by the Philippines entitled, *20 Million Farmers are Victims of Levy Racket* (1992), by retired Brigadier General Virgilio M. David, who was Philippine Deputy Military Supervisor of the Coconut Industry from 1974-77, and is currently the Administrator of the Philippine agency, the Philippine Coconut Authority, that principally oversees the industry.

pine Government's efforts to recover the levy funds and to rectify their prior misuse.[39] In particular, the Philippines believed it was proper for the Government to finance post-February 1986 programmes with levy funds that the Government had so far traced, such as those in the United Coconut Planters Bank, or recovered, with some limited advances, especially for rehabilitation programmes that alleviate the plight of farmers after natural calamities. Thus, in the Philippines' view, there was no factual and legal basis for characterizing the levy redistribution programmes as subsidies.

111. The Philippines also maintained that the Agrarian Reform Programme, which was of general application to all poor Philippine farmers, and was not specific to coconut lands, which were not even included in the programme until 1988, was not a subsidy. In response to a question from the Panel whether the Philippines considered that a subsidy must be specific in order to be countervailable under Article VI of GATT 1994, the Philippines responded in the affirmative, that it had been the practice in countervailing cases by some GATT Contracting Parties even before Article VI of GATT 1994, but such a specificity requirement was now expressly articulated only in Article 2 of the SCM Agreement.

112. The Philippines further contended that Brazil had not found that the programme's compensation scheme was concessionary to the farmers. The Philippine position was that the Agrarian Reform Programme could not be considered a subsidy since all the farmers had to pay for the lands distributed. The Philippines noted in this regard that the Ordinance stated no basis for determining the existence of a subsidy, and instead focused on the purported lack of information about the land area covered by the programme for purposes of calculating the amount of the alleged subsidy. Brazil had acknowledged that the Philippines had provided information about land valuation and payment forms, but had made no explicit determination that the land reform programme's compensation scheme had the features of a subsidy. Consequently, in the Philippines' view, Brazil had not had any basis for addressing the total land area covered by the programme. The Philippines asserted that if the compensation scheme was not found unduly concessionary, it could not be deemed a subsidy, and it did not matter how much coconut land was included in the programme. The Philippines also challenged Brazil's characterization of data on the total land area covered by the programme as "non-official," and therefore insufficient to enable calculation of the amount of the subsidy. The Philippines noted that the source of the data was the Philippine

---

[39]   In this regard the Philippines requested the understanding of the Panel in regard to the Philippines' restrained discussion of factual and legal issues about the involvement of the family and close associates of the late President Marcos in the improper diversion of the levy funds. These issues were currently under litigation in Philippine courts, which are the appropriate fora for resolving those issues. Consequently, in this dispute the Philippines limited itself to pointing out Brazil's failure to give these matters due consideration; the Philippines did not seek the Panel's definitive resolution of issues pending before Philippine courts.

Coconut Authority, the government agency principally in charge of the coconut industry. The Philippines argued that Brazil should have accepted this information, and if it had, it would have found the programme's effects on coconut lands too insubstantial even if there had been a determination that the programme's compensation scheme was unduly concessionary.

113. Finally, the Philippines asserted that Brazil erred in treating as an actual subsidy the potential grant of future investment incentives under the Omnibus Investment Code of the Philippines, despite recognizing that coconut products were not eligible for such benefits. Article VI:6(a) allows countervailing duties to offset only subsidies that have actually been "bestowed", while grants under the Omnibus Investment Code were only potential. Moreover, the investment incentives were in fact available only to products that were "new" in the sense of being qualitatively different from the non-eligible traditional coconut products, which included desiccated coconut.

114. Brazil maintained that the information submitted by the Philippines was insufficient to demonstrate that the investigated programmes were not countervailable subsidies. Brazil argued that, even assuming *arguendo* that programmes aimed at increasing coconut production funded by a levy on the coconut producers themselves did not constitute subsides, documents submitted by the Philippine government in the countervailing duty proceeding contradicted the claim that the programmes were levy-funded. According to the documentation provided by the Philippines concerning the collection and disbursement of the coconut levy, which terminated in August 1982, the amount collected was fully disbursed between August 1973 and June 1984. With the exception of Presidential Decree 582, all the programmes under investigation were initiated after June 1984. Brazil asserted that the Philippines never explained how this levy could have financed any programme during the period of investigation (1993-1994), much less programmes initiated after 1984, when it was fully disbursed by June 1984. In addition, Brazil argued that other information provided by the Philippines also contradicted the statements that all programmes were financed by the levy. For example, the information provided by the Philippines indicated that, for the Farm Assistance and Livelihood Project, P 88.7 million of the total P 113.6 million was funded by government sources other than the levy. Given these contradictions that were never explained, Brazil considered that it was fully justified in its finding that the programmes at issue were not financed by the levy, especially in light of the fact that the levy collections had been fully disbursed by June 1984.

115. Brazil considered extraordinary the Philippines' argument that Brazil should not have relied on the submitted document showing that the levy funds were fully disbursed by June 1984 because the accounting in it was false and used to hide the misappropriation of these funds by the Marcos government. In Brazil's view, this argument suggested that Brazil had violated its obligations because it relied on information submitted by the government of the exporting country. Moreover, Brazil asserted that this was the only document submitted that provided any evidence, beyond unsupported assertions, on how the funds were allocated. Finally, even assuming the Philippines was correct that the Mar-

cos regime had misappropriated the funds and did not pass them on to the coconut growers, Brazil maintained that this did not explain how, under the current government, levy funds that had already been misappropriated by 1984 could be disbursed to the growers in the 1990's. In Brazil's view, the Philippines' line of reasoning supported Brazil's finding that the programmes were not funded by the coconut levy.

116.   With respect to the Agrarian Reform Programme, Brazil asserted that it had considered this programme to confer a subsidy because the information provided by the Philippines in response to Brazil's questions was inadequate to determine whether or not a subsidy existed. Brazil had noted that the Philippines had provided data as to the assessment and forms of payment, but asserted that the Philippines had not submitted official or substantiated information on the acreage covered and on the expenses and objectives reached. Brazil maintained that a respondent which did not supply that information could not have expected a no subsidy determination. Brazil noted that the record indicated that persons buying land under the programme could obtain government loans to pay for the purchase at 6 per cent interest, and that therefore those loans were not at commercial interest rates. Moreover, Brazil maintained that the Philippines had not presented any official information on the costs of the programmes, on the total amount loaned out, or on the acreage covered. Therefore, Brazil had been unable to determine from the information provided that the administrators of the programme were covering their costs for administering the programme. Brazil stated that all this information had been requested, and that therefore, on the basis of best information available Brazil had found that this programme provided a subsidy but was unable to determine on a programme-specific basis the effect or amount of the subsidy.

117.   In response to a question by the Panel, Brazil stated that it did not consider that the Omnibus Investment Code provided a subsidy to either the coconut growers or the producers/exporters of desiccated coconut.

118.   The Philippines asserted that Brazil's statement cast serious doubt on the fairness and reliability of the Ordinance as a public statement of Brazil's subsidy determinations. In the Philippines' view, the Ordinance clearly states that Brazil had identified a set of Philippine programmes that were not subject to action, and considered the other programmes, including the Omnibus Investment Code, to have granted subsidies. The Philippines maintained that, if as Brazil now asserted, no subsidy finding could be inferred from the Ordinance's discussion of the Omnibus Investment Code, then the Ordinance should have explicitly identified the Omnibus Investment Code with the other programmes not subject to action. Instead, the Omnibus Investment Code was listed together with the other programmes Brazil had found granted subsidies and thus actionable.

3. Downstream Subsidy Analysis

(a) The Pork Panel

119. The Philippines contended that, even if the Philippine programmes were deemed to constitute subsidies on the production of coconut fruit, Brazil had no legal and factual basis for imputing those subsidies to the production of desiccated coconut. To justify a countervailing duty on desiccated coconut, Brazil was required to determine the existence and extent of a subsidy on desiccated coconut, and could not simply impute the subsidies for coconut fruit to desiccated coconut. Article VI:3 of GATT 1994 prohibits the amount of a countervailing duty from exceeding the amount of the corresponding subsidy allegedly bestowed directly or indirectly on the production of the product that is the object of the countervailing investigation. The *Pork* Panel had considered the imposition by the United States of a countervailing duty on imports of pork based on the subsidies provided to producers of live swine. The Panel, in considering the United States' analysis of the amount of the subsidy on pork, found the United States' decision, which imputed the subsidy on live swine to pork, based on the close inter-relationship between the two products, to be inconsistent with Article VI of GATT 1947, since Article VI:3 mandated that a countervailing duty be based on a subsidy to the specific product under investigation.[40] The Panel ruled that a subsidy determination must be predicated on an examination of all relevant facts,[41] and where the alleged subsidies are provided to a separate industry producing the upstream product, operating at arm's length from the industry producing the downstream product subject to the investigation, the investigating authorities must at a minimum perform an analysis of the price effect of factors relating to the price paid for the upstream product by producers of the downstream product.[42] Based on the Panel decision in *Pork*, the Philippines argued that any subsidies on coconut fruit production could not simply be imputed to the production of desiccated coconut, because these are two different products that belong to two different industries. The Philippines maintained that Brazil failed to do any analysis of the specific effects of the programmes at issue on desiccated coconut.

120. The Philippines asserted that Brazil acknowledged that coconut fruit is an upstream product, whereas desiccated coconut is a downstream product, and that the two products were produced by separate industries operating at arms' length. In the Philippines' view, Brazil's countervailing duty on desiccated coconut was thus subject to the requirements established by the Panel in *Pork*. The Philippines read *Pork* to require, in this situation, that the investigating authorities conduct a

---

[40] *Pork*, paras. 4.6 and 4.8.
[41] *Pork*, para. 4.8. The Panel noted that such "practices" were "reflected in Part I of the [Tokyo Round] SCM Code". *Id.* Thus, the Philippines argued that the pertinent principles articulated by *Pork* would apply to the instant matter even if it were considered under that Code.
[42] *Pork*, paras. 4.9 and 4.10.

"price effect" analysis that examines, at a minimum, whether the alleged subsidies to the raw material led to a decrease in the level of prices for that raw material paid by the processed product's producers below the level they would have had to pay for the raw material from other commercially available sources of supply. The Philippines also considered that *Pork* required two further relevant factors to be considered: (a) whether the raw material was internationally traded, since it is less likely that subsidies will cause the domestic price of such material to decline by the full amount of the subsidies if the producers of the raw material can export at international prices; and (b) the per unit cost of producing the additional output of the raw material that the subsidies may have caused, since the extent to which such additional output affects the price for the raw material will depend in part on the cost of producing the output.

121.   The Philippines maintained that Brazil did not conduct an examination of any of the factors set forth in *Pork*, nor of any other factors showing a price effect of the alleged subsidies on desiccated coconut. In this regard, the Philippines noted that other relevant considerations could affect the international market. For instance, international market conditions could depress the price of the downstream product so as to in turn depress the price of the upstream product even in the absence of subsidies. The Philippines argued that an investigation of subsidies on downstream products would have to consider such factors in order to avoid attributing such price depression to subsidies on the upstream product in a case where international market conditions appeared to act in conjunction with the subsidies to affect the price of the upstream product in the exporting country.

122.   The Philippines argued that, because it was improper for Brazil to have directly imputed subsidies on coconut fruit to desiccated coconut production, Brazil had no basis for resorting to a "constructed value" methodology to calculate the amount of the coconut fruit subsidy. The Philippines argued that, in accordance with Article VI:1(b)(ii) of GATT 1994, a constructed value methodology can sometimes be allowed in an anti-dumping context where a country "has a complete or substantially complete monopoly of its trade and where all domestic prices are fixed by the State".[43] However, the Philippines maintained that this approach was wholly inapplicable in the investigation at hand. First, the methodology was envisioned for an anti-dumping investigation and made little sense in a countervailing duty investigation. Second, Brazil made no effort to establish the predicate for the method's application; Brazil did not examine, and made no findings on, whether the Philippines had a complete or substantially complete monopoly of the trade in desiccated coconut or whether all domestic prices are fixed by the State. In fact, the Philippines noted that the evidence was to the contrary, as the Philippine domestic price for desiccated coconut is governed by the international price for the product, and there was no government intervention in

---

[43]   Note 2 to Article VI:1(b)(ii) of GATT 1994. The Philippines noted that same limitation applied under the corresponding provision in GATT 1947, and Article 15:1 and Article 15:2(b) of the Tokyo Round SCM Code.

market pricing. Thus, the Philippines contended that Brazil's constructed value methodology had no legal basis in GATT 1994 and was invalid as a basis for imposing countervailing duties under Article VI of GATT 1994.

123.   The Philippines also argued that the constructed value approach violated Article VI:3 of GATT 1994 because it lacked any mechanism for adjusting the purported subsidy amount to ensure its proportionality to the number and extent of the alleged upstream subsidies. Such a constructed value calculation would yield the same subsidy amount no matter how many of the programmes were considered to be subsidies, and regardless of the funding levels of such programmes. Ostensibly, the subsidy amount would remain unchanged even if only one out of the seven programme categories were deemed to be a subsidy, and even if the funding levels of all the programmes were much lower. In the Philippines' view, this methodological inflexibility rendered the constructed value approach inconsistent with Article VI:3 of GATT 1994, under which the amount of a subsidy must be determined rationally, not indiscriminately.

124.   Brazil took the position that its calculation of the level of subsidization on desiccated coconut was fully consistent with its obligations under either Article VI:3 of GATT 1994 or the Tokyo Round SCM Code. Brazil noted that neither Article VI nor the Tokyo Round SCM Code contained any guidance on the method of calculation of the amount of the subsidy. Brazil contended that, as long as its approach reasonably calculated the subsidy bestowed on the exported product, it was consistent with Article VI:3. Brazil agreed with the report of the *Pork* Panel that a "price effects" test was a reasonable method of determining whether a subsidy to an upstream product was bestowed on the exported downstream product, observing in addition that there may be other reasonable methods but it was unnecessary to consider them in this case.

125.   Brazil agreed that the situation in this case was similar to the situation in the *Pork* case. Brazil had determined that coconut fruit and desiccated coconut are separate products and that the coconut fruit is the raw material for the desiccated coconut. The Philippines had submitted information that showed that coconut fruit production and desiccated coconut production are two separate industries that operate at arm's length. Thus, the situation in this case comported with the requirements set out in *Pork* that where separate industries are operating at arm's length the downstream industry cannot be considered subsidized unless the subsidy bestowed on the coconut fruit (the upstream product) has had a price effect on the desiccated coconut (the downstream product). Brazil maintained that in this case, a price effects test was a reasonable method available for Brazil to measure the subsidies that were indirectly bestowed on desiccated coconut, since the Philippines did not provide much of the information Brazil had requested. Had the Philippines provided the information requested, Brazil asserted that it could have determined the programme-specific subsidies provided to coconuts and then conducted a more detailed analysis, based on respondent's information, to determine how much of the programme-specific subsidies on coconuts flowed downstream to the production of desiccated coconut.

126.   Brazil asserted that its analysis was consistent with the approach advocated by the *Pork* Panel. Brazil asserted that in order to determine the price effect, it had used a constructed unsubsidized price for coconut fruit and calculated an unsubsidized price for desiccated coconut. Brazil then compared this price for unsubsidized desiccated coconut to a subsidized price for desiccated coconut, calculated using the price in the Philippines of the subsidized fruit. The difference between the subsidized and unsubsidized prices for desiccated coconut determined the price effect of the subsidies and measured the subsidies indirectly bestowed on desiccated coconut. Only after finding that there were subsidies to the upstream product, coconut fruit, that were passed through to the downstream producers in the form of reduced input prices, did Brazil look at whether these indirect subsidies benefitted desiccated coconut production. Brazil determined that they did and that the subsidy was bestowed on the imported product in the form of reduced prices. Brazil asserted that it had considered all relevant facts, within the constraints of an analysis based on the best information available.

127.   Brazil argued that its construction of an unsubsidized price was reasonable and logical. Brazil asserted that the Philippines arguments concerning the use of "constructed value" in the dumping context were completely irrelevant to this dispute. Brazil maintained that it had not conducted a "constructed value" analysis, but rather had attempted to measure the price effect of the subsidies using the best information available in light of the Philippines' failure to provide necessary information.

(b)   Commercial Availability Issue

128.   The Philippines asserted that the *Pork* Panel treated consideration of other commercially available sources of supply as a means of determining whether factors other than the alleged upstream subsidies may have affected the price at which upstream producers sold the raw material to downstream producers. In the Philippines' view, unless such other factors were considered, there could be no reliable finding that the price of the raw material was determined solely or principally by the alleged upstream subsidies. The Philippines noted other relevant considerations pertaining to the conditions of international market demand and competition that, while not enumerated in *Pork*, could be considered. For example, international conditions could depress the price of the downstream product in a way that in turn also depressed the raw material's price in the exporting country even if there were no subsidies.

129.   In this regard, the Philippines referred to the Panel decision in *Canada - Countervailing duties on Grain Corn from the United States*, SCM/140 (adopted 26 March 1992) ("*Grain Corn*"), BISD 39S/411, para. 5.2.7. The Philippines argued that, although *Grain Corn* involved prices in the importing country, it illustrated the possible effects of international conditions on domestic prices:

> "Clearly, if there is a general and dramatic decline in world market prices for grain corn, this will affect Canadian producers. It will affect Canadian producers even if Canada

does not import any grain corn from the United States, even if it imports grain corn from third countries, even if it is completely self-sufficient in grain corn or, indeed, even if it is a net exporter of grain corn, as it was in some crop years. ... In each case, the Canadian price for corn would still be directly impacted - in a material way - by the world price decline...".

Grain Corn, para. 5.2.9. Just as it could affect domestic prices in an importing country, the Philippines argued that an international price decline could also depress domestic prices in an exporting country.

130.   The Philippines also argued that, where alleged subsidies and international conditions appeared to be concurrent causes of low domestic prices in an exporting country, the investigating country bore the further burden of carefully analysing the international conditions so as to avoid attributing to alleged upstream subsidies any price depression, or degrees of any such price depression, actually caused by international conditions. The Philippines maintained that if the international conditions would, by themselves, have been sufficient to depress raw material prices, e.g., by depressing the prices of the downstream product derived therefrom, even in the absence of upstream subsidies, then the depression of the raw material price cannot be deemed a benefit "bestowed" by the upstream subsidies.

131.   The Philippines maintained that Brazil's price effect analysis entailed an a priori disregard of all factors other than the alleged upstream subsidies. In other words, Brazil's comparison between the subsidized fruit price and the constructed unsubsidized fruit price yielded a price differential that Brazil simply treated as the price effect, uninfluenced by any other factors. Thus, in the Philippines' view, Brazil had ruled out by definition the relevance of other factors in its price effect analysis, contrary to the guidance of *Pork*.

132.   Brazil asserted that the *Pork* Panel's use of the phrase "other commercially available sources of supply" indicated one possible means to assess what the price of the subsidized upstream product, in this case, the fruit, would have been in the absence of the subsidies, but that this was not necessarily the only means available. Brazil maintained that it had considered international trading in the product. However, because the five largest world suppliers of coconuts were under investigation for subsidies, Brazil did not consider the international price to reflect an unsubsidized price. Thus, that Philippine coconut producers could sell in the international market did not mean they would be able to sell at a higher, unsubsidized price. Moreover, Brazil argued that the Philippines had provided no information on coconut prices in countries that did not subsidize coconut fruit production, and that even if an international price existed, there might not be commercially viable access to the upstream product by the producer of the downstream product. Thus, Brazil had considered the constructed price as the most reliable unsubsidized coconut price for comparison purposes.

133. In Brazil's view, the phrase "other commercially available sources of supply" in the *Pork* Panel report was intended to allow flexibility to determine the appropriate analysis on a case-by-case basis. Brazil asserted that such flexibility was imperative in cases, such as this one, where there was no unsubsidized commercially available source for the upstream product. Brazil noted that there were a number of reasons not to consider international prices in this case. First, Brazil determined in its investigation that the five largest producers of coconuts were subsidizing their coconut production.[44] The Philippines provided no information about coconut fruit prices in countries not found to subsidize coconut fruit production. Thus, if the major suppliers of coconut fruit received subsidies, the international price would show the effects of those subsidies. Brazil asserted that subsidies to a product in one country can affect the world market price for a product in at least three different possible ways. If subsidies are bestowed on a product by Country X are substantial and Country X is an exporter of that product, the subsidized prices can, and would be expected to, lower the world market price for that product. If subsidies are bestowed on a product by Country X, which accounts for a significant portion of the world production of that product, the subsidized prices can lower the world market price for that product. If subsidies are bestowed on a product by a number of countries whose production of the product accounts for a significant portion of the world production, the subsidized prices can lower the world market price for that product. Brazil argued that the third possibility was the case during the Brazilian investigation of desiccated coconut from the Philippines. Brazil also noted that an international price must be adjusted to include import duties and other expenses.[45] Finally, although an international price may exist, there may not be commercially viable access to the international product because of import restrictions, unreliable suppliers, shipment delays, quality differences, or other reasons. Thus, in this case, Brazil had determined to rely, for comparison purposes, on a constructed price for the Philippines, based on cost information provided by the Philippines, as the most reliable unsubsidized coconut price.

134. Brazil also argued that, to determine the competitive benefit or price effect that the subsidization of the input product (coconut fruit) has on the price of the downstream product (desiccated coconut) the price of the subsidized input must be compared to the price of an unsubsidized input. In other words, the investigating country must determine what it would have cost a producer to purchase the input product in the absence of subsidies. Without such a benchmark,

---

[44] Brazil stated that it was the practice of other countries conducting an upstream subsidy analysis to refuse to use potentially subsidized prices as a benchmark against which to compare the price in question to determine whether the subsidy was passed-through. *See, e.g., Final Affirmative Countervailing Duty Determination on Steel Wheels From Brazil*, 54 Federal Register 15523 (U.S. Department of Commerce 18 April 1989).

[45] Brazil argued that the fact that Brazilian coconut prices were above the price paid by the Philippine processors was one indication that the prices available to those processors were affected by subsidies.

no determination of a price effect or competitive benefit can be made. The issue of subsidies was relevant to the issue of the use of an international price benchmark. A respondent would always argue that a lower subsidized benchmark price should be used for comparison purposes because that would lower any subsidy rate determined by the investigating country. On the other hand, the investigating country's producers would be hurt by the use of a lower subsidized benchmark price especially if the lower benchmark price erroneously resulted in a finding of no pass-through of the subsidies. Moreover, once the subsidies were eliminated, the international prices would rise to the unsubsidized price and this unsubsidized international price could once again be used as an unsubsidized benchmark.

135.   The Philippines considered as *ex post facto* Brazil's assertion that it considered international trading, but did not consider the international price to reflect an unsubsidized price because the five largest world suppliers of coconuts were under investigation. The Philippines noted that Brazil did not cite to either the Ordinance or to DTIC Opinion 006/95 in proffering this explanation, and urged the Panel to disregard it. The Philippines also observed that, in theory, subsidies to a product in one country could conceivably affect the world market for that product, and the international price thereof. However, a subsidy determination could not be based on such a mere theoretical possibility. Rather, the investigating authorities must establish the existence of all factors that could possibly affect the world market for the product under investigation. The Philippines asserted that the Ordinance did not contain an assessment, let alone a determination, regarding the existence of such factors. Thus, Brazil's subsidy determination was flawed by its disregard of international pricing factors, and Brazil's belated rationalizations for such disregard must be rejected as both *ex post facto* and without merit.

136.   Moreover, the Philippines contended that Brazil's explanation was without merit. The Philippines contended that the mere involvement of several of the largest suppliers of coconut products in the investigation did not have any automatic effect, either upward or downward, on the international price at which coconut producers could sell their product. In the Philippines' view, Brazil should have investigated and analyzed the actual price effects of other international trading factors, rather than *a priori* ruling out the possibility of any price effects.[46] In addition, the Philippines argued that Brazil did not even assert that it considered the other relevant factor identified in *Pork*, the per unit cost of producing the additional output of raw material that the subsidies may have caused.

137.   Brazil also maintained that, in a comparison of the actual price of coconuts to the constructed unsubsidized price of coconuts, the difference necessarily reflected the price effect of the subsidies on the raw material. Brazil argued that it

---

[46]   In this regard, the Philippines argued that, since Brazil's questionnaires did not request information concerning relevant facts about international trading, Brazil had no basis for relying on best information available.

did not presume a full pass-through of the subsidies on coconuts to desiccated coconut. The extent of the pass-through calculated consisted only of the difference between the subsidized and the constructed unsubsidized price of coconut fruit. To the extent that the actual subsidized price did not reflect the full amount of the subsidies bestowed on coconut production, those subsidies were not considered to be passed through to the coconut processors.[47]

138. The Philippines asserted that Brazil's determination was undercut by evidence presented by the Philippines showing that Philippine coconut farmers sell coconut fruit to producers of products other than desiccated coconut, such as coconut oil, copra, fatty chemicals and foodnuts, and that desiccated coconut represents only a small percentage of Philippine exports of coconut products, as coconut exports are dominated by coconut oil. The Philippines considered that the *Pork* Panel had rejected an imputed subsidy analysis even when the downstream product (pork) "constitute[d] the primary product" of the upstream product (swine),[48] and asserted that there was even less legal or factual support for the use of such an analysis in this case, because desiccated coconut is not even the "primary product" of coconut fruit in the Philippines.

139. Likewise, the Philippines asserted that Brazil's determination was undermined by evidence showing that the export price of Philippine coconut products other than coconut oil, including desiccated coconut, and the Philippine domestic price of coconut fruit "husked nuts", the raw material for desiccated coconut, closely tracked the international price of coconut oil, which in turn followed the price trends in the worldwide market for oils and fats, where Philippine coconut oil has only a 5 per cent share. The Philippines argued that Brazil had wrongly ignored information on the dependence of coconut prices on world supply and demand for coconut oil. The Philippines maintained that this evidence, the "Coconut Industry Kit-Series of 1993", prepared by a coconut industry association before the initiation of Brazil's investigation, and the document prepared by the Philippines' National Economic Development Authority, a formal paper for the 1994 Proceedings of the World Conference on Lauric Oils, had been submitted during the investigation, and was not generated specifically in response to Brazil's questionnaires. Thus, Brazil had no basis for completely ignoring these documents. Moreover, the Philippines noted that these documents were not addressed by Brazil in either the Ordinance or DTIC Opinion 006/95, and thus Brazil's explanation for disregarding them was an *ex post facto* rationalization that the Panel should not consider.

140. The Philippines also argued that Brazil improperly disregarded the formal testimony of a high ranking Philippine government official during the 13 June

---

[47] As an example, Brazil asserted that if the actual subsidized price of coconuts were 25 pesos, the calculated "unsubsidized price" were 40 pesos, and the subsidies equalled 20 pesos, Brazil would have considered only 15 pesos of the subsidy to be passed through to the Philippine coconut processors.

[48] *Pork*, paras. 2.8.a, 4.9, and 4.10.

1995 meeting, at which he explained the relationship between the price of husked nuts and the international price of soybean oil. In the Philippines's view, even oral evidence, as long as subsequently reduced into writing, is admissible in countervailing investigations.

141.   Brazil contended that the Philippines' claim that the subsidies could have no price effect because the price of coconuts is dependent on the price of coconut oil was not supported by evidence submitted in the course of the investigation. Therefore, Brazil had no basis to conclude that coconut prices were unaffected by the subsidies. In this regard, Brazil objected to the Philippines' submission to the Panel of information on the relationship between soybean and coconut oil prices[49] that had not been submitted during the investigation.

142.   The Philippines maintained that Brazil had set artificially high evidentiary hurdles on the international trade issue in an attempt to obscure the fact that it had failed to address that issue at all in its determination. In this regard, the Philippines asserted that the graphs and tables it submitted to the Panel were intended only to further exemplify the type of information that Brazil should have sought and examined as part of the "other factors" analysis required by *Pork*.

143.   Brazil argued that it did consider the information provided by the Philippines about the price relationship between the various oils and desiccated coconut, but concluded that the information did not support the Philippines' claim. For example, Brazil asserted that the data in the "Coconut Industry Kit" referred to by the Philippines did not demonstrate a correlation in prices of coconut fruit and oil. Moreover, Brazil argued that some of the information was uncorroborated statements by the Philippine government, which Brazil was not obliged to rely upon. Brazil also maintained that it was not clear that information on the relationship between the price of coconuts and the price of coconut oil was relevant. Brazil posited that, if subsidies were necessary to keep the coconut producers in operation given the low price of coconut oil, this still meant that the coconut producers benefitted from the subsidies and that downstream purchasers benefited from the lower prices that could be charged because of the subsidies, asserting that, if prices drop below a profitable level in the absence of subsidies, the supply of coconut will decline and the users of coconuts will have to pay increasingly higher prices for coconuts in the fact of dwindling supply. Moreover, Brazil considered the relevance of the fact that there are many competing uses for coconuts unclear. Brazil posited that it could mean that desiccated coconut processors did not have the market power to force a pass-through of the subsidy or some portion thereof to themselves alone. It did not mean that the interplay of all supply and demand factors did not result in at least some portion of the subsidy being passed through to all consumers of coconuts, including the desiccated coconut processors.

---

[49]   Attachments 1 and 2 to the first submission of the Philippines.

144.   In the Philippines's view, Brazil had adopted the type of imputation analysis that was rejected by the Panel in *Pork*. In *Pork*, the issue was the propriety of the United States' imputation of upstream subsidies (whose actual value was unchallenged) to the downstream product using a conversion factor based on the ratio of the hog carcass to the weight of the live hog. In this case, the Philippines argued that Brazil constructed the value of the upstream subsidies, and then improperly imputed those subsidies to desiccated coconut using a conversion factor of 7.5 coconuts per kilogram of desiccated coconut. Although Brazil sought to distinguish its methodology from an imputation approach, claiming that by constructing the "unsubsidized" cost and price of coconut fruit it had measured the price effect of the subsidies on coconuts and limited the extent of the pass-through to the difference between the subsidized and the unsubsidized price of the coconuts, in the Philippines' view, this methodology still constituted the sort of upstream-downstream imputation rejected by the Panel in *Pork*, because Brazil failed to consider other factors, aside from the effect of upstream subsidies on the raw material's price, to complete the downstream price effect analysis.

145.   Brazil considered that the Philippines appeared to allege that the "improper imputation methodology" in *Pork* was the use of a conversion factor. In Brazil's view, the conversion factor was not the problem in the *Pork* calculation, the problem was that the United States merely applied a subsidy to swine directly to pork production without determining whether that subsidy passed through. Brazil asserted that it was obvious that, if the subsidy is passed through to a downstream product, a conversion factor will have to be used to convert the upstream product into the downstream product. Brazil noted that presumably the Philippines intended to argue that the methodology found improper in *Pork* was the one step pass-through without analysis, which in *Pork* was done by taking the subsidy to swine and multiplying by the conversion factor to arrive at the subsidy for pork. However, Brazil maintained that it did not conduct such a one step pass-through without analysis. Brazil first considered the price difference between subsidized and unsubsidized coconuts to determine whether there was a price effect from the subsidies. Then, finding that there was a price effect, Brazil compared the costs/prices of desiccated coconut based on subsidized coconut costs with the costs/prices of desiccated coconut based on unsubsidized coconut costs to determine the effect of the subsidy on the exported product. To determine the cost of producing one kilogram of desiccated coconut, it was necessary to determine how much coconut goes into one kilogram of desiccated coconut, requiring a conversion factor.

4.   Calculation Issues

146.   The Philippines asserted that even if Brazil's "constructed value" approach were deemed appropriate, the Panel should rule that Brazil's calculation was erroneous and lacked adequate explanation. The Philippines described the steps followed by Brazil in its constructed value calculations as follows: (1) based on a 1993 Philippine "Cost Worksheet" for hybrid coconut fruit, Brazil calculated the

annual per hectare production cost by assuming that each tree would be productive in the 8th year after planting, that annual costs would be fully amortized within 15 years from the 8th year at a 12 per cent annual rate, and that the same 12 per cent rate could be used to discount the annual cost, to arrive at a present value of US$ 821.41 per hectare; (2) while recognizing that the prevailing variety of coconut tree in the Philippines was tall trees, Brazil treated the per hectare production costs of hybrid and tall trees as equal, citing a Brazilian study showing a difference of less than three percent. Brazil divided the per hectare production cost of new hybrid coconut trees (US$ 821.41 per hectare) by the per hectare annual fruit yield of old tall coconut trees (3,910 per year), added an 8 per cent profit margin and US$ 0.015 for freight cost, to arrive at a constructed unsubsidized price of US$ 0.242 per fruit. (3) Brazil then applied a conversion ratio of 7.5 nuts per kilogram of desiccated coconut, and added an 8 per cent profit margin, to arrive at a constructed unsubsidized price for desiccated coconut of US$ 2.348 per kilogram. (4) Based on the "coconut fruit price effectively paid" by a Philippine exporter, US$ 0.051, and presumably also using at least the 7.5 nuts per kilogram conversion ratio, Brazil arrived at a subsidized price for desiccated coconut of US$ 0.800 per kilogram. (5) Brazil then deducted the subsidized price of desiccated coconut (US$ 0.800 per kilogram) from the unsubsidized price of desiccated coconut (US$ 2.348 per kilogram) to arrive at a subsidy amount of US$ 1.548 per kilogram. (6) Finally, Brazil divided the subsidy amount for desiccated coconut (US$ 1.548 per kilogram) by the "average weighted CIF export price" of desiccated coconut exported to Brazil (US$ 1.274 per kilogram), thereby deriving a 121.5 per cent countervailing duty.

147.   Brazil asserted that there were several problems with the Philippines' description of Brazil's calculation. Brazil objected to the Philippines' insinuations that it had overstated the constructed fruit price. Brazil noted that the Ordinance described how Brazil calculated the price, and that DTIC Opinion 006/95 provided the exact figures and a more detailed description which showed the exact numbers involved to result in the US$ 2.348 figure. The processing cost that the Philippines questioned was provided by a Philippine exporter. Moreover, Brazil noted that in questioning the calculations of the price for the subsidized desiccated coconut, the Philippines failed to account for the processing costs used by Brazil.

(a)   Constructed Price

148.   In the Philippines' view, Brazil's calculation was defective in several respects. First, it was inherently inconsistent to use the actual production cost of allegedly subsidized hybrid coconut trees to derive an unsubsidized price. To the extent that the Brazilian countervailing duty purported to have been imposed on existing Philippine subsidies, and subsidies typically reduce production cost, then the actual production cost of hybrid coconut trees must have presumably been reduced by the alleged Philippine subsidies. By using the actual production cost to construct a price that is higher than an actual price paid by a Philippine ex-

porter, the decision suggested some variant of a dumping charge - that is, that the Philippines exported desiccated coconut at a price that was lower than it would otherwise have been had the actual production cost of coconut fruit been passed on in the price to desiccated coconut producers, and exports of desiccated coconut.

149. The Philippines contended that Brazil had either (a) considered the actual production cost of hybrid trees unaffected by the alleged subsidies, in which event the countervailing investigation should have ended without finding any subsidy; or (b) considered the production cost reduced by the alleged subsidies, in which case it was, in the Philippines' view, incomprehensible how a subsidy-reduced production cost could be the basis for constructing an unsubsidized fruit price that was lower than the actual fruit price. The Philippines maintained that Brazil had resorted to an inappropriate anti-dumping methodology in this countervailing duty investigation, resulting in figures that were meaningless and could not support the imposition of countervailing duties.

150. Brazil asserted that it relied on the cost information submitted by the Philippines, which contained *estimated* costs. Brazil assumed those costs were estimated rather than actual because they reflected production costs absent the subsidies. Brazil noted that it could have chosen to rely on Brazilian prices, rather than seeking to construct a Philippine price, which would have resulted in a much higher rate of subsidy being found, since Brazilian coconut prices were higher than the cost information submitted by the Philippines.

151. The Philippines asserted that Brazil had presented no credible reason for considering that the Philippines' estimate of the cost for hybrid trees, relied on in the construction of the per hectare production cost of coconut fruit, represented unsubsidized costs. The Philippines had been asked for, and had provided, estimates about the actual cost and price of coconut fruit. Brazil's assertion that it could have relied on Brazilian coconut prices in constructing the cost of production of Philippine coconut fruit was unjustified, in the Philippines view, and was an *ex post facto* rationalization that was not mentioned in Brazil's determination. In any event, the Philippines argued that Brazil conceded that its production costs were unusually high by international standards, and those costs would therefore not have been an appropriate basis for calculating Philippine production costs.

(b)   Costs and Yields of Hybrid and Tall Trees

152. The Philippines argued that Brazil did not have an adequate basis for treating the per hectare production costs of hybrid and tall Philippine coconut trees as "equal". Moreover, even if the per hectare production cost of hybrid and tall trees were deemed to be equal, Brazil had no basis for treating the per fruit production cost as equal by disregarding the contrast in production costs of new and old trees, and the actual difference in the average annual fruit yields of the two types of trees. The Philippines contended that Brazil's calculation was distorted by the use of the per hectare production cost of new hybrid trees, while using the per hectare fruit yield of old or senile tall trees which had much lower

fruit yields, involved practically no maintenance costs, and comprised the over-whelming majority of coconut trees in the Philippines. The Philippines further asserted that Brazil ignored the difference in fruit yields when it divided the per hectare production cost of hybrid trees by the lower per hectare fruit yield of tall trees (3,910), instead of dividing that per hectare cost by the higher per hectare fruit yield of hybrid trees (15,000), despite the fact that the latter yield was mentioned in the "Cost Worksheet" from which Brazil derived the actual production cost of hybrid trees. In the Philippines' view, this mixing of figures for new hybrid and old tall trees reflected an unfair manipulation of data. Thus, the calculation must be deemed inconsistent with Article VI:3 of GATT 1994, which requires a rational and reliable determination of the amount of an alleged subsidy.

153. Brazil responded to the Philippines' objections to the information and assumptions underlying the calculation by noting that, with respect to "Step 1" of the calculation, Brazil did, in fact, rely on information supplied by the Philippines, the "Cost Worksheet - Coconut Production; Cost of Planting and Maintenance per Hectare of Coconut" that described the stages, timing, and costs of producing coconuts. The assumption that the trees would be productive in their 8th year and would be productive over 15 years (for amortization purposes) was derived from information supplied by the petitioners and used as best information. Regarding the consideration of costs for hybrid trees when the bulk of the Philippine trees were tall trees, Brazil noted that the cost information provided by the Philippines contained estimated costs for one farm producing hybrid trees on one acre of land. Thus, the only information the Philippines supplied on costs was for hybrid, not tall, trees. Nevertheless, Brazil attempted to check whether such information reasonably reflected costs throughout the Philippines, by considering a comparison of costs done by the Brazilian Institute for Agricultural Research comparing the costs of the two types of trees. Based on that comparison, Brazil calculated a less than 3 per cent difference in costs between the two tree types. Regarding the consideration of production cost of new trees when most of the Philippine trees were old, Brazil asserted that it had again based its calculation on information supplied by the Philippines. Brazil calculated the average yield in the Philippines by dividing the total number of trees by total production as supplied by the Philippines in response to the supplemental questionnaire. Brazil noted that the Philippine government had not submitted any information on profit that could be used in the calculation, but one Philippine exporter had submitted information that indicated a profit significantly higher than 8 per cent. Therefore, in Brazil's view, the use of an 8 per cent profit figure was more favourable to the Philippines than other record evidence would have been.

154. The Philippines argued that Brazil had not identified any factor which would indicate that the Philippine and Brazilian crops were comparable, so as to justify treatment of the production costs of Philippine hybrid and tall trees as the same based on an alleged 3 per cent difference between the production costs of two Brazilian crops, which the Philippines asserted were in any event unspecified. Likewise, Brazil had failed to explain why its subsidy calculation divided the per hectare production cost of hybrid trees by the per hectare fruit yield of tall

trees (i.e., 3,910) despite the fact that the substantially higher per hectare fruit yield of hybrid trees (i.e., 15,000) was stated in the very cost worksheet Brazil used to calculate per hectare production cost. This glaring error, by itself, in the Philippines' view rendered Brazil's subsidy calculation fundamentally indeterminate and thus unreliable.

155.   Brazil maintained that it had used the average yield of all trees in the Philippines, not only the yield for tall trees, and moreover, that the yield figure was based on the information supplied by the Philippines. Brazil also noted that the Philippines never supplied any production cost information for tall trees.

156.   The Philippines argued that it was misleading for Brazil to state that the Philippines supplied information only on costs for hybrid, not tall, trees. Brazil's questionnaires had inquired about production costs that included original planting expenses. Because only hybrid trees were being freshly planted in the Philippines, and all the replanting programmes examined by Brazil involved hybrid trees, the Philippines, in response to Brazil's questions, provided the production cost of hybrid trees. However, the Philippines explained that those types of costs were neither currently nor recently incurred by the tall trees, which were 40 years old or older. Thus, it was improper for Brazil to impute to extremely old tall trees the original replanting and other costs of new hybrid trees. Indeed, during the investigation the Philippines had stressed that tall trees should not be deemed benefited by replanting programmes that only involved hybrid trees. Moreover, because hybrid trees constituted only a tiny minority of Philippine coconut trees, it would be manifestly unreasonable to assume that Philippine exporters of desiccated coconut obtained their raw material solely or mostly from hybrid trees. The Philippines suggested that Brazil should have limited its subsidy calculation to the portion of the Philippine coconut tree population affected by alleged upstream subsidies - hybrid trees. Since the only data Brazil had concerning a Philippine exporter showed that the exporter purchased only the output of tall coconut trees, Brazil had no basis for concluding that Philippine exports were the product of coconut fruit from subsidized hybrid trees.

D.   Injury Issues

1.   Like Product

157.   The Philippines contended that, in order to impose a countervailing duty under Article VI of GATT 1994, Brazil must show through positive evidence that the alleged subsidization caused material injury to the relevant "domestic industry", which is in turn determined by the definition of the "like product". However, in the Philippines' view, the definition of the "like product" in Brazil's determination was ambiguous and contradictory. The Philippines asserted that the Ordinance variously defined the domestic "like product" to include: (1) all desiccated coconut, whether destined for the industrial market (where it is processed as a raw material) or for the retail market (where it is consumed as a finished product); (2) only desiccated coconut destined for industrial use; (3) only desiccated

coconut destined for industrial use, and coconut fruit; and (4) all desiccated coconut destined for the industrial and retail markets, and coconut fruit. As a consequence of this failure to define the like product clearly and consistently, the Philippines argued that the scope of the relevant domestic industry varied throughout the Ordinance, specifically in the sections analysing apparent consumption, capacity and employment, industrial demand, and unit cost/price. By alternately narrowing and broadening the range of data to be considered, the shifting definition of the domestic industry made the evaluation of the alleged injury unclear.

158. In support of this contention, the Philippines noted that the Ordinance at one point referred to alleged injury suffered by coconut fruit producers who were supposedly unable to participate in a 19 per cent increase in industrial demand for desiccated coconut, and elsewhere stated that the coconut fruit producers themselves cut down the supply of fruit to desiccated coconut producers because an alternative market offered higher prices for the fruit. Thus, the Philippines questioned whether Brazil had considered coconut fruit production part of the domestic industry. In addition, the Philippines contended that the unclear definitions of the like product and the domestic industry undermined the reliability of the data and analysis regarding material injury and causation set forth in the Ordinance.

159. Brazil took issue with the Philippines' position that it had failed to make a clear determination of like product.[50] Brazil asserted that it had clearly determined that the like product was domestically produced desiccated coconut, and that the like product was not subdivided based on the market in which desiccated coconut was sold. Brazil also maintained that it had clearly determined that the domestic industry consisted of the domestic producers of the like product, desiccated coconut, with the exclusion of one domestic producer, found to be a significant importer of the subject product. Brazil had included all other domestic producers in the definition of domestic industry, two of whom (the co-petitioners) accounted for on average 49 per cent of the national production (and 52 per cent of the production of the domestic industry) during the period of the injury investigation. Brazil noted that, in its consideration of injury, it used information from the co-petitioners, the only producers to respond to its questionnaires, where information for the entire domestic industry was not available.

160. Brazil asserted that Article VI does not refer to the concept of like product in the context of countervailing duties or injury, or specifically address the definition of domestic industry. Nevertheless, Brazil agreed that Article VI requires a determination of like product in order to define the domestic industry. Brazil suggested that guidance as to the meaning of the term like product in relation to

---

[50] Brazil reiterated its position that the injury arguments, including the like product arguments raised by the Philippines, were beyond the scope of the Panel's terms of reference.

Article VI of GATT 1947 can be found in the First Report of the Group of Experts:

> "the Group agreed that this term should be interpreted as a product which is identical in physical characteristics subject, however, to such variations in presentations which are due to the need to adapt the product to special conditions in the market of the importing country".[51]

In addition, Brazil referred to the Tokyo Round SCM Code, which defines the term "like product" to mean "a product which is identical, i.e., alike in all respects to the product under consideration or in the absence of such product, another product which although not alike in all respects, has characteristics closely resembling those of the product under consideration". Under both Article VI and the Tokyo Round SCM Code, therefore, Brazil argued that like product is defined on the basis of physical characteristics. In Brazil's view, the Philippines misread the Ordinance in claiming that Brazil had defined like product four different ways. The portion of the Ordinance cited by the Philippines to support this claim, Brazil argued, was the analysis of physical characteristics and the conditions of competition Brazil had relied upon in order to define the like product.

161. In examining the issue of like product, Brazil asserted that it had found that the domestic product was not alike in all respects to the imported product. There were differences in the amounts of sugar and fat contained in the products and in the size and dryness of the flakes between the two. Nevertheless, both were similar in that they were dried, grated coconut with physical characteristics that permitted overlapping uses. Therefore, Brazil determined that the product most "like" the imported product in terms of physical characteristics was the domestic desiccated coconut, but also concluded that competition between imported desiccated coconut and Brazilian coconut was a significant condition of the Brazilian market that had to be considered in the injury determination. Brazil noted that in its discussion of the like product in the Ordinance, item B, para. 4 was the only place in which it stated what product was "similar" or "like" the imported product. In Brazil's view, this confirmed its position that Item B discussed the analysis of like product in four paragraphs but only provided *one* definition of like product, and that definition of like product was based on physical characteristics as required by Article VI - to the extent that Article VI could be interpreted as establishing a "like product" requirement.

162. The Philippines argued that the ambivalence of Brazil's like product determination was demonstrated by what it termed Brazil's apparent confusion about the effect of considering only desiccated coconut for retail sale in evaluating apparent consumption data that included non-competing desiccated coconut for retail sale. In the Philippines' view, the Ordinance states that this would make the share of imports more accentuated, while Brazil argued in its first submission

---

[51] L/978 (adopted 13 May 1959), BISD 8S/145, para. 12.

that the share of imports was understated by this comparison. The Philippines argued that Brazil had also argued in its first submission that the like product included desiccated coconut for both the retail and non-retail markets, but continued to describe the data on apparent consumption as overstated due to the inclusion of desiccated coconut for retail sale. In the Philippines' view the inclusion of desiccated coconut for retail sale in the apparent consumption data would simply make the data fit the definition of like product if the like product included desiccated coconut for both retail and non-retail sale.

2.   *Material Injury*

163.   The Philippines referred to several factors, acknowledged in the Ordinance, which in its view undermined the finding of material injury. The Philippines noted that, after an 8 per cent decrease in 1991, the domestic price of Brazilian desiccated coconut increased by 23 per cent in 1992-93, and by 5 per cent in 1993-94. In addition, the operating profits of the Brazilian co-petitioners averaged 25 per cent for the 1991 to 1994 period. One co-petitioner's gross margin was constant from 1990 to 1993, indicating that its sales were not affected by price pressures and its operating margins were also reasonably stable. The other co-petitioner's operating margins were also stable. The production of the co-petitioners increased by 30 per cent from 1991-94, and one co-petitioner expanded its production capacity.

164.   In the Philippines' view, such increases in production, stability in profits and operating margins, and substantial price increases belied the existence of any material injury, and instead indicated that the co-petitioners themselves had been thriving. Moreover, given that the co-petitioners were actually able to increase their production significantly from 1991-94, the Philippines considered it obvious that imports of desiccated coconut from the Philippines did not cause the co-petitioners to reduce their prior level of production. Rather, the Philippines considered that the co-petitioners were apparently complaining that the lower-priced imports allegedly limited their ability to increase their production at projected rates. However, the Ordinance did not identify any data supporting such projected increases, and did not even provide figures for the anticipated increase in production rates. As a result, there was nothing on record to show that the co-petitioners' growth and profit projections were reasonable and realistic, rather than merely speculative. The Philippines asserted that these growth projections seemed to be based on information unreliable on its face. The co-petitioners' data on installed capacity were aggregated for desiccated coconut and other products (such as coconut fruit and coconut milk). Consequently, it was possible that any allegedly unsatisfactory growth in production was attributable to those other products, not to desiccated coconut.

165.   Brazil maintained that it looked at relevant factors that indicated that the domestic industry was injured. Brazil found that national production (including production by the importing company) fell by 45 per cent in the period 1989 to 1994, while production of the domestic industry (excluding production by the

importing company) declined by 31 per cent during the period 1991 to 1994. There was a decrease in capacity utilization throughout the period. The level of employment in the industry declined 13 per cent between 1991 and 1994. Finally, the domestic industry's share of apparent consumption dropped from 63.9 per cent in 1991 to 37.7 per cent in 1994. Brazil also argued that the fact that the production of the two co-petitioners increased during that period did not indicate no injury to the domestic industry. Injury was to the industry as a whole not to individual producers. Therefore, the fact that one of the co-petitioners obtained a greater share of a declining national production did not indicate a lack of injury to the domestic industry as a whole.

166.   Thus, Brazil argued, there was substantial evidence that the domestic industry was injured. Brazil noted that the requirement of an objective examination of positive evidence was found in Article 6:1 of the Tokyo Round SCM Code but not in Article VI of GATT 1994. Brazil argued that it nonetheless considered all relevant economic factors, some of which indicated injury, such as declining production, employment, and capacity utilization, others of which, such as operating results, did not. That not all indicators were negative did not detract from its finding. Brazil argued that previous Panel decisions recognized that a finding of injury may be based on an objective examination of positive evidence even where not all factors are negative.[52] In Brazil's view, the Philippines' arguments sought to have the Panel substitute its judgement for that of the investigating authorities as to which factors were more important indicators of injury in this case, which Brazil asserted was beyond the authority of the Panel.

167.   The Philippines argued that it was misleading for Brazil to rely on the employment trends and capacity utilization data of the two co-petitioners alone as being those of the industry. More importantly, in the Philippines' view, Brazil did not explain how such data could be a reliable basis for drawing any conclusions about the desiccated coconut industry, when Brazil conceded in the Ordinance that the data could not be disaggregated by product. In the Philippines' view, the data were indeterminate, and therefore could not support conclusions about capacity utilization and employment levels in the desiccated coconut industry.

3.   Causation

168.   The Philippines considered that, even if the domestic industry were deemed to have suffered some material injury, Brazil had failed to show that such injury was caused by the alleged subsidies on desiccated coconut imports from the Philippines. The Philippines asserted that, pursuant to Article VI:6(a) of GATT 1994, an alleged injury must be "the effect of the ... subsid[y]" in order to justify any countervailing action, and Brazil was therefore required to analyze the allegedly subsidized imports' volume, price effect and impact on the domestic

---

[52]   In this regard, Brazil referred to the reports of the Panels in *Cotton Yarn*, para. 524, *Audiocassettes*, para. 422, and *Salmon*, para. 305.

market. The Philippines argued that Brazil relied on data referring to different time periods for different aspects of its analysis, inconsistent data, and random presentation of prices, quantities and ratios, which left its analysis unclear and unsupported.

169. Brazil argued that the consideration of the volume, price effect, and impact on the domestic market, was a requirement of the Tokyo Round SCM Code, not Article VI, which did not contain any guidance on the elements of an injury determination. Nonetheless, Brazil asserted that it had properly considered those factors in making its determination.

170. Brazil also maintained that it did not rely on data for different periods in its evaluation of injury, as argued by the Philippines. Brazil acknowledged that data regarding longer periods, from 1989 through 1994, were also considered where available, but asserted that data for the period of investigation, 1991 through 1994, were considered in all cases. The only exception was where Brazil looked at the imports authorized in the first months of 1995, which Brazil asserted was a reasonable examination aimed at using the most up to date data possible.

(a)   Volume

171. The Philippines argued that Brazil's evaluation of the volume of imports was unclear. For instance, the Philippines noted that the Ordinance referred to an 89.93 per cent increase in imports of all "coconut products" from 1991-94, but did not indicate what part of that increase was desiccated coconut (as distinguished from other types of coconut products), and did not break down desiccated coconut imports by country, by month, or by year. In the Philippines' view, it was impossible to determine from this data the proportion of the total increase in imports accounted for by desiccated coconut, and the proportion accounted for by imports of desiccated coconut from the investigated countries, as distinguished from those not under investigation. While the Ordinance stated that the investigated countries accounted for 80 per cent of imports from 1989-94, in the Philippines' view, this percentage was meaningless because the Ordinance failed to establish the share of the total increase in coconut product imports accounted for by desiccated coconut imports. Moreover, the Philippines asserted that it was improper to use a 1989-94 time frame in calculating the investigated countries' share in desiccated coconut imports, and a 1991-94 time frame in calculating the increase of total coconut imports, because the difference in time periods precluded any accurate comparison.

172. Similarly, the Philippines contended, the Ordinance failed to distinguish desiccated coconut from other coconut products in the analysis of apparent consumption. The Philippines asserted that Brazil had determined that the like product was limited to desiccated coconut destined for the industrial market, excluding desiccated coconut for retail sale, but the Ordinance acknowledged that data on apparent consumption were overstated by the inclusion of desiccated coconut for retail sale, noting that it was not possible to obtain production data by market

destination. In the Philippines' view, it was thus impossible to determine whether the like product, desiccated coconut for industrial sale, had an increasing or decreasing share in apparent consumption. As a result, even if import share in domestic consumption increased in absolute terms, it was not possible to determine whether import share also increased relative to the domestic like product. This indeterminate information on apparent consumption thus obscured any causal relationship between the share of imports and the share of the domestic like product in apparent consumption. Moreover, the Philippines noted that, if the like product excluded desiccated coconut for retail sale, then imports for retail sale should have been excluded from the import volume data. However, the Ordinance did not identify the proportion of total imports accounted for by imports for retail sale. On the other hand, if the like product included all desiccated coconut, regardless of the market in which it was sold, then the apparent consumption data were not overstated.

173.   Brazil asserted that, in determining the effects of imports, it had cumulated the imports from the five countries under investigation, and found that imports of the subject product increased substantially during the period of investigation. Brazil asserted that DTIC Opinion 006/95 made clear that the only products considered in the analysis were desiccated coconut and coconut milk, the products subject to the investigation. Moreover, Table 10 in DTIC Opinion 006/95 showed both that cumulated imports of desiccated coconut, and the imports from the Philippines alone, increased significantly. The Ordinance also indicated, based on import licenses granted for the period January through May 1995, that imports were likely to increase. Thus, Brazil argued that the data showed both an increase during the period of investigation and in the imminent future of imports in absolute terms. Brazil asserted that it had found that the countries accounting for most of the increase in imports of desiccated coconut were the Philippines, the Ivory Coast, Sri Lanka, and Indonesia (all subject to investigation) which together accounted for 81.2 per cent of the total imports from 1989 to 1995. Brazil also argued that the information showed that imports increased significantly in relative terms. Brazil had found that apparent consumption overall increased 17 per cent in the period 1991 through 1994, while imports represented 35.8 per cent of the consumption in 1991 and 53.8 per cent in 1994. Thus, Brazil argued that the information supported its determination that the increase in subject imports in both absolute and relative terms was significant.

(b)   Price

174.   The Philippines argued that Brazil's consideration of price data was fundamentally flawed by its failure to examine actual import and domestic prices. Instead of considering actual import prices over a defined time period, the Philippines asserted that Brazil had relied on a single average price for imports from each country, calculated from CIF import prices, without reference to any time period. Referring to DTIC Opinion 004/95, the Philippines argued that there was no breakdown of prices by month and by year, that the only time frame men-

tioned was the period from May 1993 to April 1994, and that, with the exception of the data for Sri Lanka, the CIF prices cited in the Ordinance differed from those reported in DTIC Opinion 004/95.

175.   The Philippines observed that Brazil had constructed domestic desiccated coconut prices based on the average coconut fruit price, a conversion ratio of fruit to processed product, a markup for additional processing costs, and a 15 per cent profit rate, virtually twice as much as the 8 per cent rate used to construct the unsubsidized Philippine price in the subsidy analysis, resulting in domestic prices that in the Philippines' view were artificially higher than import prices. The Philippines argued that there was no justification for the use of a constructed domestic price in lieu of actual prices. Because a countervailing duty could be validly imposed only if the investigated imports directly competed with the domestic product, the imposition of a duty implies that there was in fact such competition, in which case the actual selling prices of both the imports and the domestic product in the Brazilian market should have been available. Yet, such prices were not obtained, and the failure to do so was not explained. In the Philippines' view, it was not possible to determine any price trends or price comparisons between imported and domestic prices in the absence of actual prices.

176.   The Philippines also asserted that the price and import volume data available actually indicated that there was no depression of domestic prices. In the Philippines' view, if lower priced imports had been affecting domestic prices, there would have been an inverse relationship between domestic price levels and import volume, as domestic producers would have had to cut prices to prevent their market share from being eroded by cheaper imports. However, on the contrary, the Philippines asserted that domestic prices and import quantities moved in the same general direction - both domestic prices and import volume decreased in 1991, and in each of the next two years. Thus, according to the Philippines, the data indicated that desiccated coconut imports did not depress domestic desiccated coconut prices.

177.   Brazil argued that the information supported its conclusion that there had been price undercutting by the cumulated imports, varying from 70 per cent for the Philippines to 104 per cent for Indonesia. In order to determine the price undercutting, Brazil had relied on a constructed domestic price in making the comparison. Brazil argued that it had constructed the domestic prices because there were no domestic prices unaffected by the subsidized imports, because the volume of subsidized imports was such that the domestic price could not remain unaffected, and because the imported product was at a different stage of production from the Brazilian desiccated coconut. Brazil asserted that if the purpose of analysing the prices was to determine the effect the subsidies had on the domestic prices, it was reasonable to attempt to determine what the price would be absent those subsidies. Constructing a price based on the cost of production plus the normal profit, was, in Brazil's view, a reasonable approach to measuring that effect.

178. Therefore, Brazilian prices were not comparable without adjustment. Brazil argued that the Philippines' complaint that the margin of profit used to construct Brazilian prices was 15 per cent while an 8 per cent profit margin was used to construct Philippine prices was a false complaint. Brazil asserted that the 15 percent margin reflected commercial reality in Brazil. Moreover, since Brazil never compared the unsubsidized Philippine price calculated for the subsidy analysis with the constructed domestic price, the Philippine price that Brazil constructed for purposes of determining the level of subsidization had no effect on the injury determination. Brazil asserted that the Brazilian domestic price was then compared to the actual CIF prices of the imports, adjusted to reflect the same level of trade as the Brazilian prices. Brazil asserted that it calculated the import price by adjusting CIF prices from import documents for freight and other expenses associated with bringing the product to the Brazilian market. This resulted, in Brazil's view, in an appropriate comparison at the same level of trade.

179. Brazil asserted that it had also found that average domestic prices had decreased in the first two years of the period of the injury investigation, then increased in the later part of the period of the injury investigation. However, Brazil asserted that it determined that such increases were accounted for by the initiation of the investigation and the implementation of the Plan Real, a currency stabilization plan that led to significant price increases. Therefore, Brazil concluded that these increases did not indicate a lack of price effect by the imports. In addition, Brazil asserted that the price information had been accorded less significance in its determination than other factors.

180. Brazil asserted that, as indicated in the Ordinance, it had placed the most importance on the volume of imports, the decline in production, and the increasing share of apparent consumption accounted for by the imports, in reaching its determination that the subsidized imports caused injury. In Brazil's view, this analysis was consistent with the requirements of both Article VI of GATT 1994 and the Tokyo Round SCM Code. Brazil again noted that Article VI provided no guidance as to what factors to consider in determining injury, and asserted that therefore, a consideration of reasonable factors was sufficient to meet the requirements of Article VI. Brazil argued that its analysis considered all relevant economic factors in making the determination.

181. The Philippines asserted that Brazil's proffered explanations underlying its consideration of constructed prices in evaluating price effects should be disregarded by the Panel because they were *ex post facto* rationalizations. In addition, the Philippines asserted that Brazil's explanations were in any event flawed. First, by assuming that there were no Brazilian prices unaffected by the subsidized imports, Brazil began its price effect analysis having already assumed such a price effect. Second, Brazil's proffered explanation that prices had to be constructed because the domestic and imported products were at different stages of production, and were thus not comparable without adjustment, was without merit, given that Brazil's formula for constructing the domestic price contained no adjustment for differing stages of production. In addition, the Philippines argued that Brazil had failed to explain or justify its calculation of a single average import price per

country. The Philippines had pointed out the difference between virtually all the CIF prices referred to in the Ordinance and those referred to in DTIC Opinion 004/95. Brazil's argument that DTIC Opinion 006/95 was the appropriate reference did not address this concern, since DTIC Opinion 006/95 referred to the same set of import documents as DTIC Opinion 004/95. However, in DTIC Opinion 006/95, different CIF prices were derived from those documents, without any explanation. Thus, in the Philippines' view, Brazil's calculation of import prices was highly suspect, and therefore the evaluation of price effects was not based on positive evidence.

182.   Brazil noted that the data contained in DTIC Opinion 004/95 was not necessarily final information used as a basis for the determination in the investigation and differed from the data contained in DTIC Opinion 006/95. Brazil noted that, as stated in the final Ordinance, after the meeting with the Technical Consultative Counsel at which DTIC Opinion 004/95 was discussed, it was decided to collect additional injury information.

183.   The Philippines also argued that even DTIC Opinion 006/95 does not state any determination concerning the cause of price increases, but merely notes that price increases "may have" been occasioned by the two factors referred to by Brazil. In the Philippines' view, this was insufficient to constitute a finding on the question. Moreover, Brazil's argument failed to explain how price increases in 1993-94 could be accounted for by the countervailing investigation initiated on 21 June 1994.

(c)   Impact of Imports and Other Factors

184.   In the view of the Philippines, the finding of causation ultimately hinged on the mere juxtaposition of the following two factors: the decrease of the market share of the domestic producers of desiccated coconut, which in turn supposedly decreased domestic production due to the lesser demand, and the increase in import volume and in import participation in domestic consumption. However, the Philippines argued that there was no reliable evidence that desiccated coconut imports caused the difficulties allegedly experienced by the Brazilian desiccated coconut producers. Instead, the Philippines argued that the evidence on record indicated that the problems of the domestic producers were caused by other factors wholly peculiar to Brazil's coconut industry.

185.   The Philippines argued that, contrary to the requirements of Article VI of GATT 1994, Brazil had ignored those other factors, and had merely listed them without assessing their impact or making any findings to ensure that their adverse effects on the domestic industry were not blamed on the allegedly subsidized imports. Among the factors Brazil assertedly disregarded were Brazil's unusually high domestic raw material and production costs. In this regard, the Philippines cited DTIC Opinion 004/95, referring to Brazil's unusually high production cost. The Philippines maintained that the co-petitioners had admitted that high costs and social benefits made Brazil's production cost higher than that of imported products. The Philippines asserted that, in light of the admissions of the co-

petitioners regarding the significance of high domestic production costs, the failure to evaluate the extent to which those costs caused the alleged injury was improper. Moreover, the Philippines argued the cost of coconut fruit became prohibitive for producers of desiccated coconut when an alternative market, the "in natura" market, offered coconut fruit prices higher than desiccated coconut producers. Yet, the Philippines asserted that Brazil had failed to assess how these prohibitive raw material costs affected domestic prices during the period under investigation.

186.   The Philippines asserted that the Ordinance listed several other non-import factors that adversely affected the production of coconut fruit, and as a result, the production of desiccated coconut. However, Brazil had not explained why any one or combination of those other factors could not have caused the alleged decrease in the production of coconut fruit and desiccated coconut. Among the other factors the Philippines asserted Brazil had admitted affected the coconut industry were: (1) a considerable number of farmers had opted to change from giant or hybrid trees to dwarf trees; (2) many farmers had converted their farms to non-coconut crops such as sugarcane, especially in Brazil's Northeastern region, where Brazil's coconut fruit production was most heavily concentrated; (3) all coconut farmers chose not to replant senile trees, whose percentage of all of Brazil's coconut trees was not identified; (4) farmers sold coconut lands to non-coconut industries that were widely expanding in Brazil's Northeastern region; (5) the high prices offered by the "in natura" market to fruit producers caused a decrease in the offer of fruit to the processors of desiccated coconut; and (6) a drought lasted for years during the period under review. In the Philippines' view, the drought alone could account for much of the decrease in desiccated coconut production due to the resulting fruit shortage, which in turn caused, rather than was caused by, a corresponding increase in imports to remedy that shortage.

187.   Brazil argued that Article VI does not require an examination of other factors in determining whether there is a causal connection between the injury and the subsidized imports. Under Article VI, it was sufficient that the subsidized imports were found to cause injury. However, Article 6:4 of the Tokyo Round SCM Code does require the consideration of other factors, and Brazil asserted that it had examined other factors that might be causing injury but found that the imported product was nevertheless causing material injury to the domestic industry. Referring to the Panel report in *Salmon*, Brazil argued that past panel practice indicated that the consideration of other factors need not be extensive. Brazil found that, as stated during the investigation, given the importance of the raw material in the total cost of fabrication of the desiccated coconut and the effect of the subsidies on the imported desiccated coconut, the subsidized imports were by themselves the cause of the injury to the domestic industry.

188.   The Philippines argued that Brazil erred in taking the position that Article VI does not require an examination of other factors in determining whether there is a causal connection between the injury and the subsidized imports. The Philippines questioned how investigating authorities could be sure that the injury was

caused by subsidized imports, rather than by other factors, other than by considering the latter. Referring to the Panel report in *Grain Corn*, the Philippines argued that it was not enough for an investigating country to have "acknowledged the existence of factors other than subsidized imports having an effect" on the domestic industry, if that country "made no effort to ensure that the injuries caused by other factors were not attributed to the subsidized imports".[53] The Philippines also took issue with Brazil's statement that the analysis of other factors need not be extensive, arguing that while the public summary of that analysis could be brief, the analysis itself should be extensive. Moreover, the Philippines asserted, the explanation of the analysis should be more extensive if the investigation showed that there were significant other factors present that could have caused injury to the domestic industry. A mere listing of the "other factors" was insufficient, in light of the Panel report in *Grain Corn*. For example, the Philippines asserted that the drought and the availability of an alternative market for coconut fruit, the "in natura" market, could very well account for all three elements which Brazil claimed supported its determination, the volume of imports, declines in domestic production, and the increasing share of apparent consumption accounted for by the imports. Indeed, information on the record indicated a correlation between import volume and drought-induced fruit shortages.

E.   Agreement on Agriculture

189.   Even assuming that the investigated programmes constituted subsidies on the production of coconut fruit, the Philippines asserted that they were not countervailable because they fully complied with the developing country and *de minimis* exemptions under Article 6 of the Agreement on Agriculture.

190.   The Philippines referred to Article 6.2 of the Agreement on Agriculture as recognizing that "government measures of assistance, whether direct or indirect, to encourage agricultural and rural development are an integral part of the development programmes of developing countries ...", and that

> "investment subsidies which are generally available to agriculture in developing country Members and agricultural input subsidies generally available to low-income or resource-poor producers in developing country Members shall be exempt from domestic support reduction commitments ... ".

The Philippines maintained that, as evidenced in the information furnished to Brazil, the Philippine programmes, which in the Philippines' view involve investment subsidies, e.g, replanting, and input subsidies, e.g, fertilizers and affordable interest rates, complied with Article 6. These forms of assistance were generally available, to the extent funds permitted, to the agricultural sector, including the most disadvantaged sectors such as coconut farming. The Philippines

---

[53]   *Grain Corn*, para. 5.2.8.

argued that in recognition of the special needs of developing countries, these programmes are exempt from any reduction commitments in the Agreement on Agriculture.

191.   The Philippines also asserted that the *de minimis* provision of Article 6.4 of the Agreement on Agriculture further exempts from reduction commitments even Philippine support measures which do not meet the criteria in Article 6.2. Article 6.4 of the Agreement on Agriculture provides:

> "(a)   A member shall not be required to include in the calculation of its Current Total AMS and shall not be required to reduce:
>
> (i)   product-specific domestic support which would otherwise be required to be included in a Member's calculations ... where such support does not exceed 5 per cent of ... total value of production of a basic agricultural product during the relevant year; and
>
> (ii)   non-product-specific domestic support ... where such support does not exceed 5 per cent of the value of that Member's total agricultural production.
>
> (b)   For developing country Members, the *de minimis* percentage under this paragraph shall be 10 per cent".

The Philippines argued that Brazil failed to estimate the amount of the alleged subsidy and to show that the Philippines provided domestic support up to, or near, the corresponding *de minimis* amount.

192.   Thus, the Philippines argued, since the Philippine programmes complied with Article 6 of the Agreement on Agriculture, Brazil could not impose countervailing measures on imports of Philippine desiccated coconut without demonstrating that such imports caused material injury to the relevant Brazilian industry. However, the Philippines maintained that Brazil had failed to demonstrate that the domestic industry suffered material injury, or that any injury that allegedly occurred could be attributed to Philippine desiccated coconut imports, and not to other causes. Thus, Brazil's countervailing duty on Philippine imports of desiccated coconuts was inconsistent with Brazil's obligations under the Agreement on Agriculture.

193.   Brazil asserted that the limitations on actionability provided for in Article 13 of the Agreement on Agriculture did not apply in this case. First, the countervailing duties imposed by Brazil were not subject to the limitations of Article 13, which applies to countervailing duties covered both by Article VI of GATT 1994 and by Part V of the Agreement on Subsidies and Countervailing Measures. Brazil asserted that the Philippines had conceded that the SCM Agreement did not apply to this dispute by virtue of Article 32.3. Therefore, Bra-

zil argued that the Agreement on Agriculture similarly did not apply, and the countervailing duties in this case were not subject to any of the limitations on actionability provided in Article 13.

194.   Brazil also maintained that the Philippines' arguments that its subsidy programmes were not countervailable because they complied with developing country and *de minimis* exemptions under Article 6 of the Agreement on Agriculture were superfluous. Brazil asserted that the Philippines had recognized that the Agreement on Agriculture merely required that Brazil make a finding of material injury to the relevant Brazilian industry before imposing countervailing duties on these products. Brazil read the Philippines' argument to claim that its programmes were covered by Article 13(b)(i), which requires Brazil to make an injury finding.[54] Thus even if the Philippines were correct in arguing that the Agreement on Agriculture is applicable, and that the Philippine programmes complied with that Agreement, Brazil had made the requisite injury finding, consistent with the requirements of the Agreement on Agriculture.

195.   Brazil also contended that, even assuming, *arguendo*, that Article 13(b)(i) were applicable in this case, the Philippines had failed to demonstrate that its programmes met the requirements of that provision. Because Article 13 of the Agreement on Agriculture is an exception to the SCM Agreement, in Brazil's view the Philippines bore the burden of demonstrating that its programmes qualified for that exception. Brazil considered that the Philippines' argument, that its programmes fell within Article 13(b) because they provide domestic support within *de minimis* levels and in conformity with Article 6, was insufficient. In Brazil's view, the Philippines provided no specific evidence that its programmes complied with the requirements of Article 6.2.[55] Brazil asserted that, lacking any specific factual support, the conclusory statements of the Philippines failed to meet the Philippines' burden of demonstrating compliance with Article 6.2. Moreover, the conclusory statements themselves failed to state the required conclusions: the Philippines did not state that the subsidies were generally available to "low-income or resource-poor producers," but that they were generally available to the agricultural sector, "including the most disadvantaged sectors such as coconut farming".[56] In Brazil's view this made clear that the programmes were not limited to "low-income or resource-poor producers". Moreover, Brazil argued that the Philippines' statement that the programmes were generally available, whether to the agricultural sector or to low-income or resource-poor pro-

---

[54]   In Brazil's view, the Philippines was not arguing that the Philippine programmes were non-actionable under Article 13(a) Agreement on Agriculture, as meeting the requirements of Annex II of the Agreement on Agriculture, the so-called "green box".

[55]   Brazil asserted that the Philippines had not provided this information during the investigation, either.

[56]   Brazil noted that this argument contradicted the Philippines' claim that the subsidies to the coconut growers were funded by the coconut levy. If the programmes were generally available to the agricultural sector, there would be no possibility that a levy on the coconut producers entirely funded the programmes.

ducers, was inaccurate. Most of the investigated programmes were available only to those growing coconuts, and others (e.g., the Agrarian Reform Programme) were available only for a limited number of products. Other low-income and re-source-poor producers did not receive the subsidies in question. Thus, Brazil asserted that the subsidies did not fully conform to the requirements of Article 6.2.

196.   Brazil also argued that the Philippines had failed to demonstrate that its subsidies were *de minimis*. Instead, the Philippines had simply asserted that Brazil had failed to show that the Philippine programmes exceeded *de minimis* levels. Brazil considered that the Philippines mistakenly assumed that the burden was on Brazil to demonstrate that the Philippines did not qualify for the exception. In Brazil's view, the Philippine argument highlighted the fundamental flaw of the position that the terms of the Agriculture Agreement applied to Brazilian activity that pre-dated the Agreement, by requiring Brazil to have applied the terms of an agreement that was not even in force at the time that Brazil initiated the investigation that resulted in the imposition of duties.

V.   ARGUMENTS PRESENTED BY THIRD PARTIES

A.   Canada

197.   Canada argued that, notwithstanding Article 32.3 of the SCM Agreement, Articles I, II, and VI of GATT 1994 were applicable to existing countervailing measures, even if those measures were first enacted or imposed before the entry into force of the WTO. In Canada's view, there was nothing retroactive in requiring WTO Members to continue to maintain only those tariff and non-tariff measures that were consistent with their GATT 1994 obligations. Moreover, the inapplicability of the SCM Agreement to an investigation did not prevent the application of Article VI of GATT 1994 to existing countervailing measures imposed as a result of such investigations. In Canada's view, the possible applicability of the Tokyo Round SCM Code, and the potential inapplicability of the SCM Agreement, were not germane to the question of whether the Brazilian measure in question could be justified as a countervailing duty under Article VI.

198.   Canada argued that the obligations of Articles I and II of GATT 1994 applied to all measures of a WTO Member, including measures that were initiated or imposed before the entry into force of the WTO for that Member. Accordingly, the exceptions to those Articles, in particular Article VI of GATT 1994, were equally available to a Member complained against to justify a measure, provided that it met the criteria set out in Article VI.

199.   Canada noted that under the GATT 1947, Contracting Parties enjoyed the protection of Articles VI and XVI of GATT 1947, and the benefits of GATT 1947 dispute settlement, while the signatories to the Tokyo Round SCM Code had additional rights and obligations that they could enforce under the dispute settlement mechanism of that Code. Contracting Parties which were also signatories to the Tokyo Round SCM Code had the choice of proceeding under the Code

or the GATT, and the choice of forum depended on the nature of the asserted inconsistency, the nature of applicable obligations, and the remedies available.

200. With the entry into force of the WTO Agreements, the various Agreements that have superseded the Tokyo Round Codes are integral to the WTO and apply to all Members, with the DSB as the single forum for enforcement of rights and obligations under any of the Agreements. However, the fact that a WTO Agreement, in this case the SCM Agreement, may not be applicable to the specific circumstances of a case did not preclude the application of GATT 1994, in this case Article VI, to the same circumstances. In Canada's view, the text of Article 32.2 of the SCM Agreement expressly limited the application of that Agreement only, and not the application of Article VI of GATT 1994. Moreover, there was nothing in GATT 1994 itself that limited its application to measures or practices imposed or enacted after the entry into force of the WTO for the Members concerned. Canada maintained that nothing in the SCM Agreement or GATT 1994 prevented the application of GATT 1994 obligations to existing measures. In Canada's view, the Panel has jurisdiction to examine all existing measures for consistency with obligations that have not been expressly excluded from its jurisdiction. The inapplicability of the SCM Agreement or the applicability of the Tokyo Round SCM Code should not preclude a panel from reviewing the existing measures of a Member for consistency with that Member's ongoing GATT 1994 obligations. The fact that enactment or imposition of a measure antedated the entry into force of the WTO should not preclude review of the measure as currently applied in accordance with WTO norms due to concerns over retroactivity or the legal distinctiveness of GATT 1994 and GATT 1947.

201. Canada also argued that the existence of potential recourse to the Tokyo Round SCM Committee for dispute settlement under the Tokyo Round SCM Code was not dispositive of the issue - the availability of one forum and legal instrument did not foreclose the availability of other fora or instruments to WTO Members, and in particular did not foreclose reliance on basic GATT obligations by WTO Members. Similarly, the possibility of domestic review proceedings in Brazil was not dispositive of the issue. Nothing in the Tokyo Round SCM Code, the SCM Agreement, or GATT 1994 required the Philippines to challenge existing measures through domestic review mechanisms to the exclusion of the WTO dispute settlement process.

202. Canada also agreed that Brazil's failure to consult with the Philippines constituted a violation of Brazil's obligations under Article 4.3 of the DSU. In Canada's view, whatever Brazil's view of the appropriate terms of consultations, the refusal to consult without first establishing those terms constituted a refusal to consult in violation of Brazil's obligations. Entering into consultations where a request is made was a basic procedural obligation of every WTO Member. Brazil should have presented its substantive or procedural objections to the Philippines during consultations, and at the meetings of the DSB, and ultimately to a panel, rather than frustrating the consultative process.

B.   European Communities

203.   On the question of the law applicable to this dispute, the EC took the position that the Philippines had brought its complaint to the wrong forum under the wrong law. The EC argued that the principle of non-retroactivity of treaty obligations, embodied in Article 28 of the Vienna Convention, precluded the application of Article VI of GATT 1994 to the Brazilian countervailing measures in question. This interpretation was, in the EC's view, consistent with the transitional provisions of Article 32.3 of the SCM Agreement, as well as the Tokyo Round SCM Committee's Decision on Consequences of Termination. In the EC's view, the principle of non-retroactivity required that the determination made by Brazil be challenged only under the provisions of the law in force between the parties at the time the application was filed, i.e., GATT 1947 and the Tokyo Round SCM Code. The EC noted that the Philippines continued to have recourse to dispute settlement under the Tokyo Round SCM Code, and in addition, if it considered the collection of countervailing duties after 1 January 1995 inconsistent with GATT 1994, it could seek a review under Brazilian law, which review would be conducted in accordance with the SCM Agreement and GATT 1994. Finally, the EC argued that Article 13 of the Agriculture Agreement applies only with respect to investigations covered by both Article VI of GATT 1994 and the SCM Agreement. Pursuant to Article 32.3 of the SCM Agreement, that Agreement did not apply to the Brazilian countervailing duty. Consequently, regardless of the Panel's decision whether Article VI applied to this dispute, Article 13 of the Agreement on Agriculture did not apply, and the Philippines' claim relating to that provision should be deemed inadmissible. The EC also supported the Brazilian request for a preliminary ruling on the question of the admissibility of the Philippines' claims, particularly since Brazil's objections covered all the claims raised by the Philippines.

204.   The EC rejected the Philippines' argument that Article 30.3 of the Vienna Convention required the application of GATT 1994 to this dispute. The EC argued that there was no conflict between the Tokyo Round SCM Code and GATT 1994 with respect to the Brazilian investigation, since Article VI of GATT 1994 did not apply to that investigation. Consequently, there was no need to resort to Article 30.3 to determine the applicable law, as there was no conflict between successive treaties dealing with the same subject matter.

205.   The EC supported Brazil's view that Article 28 of the Vienna Convention precluded the application of Article VI of GATT 1994 to this dispute, since the investigation was initiated pursuant to an application made prior to the entry into force of the WTO Agreements, including the SCM Agreement. In the EC's view, the operative act in this case was the application for countervailing duty, filed in 1994. The investigation, and the resulting duties, all flowed from that act, and must all be judged in light of the law in effect at the time of that act. The EC noted that the WTO Agreement did not contain any express provision requiring the retroactive application of Article VI of GATT 1994, nor was there any other basis on which such an intention could be established. To the contrary, the terms

of the SCM Agreement, and the decisions of the Tokyo Round SCM Committee supported the conclusion that no retroactive application was intended.

206.   The EC also noted that, unlike the Tokyo Round SCM Code and GATT 1947, which were distinct agreements with their own dispute settlement procedures and differing membership, Article VI of GATT 1994 and the SCM Agreement are part of the same agreement, the WTO Agreement, bind all Members, and are covered by the same dispute settlement arrangements. The EC asserted that the title and wording of Article 10 of the SCM Agreement evidence the intention of the parties that Article VI of GATT 1994 should apply only in conjunction with the more detailed rules contained in the SCM Agreement. Moreover, the EC asserted that this same intention is reflected in Article 32.1 of the SCM Agreement, and was further confirmed by the language of Article 13 of the Agreement on Agriculture. Article 13 of the Agreement on Agriculture exempted from the imposition of countervailing duties those countervailing duties covered by Article VI of GATT and Part V of the SCM Agreement. The EC argued that this indicated that the drafters of the WTO Agreement did not envisage the autonomous application of Article VI of GATT 1994. The EC maintained that, had such an eventuality been contemplated, it would have been anomalous not to extend the exemption to the imposition of countervailing duties which are covered only by Article VI of GATT 1994.

207.   The EC distinguished between the application, investigation, and imposition of duties, and the continued collection of duties. The EC argued that the collection of countervailing duties on individual shipments could be characterized as a situation arising out of a previous act. As such, the law applicable to continuing collection of duties was that in effect at the time duties were actually collected. Thus, for duties collected after the entry into force of the WTO, Article VI of GATT 1994 would apply. In the EC's view, however, in that case, the only obligation of the importing country would be to open, upon request, a review of the measures, in light of the new requirements of Article VI of GATT 1994, which review would be conducted under the SCM Agreement. The EC cited the decision of the Panel in *Non-Rubber Footwear* in support of its view, arguing that the situation in that case involved a similar issue, and the Panel in that case concluded that although the determinations underlying the duties could not be invalidated, the collection of duties pursuant to those determinations was subject to the new requirements of the Tokyo Round SCM Code. However, the Panel had further concluded that the importing country's obligations in this regard were satisfied if a right to request a review of the determination was afforded.

208.   Regarding the issue of the scope of the terms of reference, in response to a question from the Panel, the EC argued that a precise statement of claims in the request for establishment of a panel was essential to safeguard the defense rights of the respondent as well as the right of third parties to intervene in the dispute. Moreover, a precise definition of claims was necessary to ensure that the parties had been given an opportunity to reach a satisfactory solution of the matter during the consultation stage. The EC considered that the Panel reports referred to by Brazil on this matter provided a correct view of what constitutes a claim, and

of the degree of specificity required for a claim to be considered by a panel. The EC also argued that the principles developed by these Panels had been confirmed by Article 6.2 of the DSU. The EC considered that, in accordance with the terms of Article 6.2 of the DSU and the principles derived from previous Panel reports, the request for establishment of a panel should include, with respect to each particular claim, at least the following elements: (a) the infringing measure, (b) the obligation under the WTO Agreement which the complainant considered to have been violated, and (c) a brief explanation of the way in which the measure infringed the legal obligations. With respect to element (b), the EC maintained that a simple reference to one of the WTO Agreements without further specification was clearly insufficient, and a reference to a particular Article might be insufficient if the Article laid down more than one obligation. With respect to element (c), the EC stated that the explanation was to be distinguished from the arguments, i.e. the legal or factual reasoning advanced to support, clarify, or explain the claim. The EC noted in this regard that a claim might be supported by one or more arguments, and the same argument might support one or more claims. Furthermore, the EC maintained that the claims should be specifically identified as such in the request for establishment of a panel. The EC asserted that practice under the DSU, while still very limited, confirmed these principles, referring in this regard to the report of the Panel in *Reformulated Gasoline*, para. 6.19, and the interim report issued to the parties in *Japan - Taxes on alcoholic beverages*, WT/DS8, 10, 11, para. 6.

C. Indonesia

209. Indonesia supported the Philippines' position that the countervailing duty imposed by Brazil was inconsistent with Articles VI:3 and 6(a) of GATT 1994 and the Agreement on Agriculture. In Indonesia's view, the Philippine programmes, although they could be categorised as subsidies, were not countervailable, as they were fully in compliance with developing countries' rights and the *de minimis* exception of Article 6 of the Agriculture Agreement. Indonesia argued that since Brazil's determination was made in August 1995, the Agreement on Agriculture was applicable. Indonesia also argued that Brazil erred in relying on the best information available, and failed to take account of relevant information submitted by the Philippines.

D. Sri Lanka

210. Sri Lanka took the view that the countervailing duty in question, as applied both to imports of desiccated coconut from the Philippines, and to imports of desiccated coconut and coconut milk powder from Sri Lanka, was inconsistent with the provisions of GATT 1994 and the Agreement on Agriculture. Sri Lanka asserted that, in imposing that duty, Brazil had violated Articles I and II of GATT 1994. In Sri Lanka's view, the countervailing duty could not be justified under Article VI of GATT 1994. Sri Lanka asserted that the Sri Lankan programmes investigated by Brazil were not subsidies, since they were paid for by a

mandatory levy on exports of coconut products. In addition, the Philippine domestic support measures found by Brazil to constitute subsidies, like the Sri Lankan domestic support measures also found by Brazil to constitute subsidies, fell into the "green box" category of non-actionable subsidies under Article 13 of the Agreement on Agriculture.

E.   United States

211.   The United States took the position that the Philippines was entitled to invoke Article VI of GATT 1994. In the United States' view, Brazil improperly relied on the fact that it commenced its countervailing duty investigation on imports of desiccated coconuts before 1 January 1995 to argue that GATT 1994 does not apply to that investigation. However, when Brazil became a WTO Member, it assumed the obligation not to levy countervailing duties after that date in a manner inconsistent with Article VI of GATT 1994. Brazil accepted this obligation notwithstanding its already-initiated countervailing duty investigation on desiccated coconut. The United States asserted that, should Brazil fail to respect its obligation to levy countervailing duties in a manner consistent with Article VI of GATT 1994, and levy duties in a manner inconsistent with its schedule of tariff concessions, it would impair its tariff bindings in violation of Article II of GATT 1994, which it also accepted when it became a WTO Member. In the United States' view, for purposes of determining Brazil's obligations under Article VI of GATT 1994, it was irrelevant when Brazil had commenced its countervailing duty investigation. The United States argued that while the SCM Agreement did not apply to this dispute, that situation did not affect the application of Article VI of GATT 1994. The United States, in response to a question from the Panel, indicated that the provisions of Article 10 of the SCM Agreement did not affect its analysis of the issue of applicable law. The United States asserted that Article 10, requiring that countervailing duties be imposed pursuant to the provisions of Article VI of GATT 1994 and the SCM Agreement, was applicable only in the case of investigations initiated pursuant to applications made after 1 January 1995, which was not the case here.

212.   The United States argued that the application of Article VI of GATT 1994 in this case did not represent the imposition of a new treaty obligation in respect of past acts, facts or situations in violation of Article 28 of the Vienna Convention. The act of *imposing* a countervailing duty was the act, fact or situation that is relevant. That act - the imposition of the countervailing duty - occurred after 1 January 1995. As such, Brazil was obligated to impose duties in accordance with its commitments under GATT 1994.

213.   The United States contended that, if GATT 1994 were not interpreted in this fashion, unacceptable, and unintended, results would ensue. For example, Members of the WTO which had not been signatories to the Tokyo Round SCM Code would have no basis upon which to enforce their rights if they were denied an injury test in a countervailing duty investigation commenced before 1 January 1995. GATT 1994 was the applicable provision in such instances and

its stand-alone character must be preserved. The United States observed that Brazil itself had brought disputes under GATT 1994, for instance against the United States concerning regulations on conventional and reformulated gasoline.

214.   The United States also took the position that, should the Panel find that the Philippines was within its rights to bring this dispute under GATT 1994, the Panel must conduct its examination of this matter in light of the provisions of Article VI of GATT 1994, without reference to the SCM Agreement or the Tokyo Round SCM Code. The United States observed that the terms of reference for this dispute referred to the relevant provisions in GATT 1994 and the Agreement on Agriculture, as well as the Philippines' request for establishment of a panel, Brazil's communication to the DSB and the record of discussions at the meeting of the DSB on 21 February 1996. Article 7.2 of the DSU states that "[p]anels shall address the relevant provisions in any covered agreement or agreements cited by the parties to the dispute." Thus, the only trade agreements which the Panel is free to use as guidance in determining the legal rights and obligations of the parties in this case are those which are covered agreements and are cited by the parties. Since the Tokyo Round SCM Code is not a "covered agreement" listed in Appendix 1 of the DSU, the United States argued that the Panel has no authority to apply the Tokyo Round SCM Code. Further, the SCM Agreement was equally unavailable as guidance for the Panel. By its own terms, Article 32.3, the SCM Agreement applied only to investigations initiated pursuant to applications made after 1 January 1995. Given the DSU mandate in Articles 3.2 and 19.2 that panels "cannot add to or diminish the rights and obligations provided for in the covered agreements," it was important that the Panel not consider agreements that were neither covered agreements nor cited by the parties. To do so would affect the rights and obligations of the parties in contravention of the terms of Article 3.2 and 19.2.

215.   The United States asserted that the Philippines' first submission referred, without directly citing, to concepts which mirror those contained in the Tokyo Round SCM Code and/or the SCM Agreement, but to which Article VI of GATT 1994 makes no reference. The United States argued that if the Philippines cannot rely on these Agreements directly, it may not incorporate their principles by indirect reference.

216.   In support of its position, the United States referred to the report of the Panel in the *Oilseeds* case. That Panel found that it could only make findings in respect of GATT 1947 and could not interpret the Tokyo Round SCM Code:

> "The Panel was established to make findings 'in the light of the relevant GATT provisions'; it therefore does not have the mandate to propose interpretations of the provisions of

the Subsidies Code which the Community invokes to justify
its position".[57]

217. The United States identified specific passages in the Philippines' first
submission which referred to concepts in the Tokyo Round SCM Code and/or the
SCM Agreement, which were not found in Article VI of GATT 1994, and asserted that with regard to these arguments, the Panel should take care to insure
that its examination did not extend beyond the concepts as envisaged under Article VI of GATT 1994 to an assessment of the elaborations of concepts in either
the Tokyo Round SCM Code or the SCM Agreement. The Panel should, in the
United States' view, take a "clean slate" approach to the concepts in Article VI of
GATT 1994 and determine on the basis of the information at its disposal whether
Brazil's conduct of this investigation was in compliance with the standards of
Article VI of GATT 1994 or not. It was imperative that the Panel refrain from
creating new rights and obligations that are not included in the text of Article VI
or that cannot be fairly said to flow directly from it. To do otherwise would affect
the balance of the parties' rights and obligations under GATT 1994, contrary to
DSU Articles 3.2 and 19.2.

218. The United States also argued that there were two fundamental flaws in
Brazil's injury determination, which made it inconsistent with Article VI of
GATT 1994, without reading into that Article the refined standards provided in
the Tokyo Round SCM Code or the SCM Agreement. First, Article VI:6(a) requires a causal nexus between the subsidized imports and material injury. However, in the United States' view, Brazil's injury determination did not discuss why
such a causal nexus might exist. This was not a question of the adequacy of the
analysis; the Brazilian determination effectively had no analysis of causation.
This absence of causal analysis was inconsistent with Article VI.

219. Second, Article VI:6(a) refers to material injury to "an" established domestic industry. However, the United States asserted that the injury determination
in this case did not use a consistent definition of domestic industry for its conclusions concerning material injury. The failure to base conclusions concerning material injury on a consistent industry definition, with no plausible reasons for this
inconsistency, was impermissible in the light of the requirement in Article VI to
assess material injury to "an" established domestic industry.

220. The United States also argued that the Panel should reject the Philippines'
request for specific and retroactive remedies, i.e., that Brazil revoke its countervailing duty on desiccated coconut exports from the Philippines and reimburse
any duties collected. In the United States' view, such specific and, in the case of
reimbursement retroactive remedies were inconsistent with established GATT
practice and the DSU. Instead, the United States argued that the Panel should
make a general recommendation, consistent with the DSU and established GATT
practice, that Brazil bring its countervailing duty order into conformity with Arti-

---

[57] *Oilseeds*, para. 154.

cle VI of GATT 1994.[58] In the United States' view, GATT rules and remedy recommendations are designed to protect expectations on the competitive relationship between imported and domestic products, rather than expectations on export volumes.

221.   The United States also argued that the *only* support for granting specific and retroactive remedies lay in three pre-WTO adopted panel reports involving anti-dumping and countervailing duties. However, the United States argued, a careful analysis of the DSU demonstrated that, insofar as remedies are concerned, the drafters of the DSU did not intend that anti-dumping and countervailing duty disputes be treated any differently than other types of disputes. In addition, even if the DSU were not dispositive on this issue, the Panel should not accord the three adopted panel reports any weight, because (1) the reports themselves were devoid of any justification for treating anti-dumping and countervailing disputes differently than other types of disputes, and (2) a review of the history of unadopted anti-dumping and countervailing duty panel reports indicated that there was no consensus under the pre-WTO regime that specific and retroactive remedies were ever appropriate.

222.   Regarding the issue of the scope of the terms of reference, in response to a question from the Panel, the United States stated that the Panel was required to examine "the matter" before it, which in the United States' view referred to the subject matter of the dispute as described in the request for establishment of a panel. Referring to Article 6.2 of the DSU, the United States asserted that, while the complaining party must identify the measures at issue, it need not put the contents of its first panel submission into its request for establishment of a panel, and need only provide a summary of the legal basis sufficient to present the problem clearly. In the United States' view, it followed that particular legal claims did not need to be identified with specificity, for instance by article of the agreement concerned. However, it was necessary to identify the legal basis for the request for establishment of a panel sufficiently to provide fair notice to the defending party and potential third parties. The United States asserted that the degree of specificity needed could best be judged in the context of the particular case, guided by the requirement of provision of fair notice. The United States maintained that an exact description of issues was not required under previous dispute settlement procedures, and to extent it may have been, this practice had been overruled by the terms of Article 6.2 of the DSU. The United States indicated that guidance on the principle it put forward could be taken from the reports of the Panels in the two *Salmon* disputes.

---

[58]   The United States noted, with respect to the Philippines' claim that Brazil's failure to revoke the countervailing duty on desiccated coconut and to reimburse any duties paid was inconsistent with Brazil's obligations under Article VI:3 and 6(a) of the GATT 1994, that it agreed with Brazil's statement and similarly did not understand how failure to revoke and reimburse, in the absence of a finding that the imposition was inconsistent with Brazil's obligations, could possibly constitute a violation in its own right.

223. In the United States' view, the resolution of the question whether specific issues were within the terms of reference required examination of the precise terms contained in the request for establishment of a panel. Referring specifically to the instant dispute, the United States argued that, since the legal basis of the complaint referred exclusively to specific articles of GATT 1994, it would not seem to be appropriately within the terms of reference of the Panel to now expand the legal basis of the complaint to entirely new provisions or to new measures, since the DSB would not have been on notice. However, if the claims in dispute merely involve particular arguments regarding the matter referred to in the request for establishment of a panel, and those arguments were based on the legal basis stated in that request, then the Panel could consider those arguments consistent with the terms of reference.

224. The United States took no position with respect to the applicability of the Agreement on Agriculture in this dispute.

VI. FINDINGS

A. Applicable Law

225. The first issue confronting this Panel is to determine whether the legal obligations cited by the Philippines are applicable to the disputed measure. The Philippines alleges that the imposition by Brazil of a countervailing duty on desiccated coconut from the Philippines was inconsistent with Articles I, II and VI of GATT 1994 and Article 13 of the Agreement on Agriculture. Brazil contends that under customary principles of international law and the terms of the WTO Agreement itself, neither GATT 1994 nor the Agreement on Agriculture apply to this dispute, as the investigation leading to the imposition of the measure was initiated pursuant to an application received prior to the date of entry into force of the WTO Agreement. Accordingly, this Panel is required to address, as a threshold matter, whether Articles I, II, and VI of GATT 1994 and Article 13 of the Agreement on Agriculture are applicable to this dispute. It should be emphasized that because this issue relates to the entry into force of the new WTO regime, the question of applicable law facing this Panel will cease to be relevant as this type of dispute becomes rarer and eventually disappears altogether.

1. Applicability of GATT 1994

226. Within the WTO system, the use of countervailing measures is governed principally by GATT 1994 and the WTO Agreement on Subsidies and Countervailing Measures ("the SCM Agreement"). Although the Philippines does not invoke the SCM Agreement in this case and, of course, is not required to do so, its applicability or otherwise to this dispute is highly relevant to the broader issue of applicable law. If we were to conclude that the SCM Agreement did not constitute applicable law in this dispute, in the sense that neither the parties nor this Panel could invoke it in construing the rights and obligations in dispute, we

would be presented with the issue whether Article VI of GATT 1994 and Article 13 of the Agreement on Agriculture could apply on their own, independently of the SCM Agreement. If, in turn, we were to find that Article VI of GATT 1994 and Article 13 of the Agreement on Agriculture could not apply on their own, then the non-applicability of the SCM Agreement would render Article VI of GATT 1994 and Article 13 of the Agreement on Agriculture inapplicable as well. In this case, the Philippines' claims under these provisions could not succeed.

227.   This Panel should make clear that if we were to find that, because of the non-applicability of the SCM Agreement, Article VI of GATT 1994 and Article 13 of the Agreement on Agriculture do not apply to this dispute, this would not mean that the SCM Agreement supersedes Article VI of GATT 1994 as the basis for the regulation by the WTO Agreement of countervailing measures. It is evident that both Article VI of GATT 1994 and the SCM Agreement have force, effect, and purpose within the WTO Agreement. That GATT 1994 has not been superseded by other Multilateral Agreements on Trade in Goods ("MTN Agreements") is demonstrated by a general interpretive note to Annex 1A of the WTO Agreement.[59] The fact that certain important provisions of Article VI of GATT 1994 are neither replicated nor elaborated in the SCM Agreement further demonstrates this point.[60] Thus, the question for consideration is not whether the SCM Agreement supersedes Article VI of GATT 1994. Rather, it is whether Article VI creates rules which are separate and distinct from those of the SCM Agreement, and which can be applied without reference to that Agreement, or whether Article VI of GATT 1994 and the SCM Agreement represent an inseparable package of rights and disciplines that must be considered in conjunction.

(a)   Applicability of the SCM Agreement

228.   Article 32.3 is a transition rule which defines with precision the temporal application of the SCM Agreement. Article 32:3 provides that:

> "Subject to paragraph 4, the provisions of this Agreement shall apply to investigations, and reviews of existing measures, initiated pursuant to applications which have been

---

[59]   The general interpretive note to Annex 1A provides that, "[i]n the event of a conflict between a provision of the General Agreement on Tariffs and Trade 1994 and a provision of another agreement in Annex 1A of the Agreement Establishing the World Trade Organization ... the provision of the other agreement shall prevail to the extent of the conflict". Such an interpretive note would be unnecessary if the MTN agreements superseded GATT 1994.

[60]   For example, the SCM Agreement does not replicate or elaborate on Article VI:5 of GATT 1994, which proscribes the imposition of both an anti-dumping and a countervailing duty to compensate for the same situation of dumping and export subsidization, nor does it address the issue of countervailing action on behalf of a third country as provided for in Article VI:6(b) and (c) of GATT 1994. If the SCM Agreement were considered to supersede Article VI of GATT 1994 altogether with respect to countervailing measures, these provisions would lose all force and effect. Such a result could not have been intended.

made on or after the date of entry into force for a Member of the WTO Agreement".

The WTO Agreement entered into force for Brazil on 1 January 1995. Although the definitive countervailing duty on desiccated coconut from the Philippines was imposed on 18 August 1995, the investigation leading to the imposition of the duty was initiated on 21 June 1994 pursuant to an application made on 17 January 1994, prior to the date of entry into force of the WTO Agreement for Brazil. Thus, in accordance with the ordinary meaning of Article 32.3, the SCM Agreement does not constitute applicable law for the purpose of the dispute before us.

229.   We do not find persuasive arguments that Article 32.3 of the SCM Agreement, by referring to "investigations," limits the application of that Agreement only with respect to the "procedural" aspects of investigations. The text of Article 32.3 itself does not indicate that that provision applies only to "procedural" as opposed to "substantive" aspects of an investigation. Rather, it provides that an investigation initiated pursuant to an application made on or after the date of entry into force shall be conducted in accordance with the provisions of the SCM Agreement in its entirety - procedural and substantive. Moreover, any effort to distinguish between the "substantive" and "procedural" obligations of the SCM Agreement would generate considerable confusion and dispute, as the distinction between the two types of obligations in practice could prove extremely difficult. We share the view of the Philippines that one object and purpose of Article 32.3 is to prevent WTO Members from having to redo investigations begun before the entry into force of the WTO Agreement in accordance with the new and more detailed *procedural* provisions of the SCM Agreement. In our view, however, this consideration is equally applicable to the *substantive* provisions of the SCM Agreement, which differ in significant respects from those of the Tokyo Round Agreement on Interpretation and Application of Articles VI, XVI and XXIII of the General Agreement on Tariffs and Trade ("the Tokyo Round SCM Code"). Throughout the course of an investigation, both procedural and substantive decisions must be made, and if an investigation were to become subject to new and different rules at some point during the investigation the investigating authorities would be required to return to the beginning and to re-examine decisions already taken.[61] Accordingly, we consider that the concept of "investigation" as expressed in Article 32.3 includes both procedural and substantive aspects of an investigation and the imposition of a countervailing measure pursuant thereto.

230.   We find equally unpersuasive the argument that, while Article 32.3 might preclude application of the SCM Agreement to the *imposition* of a countervailing duty resulting from an investigation initiated pursuant to an application made

---

[61]   As an example, the determination of the domestic industry must be made at an early stage as a prerequisite to subsequent steps in the investigation. The SCM Agreement contains provisions relating to this definition that are not part of the Tokyo Round SCM Code. If the SCM Agreement applied to ongoing investigations, a WTO Member would be required to re-examine its domestic industry determination in light of these new provisions.

before the date of entry into force of the WTO Agreement, it does not preclude the application of the SCM Agreement to the continued *collection* of duties after that date. Article 32.3 defines comprehensively the situations in which the SCM Agreement applies to measures which were imposed pursuant to investigations not subject to that Agreement. Specifically, the SCM Agreement applies to "reviews of existing measures" initiated pursuant to applications made on or after the date of entry into force of the WTO Agreement. It is thus through the mechanism of reviews provided for in the SCM Agreement, and only through that mechanism, that the Agreement becomes effective with respect to measures imposed pursuant to investigations to which the SCM Agreement does not apply. If, as the Philippines argues, a panel could examine in the light of the SCM Agreement the continued *collection* of a duty even where its imposition was not subject to the SCM Agreement, and if, as the Philippines argues, that examination of the collection of the duty extended to the basis on which the duty was imposed, then in effect the determinations on which those duties were based would be subject to standards that did not apply - and which, in the case of determinations made before the WTO Agreement was signed, did not yet even exist - at the time the determinations were made. In our view, such an interpretation would be contrary to the object and purpose of Article 32.3 and would render that Article a nullity.

231.   In conclusion, we find that the SCM Agreement does not constitute applicable law for the purposes of this dispute.

(b)   Separability of Article VI of GATT 1994 and the SCM Agreement

232.   Having concluded that the SCM Agreement does not constitute applicable law for the purposes of this dispute, we next examine the implications of this conclusion for the Philippines' claims under GATT 1994. The question presented is whether Article VI of GATT 1994 can apply to a dispute in circumstances where, pursuant to Article 32.3, the SCM Agreement does not apply. In other words, we are confronted with the issue whether the provisions of Article VI of GATT 1994 relating to countervailing duties are susceptible of application and interpretation independently of the SCM Agreement. If the answer to this question is yes, then Article VI of GATT 1994 represents the law applicable to this dispute. If, by contrast, we conclude that, in relation to disputes concerning countervailing measures, Article VI of GATT 1994 is inseparable from the SCM Agreement and cannot be interpreted and applied independently of that Agreement then, pursuant to Article 32.3, the SCM Agreement, and any other provisions that depend on it, do not apply, and we cannot consider the Philippines' claims under Article VI of GATT 1994 in this dispute.

233.   As a first step, we will review whether the textual provisions defining the relationship between Article VI of GATT 1994 and the SCM Agreement, in their ordinary meaning, shed light on this issue. We will thereafter consider whether an interpretation whereby Article VI of GATT 1994 applies independently in situations where the SCM Agreement does not apply would be supported by a consid-

eration of the object and purpose of the relevant provisions. After examining precedents under GATT 1947 potentially relevant to the issue of the independent application of Article VI of GATT 1994, we will consider whether there are any consequences of a conclusion that Article VI of GATT 1994 cannot apply independent of the SCM Agreement which would cast doubt on this interpretation.

(i) Textual Analysis

234. The reference in Article 32.3 of the SCM Agreement to "this Agreement" in its ordinary meaning would appear to be a reference to the SCM Agreement, thereby suggesting that while the SCM Agreement does not apply to investigations and reviews initiated pursuant to applications made before the date of entry into force of the Agreement for a Member, Article VI of GATT 1994 would nevertheless continue to be applicable in these circumstances. However, a strict application of the term "this Agreement" as used elsewhere in the SCM Agreement could produce manifestly unreasonable results. For example, Article 1.1 of the SCM Agreement contains a definition of "subsidy" and Article 16.1 of the SCM Agreement contains a definition of "domestic industry" both of which are "for the purposes of this Agreement". However, the terms "subsidy" and "domestic industry" are used both in Article VI of GATT 1994 and the SCM Agreement. If the term "this Agreement" were interpreted *strictu sensu* to mean the SCM Agreement, then the definitions of these key terms in the SCM Agreement would be inapplicable to the same terms as used in Article VI of GATT 1994. Such a result could not have been intended.

235. In any event, while Article 32.3 of the SCM Agreement might, taken on its own, most naturally be construed to govern the temporal application of the SCM Agreement and not Article VI of GATT 1994, it might have another meaning when taken in its context. If, for example, it were understood from other provisions of the WTO Agreement that Article VI of GATT 1994 could not be applied independently of the SCM Agreement, the mere fact that Article 32.3 of the SCM Agreement refers only to "this Agreement" could not, in and of itself, sever that linkage. If it were established, by reference to other language elsewhere in the WTO Agreement, that there is an inseparable link between Article VI of GATT 1994 and the SCM Agreement, then the ordinary meaning of Article 32.3, read in conjunction with other relevant provisions, would be that the SCM Agreement, and any other provision of the WTO Agreement that depended on it, would not apply if the terms of Article 32.3 were not met. Under this construction, the term "this Agreement" in Article 32.3 of the SCM Agreement would beg the question rather than answer it.

236. In light of these considerations, we consider that the use by the drafters of the term "this Agreement" does not provide decisive guidance regarding the im-

plications of Article 32.3 for the applicability of Article VI of GATT 1994 to this dispute.[62]

237. Another provision relevant to the relationship between Article VI of GATT 1994 and the SCM Agreement is Article 10 of the SCM Agreement, which provides as follows:

"Application of Article VI of GATT 1994[35]

Members shall take all necessary steps to ensure that the imposition of a countervailing duty[36] on any product of the territory of any Member imported into the territory of another Member is in accordance with the provisions of Article VI of GATT 1994 and the terms of this Agreement. Countervailing duties may only be imposed pursuant to investigations initiated[37] and conducted in accordance with the provisions of this Agreement and the Agreement on Agriculture.

---

[36] The term "countervailing duty" shall be understood to mean a special duty levied for the purpose of offsetting any subsidy bestowed directly or indirectly upon the manufacture, production or export of any merchandise, as provided for in paragraph 3 of Article VI of GATT 1994". (footnotes 35 and 37 omitted).

In our view, Article 10 means that, in cases where the SCM Agreement applies, both Article VI of GATT 1994 and the SCM Agreement are applicable and any countervailing measure must comply with both. This is clear from the language stating that countervailing duties must be imposed in accordance with the provisions of Article VI *and* the SCM Agreement. Article 10 further requires that, in cases where the SCM Agreement applies, countervailing duty investigations must be conducted in accordance with that Agreement. It could be argued that Article 10 only applies in cases where the SCM Agreement applies, and therefore does not expressly address the applicability of Article VI of GATT 1994 in situations where, pursuant to Article 32.3, the SCM Agreement does not apply. On this reading, Article 10 would be neutral, providing little guidance on the issue of separability. However, the title of Article 10 indicates that that Article informs

---

[62] Interestingly, the Tokyo Round SCM Code contains a note that, if reproduced in the SCM Agreement, might well have been decisive on this point. Note 2 to the Preamble of the Code states that:

"Wherever in this Agreement there is reference to "the terms of this Agreement" or the "articles" or "provisions of this Agreement" it shall be taken to mean, as the context requires, the provisions of the General Agreement as interpreted and applied by this Agreement".

The Panel is uncertain why this provision was not reproduced in the SCM Agreement. However, one possible explanation is that such a provision was considered unnecessary in the light of the integrated nature of the WTO Agreement, and the provisions regulating the relationship of GATT 1994 and the MTN agreements. In any event, we do not consider that the exclusion of this provision from the SCM Agreement sheds much light on the question before us.

regarding how Article VI of GATT 1994 is to be applied. Article 10 thus suggests that Article VI and the SCM Agreement represent an inter-related package of rights and obligations relating to countervailing measures.

238.   Another provision relevant to the relationship of Article VI of GATT 1994 and the SCM Agreement is Article 32.1 of the SCM Agreement, which provides that:

> "No specific action against a subsidy of another Member can be taken except in accordance with the provisions of GATT 1994, as interpreted by this Agreement.[56]" (footnote 56 omitted).

Article 32.1, like Article 10, makes it very clear that in cases where the SCM Agreement applies, Article VI of GATT 1994 cannot be invoked as the basis for the imposition of a countervailing duty without reference to the SCM Agreement. As with respect to Article 10, it could be argued that Article 32.1 only applies where the SCM Agreement applies pursuant to Article 32.3, and that it therefore does not instruct as to whether Article VI of GATT 1994 applies where the SCM Agreement does not. It is significant, however, that Article 32.1 refers to the SCM Agreement as *interpreting* Article VI of GATT 1994. Article VI of GATT 1994 sets forth a series of core concepts central to WTO regulation of countervailing measures (e.g., subsidy, material injury, domestic industry). These concepts are, however, expressed in only the most general terms, and are thus susceptible of a wide range of interpretations. In our view, the Tokyo Round SCM Code and its successor the SCM Agreement were developed in part to lend greater precision and predictability to the rights and obligations under Article VI. Article 32.1 makes clear that where the SCM Agreement applies the meaning of Article VI of GATT 1994 cannot be established without reference to the provisions of the SCM Agreement. It is apparent from Article 32.1 that Article VI of GATT 1994 might have a different meaning if read in isolation than if read in conjunction with the SCM Agreement. The drafters clearly foresaw the possibility of conflict between GATT 1994 and the MTN agreements, as evidenced by the general interpretive note to Annex 1A. If there could be conflicts between GATT 1994 and the MTN agreements, there could also be conflicts between GATT 1994 taken in isolation and GATT 1994 interpreted in conjunction with an MTN agreement.

239.   We considered whether the potential for two different meanings of Article VI of GATT 1994 could be eliminated by insisting that it should always be interpreted in the light of the SCM Agreement or another such interpretive device. We rejected such a possibility.

240.   The clear non-applicability of the SCM to this dispute means that if we were to conclude that Article VI of GATT 1994 may apply on its own, we would be obliged to interpret it as if the SCM Agreement did not exist. In the words of one third party, it would be our duty to take a "clean-slate" approach to the interpretation of Article VI of GATT 1994, avoiding concepts which could not fairly be deemed to flow directly from a proper, self-contained Article VI analysis. It

would be legally improper to seek to reconcile any emergent differences between Article VI applied on its own and Article VI as it would be understood in conjunction with the SCM Agreement by reverting to the SCM Agreement, not as applicable law but as an interpretive aid - even though the latter Agreement by its own terms does not apply to this dispute. Such an approach would be contrary to the ordinary meaning of Article 32.3 of the SCM Agreement. It would not be appropriate for this Panel to incorporate the requirements of the SCM Agreement indirectly where the SCM Agreement does not apply directly. If, then, we interpret the relevant provisions of the WTO Agreement as permitting the application of Article VI of GATT 1994 on its own, there would be a real and altogether serious possibility that Article VI of GATT 1994 would be imbued with one meaning where applied independently, and with a different, and potentially conflicting, meaning where applied in conjunction with the SCM Agreement as required by Article 32.1.[63]

(ii)   Object and Purpose

241.   What is the relevance of this possibility to the question of interpretation before us? An interpretation which allows this possibility strikes us as contrary to one of the central objects and purposes of the WTO Agreement. This adds considerable weight to the interpretation which regards the provisions concerning countervailing measures in Article VI of GATT 1994 and the SCM Agreement as an inseparable whole.

242.   In our view, one of the central objects and purposes of the WTO Agreement, as reflected in the Preamble to that Agreement, is to "develop an integrated, more viable and durable multilateral trading system encompassing the General Agreement on Tariffs and Trade, the results of past liberalization efforts, and all of the results of the Uruguay Round of Multilateral Trade Negotiations...". This is one of the reasons that the WTO Agreement is a single undertaking, accepted by all Members. Unlike the pre-WTO regime, where contracting parties to GATT 1947 could elect whether or not to adhere to the Tokyo Round SCM Code, such option has been removed in the present regime. The integrated nature of the WTO system is reflected in Article II.2, which states that "[t]he agreements and associated legal instruments included in Annexes 1, 2 and 3 ... are integral parts of this Agreement, binding on all Members". Essential to this integration is the creation of a single Dispute Settlement Body governed by a single Understanding on Rules and Procedures Concerning the Settlement of Disputes ("the DSU"). A panel established pursuant to the DSU may under Article 7.1 examine any covered agreement(s) cited by the parties to the dispute. This integrated dispute settlement system avoids the problem of legal and procedural fragmentation that characterized the pre-WTO dispute settlement system, and allows a panel to interpret provisions of covered agreements in the light of the

---

[63]   Specific examples are discussed in the context of a related argument in paragraphs 248-252.

WTO Agreement as a whole. To revert to a situation where Article VI of GATT 1994 could have different meanings depending upon whether or not it was applied in conjunction with the SCM Agreement would perpetuate in part the legal fragmentation that the integrated WTO system was intended to avoid.

243. To repeat, this consideration regarding the object and purpose of the WTO Agreement argues strongly in favour of the conclusion that Article VI of GATT 1994 cannot be applied to a dispute regarding countervailing measures where the SCM Agreement is not applicable.

244. This conclusion is further strengthened by additional consequences which would result from an interpretation that Article VI of GATT 1994 could apply in disputes such as this one where the SCM Agreement does not. As explained below, a signatory to the Tokyo Round SCM Code could find itself subject to obligations under Article VI of GATT 1994 applied alone which are more onerous than those to which it was subject pursuant to Article VI of GATT 1947 applied in conjunction with the Tokyo Round SCM Code and which are also more onerous than those to which it will be subject at such time as the SCM Agreement applies. This would represent a result which is both manifestly absurd and unreasonable.

245. The Philippines and certain third parties appear to assume that Article VI of GATT 1994 and its predecessor in GATT 1947 represent a set of core obligations relating to countervailing measures, and that the SCM Agreement and Tokyo Round SCM Code merely add further substantive and procedural obligations *in addition to* these core obligations. It follows from this assumption that, since Brazil is required under Article VI of GATT 1947 and the Tokyo Round SCM Code to comply with the relevant provisions of Article VI of GATT 1947, and since the text of Article VI of GATT 1994 is identical to that of Article VI of GATT 1947, Brazil's material obligations under the two Articles are identical. In addition, if this assumption is correct, application of Article VI of GATT 1994 in circumstances where the SCM Agreement does not apply would not place any obligations on Brazil *beyond* those with which it will eventually have to comply at such time as Article VI of GATT 1994 in conjunction with the SCM Agreement applies. Thus, while the need for a transition rule regulating the application of the new and different provisions of the SCM Agreement is clear, there was no reason for the drafters of the WTO Agreement to apply that transition rule to Article VI of GATT 1994.

246. This Panel considers, however, that this view of the relationship between Article VI and the respective SCM Agreements is erroneous. Article VI of GATT 1947 and the Tokyo Round SCM Code represent, as among Code signatories, a package of rights and obligations regarding the use of countervailing measures, and Article VI of GATT 1994 and the SCM Agreement represent a new and different package of rights and obligations, as among WTO Members, regarding the use of countervailing duties. Thus, Article VI and the respective SCM Agreements impose obligations on a potential user of countervailing duties, in the form of conditions that have to be fulfilled in order to impose a duty, but they also

confer the right to impose a countervailing duty when those conditions are satisfied. The SCM Agreements do not merely impose *additional* substantive and procedural *obligations* on a potential user of countervailing measures. Rather, the SCM Agreements and Article VI together define, clarify and in some cases modify the whole package of *rights* and obligations of a potential user of countervailing measures.

247.   It is therefore not correct to view Article VI of GATT 1947 and Article VI of GATT 1994 as representing a core of identical rights and obligations. To the contrary, Article VI of GATT 1947 in conjunction with the Tokyo Round SCM Code, Article VI of GATT 1994 in isolation, and Article VI of GATT 1994 in conjunction with the SCM Agreement, each represent a potentially differing set of rights and obligations. Further, it is by no means clear that a measure imposed consistently with Article VI and the Tokyo Round SCM Code or the SCM Agreement would be found to be consistent with Article VI of GATT 1994 in isolation. Thus, if we were to find that Article VI of GATT 1994 applies in cases where neither the Tokyo Round SCM Code nor the SCM Agreement apply, a Member's actions could potentially be found to be inconsistent with Article VI of GATT 1994 even though those actions were consistent with Article VI of GATT 1947 in conjunction with the Tokyo Round SCM Code and/or would have been consistent with Article VI of GATT 1994 in conjunction with the SCM Agreement, had the latter agreement applied.

248.   A few examples may assist to demonstrate this point. In the dispute under consideration, Brazil in its determination stated that the Philippine government had submitted insufficient data regarding the existence and amount of subsidies to coconut fruit and their pass-through to desiccated coconut producers, and that it had therefore arrived at a level of subsidization for desiccated coconut producers on the basis of the data available. The report by Brazil's investigating authority recommending the imposition of the duties explicitly referred to Article 2.9 of the Tokyo Round SCM Code as its justification for resort to the data available. Article 2.9 states that:

> "In cases in which any interested party or signatory refuses access to, or otherwise does not provide, necessary information within a reasonable period or significantly impedes the investigation, preliminary or final findings[12], affirmative or negative, may be made on the basis of the facts available". (footnote 12 omitted).

In its submissions to the Panel, Brazil relies on its right to use of best information available in justifying its determination. In support of the proposition that the use of best information available is permitted by Article VI of GATT 1994, Brazil cites to language in the Second Report of the Group of Experts on Anti-Dumping and Countervailing Duties,[64] and (contrary to assertions elsewhere that the Tokyo

---

[64]   L/1141 (adopted 27 May 1960), BISD 9S/1994.

Round SCM Code cannot be used to interpret Article VI of GATT 1994) to Article 2.9 of the Tokyo Round SCM Code. While the Philippines does not challenge the practice of resorting to best information available *per se*, it does contend, relying in part on panel reports decided under Article 2.9 of the Tokyo Round SCM Code, that the use of best information available in this case was improper.

249. Article VI of GATT 1947 does not specifically provide for the use of best information available. By contrast, Article 2.9 of the Tokyo Round SCM Code authorizes the use of best information available, and a number of panel reports pursuant to the Tokyo Round SCM Code have applied that provision. Article 12.7 of the SCM Agreement contains language which is virtually identical to Article 2.9. This Panel does not express any view as to whether and to what extent, had it reached the issue, it would have found that the use of best information available is implicitly authorized by Article VI of GATT 1994. It is clear, however, that the Panel could in principle have reached a different conclusion on that question from that which it would have reached had it applied either the Tokyo Round SCM Code or the SCM Agreement. Under these circumstances, Brazil could have been in the situation where its actions were found to be inconsistent with Article VI of GATT 1994 in isolation, even though those actions were consistent with Article VI of GATT 1947 in conjunction with the Tokyo Round SCM Code and would have been consistent with Article VI of GATT 1994 in conjunction with the SCM Agreement had the latter agreement applied. The Panel considers that an interpretation of the WTO Agreement that could lead to such a result would be manifestly unreasonable.

250. A second example relates to the nature of the examination of causation of injury. Article VI:6(a) of GATT 1994 provides (as did its GATT 1947 predecessor) that:

> "No contracting party shall levy any anti-dumping or countervailing duty on the importation of any product of the territory of another contracting party unless it determines that the effect of the dumping or subsidization, as the case may be, is such as to cause or threaten material injury to an established domestic industry, or is such as to retard materially the establishment of a domestic industry".

Article 6.1 of the Tokyo Round SCM Code provides that "a determination of injury[17] for the purposes of Article VI of the General Agreement" (footnote 17 omitted) shall involve an objective examination of the volume and price effects of imports. Article 6.4 of the Tokyo Round SCM Code further provides that "[i]t must be demonstrated that the subsidized imports are, through the effects[19] of the subsidy, causing injury within the meaning of this Agreement". Note 19 defines those effects to be "[a]s set forth in paragraphs 2 and 3 of this Article"; paragraphs 2 and 3, in turn, refer to the volume and price effects of "subsidized imports". The SCM Agreement contains language virtually identical to that of the Tokyo Round SCM Code. On the basis of note 19, a Tokyo Round Panel determined that the analysis of causation required by Article VI in conjunction with the Tokyo Round SCM Code relates to injury caused by "subsidized imports" rather than by "subsidization" itself. *United States - Imposition of Countervailing Duties on Imports of Fresh and Chilled Atlantic Salmon from Norway*, SCM/153 (adopted 24 April 1994), paras. 328-337.

251.   The question whether an assessment of causation of injury should relate to injury caused by subsidization or to injury caused by subsidized imports is a methodological issue with significant implications. The issue is not before us and we therefore are not expressing any view as to how this question would properly be resolved under Article VI of GATT 1994 in isolation, Article VI of GATT 1947 in conjunction with the Tokyo Round SCM Code, or Article VI of GATT 1994 in conjunction with the SCM Agreement. However, the conclusions of the *Salmon* Panel are based on language in the Tokyo Round SCM Code which does not appear in Article VI itself. Thus, it is evident to the Panel that Article VI of GATT 1994 in isolation could be interpreted differently from Article VI in conjunction with either the Tokyo Round SCM Code or the SCM Agreement. Further, the application of Article VI of GATT 1994 in isolation with respect to this issue could result in obligations on an investigating country which are more stringent than those imposed by Article VI in conjunction with either the Tokyo Round SCM Code or the SCM Agreement.

252.   There are numerous additional examples of provisions of the Tokyo Round SCM Code and/or the SCM Agreement which define or clarify, and potentially modify, the meaning of Article VI. In many such cases, it is by no means inevitable that the obligations imposed by Article VI in isolation would be less than those imposed by Article VI in conjunction with either the Tokyo Round SCM Code or the SCM Agreement. For example, both the Tokyo Round SCM Code and the SCM Agreement authorize an investigating authority to exclude from the domestic industry when assessing material injury domestic producers which are also importers or which are related to importers. No such explicit authorization exists in Article VI of GATT 1994. Similarly, the SCM Agreement explicitly authorizes the cumulative assessment of the effects of subsidized imports from more than one country where certain criteria are satisfied. By contrast, neither Article VI of GATT 1947, Article VI of GATT 1994 nor the Tokyo Round SCM Code explicitly authorize cumulation. Indeed, the issue of cumulation under GATT 1947 and the Tokyo Round SCM Code was a matter of controversy among signatories to that Code.

253.   In light of the foregoing analysis, it is clear that the application of Article VI of GATT 1994 in isolation could impose on a WTO Member for a certain period of time obligations which in some respects might be more onerous than those to which it would be subject once the SCM Agreement became applicable. This aggravates the problem of differing and inconsistent interpretations identified in paragraphs 238 to 240 above. However, the implications of this analysis extend further. When Brazil initiated its countervailing duty investigation in this case, the WTO Agreement had not yet entered into force and Brazil could legitimately have expected to be able to proceed, and to have its actions adjudicated, on the basis of Article VI of GATT 1947 in conjunction with the Tokyo Round

SCM Code. Brazil would further have been aware that the SCM Agreement would not apply to the investigation pursuant to Article 32.3 of that Agreement. If the Panel were to determine that Article VI of GATT 1994 was independently applicable to disputes initiated under the Tokyo Round SCM Code, the Panel would not only be opening a risk of conflicting interpretations of Article VI of GATT 1994 but would be holding WTO Members to a package of rights and obligations that were potentially more onerous than those to which they were subject under Article VI in conjunction with the Tokyo Round SCM Code when they initiated the investigation.

254.   We note the Philippines' apparent view that Article VI of GATT 1994 can be interpreted in light of the Tokyo Round SCM Code and practice thereunder. It could be argued that, if this were the case, there would be no risk that Article VI of GATT 1994, in isolation, would be found to impose obligations beyond those imposed by Article VI of GATT 1947 in conjunction with the Tokyo Round SCM Code. We do not accept this view. First, this would require stretching the concept of "interpretation in light of the Tokyo Round SCM Code" too far. Even if Article VI of GATT 1994 could be interpreted in light of the Tokyo Round SCM Code, there could still be differences between Article VI of GATT 1994 by itself and the package of rights and obligations contained in Article VI of GATT 1994 and the Tokyo Round SCM Code taken in conjunction that no interpretation of Article VI of GATT 1994 could gloss over.

255.   In any event, we do not consider that it would be appropriate to interpret Article VI of GATT 1994 in light of the Tokyo Round SCM Code. Article 31:3(a) of the Vienna Convention on the Law of Treaties ("the Vienna Convention"), which is generally held to reflect customary principles of international law regarding treaty interpretation, provides that "any subsequent agreement between the parties to a treaty regarding its interpretation or the application of its provisions" may be taken into account when interpreting a treaty. The Tokyo Round SCM Code may constitute such a subsequent agreement among Tokyo Round SCM Code signatories regarding the interpretation of Article VI of GATT 1947. However, Article II:4 of the WTO Agreement provides that the GATT 1994 is "legally distinct" from the GATT 1947. While GATT 1994 consists of, *inter alia*, "decisions of the CONTRACTING PARTIES to GATT 1947," the Tokyo Round SCM Code is not a "decision" of the CONTRACTING PARTIES. Thus, the Tokyo Round SCM Code does not represent a *subsequent* agreement regarding interpretation of Article VI of *GATT 1994*. For the Panel to conclude to the contrary would in effect convert that Code into a "covered agreement" under Appendix 1 of the DSU. If such an approach were followed, WTO Members that were Tokyo Round Code signatories would find that their Code obligations were now enforceable under the WTO dispute settlement system.

256.   Article XVI:1 of the WTO Agreement provides that, "[e]xcept as otherwise provided under this Agreement or the Multilateral Trade Agreements, the WTO shall be guided by the decisions, procedures and customary practices followed by the CONTRACTING PARTIES to GATT 1947 and the bodies established in the framework of GATT 1947". We recognize that the *Pork* Panel had

indicated, in passing, that the Tokyo Round SCM Code represents "practice" under Article VI of GATT 1947. Article 31.3(b) of the Vienna Convention provides that there may be taken into account, when interpreting a treaty, "[a]ny subsequent practice in the application of the treaty which establishes the agreement of the parties regarding its interpretation". Article 31.3 clearly distinguishes between the use of subsequent *agreements* and of subsequent *practice* as interpretive tools. The Tokyo Round SCM Code is, in our view, in the former category and cannot itself reasonably be deemed to represent "customary practice" of the GATT 1947 CONTRACTING PARTIES. In any event, while the practice of Code signatories might be of some interpretive value in establishing their agreement regarding the interpretation of the Tokyo Round SCM Code (and arguably through Article XVI:1 of the WTO Agreement in interpreting provisions of that Code that were carried over into the successor SCM Agreement), it is clearly not relevant to the interpretation of Article VI of GATT 1994 itself; rather, only practice under Article VI of GATT 1947 is legally relevant to the interpretation of Article VI of GATT 1994.

257.   In conclusion, consideration of the relevant textual provisions of the SCM Agreement in their context and in the light of both their own object and purpose, and one of the central objects and purposes of the WTO Agreement as a whole, strongly supports the conclusion that the proper interpretation of the SCM Agreement would not allow Article VI of GATT 1994 to apply independently in situations in which the SCM Agreement does not apply.

(iii)   GATT Precedents

258.   It was argued before us that the *Pork* Panel[65] constitutes precedent for resolving one of the key questions regarding applicable law - the separability or otherwise of Article VI of GATT 1994 and the SCM Agreement. That Panel concerned a dispute between two signatories to the Tokyo Round SCM Code. Nevertheless, the Panel was established pursuant to Article XXIII of GATT 1947 and seemed to proceed on the basis of Article VI of GATT 1947 as the law applicable to the dispute in question. It could thus be argued on this basis that past practice indicated that Article VI of GATT 1947 could be applied independently of the Tokyo Round SCM Code. Given that several of the relevant provisions of the Tokyo Round SCM Code are similar to those in the SCM Agreement,[66] it

---

[65]   *United States - Countervailing Duties on Fresh, Chilled and Frozen Pork from Canada* (adopted 11 July 1991), BISD 38S/30.

[66]   Article 1 of the Tokyo Round SCM Code is virtually identical to the first sentence of Article 10 of the SCM Agreement (quoted in para. 237 above), providing as follows:

"*Application of Article VI of the General Agreement*[3]

Signatories shall take all necessary steps to ensure that the imposition of a countervailing duty[4] on any product of the territory of any signatory imported into the territory of another signatory is in accordance with the provisions of Article VI of the General Agreement and the terms of this Agreement.

could be further argued that a similar result should be reached in a dispute in the WTO under GATT 1994. Here too we are mindful of Article XVI:1 of the WTO Agreement, which provides that, "[e]xcept as otherwise provided under this Agreement or the Multilateral Trade Agreements, the WTO shall be guided by the decisions, procedures and customary practices followed by the CONTRACTING PARTIES to GATT 1947 and the bodies established in the framework of GATT 1947". Moreover, whilst panel reports do not constitute formal precedent that subsequent panels must follow, where relevant they constitute useful and persuasive guidance. After careful consideration, however, we have concluded that the circumstances of the *Pork* Panel are of very limited relevance to the issue of applicable law before us.

259. In the *Pork* Panel the complainant chose as the forum in which to pursue dispute settlement a panel established pursuant to Article XXIII of GATT 1947 rather than pursuant to Article 18 of the Tokyo Round SCM Code. Article 18.1 of the Tokyo Round SCM Code provides that a panel established thereunder "shall present to the Committee its findings concerning the rights and obligations of the signatories party to the dispute under the relevant provisions of the General Agreement as interpreted and applied by this Agreement". Thus, the dispute in *Pork* could have been referred to a panel under the Tokyo Round SCM Code. However, the propriety of Article XXIII dispute settlement as a forum for that dispute was not raised by the parties, perhaps because the issues in question focused on concepts in Article VI which were not further elaborated in the Tokyo Round SCM Code. In other words, the central contentious issue before us was neither argued before the *Pork* Panel nor formed part of its deliberations and findings. Little weight can be given to the Panel's failure to consider the issue *sua sponte*. In any event, it is doubtful whether, given the fragmented nature of dispute settlement in the GATT system, a panel established under Article XXIII of GATT 1947 would have had the authority under its terms of reference to determine, in the light of provisions of the Tokyo Round SCM Code, that GATT Article XXIII was not the proper basis on which to pursue an application.[67]

---

[4] The term "countervailing duty" shall be understood to mean a special duty levied for the purpose of off-setting any bounty or subsidy bestowed directly or indirectly upon the manufacture, production or export of any merchandise, as provided for in paragraph 3 of Article VI of the General Agreement". (footnote 3 omitted).
Similarly, Article 19.1 of the Tokyo Round SCM Code is virtually identical to Article 32.1 of the SCM Agreement (quoted in para. 238 above), providing as follows:
"No specific action against a subsidy of another signatory can be taken except in accordance with the provisions of the General Agreement, as interpreted by this Agreement.[38]"
(footnote 38 omitted).
[67] As provided in the Montreal *Improvements to the GATT Dispute Settlement Rules and Procedures*, L/6489, dated 13 April 1989, the terms of reference of the *Pork* Panel were to examine the matter "in the light of the relevant GATT provisions".

260.   Even if the issue of the choice of GATT Article XXIII dispute settlement had been argued, and if a panel established pursuant to Article XXIII had considered and decided that Article VI of GATT 1947 could be invoked independently of the Tokyo Round SCM Code, this decision would be of limited precedential effect for a panel established under the WTO. It is obvious that under the GATT system, Article VI of GATT 1947 would perforce apply on its own with respect to relations, and potential disputes, between Contracting Parties where one or both of those Contracting Parties was not a signatory to the Tokyo Round SCM Code. The pre-WTO system was, after all, characterized by a fragmentation both as regards applicable law and dispute resolution fora and procedure. We have, as noted, taken the view that one of the central objects and purposes of the WTO Agreement is to eliminate, as far as possible, that fragmentation through the creation of an integrated WTO system. Thus, the relevant provisions of the SCM Agreement being examined by this Panel must be interpreted in an altogether new and different legal context than the comparable provisions of the Tokyo Round SCM Code.

261.   Consequently, the decision of the *Pork* Panel, made in different circumstances under a different regime of obligations, does not persuade us that we should reach a different interpretation of the relevant textual provisions of the WTO Agreement to the one we have reached.

> (iv)   *Transition to the WTO System and the Consequences of a Finding of Non-Separability*

262.   We wish now to examine some of the alleged consequences of an interpretation of the WTO Agreement under which we would find that Article VI of GATT 1994 does not constitute applicable law in the circumstances of this dispute and the contention that such consequences must cast doubt on such an interpretation. One consequence, it is argued, would be to deny access to WTO dispute settlement with respect to a duty imposed as a result of a determination made after the entry into force of the WTO Agreement if that determination was the result of an investigation initiated pursuant to an application made before the entry into force of the WTO Agreement. Surely, it is argued, if the act of determination took place after the date of entry into force of the WTO Agreement it should be subject to the WTO regime. The other consequence, it is claimed, would be that some WTO Members could be left without a forum to pursue their rights under either the GATT or WTO systems with respect to countervailing measures imposed as a result of investigations initiated pursuant to applications made before the date of entry into force of the WTO Agreement.

263.   In examining these alleged consequences and their possible significance it is important to recall that the issue of applicable law arises because of the particular temporal aspects of this dispute. The WTO Agreement entered into force for Brazil on 1 January 1995. The investigation resulting in the imposition of the duty was initiated on 21 June 1994, pursuant to an application made on

17 January 1994, prior to the date of entry into force of the WTO Agreement for Brazil. The definitive countervailing duty on desiccated coconut from the Philippines was imposed, however, on 18 August 1995 after the Agreement entered into force for Brazil.

264.   The transition into a new legal regime, especially in relation to disputes such as this one which straddle the date of entry into force, frequently raises delicate legal issues. Transitional provisions typically try to balance the objective of a swift entry into force of the new agreement with the objective of safeguarding pre-existing and legitimate expectations surviving from its predecessor. In selecting a transitional regime States will balance these oft conflicting objectives. They may, at one extreme, apply the new regime fully to all measures existing at the date of entry into force of the new agreement. They may, at the other extreme, "grandfather" all measures existing at the date of entry into force of the new agreement. They may choose some "in-between" regime. The practice of States varies from agreement to agreement and, often, even within the same agreement, parties may agree on multiple transitional regimes for different subject matters. Delicate and difficult as these legal issues are, their importance abates since in time, as the new Agreement comes fully into force the transitional problems disappear.

265.   The transition into the WTO system is clearly characterized by a multiple approach to the problem. In some areas of the Agreement, WTO substantive requirements became operative and dispute resolution became available from the date of its entry into force even in relation to pre-existing measures. *E.g.*, *United States - Standards for Reformulated and Conventional Gasoline*, WT/DS2/R (29 January 1996), WT/DS2/AB/R (22 April 1996) (both adopted 20 May 1996). With respect to countervailing measures, immediate and full applicability of the WTO Agreement would mean that all existing measures, even those based on investigations and determinations completed before the WTO Agreement entered into force, could be immediately open to challenge in WTO dispute settlement proceedings, without the importing Member even having had an opportunity to assess the consistency of such existing measures with the new regime. At the other end of the spectrum, full grandfathering would permanently immunize existing measures from scrutiny under the new regime, even with respect to reviews of those measures. It is, however, abundantly clear that in relation to countervailing measures neither of these two extremes was adopted. The Members of the WTO constructed a more differentiated and gradual transitional regime for its entry into force. Perhaps this was because, unlike a measure whose consistency with the new regime can be evaluated without consideration of the process leading to its adoption, in the case of countervailing duties, procedural and substantive requirements are inextricably intertwined, and in assessing the consistency of a countervailing duty with the new regime, the process leading to its imposition must also be considered. The contours of this regime result from both the temporal provisions of the SCM Agreement and various instruments concerning the termination of GATT 1947 and the Tokyo Round SCM Code.

266.   We now return to the two alleged consequences of a finding that Article VI of GATT 1994 does not constitute applicable law to this type of dispute. One result, it is argued, would be to deny access to WTO dispute settlement with respect to a duty imposed pursuant to a determination made after the entry into force of the WTO Agreement if that determination was the end stage of an investigation following an application made before the entry into force of the WTO. Surely, it is argued, if the act of determination took place after the entry into force of the WTO it should be subject to that regime. The other result, it is claimed, would be that some WTO Members could be left without a forum to pursue their rights under either the GATT or WTO systems with respect to countervailing measures imposed pursuant to investigations initiated in response to applications made before the date of entry into force of the WTO Agreement. These results, it could be argued, are so manifestly absurd and unreasonable as to undermine the plausibility of an interpretation which would hold that Article VI of GATT 1994 does not constitute applicable law to a dispute such as the one before us.

267.   After careful consideration this Panel does not accept this proposition for the following principal reasons, which are elaborated further below.

268.   In the first place it rests on a simple misconception of the true effect of a finding that Article VI of GATT 1994, standing alone, does not constitute applicable law to a dispute of the type before us. The WTO substantive provisions and dispute resolution procedure are not, in fact, fully denied in either situation. They are, instead, phased in by the transitional provisions in the WTO. Under the WTO countervailing regime (Article VI of GATT 1994 and the SCM Agreement) Members may seek a review of duties imposed pursuant to a determination made after the entry into force of the WTO Agreement. Such a review, if conducted, must comply with the WTO regime even if the duties resulted from an investigation initiated pursuant to an application made before the date of entry into force of the WTO Agreement. Further, under a "sunset" provision, all measures are to be brought under the WTO regime, automatically, no later than five years after the entry into force of the WTO Agreement or the date of imposition of the measure, whichever is later.[68] Likewise, no WTO Members could be left totally without a forum to vindicate their rights with respect to countervailing measures imposed pursuant to investigations initiated as a result of applications made before the date of entry into force of the WTO Agreement. They too would have similar WTO rights through these reviews.

---

[68]   In many cases, the WTO will become effective for existing measures through a sunset review *less* than five years after the date of entry into force of the WTO Agreement. Specifically, for Members which maintained a sunset provision before the date of entry into force of the WTO Agreement, Article 32.4 of the SCM Agreement provides that a sunset review pursuant to WTO norms must be conducted not later than five years after the date of imposition of the measure, even if the measure was imposed before the date of entry into force of the WTO Agreement.

269.   We readily acknowledge that the rights and remedies under this phase-in regime are in several respects less extensive and less effective than would be the case had the Agreement provided for a more accelerated transitional regime (say two years instead of five years), or no transitional regime at all, in the field of countervailing measures. But it is surely not for us to comment on the choices made by the framers of the WTO in this regard except as it bears on our interpretation of the WTO Agreement in relation to the non-applicability of Article VI and the SCM Agreement to disputes of the type before us. Even if an interpretation which excluded Article VI would mean, *quod non*, that some measures would be totally immunized from the new regime, this would not constitute in our view, given the wide variety in State practice regarding transitional regimes, a result so manifestly absurd or unreasonable as to throw doubt on such an interpretation, if it were otherwise strongly supported, as is the case here, by the text itself in its context and in the light of the object and purpose of the Agreement. That no measure or Member is, in fact, totally deprived of WTO rights and remedies clearly removes any doubt in this respect.

270.   This is further confirmed if one examines the alleged consequences in the context of the overall transition regime to the WTO, which also comprises remedies under special arrangements made in relation to the previous regime. This could not have a direct bearing on the matter of interpretation before us. But, as will emerge, the sequence of negotiating and concluding these special arrangements lends some indirect support to this conclusion. It will also emerge that in some respects any shortcomings that Members may have in relation to measures resulting from investigations initiated pursuant to applications made under GATT 1947 and the Tokyo Round SCM Code, do not arise as a result of the transition rules governing the application of WTO rules to countervailing measures as such. Rather, any loss of existing rights arises out of the termination of GATT 1947 and the Tokyo Round SCM Code. At the time the WTO Agreement was signed, no understanding had been reached regarding if and when GATT 1947 and the Tokyo Round SCM Code would be terminated. Thus, we are hesitant, in interpreting the WTO Agreement, to give great weight to the effect of decisions that had not yet been taken at the time the WTO Agreement was signed.

271.   Transitional issues, including how and when to terminate the GATT 1947 and the Tokyo Round Codes, were the subject of decisions taken by the Preparatory Committee for the World Trade Organization ("the Preparatory Committee"), the CONTRACTING PARTIES to GATT 1947 and the Tokyo Round SCM Committee after the WTO Agreement was signed but before its date of entry into force. One such decision, adopted by the Tokyo Round SCM Committee at the invitation of the Preparatory Committee, recognizes that, if signatories withdrew from the Tokyo Round Code or the Code were terminated immediately, certain countervailing measures might be subject neither to the Tokyo Round SCM Code nor to the SCM Agreement. In order to resolve this situation, the Decision provides that, in the event of withdrawal from or termination of the Tokyo Round Subsidies Code, the Code nevertheless will continue to apply with respect to any countervailing duty investigation or review which is not subject to

application of the SCM Agreement pursuant to the terms of Article 32.3 of that Agreement. The Decision, which is to remain in effect for two years from the date of entry into force of the WTO Agreement, also provides that the Tokyo Round SCM Committee will remain in operation for the purpose of dealing with any dispute arising out of such an investigation or review. Finally, signatories undertake to make best efforts to expedite to the extent possible such investigations and reviews and procedures for the settlement of disputes so as to permit Committee consideration of any such dispute within the period of validity of the Decision.[69] Article 2.14 of the Tokyo Round SCM Code provides that investigations shall, except in exceptional circumstances, be concluded within one year of initiation. Thus, it appears that, even where the initiation of an investigation occurred after the date of entry into force of the WTO Agreement, pursuant to an application filed before that date, this Decision generally would allow a signatory an adequate opportunity to pursue dispute settlement under the Tokyo Round SCM Code with respect to any investigation or review not covered by the SCM Agreement.

272.	The Philippines and Brazil are both signatories of the Tokyo Round SCM Code, and the Philippines could thus have invoked the dispute settlement provisions of that Code. We do not mean to suggest by this observation that this Decision in itself forecloses the Philippines from pursuing a claim under Article VI of GATT 1994. The availability of Article VI of GATT 1994 as applicable law in this dispute is a matter to be determined on the basis of the WTO Agreement, rather than on the basis of a subsequent decision by the signatories of the Tokyo Round SCM Code taken at the invitation of the Preparatory Committee. However, the invitation by the Preparatory Committee to the Tokyo Round SCM Committee to take this decision appears to represent an acknowledgement that Article 32.3 might leave WTO Members without a remedy with respect to certain countervailing measures, and provides at least a partial resolution to that situation.

273.	The Philippines argues, and we acknowledge, that the foregoing Decision does not apply to all countervailing measures not subject to the SCM Agreement pursuant to Article 32.3 of the Agreement. Specifically, where one of the parties to a dispute involving countervailing measures is not a signatory to the Tokyo Round SCM Code, relations between the parties are governed only by GATT 1947. These parties cannot of course rely on the transition mechanism created by the Tokyo Round SCM Committee. We note, however, that a transitional decision of the CONTRACTING PARTIES to GATT 1947 resolved in part the dilemma confronting these parties. Pursuant to the Decision on the Transitional Co-Existence of the GATT 1947 and the WTO Agreement, L/7583 (adopted 8 December 1994), the GATT 1947 continued in force for one year after the date of

---

[69]	See Decision on Consequences of Withdrawal from or Termination of the Agreement on Interpretation and Application of Articles VI, XVI and XXIII of the General Agreement on Tariffs and Trade, SCM/187 (adopted 8 December 1994).

entry into force of the WTO Agreement. The Decision further provided that, in the light of unforseen circumstances, the CONTRACTING PARTIES could decide to postpone the date of termination of GATT 1947 by no more than one additional year. As a result, Contracting Parties to GATT 1947 which desired to pursue dispute settlement with respect to a countervailing measure to which neither the Tokyo Round SCM Code nor Article VI of GATT 1994 in conjunction with the SCM Agreement applied had an additional year in which to invoke GATT 1947 dispute settlement.

274.   The Panel is aware that Article 32.3 of the SCM Agreement, in conjunction with the transition decisions discussed above, does not create a seamless transition from the GATT 1947 to the WTO system. Under Article 32.3 of the SCM Agreement, countervailing duty investigations that were ongoing or with respect to which an initiation decision had not yet been made as of the date of entry into force of the WTO Agreement are not subject to Article VI of GATT 1994 in conjunction with the SCM Agreement. We are aware of several such countervailing duty investigations, as well as of a number of anti-dumping investigations that are similarly situated as a result of Article 18.3 of the WTO Agreement on Implementation of Article VI of GATT 1994 (the Anti-Dumping Agreement), which is the counterpart in that Agreement to Article 32.3 of the SCM Agreement. However, the Sub-Committee on Institutional, Procedural and Legal Matters of the Preparatory Committee for the World Trade Organization considered a two-year period of co-existence between the GATT 1947 and the WTO Agreement. Had the Preparatory Committee ultimately recommended such a decision to the CONTRACTING PARTIES to the GATT 1947, this potential gap in coverage would not exist. Thus, the gap in coverage identified by the Philippines results from the terms on which the GATT 1947 was terminated, rather than from Article 32.3 of the SCM Agreement. Therefore, little interpretive emphasis can be placed on the existence of such a gap when interpreting the WTO Agreement.

275.   In any event, the SCM Agreement by its own terms enters into effect with respect to existing measures over time. In this respect, we note that reviews of existing measures initiated pursuant to requests made after the date of entry into force of the WTO Agreement are subject to the SCM Agreement. Article 21.2 of the Agreement provides that:

> "The authorities shall review the need for the continued imposition of the duty, where warranted, on their own initiative or, provided that a reasonable period of time has elapsed since the imposition of the definitive countervailing duty, upon request by any interested party which submits positive information substantiating the need for a review. Interested parties shall have the right to request the authorities to examine whether the continued imposition of the duty is necessary to offset subsidization, whether the injury would be likely to continue or recur if the duty were removed or varied, or both. If, as a result of the review under

this paragraph, the authorities determine that the countervailing duty is no longer warranted, it shall be terminated
immediately".

276. We further note that there is an outer limit to the non-applicability of Article VI of GATT 1994 in conjunction with the SCM Agreement in the form of a
sunset clause. Article 21.3 of the SCM Agreement provides that:

"any definitive countervailing duty shall be terminated on a
date not later than five years from its imposition (or from
the date of the most recent review under paragraph 2 if that
review has covered both subsidization and injury, or under
this paragraph), unless the authorities determine, in a review
initiated before that date on their own initiative or upon a
duly substantiated request made by or on behalf of the domestic industry within a reasonable period of time prior to
that date, that the expiry of the duty would be likely to lead
to continuation or recurrence of subsidization and injury.[52]"
(footnote 52 omitted).

Article 32.4 of the SCM Agreement specifies the manner in which this provision
will enter into force under the Agreement's transitional regime:

"For the purposes of paragraph 3 of Article 21, existing
countervailing measures shall be deemed to be imposed on
a date not later than the date of entry into force for a Member of the WTO Agreement, except in cases in which the
domestic legislation of a Member in force at that date already included a clause of the type provided for in that
paragraph".

277. We recognize that these provisions regarding review are not comparable
in effect to the immediate application of the WTO Agreement to all countervailing measures. The effect of reviews regarding the continued need for imposition
of countervailing measures will likely be prospective and, depending on the date
of imposition of the measure and the circumstances subsequent to its imposition,
the exporting country Member may or may not be entitled to an immediate review. Nevertheless, it is clear from this provision that measures to which the
WTO Agreement is not immediately applicable will nevertheless be brought under WTO disciplines over time pursuant to reviews under Article 21.2 of the
SCM Agreement. Further, even measures maintained and imposed under the pre-
WTO regime, and not subject to a review under Article 21.2 of the SCM Agreement, will ultimately be brought under WTO disciplines under this sunset provision.[70]

---

[70] We note that there are virtually identical provisions in the Anti-Dumping Agreement governing
reviews of the need for continued imposition of duties and sunset. We further note that Article 9 of
the Anti-Dumping Agreement requires that Members have either a prospective or retrospective duty

278. From the foregoing analysis, it is apparent that the WTO Agreement, in conjunction with the arrangements for the termination of GATT 1947 and the Tokyo Round SCM Code, create a transitional regime under which WTO disciplines and WTO dispute resolution become applicable to countervailing measures in a determined, phased-in manner. In other words, measures that are not immediately subject to the WTO regime are, for a limited period of time, insulated from scrutiny under that regime, although they may be subject to scrutiny under the old regime. The principal features of the transition to the WTO regime are as follows:

-   Any countervailing measure imposed as a result of an application made on or after the date of entry into force of the WTO Agreement for a Member is immediately subject to WTO rules, and WTO dispute settlement, as is any review of a measure initiated as a result of an application made on or after the date of entry into force of the WTO Agreement for a Member.

-   With respect to measures imposed as a result of investigations initiated pursuant to applications made before the date of entry into force of the WTO Agreement:

    -   Between Members which were signatories to the Tokyo Round SCM Code access to dispute settlement under that Code remains available for two years after the entry into force of the WTO Agreement. If dispute resolution under the Code is not sought, or in the unusual case where the two-year period is insufficient, WTO dispute resolution will become available following reviews initiated pursuant to applications made on or after the entry into force of the WTO Agreement. At the outer limits, obligatory sunset reviews will bring measures under WTO disciplines and WTO dispute resolution will become available.

    -   For disputes among Members one or both of which were not signatories to the Tokyo Round SCM Code, dispute resolution under GATT 1947 was available for one year after the entry into force of the WTO Agreement. Otherwise, the WTO regime becomes effective for such disputes through reviews, the operation of the sunset clause, and the eventual

---

assessment system. At least one Member with a retrospective duty assessment system applies WTO norms to such retrospective duty assessments. In such cases, the provisions of the Anti-Dumping Agreement would apply to the collections of all duties for the period covered by the retrospective duty assessment, which may include duties for periods prior to the entry into force of the WTO Agreement. Because the issue is not before us, this Panel expresses no opinion as to whether this is a requirement of the Anti-Dumping Agreement, nor as to whether a duty assessment system is required by the SCM Agreement.

availability of WTO dispute resolution in the same manner as for Tokyo Round SCM Code signatories.

It is not for us to comment on the choices made by the parties in setting up the regime for transition to the WTO regime in the field of countervailing measures - save to mention that any transitional regime involves compromises. There is, in our view, nothing in this construction that is so unreasonable as to undermine this Panel's conclusion, based on our interpretation of the relevant textual provisions, that Article VI of GATT 1994 is not independently applicable to a dispute to which the SCM Agreement is not applicable.

279.   It has been argued that it would be inconsistent with the object and purpose of the WTO Agreement to interpret that Agreement in a manner that denies a Member access to WTO dispute settlement with respect to a countervailing duty imposed after the entry into force of the WTO Agreement. The imposition of that duty, it is argued, constitutes an independent act which, since it takes place after the entry into force of the WTO Agreement, should be subject to its strictures. The problem in this case is that the circumstances underlying Brazil's imposition of a countervailing duty on imports of desiccated coconut are part of a process which straddled the date of entry into force of the WTO Agreement. It is an accepted principle of customary international law, reflected in Article 28 of the Vienna Convention, that rights and obligations under a new treaty do not apply retroactively. How to apply that principle to the particular case of a countervailing measure based on a process begun before, but completed after, the date of entry into force of the WTO Agreement, is a matter of great legal delicacy. We note that the parties to the dispute and certain third parties presented extensive arguments regarding the application in this case of the principle reflected in Article 28 of the Vienna Convention. But it should be noted that the principle set forth in Article 28 applies "[u]nless a different intention appears from the treaty or is otherwise established...". In this case, the Panel has reached its conclusions on the basis of the intention of the drafters as evidenced in the text of the WTO Agreement itself. Accordingly, we have not addressed the parties' arguments regarding customary principles of international law, nor do we express any view regarding the application of such principles in other contexts under the WTO Agreement. In our view, the SCM Agreement recognizes the principle of non-retroactivity, and taking into account the complexities of applying this general principle in the context of countervailing duties, resolves the difficult question of the operation of the general principle in this specific context through transition rules which spell out the precise temporal application of the SCM Agreement, as described above. By virtue of our conclusion that Article VI of GATT 1994 does not apply where the SCM Agreement does not apply, the same resolution of this problem would apply to Article VI of GATT 1994. In our view, this result is neither manifestly absurd nor unreasonable. Indeed, we consider it to be fully consistent with the purpose identified in the Preamble of the WTO Agreement to develop an integrated multilateral trading system. Even if the text allowed any interpretive leeway on this issue, which in our view it does not, any possible advantages of an interpretation which allowed immediate recourse to WTO dispute

resolution under Article VI alone with respect to any countervailing duty imposed after the date of entry into force of the WTO Agreement is far outweighed by all the problems and difficulties flowing from such an interpretation, which, as discussed above, would lead to manifestly absurd and unreasonable results.

280.   We recognize that Articles I, II and VI of GATT 1994 are interrelated, and that Article VI allows measures which might otherwise be inconsistent with Articles I and II of GATT 1994.[71] Clearly, the fact that the WTO Agreement creates a transition regime in which Article VI of GATT 1994 and the SCM Agreement become effective in a phased manner with respect to certain countervailing measures does not mean that, until those provisions become effective, such measures are inconsistent with Articles I and II of GATT 1994. It could not have been the intention of the drafters in creating a gradual, phased-in entry into force of Article VI and the SCM Agreement to render all measures subject to the phase-in immediately invalid. To the contrary, as explained above, this Panel concluded that the effect of this transition regime is to insulate countervailing measures imposed as a result of an investigation initiated pursuant to an application made before the date of entry into force of the WTO Agreement for a Member until such time as the measures are subject to a review to which Article VI of GATT 1994 and the SCM Agreement apply. Needless to say, this result has no bearing on the force and effect of Articles I and II of GATT 1994 with respect to measures other than those countervailing measures subject to the transition rule set forth in Article 32.3 of the SCM Agreement.

281.   In light of the provisions of the WTO Agreement, interpreted in their context and in light of their object and purpose, as discussed above, this Panel concludes that Article VI of GATT 1994 does not constitute applicable law for the purposes of this dispute. As a result, the Philippines' claims under Articles I and II, which derive from their claims of inconsistency with Article VI of GATT 1994, cannot succeed.

2.   Applicability of the Agreement on Agriculture

282.   This Panel now turns to the question of the applicability of the Agreement on Agriculture to disputes such as this one, which involve countervailing measures imposed as a result of investigations initiated pursuant to applications made before the date of entry into force of the WTO Agreement for a Member. The

---

[71]   Reflective of this relationship is Article II:2(b), which provides that "[n]othing in this Article shall prevent any contracting party from imposing at any time on the importation of any product ... any anti-dumping or countervailing duty applied consistently with the provisions of Article VI*" (note omitted). We note that the application of this provision requires a judgement regarding whether a countervailing duty is "applied consistently with Article VI". Here the measures are neither "consistent" nor "inconsistent" with Article VI of GATT 1994; rather, they are simply not subject to that Article, and any assessment of their consistency should be performed by reference to Article VI of GATT 1947 and, with respect to Tokyo Round SCM Code signatories, also with reference to that Code.

Philippines claimed that, even if the programmes at issue in Brazil's investigation constitute subsidies on coconut fruit, the programmes fully comply with the developing country and *de minimis* exemptions from domestic support commitments under Article 6 of the Agreement on Agriculture. Thus under Article 13(b)(i) of that Agreement the programmes are exempt from the imposition of countervailing duties unless a determination of injury or threat thereof is made in accordance with Article VI of GATT 1994 and Part V of the SCM Agreement. Brazil contends that Article 13 of the Agreement on Agriculture only applies to countervailing duties subject both to the Article VI of GATT 1994 and the SCM Agreement, and that this is not the case here.

283.   Article 13 of the Agreement on Agriculture provides that:

> "During the implementation period, notwithstanding the provisions of GATT 1994 and the Agreement on Subsidies and Countervailing Measures (referred to in this Article as the "Subsidies Agreement"):
>
> . . .
>
> (b)   domestic support measures that conform fully to the provisions of Article 6 of this Agreement including direct payments that conform to the requirements of paragraph 5 thereof, as reflected in each Member's schedule, as well as domestic support within *de minimis* levels and in conformity with paragraph 2 of Article 6, shall be:
>
> > (i)   exempt from the imposition of countervailing duties unless a determination of injury or threat thereof is made in accordance with Article VI of GATT 1994 and Part V of the Subsidies Agreement, and due restraint shall be shown in initiating any countervailing duty investigations...".

Note 4 to Article 13 provides that:

> "'Countervailing duties' where referred to in this Article are those covered by Article VI of GATT 1994 and Part V of the Agreement on Subsidies and Countervailing Measures".

284.   We have previously concluded that neither Article VI of GATT 1994 in isolation, nor Article VI of GATT 1994 in conjunction with the SCM Agreement, apply to the measures at issue in this dispute. Countervailing duties are subject to Article 13 of the Agreement on Agriculture only if they are "covered by Article VI of GATT 1994 and Part V of the Agreement on Subsidies and Countervailing Measures". Thus, we conclude that Article 13 of the Agreement on Agriculture does not apply to this dispute.

285.   We further note that Article 13 of the Agreement on Agriculture reinforces our conclusions regarding the non-applicability of Article VI of GATT

1994 to this dispute. First, it appears from the text of Article 13 (specifically, to the consistent references to Article VI of GATT 1994 *and* the SCM Agreement) that the drafters expected that Article VI of GATT 1994 and the SCM Agreement would operate only in conjunction. Thus, Article 13 demonstrates that the WTO Agreement establishes an integrated package of rights and obligations relating to the use of countervailing measures. These rights and obligations are found in Article VI of GATT 1994, the SCM Agreement, and the Agreement on Agriculture. We do not consider that this package of rights and obligations would operate as intended if portions of the package were found to apply to a countervailing measure when other portions did not.

B.   Failure to Consult

286.   The Philippines requests a finding that Brazil's refusal to hold consultations under Article XXIII:1 of GATT 1994 in this matter is inconsistent with its obligations under that Article and Articles 4.1, 4.2 and 4.3 of the DSU. Brazil in response argues that the Philippines has failed to state a claim in this regard, and that therefore this issue is not within the Panel's terms of reference.

287.   The Philippine's request concerns a matter which this Panel views with the utmost seriousness. Compliance with the fundamental obligation of WTO Members to enter into consultations where a request is made under the DSU is vital to the operation of the dispute settlement system. Article 4.2 of the DSU provides that "Each Member undertakes to accord sympathetic consideration to and afford adequate opportunity for consultation regarding any representations made by another Member concerning measures affecting the operation of any covered agreement taken within the territory of the former[3]". Moreover, pursuant to Article 4.6 of the DSU, consultations are "without prejudice to the rights of any Member in any further proceedings". In our view, these provisions make clear that Members' duty to consult is absolute, and is not susceptible to the prior imposition of any terms and conditions by a Member.

288.   This Panel is bound to examine only those claims which fall within the scope of our terms of reference. In this case, the parties agreed to special terms of reference, directing the Panel to examine the "matter" referred to the DSB for settlement by the Philippines in the request for establishment of a panel, taking into account Brazil's submission in document WT/DS22/3 and the record of discussions at the meeting of the DSB on 21 February 1996.

289.   The parties disagreed concerning the standard by which a panel should evaluate whether a claim is within the terms of reference of a panel under the provisions of the DSU. Article 6.2 of the DSU requires that a request for establishment of a panel "shall indicate whether consultations were held, identify the specific measures at issue and provide a brief summary of the legal basis of the complaint sufficient to present the problem clearly". In our view, at a minimum, it should have been possible, based on a reasonable reading of the documents determining the scope of the terms of reference, to conclude that this Panel would be asked to make findings regarding Brazil's failure to consult.

290.   We examined the Philippines' request for establishment of a panel, and the additional documents the Panel was directed to take into account, in order to determine whether the Philippines had stated a claim regarding Brazil's failure to consult sufficiently to bring it within the scope of the Panel's terms of reference. The Philippines' request for establishment of a panel clearly fulfils the first requirement of Article 6.2, by indicating the Philippines' view that consultations were not held because Brazil refused to consult. It also identifies the countervailing measures imposed by Brazil, the Philippines' assertions of various violations with regard to those measures, and requested findings with respect to those measures. However, there is nothing in the request for establishment of a panel that would lead to the conclusion that the requested panel would be asked to make any finding regarding Brazil's failure to consult. We consider it self-evident that Brazil's submission in document WT/DS22/3 does not state a claim on behalf of the Philippines. Finally, while the record of the discussions in the DSB meeting of 21 February 1996 repeats the Philippines' view that consultations were not held because Brazil refused to consult, there is again nothing in that record that would lead to the conclusion that the requested panel would be asked to make any finding regarding Brazil's failure to consult. In our view, it would not have been possible, based on a reasonable reading of the documents determining the scope of the Panel's terms of reference in this dispute, to conclude that the Panel would be asked to make any finding regarding Brazil's failure to consult. We therefore conclude that the Philippines' claim regarding Brazil's failure to consult is not within our terms of reference.

C.   Translation of DTIC Opinion 006/95

291.   On 12 June 1996, the second day of the Panel's first meeting with the parties, Brazil submitted a two-page document setting forth corrections to its translations of Interministerial Ordinance No. 11 and DTIC Opinion 006/95, indicating that the initial translation did not properly reflect the original Portuguese-language determinations. The Philippines objected to consideration of the corrected translations of the two texts, asserting that there were substantive differences between the initial and corrected translations. The Philippines subsequently submitted a letter objecting to the "acceptance" of the corrected translations, objecting to Brazil's failure to provide advance warning of the pending corrections, and inferring that the corrections were made in response to arguments made during the oral presentations of the Philippines and third parties and/or to address some of the concerns expressed in our questions to Brazil. The Philippines indicated three instances in which it considered that Brazil had gone beyond translation corrections to change the substance of the documents.

292.   On 17 July 1996, at the Panel's second meeting with the parties, we issued the following ruling concerning this issue:

> "The Panel takes note of the Philippine's request that the Panel 'not accept' the corrected translation, and in par-

ticular of the objections of the Philippines regarding corrections 1, 7 and 9 to Interministerial Directive no. 11.

"The Panel considers that it would have been preferable had Brazil confirmed the accuracy of its translations prior to submitting them to the Panel. However, for the Panel to decline to accept any linguistic corrections on the grounds they differed from the initial translation would prevent the Panel from reviewing should it become necessary the countervailing duty in light of the actual determination made by Brazil.

"The Panel has before it the original Portuguese-language text of Interministerial Directive no. 11 and translations prepared by both parties. The Panel will refer to both the Philippine and corrected Brazilian translations should it be required to consider the language of that Directive. Should there be any material difference between the two translations with respect to relevant language in the Directive, the Panel will if and as required resolve any such difference by reference to the original Portuguese-language Directive.

"The Panel has before it the original Portuguese-language text of DTIC Notice 06/95. Should the Panel be required to refer to DTIC Notice no. 06/95, and if the language considered was subject to correction by Brazil, the Panel will confirm the accuracy of the corrected translation by reference to the Portuguese-language text of the Notice. The Philippines may inform the Panel if it considers that any of the corrections inaccurately reflects the original Portuguese-language Notice.

"Should the Philippines consider that any modification to the Panel's procedures is required to accommodate these circumstances, the Panel is prepared to entertain any request for such a modification".

VII. CONCLUDING REMARKS

293.   The substantive questions raised by the Parties to this dispute are a matter of major concern and would merit serious consideration. However, because the issue of applicable law was dispositive in this dispute, this Panel did not reach any conclusion with respect to those substantive questions.

VIII. CONCLUSIONS

294.   In light of the findings above, the Panel makes the following conclusions:

(a)   Article VI of GATT 1994 does not constitute applicable law for the purposes of this dispute. As a result, the substance of the Philippines' claims under that Article, and of its claims under Articles I and II of GATT 1994 which derive from their claims of inconsistency with Article VI of GATT 1994, cannot be considered by this Panel.

(b)   The Agreement on Agriculture does not constitute applicable law for the purposes of this dispute. As a result, the substance of the Philippines' claims under that Agreement cannot be considered by this Panel.

(c)   The Philippines' claim regarding Brazil's failure to consult is not within the terms of reference of this Panel and therefore its substance cannot be considered.

295.   The Panel, having concluded that the substance of the Philippines' claims are not properly before it, recommends that the Dispute Settlement Body make such a ruling.

RESTRICTED

WORLD TRADE
ORGANIZATION

WT/DS22/3

29 January 1996

(96-0276)

Original: English

BRAZIL - MEASURES AFFECTING DESICCATED COCONUT

Communication from Brazil

The following communication, dated 24 January 1996, from the Permanent Mission of Brazil to the Chairman of the Dispute Settlement Body, is circulated at the request of that Delegation.

———————

I have the honour to convey to you herewith a copy of document SCM/193 on the issue of countervailing duties imposed by Brazil on imports of processed desiccated coconut from the Philippines. The matter was referred to during the Tokyo Round Committee held on 31 October 1995.

As you will learn from the paper, during the past few months Brazil and the Philippines have faced, besides substantive issues relating to the Brazilian measure, the question of the applicable law under which consultations ought to be requested. Brazil understands, for the reasons indicated in the position paper, that the Tokyo Round Code on Subsidies and Countervailing Measures should be the only legal framework applicable to the dispute, whereas the Philippines espouse the opposite view.

In order to clarify the matter and to seek transparency on the subject with all the Tokyo Round Committee Members, the Brazilian Mission requested that said position paper be circulated, as a Committee document, among Members of the Committee on Subsidies and Countervailing Measures of the Agreement on Interpretation and Application of Articles VI, XVI and XXIII of the General Agreement on Tariffs and Trade (the Tokyo Round Committee on Subsidies and Countervailing Measures) before 31 January.

Considering that, at the request of the Philippine Mission, the issue has been included in the agenda for the next meeting of the Dispute Settlement Body to be held on 31 January, I kindly request that the present letter and its attached document SCM/193 be circulated as a WTO document under a DS symbol, to all WTO Members before the DSB meeting.

Brazil understands that the DSB is not the appropriate forum for the discussion on the dispute with the Philippines and wishes to circulate document SCM/193 among WTO Members for information purposes only and without prejudice to its rights under the Tokyo Round Code on Subsidies and Countervailing Measures and to its position on the applicable law.

GENERAL AGREEMENT	RESTRICTED
	SCM/193
ON TARIFFS AND TRADE	26 January 1996
	Special Distribution
	(96-0274)
Committee on Subsidies and	Original: English
Countervailing Measures	

BRAZIL - IMPOSITION OF COUNTERVAILING DUTIES ON IMPORTS
OF PROCESSED DESICCATED COCONUT FROM THE PHILIPPINES

Communication from Brazil

The following communication, dated 24 January 1996, has been received from the Permanent Mission of Brazil.

———————

I have the honour to convey to you herewith a position paper prepared by Brazil on the issue of countervailing duties imposed by Brazil on imports of processed desiccated coconut from the Philippines. The matter was referred to during the Tokyo Round Committee held on 31 October 1995.

As you will learn from the paper, during the past few months Brazil and the Philippines have faced, besides substantive issues relating to the Brazilian measure, the question of the applicable law under which consultations ought to be requested. Brazil understands, for the reasons indicated in the position paper, that the Tokyo Round Code on Subsidies and Countervailing Measures should be the only legal framework applicable to the dispute, whereas the Philippines espouse the opposite view.

In order to clarify the matter and to seek transparency on the subject with all the Committee Members, I kindly request that the said position paper be circulated, as a Committee document, among Members of the Committee on Subsidies and Countervailing Measures of the Agreement on Interpretation and Application of Articles VI, XVI and XXIII of the General Agreement on Tariffs and Trade (the Tokyo Round Committee on Subsidies and Countervailing Measures) before 31 January.

———————

The Permanent Mission of Brazil in Geneva hereby submits relevant information concerning the adoption of countervailing duties on imports of desiccated coconut from the Philippines.

I.   Summary of the Investigation and the Legal Framework

1.   The Brazilian authorities initiated investigations on subsidies granted to coconut processors in the Philippines and four other countries through Public Notice SECEX No. 40, dated 21 July 1994.

2.   The investigations were based on the Agreement on Interpretation and Application of Articles VI, XVI and XXIII of the General Agreement on Tariffs and Trade (the Tokyo Round Agreement on Subsidies and Countervailing Measures), to which the Philippines and Brazil are parties.

3.   After preliminary findings, the Brazilian authorities imposed provisional countervailing duties on imports of Philippine desiccated coconut through Public Notice No. 113, dated 23 March 1995. Later, the Brazilian authorities concluded that subsidies actually existed and imposed definitive countervailing measures on imports of processed desiccated coconut from the Philippines through Public Notice No. 11, dated 10 August 1995.

II.   Discussions with the Philippine Side

4.   On 10 November 1995, the Permanent Representative of the Philippines in Geneva addressed a letter to the Chairman of the Committee on Subsidies and Countervailing Measures in which she informed that the "Government of the Republic of the Philippines wishes to initiate procedures under Article 17 of the Tokyo Round Agreement on Subsidies and Countervailing Measures ...". Brazil replied on 14 November that since formal consultations under the Tokyo Round Code had not been requested nor had taken place, it would be improper to jump to the conciliation process of Article 17. Brazil also indicated that it was ready to start formal consultations upon request by the Philippines.

5.   On 27 November 1995, the Permanent Representative of the Philippines addressed a letter to the Permanent Representative of Brazil requesting formal consultations under Article XXIII:1 of GATT 1994. The Brazilian answer, dated 8 December 1995 stated that the Permanent Mission of Brazil was ready for consultations "as long as it was mutually understood that those consultations will be undertaken exclusively under the Code on Subsidies and Countervailing Measures [...] resulting from the Tokyo Round, under which auspices coconut subsidies investigations were conducted and countervailing duties imposed".

6.   On 13 December 1995, the Philippines replied that the Brazilian answer constituted a refusal of their request for consultations under Article XXIII.1 of GATT 1994.

7.   On 10 January 1996, Brazil once again reiterated the contents of its previous letter dated 8 December, in which it was informed that Brazil was "prepared to enter into consultations with the Philippines on the matter of countervailing duties imposed by Brazil on imports of desiccated coconut from the Philippines. Since the investigation and the imposition of definitive countervailing duties were held under the Tokyo Round Code on that specific matter [...]. Brazil considers that the legal framework for consultations on the

subject is the same Tokyo Round Code, which is still in place until the end of the current year for dispute settlement purposes".

8.   Brazil has, therefore, for three times offered formal consultations to the Philippines. No reply in the sense of the acceptance of those offers ever reached the Brazilian mission.

9.   In a letter dated 16 January 1996 the Government of the Philippines informed the Government of Brazil that they had decided to request a panel.

III.   Brazilian Arguments

10.   The Brazilian position on this matter is as follows:

(a)   The Philippines stand in favour of the application of Article VI of GATT 1994 to this dispute is unacceptable to Brazil and raises relevant systemic issues of interest to all Members of the WTO;

(b)   The Brazilian investigation started in 1994, under the Tokyo Round Code on Subsidies and Countervailing Measures;

(c)   The Tokyo Round Code is in force until 31 December 1996 and may be invoked by the Philippines;

(d)   Furthermore, the scope of Article VI of GATT 1947 is legally distinct from that of Article VI of GATT 1994. Article VI of GATT 1947, as interpreted by the Tokyo Round Agreements, embodied a specific set of rights and obligations; Article VI of GATT 1994, as interpreted by the Agreement on Subsidies and Countervailing Measures, embodies another specific set of rights and obligations. To invoke Article VI of GATT 1994 implies the adoption of the specific views of the WTO agreements as opposed to those of the Tokyo agreements. Therefore, to invoke now Article VI of GATT 1994 to a dispute started under the Tokyo Round Code would constitute an attempt to apply an inappropriate legal framework;

(e)   Any attempt to frame the present case within the scope of the WTO agreements constitutes an attempt to circumvent the application of the appropriate law;

(f)   No formal consultations ever took place between the Brazilian and the Philippine Missions in Geneva, in spite of reiterated Brazilian offers to do so.

VI.   Conclusions

11.   In summary, Brazil reiterates its disposition to consult with the Philippine Mission on the basis of the relevant provisions of the Tokyo Round Code on Subsidies and Countervailing Measures.

12.   Brazil considers this issue of particular interest to all WTO Members because in substantive terms it goes well beyond the question of the adoption of a certain level of countervailing duties. In fact, the central issue is the question of the application of the appropriate legal framework.

ANNEX 2

WORLD TRADE
ORGANIZATION

WT/DS22/5

8 February 1996
(96-0478)

Original: English

BRAZIL - MEASURES AFFECTING DESICCATED COCONUT

Request for the Establishment of a Panel by the Philippines

The following communication, dated 5 February 1996, from the Permanent Mission of the Philippines to the Chairman of the Dispute Settlement Body, is circulated at the request of that delegation.

———————

On 27 November 1995, the Government of the Philippines requested the Government of Brazil to enter into consultations pursuant to Article XXIII:1 of the 1994 General Agreement on Tariffs and Trade (GATT 1994). A copy of this request was notified to the Dispute Settlement Body (DSB) as well as to the Council on Trade in Goods, the Committee on Subsidies and Countervailing Measures, and the Committee on Agriculture, in accordance with Article 4:4 of the Dispute Settlement Understanding.

The Philippines requested consultations under Article XXIII:1 because benefits under GATT 1994 are being nullified and impaired as a result of the 121.5 per cent countervailing duty imposed on Philippine exports of processed desiccated coconut products, which is inconsistent with Brazil's obligations under Article VI of GATT 1994, in particular with respect to paragraphs 3 and 6(a).

Even if assuming the development assistance extended to coconut farmers were to be considered subsidies, and that these were passed on entirely to benefit independent desiccated coconut processors, the Brazilian measure would also be inconsistent with Brazil's obligations under Article 13 of the Agreement on Agriculture.

Additionally, the Philippines is of the view that:

1. Brazil did not give the Philippines reasonable opportunity, throughout the investigation, to clarify the factual situation. As previously stated by the Philippine Government, there is no subsidy granted to desiccated coconut processing. Development assistance was provided to coconut farmers

through a levy collected from them, and not through the government budget. These were private funds of the coconut farmers.

2. In calculating the amount of the subsidy and the countervailing duty, Brazil relied on *'information available'* which excluded data and information on the type of assistance programmes to the coconut producers that was provided by the Philippines.

3. Brazil calculated the amount of the alleged subsidy and countervailing duty by treating the coconut fruit as substitutable for desiccated coconut when these two products are not like products. Moreover, Brazil is a producer of coconuts and desiccated coconut, both of which are available in the domestic market of Brazil, and should therefore not have treated the coconut fruit as a substitute for desiccated coconut.

4. In investigating the assistance programmes to the Philippine coconut industry, Brazil failed to recognize that these programmes, as implemented by a developing country like the Philippines, should not have been considered as subsidies *per se*. Moreover, as the Philippines had previously testified, the source of funds for the assistance programmes came from a levy on coconut production, and not from any government budget.

For the further information of the DSB, we understand that Brazil has only recently notified the WTO of the instruments that imposed the provisional countervailing duty of 14.1 per cent on 28 March 1995, and the definitive countervailing duty of 121.5 per cent on 21 August 1995.

In its response dated 8 December 1995, Brazil stated that it was prepared to enter into consultations with the Philippines as long as it was mutually understood that those consultations would be undertaken exclusively under the 1979 Agreement on Interpretation and Application of Articles VI, XVI, and XXIII of the General Agreement on Tariffs and Trade (or, Tokyo Round Code on Subsidies and Countervailing Measures), under which auspices the coconut subsidies investigations were conducted and the countervailing duties imposed.

In a letter dated 13 December 1995, the Philippines replied that Brazil's response constituted a refusal of the request for consultations under Article XXIII:1, but that it hoped that Brazil would be able to engage the Philippines in such consultations within the 30-day period provided in Article 4:3 of the Dispute Settlement Understanding (DSU).

Unfortunately, Brazil has failed to enter into consultations with the Philippines within the period prescribed in the DSU.

The Government of the Philippines requests the establishment of a Panel pursuant to Article XXIII:2 of GATT 1994 and Articles 4 and 6 of the DSU, and under the standard terms of reference provided in Article 7.1 of the DSU. The Philippines requests that the Panel consider and find that:

1. The countervailing duty imposed by Brazil is inconsistent with paragraphs 3 and 6(a) of Article VI of GATT 1994.

2.   Brazil should desist from further imposing the countervailing duty on desiccated coconut exports of the Philippines, and reimburse whatever duties were collected.

The Philippines submits this request for the establishment of a Panel for inscription in the agenda of the next meeting of the DSB on 21 February 1996, and further requests that a special meeting of the DSB be convened not later than 15 days after the meeting of 21 February.

ANNEX 3

RESTRICTED

WORLD TRADE
ORGANIZATION

WT/DSB/M/11

19 March 1996

(96-0987)

DISPUTE SETTLEMENT BODY
21 February 1996

MINUTES OF MEETING

Held in the Centre William Rappard
on 21 February 1996

Chairman: Mr. C. Lafer (Brazil)

1.   Brazil - Measures affecting desiccated coconut

      -    Request by the Philippines for the establishment of a panel
           (WT/DS22/5)

The Chairman recalled that this matter had been proposed for inscription
on the Agenda of the DSB meeting on 31 January. Its consideration was,
however, postponed to the next meeting of the DSB. He then drew attention to
the communication from the Philippines in document WT/DS22/5.

The representative of the <u>Philippines</u> said that since her country's request for the establishment of a panel was explained in WT/DS22/5 she wished only to point out that the 121.5 per cent countervailing duty imposed by Brazil on Philippine's exports of desiccated coconut was inconsistent with Brazil's obligations under Article VI of GATT 1994 and other related covered agreements. The measure nullified Philippine's benefits under the GATT 1994. In was her country's view that an investigation should not have been initiated by Brazil nor a countervailing duty have been imposed. Although several meetings had been held with Brazil over the last few months on this matter, it had not been possible to arrive at a mutually agreed solution. Therefore, the Philippines requested that a panel be established at the present meeting and hoped that Brazil would be able to agree to this request.

The representative of <u>Brazil</u> recalled that his country's arguments concerning this dispute were contained in WT/DS22/3. During the last few months, Brazil and the Philippines had been discussing the question of applicable law, i.e., the legal framework to examine a countervailing measure imposed by Brazil on coconut imports from the Philippines. Brazil firmly believed that a measure should be reviewed against the same standards which had been used for its adoption. This principle was contained in Article 32.3 of the Uruguay Round Agreement on Subsidies and Countervailing Measures (SCM). Members had also agreed on that principle in the transitional arrangements negotiated in 1994.[72] Overturning this principle would not be very constructive and might cause serious problems for the WTO system. Members were formally and morally requested to abide by the rules which they had established. This issue involved important standards such as fairness, reasonableness and legality. Fairness, because all procedures, decisions and practices under a certain legal system ought to be examined. Reasonableness, since the Philippines had an effective remedy for their complaint in the Tokyo Round Subsidies Code which was in place for dispute settlement purposes until the end of 1996. Brazil was not against the reasonable right of the Philippines to seek redress to what it perceived as nullification and impairment of its benefits. Legality, because decisions had been taken to avoid "contamination" of the WTO with GATT cases. In December 1994, Members had decided that the Tokyo Round Code would be extended until December 1996 in order to deal with cases initiated under that Code, prior to the establishment of the WTO, and that the SCM Agreement would not apply to investigations initiated before 1 January 1995. Brazil and the Philippines were still discussing this matter. Brazil therefore considered that it was premature to establish a panel at the present meeting and wished the DSB to revert to this matter at its next meeting.

The representative of <u>Indonesia, speaking on behalf of ASEAN countries,</u> said that ASEAN countries supported the request for the establishment of a

---

[72] PC/15-L/7586 and PC/16-L7587

panel. The Philippines had only invoked its rights under Article VI of GATT 1994 to which Brazil was also bound. It had chosen neither to invoke the Tokyo Round Subsidies Code nor its rights under the SCM Agreement. Therefore, ASEAN countries did not support Brazil's view that the question of the applicable law should first be resolved. The Philippines had complied with the DSU requirements and the DSB would have to establish a panel. Indonesia and Malaysia had also been affected by the same measure taken by Brazil on 21 August 1995. The investigation initiated by Brazil on desiccated coconut was inconsistent with its obligations under Article VI of GATT 1994 and the WTO. This had resulted in definitive countervailing duties of 155.57 and 196.5 per cent for Indonesia and Malaysia respectively. He reiterated that Brazil had neither conducted the investigation transparently nor had it provided a reasonable opportunity for Indonesia and Malaysia to clarify the factual situation. Although a set of questionnaires had been answered, and some statistical data and various legal dispositions submitted, Brazil had neglected to take this information into account since it was not supplied in Portuguese. Brazil's Government which should have determined and calculated the subsidy margin on the basis of information available, had violated Article VI of the GATT 1994. Malaysia and Indonesia reserved their right to actively participate in the panel as third parties.

The representative of Sri Lanka said that his delegation supported the Philippines' request for the establishment of a panel. His country agreed with the Philippines on the rationale for a panel to examine the countervailing duties imposed by Brazil on exports of desiccated coconut from the Philippines. Sri Lanka was one of the countries which had also been severely affected by Brazil's action on desiccated coconut and coconut milk powder. The countervailing duty imposed by Brazil on 21 August 1995 on imports of desiccated coconut and coconut milk powder amounted to 81.4 per cent and 175.8 per cent respectively. Sri Lanka considered Brazil's action as unjustifiable and unreasonable because it violated Sri Lanka's rights under the GATT 1994. Consultations had been held with Brazil with a view to arriving at a mutually acceptable solution, but the outcome of these consultations had not been positive. Sri Lanka would hold further consultations with Brazil until all prospects of arriving at a mutual settlement were exhausted. Sri Lanka's exports of desiccated coconut and coconut milk powder had come to a halt as a result of Brazil's action. As his country had a direct trade interest in the matter, it reserved its third-party rights.

The representative of the Philippines thanked Brazil for elaborating on its position with respect to the application of Article VI of GATT 1994 contained in WT/DS22/3 and wished to make the following points. First, in past GATT practice it had been recognized that it was up to the complainant to decide whether it wanted to invoke the general GATT provisions - in this case Article VI - or the specific Tokyo Round Code provisions. There had been disputes in the past where parties had invoked their rights with respect to Article VI and not the Tokyo Round Codes. Second, the fact that Brazil's investigation had started in 1994 under the Tokyo Round Subsidies Code did not deprive the Philippines of their rights under GATT 1994 and the DSU. The Philippines' view was that the transitional provision in Article 32.3 of the SCM Agreement applied to the said Agreement itself and did not govern the application of Article VI of GATT 1994 which, since its entry into force in 1995, required Brazil to implement countervailing measures only in conformity with Article VI. Third, although the Tokyo Round Committee continued to be in place until the end of 1996, this did not preclude the Philippines from invoking its rights under GATT 1994. Moreover, the Decision of 8 December 1994 on Transitional Co-existence of the Tokyo Round Subsidies Code and the WTO Agreement confirmed the priority of WTO dispute settlement procedures over the Tokyo Round Subsidies Code. The Decision of 8 December 1994 on the consequences of termination of, or withdrawal of, the Tokyo Round Subsidies Code governed only the transition from the Tokyo Round Subsidies Code to the 1994 SCM Agreement. This Decision did not prevent the right of Members to invoke Article VI of GATT 1994 and the DSU. Fourth, Brazil had stated that Article VI of GATT 1947, as interpreted by the Tokyo Round Subsidies Code, was legally distinct from Article VI of GATT 1994, which in turn was interpreted by the 1994 SCM Agreement. To invoke Article VI of GATT 1994 "implied the adoption of the specific views of the WTO agreements as opposed to those of the Tokyo Round Agreements."[73] It was the Philippines' position that Article VI of GATT 1994 and the SCM Agreement were two distinct legal instruments and the Philippines was simply invoking its rights under Article VI of GATT 1994. Brazil also alleged that in spite of its repeated offers to consult no formal consultations ever took place. Consultations had not been held because Brazil refused to consult. She reiterated that on 27 November 1995 the Philippines had requested consultations under Article XXIII:1 on the consistency of Brazil's measure with respect to Article VI of GATT 1994. On 29 November the Philippines had notified the DSB, the Council for Trade in Goods, the Committee on Subsidies and Countervailing Measures and the Committee on Agriculture of its request. On 8 December, Brazil had offered to consult only under the Tokyo Round Subsidies Code. In a letter dated 13 December, the Philippines had stated that Brazil's response of 8 December constituted a refusal to consult under Article XXIII:1. Therefore the Philippines hoped that Brazil would be able to engage in Article XXIII:1 consultations within the 30-day period provided for in Article 4.3 of the DSU. On 10 January 1996 Brazil had responded to the Philippines' letter of 13 December 1995 and had reiterated its offer to consult only under the Tokyo Round Subsidies Code. On 15 January the Philippines had informed Brazil that, since Brazil maintained its position, the Philippines had no other recourse but to invoke Article XXIII:2 of GATT 1994 and Articles 4.3, 6 and 7.1 of the DSU. Thus, on 17 January the Philippines had requested the establishment of a panel. The Philippines sought redress from the actions of Brazil under Article VI of GATT 1994. It had faithfully adhered to the requirements in the DSU, and now requested the establishment of a panel. Since Brazil's did not agree with the

---

[73]   SCM/193, p.3.

establishment of a panel at the present meeting the Philippines requested a DSB meeting within 15 days in order to consider its request for the establishment of a panel.

The representative of <u>Brazil</u> said that his delegation noted all the statements made at the present meeting. He reiterated that this issue involved such important standards as fairness, reasonableness and legality as he had stated in the statement made earlier. He stressed that Brazil had never refused to consult. It had only insisted that consultations should be held under the Tokyo Round Code provisions. The question of applicable law was central to this case and if a panel was established Brazil would request a preliminary ruling on the question of the applicable law.

The DSB <u>took note</u> of the statements and <u>agreed</u> to convene its next meeting on 5 March in order to revert to this matter.

2.   <u>United States - Standards for reformulated and conventional gasoline</u>
-      <u>Panel report</u> (WT/DS2/R)

The <u>Chairman</u> recalled that at its meeting on 10 April 1995, the DSB had established a Panel to examine the complaint by Venezuela. On 31 May 1995 the DSB had established a Panel to examine the complaint concerning the same matter by Brazil. At that meeting, pursuant to Article 9 of the DSU in respect of multiple complaints the DSB had decided, with the agreement of all parties, that for practical reasons this matter be examined by the panel already established at the request of Venezuela on 10 April 1995. The Panel report, contained in document WT/DS2/R and circulated on 29 January 1996, was now before the DSB for adoption at the request of Venezuela.

<u>Mr. Harbinson</u> (Hong Kong), <u>speaking in his personal capacity on behalf of Mr. Wong</u>, Chairman of the Panel, said that the Panel had been established by the DSB on 10 April 1995 at the request of Venezuela. The Panel had been given standard terms of reference, with Mr. Joseph Wong as Chairman and Mr. Crawford Falconer and Mr. Kim Luotonen as panelists. Australia, Canada, the European Communities and Norway had reserved their rights to participate in the Panel proceedings as third parties. On 31 May 1995, the DSB had established a Panel on the same matter at the request of Brazil. Pursuant to Article 9 of the DSU in respect of multiple complainants the DSB had decided, with the agreement of all the parties, that for practical reasons this matter be examined by the Panel already established at the request of Venezuela. The Panel had met with the parties to the dispute from 10 to 12 July 1995 and from 13 to 15 September 1995. It had also met with the interested third parties on 11 July 1995. The Panel had issued its interim report to the parties on 11 December 1995. Following a request made by the United States pursuant to Article 15.2 of the DSU, the Panel had held a further meeting with the parties on 3 January 1996. The Panel had issued its final report to the parties to the dispute on 17 January 1996. The Panel had examined the final decision adopted on 15 December 1993 by the United States Environmental Protection Agency, "Regulation of Fuels and Fuel

Additives: Standards for Reformulated and Conventional Gasoline" (the Gasoline Rule). After a thorough analysis of the underlying facts and arguments of the parties, and in the light of the findings contained in the final report, the Panel had concluded that the baseline establishment methods contained in the Gasoline Rule were not consistent with Article III:4 of the General Agreement, and could not be justified under paragraphs (b), (d) and (g) of Article XX of the General Agreement. The Panel had therefore recommended that the DSB request the United States to bring the measures in question in conformity with its obligations under the General Agreement. In concluding, the Panel had underlined that it was not its task to examine generally the desirability or necessity of the environmental objectives of the Clean Air Act or the Gasoline Rule. Its examination was confined to those aspects of the Gasoline Rule that had been raised by the complainants under specific provisions of the General Agreement. Under the General Agreement, Members were free to set their own environmental objectives but they were bound to implement these objectives through measures consistent with its provisions, notably those on the relative treatment of domestic and imported products.

The representative of <u>Venezuela</u> expressed his delegation's gratitude to the panelists and the Secretariat for their meticulous and well-structured work. His country appreciated the time and efforts devoted to reviewing and analysing the facts and the legal arguments submitted by the parties during the proceedings, and the efforts in the search for a satisfactory settlement of the dispute. Parties to the dispute had been given equitable opportunity to participate in the proceedings both orally and in writing. The Panel's conclusions followed the same line of reasoning as that of other panels in GATT history. Several aspects of the Panel report deserved special mention. First, the report recognized explicitly that no rule or provision of the WTO Agreement prevented the United States from setting its own clean air standards. Members had sovereign authority in setting their own environmental objectives but they were bound to ensure that national standards and regulations accorded treatment to imported products which was no less favourable than that granted to like domestic products. Second, the report acknowledged what Venezuela had repeatedly stated to the United States namely, that the objectives of the Clean Air Act aimed at improving air quality were not questioned. Venezuela had brought the matter to the Panel to demonstrate that those objectives could be achieved without discriminating against imported gasoline and were in full conformity with the principle of national treatment laid down in Article III of the General Agreement. In this connection, the Panel upheld Venezuela's argument that there was no justification for the discriminatory aspects of the Gasoline Regulation, since several alternative methods were available to the United States to meet environmental objectives without distorting the competitive conditions between imported and domestically-produced gasoline. Far from seeking privileges or special treatment, all that Venezuela had asked of the United States was treatment for Venezuelan gasoline which was not less favourable than the treatment established in the Regulation for the like product of US origin. Therefore, the settlement of this dispute by means of the WTO procedures, had occurred despite Venezuela's wish.

From the beginning of the process of elaboration of the Gasoline Regulation in 1992 until 1994 his country had been proposing alternatives to the United States enabling to avoid all discrimination against imported gasoline. One of these alternatives was an agreement between the two countries to be applied in conformity with the most-favoured-nation principle. Unfortunately the US Congress, when enacting the Gasoline Regulation, had refused funds for putting that proposal into effect. Therefore Venezuela had decided to bring its complaint to the DSB. Thereafter, in the framework of the WTO dispute settlement proceedings, alternatives had been presented to the Panel which, after subjecting them to a thorough and balanced examination, had agreed with Venezuela that they were feasible both practically and legally. Some of the measures were fully consistent with the General Agreement, while others, which were less clearly consistent, at least had the virtue of generating a less trade restrictive effect. In the light of these considerations and in accordance with Article 16.4 of the DSU Venezuela had requested that the adoption of the report be included in the Agenda of the present meeting. However, the United States had notified its intention to apply for a review by the Appellate Body of certain legal aspects of the report. While recognizing that the United States had the right to appeal, its decision to do so could set a pattern which might be followed by Members where panel reports were unfavourable to them. Clearly, this would adversely affect the credibility of panel reports.

The representative of the <u>United States</u> said that the Panel report had been inscribed on the Agenda of the DSB for consideration at the present meeting. However since the United States had notified its decision to appeal certain legal issues, Article 16 of the DSU prevented consideration of the report for adoption at the present meeting. The DSB was not the appropriate forum to discuss the legal issues of the report that the United States had asked the Appellate Body to review which concerned the panel's consideration of Article XX of the General Agreement. However, the United States had serious concerns about the panel's treatment of issues not covered by this appeal. He was referring to what the United States considered a significant and inappropriate deviation from the customary practice that panels had followed in the past under the GATT 1947. Under past practice, panels had carefully avoided discussing legal issues that were uncontested during the panel proceedings, or unnecessary to the panel's findings in a particular dispute. Since Article XVI:1 of the WTO Agreement affirmed that the WTO shall be guided by the customary practices of the bodies established in the framework of the GATT 1947, it was the United States' expectation that this panel would follow that practice. Regrettably, it did not. In responding to the claim that the US measure in question was inconsistent with Article III:4 of the GATT 1994, the United States did not contest that the measure openly treated imports differently than like domestic products, and the panel acknowledged this position. Nonetheless, the panel proceeded to discuss at length the issue of like products with reference to hypothetical situations not presented, and it did so in a manner that appeared to offer opinions on arguments and issues that had arisen or might arise in the context of disputes other than this one. Such discussion was inappropriate and should serve as a model for what future panels should not do. Article 11 of the DSU clearly set out the limited role of panels, which was "to make an objective assessment of the matter before it, including the facts of the case." By opining on matters that were neither contested nor necessary to reach its conclusions, the panel exceeded these limits. The GATT 1947 panel process gained the confidence of delegations negotiating the DSU in part because of the conservative approach panels generally took in confining themselves strictly to the issues presented for resolution. The departure of this panel from that principle, and its foray into unnecessary *obiter dicta*, did not set a good example for the new WTO system. The United States expected that future panels would refrain from such wandering into policy issues. It simply was not appropriate in the context of dispute settlement.

The representative of Brazil wished to express its gratitude to the panelists, who had put tremendous efforts in understanding and deciding this case, and to the Secretariat who had been efficient and reliable as usual. The decision by the United States to appeal did not, in Brazil's opinion, diminish the merits of this report. One of these merits was the finding that discrimination could not be justified if the disciplines were not respected. One of the other merits of the report was that, "under the General Agreement WTO Members are free to set their own environmental objectives, but they are bound to implement these objectives through measures consistent with its provisions, notably with those on the relative treatment of domestic and imported products".[74] Since the beginning of this dispute settlement procedure, his delegation had expressed its view that this was not an environmental case. Brazil continued to hold this view, and agreed with the conclusions of the panel in this respect.

The DSB took note of the statements and of the US decision to appeal to the Appellate Body the panel report in DS2/R.

3.   Turkey - Action on imports of textiles and clothing

-       Statement by Hong Kong

The Chairman drew attention to the request for consultations by Hong Kong contained in WT/DS29/1.

The representative of Hong Kong said that his authorities fully respected the rights of Members to form customs unions or free-trade areas in accordance with the relevant provisions of the multilateral instruments which governed such matters. Nonetheless, Hong Kong was very much concerned that the implementation of customs unions or free-trade areas should not adversely affect other Members. He wished to raise Hong Kong's serious concern over a specific

---

[74]   DS2/R para. 7.1.

issue associated with the implementation of the Customs Union between Turkey and the European Community. On 1 January 1996, quantitative restrictions had been imposed by Turkey on the import of a broad range of textile and clothing products from Hong Kong and other sources i.e. a total of twenty-five suppliers. The imposition of these restrictions was unilateral and without prior notification. Hong Kong had written to the Turkish authorities requesting details of the measures taken and their justification under the WTO Agreement. The response had not provided satisfactory or complete answers to the questions raised. Although the volume of trade affected was relatively small, at stake were important points of principle. The quantitative restrictions violated Article XI of the GATT 1994, which provided for their general elimination, and Article XIII, which required that any such restrictions be administered in a non-discriminatory manner. These restrictions were also inconsistent with Turkey's obligation under Article 2 of the Agreement on Textiles and Clothing (ATC), which stipulated that new restrictions shall not be introduced except under the relevant provisions thereof or GATT 1994. The objective of the ATC was to bring trade in textiles under the GATT disciplines over a period of ten years. During the transitional period, safeguards could only be invoked if serious damage, or actual threat thereof, could be demonstrated. Turkey's action had not met the above-mentioned criteria and the transitional safeguard provisions of the ATC had not been invoked. In the view of Hong Kong Article XXIV could not be interpreted to justify the introduction of the quantitative restrictions by Turkey. In an effort to resolve this issue, Hong Kong had requested consultations with Turkey on 12 February 1996, under Article XXII:1 of the GATT 1994 pursuant to Article 4 of the DSU. It hoped that Turkey would fully discharge its obligations under the GATT and the WTO and urged that the action taken by Turkey be rescinded. In light of the outcome of these consultations, it reserved its rights to take the matter further, should this prove to be necessary.

The representative of the <u>Philippines, speaking on behalf of certain ASEAN countries</u>, namely Malaysia, the Philippines and Thailand which had been affected by the unilateral imposition of quantitative restrictions by Turkey on certain textile and clothing products. At the meeting of the Council for Trade in Goods on 29 January, ASEAN countries had registered their serious concern with the measure taken by Turkey and had stated that they reserved their rights to pursue the matter under the relevant WTO provisions, including GATT 1994 and the ATC. Like Hong Kong, ASEAN countries respected the rights of a Member to form customs unions or free-trade areas in accordance with the relevant multilateral trade agreements. While they welcomed the implementation of the Customs Union between Turkey and the European Community, they believed that Turkey should have ensured that the implementation of the agreement was not at the expense of other Members' rights under relevant WTO provisions. The WTO was a rule-based institution and one expected reasonable compliance with all that was agreed to and that Members would not take actions which would undermine the credibility of the WTO. At the conclusion of the Uruguay Round, Members had committed themselves to bring trade in textiles under the disciplines of GATT 1994 and the ATC. Malaysia, the Philippines and Thailand wished to reserve their rights to participate in consultations requested by Hong Kong. They would also prefer Turkey to withdraw the quantitative restrictions that it had imposed.

The representative of India said that his delegation wished to be associated with the statement made by Hong Kong. India requested Turkey to take into account the serious concerns of Hong Kong and to withdraw the quantitative restrictions it had imposed. Should this not happen, India wished to reserve its rights under the WTO Agreement and, in parallel, wished to express its interest to be joined in consultations requested by Hong Kong.

The representative of Korea shared the concerns expressed by Hong Kong. As a matter of principle, a number of questions remained to be answered concerning the compatibility of this measure with Turkey's commitments under the WTO Agreement. His authorities were currently reviewing the substantive effect the Turkish measure had on Korea's trade, as well as the legal implications thereof. Pending the results of this review, Korea reserved its rights, including that under Article 4.11 of the DSU concerning the request, to be joined in consultations.

The representative of Peru said that his delegation echoed the views expressed by Hong Kong and wished to reserve its rights, including those under Article 4.11 of the DSU.

The representative of Argentina said that his country shared Hong Kong's concerns regarding the conformity of the unilateral measures adopted by Turkey which also affected imports from Argentina. Consultations were ongoing and Argentina wished to reserve its rights on this matter.

The representative of Colombia said that the concerns raised by Hong Kong deserved careful consideration. Colombia would be following these consultations very closely. It hoped that this matter could be resolved in the best possible manner.

The representative of Brazil said that its exports of textiles and clothing had also been affected by the unilateral measure taken by Turkey. Brazil, therefore, wished to reserve its rights on this issue, including those under Article 4.11 of the DSU.

The representative of Pakistan said that the issue raised by Hong Kong had been discussed by the Committee on Trade and Development (CTD) at its meeting on 29 January. On that occasion, Pakistan had understood Turkey's natural disposition to forge closer relations with the European Communities located in close proximity of that market. His country however noted with disappointment that the formation of the Customs Union had resulted in raising discriminatory barriers against the trade of third countries including Pakistan. Pakistan felt that this raised valid questions about the compatibility of such restrictions with the requirements of the relevant provisions of the GATT. Pakistan noted Hong Kong's statement and would follow with deep interest the consultations requested by it.

The representative of <u>Turkey</u> said that his country had accepted to enter into bilateral consultations with Hong Kong in order to discuss this matter which was covered by Article XXIV:8(a) of the GATT 1994. Turkey was ready to fix a mutually agreed date for consultations with Hong Kong. His delegation noted the statements made at the present meeting and would consider the possible further requests, taking into account the relevant provisions of the WTO Agreement.

The representative of the <u>European Communities</u> informed the DSB that the Communities wished to be joined in the consultations requested by Hong Kong. The measures, as indicated by Turkey, resulted from the implementation of treaty establishing the Customs Union between Turkey and the European Community and were, in the view of the Communities, consistent with the provisions of the General Agreement and in particular were covered by Article XXIV:8.

The representative of <u>Hong Kong</u> said that his delegation noted the request of the Communities to be joined in consultations in accordance with Article 4.11 of the DSU. The language of Article 4.11 was clear in that any claim of substantial interest would be for the responding party, in this case Turkey, to agree. Also, if the request to join consultations was denied then the Member requesting to join consultations might proceed to initiate their own consultations. In the present case, any such request to join consultations were requests to join Hong Kong in consultations with Turkey. The purpose of such requests could not be to join Turkey in consultations with Hong Kong. Otherwise, the decision as to whether the requesting party should be joined in the consultations would be in the hands of Hong Kong rather than Turkey. Hong Kong had no wish to be difficult in this, but hoped that due consideration would be given to the above view on the systemic aspects of this case. Hong Kong was glad that Turkey agreed to bilateral consultations. He referred to a letter from the Turkish authorities indicating that it would not be convenient for them to consult in Geneva in the week beginning of the 11 March, which was the date suggested by Hong Kong. He hoped that in light of the interest which had been expressed by a number of delegations, Turkey might reconsider this matter because given the number of delegations interested, and given the fact that this dispute was taking place under multilateral instruments, it would be far more convenient for consultations to take place on neutral ground.

The DSB <u>took note</u> of the statements.

4.   <u>United States - Restrictions on imports of cotton and man-made fibre underwear</u>

- <u>Statement by Costa Rica</u>

The representative of <u>Costa Rica, speaking under "Other Business"</u>, recalled that at the DSB meeting on 31 January his delegation had informed the DSB that on 22 December 1995 Costa Rica had requested consultations with the United States with regard to the restrictions on Costa Rica's exports of cotton and man-made fibre underwear (category 352/652). However, these consultations did not arrive at a mutually satisfactory solution. Since the 60-day period for consultations had already expired, Costa Rica would soon request the establishment of a panel to examine this matter. In order for the panel to be established as quickly as possible, Costa Rica wished to request that a meeting of the DSB be convened for this purpose as provided for in footnote 5 of Article 6 of the DSU.

The DSB took note of the statement.

5.   Appellate Body - Working Procedures for Appellate Review

-    Statement by the Chairman

The Chairman, speaking under "Other Business", recalled that the Appellate Body's Working Procedures for Appellate Review which came into force on 15 February, had been circulated in WT/AB/WP/1. On 19 February informal consultations had been held for the purpose of providing a technical briefing on the Working Procedures during the course of which questions and comments had been made by Members. The package circulated on 15 February contained both the Working Procedures adopted by the Appellate Body and a covering letter from the Chairman of the Appellate Body to the DSB Chairman. The letter addressed the issues raised by Members which had been conveyed to the Appellate Body during the consultations held by the outgoing and incoming Chairmen of the DSB in accordance with the Decision on the Establishment of the Appellate Body contained in WT/DSB/1. It also explained the Appellate Body's reasons for its conclusions on certain key elements of the Working Procedures. For example, on issues of establishment of divisions, rotation and collegiality.

The consultations that he had held on behalf of Members with the Appellate Body, pursuant to Article 17.9 of the DSU and the DSB Decision on the Establishment of the Appellate Body, had the objective of making the Appellate Body aware of the concerns of Members. It was important to familiarize the Appellate Body with the sensitivities of the WTO and its "climate of opinion". Article 17.9 of the DSU contemplated neither a negotiations process nor a formal approval by the DSB of the Appellate Body's working procedures. The consultations contemplated in the DSU and the DSB Decision on the Establishment of the Appellate Body were in the nature of an advice - *consilium* - counsel to, and for the benefit of, the Appellate Body, but not a command *praeceptum* - that obliged the Appellate Body. Aquinas - distinguished between *praeceptum* - command and *consilium* - advice, by saying that *praeceptum* implied necessity to obey, while *consilium* provided options for those to whom they were given. The Working Procedures for Appellate Review were legally in effect, as of 15 February. They could be modified through the amendment procedure set out in Rule 32 of the Working Procedures. Finally, he drew the attention of Members to the fact that the Appellate Body had decided that the Working Procedures for Appellate Review would be issued as an unrestricted document.

The representative of <u>Mexico</u> recalled that in accordance with Article 17.9 of the DSU "working procedures shall be drawn up by the Appellate Body in consultation with the Chairman of the DSB and the Director-General, and communicated to the Members for their information". Mexico had hoped that its concerns, as well as other Members' concerns expressed during the informal consultations, would be reflected in the Appellate Body's Working Procedures. However, he noticed that this was not the case. His country's concerns pertained to the issues of collegiality and nationality of Appellate Body members which might affect the integrity and credibility of the dispute settlement mechanism. In accordance with Rule 4.3 of the Working Procedures "the division responsible for deciding each appeal shall exchange views with the other members before the division finalizes the appellate report for circulation to WTO Members". In other words, the seven members of the Appellate Body would influence the final decision through an exchange of views before the appellate report is finalized. However, Article 17.1 of the DSU provided that "the Appellate Body shall hear appeals from panel cases. It shall be composed of seven persons, three of whom shall serve on any one case. Persons serving on the Appellate Body shall serve in rotation". He recalled that collegiality was a new concept alien to the issues negotiated in the Uruguay Round. When Article 17 of the DSU was negotiated the idea was that each appellate review would be carried out only by three members of the Appellate Body. On the one hand, Article V:4(b)(i) of the Rules of Conduct stated that persons serving on the Standing Appellate Body who, through rotation, are selected to hear the appeal of a particular panel case (i.e. the three persons) shall review the factual portion of the panel report and complete the form at Annex 3. On the other hand, Rule 9.1, of the Working Procedures of the Appellate Body stated that each member (i.e. each of the seven members) shall take the steps set out in Article V:4(b)(i) of the Rules of Conduct.

Mexico was also concerned that Rule 6.2 of the Working Procedures provided for the "opportunity for all members to serve regardless of their national origin". He recalled that GATT practice, as well as Article 8.3 of the DSU were clear that "citizens of Members whose governments are parties to the dispute or third parties...shall not serve on a panel concerned with that dispute, unless the parties to the dispute agree otherwise". This was the best way to avoid possible direct or indirect conflict of interest. His authorities did not doubt the impartiality, honesty and moral integrity of the Appellate Body members. However, it would be very difficult for Mexico, and perhaps for other Members, to explain to some sectors of its national public opinion, in particular those who disagree with free trade, that in a lost dispute a citizen of the other party was a member of the Appellate Body, while no Mexican citizen had the same possibility.

His delegation hoped that the members of the Appellate Body would urgently reconsider the need to maintain the concepts of collegiality and nationality. Mexico reserved its rights under Article 17.1 of the DSU with regard to collegiality. It would also seek, if it considered appropriate, to define more precisely the notion "direct or indirect conflict of interest" in Article 17.3 of the DSU through the Rules of Conduct which were still subject to negotiations.

The representative of Egypt welcomed the fact that the Appellate Body finalized its Working Procedures. His delegation would have wished to have been consulted further in the process of the preparation of the Working Procedures. However, the covering letter from the Chairman of the Appellate Body explained the various issues which would have raised some concerns. Egypt was not concerned over collegiality or over nationality. Appellate Body members would be receiving documents related to all appeals. In accordance with Rule 4.3 of the Working Procedures, the division deciding each appeal shall exchange views - not consult - with other members. Working Procedures required only an exchange of views not that due consideration be given to the views expressed. However, the seven members would be overburdened with work since they would have to work as if they were involved in each and every case. They would have to study and reflect on documents circulated to them and in due course exchange their views. As to the question of nationality of members, all precautions had already been taken prior to their selection. Although the Rules of Conduct had not yet been adopted, the Appellate Body should be bound by these same rules since there were not other such rules available. In connection with Rule 8.1 of the Working Procedures which indicated that the Rules of Conduct for the DSU had only been adopted on a provisional basis, Egypt's position was that the same rules would govern not only the Appellate Body but also the Textiles Monitoring Body. In case these rules were amended in future, ag greater transparency should be observed. While Members would not be involved in negotiating amendments, at least their views would be made known to the Appellate Body members.

The representative of India said his country had already raised some concerns with regard to the Working Procedures and the letter from the Chairman of the Appellate Body during the informal consultations on 19 February. At the present meeting he wished to share some systemic concerns and to draw attention to the substance of the Working Procedures. He recognized that not all concerns could be dealt with by the Appellate Body and that some of them would have to be dealt with by the DSB. At the present meeting he wished only to enumerate those concerns so that in the future Members would be able to deal with them in a manner consistent with the roles that the DSU assigned to the DSB and the Appellate Body.

On the issue of collegiality Members had had different views regarding the extent to which the four members not serving on a division should influence the decision of the division. In his view any process which would enable the four members not serving on the division to be involved in the dispute was contrary to the letter and spirit of Article 17.1 of the DSU. He also mentioned that the circumstances under which the concept of collegiality was brought to the forefront could not be ignored. Rule 4.3 of the Working Procedures was not in accordance with Article 17.1 of the DSU and this problem could not be resolved through Rule 4.4 which is clearly inconsistent with Rule 4.3.

With regard to the question of nationality, there were some practical reasons which made it difficult to have a requirement that a member of the Appellate Body should stand aside in an appeal involving that member's country of origin. Article 17.3 of the DSU stipulated that the Appellate Body members should not participate in the consideration of any dispute that would create a direct or indirect conflict of interest. It was a moot point whether the nationality of a member created a conflict of interest. While one should not attach nationality tags to the Appellate Body members it would have been better for the credibility of the system if a mechanism had been devised to enable an appellant or appellee to convey informally his concerns about an Appellate Body member who was a citizen of a country involved in the dispute. Disputes brought to the Appellate Body were bound to acquire high political visibility and media attention. Therefore, it would not be wise to ignore perceptions. Although Rule 6.2 of the Working Procedures specified the principle of rotation, its mechanics were not spelled out. The DSB needed to be assured that the mechanism for ensuring rotation was reliable.

Rules 8, 9, 10 and 11 had been adopted on a provisional basis and Rule 8.1 implied that Rules of Conduct were not yet approved by the DSB. India was concerned that certain rules acquired legitimacy even before they were brought before the DSB and Members had to find ways of ensuring that this did not recur in the future. He noted that there was some dichotomy. The Appellate Body believed that dealing with the issue of nationality in any other way would be unnecessary in view of the qualifications required for membership of the Appellate Body and undesirable because it would cast doubts on the capacity of the Appellate Body members to be independent and impartial. However, the Appellate Body was willing to accept a situation where there would be a challenge on the basis of financial or professional interests. If the qualifications of the Appellate Body members and their selection process had ensured independence and impartiality in decision-making then there would be not need for the Appellate Body members to have Rules of Conduct.

Rule 32.2 of the Working Procedures stipulated that the Appellate Body might amend its rules in compliance with Article 17.9 of the DSU. In accordance with WT/DSB/1 the DSB Chairman should consult with the Members in order to obtain their views prior to advising the Appellate Body on the working procedures. It would be an anomalous situation if the Members were consulted by the Chairman at the initial stage of preparation of the Working Procedures but not when they would be subsequently amended.

He also had a systemic concern with regard to Rule 15 which implied that the Appellate Body could authorize a member to continue to be a member after it ceased to be a member. This was contrary to Article 17.1 of the DSU which, *inter alia*, provided that a standing Appellate Body shall be established by the DSB and that it shall be composed of seven persons. Rule 15 would lead to a situation where the Appellate Body could consist of more than seven members or an Appellate Body member continued after the expiry of his term without the approval of the DSB. While the practical need for the provision contained in

Rule 15 was understandable, he would be seriously concerned if a member of the Appellate Body could continue without concurrence or approval by the DSB. This Rule provided for notification to the DSB instead of approval and therefore was in violation of Article 17.1 of the DSU. As to Rule 29 regarding failure to appear, it was not clear as to how the views of a participant who failed to make a written submission and to appear could be heard.

He also noted that the letter of the Chairman of the Appellate Body indicated that the Appellate Body had held consultations with the Chairman of the DSB in December 1995 and January and February 1996. However, the first informal consultations with the Members on this subject had been held on 1 February. It would have been appropriate and useful if informal consultations on this subject had been initiated in December. The Appellate Body members would have been sensitized to various concerns and issues prior to drawing up of their working procedures. If consultations had been held in time Members would probably not face the difficulties at the present meeting. He recalled that the Chairman of the DSB, whenever provided an input to the Appellate Body regarding working procedures was performing an official duty assigned to him in the DSU. It would not be unfair for the collectivity of the DSB to expect that the Chairman would consult Members before providing an input to the Appellate Body, even if there had been no decision by the DSB that the Chairman should consult Members before advising the Appellate Body. He was glad that the Appellate Body had expressed formally its strong commitment to the dispute settlement system as a whole. Countries involved in the Uruguay Round negotiations had the vision and courage to opt for a strengthened dispute settlement system with the Appellate Body at the apex of that system. Members were unlikely to be less committed to the integrity of the dispute settlement system as a whole than anybody else.

The representative of the United States thanked the Chairman for holding the informal meeting on 19 February concerning the Working Procedures for Appellate Review. The technical briefing provided at that meeting had been very useful. On that occasion the United States had expressed some concerns, and in view of the Chairman's commitment to relay those concerns to the Appellate Body, he did not see the need to reiterate them at the present meeting. However, he wished to register some of the clarifications that delegations had received concerning two issues. First, the Appellate Body Secretariat had confirmed that the decisions of the Appellate Body might only "uphold, modify or reverse" the legal findings or conclusions of the panel as provided for in Article 17.13 of the DSU. The United States fully understood that the Appellate Body Secretariat did not presume to speak for the Appellate Body itself, but this helped to clarify the references in Rules 21 and 22 to "the nature of the decision or ruling sought". Second, the proof of service requirement in the Working Procedures could lead to a needless waste of paper. His country noted that the Appellate Body Secretariat had confirmed that proof of service might be provided in a manner consistent with the current practice of indicating on the document itself the parties to whom copies had been sent. He further noted that the Working

Procedures were far from perfect. In particular Rule 29 was disturbing in its implications for possible sanctions against Members. However, it would be better to live for a while with the problems that these rules presented rather than have the Appellate Body entering into a series of too frequent modifications of these new rules.

The representative of <u>Chile</u> supported the statements made by Mexico and India with regard to the question of collegiality. Rule 4.3 of the Working Procedures went beyond what was authorized under the DSU. A division consisting of three members was to decide an appeal and under no circumstances was an exchange of views with other members to take place. An attempt had been made to ensure flexibility in time periods provided for in Rules 18.1 and 29. However, this should not be turned to the disadvantage of the parties. He recalled that the DSU had not authorized the Appellate Body to establish time-periods or to consider the failure to submit a written submission. While Chile was aware that the Working Procedures had been established in accordance with Article 17.9 of the DSU. It wished the Appellate Body to take into consideration the concerns expressed by Members in order to ensure fairness in the implementation of procedural aspects of the Appellate Body.

The representative of <u>Canada</u> said that her country was very interested in the Appellate Body's Working Procedures and had made several suggestions with regard to some important elements of these procedures. The Working Procedures as presently drafted incorporated worthy principles. However, Canada identified some questions and concerns with regard to a few aspects of these procedures. Her country intended to follow closely the application of these procedures. It expected that they would be applied in a practical and flexible manner and that with time Canada's questions would be answered and its concerns would turn out to be unjustified. Her delegation was certain that the Appellate Body would also be closely watching how these procedures worked in practice and would be receptive to the comments and concerns which Members might express at a later date prior to any review of these procedures by the Appellate Body.

The representative of the <u>European Communities</u> said that, like other delegations, the Communities clearly accepted the premise on which the debate in this forum was taking place. The Working Procedures were indeed now operational as indicated in the informal meeting on 19 February and Members were not involved at this stage in any negotiating process. However, the Communities had a number of concerns. The practical concern had already been addressed by the United States and the Communities shared the United States' views. His delegation was concerned in particular with the question of the service of documents as required by Rule 18 and was grateful for the confirmation that, as far as possible, the existing practice would continue. However, Rule 18 should be applied with a degree of flexibility which would indeed allow for the use of technology, the fax machine and copying which would facilitate what could otherwise be a burdensome extra obligation. The legal and judicial concern related to Rule 29; the Communities had a very genuine concern that, in fact, a new law had been created in the sense that failure to make a submission within a prescribed time-limit or to appear in an oral hearing could have the result of the dismissal of the appeal. This was a serious issue which should be drawn to the attention of the Appellate Body. The Community hoped that judgement by default would be the rare exception to the rule and that those concerns be communicated to the Appellate Body. The linguistic concern related to the French and Spanish language versions of the text. The Communities would be submitting some comments in writing as soon as they were available. He stressed that these comments did not relate to substance. The objective was only to ensure conformity as between one language version and another. Rule 8.1 of the working procedures stipulated that on a provisional basis the Appellate Body would adopt only those rules which are applicable to it. But the text of the Rules of Conduct was clear in all cases as to which rules were applicable to it. In other words a rule of *mutatis mutandis* could well apply but one had to be certain what the *mutandis* element contained. For example, on page 17 of the document WT/AB/WP/1 would the footnote on that page fall into the category of the *mutandis*? The Communities would be watching the application of the rules of procedure in the light of experience and hopefully some of the concerns would dissipate. They would be grateful if those concerns could be conveyed to the Appellate Body.

The DSB took note of the statements.

UNITED STATES - MEASURE AFFECTING IMPORTS OF WOVEN WOOL SHIRTS AND BLOUSES FROM INDIA

Report of the Appellate Body
WT/DS33/AB/R *

Adopted by the Dispute Settlement Body on 23 May 1997

India, Appellant

United States, Appellee

Present:

Beeby, Presiding Member

Bacchus, Member

Matsushita, Member

I. INTRODUCTION

India appeals from certain issues of law and legal interpretations in the Panel Report, *United States - Measure Affecting Imports of Woven Wool Shirts and Blouses from India*, WT/DS33/R (the "Panel Report"). That Panel was established on 17 April 1996 to consider a complaint by India against the United States relating to a transitional safeguard restraint imposed on imports of woven wool shirts and blouses (category 440) from India.

The measure was imposed by the United States on 14 July 1995 after bilateral consultations with India in April and June 1995 did not result in a mutually-agreed solution. The restraint was effective as from 18 April 1995 for one year and was later extended through 17 April 1997. The United States took this transitional safeguard action pursuant to Article 6 of the *Agreement on Textiles and Clothing* (the "*ATC*"). As required by Article 6.10 of the *ATC*, the United States referred the matter to the Textiles Monitoring Body (the "TMB"), which concluded and confirmed upon review that the transitional safeguard action in this case was imposed in accordance with the requirements of the *ATC*. The TMB found that "actual threat of serious damage had been demonstrated" and that "this actual threat could be attributed to the sharp and substantial increase in imports from India".[1] At India's request, the Dispute Settlement Body (the "DSB") established a panel (the "Panel") to examine the legality of the United States' transitional safeguard measure.

---

* WT/DS33/AB/R/Corr.1
[1] G/TMB/R/3, confirmed in G/TMB/R/6.

After the release of the interim report of the Panel, the United States announced that it would withdraw the transitional safeguard measure, effective as of 22 November 1996, "due to a steady decline in imports of woven wool shirts and blouses from India and the adjustment of the industry". Nevertheless, India requested that the Panel continue its work and produce a comprehensive report on the dispute. The Panel Report in *United States - Measure Affecting Imports of Woven Wool Shirts and Blouses from India* was circulated to the Members of the World Trade Organization (the "WTO") on 6 January 1997. The Panel Report contains the following conclusions and recommendations:

> 8.1   We conclude that the US restraint applied as of 18 April 1995 on imports of woven wool shirts and blouses, category 440, from India and its extensions violated the provisions of Articles 2 and 6 of the ATC. Since Article 3.8 of the DSU provides that "In cases where there is an infringement of the obligations assumed under a covered agreement, the action is considered *prima facie* to constitute a case of nullification and impairment", we conclude that the said US measure nullified and impaired the benefits of India under the WTO Agreement, in particular under the ATC. The Panel recommends that the Dispute Settlement Body make such a ruling.

On 24 February 1997, India notified the DSB[2] of its decision to appeal certain issues of law covered in the Panel Report and certain legal interpretations developed by the Panel, pursuant to Article 16.4 of the *Understanding on Rules and Procedures Governing the Settlement of Disputes* (the "*DSU*"), and filed a notice of appeal with the Appellate Body pursuant to Rule 20 of the *Working Procedures for Appellate Review* (the "*Working Procedures*"). Pursuant to Rule 21 of the *Working Procedures*, India filed an appellant's submission on 6 March 1997. At the request of the United States, pursuant to Rule 16(2) of the *Working Procedures*, the Appellate Body extended the time for the United States to file its appellee's submission to 24 March 1997. On that date, the United States filed its submission pursuant to Rule 22 of the *Working Procedures*.

The oral hearing provided for in Rule 27 of the *Working Procedures* was held on 7 April 1997. The participants presented their arguments and answered questions from the Division of the Appellate Body hearing the appeal.

---

[2]   WT/DS33/3, 24 February 1997.

II.   ARGUMENTS OF THE PARTICIPANTS

A.   *India*

India agrees with the overall conclusions of the Panel Report, but alleges that the Panel erred in law when making its findings on the burden of proof, on the TMB and on the issue of judicial economy.

1.   *Burden of Proof*

India notes that the Panel made statements on the burden of proof in its findings in paragraph 7.12 of the Panel Report as well as in its comments on the interim review in paragraph 6.7 of the Panel Report. India argues that both statements are incorrect, and furthermore, are contradictory. India asserts that the specific interim review comments at issue are part of the findings to be reviewed by the Appellate Body.

India asserts that the fact that India had initiated dispute settlement proceedings did not impose upon India the obligation to establish that the United States had violated Article 6 of the *ATC*, as the Panel stated in paragraph 7.12, nor the obligation to present a *prima facie* case to that effect, as the Panel stated in paragraph 6.7. According to India, the issue of the burden of proof is an issue of substantive law and must be answered solely on the basis of the substantive law of the WTO in the light of the customary rules of interpretation of public international law. India maintains that the question of whether it is up to a particular Member to demonstrate an inconsistency with the *Marrakesh Agreement Establishing the World Trade Organization*[3] (the "*WTO Agreement*") does not depend on whether the Member is a complaining or a respondent party in the proceedings in which the inconsistency is at issue, but rather on the nature of the provision invoked. In India's view, the rules on the burden of proof determine which party in the dispute must make a legal claim and supply the evidence; the function of the rules is to ensure that a dispute can be settled even if the legal claims and factual information before the panel are incomplete. As India reads it, according to the Panel's comments on the interim review, both parties bear a burden of proof of different degrees.

Moreover, India argues that the Panel's finding on the distribution of the burden of proof is inconsistent with the finding on the same issue by the concurrent WTO panel in *United States - Restrictions on Imports of Cotton and Manmade Fibre Underwear*.[4] India points to that panel's statement that the principle that the party invoking the exception carries the burden of proof is well-

---

[3]   Done at Marrakesh, Morocco, 15 April 1994.
[4]   Adopted 25 February 1997, WT/DS24/R, para. 7.16.

established in the GATT 1947 practice.[5] Thus, India argues that in making its finding on burden of proof in this case, the Panel failed to take into account the customary practice of the CONTRACTING PARTIES under the GATT 1947. India maintains that the *ATC* is an exception to the GATT 1994 because it authorizes the temporary maintenance of measures inconsistent with Articles XI and XIII of the GATT 1994. India argues that within that temporary and exceptional regime deviating from basic GATT principles, Article 6 of the *ATC* establishes an exception from the general principles of trade in textiles and clothing that are set out in Article 2.4 of the *ATC* by authorizing the introduction of new and discriminatory quantitative restraints within the framework of what Article 6.1 of the *ATC* describes as "a specific transitional safeguard mechanism" that "should be applied as sparingly as possible". India concludes that the principles applied to the exceptions in the GATT 1994, therefore, apply with even greater force to Article 6 of the *ATC*. In India's view, the Panel's finding on burden of proof changes the operation of the substantive requirements under Article 6 of the *ATC*, upsetting the negotiated balance of interests between importing and exporting Members under the *ATC*.

2.   The TMB

India asserts that the Panel's finding in paragraph 7.20 of the Panel Report that the TMB, when examining a transitional safeguard measure in accordance with Article 6.10 of the *ATC*, "is not limited to the initial information submitted by the importing Member as parties may submit additional and other information in support of their positions, which, we understand, may relate to subsequent events",[6] was requested neither by India nor by the United States. India contends that this finding attributes to the TMB discretionary powers that neither of the parties to the dispute suggested the TMB had.

India argues that the *ATC* and the *DSU* accord exporting Members three important procedural rights: (i) the right to hold consultations on the proposed transitional safeguard action on the basis of specific and factual information; (ii) the right to a review of a transitional safeguard action by the TMB; and (iii) the right to refer the matter to the DSB for examination by a panel. In India's view, the Panel's finding denies Members the benefit of the first two of these three rights.

India submits that the Panel bases its finding on the erroneous notion that the *ATC* and the *DSU* establish a "two-track process" for the review of transitional safeguard actions, and that therefore the matter on which the TMB makes a recommendation and the matter submitted to the DSB can be different. In India's view, the *ATC* and the *DSU* establish a two-stage procedure under which the

---

[5]   India cites seven GATT 1947 panel reports to demonstrate that there has been a consistently applied and well-established practice that the party invoking an exception bears the burden of proof.
[6]   Panel Report, para. 7.20.

same measure is first submitted to the TMB and, if its recommendations are not acceptable, to the DSB. India stresses that the TMB review is a substitute for consultations normally held before the request for the establishment of a panel, and India argues that information that was not available at the time when the safeguard determination was made is not information that is "relevant" in the TMB's review of that determination under Article 6.10 of the *ATC*.

India further asserts that the task of the TMB is to deal with disputes arising from measures actually taken and to carry out those functions that are specifically assigned to it by the *ATC*. According to India, the expression of views on transitional safeguard actions that have not yet been taken is not part of this task. India maintains that by attributing to the TMB this additional competence, even when the Members did not agree to seek views on that matter, the Panel attributed to the TMB the authority to conciliate without the consent of the Members concerned, which is not consistent with the *DSU*.

Finally, India asserts that a comparison of the provisions of the *ATC* on the TMB and the provisions of the Multi-Fibre Arrangement (the "MFA") on the Textiles Surveillance Body (the "TSB"), reveals that the TMB, in contrast to the TSB under the MFA, has a well-defined, limited function of a legal nature.

In response to the argument by the United States that the Panel's statement on the role of the TMB is merely *obiter dicta* on which the Appellate Body need not rule, India argues that Articles 17.6, 17.12 and 17.13 of the *DSU* do not distinguish between *dicta* and findings. According to India, the right to appellate review would be seriously impaired if panels could express legal opinions on any point other than the issues involved in the case before them and Members of the WTO could not seek an appellate review of those opinions.

3. Judicial Economy

India points out that the Panel did not make findings on two of the four issues India submitted to the Panel for examination: namely, whether the United States' failure to specify in its request for consultations whether the proposed transitional safeguard action related to serious damage or the actual threat of serious damage was consistent with Article 6 of the *ATC*; and whether the retroactive application by the United States of its transitional safeguard action was consistent with Article 2 of the *ATC*.

India argues that, within the framework of the *ATC*, the determination, the request for consultations on a proposed transitional safeguard action and the actual application of the transitional safeguard action must be regarded as distinct measures that can be contested separately. India states that it contested these measures separately *not* for the purpose of making the panel address theoretical issues, but rather out of a practical concern relating to the implementation of the Panel's recommendations by the United States. India argues that by defining the three factually and legally distinct measures as a single, "contested measure", the Panel denied India the right to an objective assessment of the request for consultations and the application of the transitional safeguard action in accordance with

Article 11 of the *DSU*.[7] India insists that it is not arguing that panels have to address in all instances all legal claims made by the parties. India acknowledges that there are many instances in which a finding on one matter resolves the dispute on another matter. In the present case, however, India maintains that the Panel's findings did not resolve the dispute on the two matters referred to above.

India asserts that the Panel failed to distinguish the contested "measure" from the matter to be examined. India explains that any dispute brought by a WTO Member under Article XXIII:1(a) of the GATT 1994 concerns an act or omission of another Member, that is a "measure". India notes that the dispute settlement procedures of the WTO begin with consultations on a specific measure and end with a recommendation on that measure. However, India maintains that the matter the panel must examine in accordance with Articles 6, 7 and 11 of the *DSU* is not the measure by itself, but rather the legal claims which the parties to the dispute make in connection with the measure. India concludes that the function assigned to a panel under Article 11 of the *DSU* is, thus, to examine all legal claims made relating to all measures at issue. India concludes that by defining its task solely in terms of the measure to be brought into conformity with the *ATC*, the Panel curtailed India's right to an objective assessment of all the legal claims it had made in its request for a panel. India also observes that while a panel must examine all claims made by the parties to the dispute and cannot go beyond these claims, it need not examine all arguments of the parties and can develop its own arguments.

India asserts that the panels established under the GATT 1947 did not apply the concept of judicial economy as suggested by the Panel in the Panel Report. India contends that those previous panels did not systematically end their legal analysis as soon as they had found the contested measure to be inconsistent with the GATT 1947, but instead determined the scope of their examination in the light of the objectives and legal interests of the parties to the dispute. India argues that had the Panel in this case been guided by the customary practice of the CONTRACTING PARTIES to the GATT 1947, it would have determined the scope of its examination in the light of India's expressed legal interest in findings on which the Panel failed to rule. Because the Panel in this case was not guided by this customary practice, India argues that matters that could be resolved in one proceeding will have to be resolved instead in multiple proceedings if future panels apply this Panel's concept of judicial economy.

Therefore, India submits that the Panel's application of the notion of judicial economy undermines the objectives of the *DSU*, which are described in Article 3.2 of the *DSU* and in India's view, include both dispute resolution as well as dispute prevention. India maintains that these objectives can only be achieved if

---

[7] India also asserts that the question of what constitutes the "measure" that may be maintained in accordance with Article 6.12 of the *ATC* for a period of up to three years and the question of what constitutes "the specific measures at issue" within the meaning of Article 6 of the *DSU* are obviously completely different issues.

panels resolve both the dispute over the particular contested measure and the issues of interpretation arising from all legal claims made in connection with that measure.

B.   United States

With respect to each of the three issues raised in this appeal, the United States argues that the Panel acted correctly. The United States asks the Appellate Body to affirm the Panel Report.

1.   Burden of Proof

The United States argues that the Panel properly addressed the issue of burden of proof in paragraphs 6.7 and 7.12 of the Panel Report. Unlike India, the United States does not see any contradiction between the Panel's statements in paragraphs 6.7 and 7.12 of the Panel Report, and considers paragraph 6.7 to be the final interpretative word on this issue by the Panel. As the United States sees it, the Panel found, consistently with the *DSU*, that both India and the United States had differing burdens to present factual and legal arguments: first, as the complaining party, India had the initial burden of establishing "a *prima facie* case of violation of the ATC, namely, that the restrictions imposed by the United States did not respect the provisions of Article 2.4 and 6 of the ATC"; then, after India had established a *prima facie* case, the United States had the burden "to convince the Panel that, at the time of its determination, it had respected the requirements of Article 6 of the ATC".

The United States argues that the Panel did not assign any burden of proof, in the sense of burden of persuasion, to either India or the United States. The United States contends that India distorts the findings of the Panel when it claims that the Panel held that India had the ultimate burden of persuasion. According to the United States, the Panel merely required India to meet the burden of going forward with the evidence. The United States argues that it is clear from the ordinary meaning of Articles 3.8, 6.2 and paragraph 5 of the working procedures for panels in Appendix 3 of the *DSU* that India had the obligation to initiate and commence the legal and factual issues, not only at the stage of a request for a panel, but also at the first substantive meeting of the parties. In other words, India had to make a *prima facie* demonstration that the United States' measure violated provisions of the *ATC*. The United States stresses that, in fact, India did so successfully in the present case.

The United States argues that India incorrectly asserts that there is a "consistently applied" and "well-established" GATT practice that the party invoking an exception carries the burden of proof of justifying the use of the exception. According to the United States, the panel reports cited by India in its appellant's submission do not reflect GATT practice justifying India's arguments that: (1) everything other than India's "core rules" are exceptions; (2) all "exceptions" are required to be construed narrowly; and (3) the complaining party has no burden to demonstrate that a so-called "exception" was improperly invoked. The United States maintains that the reports cited are either distinguishable, irrelevant, or contradicted by other reports, and that only in a few special situations involving the general exceptions of the GATT 1994 and other isolated exceptions of the GATT 1994 have panels consistently assigned the ultimate burden of persuasion to a particular party.

According to the United States, in disputes involving the vast majority of GATT provisions, it is well-established practice that the complaining party has the burden of making a *prima facie* case. Furthermore, the United States argues that India's legal taxonomy is overly simplistic in that it treats all so-called "exceptions" identically and fails to consider the reasons why such so-called "exceptions" exist. The United States argues that India also ignores the fact that, in addition to "obligations", WTO Member also have "rights", and that many, if not most, of what would be considered "exceptions" under India's taxonomy are more properly viewed as "rights". The United States argues that India's approach results in a "crude" method of treaty interpretation that is at odds with what the Appellate Body said in *United States - Standards for Reformulated and Conventional Gasoline*, in the sense that India's treatment of so-called "exceptions" is not case-by-case, but instead is a simplistic, "one-size-fits-all" mechanical approach to treaty interpretation.[8]

Finally, the United States argues that India's theory, if accepted, would alter significantly the rights and obligations of WTO Members with respect to a multitude of provisions of the GATT 1994 and other WTO agreements.[9]

Assuming *arguendo* that India correctly asserts that there is a "consistently applied" and "well-established" GATT practice that the party invoking an exception carries the burden of proof, the United States argues that Article 6 of the *ATC* is not such an exception. The non-exceptional nature of Article 6 is reflected in Article 2.4 of the *ATC*, which states two very general rules, namely, that textile restrictions existing before the *ATC* came into force would be grandfathered, and that new restrictions may be introduced only in accordance with the provisions of the *ATC* and other relevant provisions of the GATT 1994. The United States contends that the term "except" used in Article 2.4 of the *ATC* is in this context a synonym for "only", "provided that", or "unless" and cannot be read as an indication that Article 6 of the *ATC* is an exception. The United States

---

[8] Referring to the Appellate Body Report in *United States - Standards for Reformulated and Conventional Gasoline*, AB-1996-1, adopted 20 May 1996, WT/DS2/9, DSR 1996:I, 3, at 16, the United States argues that India's approach ignores the "object and purpose" of provisions, it provides for no "scrutiny of the factual and legal context in a given dispute" and it disregards "the words actually used by WTO Members themselves to express their intent and purpose".

[9] The United asserted that under India's theory, all of the WTO provisions providing special and differential treatment for developing countries would be labelled as exceptions and that, therefore, the burden of persuasion would be on the developing country seeking to rely on one of these provisions.

adds as well that the text, context and object of Article 6 of the *ATC* support the conclusion that Article 6 is not a provision that compels a shifting of the burden of proof. The United States argues that for importing countries, Article 6 constituted a critical *quid pro quo* for the acceptance of the *ATC*'s phase-out of pre-existing quotas and integration of textiles and clothing trade into the multilateral trading system. The United States asserts that as an integral *ATC* provision, the transitional safeguard mechanism is on an equal footing with the other provisions of the *ATC*, such as the integration schedule of Article 2. Therefore, the United States concludes, the phrase "should be applied as sparingly as possible" in Article 6.1 of the *ATC* does not provide support for the notion that Article 6 is an exceptional provision; rather, that phrase merely reminds Members not to abuse their right to use temporary, transitional safeguard measures.[10] The United States asserts that the treatment of Article 6 of the *ATC* as an exception would upset the carefully negotiated balance of rights and obligations of Article 6.[11]

2. The TMB

The United States argues that the Panel's discussion of the TMB was mere *obiter dicta* which had no effect on the outcome of the case, and that it is difficult to see how India's procedural rights under the *ATC* have been denied in any way by this *dicta*. The United States considers that the appropriate manner of "addressing" this Panel's *dicta* on an issue raised by neither of the parties would be for the Appellate Body simply to declare this aspect of the report to be *dicta* and not to offer any additional *dicta* of its own with respect to the role of the TMB.

Furthermore, the United States observes that nothing in the text of the *ATC* supports India's assertion that the information considered by the TMB in its examination of the transitional safeguard action must be limited to the information used by the importing Member in making its determination to take the transitional safeguard action. According to the United States, Article 6.10 of the *ATC*, and in particular the phrase, "any other relevant information", clearly contemplates the consideration of information that is not the same as that used by the importing Member at the time of the determination to take the action. The United States also argues that nothing in the *ATC* supports India's assertion that the TMB, in contrast to the TSB, has a well-defined, limited function of a legal nature.

---

[10] The United States notes that the Appellate Body in *United States - Restrictions on Imports of Cotton and Man-made Fibre Underwear*, AB-1996-3, adopted 25 February 1997, WT/DS24/AB/R, DSR 1997:I, 11, at 23, did not interpret Article 6 of the *ATC* either narrowly or broadly and indicated that the "as sparingly as possible" language could not be examined in isolation.

[11] The United States notes that the Appellate Body in *United States - Restrictions on Imports of Cotton and Man-made Fibre Underwear*, did not "loosen up the carefully negotiated language of Article 6.10, which reflect an equally carefully drawn balance of rights and obligations of Members ...".

3.   Judicial Economy

The United States argues that the Panel did not err by declining to rule on all claims made by India. According to the United States, nothing in the *DSU* or elsewhere in the *WTO Agreement* requires a panel to rule on every claim raised by a party. The United States argues that the text of Article 11 of the *DSU* does not impose such obligation. The United States cites Article 3.7 of the *DSU* for the proposition that the primary function of the dispute settlement system is to resolve disputes by achieving the withdrawal of WTO-inconsistent measures, not to render interpretations or to generate opinions on any issue. The United States notes that Article IX of the *WTO Agreement* provides a mechanism for obtaining authoritative interpretations, as recognized in Article 3.9 of the *DSU*.[12] The United States does not accept India's argument that WTO dispute settlement has the "twin objective" of "dispute resolution" and "dispute prevention". According to the United States, this argument is at odds with Articles 3.7 and 3.9 of the *DSU*. The United States maintains that "dispute prevention" is, at most, a subsidiary function under the *DSU*, and one which does not translate into a legal requirement that a panel address every claim raised by a party.

With respect to India's argument that there are three "measures", rather than one, at issue in this case,[13] the United States observes that it is clear from Article 6.12 of the *ATC* that the "measure" is in fact the transitional safeguard action, not the procedures leading up to the imposition of the transitional safeguard action. In the opinion of the United States, India's interpretation of "measure" constitutes the sort of arbitrary subdivision of a measure that the Appellate Body criticized in *United States - Standards for Reformulated and Conventional Gasoline*. The United States also argues that India's belated identification of three measures, rather than one measure, is nothing more than a *post hoc* argument presented for the first time in this appeal.

The United States points out that in addition to being consistent with the text of the *DSU*, the Panel's decision to refrain from ruling on certain issues raised by India was consistent with the well-established practice of the GATT 1947 panels, which frequently declined to address claims in situations where the resolution of a claim was unnecessary for the purpose of resolving a dispute. The United States asserts that this practice has been continued under the *DSU* and the *WTO Agreement* by both WTO panels and the Appellate Body.

The United States also suggests that, as an alternative to finding that the Panel did not err when it declined to make findings on certain issues, the Appellate Body, as it did in *Brazil - Measures Affecting Desiccated Coconut*, could

---

[12]   The United States refers in this context to the Appellate Body Report in *Japan - Taxes on Alcoholic Beverages*, AB-1996-2, adopted 1 November 1996, WT/DS8/AB/R, WT/DS10/AB/R, WT/DS11/AB/R, DSR 1996:I, 97, at 106-108.

[13]   India argues that not only the United States' determination, but also the United States' request for consultations and the backdating of the United States' restraint each constitute a distinct "measure" that can be contested separately.

simply address the issue by deciding that it is unnecessary to resolve the procedural issue raised by India since it will have absolutely no effect on the previous conclusion by the Panel that the transitional safeguard measure imposed by the United States was inconsistent with the *ATC*.

Finally, the United States observes that the practice of panels and the Appellate Body in refraining from making findings that are unnecessary to the resolution of disputes has been described as being based on concerns of judicial economy. The United States argues that to the extent such concerns were valid under the pre-WTO regime, they are, in view of the number of matters now referred to the DSB, even more valid today. In order to preserve the integrity of the WTO system in general, and the dispute settlement mechanism in particular, the United States argues that both panels and the Appellate Body should focus only on those claims that must be addressed to resolve a dispute.

III.   ISSUES RAISED IN THIS APPEAL

This appeal raises the following legal issues:

(a)   Whether a party claiming that a transitional safeguard action violates Article 6 of the *ATC* has the burden of demonstrating that there has been an infringement of the obligations assumed under the *ATC*;

(b)   Whether the TMB is limited in its examination of a transitional safeguard action pursuant to Article 6.10 of the *ATC* to the evidence used by the importing Member in making its determination to take such action, or may also consider developments and information subsequent to that determination; and

(c)   Whether, under Article 11 of the *DSU*, a complaining party is entitled to a finding on all of the legal claims it makes to a panel relating to the measure in dispute.

IV.   BURDEN OF PROOF

On the issue of burden of proof, the Panel concluded the following at paragraph 7.12 of the "Findings" section of the Panel Report:

The parties seem to have addressed two different aspects of what one might call the "burden of proof" issue. We believe that a distinction should be made. First, we consider the question of which party bears the burden of proof before the Panel. Since India is the party that initiated the dispute settlement proceedings, we consider that it is for India to put forward factual and legal arguments in order to establish that the US restriction was inconsistent with Article 2 of the ATC and that the US determination for a safeguard action was inconsistent with the provisions of Article 6 of the ATC. Second, we consider the question of what the importing

Member must demonstrate at the time of its determination. Concerning the substantive obligations under Article 6 of the ATC, it is clear from the wording of Article 6.2 and 6.3 of the ATC that, in its determination of the need for the proposed restraint, the United States had the obligation to demonstrate that it had complied with the relevant conditions of application of Article 6.2 and 6.3 of the ATC.

The Panel illuminated this finding at paragraph 6.7 in the "Interim Review" section of the Panel Report:

Concerning India's comment about burden of proof, it was for India to submit a *prima facie* case of violation of the ATC, namely, that the restriction imposed by the United States did not respect the provisions of Articles 2.4 and 6 of the ATC. It was then for the United States to convince the Panel that, at the time of its determination, it had respected the requirements of Article 6 of the ATC.

Although the Panel's finding at paragraph 7.12 and comments on interim review at paragraph 6.7 of the Panel Report are not a model of clarity, we do not believe the Panel erred in law. We agree with the Panel that it was up to India to present evidence and argument sufficient to establish a presumption that the transitional safeguard determination made by the United States was inconsistent with its obligations under Article 6 of the *ATC*. With this presumption thus established, it was then up to the United States to bring evidence and argument to rebut the presumption.

The foundation of dispute settlement under Article XXIII of the GATT 1994 is the assurance to Members of the benefits accruing directly or indirectly to them under the GATT 1994. This was true as well of dispute settlement under the GATT 1947. If any Member should consider that its benefits are nullified or impaired as the result of circumstances set out in Article XXIII, then dispute settlement is available. With respect to complaints of violation of obligations pursuant to Article XXIII:1(a) of the GATT 1994, Article 3.8 of the *DSU* codifies previous GATT 1947 practice:

In cases where there is an infringement of the obligations assumed under a covered agreement, the action is considered *prima facie* to constitute a case of nullification or impairment. This means that there is normally a presumption that a breach of the rules has an adverse impact on other Members parties to that covered agreement, and in such cases, it shall be up to the Member against whom the complaint has been brought to rebut the charge.

Article 3.8 of the *DSU* provides that in cases where there is an infringement of the obligations assumed under a covered agreement - that is, in cases where a violation is established - there is a presumption of nullification or impairment. Article 3.8 then goes on to explain that "the Member against whom the complaint has been brought" must rebut this presumption. However, the issue in this case is not what happens after a violation is established; the issue in this case is which party must first show that there is, or is not, a violation. More specifically, the issue in this case is which party has the burden of demonstrating that there has, or has not been, an infringement of the obligations assumed under Article 6 of the *ATC*.[14]

In addressing this issue, we find it difficult, indeed, to see how any system of judicial settlement could work if it incorporated the proposition that the mere assertion of a claim might amount to proof. It is, thus, hardly surprising that various international tribunals, including the International Court of Justice, have generally and consistently accepted and applied the rule that the party who asserts a fact, whether the claimant or the respondent, is responsible for providing proof thereof.[15] Also, it is a generally-accepted canon of evidence in civil law, common law and, in fact, most jurisdictions, that the burden of proof rests upon the party, whether complaining or defending, who asserts the affirmative of a particular claim or defence. If that party adduces evidence sufficient to raise a presumption that what is claimed is true, the burden then shifts to the other party, who will fail unless it adduces sufficient evidence to rebut the presumption.[16]

In the context of the GATT 1994 and the *WTO Agreement*, precisely how much and precisely what kind of evidence will be required to establish such a presumption will necessarily vary from measure to measure, provision to provision, and case to case.

A number of GATT 1947 panel reports contain language supporting the proposition that the burden of establishing a violation under Article XXIII:1(a) of the GATT 1947 was on the complaining party. As early as 1952, in *Treatment by Germany of Imports of Sardines*, concerning a complaint by Norway, the panel clearly put the burden of establishing a violation of the GATT 1947 obligations at issue on the complaining party, when it concluded:

---

[14]   Article 8.10, last sentence, of the *ATC*, allows a Member to invoke Article XXIII of the GATT 1994.

[15]   M. Kazazi, *Burden of Proof and Related Issues: A Study on Evidence Before International Tribunals* (Kluwer Law International, 1996), p. 117.

[16]   See M.N. Howard, P. Crane and D.A. Hochberg, *Phipson on Evidence*, 14th ed. (Sweet & Maxwell, 1990), p. 52: "The burden of proof rests upon the party, whether plaintiff or defendant, who substantially asserts the affirmative of the issue." See also L. Rutherford and S. Bone (eds.), *Osborne's Concise Law Dictionary*, 8th ed. (Sweet & Maxwell, 1993), p. 266; Earl Jowitt and C. Walsh, *Jowitt's Dictionary of English Law*, 2nd ed. by J. Burke (Sweet & Maxwell, 1977), Vol. 1, p. 263; L.B. Curzon, *A Directory of Law*, 2nd ed. (Macdonald and Evans, 1983), p. 47; Art. 9, Nouveau Code de Procédure Civile; J. Carbonnier, *Droit Civil*, Introduction, 20th ed. (Presses Universitaires de France, 1991), p. 320; J. Chevalier and L. Bach, *Droit Civil*, 12th ed. (Sirey, 1995), Vol. 1, p. 101; R. Guillien and J. Vincent, *Termes juridiques*, 10th ed. (Dalloz, 1995), p. 384; O. Samyn, P. Simonetta and C. Sogno, *Dictionnaire des Termes Juridiques* (Editions de Vecchi, 1986), p. 250; J. González Pérez, *Manual de Derecho Procesal Administrativo*, 2nd ed. (Editorial Civitas, 1992), p. 311; C.M. Bianca, S. Patti and G. Patti, *Lessico di Diritto Civile* (Giuffré Editore, 1991), p. 550; F. Galgano, *Diritto Privato*, 8th ed. (Casa Editrice Dott. Antonio Milani, 1994), p. 873; and A. Trabucchi, *Istituzioni di Diritto Civile* (Casa Editrice Dott. Antonio Milani, 1991), p. 210.

The examination of the evidence submitted led the Panel to the conclusion that no sufficient evidence had been presented to show that the German Government had failed to carry out its obligations under Article I:1 and Article XIII:1.[17]

In 1978, in *EEC - Measures on Animal Feed Proteins*, concerning a complaint by the United States, the panel made it equally clear that the burden of proof in that case was on the complaining party. In the final paragraph of that panel report, the panel stated:

> Having heard no evidence that either the purchasing obligation, the security deposit or the protein certificate discriminated against imports of "like products" from any contracting party, the Panel concluded that the EEC measures were not inconsistent with the EEC obligations under Article I:1.[18]

Two recent panel reports under the GATT 1947 which follow this approach are the 1992 report in *Canada - Import, Distribution and Sale of Certain Alcoholic Drinks by Provincial Marketing Agencies*[19] and the 1994 report in *United States - Measures Affecting the Importation, Internal Sale and Use of Tobacco.*[20] In the first case, the United States claimed that Canada had not fully eliminated the listing and delisting practices that a prior GATT panel report had found to be inconsistent with Article XI of the GATT 1947. The panel concluded, however, that with the exception of the listing and delisting practices of the province of Ontario, the United States had not substantiated its claim that Canada still maintained listing and delisting practices inconsistent with Article XI of the GATT 1947. In the second case, the complainants claimed, *inter alia*, that the penalty provisions of the Domestic Marketing Assessment legislation enacted by the United States were separate taxes or charges within the meaning of Article III:2 of the GATT 1947, and that Section 1106(c) of the 1993 Budget Act of the United States, mandated action inconsistent with Article VIII:1(a) of the GATT 1947. With regard to both claims, the panel concluded that the evidence submitted to it did not support the complainants' claims of inconsistency with the GATT 1947 obligations involved.

---

[17] Adopted 31 October 1952, BISD 1S/53, para. 15. See also the report of the Working Party in *The Australian Subsidy on Ammonium Sulphate*, adopted 3 April 1950, BISD Vol. II/188, para. 11.

[18] Adopted 14 March 1978, BISD 25S/49, para. 4.21. See also *European Communities - Refunds on Exports of Sugar, Complaint by Brazil*, adopted 10 November 1980, BISD 27S/69, para. (e) of the Conclusions; *Canada, Administration of the Foreign Investment Review Act*, adopted 7 February 1984, BISD 30S/140, para. 5.13; and *Japan - Tariff on Import of Spruce, Pine, Fir (SPF) Dimension Lumber*, adopted 19 July 1989, BISD 36S/167, para. 10.

[19] Adopted 18 February 1992, BISD 39S/27, paras. 5.2-5.3.

[20] Adopted 4 October 1994, DS44/R, paras. 82 and 124.

India has argued that it is "customary GATT practice" that the party invoking a provision which is identified as an exception must offer proof that the conditions set out in that provision are met. We acknowledge that several GATT 1947 and WTO panels have required such proof of a party invoking a defence, such as those found in Article XX[21] or Article XI:2(c)(i),[22] to a claim of violation of a GATT obligation, such as those found in Articles I:1, II:1, III or XI:1. Articles XX and XI:(2)(c)(i) are limited exceptions from obligations under certain other provisions of the GATT 1994, not positive rules establishing obligations in themselves. They are in the nature of affirmative defences. It is only reasonable that the burden of establishing such a defence should rest on the party asserting it.[23]

We do not believe that these particular previous GATT 1947 panel reports are relevant in this case. This case concerns Article 6 of the *ATC*. The *ATC* is a transitional arrangement that, by its own terms, will terminate when trade in textiles and clothing is fully integrated into the multilateral trading system. Article 6 of the *ATC* is an integral part of the transitional arrangement manifested in the *ATC* and should be interpreted accordingly. As the Appellate Body observed in *United States - Restrictions on Imports of Cotton and Man-made Fibre Underwear* with respect to Article 6.10 of the *ATC*, we believe Article 6 is "carefully negotiated language ... which reflects an equally carefully drawn balance of rights and obligations of Members ... ."[24] That balance must be respected.

The transitional safeguard mechanism provided in Article 6 of the *ATC* is a fundamental part of the rights and obligations of WTO Members concerning non-integrated textile and clothing products covered by the *ATC* during the transitional period. Consequently, a party claiming a violation of a provision of the *WTO Agreement* by another Member must assert and prove its claim. In this case, India claimed a violation by the United States of Article 6 of the *ATC*. We agree

---

[21] *Canada - Administration of Foreign Investment Review Act*, adopted 7 February 1984, BISD 30S/140, para. 5.20; *United States - Section 337 of the Tariff Act of 1930*, adopted 7 November 1989, BISD 36S/345, para. 5.27; *United States - Measures Affecting Alcoholic and Malt Beverages*, adopted 19 June 1992, BISD 39S/206, paras. 5.43 and 5.52; and Panel Report, *United States - Standards for Reformulated and Conventional Gasoline*, as modified by the Appellate Body Report, AB-1996-1, adopted 20 May 1996, WT/DS2/9, para. 6.20.

[22] *Japan - Restrictions on Imports of Certain Agricultural Products*, adopted 22 March 1988, BISD 35S/163, para. 5.1.3.7, *EEC - Restrictions on Imports of Dessert Apples*, Complaint by Chile, adopted 22 June 1989, BISD 36S/93, para. 12:3; and *Canada - Import Restrictions on Ice Cream and Yoghurt*, adopted 5 December 1989, BISD 36S/68, para. 59.

[23] Furthermore, there are a few cases that are similar in that the defending party invoked, as a defence, certain provisions and the panel explicitly required the defending party to demonstrate the applicability of the provision it was asserting. See, for example, *United States - Customs User Fee*, adopted 2 February 1988, BISD 35S/245, para. 98, concerning Article II:2 of the GATT 1947; *Canada - Import, Distribution and Sale of Certain Alcoholic Drinks by Provincial Marketing Agencies*, adopted 22 March 1988, BISD 35S/37, para 4.34, concerning Article XXIV:12 of the GATT 1947; and *United States - Measures Affecting Alcoholic and Malt Beverages*, adopted 19 June 1992, BISD 39S/206, para. 5.44, concerning the Protocol of Provisional Application.

[24] AB-1996-3, adopted 25 February 1997, WT/DS24/AB/R, DSR 1997:I, 11, at 23.

with the Panel that it, therefore, was up to India to put forward evidence and legal argument sufficient to demonstrate that the transitional safeguard action by the United States was inconsistent with the obligations assumed by the United States under Articles 2 and 6 of the *ATC*. India did so in this case. And, with India having done so, the onus then shifted to the United States to bring forward evidence and argument to disprove the claim. This, the United States was not able to do and, therefore, the Panel found that the transitional safeguard action by the United States "violated the provisions of Articles 2 and 6 of the ATC".[25]

In our view, the Panel did not err on this issue in this case.

V. THE TMB

India appealed the following statement relating to Article 6.10 of the *ATC* at paragraph 7.20 of the Panel Report:

> During the review process, the TMB is not limited to the initial information submitted by the importing Member as parties may submit additional and other information in support of their positions, which, *we understand*, may relate to subsequent events. (emphasis added)

In our view, this statement by the Panel is purely a descriptive and gratuitous comment providing background concerning the Panel's understanding of how the TMB functions. We do not consider this comment by the Panel to be "a legal finding or conclusion" which the Appellate Body "may uphold, modify or reverse".[26]

VI. JUDICIAL ECONOMY

With respect to the issue of whether Article 11 of the *DSU* entitles a complaining party to a finding on each of the legal claims it makes to a panel, the Panel stated in paragraph 6.6 of the Panel Report:

> Concerning India's argument that Article 11 of the DSU entitles India to a finding on each of the issues it raised, we disagree and refer to the consistent GATT panel practice of judicial economy. India is entitled to have the dispute over the contested "measure" resolved by the Panel, and if we judge that the specific matter in dispute can be resolved by addressing only some of the arguments raised by the complaining party, we can do so. We, therefore, decide to address only the legal issues we think are needed in order to

---

[25] Panel Report, para. 8.1.
[26] Within the meaning of Article 17.13 of the *DSU*.

make such findings as will assist the DSB in making recommendations or in giving rulings in respect of this dispute.

The function of panels is expressly defined in Article 11 of the *DSU*,
which reads as follows:

> The function of panels is to assist the DSB in discharging its
> responsibilities under this Understanding and the covered
> agreements. Accordingly, a panel should make an objective
> assessment of the matter before it, including an objective
> assessment of the facts of the case and the applicability of
> and conformity with the relevant covered agreements, and
> *make such other findings as will assist the DSB* in making
> the recommendations or in giving the rulings provided for
> in the covered agreements ... (emphasis added).

Nothing in this provision or in previous GATT practice *requires* a panel
to examine *all* legal claims made by the complaining party. Previous GATT 1947
and WTO panels have frequently addressed only those issues that such panels
considered necessary for the resolution of the matter between the parties, and
have declined to decide other issues. Thus, if a panel found that a measure was
inconsistent with a particular provision of the GATT 1947, it generally did not go
on to examine whether the measure was also inconsistent with other GATT provisions that a complaining party may have argued were violated.[27] In recent
WTO practice, panels likewise have refrained from examining each and every
claim made by the complaining party and have made findings only on those
claims that such panels concluded were necessary to resolve the particular matter.[28]

Although a few GATT 1947 and WTO panels did make broader rulings,
by considering and deciding issues that were not absolutely necessary to dispose

---

[27] See, for example, *EEC - Quantitative Restrictions Against Imports of Certain Products from
Hong Kong*, adopted 12 July 1983, BISD 30S/129, para. 33; *Canada - Administration of the For-
eign Investment Review Act*, adopted 7 February 1984, BISD 30S/140, para. 5.16; *United States -
Imports of Sugar from Nicaragua*, adopted 13 March 1984, BISD 31S/67, paras. 4.5-4.6; *United
States - Manufacturing Clause*, adopted 15/16 May 1984, BISD 31S/74, para. 40; *Japan - Measures
on Imports of Leather*, adopted 15/16 May 1984, BISD 31S/94, para. 57; *Japan - Trade in Semi-
Conductors*, adopted 4 May 1988, BISD 35S/116, para. 122; *Japan - Restrictions on Imports of
Certain Agricultural Products*, adopted 22 March 1988, BISD 35S/163, para. 5.4.2; *EEC - Regula-
tions on Imports of Parts and Components*, adopted 16 May 1990, BISD 37S/132, paras. 5.10, 5.22,
and 5.27; *Canada - Import, Distribution and Sale of Certain Alcoholic Drinks by Provincial Marketing Agencies*, adopted 22 March 1988, BISD 35S/37, para. 5.6; and *United States - Denial of
Most-Favoured-Nation Treatment as to Non-Rubber Footwear from Brazil*, adopted 19 June 1992,
BISD 39S/128, para. 6.18.
[28] See, for example, Panel Report, *Brazil - Measures Affecting Desiccated Coconut*, adopted 20
March 1997, WT/DS22/R, para. 293; and Panel Report, *United States - Standards for Reformulated
and Conventional Gasoline*, as modified by the Appellate Body Report, AB-1996-1, adopted 20
May 1996, WT/DS2/9, para. 6.43.

of the particular dispute, there is nothing anywhere in the *DSU* that requires panels to do so.[29]

Furthermore, such a requirement is not consistent with the aim of the WTO dispute settlement system. Article 3.7 of the *DSU* explicitly states:

> The aim of the dispute settlement mechanism is to secure a positive solution to a dispute. A solution mutually acceptable to the parties to a dispute and consistent with the covered agreements is clearly to be preferred.

Thus, the basic aim of dispute settlement in the WTO is to settle disputes. This basic aim is affirmed elsewhere in the *DSU*. Article 3.4, for example, stipulates:

> Recommendations or rulings made by the DSB shall be aimed at achieving a satisfactory settlement of the matter in accordance with the rights and obligations under this Understanding and under the covered agreements.

As India emphasizes, Article 3.2 of the *DSU* states that the Members of the WTO "recognize" that the dispute settlement system "serves to preserve the rights and obligations of Members under the covered agreements, and *to clarify the existing provisions of those agreements* in accordance with customary rules of interpretation of public international law" (emphasis added). Given the explicit aim of dispute settlement that permeates the *DSU*, we do not consider that Article 3.2 of the *DSU* is meant to encourage either panels or the Appellate Body to "make law" by clarifying existing provisions of the *WTO Agreement* outside the context of resolving a particular dispute. A panel need only address those claims which must be addressed in order to resolve the matter in issue in the dispute.[30]

We note, furthermore, that Article IX of the *WTO Agreement* provides that the Ministerial Conference and the General Council have the "exclusive authority" to adopt interpretations of the *WTO Agreement* and the Multilateral Trade Agreements.[31] This is explicitly recognized in Article 3.9 of the *DSU*, which provides:

> The provisions of this Understanding are without prejudice to the rights of Members to seek authoritative interpretation of provisions of a covered agreement through decision-

---

[29] See, for example, *EEC - Restrictions on Imports of Dessert Apples*, Complaint by Chile, adopted 22 June 1989, BISD 36S/93, para.12.20, where the panel explicitly stated that given its finding that the EEC measures were in violation of Article XI:1 of the GATT 1947 and were not justified by Article XI:2(c)(i) or (ii) of the GATT 1947, no further examination of the administration of the measures would normally be required. In that case, the panel nonetheless considered it "appropriate" to examine the administration of the EEC measures in respect of Article XIII of the GATT 1947 in view of the questions of great practical interest raised by both parties.

[30] The "matter in issue" is the "matter referred to the DSB" pursuant to Article 7 of the *DSU*.

[31] *Japan - Taxes on Alcoholic Beverages*, AB-1996-2, adopted 1 November 1996, WT/DS8/AB/R, WT/DS10/AB/R, WT/DS11/AB/R, DSR 1996:I, 97, at 107.

making under the WTO Agreement or a covered agreement which is a Plurilateral Trade Agreement.

In the light of the above, we believe that the Panel's finding in paragraph 6.6 of the Panel Report is consistent with the *DSU* as well as with practice under the GATT 1947 and the *WTO Agreement*.

VII.   FINDINGS AND CONCLUSIONS

For the reasons set out in this Report, the Appellate Body upholds the legal findings and conclusions of the Panel.

The Appellate Body *recommends* that the Dispute Settlement Body make a ruling consistent with the legal findings and conclusions in the Panel Report and this Report.

UNITED STATES - MEASURE AFFECTING IMPORTS OF WOVEN WOOL SHIRTS AND BLOUSES FROM INDIA

Report of the Panel
WT/DS33/R

*Adopted by the Dispute Settlement Body on 23 May 1997
as upheld by the Appellate Body Report*

TABLE OF CONTENTS

I.   INTRODUCTION

1.1   In a communication dated 14 March 1996, India requested that a panel be established at the next meeting of the Dispute Settlement Body (DSB) pursuant to Article XXIII:2 of GATT 1994, Article 6 of the Understanding on Rules and Procedures Governing the Settlement of Disputes (DSU) and Article 8.10 and other relevant provisions of the Agreement on Textiles and Clothing (ATC) (WT/DS33/1). This arose from a restraint introduced by the United States in respect of India's exports of woven wool shirts and blouses (US category 440), under Article 6 of the ATC.

1.2   India noted that the matter had remained unresolved in spite of bilateral consultations between India and the United States held under Article 6.7 of the ATC in April and June 1995; the examination of the matter by the Textiles Monitoring Body (TMB) under Article 6.10 of the ATC in August and September 1995; the communication sent to the TMB under Article 8.10 of the ATC, within one month of the TMB recommendation under Article 6.10 of the ATC, explaining the reasons for India's inability to conform to the TMB recommendations; and the review of the matter by the TMB under Article 8.10 of the ATC in November 1995. Consequently, India considered that it had met all requirements in Article 8.10 of the ATC for direct recourse to Article XXIII:2 of GATT 1994. At its meeting held on 17 April 1996, the DSB established a panel pursuant to the request of India, with standard terms of reference, in accordance with Article 6 of the DSU (WT/DSB/M/14).

1.3   On 27 June 1996, the DSB informed Members that the terms of reference and the composition of the panel (WT/DS33/2) were as follows:

Terms of Reference

> "To examine, in the light of the relevant provisions of the covered agreements cited by India in document WT/DS/33/1, the matter referred to the DSB by India in that document and to make such findings as will assist the DSB in making the recommendations or in giving the   rulings provided for in those agreements."

Composition

Chairman: Mr. Jacques Bourgeois

Panelists: Mr. Robert Arnott

Mr. Wilhelm Meier

Five Members reserved their rights to participate in the Panel proceedings as third parties; namely Canada, the European Communities, Norway, Pakistan and Turkey.

1.4   The Panel met with the parties to the dispute on 9 and 10 September and on 4 October 1996. The Panel submitted its complete findings and conclusions to the parties to the dispute on 12 November 1996.

* * * * *

II.   CHRONOLOGY OF EVENTS

United States   Requests   Consultations   under   the   MFA[1]   in December 1994

2.1   Since the inception of the MFA in 1974, exports of textile and clothing products from India to the United States had been regulated by bilateral textile agreements under Article 4 of the MFA. The last bilateral textile agreement between India and the United States expired on 31 December 1994 and, effective from 1 January 1995, trade in textiles and clothing between the two Members has been governed by the ATC.

2.2   In the last bilateral textiles agreement between India and the United States, India's exports of several cotton and man-made fibre product categories had been subject to specific quota limits (Group I) and those product categories

---

[1]   Arrangement Regarding International Trade in Textiles (the "Multifibre Arrangement" or "MFA").

that were not so designated, plus all silk-blended garments and vegetable fibre garments, were subject to a group limit (Group II). Wool products (Group III) were not subject to specific or group limits, but were subject to the consultation mechanism in the bilateral agreement.

2.3   On 30 December 1994, the United States issued a request for consultations with India under paragraphs 19 and 20 of the bilateral agreement for the purpose of establishing restraints on India's exports to the United States of woven wool shirts and blouses (category 440 in Group III).[2] The request for consultations, accompanied by a statement entitled "Market Statement, Wool Woven Shirts and Blouses: Category 440", stated that the United States had concluded that the level of imports from India in this category was creating a real risk of disruption in the United States' domestic industry.

2.4   Consultations between India and the United States were held in Geneva on 18 April 1995 pursuant to the request issued in December 1994. India considered that the request for consultations, issued one day before the expiry of the MFA and the bilateral textiles agreement, was no longer valid in April 1995; from 1 January 1995 the framework for international trade in textiles was provided by the ATC and the other WTO agreements.

United States Requests Consultations Under the ATC in April 1995

2.5   On the same day, 18 April 1995, the United States requested new consultations with India on, *inter alia*, category 440 under the transitional safeguard mechanism in Article 6 of the ATC. The United States withdrew its previous consultation request issued on 30 December 1994 as India considered that the request was no longer valid due to the entry into force of the ATC. The consultation request in the form of a diplomatic note stated that the United States had concluded that the sharp and substantial increase in imports from India in this category "is causing serious damage, or actual threat thereof to the United States industry", and was accompanied by a "Statement of Serious Damage" (hereinafter referred to as the Market Statement) which claimed that a "sharp and substantial increase in imports of woven wool shirts and blouses, Category 440, is causing serious damage to the US industry producing woven wool shirts and blouses. The United States proposed a quota limit for exports of category 440 of 76,698 dozen. The request for consultations was officially published in the US Federal Register on 23 May 1995 (60 Fed. Reg. 27274).

2.6   Further discussions were held between the two delegations in Geneva on 19 April 1995 at the request of the United States. However, as the request for consultations had been issued only on the previous day, India had not had time to

---

[2]   The action by the United States also covered two other product categories, wool coats etc. for men and boys (category 434 of Group III) and wool coats etc. for women and girls (category 435 of Group III) which are not part of this matter.

complete its review of the Market Statement and, therefore, considered these consultations to be preliminary. In the course of these consultations, India sought clarification from the United States on a number of technical points raised by the Market Statement. Further consultations were held in Washington on 14-16 June 1995 which did not result in a mutual settlement of the matter.

United States Imposes Restraints on Imports from India in July 1995

2.7   On 14 July 1995, as no mutual settlement was reached within the 60-day consultation period provided in the ATC, India was informed by the United States that a restraint would be applied on imports from India of the products covered by US category 440, effective from 18 April 1995 and extending through 17 April 1996. The level of the restraint was set at 76,698 dozen for the first 12-month period.

Review by the Textiles Monitoring Body

2.8   Pursuant to Article 6.10 of the ATC, the United States notified the TMB of the restraint. The TMB examined the matter at its sessions from 28 August to 1 September and 12-15 September 1995 and heard presentations from the United States and India.[3] With respect to category 440, the United States submitted to the TMB a document entitled "Other Relevant Information", containing information on the situation of the United States industry producing woven wool shirts and blouses.

2.9   With respect to category 440, the TMB found:

> "During its review under paragraphs 2 and 3 of Article 6, of the safeguard action taken by the United States against imports of category 440 from India, the TMB found that the *actual threat of serious damage* had been demonstrated, and that, pursuant to paragraph 4 of Article 6, this actual

---

[3]   Restraints were also applied on categories 434 and 435, and at its session on 28 August to 1 September 1995, the TMB examined all three actions. For category 434, the TMB found that "serious damage, or actual threat thereof, had not been demonstrated and recommended that the United States rescind the measure". The United States rescinded the measure. For category 435, the TMB found that serious damage had not been demonstrated, but could not reach consensus on the existence of actual threat of serious damage. The TMB again reviewed the matter relating to category 435 which had been referred to it by India under Article 8.6 of the ATC during its meeting on 13-17 November 1995. However, the Body could not make any recommendations in addition to the conclusions it had reached during its earlier meeting. Since the matter relating to category 435 remained unresolved by the TMB, India brought the matter before the Dispute Settlement Body (DSB). On 23 April 1996, India was informed that the United States had removed the restraints on category 435 through a notification in the Federal Register on 23 April 1996. In the light of this, India terminated further action under the DSU without prejudice to its stand on the inconsistency of the US measure or on the various factual and legal issues outlined by India in its request for establishment of a panel.

threat could be attributed to the sharp and substantial increase in imports from India." (G/TMB/R/3)

India Requests Review of TMB Finding in October 1995

2.10   India sent a communication on 16 October 1995 to the TMB informing that Body of its inability to conform with its recommendations and explaining the reasons therefor, as provided in Article 8.10 of the ATC. India requested the TMB to give a thorough consideration to the reasons it had given and to recommend that the United States rescind the restraint on India's exports in category 440.

2.11   The TMB reviewed the matter raised by India at its meeting on 13-17 November 1995, and made the following statement in its report:

> "The TMB reviewed the matter referred to it by India under Article 8.10 in its letter dated 16 October 1995. The TMB heard the presentation made by India and considered the elements put forward. The Body could not make any recommendation in addition to the conclusions it had reached at its meeting on 12-15 September 1995 (G/TMB/R/3, paragraph 26). The TMB therefore considered its review of the matter completed". (G/TMB/R/6)

India Requests the Establishment of a Panel in March 1996

2.12   Since the matter relating to category 440 remained unresolved, India brought the matter before the DSB. India filed a request with the DSB on 14 March 1996 for the establishment of a panel on the restraint, pursuant to Article XXIII:2 of GATT 1994, Article 6 of the DSU and Article 8.10 and other relevant provisions of the ATC. India requested that the panel be established with standard terms of reference as set out in Article 7 of the DSU (WT/DS33/1). At the meeting held on 17 April 1996, the DSB agreed to establish the panel in respect of category 440 with standard terms of reference as requested by India (WT/DS33/2).

2.13   On 18 April 1996, the United States announced the continuation of the restraint on category 440 until 17 April 1997.

2.14   On 24 June 1996, the present Panel was constituted. (WT/DS33/2 dated 27 June 1996.)

* * * * *

III. CLAIMS OF THE PARTIES

The Request of India

3.1   In its request for the establishment of a panel (WT/DS33/1), India requested that the Panel consider and find that:

(i)   The restraint introduced by the United States on 14 July 1995 on imports of category 440 (woven wool shirts and blouses) from India effective from 18 April 1995 was inconsistent with Articles 6, 8 and 2 of the ATC.

(ii)   The action of the United States in imposing the restraint on imports of category 440 from India nullified or impaired the benefits accruing to India under the WTO Agreement and under GATT 1994 and the ATC in particular.

(iii)   The Government of the United States should have brought the measure into conformity with the ATC by withdrawing the restraint imposed by it on imports of category 440 from India.

3.2   *India* also requested a supplementary finding by the Panel that:

(i)   According to the ATC, notably Article 6, the onus of demonstrating serious damage or its actual threat was on the United States, as the importing Member. It had to choose at the beginning of the process whether it would claim the existence of "serious damage" or "actual threat". These were not interchangeable because the data requirement would vary with the chosen situation. It would not be valid to transfer a transitional safeguard to a situation of actual threat when the claim of serious damage had failed to gain acceptance.

(ii)   There was no provision in the ATC under which the United States, as the importing Member, could have imposed a restraint with retrospective effect.

The Request of the United States

3.3   The *United States* requested the Panel to find that:

(i)   the United States' application and maintenance of a safeguard restraint on woven wool shirts and blouses from India was consistent with Article 6 of the ATC;

(ii)   the restraint was not inconsistent with Article 2 or any other provision of the ATC; and

(iii)   the measure did not nullify and impair benefits accruing to India under the ATC or GATT 1994.

Comments on the Request to the Panel

3.4   The *United States* referred to India's request to the Panel which appeared to be seeking a specific remedy in this dispute and expressed the opinion that such a remedy fell outside the scope of the Panel's mandate as provided in the DSU. India had requested that the Panel interpret Article 19.1 of the DSU to require removal of a restraint to bring the action "in conformity" with the relevant agreement. The United States had taken issue with India's assertion that bringing a safeguard action into conformity with the ATC or, allegedly, with GATT 1994, to the extent it was relevant, required withdrawing the restraint. What was clear was that the DSU gave WTO panels explicit instructions with respect to the one and only recommendation that properly may be offered if the measures of a Member were found to be inconsistent with its obligations: to bring the measures into conformity with its obligations. The avoidance of granting specific remedies, such as the withdrawal or modification of a measure, was a well-established practice under GATT 1947 and had been codified in Article 19.1 of the DSU, which provided: "Where a panel or the Appellate Body concludes that a measure is inconsistent with a covered agreement, it shall recommend that the Member concerned bring the measure into conformity with that agreement," rather than that the Member "withdraw" the measure.

3.5   *India* noted the US views in the preceding paragraph with concern and asked the United States which legal options it wished to preserve by presenting them. India stressed that it had not asked the Panel to make a recommendation on the issue of implementation in accordance with Article 19.1, first sentence, of the DSU, but to exercise the discretion that the second sentence of Article 19.1 conferred upon it, namely, that it could, in addition to its recommendations, "suggest ways in which the Member concerned could implement the recommendations". In the view of India, there were no alternatives as to how a safeguard action taken inconsistently with Article 6 of the ATC could be brought into conformity and the United States had not been able to indicate any such alternatives. The rationale of the second sentence of Article 19.1 of the DSU was procedural economy; it was designed to reduce the likelihood of a second proceeding about the implementation of the results of the first. It would thus be perfectly consistent not only with the wording but also the spirit of that provision if the Panel were to find that there were no alternatives to withdrawal in the present case and to suggest, therefore, that the United States implement the Panel's recommendation by withdrawing the measure.

* * * * *

IV.   THIRD PARTY SUBMISSIONS

4.1   At the first substantive meeting of the Panel on 10 September 1996, four Members (Canada, EC, Norway and Pakistan) which had indicated their interests in this matter as third parties at the DSU meeting on 17 April 1996 (DS33/2, paragraph 4) made submissions. Turkey had also indicated its third party interests and attended the Panel meeting but did not provide a submission.

Submission of Canada

4.2   *Canada* pointed out that it had a substantial interest in several issues relating to the interpretation of the ATC raised by the parties to the dispute; namely, (i) the question of the ability of a Member to maintain a restraint in the absence of an "endorsement" by the TMB; (ii) the appropriate effective date for the application of a restraint measure; (iii) the type of information a Member had to submit to the TMB to justify a request for consultations and the treatment given to additional information provided to the TMB; and (iv) whether the Member making the request had to specify from the outset the basis for the request.

4.3   *Canada* noted that India had requested, *inter alia*, a supplementary finding by the Panel that because the TMB had not specifically upheld the safeguard action taken by the United States, this implied that the TMB had not found the safeguard action to be justified and, therefore, the United States had a legal obligation to withdraw the restraint. It was Canada's view that such an interpretation was too narrow and would unduly circumscribe the ability of Members to take safeguard actions as provided for in the ATC. While the TMB had a significant role to play in the review of the safeguard actions, there was no requirement in the ATC that the TMB had to "endorse" a safeguard action in order for it to be maintained. On the contrary, during the Uruguay Round negotiations leading to the ATC, several participants had made proposals to require a positive decision of the multilateral reviewing body (now the TMB) in order for a restraint measure to remain in place. Canada noted that none of these proposals had been incorporated into the ATC which reflected an implicit rejection of the approach now advocated by India.

4.4   In the view of *Canada*, if the TMB was required to specifically approve every safeguard action taken, it would rarely be possible for any Member to avail itself of the ATC safeguard clause because a single TMB member could block a consensus. Such a result would clearly be at odds with the intention of the ATC, which explicitly provided to the Members the authority to make the determination of whether a safeguard action was required.

4.5   *Canada* recalled that India had submitted that the United States was incorrect in imposing the restraint measure from the date of the request for consultations with India under Article 6 of the ATC. In this regard Canada noted that the ATC was silent with respect to the appropriate effective date of implementation of a safeguard action. In the absence of any specific prohibition, it was open to an importing Member to apply the safeguard action from the date of the request. It was more appropriate to implement the restraint as close as possible to the date of the request so as to avoid the possibility of having the domestic market flooded with imports after the request, but before the consultations were completed. A further element was that the calculation of the restraint level, pursuant to Article 6.8 of the ATC, was based on the MFA formula of the first 12 of the last 14 months preceding the month in which the request for consultations was made. The rationale for this calculation was to avoid including in the base level what was usually the most severe part of the import surge that had led to the request for consultations. The calculation of this formula supported the argument that it was more appropriate to implement any restraint as close as possible to the date of the request for consultations.

4.6   *Canada* also referred to India's submission that the review by the TMB should have been conducted only on the basis of the information provided to India at the time of the consultation request, rather than on supplementary information provided by the United States to the TMB at the time of its review. In this regard, Article 6.10 of the ATC stated that in examining a safeguard action, the TMB shall have at its disposal the factual data accompanying a request for consultations as provided to the Chairman of the TMB at the time of the request, pursuant to Article 6.7 of the ATC, "as well as any other relevant information provided by the Members concerned". The plain meaning of Article 6.10 of the ATC was that the TMB, in conducting its examination, may consider not only the information that was provided to it pursuant to Article 6.7 of the ATC, but also any additional submissions of a Member concerned. As a practical matter, this allowed the TMB to consider the most up-to-date data in its examination of the safeguard action, including data that were not available at the time of the request for consultations.

4.7   With reference to India's view that the onus of demonstrating serious damage or actual threat was on the importing Member which must choose at the outset whether it would claim the existence of "serious damage" or of "actual threat thereof" and that these two categories were not interchangeable because each category required different supporting data, *Canada* noted that no distinction was made between the definition of "serious damage" or "actual threat thereof" in Article 6 of the ATC, nor in the list of factors to be considered by a Member in making a determination under Article 6.2 of the ATC. Accordingly, the practice under the ATC had been for the Member taking such safeguard action to allege "serious damage or actual threat thereof" as a whole and to permit the TMB in its review under Article 6.10 of the ATC to determine whether either element, or both elements of the standard had been satisfied. Canada considered that, when reviewing an allegation of "serious damage or actual threat thereof" the TMB must base its recommendations on the evidence before it. It may find that the evidence supports a determination of "serious damage" alone, of "actual threat" alone, of both, or of neither. However, it did not follow that an importing Member should be required to choose which component of the standard to allege at the commencement of the Article 6 process. To impose such a requirement on an importing Member would unreasonably restrict the scope of its case, and would infringe upon the discretion of the TMB to conduct its examination and base its recommendations on all the evidence before it.

4.8   In a subsequent submission, *India* disagreed with the point in the first sentence of paragraph 4.3, recalling that, under the MFA, the exporting country had the right to refuse to accept a discriminatory restraint while under the ATC, the exporting Members had lost that right. The counterpart to that loss was the requirement of a TMB examination and recommendation. The recourse available to importing Members under the ATC was, therefore, not significantly different from the recourse available to them under the MFA: the consent of the exporting country was required under the MFA while under the ATC, it was a TMB examination and recommendation that was required.

4.9   On the above point, the *United States* disagreed with India's assertion as the MFA required TSB examination of unilateral restraints and that the TSB make recommendations, just as required of the TMB.

Soumission of the European Communities

4.10   The *European Communities* expressed the opinion that a restraint could be justified for either a case of imports having caused serious damage or for a case of imports actually threatening to cause serious damage pursuant to Article 6.2 of the ATC. Nowhere in the ATC was there any obligation on the importing Member to choose at the beginning of the process whether it would claim "serious damage" or "actual threat". This was because any such obligation would create consequences which were clearly not intended by the ATC negotiators, namely: (i) that an importing Member claiming "serious damage" might be persuaded by the exporting Member during their consultations that the situation was really one of "actual threat" but that no restraint could be established simply because the importing Member had initially claimed only "serious damage"; (ii) that importing Members would, therefore, have simultaneously to request two parallel sets of consultations, the first to discuss a restraint based on "serious damage" and the second to discuss one based on "actual threat". Clearly such situations did not follow from the actual wording of the ATC and neither were they intended by the negotiators. At another level, if the consultations resulted in agreement under Article 6.9 of the ATC then presumable the two parties were satisfied on this point. On the other hand, if the consultations did not reach agreement then it would be up to the TMB to "promptly conduct an examination of the matter, including the determination of serious damage, or actual threat thereof pursuant to Article 6.10 of the ATC". In this case it would be the TMB's determination which would matter and the option "chosen" by the importing Member would be irrelevant.

4.11   The *European Communities* considered the question of the standard of review to be of great importance. The EC reminded the Panel that one of the most thorough discussions of the problems relating to the standard of review in cases involving the legal appreciation of facts in the light of evidentiary requirements laid down in the Tokyo Round Subsidies Code,[4] took place before the panel on the US countervailing duties imposed on lead and bismuth steel origi-

---

[4]   Agreement on Interpretation and Application of Articles VI, XVI and XXIII of the General Agreement on Tariffs and Trade.

nating in France, the UK and Germany. Although that panel report was never adopted, it contained valuable insights into the difference between the issues to which the normal rules of treaty interpretation were to be applied and the issues involving legal appreciation of the facts in the light of evidentiary requirements laid down in the relevant agreement (paragraphs 368 and 369).

4.12   The *European Communities* also considered it important for the Panel to take account of the fact that the test of reasonableness proposed by the US, even though it was taken from the *Fur Felt Hat* case carried for the US connotations of extreme deference to the judgement of the national government. It should be noted that the panel in *Lead and Bismuth Steel* said that:

> "...the criteria for a review by a panel of factual assessments
> by domestic investigating authorities of signatories against
> the requirements of the agreement could not be based on a
> simple transposition of standards applied in domestic ad-
> ministrative law of signatories."

The *European Communities* attached great importance to an approach in these issues in the spirit of the panel report on *Lead and Bismuth Steel*. It should be clear that in the case of factual assessments by national investigating authorities of Members in the light of the requirements of the agreement (as interpreted in accordance with the customary rules of interpretation of international law), a margin of discretion should be left to these authorities, but the Panel could not borrow from one particular legal system in circumscribing this margin of discretion. In this case the Panel must be inspired by the administrative law systems of the Members.

Submission of Norway

4.13   *Norway* stated that its concern in this case was primarily of a systemic nature and noted that the Panel was considering a dispute which twice, and with consensus recommendations, had been dealt with by the TMB. It was concerned that the effect of the case might not only be the positive resolution of a dispute, but the undermining of future TMB recommendations and thus the TMB's efficiency. The result of this efficiency so far had been that quotas had been dismantled considerably faster than what would have been possible by way of panels. Norway questioned India's asking the panel to address the issues of "TMB endorsement" and of "serious damage" as opposed to "actual threat of serious damage". On the question of retroactive implementation, it accepted India's request for clarification.

4.14   It was the view of *Norway* that both the TMB and India were wrong in claiming, with respect to the introduction of a safeguard action, that the ATC did not provide any indication with respect to the effective date of implementation of a measure, although India was right in saying that there was no "explicit authorization in the ATC's transitional safeguard clause to impose the additional burden of retroactive application". Norway was of the opinion that there were sufficient indications to be found and that it was unnecessary as well as unjustifiable to resort to Article XIII:3(b) of GATT 1994. Article 6.10 of the ATC suggested that the term "apply" was distinct from the term "implement". Saying that a Member "... may apply the restraint by date of import or date of export ..." could not be read to mean the same as if the sentence had substituted the word "implement" for "apply". The term "apply" was concerned more with the manner of implementation than with its effective timing. It was perfectly reasonable to require that a measure be applied only after certain procedures had been completed and then to allow discretion to implement the same measure in such a way as to give it effect from a different date. This was also indirectly supported by the fact that a measure may be applied "within 30 days following the 60-day period for consultations". In the view of Norway it was, therefore, legitimate to question whether one was, in fact, dealing with a case of retroactive implementation. Another argument, if one were indeed dealing with a retroactive measure, was the fact that there was provision for it in the predecessor agreement, suggesting that an explicit provision to the contrary would have been included in the ATC if negotiators were concerned with making a clean break with the past in this respect.

4.15 *Norway* also pointed out that Article 6.10 of the ATC should be read in conjunction with Article 6.11. If one were to accept India's arguments, it would in all likelihood undermine the valuable consultation procedure in Article 6.10 of the ATC and encourage importers to introduce quotas without prior consultation, under Article 6.11 of the ATC. Norway also agreed with the US argument that India's position would encourage an exporter to flood the importing market with imports after the request and before consultations were completed. Norway supported India to the extent that the matter needed clarification; however, it disagreed with India's interpretation of the ATC on several points and respectfully asked the Panel to give favourable consideration to the interpretations and arguments it put forward.

Submission of Pakistan

4.16 *Pakistan* pointed out that the ATC represented a balance of rights and obligations between the exporting Members and the importing Members. The ATC was an improvement over the MFA and even during the transitional period the progress made in the negotiation of the ATC could not be nullified. Pakistan urged the Panel to consider the systemic implications of the present case from this perspective and to reach a decision which did not in any way retard the progress already made or impair the benefits accruing to the exporting Members. Pakistan considered that the Panel should look into the element of good faith on the part of authorities initiating a safeguard action, including (a) whether the authorities had based their decision on all available data; (b) whether the analysis of available data was in accordance with normal and generally recognized principles and procedures; (c) whether there was an element of arbitrariness; and (d) whether any action was taken on unsubstantiated presumptions. In examining the different stages of the case it would be important to examine whether the authorities had adopted a consistent position throughout the different stages or whether they had changed their position or introduced new elements at different stages of the process. Good faith could not and should not co-exist with ex-post justifications.

4.17   *Pakistan* considered that the Panel was required to pronounce on the distinction between "serious damage" and "actual threat of serious damage". While Article 6.2 and 6.3 of the ATC listed the same economic variables to be considered in both cases, it was also true that different analysis and information in respect of the same economic variables would be required to prove either serious damage or actual threat of serious damage, as the case may be. In a case of serious damage, the analysis should clearly demonstrate the damage that had already occurred, while in case of a claim for actual threat of serious damage, the analysis should include the reasons which may lead to serious damage. The Panel should also determine what effect the introduction of new information by parties could have on the legality of the whole proceeding. An important step in the ATC was the consultations, which must be based on the "specific and relevant" information provided by the importing Member to the exporting Member under Article 6.7 of the ATC. Any new information supplied at the TMB's review of the safeguard action would put the exporting Member at a great disadvantage. According to Article 6.10 of the ATC, the TMB may have "any other relevant information provided by the Member concerned", but this could not be interpreted to mean new information. Whenever any new information was introduced, the legal process should start afresh. New information introduced at the time of the TMB's review could be: (i) information pertaining to the period after the request for consultations was issued and should not be relevant to the case in question; (ii) information available earlier but not used, which demonstrated a lack of serious effort which would not support the contention of good faith; or (iii) information pertaining to the period before the request for consultations was issued but not available at the time of the request. This would also be an ex-post justification and would put the exporting Member at a disadvantage which could be rectified only by issuing a fresh request for consultations.

* * * * *

V.   MAIN ARGUMENTS OF THE PARTIES

A.   Introduction

5.1   The Panel noted that India had arranged its first submission in a sequence beginning with general points on the safeguard mechanism followed by arguments on burden of proof and standard of review (Part A). This was followed by an argument that the safeguard action on which the United States sought consultations was not the safeguard action endorsed by the TMB (Part B). There then followed the claim that the United States had failed to demonstrate serious damage in the consultations and, therefore, had acted inconsistently with Article 6 of the ATC (Part C); a consideration of supplementary information (Part D) and retroactive application (Part E). In this descriptive part of the Panel's report, much of India's structure has been used, but not fully. Rather, the descriptive part follows the approach adopted by the Panel in setting out its findings which, it was considered, would facilitate in relating the arguments of the parties to the Panel's findings on these arguments.

B. Burden of Proof

5.2   *India* argued that the United States bore the burden of proving that it had met the requirements of Article 6 of the ATC. The CONTRACTING PARTIES to GATT 1947 had consistently found that exceptions must be interpreted narrowly and that the party invoking an exception bore the burden of proving that it had met the legal requirements justifying the invocation. India referred to two documents in this context (BISD 30S/140 and 36S/345). Based on this principle alone, the Panel would need to find that it was the United States that bore the burden of proving that it had made the determination in accordance with Article 6 of the ATC. Moreover, Article 6.2 of the ATC clearly permitted safeguard action only if it was demonstrated that an increase in imports caused serious damage or actual threat thereof. It was, consequently, up to the Member taking safeguard action to make that demonstration. This followed not only from the general principle of law recognized by panels but also from the text of Article 6.2 of the ATC itself. It permitted safeguard action by a Member when "... it is demonstrated that a particular product is being imported into its territory in such increased quantities as to cause serious damage, or actual threat thereof ..." and goes on to state that "[s]erious damage or threat thereof must demonstrably be caused by such increased quantities ...". The requirement to demonstrate an increase in imports, serious damage and the causal link between the two was clearly a requirement imposed on the Member that chose to apply the safeguard action, not on the Member(s) against which the action was directed.

5.3   *India* also considered that the Member invoking Article 6 of the ATC had the possibility to make the demonstration by submitting positive evidence on the basis of data it had collected. If the Member against which the action was taken had to bear the burden of proof, it would have to demonstrate the negative, which was often impossible, on the basis of the data available to it which were likely to be more limited than those available to the importing Member. The purpose of Article 6 of the ATC, which was to impose a strict discipline on the use of safeguards could, therefore, not be achieved if the burden of proof was shifted from the importing to the exporting Members.

5.4   The *United States* argued that, consistent with accepted GATT 1947 dispute settlement practice which had been carried over in the WTO, the burden was on India in the first instance to make a *prima facie* case that the United States' application of a transitional safeguard on imports of woven wool shirts and blouses from India had been inconsistent with the ATC. The language of Article XXIII of GATT 1994 and practice under GATT 1947 supported this principle. Article XXIII of GATT 1994, as referenced in Article 8.10 of the ATC, provided recourse to a dispute settlement proceeding when a Member considered that any benefit accruing to it directly or indirectly was being nullified or impaired as a result of the failure of another Member to carry out its obligations under that Agreement. In this case, India had the initial burden of demonstrating that the United States had failed to carry out its obligations under the ATC and, in the view of the US, India had failed to sustain that burden.

5.5   The *United States* further argued that the burden was not on the US to re-demonstrate that its actions were justified. The ATC allowed a Member to impose a safeguard when it had determined that imports were causing or threatened to cause serious damage to its market. It was the view of the United States that the task of the Panel was to determine whether India had advanced facts which provided convincing evidence that it was unreasonable for the United States to determine, in accordance with Article 6.2 and 6.3 of the ATC, that the adverse effects of increased woven wool shirt and blouse imports on the US domestic industry amounted to serious damage or actual threat thereof. If India had not advanced such evidence, then the Panel should find that the determination under Article 6.2 of the ATC had been properly made and was consistent with the United States' obligations under the ATC. A similar examination should be applied with respect to determinations under Article 6.4 of the ATC.

5.6   The *United States* considered that India's argument that the ATC was an exception to GATT 1994 and that this "inconsistency" was sufficient to place the burden on the defending Member to establish conformity with ATC obligations would overturn the balance of this Agreement and many of the other Multilateral Trade Agreements. In this respect the ATC was similar, for example, to the Agreement on the Application of Sanitary and Phytosanitary Measures, the Agreement on Technical Barriers to Trade and the Agreement on Safeguards and the Agreement on Trade-Related Aspects of Intellectual Property Rights.

C.   *Standard of Review*

5.7   In the view of *India*, there was no standard of reasonableness foreseen in the ATC and given the highly exceptional character of the ATC's safeguard provisions, it would be legally inadmissible to "import" into the ATC the standard of review included at the request of the United States in the Anti-Dumping Agreement.[5] In fact, the Ministerial Decision on Review of Article 17.6 of the Agreement on Implementation of Article VI of the General Agreement on Tariffs and Trade 1994 clearly implied that this standard was relevant only for the Anti-Dumping Agreement and that it had no general applicability. According to the DSU, the dispute settlement system served, *inter alia*, to clarify the provisions of the WTO agreements "in accordance with the customary rules of interpretation of

---

[5]   Agreement on Implementation of Article VI of the General Agreement on Tariffs and Trade 1994.

public international law".[6] According to general principles of international law, every treaty must be performed in good faith.[7] The task of the Panel was, consequently, to ascertain whether the United States had carried out its obligations under Article 6 of the ATC in good faith. India was not requesting the Panel to conduct a *de novo* review of the matter and to replace the United States' determination by its own, but was asking the Panel to objectively assess, in accordance with Article 11 of the DSU, whether the United States had made its determination in accordance with its obligations under Article 6 of the ATC.

5.8   In a response to the Panel, *India* pointed out that in applying the United States' domestic law, in particular the law governing the review of anti-dumping and countervailing duty actions, courts had accorded deference to administrative agencies in accordance with the "Chevron doctrine". Courts did not review whether the agency administering anti-dumping or countervailing duties had interpreted the law correctly, but whether its interpretation was reasonable. Similarly, United States courts did not examine whether the agency had applied the law correctly but whether their application was reasonable. The notion of "reasonableness" was, thus, used to define the scope of a legal doctrine that had created considerable scope of discretion for agencies and a significant shift of power from the courts to the executive branch. Article 17 of the Anti-Dumping Agreement was a reflection of the "Chevron doctrine". During the course of the proceedings of this Panel, the United States, without referring to Article 17 of the Anti-Dumping Agreement directly, had presented arguments to the Panel which, if accepted, would constitute an incorporation of the principles of that provision into the ATC.

5.9   The *United States* argued that all parties to an agreement must apply it in good faith. This was an important principle in treaty and domestic contract law. Making a determination in a reasonable manner and in good faith followed from the first step of applying a treaty in good faith. It did not "replace" the obligation to apply a treaty in good faith. The United States had stated that, in applying the provisions of Article 6 of the ATC in good faith, it had made a reasonable determination after examining relevant data that a transitional safeguard was necessary. It had also followed Article 6.7 of the ATC and ultimately Article 6.10 when no mutual solution was reached with India. The TMB findings required under Articles 6.10 and 8 of the ATC had supported the US application of the safeguard.

5.10   The *United States* further argued that there was no need for a specific provision on standard of review in the ATC or in any other agreement, although the negotiators of the Anti-Dumping Agreement had seen the need to negotiate a specific standard of review for those cases because of the nature and problems found in the anti-dumping area. The standard of review in Article 17.6 of that

---

[6]   Article 3:2 of the DSU.
[7]   See Article 26 of the Vienna Convention on the Law of Treaties.

Agreement was not relevant in this matter and the United States had not advanced that standard for this case. The US had not cited any anti-dumping or subsidy case law, as India had done. India's assertion that the United States had sought to apply anti-dumping and subsidy standards to this case was incorrect.

5.11   *India* recalled that the role of panels was, according to Article 3.2 of the DSU, to preserve the rights and obligations of WTO Members. If this Panel were to sanction "reasonable" deviations from the requirements set out in Article 6 of the ATC rather than determine whether they had been observed in good faith or if it were to sanction an exercise of discretion on the grounds that it was "reasonable" rather than determine whether the Member had exercised it in good faith, it would effectively diminish the rights and obligations of Members and, therefore, act inconsistently with that basic principle of the DSU. The text of the ATC clearly delineated the range of discretion available to Members making determinations for the purpose of imposing safeguard actions. If the Panel were to expand that range by applying the notion of reasonableness, it would be acting without any basis in the text of the ATC and contrary to the general principles of international law and it would, therefore, not be finding and confirming the existing WTO law, as was its task. Rather, it would be inventing new law which no Member had accepted. This could not, in India's view, but undermine the Members' confidence in the newly established dispute settlement procedures.

5.12   The *United States* reiterated that the appropriate standard of review was one of reasonableness and good faith examination of the data. The principle of "good faith" application of treaties was relevant, but it was argued that this principle was integral to the standard of reasonableness. One resulted from the other. The US considered it self-evident that all Members must follow the international law principle of good faith application of treaties and in doing so they must come to "reasonable" conclusions based on the examination conducted. The United States had applied the ATC consistently with that entire precept. Referring first to the relevant Uruguay Round principles other than under the ATC, it was noted that Article 3.1 of the DSU provided that: "Members affirm their adherence to the principles for the management of disputes ... applied under Articles XXII and XXIII of GATT 1947, and the rules and procedures as further elaborated and modified herein." Article XVI:1 of the Agreement Establishing the WTO also provided that "[e]xcept otherwise provided under this Agreement or the Multilateral Trade Agreements, the WTO shall be guided by the decisions, procedures and customary practices followed by the CONTRACTING PARTIES to GATT 1947 and the bodies established in the framework of GATT 1947".

5.13   The *United States* also noted that Article 3.2 of the DSU provided, in part, that:

> "The Members recognize that [the dispute settlement system of the WTO] serves to preserve the rights and obligations of Members under the covered agreements, and to clarify the existing provisions of those agreements in accordance with customary rules of interpretation of public international law.

> Recommendations and rules of the DSB cannot add to or
> diminish the rights and obligations provided in the covered
> agreements."

It was, therefore, clear under Article 3.2 of the DSU that while WTO dispute settlement also served to clarify provisions of covered agreements, the process could not add to or diminish the rights and obligations provided in those agreements.

5.14   The United States further pointed out that Article 11 of the DSU provided, in part, that:

> "... a panel should make an objective assessment of the
> matter before it, including an objective assessment of the
> facts of the case and the applicability of and conformity
> with the relevant covered agreements, and make such other
> findings as will assist the DSB in making the recommenda-
> tions or in giving the rulings provided for in the covered
> agreements".

Article 11 of the DSU incorporated paragraph 16 of the 1979 GATT Understanding Regarding Notification, Consultation, Dispute Settlement and Surveillance.[8] The drafters of the DSU had sought to make the DSU a comprehensive text incorporating all prior codification efforts on dispute settlement. The CONTRACTING PARTIES to GATT 1947 had intended the 1979 Understanding and its annex to reflect customary practice and improvements in practice, including the standard of review enunciated in the 1951 GATT working party report concerning the withdrawal by the United States under Article XIX of a tariff concession on women's fur felt hat and hat bodies (*Fur Felt Hat* case).[9]

5.15   The *United States* argued that, in sum, an objective assessment by the Panel, in accordance with Article 11 of the DSU, required examining whether the United States had acted consistently with the requirements of the ATC and in good faith and whether the determination was reasonable in light of the data before the investigating authority.

The Fur Felt Hat Case

5.16   The *United States* argued that the *Fur Felt Hat* case provided authoritative guidance from GATT 1947 practice and procedures concerning the standard of review to apply in this case. The standard of review enunciated in that case was also consistent with principles of international law concerning the good faith application of treaties. The *Fur Felt Hat* case suggested that this Panel must determine whether the United States had applied the provisions of Article 6 of the ATC in good faith and had made a reasonable or good faith assessment of the

---

[8]   L/4907, adopted 28 November 1979.

[9]   GATT/CP/106, report adopted on 22 October 1951, Sales No. GATT/1951-3.

facts to make the determinations required of it under Article 6 of the ATC. Article 6 stated that "[s]afeguard action may be taken ... when, on the basis of a determination by a Member, it is demonstrated...". Clearly the focus of the ATC was on a determination made by the importing Member based on data available. While the *Fur Felt Hat* Working Party had examined action taken under Article XIX:1 of GATT 1947, the determination required in that case in GATT 1947 practice was similar to the determination required under Article 6.2 of the ATC.[10]

5.17   In that case the Czechoslovak Government had sought a determination that the United States invocation of Article XIX had been improper and had asserted that the United States had not met certain conditions under Article XIX to take action, seeking revocation of the measure. The Working Party had rejected the Czechoslovak argument and stated:

> "... it may be observed that the Working Party naturally could not have the facilities available to the United States authorities for examining interested parties and independent witnesses from the United States hat-making areas, and for forming judgements on the basis of such examination. ...Moreover, the United States is not called upon to prove conclusively that the degree of injury caused or threatened in this case must be regarded as serious; since the question under consideration is whether or not they are in breach of Article XIX, they are entitled to the benefit of any reasonable doubt."[11]

5.18   The *United States* argued that, just as in this case, the information examined by the *Fur Felt Hat* Working Party as a basis for its conclusions, although strong, was not perfect; for instance the US authorities had failed to separate figures on production of men's and women's hat bodies. However, the Working Party decided that "the available data support[ed] the view that increased imports caused or threatened some adverse effect on United States producers."[12]   The Working Party further determined that the United States' authorities in that case had investigated the matter thoroughly "on the basis of the data available to them at the time of their enquiry and had reached in good faith the conclusion that the proposed action fell within the terms of Article XIX ...".[13] The reasoning of the *Fur Felt Hat* Working Party applied to the standard of review the Panel must follow in the present case.

---

[10]   In fact, fur felt hats and hat bodies are listed as products covered under the ATC in the ATC Annex. Such products would have, for the United States, been subject to the ATC Article 6 safeguard mechanism, but the United States has integrated the product into GATT 1994 in accordance with Article 2 of the ATC. Article XIX now applies again to those products for the United States.

[11]   *Fur Felt Hat* at paragraph 30.

[12]   *Id.*

[13]   *Id.* at paragraph 48.

5.19   In the view of the *United States*, the regime now governing textile and clothing trade in the WTO was a safeguards regime, just as Article XIX of GATT 1994 and the Agreement on Safeguards was a safeguards regime. Both regimes permitted a Member to restrict trade in fairly traded goods on the basis of a determination made by a Member, subject to certain limitations. The textile regime diverged from Article XIX of GATT 1994 but many of its basic concepts depended on the fundamental concepts behind Article XIX. Where the negotiators had indicated their desire that the two regimes differ, the difference in rights and obligations provided in the negotiated text must be respected. However, the *Fur Felt Hat* case, an accepted precedent which predated the divergence between the two regimes, was persuasive in interpreting the provisions in both, or either, of these regimes concerning the initial decision to take a safeguard action. Guidance from that case did not involve wholesale incorporation of Article XIX of GATT 1994 or Agreement on Safeguards principles or the issue of compensation and non-discriminatory treatment as India would argue.

5.20   The *United States* noted that, in its first submission, India had argued that the standard for the Panel's review should not include any examination of the reasonableness of the determination, but should instead focus on whether the authorities had carried out their obligations "in good faith", as did the Working Party in the *Fur Felt Hat* case. Although the US disagreed with India's position with regard to the role of reasonableness, it did agree that good faith application of the ATC's provision was a relevant yardstick for Panel review. "Good faith" had been defined as "in accordance with standards of honesty, trust, sincerity etc. ...".[14] For the Panel to determine whether the authorities had carried out their obligations "in good faith", it did not need to ascertain whether the Panel would have reached the same determination as the authorities. Instead, the Panel would examine the basis for the authorities' conclusions, including an examination of the data upon which the authorities had relied, in order to determine whether the determination reflected a good faith application of the ATC standards. In this case the US authorities had exercised their discretion and followed the relevant ATC provisions in complete good faith.

5.21   The *United States* argued, therefore, that the reasoning of the *Fur Felt Hat* case applied equally to the case presented to the Panel. Since the key question was whether the determination by the US Committee on the Implementation of Textile Agreements (CITA) was consistent with the requirements of Article 6.2 and 6.3 of the ATC, the relevant question to be considered was not whether serious damage or threat of serious damage currently existed, but whether CITA had determined reasonably and in good faith that it existed at the time of the CITA determination in April 1995. The CITA determination could, therefore, only be evaluated on the basis of data existing at that time. The data presented later to the TMB in fact had corroborated the analysis done in April 1995.

---

[14]   Webster's Encyclopedic Unabridged Dictionary of the English Language (1989).

5.22   *India* pointed out that no GATT 1947 panel had followed the approach of the *Fur Felt Hat* Working Party. In fact, the panels on *New Zealand - Imports of Electrical Transformers from Finland* and *Canadian Countervailing Duties on Grain Corn from the United States* had fully reviewed the importing countries' actions without applying a standard of review and had imposed on the importing countries the duty to establish all the facts on which they had based their actions. The disciplines applied by those GATT 1947 panels in the cases of actions against dumped and subsidized trade should, as a minimum, be applied in the case of discriminatory actions against exports of textiles and clothing that were neither dumped nor subsidized. India further argued that to transpose the criteria applied in the *Fur Felt Hat* case to action under the ATC would be legally incorrect.

5.23   The *United States* rejected India's comment, above, that the *Fur Felt Hat* case was legally incorrect in these proceedings. That case involved review of safeguard action at a time when the review would have been similar in the textile context. Certainly dumping cases with a standard of review different from Article 17.6 of the Anti-Dumping Agreement were no longer applicable in dumping cases, and it was questioned why India's use of *New Zealand Transformers* or the principles it wished to interpose in this case, a textiles safeguard case, should be any better. In essence, while the standard in the *Fur Felt Hat* case might be modified by the specific provisions of the Agreement on Safeguards, principles not relevant to actions taken under that Agreement were useful here. Instead, India had resurrected the standard pre-Article 17.6 of the Anti-Dumping Agreement, in a case close to first impression, involving a special safeguard for textiles and clothing.

5.24   Also with respect to the *Fur Felt Hat* case, *India* considered that its findings had been overtaken by the Agreement on Safeguards, which declared in its Article 4 that injury determinations for the purpose of Article XIX action may only be made if an investigation by the importing Member demonstrated, on the basis of objective evidence, that a rise in imports had caused serious injury. The legal situation in which the *Fur Felt Hat* criteria were developed were, therefore, not analogous to the situation arising under Article 6 of the ATC and not even analogous to the situation arising under Article XIX as interpreted by the Agreement on Safeguards. The analogy the United States wished the Panel to draw was, for these reasons, misplaced. The criteria set out in the *Fur Felt Hat* case were, therefore, no longer part of the law of the WTO. Moreover, the findings of that Working Party related to a safeguard mechanism under which the WTO Members adversely affected by the safeguard action may take compensatory action; the ATC's safeguard mechanism, however, did not authorize textile exporting Members to take compensatory action. It would, for this reason alone, be inappropriate to accord to Members invoking the ATC safeguards provisions, under which no compensation was due, the latitudes they had under Article XIX of GATT 1994. India also considered that it had demonstrated that it would be legally incorrect and illogical if the Panel were to infer, just because both the *Fur Felt Hat* case and the case before it concerned safeguard actions, that the standard of review applied in the *Fur Felt Hat* case must also be applied in the present case.

5.25   In response to these views, the *United States* argued that this case was close to a case of first impression and it had cited and sought guidance from a GATT 1947 safeguard case that was most comparable to the situation faced in making safeguard determinations under the ATC. It was incorrect for India to state that no GATT 1947 panel had followed the approach of the *Fur Felt Hat* Working Party and that it was no longer part of the law of the WTO. GATT precedent interpreting Article XIX:1 (for instance, as recorded in the chapter on Article XIX in the GATT Analytical Index) consisted almost entirely of the findings and recommendations of this Working Party. Under Article XVI:1 of the Agreement Establishing the WTO, the WTO and its Members were to be guided by the decisions, procedures and customary practices of the GATT 1947 system. Article 3.1 of the DSU stated the same. The *Fur Felt Hat* decision had continuing relevance even after negotiation of the new Agreement on Safeguards.

5.26   The *United States* further argued that the standards for safeguard action provided in the Agreement on Safeguards reflected a shift in focus incorporating the jurisprudence of the *Fur Felt Hat* case. These standards were not phrased in terms of facts that the importing Member must prove, if necessary, to a panel. Rather, they were phrased explicitly in terms of the investigation to be undertaken by the competent authorities in the importing Member. Thus, a panel's evaluation of measures taken pursuant to the Agreement on Safeguards should follow the approach taken in the *Fur Felt Hat* case.

5.27   The *United States* also referred to India's point regarding compensation in respect of a safeguard action and noted that pursuant to Article 8.2 of the Safeguards Agreement, there was no right to compensation for a period of three years. It was no coincidence that this was the maximum duration of a restraint pursuant to Article 6 of the ATC. There was no significant loss of "GATT rights" in this respect. India's arguments regarding the need for multilateral approval if a Member wished to take a safeguard action without payment of compensation were simply incorrect. The situation was also the same in respect of dispute settlement. Under both the ATC and the Safeguards Agreement parties had recourse to Article XXIII dispute settlement. Moreover, before the Safeguards Agreement and the ATC, the MFA had permitted recourse to Article XXIII dispute settlement. The US drew the Panel's attention to Article 11.10 of the MFA. Therefore, the legal situation for safeguards under Article XIX of GATT 1994, for purposes of the discreet discussion of standard of review, was no more analogous than any other case law.

D.   Article 6 of the ATC

The ATC Safeguard Mechanism

5.28   *India* argued that the transitional safeguard mechanism established under the ATC was an exception to the basic principles of the General Agreement and the general safeguard provisions of Article XIX of GATT 1994 and it must be interpreted accordingly. Article XI of GATT 1994 provided for a general prohibition of quantitative restrictions; one of the exceptions to this general prohibition was Article XIX of GATT 1994, which permitted safeguard actions in the form of quantitative restrictions. However, such restrictions must be imposed consistently with Article XIII of GATT 1994, that is, non-discriminatorily. The textiles and clothing sector had, however, remained outside the GATT system for a long time and the ATC set out provisions to be applied by Members for the integration of the textiles and clothing sector into GATT 1994 during a transitional period. The scheme of the ATC was that all quantitative restrictions maintained under the provisions of the MFA and in effect on the day before the entry into force of the WTO Agreement would be governed by the provisions of the ATC (Article 2.1) and that no new restrictions would be introduced except under the provisions of the ATC or GATT 1994 (Article 2.4). The ATC envisaged, in respect of safeguard action, that Article XIX of GATT 1994 would apply in respect of products already integrated into GATT 1994, while Article 6 of the ATC would apply in respect of products yet to be integrated into GATT 1994. Article 6 of the ATC established a transitional safeguard mechanism that permitted WTO Members not only to impose quantitative restrictions inconsistently with Article XI of GATT 1994 but also to do so on a "Member-by-Member" basis, which were the terms used in Article 6.4 of the ATC to describe discriminatory actions inconsistent with Article XIII of GATT 1994.

5.29   *India* further argued that to impose burdens on particular exporters not because they engaged in dumping or benefitted from subsidies but merely because they were more efficient than others was contrary to the basic purpose of the multilateral trading order. There was, therefore, no other provision in the whole of the WTO legal system that permitted the imposition of restraints on imports from a particular WTO Member merely because it caused, or threatened to cause, damage to a domestic industry. The drafters of the ATC had explicitly recognized the exceptional character of the transitional safeguard in Article 6.1 of the ATC, according to which that safeguard "should be applied as sparingly as possible".

5.30   The *United States* argued that, in the present case, it had faithfully applied the procedures of, and its action was fully consistent with, Article 6 of the ATC. Article 6 should be interpreted in accordance with the ordinary meaning of its terms, in their context and in light of the ATC's object and purpose. Article 31.1 of the Vienna Convention provided that: "A treaty shall be interpreted in good faith in accordance with the ordinary meaning to be given to the terms of the treaty in their context and in the light of its object and purpose." Applying these principles, the ordinary meaning of the actual terms of Article 6.2 of the ATC was simply that a safeguard action may be taken based on a Member's determination that demonstrated that the requisite conditions of serious damage or actual threat thereof caused by increased import quantities existed and that the serious damage or actual threat thereof was properly attributable to the Member against which the measure had been applied. There was no basis in the text of Article 6 to assume that it must be interpreted narrowly or as an exceptional provision.

5.31   In the view of *India*, the highly exceptional character of the transitional safeguard in Article 6 of the ATC must be taken into account in interpreting that provision. GATT 1947 panels had repeatedly recognized that exceptions must be interpreted narrowly (see for instance BISD 30S/140 and 36S/345). This principle must be particularly strictly applied in the case of a provision which constituted not only an exception to the principles set out in Article XI of GATT 1994 but also to those set out in its Article XIII. This implied, *inter alia*, that it would be legally incorrect to weaken the disciplines established under Article 6 of the ATC by extending to the transitional safeguard mechanism, by analogy, legal principles developed under other safeguard provisions of the WTO legal system.

5.32   The *United States* argued that the safeguard mechanism in Article 6 of the ATC must be viewed as an integral part of the ATC and not as a "highly exceptional" provision. The Uruguay Round negotiators had designed the ATC to balance the interests of predominantly exporting Members and predominantly importing Members until the 10-year transitional period was over. Exporting Members were guaranteed that by 1 January 2005, all textile and clothing products would be subject to normal GATT rules. In addition, they were guaranteed that, where applicable, during the transition, products under quota would enjoy accelerated growth in access. Exporting Members were also guaranteed that specified percentages of products listed in the Annex to the ATC would be integrated into GATT 1994 in three stages. Once such products were integrated, quotas could not be maintained or placed on them except pursuant to Article XIX of GATT 1994. Importing Members, for their part, were provided with a special mechanism for safeguard actions that could be used during the 10-year transitional period if they were faced with serious damage or an actual threat thereof to their producers as a result of sharply increased imports. This balance of interests between accelerated quota growth and specified integration for the exporting Members and a special safeguard mechanism for the importing Members had enabled all sides to agree to the ATC.

5.33   *India* disagreed with the US view that importing Members had obtained the right to take safeguard action in exchange for accelerated quota growth and specified integration for the exporting Members. This argument overlooked the fact that the restraints applied under the MFA were inconsistent with the obligations of importing countries under GATT 1947. The removal of quotas provided for under the ATC in the textiles and clothing sector was not trade liberalization. Furthermore, India did not accept that the safeguard mechanism must be viewed as an integral part of the ATC and not as a "highly exceptional" provision; rather, India, while accepting that the safeguard provision was an integral part of the ATC, considered that it was also an exception to the basic principles of the GATT and the general safeguard provisions of Article XIX of the GATT and must be interpreted accordingly by the Panel.

5.34   On this aspect, the *United States* considered the context, object, and purpose of Article 6 of the ATC to be important. The ability to respond to import surges through the application of a transitional safeguard action was a key concession made in the Uruguay Round negotiations to predominantly importing Members. It counterbalanced the substantial and irreversible trade liberalization that was set out elsewhere in the ATC. For this reason, Article 6 of the ATC occupied a central position in the operation of the ATC during the 10-year transitional period. It would not be consistent with the circumstances of the negotiations to unduly circumscribe the manner in which Article 6 was interpreted. The reference in Article 6.1 of the ATC to the fact that the transitional safeguard "should be applied as sparingly as possible" did not alter this result. The phrase did not speak to how Article 6 should be interpreted with regard to a specific instance of serious damage, or actual threat thereof. The term "sparing" comes directly from Article 3.2 of the MFA. Under the MFA and now under the ATC, "sparing" did not and does not amount to abstaining from taking safeguard action when the requirements in Article 6 of the ATC were fulfilled.

5.35   The *United States* also pointed out that imports of woven wool shirts and blouses from India had increased 414 per cent from the year ending January 1994 to year ending January 1995. There was a definite decline in US domestic production concurrent with this surge in imports which compelled a finding of serious damage or actual threat thereof to the domestic industry. In making that determination, the US had followed all of the necessary procedures in the ATC in good faith taking into account some of the relevant factors listed in Article 6.3 of the ATC for which published information was available as well as information from contacts with producers on other factors for which published information was not available. The reasonableness of this determination was further illustrated by the fact that the TMB, comprised of members from exporting and importing Members, had reached a consensus supporting the application of a safeguard action by the United States.

Legal Analyses of Serious Damage or Actual Threat Thereof Suggested by the Parties

5.36   *India* argued that the onus of demonstrating serious damage or its actual threat was on the importing Member which had to choose at the beginning of the process whether it would claim the existence of serious damage or of actual threat. These were not interchangeable because the data requirements would vary with the chosen situation. Actual threat could only be established by the necessary data on imminent measurable imports, without which, the demonstration of actual threat was likely to be based on conjecture and not on concrete facts.

5.37   The *United States* argued in response that Article 6 of the ATC did not require it to choose between serious damage or actual threat thereof and there were no criteria, definitions or otherwise that separated the phrase "serious damage, or actual threat thereof". Nor had any such criteria existed under the MFA from which this phrase and the criteria in the ATC came. The tests suggested by

India which supplied criteria for serious damage and threat separately did not exist in the ATC. In particular, no separate test for actual threat was negotiated into the text of the ATC. Since the TMB must examine "serious damage, or actual threat thereof.", it was not constrained to make a finding based on whether a Member alleged both or not and the ATC did not require the TMB and the investigating authorities to choose between serious damage or actual threat. The ATC also did not require the TMB to make a finding based on the entire phrase.

5.38   *India* insisted that the ATC did delineate between serious damage and actual threat thereof. This delineation was reflected in the routine practice of the TMB to distinguish between serious damage and actual threat thereof in its recommendations. Therefore, if the TMB had actually come to the conclusion that a situation of "serious damage" existed, it would have said so in it findings. Since the TMB had not said in its finding that a situation of "serious damage" had been demonstrated, it was obvious that they did not consider that a situation of "serious damage" had been demonstrated. By comparing the manner in which the TMB had given its findings in respect of a number of other cases, it became clear that if the TMB had come to the conclusion that "serious damage" had been demonstrated, it would not have give the finding that "actual threat of serious damage" had been demonstrated.

5.39   *India* referred to the specific safeguard action on which the United States and India had held consultations in June 1995 and noted that it was an action based on a determination of serious damage while the TMB had endorsed, in August 1995, an action based on alleged actual threat of serious damage. India considered that the United States must have had doubts as to the legal justification of its determination of serious damage and the adequacy of its data because, when the US measure was reviewed by the TMB, it made the claim that imports from India had also presented an actual threat of injury and the United States had presented entirely new data. The TMB endorsed that new claim but not the one on which India and the United States had held consultations. The Diplomatic Note of the United States conveying its request for consultations had included a "Statement of Serious Damage" but it had not included any statement claiming an actual threat of serious damage. The safeguard action on which the United States had held consultations was thus an action allegedly designed to remedy the serious damage to the domestic industry which had already been caused by imports from India. The limited amount of data that had been made available during the consultations all related to the actual state of the industry and the imports that had already taken place. Besides, the Public Notice of CITA, dated 17 May 1995 (published in the US Federal Register on 23 May 1995), only mentioned "serious damage to the US industry producing woven wool shirts and blouses". Under these circumstances, the request by the United States could only be understood by India as a request concerning serious damage and India, therefore, examined the request only from that angle. Not having obtained the TMB's endorsement of the determination on which it had held consultations with India, the United States should have immediately withdrawn its safeguard action.

5.40   *India* also claimed that since the safeguard action endorsed by the TMB was an action on which the United States had never held any consultations with India, it therefore, never had any opportunity to challenge such action. India was of the view that the TMB had committed a serious error in failing to recognize that a situation of serious damage and a situation of actual threat of serious damage were two entirely different matters. A claim of serious damage must be accompanied by a demonstration that serious damage had already occurred and consequently substantiated according to Article 6.7 of the ATC by "specific and relevant factual information" related to that claim. In the case of serious damage, a retrospective analysis was required and the issue was: what damage had already been caused by imports? A claim of actual threat of serious damage must be accompanied by a demonstration that the domestic industry had reached a vulnerable stage and was on the brink of serious damage, so that any further sharp and substantial increase in imports would push the industry into a state of serious damage. In the case of actual threat, a prospective analysis must be performed and the issue was: which imports were imminent and what damage were they likely to cause? Different facts had to be demonstrated for each case and a consultation on serious damage could, therefore, not be deemed to comprise a consultation on threat of serious damage.

5.41   Furthermore, in the view of *India*, the footnote to Article 6.4 of the ATC clarified that the imminent increase in imports shall be measurable and shall not be determined to exist on the basis of allegation, conjecture or mere possibility. There were two elements in this type of situation: "imminence" in terms of time and "measurable" in terms of quantity. Imminent and measurable imports could be deduced from circumstances such as: goods were already on the high seas and due to arrive in the immediate future or when measurable quantities of goods had been delivered at the dockside for shipment or when the goods had been firmly contracted and were awaiting shipment, etc. The measurable quantities should be large enough to satisfy the stipulation of "sharp and substantial increase in imports".

5.42   The *United States* accepted that the Market Statement had referenced only "serious damage." However, the use of this shorthand phrase in the initial document was of no substantive consequence and was quickly corrected. The United States had expressly informed India in its diplomatic note that the case was based on the existence of "serious damage, or actual threat thereof" and during consultations the United States had explained to India all of the factors for its determination. India had also complained that the US had not expressly examined each and every factor listed in Article 6.3 of the ATC, but had failed to show why the US was required to do so. Article 6.3 referred to "such relevant economic variables as" those listed and that "none of [these factors] either alone or combined with other factors, can necessarily give decisive guidance". The United States clearly had examined factors "such as" the listed factors. The issue was not whether the US had discussed a particular set of factors in its entirety (even where data on some factors might not have been available), but whether the United States' examination was sufficiently meaningful so as to reasonably support the finding and to constitute a good faith application of the Article 6 standard.

5.43   In a response to the Panel, the *United States* pointed out that at no time before the TMB proceeding had India taken issue with the reference in the US diplomatic note requesting consultations on the basis of serious damage or actual threat thereof or that the shorthand had been used in the text of the Market Statement. India also had not asked the United States to clarify whether it had chosen between serious damage or threat in light of the apparent different reference in the Diplomatic Note and the April Market Statement. India had only asserted this point during the TMB proceeding. The United States Diplomatic Note to India was the official request for consultations. The reference to serious damage or actual threat thereof was always in the Diplomatic Note, therefore, no "correction" was necessary. In response to a question from India, the United States also explained that, in its view, India was aware that the entire phrase was the basis for the call, especially since neither the ATC nor the MFA, which had used the same phrase as a definition of "market disruption," separated the two or provided different criteria for each.

5.44   With respect to the above, *India* considered that no correction to the terminology in the Market Statement was possible since the Diplomatic Note which preceded the Market Statement transmitted a determination that had already been made and that determination related to serious damage only. The nature of that determination could not be changed through the Diplomatic Note transmitting it. India had to conclude, therefore, that an alleged situation of serious damage and not actual threat thereof, was the basis for the United States' request for consultations and for the substantive discussions during those consultations. The distinction between serious damage and actual threat thereof only became an issue in this case at the time of the TMB review.

5.45   The *United States* insisted that it had followed all procedures required under Article 6.2 and 6.3 of the ATC. The safeguard standard was "serious damage, or actual threat thereof."[15] Article 6.2 of the ATC provided, in part, that:

> "...safeguard action may be taken under this Article when, on the basis of a determination by a Member, [footnote omitted] it is demonstrated that a particular product is being imported into its territory in such increased quantities as to cause serious damage, or actual threat thereof, to the domestic industry producing like and/or directly competitive products. Serious damage or actual threat thereof must de-

---

[15]   Article 3 of the MFA provided that action could be taken to limit exports "causing market disruption as defined in Annex A..." Annex A of the MFA set forth a test for "market disruption," which was based on the existence of "serious damage to domestic producers or actual threat thereof". Annex A also sets forth factors for a determination similar to those found in Articles 6.3 and 6.4 of the ATC.

monstrably be caused by such increased quantities in total imports of that product and not by such other factors as technological changes or changes in consumer preferences".

5.46   The *United States* further submitted that Article 6 of the ATC provided no separate definition or separate factors applying to actual threat of serious damage as distinguished from serious damage. The phrase "serious damage, or actual threat thereof" was derived from the definition of market disruption in Article 3 of Annex A of the MFA. There, too, no separate factors for the two elements had been provided and the MFA's TSB had never supplied any. Article 6.3 of the ATC set out various factors for determining serious damage or actual threat thereof, resulting from increased quantities in total imports. That Article provided that:

> "[i]n making a determination of serious damage, or actual threat thereof, as referred to in paragraph 2, the Member shall examine the effect of those imports on the state of the particular industry, as reflected in changes in such relevant economic variables *as* output, productivity, utilization of capacity, inventories, market share, exports, wages, employment, domestic prices, profits and investment; none of which either alone or combined with other factors, can necessarily give decisive guidance".

5.47   In the view of the *United States*, the statement prepared by CITA had included sufficient information to justify its finding. Concerning serious damage or actual threat thereof caused by total imports, Article 6.2 and 6.3 of the ATC, the facts were, as provided in the Market Statement, that when CITA made its determination: (i) there was a surge in total imports of 94 per cent for the year ending January 1995 compared to the year ending January 1994; (ii) there was serious damage or actual threat thereof to US production of woven wool shirts and blouses as a result of that massive increase in total imports; (iii) the products involved were "like" and/or "directly competitive" woven wool shirts and blouses; US manufacturers competed with imports from India and other suppliers and were sold to the same stores; and (iv) there were adverse effects on investments, market share, employment (about 6 per cent of the workers in the woven wool shirt industry lost their jobs from 1994 to 1995 as a result of imports), in this small and volatile US industry. More specifically, the US found that imports of category 440 had surged from 44,363 dozen in 1992 to 141,569 dozen in 1994. At the same time data showed that production, after slightly rising in 1993, had suffered a decline of 8.4 per cent in 1994. Production continued to decline in 1995, 5.3 per cent below the year ending June 1994 level. Market share of domestic manufacturers declined, employment declined, investment, profits and capacity were adversely impacted by imports of category 440.

5.48   In a response to the Panel, the *United States* further explained that it did not consider that a finding of "actual threat of serious damage" required some sort of data, analysis or argumentation different from that required for a finding of "serious damage". In making its determination, the US was required to follow Article 6.2 and 6.3 of the ATC which provided the standard and some of the factors important in making a serious damage or actual threat thereof determination. Unlike the Agreement on Safeguards, there was nothing in Article 6 of the ATC providing different conditions to be met for serious damage on the one hand and actual threat thereof on the other hand. There were also no separate criteria. There was no requirement in the ATC spelling out the sort of analysis or argumentation required for serious damage or actual threat thereof. The United States did not believe it appropriate to read into the ATC any particular threat criteria.

5.49   In the view of *India*, there was a definite differentiation between the existence of serious damage and actual threat thereof and the absence in Article 6 of the ATC of different conditions to be met for one or the other did not remove this clear distinction. The factors contained in Article 6.3 and 6.4 of the ATC must be reviewed to determine whether or not the industry was facing a situation where serious damage existed or a situation where there was a threat of serious damage. The US Market Statement clearly identified the US determination that "serious damage" existed at the time of the request for consultations and there was no indication, or data supplied, that the limited factors reviewed by the US pointed to a condition which could be characterized as "actual threat" of serious damage to the domestic industry.

Status of the Market Statement

5.50   The *United States* stated that the information contained in the Market Statement constituted the totality of the information used by CITA in making its determination of serious damage, or actual threat thereof. Other relevant information had been supplied during consultations or pursuant to Article 6.10 of the ATC and was provided as updates or upon request to confirm the initial determination. The United States found no guidance in the ATC or DSU on whether the Market Statement should be the sole basis for the Panel to assess whether the US had acted in conformity with Article 6 of the ATC. Article 6 may lead one to conclude that the original data available at the time of the determination was legally relevant concerning the reasonableness of the determination of the importing Member. However, Article 6.10 of the ATC allowed additional or new/updated data for TMB review. Implicitly one would expect that if, during consultations, more data were requested, that data could be supplied, if available, to confirm a determination. Article 6.7 of the ATC only provided for data to accompany the request for consultations. In the context of consultations and Article 6.10 of the ATC, other relevant data and the TMB proceeding in this case, may only be persuasive information during Panel review. The United States believed that the December 1994 Market Statement had no legal status before this Panel since India had rejected the request for consultations based on that Statement and had demanded that the United States re-submit its request under the ATC. The Market Statement was the Statement accompanying the request under Article 6 of the ATC and the only Statement with status in this proceeding. However, some factual information in the December Market Statement was also reflected in the Market Statement in April 1995.

5.51   *India* argued that the United States had not fulfilled the requirements of Article 6 of the ATC in the Market Statement submitted to India in April 1995 as the basis for consultations on the proposed safeguard action. Furthermore, the US determination in this Market Statement was one of only "serious damage" which conveyed the conditions which the United States believed existed and should have been the limit of any TMB review. Also, the information contained in the Market Statement did not represent data on the "industry" which the United States claimed was experiencing "serious damage" due to increased imports but another, much larger industry and was not relevant to the economic variables to be examined in making the determination.

Sources of Data Provided By the United States

5.52   The *United States* explained that it had relied as much as possible on official data sources to assess objectively conditions in the domestic textile and clothing industries. Because the industry producing category 440, woven wool shirts and blouses, was a small one, there were limited published data available to supplement the official data on production and imports that formed the basis of CITA's determination of serious damage or actual threat thereof. Accordingly, in developing the additional information required to make its determination, CITA had relied heavily on information furnished by clothing manufacturers, particularly the two major companies that produced garments in category 440. This information had been collected by CITA through multiple phone calls and telefax exchanges. Because the information was collected from individual companies, it was treated on a business confidential basis. Further, the ATC did not provide a methodology for collecting data; it only noted in Article 6.7 of the ATC that when requesting consultations, the accompanying data must be "specific and relevant factual information, as up-to-date as possible."

5.53   While *India* accepted that Article 6.7 of the ATC required that the request for consultations be accompanied by "specific and relevant factual information, as up-to-date as possible", the requirement not to ignore the latest information available did not imply that the United States was freed of its obligation under Article 6.2 and 6.3 of the ATC to collect all the key economic data necessary to demonstrate that the domestic industry was suffering serious damage. To accept the argument of the United States on this point would turn the additional requirements set out in Article 6.7 of the ATC into an exemption from the requirements set out in Article 6.2 and 6.3 of the ATC which could not be correct.

5.54   The *United States* further pointed out that CITA had also used information and data provided by trade associations and labour unions which represented the companies and workers of this industry. The latter two sources were considered to be especially valuable because they had both an overview of industry information and a more objective perspective that the individual companies did not necessarily have. Using the above sources, CITA had identified the companies that manufactured woven wool shirts and blouses among the many manufacturers that produced woven shirts and blouses of all fibres and had questioned them on current business conditions, particularly the economic variables called for in Article 6 of the ATC. This information was then analyzed and detailed in the Market Statement. Because the textile and clothing programme was designed to adopt safeguard action expeditiously, it was not possible for the Office of Textiles and Apparel (OTEXA) to conduct any extensive, formal written surveys of manufacturers to obtain this information. Such formal surveys required advance notice and an extensive public comment period which would have prevented the adoption of a safeguard action in time to prevent serious damage or actual threat thereof to the industry in question.

5.55   *India* disagreed with some of the information in the preceding paragraph, arguing that official data on imports in category 440 were published in their entirety, including not only the aggregate imports assigned to category 440, but also the quantity, value, date of export, date of import, and country of origin for each of the HTS lines. In terms of the "official data on production", it was limited and there had been no indication that the US had been able to supplement this limited data in order to demonstrate production levels and trends of domestic production that would be comparable to all the products contained in import category 440. The specific and relevant data officially maintained by the United States on exports of products comparable to those contained in import category 440 had also been ignored by the US.

5.56   The *United States* pointed out, in response to a question from India, that in the case of the woven wool shirt and blouse industry, two firms accounted for a majority of US production, so the information reported was reasonably relied upon by CITA is indicative of conditions in the industry. Some information applied specifically to the woven wool shirt and blouse industry and some, in cases where the overall trend was reflective of conditions in the specific industry in question, reflected a broader scope.

E.   Demonstration of Serious Damage by the United States

5.57   *India* argued that the United States had failed in its Market Statement to demonstrate during the consultations that imported woven wool shirts and blouses were causing serious damage to its domestic industry and, therefore, had acted inconsistently with Article 6 of the ATC. Under Article 6.2 of the ATC, a WTO Member may take a safeguard action when

> "on the basis of a determination by a Member, it is demonstrated that a particular product is being imported into its territory in such increased quantities as to cause serious damage, or actual threat thereof, to the domestic industry producing like and/or directly competitive products".

In making such a determination, Article 6.3 of the ATC stated that a Member "shall examine the effect of those imports on the state of the particular industry, as reflected in changes in such relevant economic variables as output, productivity, utilization of capacity, inventories, market share, exports, wages, employment, domestic prices, profits and investment; none of which, either alone or combined with other factors, can necessarily give decisive guidance".

5.58   The *United States* argued that CITA had determined that high levels and surging imports of woven wool shirts and blouses coincided with a deterioration in the domestic industry's condition in terms of such factors as domestic output, market share, investment, employment, man-hours worked and total annual wages. Therefore, CITA had concluded that the surge in imports of woven wool shirts and blouses had caused serious damage or actual threat thereof to the industry. In the course of CITA's investigation into serious damage or actual threat thereof to the domestic industry producing woven wool shirts and blouses, there was no indication whatsoever that technological changes and/or changes in consumer preferences had resulted in the serious damage or actual threat thereof.

5.59   The *United States* considered that the first step for the Panel was to decide whether, pursuant to Article 6.2 of the ATC, there was evidence supporting CITA's decision that the domestic industry producing category 440 had been seriously damaged or threatened with such damage by reason of total imports not imports from India. The United States argued that it had demonstrated that total imports had caused, or actually threatened, serious damage to its highly sensitive industry producing woven wool shirts and blouses. This finding was consistent with Article 6.2 of the ATC, which provided that serious damage or actual threat thereof must demonstrably be caused by such increased quantities in "total imports" of that product and not by such other factors as technological changes or changes in consumer preference. Article 6.3 of the ATC provided that "[i]n making a determination of serious damage or actual threat thereof" the United States must examine the effect of imports on the state of the industry. In so doing the United States was to examine variables such as those listed in Article 6.3 of the ATC, "none of which, either alone or combined with other factors, can necessarily give decisive guidance." Support for the interpretation that the list was illustrative is also found in Article 6.7 of the ATC. There, data was to include "the factors, referred to in paragraph 3 [of Article 6], on which the Member invoking the action has based its determination of the existence of serious damage or actual threat thereof".

5.60   *India* considered that the list of factors included in Article 6.3 of the ATC was not meant to imply that the initiating Member was provided the liberty to select data for those "relevant economic variables" which were convenient or that the list of "relevant economic variables" was meant to be an exhaustive list of variables to be reviewed. Rather they represented the primary, minimum factors that should be available for review in order to make an informed and demonstrable determination of serious damage or actual threat thereof, to a specific industry.

5.61   *India* further argued that the issue before the Panel was not whether the ATC prescribed a specific evidentiary standard, but whether the United States had demonstrated a causal link between rising imports and declining production by noting their co-existence. India considered that rising imports and declining production must necessarily be present in all safeguard actions under the ATC, but the co-existence of the two could, therefore, not be sufficient to constitute a determination of a causal link.

India's Review of the Economic Variables

5.62   *India* argued that Article 6.3 of the ATC required a Member to examine the state of the particular industry, as reflected in changes in eleven factors: output, productivity, utilization of capacity, inventories, market share, exports, wages, employment, domestic prices, profits and investment. The United States' Market Statement on woven wool shirts and blouses provided figures on only four of these eleven factors: output, market share, wages and employment. In addition, the Statement included "industry statements" providing figures on domestic prices, and anecdotal information on investment and utilization of capacity. This left the Market Statement deficient with respect to four relevant economic variables, namely exports, profits, productivity and inventories.

5.63   *India* further argued that although Article 6.3 of the ATC indicated an illustrative list of factors, on which data had to be examined, it would be in order if an importing Member also examined other factors while making a determination. However, it would be inconsistent with Article 6.7 of the ATC if all the factors mentioned in Article 6.3 of the ATC were not taken into account by the importing Member. The "other relevant information" provided to the TMB by the US on 28 August 1995 was inconsistent with Article 6.10 of the ATC, because these were not the data supplied to the Indian delegation during the consultations. These data were also not available to the United States when it made its determination.

5.64   The *United States* noted that India had questioned the validity and relevance of some of the data in the Market Statement and the data furnished to the TMB in August 1995 and considered that these claims were without merit. With regard to India's claims that CITA's determination was invalid because it did not contain data on every factor listed in Article 6.3 of the ATC, the United States argued that CITA had examined factors for which information was available. The list of factors in Article 6.3 of the ATC was illustrative. The information supplied to India, and to the Panel, represented a strong case that would not be affected by data on other factors. Under Article 6.3 of the ATC, the issue was not whether CITA had discussed a particular set of factors in its entirety (even where data on some factors might not have been available), but whether CITA's examination was sufficiently meaningful so as to reasonably support the finding and to constitute a good faith application of the Article 6 standard.

5.65   The *United States* also pointed out that it had tried to provide information on the other, unpublished factors which India had characterized as anecdotal and unverifiable. Data on domestic prices was available from contacts with individual firms. There were about 15 firms that produced woven wool shirts and blouses in the United States and two firms accounted for at least 60 per cent of total US production. The information presented in connection with this case was based mainly on conversations with these two firms; therefore, that information was relevant and accurate.

United States Review of the Economic Variables

5.66   The *United States* argued that, in accordance with Article 6.3 of the ATC, it had reviewed relevant economic data such as output, market share loss, import penetration, employment, man-hours, wages, and domestic prices. It had also looked at other variables such as profits, investment, capacity, and sales. As described in the Market Statement, total imports of woven wool shirts and blouses had surged to 141,502 dozen in the year ending January 1995, nearly double the level of the year ending January 1994. The ratio of imports to domestic production had increased rapidly from 88 per cent in 1993 to 151 per cent during January-September 1994, thus indicating that imports had far surpassed the level of domestic production.

5.67   The *United States* further argued that these high and surging imports, at low prices, coincided with a deterioration in the industry's condition in terms of such factors as domestic output, market share, investment, employment, man-hours worked and total annual wages. Among these findings were that:

(a)   US production of clothing in category 440 had declined in the first nine months of 1994 with the level falling to 61,000 dozen 8 per cent below the 66,000 dozen produced during January-September 1993.

(b)   US producers' share of the domestic market had fallen from 53 per cent in 1993 to 40 per cent in the first nine months of 1994.

(c)   Employment in the industry producing woven shirts and blouses including shirts and blouses made from wool declined 6 per cent between 1993 and 1994.

(d)   Total annual production worker wages in the industry producing woven shirts and blouses including shirts and blouses made from wool had fallen 3 per cent over the same time period.

(e)   Average man-hours worked in the industry producing woven shirts and blouses including shirts and blouses made from wool had dropped 6 per cent between 1993 and 1994.

(f)   Prices for domestically produced woven wool shirts and blouses were substantially higher than imports.

(g)   Profit margins had deteriorated across the woven wool shirt and blouse industry as a result of raw material cost increases and the fact that companies were unable to raise prices because of low-priced imports.

(h)   Investment levels were stagnant throughout much of the industry.

(i)   Production capacity of several companies had declined, with one manufacturer of woven wool shirts and blouses reporting that the dropping of outside contracting represented the equivalent of closing four plants. That company ran at only 70 per cent of its capacity for its own manufacturing plants.

(j)   Most companies had reported sales declines as they lost market share to lower priced imports; some companies reported declines of 20 per cent or more.

The Industry and the Products

(i)   The Nature of the Wool Sector in the United States

5.68   The *United States* explained that the wool products sector of the US textile and clothing industry was very sensitive to imports. At each stage of processing, the production of wool products was more expensive and/or more complicated than production of most cotton and man-made fibre products and the sector was, therefore, more vulnerable to low-price import competition. Also, the market for wool products in the United States was very small relative to the market for cotton and man-made fibre products. Of the United States' total consumption of fibre (including the fibre content of imported products), wool accounted for only 1.9 per cent in 1995 compared to 56.9 per cent for man-made fibre and 38.5 per cent for cotton. The share of fibre consumption represented by US wool products manufacturers was even lower. With such a low share of the total textile and clothing market, US wool products manufacturers were notably exposed to serious damage or threat thereof from imports. While imports of all textile and clothing products averaged 10.0 per cent annual growth between 1990 and 1995, imports of wool products averaged 13.9 per cent annual growth.

5.69   The *United States* also advised that US firms producing wool clothing were in general much smaller compared to cotton and man-made fibre clothing manufacturers. The small size of wool clothing companies left them especially vulnerable to increased imports. Without the financial reserves of larger firms, wool clothing producers could not as readily withstand a sudden reduction in sales or a drop in prices due to import competition. The United States also noted that the sensitivity of the wool sector of the US textile and clothing industry had been recognized within the framework of the MFA and the ATC. Under the MFA regime, while growth rates for quotas on most man-made fibre or cotton products were traditionally set at 6 per cent per year, the United States had negotiated one per cent growth rates for wool quotas. The Textiles Surveillance Body (TSB) under the MFA allowed this exception to the standard growth rates for other fibre products. The negotiators of the ATC similarly had limited the growth rate to 2 per cent for wool products,[16] whereas all other products were required to be afforded a 6 per cent annual growth rate under Article 6.13 of the ATC. In the view of the US, because of this sensitivity in the wool sector, even a relatively small increase in imports could have a very pronounced and devastating impact on US producers of wool products.

5.70   In the view of *India*, there were no provisions in the ATC that would merit the wool clothing industry of the United States to be treated more favourably than any other sector of the US industry or the clothing industry of any other Member. The lower growth stipulated for restraint levels introduced under Article 6 for wool products came into operation only after the stage of justifying the restraint to the TMB and arriving at the appropriate level. Moreover, US import duties for woollen clothing were lower than the corresponding duties for woollen fabrics. Thus, it would appear that the US was more concerned about protecting its weaving industry in the wool sector rather than the clothing one. The exporters of India supplying woven wool shirts and blouses to the United States were all smaller in financial size as compared to the woven wool shirts and blouses in- dustry units of the United States. The adverse impact on such suppliers arising from a restraint had much more serious consequences than could occur to the US manufacturers from increased imports.

5.71   *India* further argued that it was not true that during the MFA regime a 6 per cent growth rate had applied to other textile products and 1 per cent growth rate had applied to wool products. In fact, some of the bilateral agreements of India had growth rates of less than 1 per cent for some items which were not wool products. There were several restraints under India's bilateral agreements with 6 per cent growth rate where woollen products were part of the restraints. Thus, growth rates ranging up to 6 per cent had operated under the MFA regime for several wool products and growth rates of 1 per cent or even less had oper- ated for non-wool products also. While an informal exception had been provided in the growth rate to be provided for restrained woollen products outside the text of the ATC, there was no other formal or informal indication in the context of the ATC that the manufacturers of woollen products were eligible for any other spe- cial consideration or exceptional treatment in protection against imports. It was also not correct for the United States to state that it had negotiated 1 per cent growth rates for wool products with all countries under the MFA. For example, the reported growth rates for selected wool clothing products from Colombia and Mexico were many times higher.

---

[16]   See *Note for the Record* dated 16 December 1993, Chairman Peter D. Sutherland, Trade Nego- tiations Committee, General Agreement on Tariffs and Trade, reprinted in G/TMB/N/107, 30 June 1995.

5.72   The *United States* considered that the above views of India did not contradict the essential truth of the US submission which was that the sensitivity of the wool sector of the United States' textile and clothing industry had been recognized within the framework of the MFA and the ATC. For US bilateral textile import restraint agreements under the MFA, growth rates for quotas on most man-made fibre or cotton products were traditionally set at 6 per cent per year, while the United States negotiated 1 per cent growth rates for wool quotas. In saying this, the United States was referring to specific limits on individual categories. US wool categories under group limit as in its bilateral agreement with India had a 6 per cent growth rate. None of these categories had specific limits applicable to it alone. Finally, India's last statement was not correct. The previous MFA Agreement with Colombia provided for one per cent growth for all wool clothing categories and the same could be said for the Mexican agreement prior to the NAFTA.

5.73   The *United States*, in response to a question from India, further argued that it had the flexibility under Article 6.6(c) of the ATC, to give to eligible Members a growth rate of more than 2 per cent, but less than 6 per cent. Thus, even Article 6.6(c) of the ATC recognized the sensitivity of importing Member's wool production to imports. The United States noted, however, that Article 6.6(c) of the ATC clearly did not apply to India since, *inter alia*, India's total textile and clothing exports did not consist "almost exclusively" of wool products. India's volume was not even comparatively small in the markets of importing Members. Further, even this provision did not mandate a 6 per cent growth rate for wool after safeguard action was taken, but allowed importing Members leeway when considering quota levels, growth rate, and flexibility.

5.74   Also in response to a question from India, the *United States* explained that the MFA had recognized the difficulties faced by importing countries with small markets, high levels of imports and correspondingly low levels of production in both its Annex B, paragraph 2 and in paragraph 12 of the 1986 Protocol of Extension. These paragraphs authorized lower positive growth rates than normally required under MFA Annex B. Although this language did not originate as a result of the US wool textile and clothing market, it had long been apparent that the language applied to this market. As a result, the United States had negotiated restraints on wool textile and clothing exports since the early 1970s, in all cases with one per cent growth rates for all specific limits covering wool textiles and clothing. The United States had negotiated growth rates of less than one per cent for wool textiles, but had never negotiated growth rates above one per cent. These rates had been accepted by the TSB after US explanations of the difficulties facing the wool textile and clothing producers. It was noted that the US' first written submission and oral statement noted that the ATC "limits" the growth rate. To clarify, the ATC, through the Sutherland Note (see footnote 16), provided that the rate shall be "no less than" 2 per cent in the context of Article 6.13 of the ATC. Similarly, Article 6.13 required that for other products the rate could be "no less than" 6 per cent. As such, the US' argument was that the minimum threshold for wool products under the ATC was considerably less than the minimum threshold for other fibres because of the import sensitivity of wool in importing Members, particularly in the United States.

5.75   *India* stressed that the MFA had not provided any explicit statements concerning the vulnerability of the wool sector to harm caused by even modest increases in imports. The MFA did recognize small markets which did not refer to particular products within the overall market. Therefore, in the absence of any data supporting the US conclusion of the vulnerability of wool products in the US' market, the application of the minimum allowable rate of two per cent and the request for consultations at low levels based on the vulnerability of the wool sector had no validity in the actions taken by the United States on category 440 from India.

(ii)   What Constitutes the Domestic Market

5.76   *India* argued that most of the facts which the United States had submitted first to India during the course of the consultations to support its claim of "serious damage", and subsequently to the TMB to support the later claim of "actual threat of serious damage", did not relate to the state of the industry producing woven wool shirts and blouses, but to the state of the industry producing woven shirts and blouses generally. These data would be irrelevant because the ATC required the United States to demonstrate that the particular industry producing woven wool shirts and blouses had suffered serious damage or threat thereof. That particular industry, however, represented less than one per cent of the employment in the industry producing woven shirts and blouses generally. The state of that industry gave, therefore, no indication of the state of the particular industry to be protected by the restraints on imports of woven wool shirts and blouses. The United States had submitted only two pieces of data that related to the particular industry designed to be protected by its safeguard action, namely, the data showing that in the first nine months of 1994, imports of woven wool shirts and blouses had increased to 92,000 dozen from a level of 43,000 dozen, i.e. an increase of 114 per cent, while domestic production of these products had marginally declined by 5,000 dozen from 66,000 dozen, that is by 8 per cent. Other information specifically related to the woven wool shirt and blouse industry on which the United States had based its determination was not positive evidence but mere allegation, including the "finding" that "production capacity of several companies had declined" without ascertaining the overall changes in capacity and the fact that it produced 5,000 dozen woven wool shirts and blouses less during a brief period of time.

5.77   *India* also noted that, with respect to market share loss, the US Market Statement stated that "the share of the US woven wool shirt and blouse market held by domestic manufacturers fell from 53 per cent in 1993 to 40 per cent in 1994". In Table II of the Market Statement, the term "market" was used to describe an artificial construct based on the sum of imports and domestic production, not the total quantity of woven wool shirts and blouses purchased by United States consumers. This resulted in misleading conclusions when a substantial share of domestic production was exported, as was the case for the United States industry. In the view of India, a portion of United States domestic production of woven wool shirts and blouses was exported and, therefore, must be subtracted from production figures to arrive at the portion of domestic production supplied to United States' consumers. In addition to the portion of domestic production that was not exported, domestic consumers may purchase from imported sources. The domestic market (consumption) for woven wool shirts and blouses, therefore, constituted domestic production minus exports plus imports. To determine changes in the share of imports in the domestic market, it was, consequently, necessary to examine not only changes in production and imports but also changes in exports.

5.78   Concerning the above, the *United States* explained that, for some time, CITA had treated the total market for a textile or clothing category as production plus imports. Similar market share findings by CITA had long been accepted by the TSB in their examination of requests by the United States. CITA had found that the market share held by domestic producers had declined in the face of surging total imports from 53 to 40 per cent. These data were public information in the Department of Commerce's publication on US imports, production, markets, import penetration rates and domestic market shares for textile and clothing product categories. India had contended that the information examined by CITA on market share was irrelevant or otherwise deficient, particularly because the market examined by CITA had not included changes in the quantity of exports The US had repeatedly informed India, the TMB and the Panel that US export quantity data was unreliable because of the low incentive of exporters to report the data. This fact was neither new nor unique to the United States as the export data from many other Members suffered from the same problems.

5.79   The *United States* also noted the comparability limitation in all of its wool clothing categories. This situation was long-standing, going back to the creation of the wool clothing category system when it was determined that imported clothing of fibres other than wool but containing greater than 17 per cent by value of wool actually competed in the same market as domestically produced wool clothing, which for production data purposes had always been defined as 51 per cent or greater of wool by weight. When the United States adopted the Harmonized Tariff Schedule (HTS) in January 1989, this definition was retained in shifting from a chief value to a chief weight system by altering the definition for imported wool clothing to those containing 36 per cent or greater of wool by weight. With full awareness of the anomaly in the data, CITA had considered the situation in the domestic woven wool shirt and blouse industry, as described in the definition of the US domestic industry production data it examined, i.e. woven wool shirts and blouses with 51 per cent or greater wool content. Although the import data included like and competitive products with a wool content as low as 36 per cent, there was no indication, in the record before CITA, the TMB or the Panel that imported lower wool content products did not compete with or negatively impact upon the domestic industry. The United States also noted that products from India were actually chiefly 51 per cent or more wool and the US industry was not producing less than 51 per cent wool.

(iii) Products Manufactured Domestically

5.80 *India* considered that the US has mischaracterized the industry that CITA had claimed as comparable to imports in category 440. In the US Market Statement, that industry was characterized as producing woven shirts and blouses of wool fabric. However, according to the US Correlation describing products assigned to imports in category 440, it was noted that woven shirts and blouses of man-made fibre fabric were included if the fabric contained 36 per cent or more by weight of wool. These man-made fibre woven shirts or blouses accounted for 15 to 25 per cent of all US imports in category 440 but none of these blended man-made fibre/wool shirts or blouses were included in the US production or employment data. According to the official Department of Commerce export data, over 35,000 dozen of the man-made fibre shirts containing 36 per cent by weight of wool were exported in 1993. The complete exclusion of export data in conjunction with the production and market data in relation to category 440 made any conclusion regarding the linkage between imports and production for the domestic market extremely questionable.

5.81 In this regard, the *United States* argued that it had not mischaracterized the industry producing woven wool shirts and blouses and that it was comparable to imports in category 440. As the US had pointed out, CITA was well aware of this comparability limitation in all of its wool clothing categories. The background of this situation was well documented in the US submission. It was important to point out that the current definitions underlying the import category system have been in place for many years, was well known to all of the major participants in international textile trade and had been explicitly accepted and agreed under the MFA and the ATC. India fully understood the US category system and was thoroughly familiar with the data that CITA employed to arrive at its determinations. It was disingenuous for India to suggest that the United States "has mischaracterized the industry" and that the information the United States provided contained "significant oversights". Furthermore, given the definition of wool clothing for production data purposes, there had never been any attempt to collect domestic production data on woven man-made fibre shirts and blouses containing 36 per cent or more by weight wool. Moreover, the United States has previously stated that the US industry, as defined by the production data corresponding to category 440, did not and had never manufactured this clothing. This fact was not controverted by the existence of a US export classification that identified man-made fibre clothing containing 36 per cent or more by weight of wool. Likewise, India's use of these export data, elsewhere shown by the United States to be erroneous, did not alter the conclusion that the US industry, as defined, did not produce such clothing.

5.82 The *United States* further explained that US domestic manufacturers of woven wool shirts and blouses did not produce this clothing in blends of greater than 36 and less than 50 per cent by weight of wool. The majority of the woven wool shirts and blouses produced in the US was 100 per cent wool; the few products with man-made fibre blends were of more than 50 per cent by weight of wool. Therefore, the production data provided in the Market Statement related only to "wool rich" woven shirts and blouses. Official data on export quantities could not be relied upon while estimates by industry sources indicated that less than 10 percent of US woven wool shirt and blouse production was exported. Therefore, since the domestic manufacturers produced only chief weight wool woven shirts and blouses, it could be concluded that no shirts of 36 per cent or more but less than 50 per cent or more by weight wool were exported. US imports of woven shirts and blouses containing 36 per cent or more by weight of wool were deemed to be wool garments, as such, they competed directly with other domestically produced or imported woven wool shirts and blouses in category 440.

Data on Domestic Production

5.83   *India* noted that, in contrast to the declining production in the wool segment of the industry, production in the industry as a whole had risen from 30,509 thousand dozen in 1993 to 32,767 thousand dozen in 1994, an increase of 7.4 per cent. Declining production in the wool sector might, in fact, be explained by the rising production in shirts and blouses made from fibres other than wool, as machines were shifted from wool production lines to other lines. A plausible explanation for the shift in production within the woven shirts and blouses industry was the commercial attraction of other product lines and not increased imports. If the United States industry had been unable or unwilling to respond to the upsurge in United States consumer demand for woven wool shirts and blouses, this was not an indication of "serious damage" from imports. Also, if high capacity utilization in the production of other fibres had made more commercial sense to the woven shirt and blouse industry than the production of wool shirts and blouses, a market which had been shrinking for twelve years, then the marginal decline in the production of wool shirts and blouses could not possibly be attributed to increasing imports. According to Article 6.2 serious damage or actual threat thereof must demonstrably not be caused by "such other factors as technological change or changes in consumer preference". The statement of serious damage clearly did not constitute a good faith effort to fulfil that requirement.

5.84   In a response to the Panel, *India* explained its view that there was a demonstrable lack of correlation between changes in imports and changes in US domestic production and that, in general, the level of US domestic production had not changed in proportion to the level of imports. It was not correct, in India's view, to assume that this decline was caused by an increase in imports. In the Market Statement it was stated that "there are approximately 748 establishments in the United States that manufacture woven shirts and blouses including shirts and blouses made from wool". The official data on US production indicated that the total production of woven shirts and blouses had increased from

29.6 million dozen in 1992 to 30.8 million dozen in 1993, an increase of 4 per cent, and production in 1994 had grown by 5.9 per cent over the 1993 level to 32.6 million dozen. These data would indicate that the US industry producing woven shirts and blouses had increased production during the period from 1992 to 1994. India argued that a decision by these establishments as to the selection of fibre and fibre blends might have changed, but the fact that the actual production of these woven shirts and blouses had increased could not be denied.

US Production, Total Imports and Imports from India
Woven Wool Shirts and Blouses
Category 440
(Dozen)

			Year Ending June		
	1993	1994	1994	1995	95/94 Per cent Change
Production	81,000	74,000	76,000	73,000	-3.9
Imports					
Total	72,302	141,569	80,456	144,034	79.0
India	14,787	76,809	22,994	70,856	208.2

Source: US Submission, 20 September 1996

5.85   *India* noted with respect to the above Table that the United States had excluded the data for 1992 which was available at the time of the Market Statement. The 1992 data would show that production had increased from 1992 to 1993 as had imports. Thus, the correlation between production declines and import increases was not demonstrated. Furthermore, if the US were to have included the export data as well, there would be significant changes in CITA's reported size of the market and perhaps different conclusions concerning the impact of declining exports on the level of US production. In India's opinion, based on the available official US data, the declining export levels would have had a greater impact on this sub-industry than any other feature. In addition, the US should have noted that the production data presented in its Table did not include any man-made fibre woven shirts and blouses containing 36 per cent or more by weight wool, while between 15 to 25 per cent of the import data contained these particular products.

5.86   In response, the *United States* explained that the 1992 production data for woven wool shirts and blouses that was available at the time of the April 1995 request was preliminary data. Since the preliminary data was being reviewed at that time and final 1992 production numbers would be published shortly thereafter, the United States chose not to include the preliminary 1992 production number in the Market Statement. Production data for wool clothing categories was small compared to production data for other clothing categories. Given the small quantities of wool clothing production, even minor revisions to the preliminary production numbers could result in significantly different final production numbers. However, in the particular case of category 440, woven wool shirts and blouses, the final 1992 production number was the same as the preliminary number: 80,000 dozen.

5.87   Commenting further on the above points, the *United States* considered that India was introducing US export data identifying shipments of man-made fibre shirts containing 36 per cent or more wool as evidence of US production of these shirts and in support of its argument that a decline in exports of these shirts accounted for the observed decline in woven wool shirt and blouse production by the US industry. The United States pointed out that it had previously stated that the US industry under consideration in this case did not and had never manufactured the clothing of low wool content defined by this export classification. Moreover, the United States had repeatedly pointed out the unreliability and inaccuracy of US export data in quantity terms, making this information unsuitable for analytical purposes.

5.88   *India* noted that the US had rejected its contention that a given decline in production might have been the result of reduced export demand but insisted that the decline in US exports was official and indicated a precipitous decline from 1992 to 1993 to 1994. These data appeared not only in the US Department of Commerce, Bureau of Census data, but also in the US Department of Agriculture data.

5.89   The *United States* replied to a question by India concerning the decline in domestic production of 5,000 dozen units in the first nine months of 1994 while imports more than doubled to 92,000 dozen in the same period in relation to the trend of the past decade when domestic production had not varied in proportion to imports. In the US view, the production data for category 440 was not comparable with data prior to 1992. However, the data made available to the TMB in August 1995 showed that for the three comparable, consecutive calendar years of production and import data, the proportion of imports to domestic production had more than tripled, increasing from 56 per cent in 1992 to 191 per cent in 1994.

5.90   The *United States* also replied to a question from India that the decline in production of 5,000 dozen units could be explained by a loss of export orders rather than an increase in import competition. The US rejected India's view that a given decline in production might have been the result of reduced export demand. CITA had found ample evidence of damage or the threat of damage occurring to US producers of woven wool shirts and blouses due to import competition and had received no information that there had been a decline in export orders. The United States also pointed out that, because of the relatively small number of woven wool shirts and blouses produced in the US, after rounding, the preliminary and final 1992 production data reflected in December 1994, April 1995, and currently were the same 80,000 dozen.

Data on Exports

5.91   *India* argued that, to determine whether the share of imports of woven wool shirts and blouses into the United States' market rose or fell in 1994, it was necessary for the United States to collect data on exports that were comparable to those for imports and production. The United States Market Statement had not included such data.[17] It was the responsibility of a Member that decided to impose a safeguard action to be in a position to provide all data relevant to an assessment of serious damage or actual threat thereof, and in particular exports. Otherwise, a safeguard action could not be taken consistently with Article 6 of the ATC. India had obtained figures on United States exports of woven wool shirts and blouses from official United States publications.[18] According to these data, virtually all the United States production of woven wool shirts and blouses was exported, leaving imports to satisfy demand. This suggested that imports had satisfied a domestic market that had not been supplied by domestic producers and that changes in the level of imports could consequently not cause damage to the domestic industry.

5.92   In addition, *India* considered that, in order to determine whether, and to what extent Indian shirts and blouses were actually competing with US-made shirts and blouses in the United States market, the US would need to examine, *inter alia*, which portion of US production was sold domestically and which portion was sold abroad. The United States had refused to do so, claiming that its official export data were unreliable and that it could proceed on the basis of the "best data available". However, under the ATC, the United States must base its determination on a demonstration that it was the increase in imports and not other factors that had caused the serious damage and the United States must, therefore, collect the data necessary to make that demonstration. If the best information available did not include export statistics, while these statistics were necessary to make that demonstration, then the United States could not take the safeguard action.

5.93   In response to India's claims that the domestic industry could not be damaged by imports because domestic producers had chosen to export virtually their entire production, the *United States* explained that because of the known inaccuracy of the US export data, which had been pointed out at the time of the TMB proceeding in August 1995, official US export data could not be used to calculate the volume of the US market. The point made by India, that the entire production of the US woven wool shirt and blouse industry had been exported, was completely false and needed to be corrected. Official data on export quantities was highly suspect and could not be relied upon to assess conditions in the industry.

---

[17]   In its August 1995 submission to the TMB, the United States provided data on the dollar value of exported wool woven shirts and blouses. These data cannot be compared to the data provided on imports and production. The reason is that the export data supplied by the United States is in value (dollar) terms while the data on imports and production is in quantity terms (dozens). The United States explained in a footnote that export quantity data are questionable due to reporting inconsistencies.

[18]   1993: Production 82,000 and Exports 85,000. 1994: Production 76,000 and Exports 76,000.

Estimates by industry sources indicated that approximately 10 per cent of US woven wool shirt and blouse production had been exported.

5.94   The *United States* expanded upon the above points, explaining that it already knew from the two largest manufacturers in the industry that only 10 per cent of their production was exported. This information had been collected on a business confidential basis and no random sampling or scientific analysis was required or could be read to be required in the ATC. Nor was it necessary in this case where only 15 firms comprised the entire domestic industry. The data covering 60 per cent of the industry was excellent coverage and certainly CITA's reliance on this data was reasonable. In terms of exports, other sources were better than the official US data and this was also a problem with export data of other countries. India was wrong in stating that if it were true that there was a weak incentive to report export data accurately, this was true also of production and import data. In the United States reporting of production data from manufacturers was required by law and better reporting of import data was also required by law for duty collection and quota monitoring purposes in particular. This was not the case for exports.

5.95   The *United States* also explained that it had not provided India with the table referred to in paragraph 43 of India's first submission to the Panel; India had evidently developed the table on its own. The US reiterated that it had pointed out during consultations with India and during the August TMB proceedings that US export quantity data could not be used to calculate the volume of the US market because of the known inaccuracies of the export data. Even after all the shortcomings of the export quantity data were explained by the US in detail during the TMB review, India continued to use the inaccurate export data it obtained to incorrectly point out that the entire production of the US wool woven shirt and blouse industry was exported.

5.96   *India* reiterated that official US export data were available and was published not only by OTEXA, but also by the US Department of Commerce, Bureau of Census and the US Department of Agriculture. The detailed, and official export data of the United States allowed for a review of the quantity, value, and trends of exports of very specific and particular products including those that would be comparable to the import data contained in category 440. The facts, as presented in the official export data, indicated a clear decline in US export levels of products comparable to those in category 440. In particular, HS number 6205.30.15.00 identified exports of man-made fibre shirts containing at least 36 per cent by weight of wool and even if, as CITA contended, the data were not accurate, it at least indicated that a significant decline in the export of these products occurred between 1992 and 1994.

5.97   In response, the *United States* further advised that estimates obtained by CITA from the two largest individual domestic producers indicated that no more than 10 per cent of US woven wool shirt and blouse production was exported. If the market was adjusted for exports, assuming exports accounted for 10 per cent of the domestic production, the domestic market share in 1993 would decline from 53 to 51 per cent and for the first nine months of 1994 would fall from 40 to 37 per cent. As a result, the import market share in 1993 would increase from 47 to 49 per cent and for January-September 1994 would increase from 60 to 63 per cent. More generally, in characterizing the US data as unreliable, India was apparently contending that an importing Member could not resort to its ATC Article 6 rights to take a safeguard action without first obtaining all of the data necessary to respond to any conceivable challenge the exporting Member might make, and that all of these data must be publicly available. Acceptance of this argument would require that the data presented by importing Members in justification be limited only to information obtainable from public sources, however limited or inapplicable that information might be. In fact, there was no such limit in the ATC.

5.98   In summing up its argumentation, *India* claimed that the responsibility for compiling, examining and supplying to the exporting country the relevant data in respect of factors referred to in Article 6.3 of the ATC was entirely that of the importing Member. In the present case, the US had not supplied any information to India either in the consultation request or during the consultations, relating to one very important element to determine the state of the US industry *vis-à-vis* the exports effected by the US industry in category 440. India had collected US export data from the figures published by the US Department of Commerce. The US termed its own published data as "inaccurate" and "unreliable" but were not in a position to furnish any more reliable and accurate export data. If the published US data could not be used to assess the volume of US exports then there was no other way of correctly doing so. Different figures on production and exports as published by the US have been tabled by India and these figures have shown that a quantity equal to the entire production of the US in category 440 was exported. The US presentation claimed that the published official data of the United States on export quantities was highly suspect and suggested that "estimate by industry sources indicate that approximately 10 per cent of wool shirts and blouses production is exported". India submitted that the estimate of approximate quantities by the industry sources could not be held more reliable than the official data published by the US.

5.99   In the view of *India*, the US submission also failed to explain whether the exports of man-made fibre/wool blended shirts containing between 50 per cent and 64 per cent of man-made fibre had been taken into account while estimating wool shirt and blouse exports, while for import purposes, these were considered under category 440. It was India's understanding that in the absence of any specified procedure for culling out the export data, these were classified as man-made fibre shirts for export purposes. US data on the export of these blended fibre shirts had been submitted to the Panel in India's response to questions on 20 September 1996 and these data had shown that the entities exporting these products had experienced a significant decline in 1994 whether reported in dollars, dozen, or raw fibre equivalents. It was, therefore, more than reasonable to assume that this decline in exports would have more of an impact on the industry data supplied by the United States than any increase in imports.

5.100 The *United States* also summed up its position which had consistently been that US export quantity data was unreliable and could not be used in assessing conditions in the US industry. India had persisted in using this flawed evidence not only to support its untrue assertion that most of US production in category 440 was exported but also to denigrate the US production data and market share calculations. The deficiency of the export data stemmed from the low incentive of exporters to properly report the data and the absence of procedures to verify its accuracy. As pointed out in an attachment to the first US submission to the Panel, the Trade Data Division of OTEXA and the Bureau of the Census conducted an investigation of US exports of woven wool shirts and blouses and found that in 53 of the 201 exportations, the quantity reported was either zero or unrealistic; the Census Bureau talked with two US exporters who said they exported clothing but had no idea of its fibre content. The 6-digit Schedule B number was reported incorrectly in 4 of the 6 records examined and the correct Schedule B number could not be determined. More recently, in response to questions raised by India regarding US exports under Schedule B number 6205.30.1500, men's and boys' shirts of man-made fibre, containing 36 per cent or more by weight of wool, the Trade Data Division had conducted a shipment-by-shipment investigation of this export data. This investigation covered 1994 shipments of 7,554 dozen shirts which were made in 32 separate shipments. Most of the shipments were small and from different companies to different countries. However, four shipments were made by the same company to Honduras and represented 51 per cent of the total exports in this particular Schedule B number, i.e. 3,840 dozen. The Trade Data Division requested the Foreign Trade Division of the Bureau of the Census to review the data reported in these shipments. They found that all the shirts in these export shipments were in fact cotton woven shirts and were incorrectly classified. The 3,840 dozen shirts should have been classified under Schedule B number 6205.20.3000, men's and boys' woven shirts of cotton, not 6205.30.1500, for wool.

5.101 In the *United States'* view, the results of this investigation supported OTEXA's previous investigations and determinations that US export quantity data were not reliable. India's assertion that the estimate of approximate quantities of exports obtained by "industry sources cannot be held more reliable than the official data published by the United States Government" was wrong. Investigations conducted by OTEXA and the Bureau of the Census clearly indicated that US export quantity data were unreliable and inaccurate, making this information unsuitable for analytical purposes. CITA had, as mentioned above, obtained estimates from the two largest individual domestic producers of woven wool shirts and blouses, representing at least 60 per cent of domestic production, and they had indicated that no more than 10 per cent of US woven wool shirt and blouse production was exported. There was no basis to contend that information specifically requested from and supplied by companies about an important component of their sales would not be more reliable than unverified data that had been proven incorrect.

5.102 *India* argued that the calculation of export levels should have been made on the basis of reliable data when the determination of serious damage was made, and not subsequently in response to a query by India in the context of a panel proceeding. The recalculations of the United States only served to highlight the point made by India that export data were essential for the calculation of market share, and that data and other information used in a determination of serious damage must be verifiable to constitute the basis of the demonstration required under Article 6 of the ATC.

5.103 *India* also noted the United States had claimed that it was consistent with the requirements of Article 6.2 and 6.3 of the ATC to collect data on total production by directly contacting the producers benefitting from the safeguard action and at the same time it claimed that the data on the exports of domestic production was not available because the official export statistics were not reliable. It was questioned why the United States considered it consistent with the ATC to collect the information favourable to domestic producers (total production) informally through direct contacts, but it was only after its determination of serious damage that the United States informally contacted two of the fifteen producers to obtain information on the share of its production exported. Why was this not done before making the determination?

Data on Employment,[19] Man-hours and Wages

5.104 *India* pointed out that, with respect to employment, man-hours and total annual wages, the information provided in the Market Statement referred to the "748 establishments in the US that manufacture woven shirts and blouses including shirts and blouses made from wool". The Statement made reference to the fact that "employment in the industry producing woven shirts and blouses including shirts and blouses made from wool had declined to 31,929 production workers in 1994, six per cent below the 1993 level and a loss of 2,125 jobs". If the loss of 2,125 jobs was placed in relation to a decline in United States production of woven shirts and blouses from wool of 5,000 dozen between January-September 1993 and January-September 1994, it implied that a decline in production of 3 dozen woven shirts and blouses on an annual basis led to the loss of one job, clearly an absurd inference. The Statement went on to claim that "the average annual man-hours worked dropped" and total annual production worker wages fell", even though both claims referred to the industry producing all woven shirts and blouses, not the portion producing woven wool shirts and blouses. The fact that data on the industry producing all woven shirts and blouses was entirely irrelevant to the sub-sector making woven wool shirts and blouses was confirmed by the information submitted by the United States to the TMB in August 1995 under "Other Relevant Information". In the August 1995 submission, it was made clear that 200 workers were employed in the production of woven wool shirts and

---

[19] See also paragraphs 5.154 to 5.156

blouses in 1994, as compared to 215 workers in 1993, a total loss of 15 positions. India considered that data on employment, wages and man-hours at a more disaggregated level for the specific industry producing woven wool shirts and blouses should have formed part of the Market Statement provided to India as the basis for the consultations in April 1995, and were requested by India at the time. Employment figures submitted by the United States in April 1995 and August 1995 were:

Year	April 1995			August 1995		
	Work-ers	Average annual man-hours	Total annual wages	Work-ers	Average annual man-hours	Total annual wages
1993	34054	62500000	$423100000	215	413000	$2713000
1994	31929	58900000	$411200000	200	382000	$2590000

Sources: April 1995 employment data from Table III of United States statement of serious damage; August 1995 employment data from Table III of United States submission to TMB.

5.105 *India* also noted that the data on employment in the wool shirt and blouse sector was specifically requested during the consultations and the Indian delegation was informed that such data did not exist. However, the data on employment in the wool shirt and blouse industry was included in the so-called "other relevant information" provided to the TMB on 28 August 1995.

5.106 *India* further pointed out that if the figures on employment provided by the United States in August 1995 were placed in relation to those provided by the United States in its April 1995 Market Statement, they indicated that the wool sub-sector accounted for 0.6 per cent of employment in the woven shirt and blouse industry. Since the sub-sector was an extremely small, if not negligible, portion of employment in the domestic woven shirts and blouses industry, the figures provided by the United States on employment, man-hours and wages in its Market Statement were totally irrelevant.

5.107 With respect to the above point, the *United States* claimed that it had indicated to India during consultations that employment data relating specifically to category 440 were not available, meaning only that such data could not be obtained directly from published sources nor was it regularly compiled for CITA. Data on employment and wages were published only at a higher level of aggregation than the woven wool shirt and blouse industry and at the time of the request the data given in the Market Statement was the most detailed that CITA was able to provide. It was not true, as India was implying, that the United States deliberately withheld such data from the Indian delegation during consultations. In actuality, when it became apparent that the justification for the request was being questioned by India because of the lack of this data and after indications from the TMB that such data would be a necessary element of their consideration of the case, CITA pursued ways of developing the requested information. Only after developing a methodology to further disaggregate the available data was OTEXA later able to provide, at the insistence of India during consultations and in accordance with the wishes of the TMB, more specific estimates based on additional information obtained from official and industry sources, which confirmed the downward trend of the broader category data reflected in April 1995.

5.108 In response to the points raised by India, the *United States* commented that it was correct that the employment-related information from the Market Statement was applicable to the industry producing woven shirts and blouses. CITA believed the more aggregated data to be generally indicative of the trend in the woven wool shirt and blouse industry at that time and received information from industry sources confirming this fact. OTEXA was later able to provide more specific estimates based on additional information obtained from official and industry sources.

5.109 *India* commented that the US had not explained why the more aggregated data of the total woven shirt and blouse industry was not indicative of the trend in terms of production, prices, profits, exports, imports, or any of the other relevant economic variables that should be reviewed prior to making a determination of serious damage or actual threat thereof. The increased production in the total woven shirt and blouse industry appeared to be ignored at the aggregate level because it contradicted the conclusion made by the United States concerning the trend in production data.

5.110 The *United States* referred to the above claim of India that the figures supplied by the United States on employment, man-hours, and wages were irrelevant because they covered the entire woven shirt and blouse industry and not just the woven wool shirt and blouse industry. The US pointed out that employment data presented in the Market Statement encompassed the entire US woven shirt and blouse industry and were derived from official Bureau of Labour Statistics (BLS) data covering even higher clothing production aggregates. This was the best information available at the time of the request for consultations. As a result of questions during consultations mandated by Article 6 of the ATC and as indicated by the TMB, the United States had provided the TMB with a breakdown of employment for category 440, woven wool shirts and blouses. CITA believed the more aggregated data to be generally indicative of the trend in the woven wool shirt and blouse industry at that time and received information from industry sources confirming this fact. CITA did not look at the trend in production for the woven shirt and blouse industry since CITA already had production data relevant to the wool sector of this industry.

5.111 The *United States* pointed to India's claim that because later data had shown that the number of jobs lost in the woven wool shirt and blouse industry was estimated at only fifteen jobs, there was no basis for the US determination of serious damage or actual threat thereof. In this regard the US recalled that the domestic industry in category 440 was very small, representing only 15 firms. Even though the loss of 15 jobs may, at first glance, appear small in absolute terms, it represented almost a 7 per cent decline in the number of production workers in one year. It would be difficult to argue that this was not a significant relative loss of employment. Furthermore, the United States found no indication in the language of Article 6.2 and 6.3 of the ATC that the term "domestic industry" was reserved for larger groupings of companies with greater numbers of workers. Indeed, the language of Article 6.2 of the ATC referred to "safeguard action" and the "domestic industry producing like and/or directly competitive products." This language placed no legal barriers on the maintenance of a safeguard action where the product may be narrowly defined or the industry small.

5.112 In response to a question from India asking if the number of production workers certified as eligible to apply for Worker Adjustment Assistance (220 workers) was more than nine times the decline of production workers (24 workers) during the April 1993-April 1995 period, the *United States* explained that the 220 workers employed in facilities producing woven wool shirts and blouses, that were certified as eligible for Workers Adjustment Assistance during the two and a half year period, January 1993-July 1995, included production workers as well as those workers employed in administrative, sales, and distribution positions associated with such production. Not all workers certified as eligible for Workers Adjustment Assistance had permanently lost their jobs; in many cases, workers were partially separated or temporarily laid off. (See also paragraphs 5.157 to 5.159.)

Information on Prices

5.113 *India* questioned if the information on domestic prices in the Market Statement could be considered to be representative of the situation of the particular segment of the industry producing woven wool shirts and blouses. According to the Market Statement, the industry statements were "based on information supplied by individual US firms domestically producing shirts and blouses", and "in general ... applies to companies producing men's and women's woven wool shirts and blouses". In other words, the information had been obtained from enterprises that manufactured woven wool shirts and blouses as part of their production of woven shirts and blouses. It was also questioned if it was appropriate to use informal surveys of enterprises as the basis for taking an action against the imports of a trading partner. During the bilateral consultations held in April and June 1995, India's delegation had sought clarifications from the United States' delegation regarding the underlying methodology that had been used. The United States delegation' had confirmed that there was no procedure for regular or periodic compilation of price data. Data relating to price and the disaggregation of employment data for specified product segments such as woven wool shirts and blouses etc. were based on informal surveys of a limited number of firms producing these items. There was no scientific random method or a stipulated sample size for such surveys. It was also noted that the firms responding to such surveys were always aware that the purpose of the survey was to initiate a safeguard action to protect that segment of the industry.

5.114 In the view of *India*, the informal methods used to survey enterprises might explain the wide variations of the results of such surveys reflected in the different industry statements furnished by United States. For example, in the December 1994 request for consultations, the average producers' price was reported as $215-225, while in the Market Statement, the average producers' price was reported as $525-550. Since it was unlikely that producer prices would double in such a short period of time, this discrepancy between the two Statements by the United States cast doubt on the consistency of information collected by informal surveys.

5.115 The *United States* explained that the difference in the two prices was not caused by an increase in domestic prices; rather, the two prices represented the average prices of two different groups of products. Prices as reported in the December 1994 market statement for category 440 under the MFA reflected the average domestic producer prices for wool shirts comparable to wool shirts imported from India which were concentrated in one of the 24, 10-digit product classifications in the Harmonized Tariff Schedule of the United States Annotated (HTSUSA) that made up category 440. This had been done because MFA determinations were based on sharp and substantial increases in products by country. The US had compared the average, landed duty-paid value of wool shirts imported from India classified under HTSUSA 6205.10.2010 men's wool shirts, other than hand loomed and folklore shirts with the average price of domestically produced men's woven wool shirts. The average US producers' price in the Market Statement issued in April 1995 under the ATC represented the average domestic price for all woven wool shirts and blouses produced in the US which competed with all woven wool shirts and blouses imported from every country in category 440. Under the ATC, the initial determination was on total imports in the category. Therefore, the $525/$550 per dozen average import price in the Market Statement was examined based on the United States' reading of Article 6.2 of the ATC requirement of an examination of "total imports". By contrast, the $215/$225 average import price in December 1994 was based on a particular product from a particular country (i.e. India) which was the analytical approach required by the MFA.

5.116 The *United States*, in response to a question by India whether the substantial price differences could be explained by quality differences (low priced imports and high priced domestic production), responded that the average landed duty-paid import value for total US imports of category 440, woven wool shirts and blouses, was $US 187.23 per dozen while such imports from India were valued at $US 133.85 per dozen or 75 per cent below the average US producers' price for domestically produced woven wool shirts and blouses, and 29 per cent below the category 440 average landed duty-paid value for total US imports of woven wool shirts and blouses. The price difference between domestically produced woven wool shirts and blouses and imports (including those from India) was primarily the result of differences in labour costs that varied among all countries producing woven wool shirts and blouses. Quality differences reflected in prices of woven wool shirts and blouses included differences in hand tailoring, the quality of wool fabric, fibre content, fibre blending, detail included, etc. which varied among all countries that produced woven wool shirts and blouses. The domestic price for woven wool shirts and blouses reflected the average price of all domestically produced woven wool shirts and blouses and was compared with the average landed, duty-paid import values at the category level (all products imported in the category) from each country supplying the US market and the average import value for all supplying countries. The United States did not accept India's assumptions that in a single market prices of competing products would "normally tend to converge" or that products of different quality and which were sold at varying retail prices could not "compete".

5.117 In response to the above point, *India* noted that the US had established a number of "quality differences" for these woven wool shirts and blouses, but offered no data on the various quantities that were produced among these various quality differences. It would have been interesting to see the trend in production of those shirts which in December 1994 were at $225 per dozen for comparable shirts being imported from India, whereas the average US price for all woven wool shirts and blouses was $550 per dozen. This would have indicated that not only was there a wide quality difference among the shirts produced in the United States, but also that those shirts which were directly comparable and competitive with the shirts from India may have increased or producers may have shifted to the higher value shirts. There must have been some discrimination in the presentation of price and production data that would indicate that US data were comparable to those products in category 440 which were claimed to be seriously damaging or actually threatening serious damage to US producers of "like and/or directly competitive products".

5.118 The *United States* noted in this regard that quality differences, as reflected in prices of woven wool shirts and blouses varied among all countries that produced woven wool shirts and blouses. The domestic price for woven wool shirts and blouses reflected the average price of all domestically produced woven wool shirts and blouses and was compared with the average landed, duty-paid import values at the category level from each country supplying the US market and the average import value for all supplying countries. Domestic producers of woven wool shirts and blouses in the relatively narrow category 440 competed with imports from India and from all the other suppliers.

Information on Investment and Capacity

5.119 *India* noted that the Market Statement had included information on investment and utilization of capacity based on industry statements. As follows:

Variable	Information provided in the April 1995 Market Statement
Investment	"Investment levels are stagnant across much of the industry."
Utilization of capacity	"Several companies reported a decline in capacity. One company reported ending all outside contracting production (formerly about 25 per cent of their manufacturing), representing the equivalent of closing four plants. The company's own manufacturing plants are now running at only 70 per cent of capacity. Furthermore, this company also operates several woollen fabric mills which supply the apparel manufacturing plants, and these mills are now running at about 65 per cent of capacity."

5.120   This information was, in the opinion of *India*, anecdotal and unverifiable. It was also unclear whether the information referred to the particular segment of the woven shirt and blouse industry producing garments made from wool. For example, the fact that "several companies reported a decline in capacity" did not appear to be significant in the context of an industry reported by the United States in its Market Statement as comprising 748 establishments. It was also argued that one company reported dropping of contracts or reduced capacity utilisation which was not an appropriate indication of the capacity utilisation for the entire industry. If the production capacities of several companies that had actually declined were related to the wool shirt and blouse industry, the decline in domestic production during 1994 should have been much more than an estimated 8 per cent. Other information provided in the Market Statement, (and reproduced below) was equally anecdotal and unverifiable. The information on "profits" was in fact on "profit margins", leaving it unclear whether total profits had declined or increased. India argued that the United States had provided no proof for the assertions in the industry statement regarding the role of "lower-priced" imports in industry developments.

Variable	Information provided in the April 1995 Market Statement
Employment	"Several companies reported declines in their employment, some of which were specifically attributed to the impact of competitive goods. Some employment declines were in the range of 25-30 per cent."
Sales	"Most companies reported sales declines as they lost market share to lower priced imports. Some companies experienced sales declines of 20 per cent."
Prices	"Prices of domestic product, manufactured mainly from US made fabric, are substantially higher than import competition."
Profits	"Profit margins have been eroded across the board in the wool shirt industry as raw materials costs increased while companies were unable to raise prices because of low-priced import competition."

5.121   In response to India's assertion that one company reporting dropping of contracts or capacity utilization was not an appropriate indication of the capacity utilization for the entire industry, the *United States* argued that, given the small size of the woven wool shirt and blouse industry, the decline in capacity utilization from this one company alone was highly indicative of what was going on in the entire woven wool shirt and blouse industry. India had also alleged that the decline in domestic production during 1994 should have been more than an estimated 8 per cent; however, the loss in capacity utilization did not necessarily correlate with a commensurate drop in production during the same time-period.

Rather, the loss in capacity utilization was an indication of deteriorating conditions in this industry that would lead to more severe production declines in the future.

F.   Causal Link Between Increased Imports and the Domestic Industry Situation

5.122 According to *India*, the Market Statement submitted by the United States in April 1995 stated that "the sharp and substantial increase in imports of woven wool shirts and blouses, category 440, is causing serious damage to the US industry producing woven wool shirts and blouses". Since the figures on market share, employment and wages were, as argued by India, irrelevant, and the figures on domestic prices and information on other relevant economic variables were based on questionable survey methods and were unverifiable, the only real evidence provided by the United States in support of its assertion of serious damage was the fact that imports of category 440 had increased in 1994 by 69,296 dozen to nearly double the previous year's level, while domestic production had dropped marginally by 5,000 dozen during January-September. While it had been claimed by the US that production had declined due to imports, no analysis was provided to link the two. Nor was the decline in production proportionate to the increase in imports. In the industry statement, there were claims of loss of employment, closure of plants, loss of profits etc. arising from imports; however, no attempt had been made to link these developments to imports. The Market Statement submitted by the United States in April 1995 never went beyond assertions.

5.123 The *United States* argued that the causation requirement in Article 6.2 of the ATC, linking serious damage, or the threat thereof to total imports, had been met in this case. As evidenced in the information provided in the Market Statement and later to the TMB: (i) imports had not only increased, but surged; there were negative industry indicators occurring contemporaneously with those surging imports; (ii) about 7 per cent of the workers in the woven wool shirt industry had lost their jobs from 1993 to 1994 (from 1994 to 1995 there was a loss of 5.9 per cent); later data supported this trend that the adverse impact of imports on employment was evidenced by the US trade adjustment assistance certifications (by US law a connection has to be made to imports to be eligible for certification); and (iii) US market share had declined as imports increased and production declined at the same time that imports increased.

5.124 In the view of the *United States*, CITA had demonstrated in the Market Statement and at the TMB proceeding the causation required under the ATC. Although India has asserted on this issue that "positive evidence" was required, the United States found no evidentiary standard in the ATC and could only conclude that India was adding to the text of the ATC provisions that were not negotiated and were not intended as an interpretation of the Agreement by the US.

5.125 The *United States* considered that India was seeking to modify the ATC by creating a proportionality requirement to establish a causal link. India had claimed that the United States must demonstrate that the decline in production evident before CITA was "proportionate to the increase in imports". The United States found no such test in Article 6.2 or 6.3 of the ATC. Nor was there a factual or economic justification that would require a finding that serious damage to the domestic woven wool shirt and blouse industry by imports would be reflected by exactly proportional changes in production and imports. The United States' imports of woven wool shirts and blouses from a number of countries were limited by quotas. There was also a sharp seasonal variation in these imports as well as differences in the timing of production and import activity.

5.126 *India* stated that it had never proposed a proportionality requirement, but had remarked that US production had never varied previously with imports and that this lack of correlation suggested that factors other than imports must have influenced the level of domestic production and, in particular, developments on the export market. India agreed that factors such as sharp seasonal variations in imports and differences in the timing of production and import activity made it impossible to conclude from the mere co-existence of rising imports and declining production that the two were causally linked.

5.127 *India* further argued that a demonstration that there had been a rise in imports and a decline in production was not a demonstration that there was a causal relationship between the two; logically, additional facts and data were necessary. Article 6.2 of the ATC explicitly stipulated that a demonstration that there had been an increase in imports and serious damage or threat thereof was not sufficient but must be supplemented by an additional demonstration that the increase in imports and not other factors were causing the serious damage or actual threat thereof. This demonstration of causality had not been attempted by the United States.

5.128 Concerning the lack of a causal link, *India* referred to the data on the dollar value of exports submitted by the United States to the TMB in August 1995 which indicated that the value of exports of woven wool shirts and blouses from the United States had increased by 41 per cent in 1993 and by nearly 30 per cent in 1994. Since a major portion of domestic production of woven wool shirts and blouses was exported, the domestic industry was, in fact, experiencing a significant improvement in the period prior to the imposition of the safeguard action in July 1995. Also, in its submission to the TMB in August 1995, India had pointed out that imports from India of category 440 were steadily dropping in 1995. This statement was confirmed by figures on imports submitted by the United States. During the first six months of 1995, imports from India had amounted to 2,887 dozen, 67 per cent below the earlier year's figure. The condition of increased imports was therefore not met in July 1995 when the United States unilaterally imposed restraints on imports of category 440 from India. During the period 18 April 1996 to 2 August 1996, i.e. the first three months of the second year of the continuation of the restraints, the actual imports from India had been less than one per cent of the restraint level imposed by the United States. Thus the subsequent data and import statistics proved beyond any doubt that the attribution of actual threat of serious damage to the domestic industry to imports from

India had been grossly misplaced and the finding of the TMB on this point was, therefore, wrong.

5.129 *India* further argued that the absence of a causal link between increased imports and declining production of woven wool shirts and blouses was demonstrated by figures over a longer time period. From 1985 to 1992, imports of woven wool shirts and blouses had fallen consistently and substantially, from 262,000 dozen in 1985 to 44,000 dozen in 1992. During the same period, production had also declined substantially, from 445,000 dozen to 80,000 dozen. Thus, declining production was accompanied by declining imports for the period 1985-92. In 1993, the United States market for woven wool shirts and blouses had begun to recover, with both production and imports rising. In 1994, imports nearly doubled, while production declined by 7.5 per cent. Since a major portion of United States production was exported, the increase in imports was obviously related to expanding domestic demand for woven wool shirts and blouses. The United States industry producing woven shirts and blouses had probably not anticipated this development in the wool segment since the market had been declining for a number of years. One explanation for a lack of correlation between imports from India and US domestic production was that Indian and US products were not actually competing with one another in the US market because they fell into different price and quality categories. Another possible explanation was that, while India supplied the US market, the US producers supplied both the domestic and the export markets. India's exports, therefore, varied solely with the demand in the US market; US production varied also with the demand in other countries.

5.130 *India* noted that, in respect of the import data going back to 1983, these data related to the imports and production of products defined in category 440, were derived by the United States Department of Commerce, OTEXA, and were contained in their periodic publications. The import data for 1983 and 1985 were the total reported imports of woven wool shirts and blouses that were in chief value wool while the reported imports from 1989 through 1994 were for woven shirts and blouses in chief weight wool and in chief weight man-made fibre if they contained 36 per cent or more by weight of wool. There was no publicly available data for production and it was assumed that this data relating to category 440 by OTEXA was derived by that agency for use by CITA in assessing the US domestic market for these products.

5.131 The *United States* considered that the reference by India to production and import data going back as far as 1983 was an effort to deflect attention away from the surge in imports from India that had occurred in the time leading up to the issuance of the request for consultations. India's proposed time series dating back to 1983 was technically flawed as the production data cited covered a time period that included two census survey benchmark years, 1987 and 1992. Data prior to those years were not comparable to the subsequent years' data due to differences in the composition of the survey sample. Import data were likewise not comparable over the period of years given, because, beginning in 1989, the United States had shifted to the Harmonized Tariff System classification. This shift involved a change in the wool shirt definition from a "chief value wool" basis to a "chief weight wool" basis, that caused the data prior to 1989 to be not comparable with subsequent years' data. On India's assertion that a major portion of US production was exported and its subsequent assumption that as a result the domestic industry was in fact experiencing improvement, the United States noted that the assertion and the assumption were false because export data was extremely unreliable. The United States had already illustrated that point by confirming that only 10 per cent of the production was exported by the industry representing 60 per cent of US production and that there were misclassifications of cotton exports under the wool heading.

5.132 *India* considered that the US' view in the first sentence of the preceding paragraph was a misrepresentation of the arguments made by India, which referred the Panel to the absence of a consistent relationship between changes in imports and changes in domestic production. This argument would remain valid irrespective of the shift in the United States data collection methods. For instance, between 1985 and 1989, a period in which data on imports and production were presumably collected on a consistent basis, both imports and production declined substantially. Starting from 1990, there was again no consistent pattern between changes in imports and domestic production, undoubtedly reflecting developments in the domestic and export markets. It was for this reason that India had asked for information on exports.

5.133 The *United States* argued that India's assertion that between 1985 and 1989, data on production had been collected on a consistent basis was not true. As stated in the US' first submission, India's data covered a time period that included one census survey benchmark year, 1987. Data prior to that year was not comparable to the subsequent years' data due to differences in the composition of the survey sample.

5.134 In response to these arguments, *India* submitted that the reliability or comparability of production data could not differ significantly from one census survey to another if all the census surveys were objectively and scientifically done. In assessing the role of imports in influencing or not influencing the production trends, it was not only justified but essential to look at the relation between imports and production during as long a period as possible. These data established the fact, over a significant period of time, that changes in import levels were not correlated proportionately or otherwise to the changes in domestic production. In terms of the US shift to the Harmonized Tariff System, the US submission was factually incorrect. The wool shirt definition prior to the Harmonized Tariff System had been based on a chief value determination. Under the Harmonized Tariff System, the classification was based on a chief weight determination, but the US had developed statistical breakdowns for both exports and imports to identify shirts and blouses in chief weight man-made fibre but containing 36 per cent or more by weight wool. The statistical breakdowns were developed and implemented in order to identify those woven shirts and blouses in chief weight man-made fibre, but, on the basis of estimates by the United States, similar to those woven shirts and blouses that were in chief value wool. Thus, these chief weight man-made fibre shirts and blouses were included as part of category 440 even though they were in fact man-made fibre shirts and blouses.

5.135 In response, the *United States* argued that India's assertion was incorrect that the reliability and comparability of production data could not differ significantly from one census survey to another. First, there was no issue of reliability but only of comparability. Comparability was lost because, in the process of revising the five-year Census of Manufacturers, new firms were identified and a new sample and sample size was established which included a different group of firms than the previous survey. As a result, the five-year Census of Manufacturers established a new benchmark, and data generated by this new survey were not directly comparable with previous years' data which were generated from reports of the old sample of firms. The Bureau of the Census production data in its quarterly Current Industrial Report (CIR) were based on data collected from firms identified in the five-year Census of Manufactures. Starting with production data collected for 1992 in the CIR, the number of firms originally identified in the 1992 Census of Manufactures was revised every year with the Annual Survey of Manufactures, which was taken during the intermediate census years. The annual revisions to the sample size were reflected in the CIR production data. This data collection process was not in effect prior to 1992.

5.136 Regarding India's statement on the US shift to the HTS, the *United States* stated that it did develop statistical breakdowns to identify wool garments that prior to the HTS were based on a chief value determination. When the wool clothing category system was created, it was determined that imported clothing of fibres other than wool but containing greater than 17 per cent by value wool actually competed in the same market as domestically produced wool clothing, which for production data purposes had always been defined as 51 per cent or greater of wool by weight. When the United States adopted the Harmonized Tariff Schedule (HTS) in January 1989, this definition was retained in shifting from a chief value to a chief weight system by altering the definition for imported wool clothing to those containing 36 per cent or greater wool by weight. The 36 per cent determination was done for all wool clothing categories, not just woven wool shirts and blouses. The fibre content that prevailed in tailored clothing had the dominant influence on the conversion from the chief value concept to the chief weight concept. For the reasons outlined above, it was not valid to compare data across time periods containing these breaks in the continuity of the reported data, even with the caveats that India proclaimed.

G. Attribution to India

5.137 The *United States* argued that, having properly established both (a) the existence of serious damage or actual threat thereof, and (b) the causal relationship between such damage or threat by reason of total imports, the next step was for CITA to determine to which Member or Members the cause of serious damage or actual threat thereof could be attributed. There was no requirement under Article 6.4 of the ATC for the US to make a determination that India was the sole cause of the serious damage or actual threat thereof. Indeed, that finding would already have been established under Article 6.2 of the ATC before it would be possible to proceed to the analysis under Article 6.4. Rather, the United States was required to determine to which of various Members' imports to attribute the damage or threat. The United States rejected any interpretation that would suggest that the test in Article 6.2 of the ATC was integral to or folded into the test in Article 6.4 of the ATC. That would not be a legitimate reading of the text in accordance with principles of international law found in Article 31 of the Vienna Convention on the Law of Treaties.

5.138 The *United States* further argued that it had followed the requirements under Article 6.4 of the ATC in attributing the serious damage or actual threat thereof to India.[20] Article 6.4 of the ATC provided that, after a Member had determined that serious damage or actual threat thereof existed, the Member must attribute that damage or threat to a Member or Members, on the basis of a sharp and substantial increase in imports from the Member, actual or imminent, and other factors. It was clear here that the phrase "actual or imminent" accompanied Article 6.4 of the ATC reference to "sharp and substantial" increases of imports from a Member or Members not the "serious damage, or actual threat thereof" examination required under Article 6.2 and 6.3 of the ATC as offered by India.

5.139 The *United States* noted that imports from India, by any relevant benchmark, had increased sharply and substantially. India was the largest supplier of woven wool shirts and blouses (category 440), to the United States during the year ending January 1995, with 54 per cent of total US imports. Imports from India had reached 76,698 dozen for the year ending January 1995, five times the 14,914 dozen imported in the year ending January 1994. In addition, imports from India for the year ending January 1995 had exceeded the quota levels the United States had in place with three other suppliers. Further, the United States had examined the levels of imports from India compared to imports of woven wool shirts and blouses from other sources, market share and import and domestic prices at a comparable stage of commercial transaction. The data had shown that imports from India for the year ending January 1995 were equal to total US production of woven wool shirts and blouses in the year ending September 1994. In 1993, imports from India in category 440 had been 20 per cent of total 1993 US imports of category 440 and was 18 per cent of US production in 1993. This information, coupled with the persistent decline in production up to that point and reports from the industry that production had continued to fall, reinforced the perception that further damage to the industry was imminent. As described in the Market Statement, the US had found that US imports of woven wool shirts and blouses from India in category 440 during 1994 had entered at an average landed duty-paid value of $133.85 per dozen, 75 per cent below the US producers' aver-

---

[20] An attribution of serious damage or actual threat thereof was also made against Hong Kong in respect of this produced category.

age price for woven wool shirts and blouses. The US' examination of such factors had fully supported its determination that serious damage or actual threat thereof was attributed to India's exports to the United States. Other relevant information provided to the TMB, some of which was provided as a result of inquiries from India during bilateral consultations, further buttressed the case for attribution. By the time the United States had presented its case to the TMB more up-to-date data showed that imports from India were 49 per cent of total US imports; 33 per cent of the total market in 1994; and 96 per cent of US domestic production in 1994 (this share increased to 98 per cent of US domestic production in the year ending June 1995). Therefore, the trend and current status described in the Market Statement was fully supported by the time of the TMB review.

TMB Review of the United States Action

5.140 The *United States* pointed out that it had presented its case to the TMB as provided in Article 6.10 of the ATC and had fully responded to all requests by the TMB for information. Furthermore, as expressly set out in Article 6.10 of the ATC, the US had provided the TMB with other relevant data on the industry's condition. The TMB had held hearings over a period of days at which the matter was addressed in considerable detail. India had presented extensive arguments and at the end of its proceedings, the TMB had determined that "actual threat could be attributed to the sharp and substantial increase in imports from India".

5.141 The *United States* considered that the TMB finding upholding the US determination and rejecting India's challenge was consistent with Article 6 of the ATC. If the consultations provided for in Article 6.7 of the ATC did not result in a mutual solution, the importing Member must exercise its option to take action to limit the relevant imports within 30 days after the 60 day time-frame noted in Article 6.10 of the ATC. Once that action was taken, Article 6 of the ATC required automatic review by the TMB. The TMB must review the case, determine whether the safeguard action was justified and make appropriate recommendations to the Members concerned. In addition to the data supplied in accordance with Article 6.7 of the ATC, Article 6.10 of the ATC also provided that the TMB "shall have available to it any other relevant information provided by the Members concerned". Importing Members must notify the Chairman of the TMB with relevant factual data at the same time the request for consultations was made. Subsequent and additional data supplied to the TMB supported the original determination and were entirely appropriate under the ATC.

5.142 In the view of *India*, the TMB had not upheld the US action; rather, the US action had been based on a situation of "serious damage" and the TMB did not find that a situation of "serious damage" was demonstrated by the data presented by the US Government.

H.   Status of Other Relevant Information

5.143 In the view of *India*, the TMB had made a serious error in permitting the United States to submit information in August 1995 designed to justify its claim before the TMB that its safeguard action was based on "actual threat of serious damage" though "actual threat of serious damage" had not formed the basis for the consultations held with India. Article 6.7 of the ATC required the importing Member seeking consultations to supply to the exporting Member "specific and relevant" information pertaining to the reference period in regard to factors on which it had based its determination of serious damage or actual threat. Once the 60-day consultation period was over, any new information could only be introduced by cancelling the request for consultations and submitting a new request for consultations on the basis of the new information; otherwise, the requirement to supply specific and relevant information during the consultation period would be meaningless.

5.144 *India* pointed out that, according to Article 6.10 of the ATC, the TMB, when reviewing the safeguard action after the expiry of the 60-day consultation period, shall have before it not only the information supplied by the Member seeking consultations in accordance with Article 6:7 but also "any other relevant information provided by the Members concerned". This "other relevant information" could, for instance, be a narrative report by the importing Member relating to the restraint imposed but could not be new data introduced to justify the determination on which the consultations had been sought. This possibility could not be construed to permit the Member initiating the action additional time after its action to develop further data. If certain information or data had either not been available to CITA or had not been considered by CITA at the time of its determination of serious damage, such information or data could not be introduced by CITA at a later stage as "other relevant information" to justify *ex post*, the application of a safeguard action.

5.145 The *United States*, in response to India's allegation that information not available to CITA or not considered by CITA at the time of its determination of serious damage could not be introduced by CITA at a later stage to justify the application of a safeguard action, stated that it had provided a submission of "other relevant information", as permitted in Article 6.10 of the ATC, in order to provide updated data to reflect the most current conditions in the domestic market and as regards imports, and also to respond specifically to concerns raised in bilateral consultations and not to "justify" the decision. The United States directed the Panel to Article 6.10 of the ATC which provided that the TMB shall have available to it not only the data submitted at the time of the request, but in addition, "any other relevant information". Further, there was no definition of that phrase.

5.146 *India* considered that, if the TMB were to give the importing Member the right to introduce new data at the time of the review by the TMB, it would effectively deny the exporting Member the right to challenge that information in prior bilateral consultations and would accord the importing Member the right to skip an important step in the procedures that had to be followed under Article 6 of the ATC before a safeguard action may be taken. Thus, by allowing the introduction of new data at the time of its review, the TMB would effectively be waiving the importing Member's obligations. The TMB, however, did not have the authority to accord Members the right to derogate from the ATC. As the TMB did not give any reasons for its decisions on the safeguard actions, it was not known why it endorsed a safeguard action based on alleged "actual threat" of serious damage on which no prior consultations had been held, and to consider information that was not the subject of consultations. India considered that this decision deprived it of the right to hold consultations with the United States, based on relevant and specific facts, on the specific safeguard action endorsed by the TMB.

5.147 *India* repeated that the data submitted to TMB on 28 August 1995 was entirely new in some of the elements such as the number of establishments, employment, wages, etc. for the woven wool shirts and blouse segment of the woven shirt and blouse industry. The United States' Market Statement furnished in April 1995 did not include any data on exports. In its August 1995 submission to the TMB, the United States provided data on the dollar value of exported woven wool shirts and blouses. In other factors many of the figures were revisions to what had earlier been supplied to the Indian delegation. Therefore, the fresh data presented before the TMB did not amount to "other relevant information" as defined in Article 6.10 of the ATC.

5.148 The *United States* disagreed with this view and pointed out that the "other relevant information" was provided in direct response to issues raised in bilateral consultations, and as petitioned by the TMB. No data on the number of establishments was made available in the submission of "other relevant information".

5.149 In a response to the Panel, the *United States* argued that Article 6.10 of the ATC expressly provided that the TMB "shall have available to it the factual data provided to the Chairman of the TMB, referred to in paragraph 7 [Article 6.7 of the ATC], as well as any other relevant information provided by the Members concerned". There was no definition of "other relevant information" and no limitation on how much or what kind of information could be supplied to the TMB. The only stipulation was that the information be "relevant". Therefore, the United States interpreted the ATC to allow new or additional data to confirm the data available at the time of the determination.

5.150 In response to the preceding, *India* argued that revisions to the data which formed the basis for the determination would require a re-examination of the basis for the determination and result in either the withdrawal of the action, or the initiation of a new action. The new data submitted by the US had not been used by it in making its initial determination, nor could it be characterized as data which clarified or confirmed the data used by the US to determine and demonstrate that its actions were consistent with Article 6 of the ATC. Article 6.7 of the ATC was very clear in requiring that the Member seeking consultations shall, at the time of requesting consultations, "communicate to the Chairman of the TMB the request for consultations, including all the relevant factual data outlined in paragraphs 3 and 4, together with the proposed restraint level". The submission of "other relevant information" could not be used to justify the absence of "all the relevant factual data" required to be submitted at the time of the request for consultations, nor could it be substituted in the review to determine if the situation of serious damage, or actual threat thereof, had been demonstrated in accordance with the criteria of Article 6 of the ATC.

5.151 *India* pointed out that with the exception of import data, there appeared to be no reliable published official sources indicating any of the data regarding a woven wool shirt and blouse industry in the United States. India further argued that even if the supplementary information submitted by the United States after the consultations was taken into account, the United States could not be deemed to have met the requirements of Article 6 of the ATC. It was the position of India that the TMB review of the United States' safeguard action should have been conducted only on the basis of the documentation provided to India in April 1995 at the time of the consultation request. The information submitted to the TMB was, therefore, irrelevant for the proceedings of the Panel. However, even if this information was taken into account, the United States could not be deemed to have fulfilled the requirements set out in Article 6.2 and 6.3 of the ATC.

5.152 The *United States* reiterated that, following the issuance of the Market Statement, there were consultations, questions were asked during consultations and during the TMB review. At the end of this extended process in July, there were additional data that CITA did not have access to in April 1995; some of the employment and employment-related data reflected in the Market Statement was not focused on the woven wool shirt and blouse industry. Some of the evidence obtained after consultations and for the TMB process was different, some of the data were more focused on the domestic industry producing woven wool shirts and blouses, but all of the data pointed in the same direction as the data originally outlined in the Market Statement (i.e. that the domestic industry was seriously damaged or actually threatened thereof as a result of total imports and that imports from India were contributing to the condition). Where there were data that clearly did not meet the test of reliability, such as exports, it was not used by CITA in reaching its determination. Even the factors that were more indicative of trends or the situation at the time, according to Article 6.3 of the ATC, did not have to be alone or together determinative for CITA. CITA had followed its normal practice and procedures in using and deriving information from reliable published official sources. CITA had also followed its normal practice by consulting with the key producers, representing a substantial percentage of domestic production, on a business confidential basis, to verify certain information.

5.153 *India* argued that it followed from the above that a Panel reviewing whether a safeguard action met the requirements of the ATC could also rely only on the information made available by the importing Member to the exporting Member during the consultations, that is, the Market Statement. If the Panel were to proceed otherwise, it would effectively deny the exporting Member the right to hold meaningful consultations on the basis of the information that had formed the basis of the determination and this would create a serious moral hazard as the importing Member would then no longer have an incentive to submit to the exporting Member all the information available to it at the time of the consultations. Moreover, it would enable importing Members to initiate a safeguard action merely on the basis of conjecture and then maintain it if subsequent information were to confirm the facts. India cited the two following instances where the US had attempted to introduce information in August 1995 that was not presented at the time the initial action was taken.

Employment in "Other Relevant Information"

5.154 *India* noted that in the first instance, the US data for employment (Table III of the Market Statement) included employment data for all production workers producing woven shirts and blouses. In August 1995, the US had presented an "updated Table III" which purported to identify those production workers producing woven shirts and blouses that were primarily engaged in producing woven wool shirts and blouses. These "newly identified" workers constituting the "woven wool shirt and blouse industry" represented 0.6 per cent of all production workers engaged in the woven shirt and blouse industry. These new data were derived from the 1992 Census of Manufacturers, Apparel Current Industrial Reports, Bureau of Labour Statistics, and industry survey. As these data were not publicly available in the Census publications, or from the Bureau of Labour Statistics, it was presumed that these data came from an industry survey that was not prescribed and possibly was not available when the determination to request consultations was made in April.

5.155 In response to the points on employment in the preceding paragraph, the *United States* explained that the processes used by CITA demonstrated the fallacy of India's argument. As a general policy, after a request was made, the efforts to collect data and other relevant information were not discontinued. CITA was satisfied that it had sufficient information at the time of the request to take action based on the existence of serious damage or actual threat thereof to the domestic woven wool shirt and blouse industry. However, during and after the consultation period, additional enquiries and analysis had been conducted to refine the existing information and to furnish more data pertaining to the case, especially after it appeared that the adequacy of CITA's information was being challenged. Unlike other regimes, there was no bar or requirement under the ATC concerning this action by CITA. By providing more information, CITA was not trying to justify its action after the fact, but rather to make this information available in response to questions from India during consultations and in an effort to reach a mutually satisfactory agreement in this case. The United States also was later informed that the TMB felt it needed employment-related data on a more specific category level basis in considering the matter.

5.156 The *United States* further explained that, regarding the US employment data made available in this case, at the time CITA requested consultations it had data on the number of workers in the woven shirt and blouse industry and information from consultations with industry sources indicating that the declining trend of employment at the broader industry level was reflective and representative of the situation in the more narrowly defined woven wool shirt and blouse industry. After further analysis and more discussions on a business confidential basis with the two major manufacturers of woven wool shirts and blouses, an employment number was computed indicating the number of employees specifically producing woven wool shirts and blouses and these data were presented as part of the other relevant information at the TMB session in August 1995.

Establishments in "Other Relevant Information"

5.157 The second instance cited by *India* involved the location of the establishments producing woven wool shirts and blouses. In the Market Statement, the "Industry Profile" stated that the establishments producing woven wool shirts and blouses were located mainly in Oregon, Washington, Nebraska, and Iowa. Nonetheless, the new data provided by the United States in its August Market Statement included, for the first time, a listing of workers certified for trade adjustment assistance in the "woven wool shirt and blouse" area. Of the 200 or so production workers that constituted a presumed "woven wool shirt and blouse industry", the United States presented data that indicated 220 workers had been certified for trade adjustment assistance between 25 April 1993 and 15 April 1995. Of interest in the US presentation was the fact that these workers were from Tennessee, Utah, Pennsylvania, and South Carolina. These States were almost a full continent removed from where the establishments producing these woven wool shirts and blouses were located. This raised significant questions as to whether or not the data reviewed by the United States in April 1995 was accurate and/or relevant in light of this new data presented in August 1995.

5.158 In regard to India's views on the location of the establishment, the *United States* noted that the two major producers of woven wool shirts and blouses, accounting for more than 60 per cent of domestic production, had wool clothing manufacturing facilities in Oregon, Washington, Nebraska, Iowa and Pennsylvania. These two manufacturers also contracted out the production of woven wool shirts and blouses. One of these producers of woven wool shirts and blouses had to end all outside contracting production due to the impact of imports. This was reported to be the equivalent of closing four plants. This reduction in contract work could account for the Workers Adjustment Assistance certification for workers at the production facilities in Tennessee, Utah and South Carolina. The other major producer of woven wool shirts and blouses had production operations in Pennsylvania, which would account for the Workers Adjustment Assistance certification for workers at the production facility in Pennsylvania.

5.159 The *United States* referred to India's arguments in this section and noted that data available to CITA in April 1995 had shown, among other things, very high levels of increased imports and declining US production and the subsequent and additional data supplied by the United States to the TMB had confirmed the validity of the original determination and constituted "relevant" data that were expressly allowed for TMB review under Article 6.10 of the ATC which was clear after the 60-day consultation period.

I.   Consultations and Endorsement of Actions by TMB: Additional Procedural Requirements

5.160 *India* argued that the safeguard action on which the United States had held consultations had not been endorsed by the TMB and the safeguard action which had received the endorsement of the TMB had not been the subject of consultations. Therefore, the safeguard action did not meet the procedural requirements in Article 6 of the ATC, which were that the safeguard action must have been the subject of bilateral consultations and have been endorsed by the TMB. As the TMB had not endorsed the safeguard action, the United States should have withdrawn it. This requirement of an endorsement by the TMB of the safeguard action ensured a multilateral examination of the conformity of the safeguard action with the provisions of the ATC; both the right to consultations and the right to a multilateral examination were extremely important shields against abuse of the ATC safeguard provisions.

5.161 *India* based its argument in this regard on the nature and purpose of the ATC and the circumstances of its conclusion. India essentially invited the Panel to interpret Article 6 in such a manner as to give effect to the pivotal role of that provision in preserving the balance of rights and obligations under the ATC. A contextualand purpose-oriented interpretation of Article 6 of the ATC must lead the Panel to the conclusion that the creation of a right to discriminatory safeguard action without any offsetting right to compensation or retaliation nor any multilateral endorsement would put exporting Members into a legal position under the ATC worse than what they had under the MFA and would consequently be contrary to the basic objectives of the ATC. India did not believe that these arguments could be dismissed merely on the ground that the ATC referred to "recommendations" and not to "decisions" when it required the TMB to act. Further, if, notwithstanding the fact that the ATC obliged WTO Members to submit all their safeguard actions to the TMB and that the TMB clearly had the obligation to examine the ATC-conformity of all safeguard actions and to make recommendations on all of them, the Panel were to rule that a failure to make a recommendation had no legal consequence, the Panel would fundamentally upset the balance of rights and obligations under the ATC. The TMB would become the only body of the WTO whose decision whether or not to make a recommendation was legally irrelevant.

5.162 The *United States* referred to India's arguments on TMB endorsement and expressed its view that CITA's determination had been based on a showing of "serious damage, or actual threat thereof", and there was no requirement that the TMB "endorse" a measure for it to be maintained. The TMB had reached consensus that the finding of actual threat of serious damage attributable to India in this case was justified. It made no finding for or against "serious damage" *per se* and the TMB was only required under the ATC to make "appropriate" recommendations after examining serious damage or actual threat thereof. Whatever a TMB finding or recommendation was, Members were only required under Article 8.9 of the ATC to "endeavour to accept in full the recommendations of the TMB." There was no further obligation concerning the maintenance of a safeguard in the ATC on that matter. For a Member to maintain a transitional safeguard, TMB approval was not required.

5.163 The *United States* also referred to India's assertion that there was no difference between "recommendations" of the TMB and this Panel, the DSB and the Appellate Body. The texts of the ATC and DSU clearly demonstrated the error of this argument. The report of this Panel or an Appellate Body Report adopted by the DSB required action on the part of a complaining party receiving a recommendation to bring its measures into conformity with its obligations. The DSU in Articles 21 and 22 specified those actions and the consequences of inaction. As already pointed out, Article 8.9 of the ATC only required with respect to TMB recommendations, that Members "endeavour to accept in full". There was no requirement in the ATC concerning TMB findings and observations. Moreover, pursuant to Article 8.10 of the ATC, Members then had recourse to GATT Article XXIII and DSU procedures.

5.164 Also concerning the need for TMB endorsement of a determination, *India* noted that under Article 1.6 of the MFA, all rights of the contracting parties under GATT 1947 had been fully reserved and, notwithstanding the existence of the MFA, they had not been legally entitled to take safeguard actions inconsistent with Article XIX of GATT 1947. If an exporting country did not agree with the determination of an importing country, it could invoke its rights under GATT 1947 and thereby force that country to take non-discriminatory action under Article XIX of GATT 1947. That possibility, though hardly made use of, was part of the checks and balances under the MFA. Given that legal situation, the TSB could only perform conciliatory functions. Under the ATC, however, the exporting Member's rights under GATT 1994 were legally curtailed. Importing Members were now legally entitled to take discriminatory safeguard action without having to compensate the exporting Member concerned. The textiles exporting Members could no longer invoke their right to non-discriminatory treatment and to compensation under Articles XIII and XIX of GATT 1994 if they disagreed with the determinations on which the importing Member had based its safeguard action. This significant loss of GATT rights had been compensated by the requirement of a formal review and endorsement by the TMB of all invocations of the ATC's safeguard provisions as well as an explicit reference in Article 8.10 of the ATC to the right of a Member to bring the matter before the DSB and invoke Article XXIII:2 in case the matter remained unresolved even after completion of the TMB process. This requirement did not take away from the importing Members any of the rights they had under the GATT or under the MFA. If the importing Member did not obtain the TMB's approval, it could exercise its right to integrate the product concerned into GATT 1994 and invoke Article XIX to protect its industry. The requirement of a TMB approval, therefore, did not mean that importing Members could take safeguard action only with multilateral approval; it meant that they needed multilateral approval if they wished to do so on a discriminatory basis and without offering any trade compensation to the exporting Member.

5.165 In response, the *United States* disputed India's claims that the US characterization of the MFA was wrong. India had claimed that the MFA was not an exception to the GATT and Article 1.6 of the MFA, saying that the MFA would not affect the rights and obligations of participating countries under the GATT. India, however, neglected to mention paragraph 7 of that same Article, which provided "[t]he participating countries recognize that, since measures taken under this Arrangement are intended to deal with the special problems of textile products, such measures should be considered as exceptional, and not lending themselves to application in other fields." It was this paragraph that the United States had in mind when it stated earlier that the MFA was established as an exception to the GATT rules regarding application of quantitative restrictions.

5.166 *India* further emphasized that the safeguard mechanism in the ATC was a compromise reached during negotiations with a stipulation that it should be applied as sparingly as possible and with disciplines which would reduce the risk of misuse. The "two-tier approach" with regard to determination as well as the requirement for review by the TMB, contained in Article 6 of the ATC, was meant to reduce the risk of misuse of the transitional safeguard mechanism. According to Article 6.9 to 11, all safeguard actions must be submitted to the TMB for examination and may be introduced or maintained by the importing Member only if they had been endorsed by the TMB. The required examination by the TMB would be meaningless and the purposes of Article 6.10 of the ATC could not be achieved if unilateral safeguard action could be taken or continued without the endorsement of the TMB. The ATC incorporated the necessary balance in Article 6 of the ATC by giving importing Members the possibility to resort to safeguard action during the transitional period and by giving the exporting Members the protection of a review of the safeguard action by the TMB, and if necessary, by a panel. This balance would be lost if the Panel were to find that the United States was entitled to take the safeguard action notwithstanding the lack of endorsement by the TMB of the specific action it proposed to take when it requested India to consult.

5.167 *India* further pointed out that, in order to be consistent with the ATC, a safeguard action must meet the procedural requirements of Article 6 of the ATC. For actions other than agreed restraints, these requirements were essentially the following:

    (i)   "The Member proposing to take safeguard action shall seek consultations" (Article 6.7).

    (ii)   This request "shall be accompanied by specific and factual information" (Article 6.7).

    (iii)   If the consultations fail and an action is taken, the TMB "shall promptly conduct an examination" (Article 6.10).

(iv)   Following that examination, the TMB "shall ... make appropriate recommendations to the Members concerned" (Article 6.10).

By using the term "shall" in all of the above-cited provisions, the text of Article 6 of the ATC made clear that a safeguard action would be consistent with the ATC only if all of the above requirements, including the requirement that the TMB make a recommendation on the safeguard action, were fulfilled. In the case before the Panel, the TMB had made no recommendation on the safeguard action on which the United States had made a determination and on which it had consulted with India and the procedural requirements listed above had, therefore, not been met.

5.168 The *United States* argued that although the TMB had an important role in reviewing safeguard actions and Members were required to endeavour to comply with its recommendations, there was no requirement that the TMB "endorse" a measure for it to be maintained. Furthermore, there was no requirement that the TMB make a finding on both serious damage and actual threat. Article 6.10 of the ATC provided that the TMB "conduct an examination of the matter, including the determination of serious damage, or actual threat thereof, and its causes, and make appropriate recommendations ...". Contrary to India's claim, there was no requirement that the TMB produce a consensus finding on the US' complete determination of "serious damage, or actual threat thereof". The TMB had not made any comment on the existence of serious damage with respect to category 440, but instead had noted that there had been a consensus in the TMB on the existence of actual threat and that such actual threat could be attributed to the sharp and substantial increase in imports from India (G/TMB/2 and G/TMB/R/3). Therefore, it was not appropriate to assume that there was any finding or conclusion by the TMB concerning serious damage one way or the other. The *United States* referred to India's claim that the ATC had specifically assigned to the TMB legal functions that had not been assigned to the TSB. The US, however, was of the view that Article 6.9 and 6.10 of the ATC virtually mirrored, to the extent of TSB responsibility, Article 3.4 and 3.5 of the MFA, respectively. Therefore, India's contention that the drafters of the ATC had given the TMB powers beyond those accorded to the TSB was without merit.

5.169 *India* pointed out that the ATC was not the only WTO agreement that attached legal consequences to the existence or non-existence of a recommendation of a WTO body. The General Council may adopt a budget only if the Committee on Budget Finance and Administration submitted a "recommendation" to it (Article VII of the WTO Agreement). The Ministerial Conference may adopt an interpretation of the GATT only on the basis of a "recommendation" by the Council for Trade in Goods (Article IX of the WTO Agreement). A WTO Member may suspend concessions under Article 22 of the DSU only if the "recommendations" of a panel or the Appellate Body were not implemented within a reasonable period of time. India concluded from this that the argumentation of the United States invited the Panel to take an extraordinary step, namely, to declare the TMB to be the only WTO body whose decision to make or not to make a recommendation would not have any legal consequence and this in spite of the fact that the ATC had specifically assigned an important legal task to this body.

5.170 *India* rejected the characterization of the TMB by the United States as a "special board and conciliation type body" similar to the TSB and the United States' contention that a safeguard action may be taken under the ATC even if the TMB failed to make a recommendation on it. India pointed out that, according to Article 8 of the ATC, the TMB was to

> "... supervise the implementation of this Agreement, to examine all measures taken under this Agreement and their conformity therewith, and to take the actions specifically required of it by this Agreement ..."

while the corresponding provision of the MFA, (Article 11) stated that the task of the TSB was to "... supervise the implementation of this Arrangement".

5.171 According to *India*, there was no reference in the above provision for a TSB examination of the MFA-consistency of all safeguard actions. Moreover, the TSB merely had the task to review, "... at the request of any participating country, ... promptly any particular measure or arrangements which that country considered to be detrimental to its interests ...". The complaints submitted to the TSB could, therefore, be complaints of a non-legal, economic nature. It clearly followed from the above that the TMB had a legal function because its central task was to examine the ATC-conformity of all safeguard actions, while the TSB had merely a conciliatory function because it was to become active only if countries requested it to consider measures detrimental to their interests. By declaring that the TMB had functions equivalent to those of the TSB, the United States had simply ignored the fact that the mandates of the TMB and the TSB were defined in completely different ways in the legal instruments establishing them.

5.172 *India* indicated, while fully reserving its position on the question of endorsement, that in the case before the Panel the question of whether the TMB must approve the safeguard action need not necessarily be answered. Given the absence of any decision of the TMB on the safeguard action on which the United States had consulted with India, it would be sufficient for the Panel to rule that a safeguard action under the ATC may only be taken if the TMB had made a recommendation and to leave aside the question of whether approval was required. This would enable the Panel to rely exclusively on the explicit wording of Article 6.10 of the ATC ("The TMB shall ... make appropriate recommendations") rather than on the contextual and purpose-oriented interpretation of that provision that India considers to be the appropriate one. Therefore, in case the Panel were to conclude that a TMB endorsement was not required or if it were to conclude that the case did not require a ruling on this point, India subsidiarily requested the Panel to find that the safeguard action of the United States was inconsistent with its obligations under the ATC because the TMB, contrary to the explicit requirement set out in Article 6.10 of the ATC, had not made any recommendation on the action on which the United States had consulted with India.

5.173 The *United States* questioned whether India could *post hoc* amend its pleadings in this case as it had done in the preceding paragraph. There, India has made a subsidiary request of the Panel not found in its original request. This was inconsistent with the DSU and WTO and GATT practice as seen in the Appellate Body Report on Reformulated Gasoline. In that dispute, the Appellate Body had refused to address issues that Venezuela did not raise in a request for appeal.

J. Date of the Safeguard action

5.174 *India* argued that the United States' retroactive application of the safeguard action violated Article XIII of GATT 1994 and was not justified by Article 6.10 of the ATC. On 14 July 1995, India was informed by the United States that a restraint would be applied on imports from India, *inter alia*, in category 440, during the period beginning on 18 April 1995 and extending through 17 April 1998. The United States, therefore, had decided that the period of restraint would begin on the date of its request for consultations with India under Article 6 of the ATC. This meant that, in determining the amount of permitted imports during the period of restraint, the imports that took place during the period of consultations were to be deducted to the detriment of Indian exporters.

5.175 In the view of *India*, Article 1.6 of the ATC specifically reserved the rights of the WTO Members under GATT 1994 "unless otherwise provided in this Agreement" (ATC). The restraint imposed by the United States was inconsistent with Article XIII of GATT 1994 and was consequently justified only if, and to the extent, permitted under the ATC. Article XIII:3(b) did not permit a retroactive application of import restraints. The GATT panel on *EEC Restrictions on Imports of Dessert Apples -Complaint by Chile* therefore considered that "backdated quotas, that is, quotas declared to have already been filled at the time of their announcement, did not conform to the requirements of Article XIII:3(b) ...".[21] The ATC did not provide for an exception to that principle. Its Article 6.10 merely provided that "the Member which proposed to take safeguard action may apply the restraint by date of import or date of export" if, "after the expiry of the period of 60 days from the date on which the request for consultations has been received", no agreement has been reached. There was nowhere in the ATC any indication that the restraints may be back-dated.

5.176 The *United States* referred to India's rationale as to why the *Dessert Apples* case was comparable to what the US had done in this matter and found it illogical. There was a distinct difference between declaring a quota to be totally filled and one partially filled. Thus, it did not comprehend India's reasoning in this matter. The US case was not the same or similar to the one in *Dessert Apples*. Therefore, the case was not even persuasive here.

---

[21]   BISD 36S/93.

5.177 *India* replied that it was true that this panel had examined an extreme case, namely a case of backdating with the effect that the total quota declared to be available for future trade had already been totally filled at the time of the announcement. However, the reasoning of the panel also applied in the case in which a quota declared to be available at the time of its announcement would be already partially filled.

5.178 The *United States* also argued that the application of the transitional safeguard from the date of the request for consultations was consistent with the ATC. The US had applied the safeguard restraint on woven wool shirts and blouses from India from the date the request for consultations was made. The ATC did not bar such a choice. Even the TMB had noted that "with respect to the introduction of a safeguard action, the [ATC] does not provide any indication with respect to the effective date of implementation of that measure."[22] Thus, in the absence of any provision to the contrary, the United States was not prohibited from applying the safeguard action from the date of the request. Indeed, application as from the request date was a practical necessity as such a request would trigger speculative trade. If traders believed that imports before completion of the consultation process would not be counted against a prospective restraint, speculative imports would aggravate the damage or bankrupt the remaining industry. Although imports in many instances continued to increase following the notification of a request, traders were informed by the US Federal Register notice that any unilateral quota established would be applied to cover exports since the date of the request. The US maintained that even though the request for consultations was officially published after the date of the request itself, the United States did not "enforce" the restraint until well after publication, albeit applying to shipments from the time of the request. Entry of those shipments would not be affected until after the restraint was enforced (after publication) and the quota for India would not be deducted until later, or after publication.

5.179 The *United States* stressed that it did not accept India's interpretation of Article 6.10 of the ATC and Articles XIII and X:2 of GATT 1994 on the issue of the effective date of a safeguard. It added to the points in the preceding paragraph made above that with respect to Article X:2 it believed that it was questionable if an ATC transitional safeguard fell under the "general application" requirement. As both parties agreed, ATC textiles safeguards were applied on a Member-by-Member basis and were not subject to the non-discriminatory application of quantitative restrictions under GATT 1994. Even so, the United States maintained that it had not "enforced" the safeguard within the meaning of GATT 1994 Article X:2 until after publication. As such, Article X:2 of GATT 1994 was likely not applicable.

5.180 *India* noted that the MFA specifically determined the beginning of the 12-month restraint period to remove any uncertainty during consultations following

---

[22] G/TMB/R/2.

a request for consultations and there was no option provided in the MFA for the country to apply the restraint from any other date than the date specified in the MFA. The ATC, unlike the MFA, allowed for a restraint to be applied for three years and explicitly stated that the application of that restraint must occur at a time, to be determined by the importing country, during the 30 days following the 60-day consultation period. It was factually incorrect for the United States to present the ATC as allowing Members the option of selecting the date upon which the 12-month restraint period would become effective.

5.181   The *United States* reiterated that in some cases, as in the case of woollen products, seasonality of shipments indicated less imports, not an unwillingness to ship when a request was announced. Nevertheless, if shipments exported after the request were not counted against the quota that would almost guarantee a surge in the trade for months immediately following the request with no subsequent price to be paid for causing additional damage to the domestic industry. If the Panel prohibited this practice, which was not prohibited by the ATC, the Panel would be signalling to traders that they could flood the market with imports before consultations were completed.

5.182   In sum, *India* argued that the United States had submitted no evidence that "speculative exports" would occur following a request for consultations. There may, or may not, be a real or imagined incentive to ship products quickly in order to export goods prior to the start of a quota, but no evidence was given demonstrating that this was, in fact, the case. The US data on shipment time was considered to be, in this instance, meaningless. In the view of India, it only indicated that transit time between India and the United States was somewhere between 48 hours and 50 days. A more meaningful examination would review the time between the placing of an order or opening an irrevocable letter of credit, receiving the appropriate export documentation, actual date of export, and date of import. None of these were indicated to have been reviewed by the United States in order to discern "actual shipping patterns" of goods prior to the start of a quota, or after the start of a quota.

Article XIII:3(b) of GATT 1994

5.183   *India* argued that the TMB had correctly noted that "with respect to the introduction of a safeguard action, the [ATC] does not provide any indication with respect to the effective date of implementation of that measure."[23] However, it would be completely erroneous to conclude from that fact that the importing Members had the right to apply their restraints retroactively. Exactly the opposite was true in the opinion of India. Because there was no explicit authorization in the ATC's transitional safeguard clause to impose the additional burden of retroactive application, the general prohibition of retroactive import restraints set out

---

[23]   G/TMB/R/2.

in Article XIII:3(b) of GATT 1994 applied and importing Members were therefore not entitled to impose that burden. The perception that appeared to be implicit in the TMB's statement was that everything that was not prohibited by Article 6 of the ATC was permitted. That perception turned the relationship between the general principles of GATT 1994 and the highly exceptional provisions of Article 6 on its head. The lack of a provision in the ATC permitting retroactivity had not been an oversight. Article 3.5(i) of the MFA explicitly stated that, if, after a period of 60 days from the date on which the request for consultations had been received, no agreement had been reached, the importing country could impose restraints at a specified level "for the twelve-month period beginning on the day when the request was received by the participating country". All the negotiators of the ATC were familiar with the MFA and nevertheless it was decided not to include a corresponding provision in the ATC.

5.184 *India* considered that the date of publication of the request for consultations was irrelevant in the context of Article 2.4 of the ATC and Article XIII of the GATT and stressed that the requirement of advance public announcement of Article XIII would not be met if the importing Member were to make, at the time of the request for consultations a public announcement of the quantity or value of the products that may be imported in a specified future period if the government were to decide to restrict imports subsequent to the consultations. The very purpose of Article XIII was to achieve predictability in trade relations by obliging WTO Members to indicate clearly the future trading regime. This interpretation would also frustrate the intent of Article X:2 of GATT 1994 because it would allow governments to enforce measures before they had announced their eventual decision to apply them.

5.185 *India* also considered the requirement of advance publication of quotas under Article XIII of GATT 1994 and the requirement of Article 6.10 of the ATC that a safeguard action may only be taken within the 30 days following the 60-day period for consultations must be interpreted consistently with one another. If the requirement of an advance publication of the quota under Article XIII could be met by merely announcing the possibility of a quota rather than the quota itself, then it would logically have to be considered to be consistent with Article 6.10 of the ATC to merely announce during the 30-day interval the possibility of a quota rather than the quota itself. These considerations made it clear that allowing WTO Members to meet their advance publication requirements under the WTO agreements by permitting them to announce the possibility of a trade action *ex ante* and the decision to actually impose it *ex post* would have far-reaching consequences undermining the role of the WTO agreements as sources of law and predictability in international trade relations. The Panel should not, therefore, arrive at a compromise between the position of India and that of the United States by declaring the date of the publication of the request for consultations as the date to which a quota may be backdated.

5.186 The *United States* cited India's argument concerning Article XIII:3(b) of GATT 1994, and argued that Article XIII was outside the terms of reference of this Panel. India had stated in its request that the Panel find that "[t]here was no provision in the ATC under which the United States ... can impose a restraint with retrospective effect". In its request for Panel review, India had made no claim under GATT 1994 concerning this issue and as such, India's argument should not at this time be addressed under GATT 1994. In any event, in the view of the United States, application of the measure in this instance would be fully consistent with the provisions of Article XIII:3(b) of GATT 1994 as public notice had been given of the total quantity (not less than 76,698 dozen woven wool shirts and blouses) that would be permitted from the date of the request for consultations, in the event that no mutual solution would be reached with India. The United States had also provided public notice that products exported or *en route* after the date of the request, but entering before the effective date of the restraint (which was 90 days after the date of the request) would not be excluded from entry, but would be charged against the earlier announced quota amount.

5.187 *India* referred to the argument of the United States that Article XIII of GATT did not form part of the Panel's terms of reference and recalled that in paragraph 12 of its request for the establishment of a Panel it had requested it to find that "There is no provision in the ATC under which the United States, as the importing Member, can impose a restraint with retrospective effect." In this regard India argued that the ATC was an exception to the basic rules of GATT 1994 and any WTO Member requesting consultations with the claim that a certain measure did not conform to the ATC was, in effect, claiming that the ATC did not justify the deviation from the basic GATT provisions. India's request for a Panel finding must, therefore, have been understood by the United States and other WTO Members as a request for a finding by the Panel that, given the absence of a rule in the ATC permitting the retroactive application of safeguard actions, India was entitled to the non-retroactive application prescribed by GATT 1994. The text of a request for the establishment of a Panel should be interpreted like any other legal text, that is, by examining not merely the words used but also their context and purpose. India considered that its request for a Panel finding on retroactivity, in the context in which it was made and given the purpose it served, must be interpreted to comprise a request for a finding under GATT 1994 in respect of the issue of retroactivity.

5.188 In response to a question as to which provision of the WTO Agreement, the GATT and the ATC, if any, India was referring to in paragraph 11.2 of its request for a panel (WT/DS33/1), *India* noted that Article 6.2 of the DSU stated that the request for the establishment of a panel shall "provide a brief summary of the legal basis of the complaint sufficient to present the problem clearly". This Article did not require that the complaining Member should indicate specific provisions of the covered agreement(s) invoked nor was this customary for Members. Article 7 of the DSU would appear to indicate that parties to the dispute were required to cite the names of the covered agreements and the Panel would examine the matter in the light of the relevant provisions in the covered agreements cited. The manner in which brackets had been used in the standard terms of reference contained in Article 7 of the DSU also appeared to confirm this. Paragraph 11.2 of India's request for establishment of a Panel and paragraph 79(ii) of India's first written submission requested the Panel to find, in accordance with Article 3.8 of the DSU, the safeguard action of the United States nullified or impaired the benefits accruing to India under the WTO Agreement, under the ATC and under GATT 1994 in particular. The phrase "WTO Agreement" referred to "Agreement Establishing the World Trade Organization" as per the standard list of abbreviations. According to Article II:2 of the WTO Agreement, the Agreement and the associated legal instruments included in Annexes 1, 2 and 3 were integral parts of the WTO Agreement. In brief, the term "WTO Agreement" also included "the Multilateral Trade Agreements". Under these circumstances, paragraph 11.2 of India's request for the establishment of a Panel and paragraph 79(ii) of India's first written submission should be understood by the Panel as a request that the Panel find in accordance with Article 3.8 of the DSU that the United States' actions, being inconsistent with the provisions of the ATC and GATT 1994, which were Multilateral Trade Agreements included in the "WTO Agreement", nullified or impaired benefits accruing to India under the provisions of these Agreements.

Speculative Rise in Imports

5.189 *India* further pointed out that the United States had indicated that it considered the retroactive application of restraints necessary to prevent a speculative rise in imports after the request for consultations. If traders believed that imports before the completion of the consultations were not counted, so they argued, the request for consultations would trigger speculative trade that would aggravate the damage to the domestic industry. In the view of India, this argument was not based on commercial realities. Most textile and clothing products were made to order and it was generally impossible to complete the process of contracting, manufacturing and shipping within a period of only 60 days. The reality was that requests for consultations, because of the uncertainty they created, more often discouraged trade and, therefore, had a commercial impact equivalent to the restraints the importing Member was proposing to take.

5.190 In a response to the Panel, *India* expanded upon its claim that it was generally impossible to produce and ship textile products on such notice as 60 days. It explained that, in India, quotas were distributed on the basis of a policy notification by the Government. During the years 1994 to 1996, one of the systems of quota allotment was called the First Come First Served (Small Order) system which was designed to provide the quickest turnaround time for servicing of export orders. Quotas were allotted against Letters of Credit obtained from the importers for small orders with the stipulation that the quantities allotted under this system should be utilized within a period of 60 days of allotment. There were persistent representations from the clothing exporting industry that the period of 60 days was insufficient for processing the export orders. Therefore, it had become necessary for India to stipulate a validity period of 75 days from 1996 onwards. Furthermore, there had been representations from the exporters of woollen clothing for extending the validity to 90 days since even the 75 days' period appeared to be insufficient for processing the export orders for woollen clothing. India's exports of woven wool shirts and blouses to the United States consisted almost entirely of regenerated wool products, that is, products made from woollen rags which required extracting and regenerating their fibre content, and converting it into yarn, fabrics and then clothing. Since export orders were for specific fabric and clothing designs most of these processes had to be carried out after receipt of the export order for clothing. It was thus obvious that for woven wool shirts and blouses to be exported to the US, the time required was even more than what was required for export of other clothing.

5.191 In a response to the Panel, the *United States* expressed the view that when a request for consultations was announced in the Federal Register, interested parties were informed that if no agreement was reached in consultations, the United States may decide to establish a limit for the 12-month period beginning from the date of the request for consultations. If the United States did not so inform the public, there would be an incentive to ship products quickly in order to export goods prior to the start of a quota. In situations of rapidly rising imports, the goal for importers to ship quickly was to avoid having their goods caught in a quota embargo. India's claim that it would take more than 60 days for importers to receive any such imports from India was contrary to the facts of actual shipping patterns. A review of shipments of category 440 exported from India during the 12-month period of 18 April 1995 to 17 April 1996, the first control period of the Article 6 action, showed a different situation. Of approximately 200 entries, 25 per cent had arrived within 48 hours of exportation from India using an air carrier. There was only one entry that had taken longer than 50 days to arrive in the United States, with most entries arriving within three to four weeks from the date of export from India. In this era of instantaneous communication, it takes very little time to handle the relatively simple business transactions for an ongoing programme. Regardless of the time needed to begin a new purchase transaction, there could be an incentive for "speculative exports" to avoid the imposition of a quota for orders already placed and waiting to be shipped. Once it was learned that there may be a quota imposed within 60 days, the concerned business entity could seek to speed up the shipping of an order or could have it shipped by air, as evidenced by the data presented above.

5.192 *India* considered, with respect to the preceding views, that a more meaningful examination of shipment time would review the time between the placing of an order, or opening an irrevocable letter of credit, receiving the appropriate export documentation, actual date of export, and date of import. None of these were indicated to have been reviewed by the United States in order to discern "actual shipping patterns" of goods prior to the start of a quota, or after the start of a quota. India explained that it had never claimed that goods could not be shipped from India to the United States by air freight within a very short period of time. India had claimed that textiles products were generally made to order and that the period between the placing of the order and the exports from India was normally longer than 60 days. The United States pointed out that it looked at the shipping pattern during the time most relevant to this issue, which was the time of the first control period of this action or between 18 April 1995 and 17 April 1996. That examination revealed that of approximately 200 entries, 25 per cent had arrived within 48 hours of export from India using an air carrier. Most entries arrived three to four weeks from the date of export from India.

Unusual and Critical Circumstances

5.193 *India* noted that the ATC provided for highly unusual and critical circumstances in which a delay in the application of restraint could cause damage that would be difficult to repair and it was not excluded that such circumstances might arise as a result of the traders' reaction to a request for consultations. In that case the importing Member had the right to resort to Article 6.11 of the ATC, and subject to the strict conditions set out in that provision, apply a safeguard action provisionally prior to the lapse of the consultation period. The circumstances that the United States invoked to justify the introduction of a new right for importing Members under the ATC were thus specifically dealt with in that provision. If the Panel were to recognize the existence of a general right to impose restraints retroactively to deal with speculative imports aggravating the damage to the domestic industry, it would effectively permit importing Members to escape the strictures of the very ATC provision that allowed Members to deal with such situations.

5.194 With respect to India's argument that safeguard action in critical circumstances under Article 6.11 of the ATC addressed the issue, the *United States* disagreed, arguing that Article 6.11 of the ATC was designed to respond to true emergency cases and not to the problem of speculative trade that existed in virtually all cases. Even under the MFA, a "critical circumstances" action was not relevant to the issue of the effective date of a safeguard action. The same provision existed in the MFA along with an express provision on application of restraints from the date of the call in regular safeguard circumstances. There was no substantive change announced in the ATC that the critical circumstances mechanism "replaced" the freedom to apply the restraint from the call date.

5.195 The *United States* further referred to India's claim that critical circumstances safeguard action under ATC Article 6.11 of the ATC was designed in any way to solve the problem addressed by the application of a restraint from the date of the request. Article 6.11 of the ATC was not a provision created for the first time under the ATC or introduced as a new concept under the ATC to address the speculative trade issue. It was merely, like some other provisions of the ATC, a carryover from the MFA for real critical circumstances safeguard cases such as cases that truly could not wait for the parties to decide on the date and place for consultations. While Article 3 of the MFA addressed the problem by expressly recognizing a country's ability to apply the safeguard in that manner, the MFA also contained Article 3.6, the predecessor to Article 6.11 of the ATC. Therefore, even under the MFA "critical circumstances" action was not relevant to the issue of when a regular safeguard could be applied and the issue of addressing speculative trade when consultations under regular safeguard action took place.

K.   Article 2 of the ATC

5.196 *India* noted that Article 2.4 of the ATC prohibited the introduction of new restraints except under the provisions of that Agreement or relevant GATT 1994 provisions. The restraints referred to in these provisions were the measures prohibited by Articles XI and XIII of GATT 1994. Any new restraint inconsistent with Articles XI or XIII and covered neither by the provisions of the ATC nor those of GATT 1994 were, therefore, also inconsistent with Article 2.4 of the ATC. In response to the argument of the United States, India requested the Panel to find that the retroactive application of the United States safeguard action was inconsistent with Article XIII of the GATT and Article 2 of the ATC or, if the Panel were to consider Article XIII of the GATT not to form part of its terms of reference, that the retroactive application was inconsistent with Article 2 of the ATC.

5.197 The *United States* argued that since the safeguard action on imports of woven wool shirts and blouses from India was fully consistent with Article 6 of the ATC, there was no violation of Article 2 of the ATC.

5.198 In sum, *India* requested the Panel to find that the retroactive application of the United States' safeguard action was inconsistent with Article XIII of the GATT and Article 2 of the ATC or, if the Panel were to consider Article XIII of the GATT not to form part of its terms of reference, that the retroactive application was inconsistent with Article 2 of the ATC.

* * * * *

VI.   INTERIM REVIEW

6.1   On 22 November 1996, the United States and India requested the Panel to review, in accordance with Article 15.2 of the DSU, precise aspects of the interim report that had been issued to the parties on 12 November 1996. Both India and the United States agreed not to request the Panel to hold a meeting for that purpose. We reviewed the arguments presented by the parties in their written submissions and issue our final report accordingly.

6.2   We note that the United States stated that the restraint, which is the object of the present dispute, was to be withdrawn "due to a steady decline in imports of woven wool shirts and blouses from India and the adjustment of the industry". This was confirmed in a Federal Register notice dated 4 December 1996 (61 FR 64342). In the absence of an agreement between the parties to terminate the proceedings, we think that it is appropriate to issue our final report regarding the matter set out in the terms of reference of this Panel in order to comply with our mandate, as referred to in paragraph 1.3 of this report, notwithstanding the withdrawal of the US restraint. A number of GATT panels have done so.[24]

6.3   Concerning the interpretation of Article 6.2 and 6.3 of the ATC, the United States argued that under the MFA it was never required to "demonstrate" at least all of the factors therein referred to; that India had admitted that Article 6.3 contained an illustrative list of such factors; and that the interpretation by the Panel of Article 6.3 of the ATC turned the provision on its head. We are of the view that the ATC is a different agreement from the MFA; that India did not make such an admission;[25] and that the wording of Article 6.3 of the ATC is clear.

6.4   Concerning the comments made by the United States regarding the US government's lack of reliable export data, we reiterate that we do not interpret the ATC so as to impose on WTO Members any method of collecting data but that it is up to each concerned Member to collect the relevant data from relevant sources, possibly including the private sector.

6.5   Concerning the requirement under Article 6.2 of the ATC that the importing Member must positively confirm that the state of the particular industry of the importing Member was not caused by "such other factors as technological changes and changes in consumer preference", we refer simply to the clear wording of Article 6.2 of the ATC. The absence of adequate reference to the issue of technological changes and changes in the consumer preference in a determination necessarily implies that the importing Member did not address this aspect of the causation requirement.

6.6   Concerning India's argument that Article 11 of the DSU entitles India to a finding on each of the issues it raised, we disagree and refer to the consistent GATT panel practice of judicial economy. India is entitled to have the dispute over the contested "measure" resolved by the Panel, and if we judge that the specific matter in dispute can be resolved by addressing only some of the arguments raised by the complaining party, we can do so. We, therefore, decide to address only the legal issues we think are needed in order to make such findings as will assist the DSB in making recommendations or in giving rulings in respect of this dispute.

---

[24]   See for instance the Panel Report on "EEC - Restrictions on Imports of Dessert Apples, Complaint by Chile" (adopted on 22 June 1989, BISD 36S/93), the Panel Report on "EEC - Restrictions on Imports of Apples, Complaint by the United States" (adopted on 22 June 1989, BISD 36S/135), the Panel Report on "United States - Prohibition of Imports of Tuna and Tuna Products from Canada" (adopted on 22 February 1982, BISD 29S/91) or the Panel Report on "EEC - Measures on Animal Feed Proteins" (adopted on 14 March 1978, BISD 25S/49).

[25]   As noted in paragraph 5.63 of this report in referring to an explicit allegation by India: " ... Article 6.3 of the ATC indicates an illustrative list of factors, on which data had to be examined, it would be in order if an importing Member also examined other factors, while making a determination. However, it would be inconsistent with Article 6.7 of the ATC if all factors mentioned in Article 6.3 were not taken into account by the importing Member. ..."

6.7   Concerning India's comment about the burden of proof, it was for India to submit a *prima facie* case of violation of the ATC, namely, that the restriction imposed by the United States did not respect the provisions of Articles 2.4 and 6 of the ATC. It was then for the United States to convince the Panel that, at the time of its determination, it had respected the requirements of Article 6 of the ATC.

6.8   Concerning India's comments on the "two-track approach" in paragraphs 7.18 to 7.21, we are not taking any position as to whether the TMB process must be exhausted before a panel process can be initiated. Concerning the different roles of the TMB and panel processes, we expand our discussion in paragraph 7.19.

6.9   Concerning India's argument that it did question US production statistics, we amend our text accordingly.

6.10   India and the United States also made other suggestions concerning language changes, which we accept and introduce in our final report.

* * * * *

VII.   FINDINGS

A.   Introduction

7.1   The principal facts that led to the present dispute are the following: On 18 April 1995, the United States requested consultations with India pursuant to Article 6.7 of the ATC regarding the proposed safeguard action on imports of woven wool shirts and blouses, category 440. The request for consultations consisted of a Diplomatic Note and a document entitled "Statement of Serious Damage: Category 440", dated 18 April 1995 (hereinafter referred to as the Market Statement). The Diplomatic Note stated that the sharp and substantial increase in imports from India of the products in the category 440 was "causing serious damage or actual threat thereof to the US industry producing wool woven shirts and blouses"; the accompanying Market Statement stated that "the sharp and substantial increase in imports of woven wool shirts and blouses, Category 440, is causing serious damage to the US industry producing woven wool shirts and blouses". On 23 May 1995, the United States published a notice in the US Federal Register stating that "the sharp and substantial increase in imports of woven wool shirts and blouses, Category 440, is causing serious damage to the US industry producing woven wool shirts and blouses", and that

> "if no solution is agreed upon in consultations with the Government of India ... , the Committee for the Implementation of Textiles Agreements may later establish a limit for the entry and withdrawal from warehouse for consumption of wool textile products in Category 440 ... and exported

during the twelve month period April 18, 1995 through
April 17, 1996, at a level of not less than 76,698 dozen ... ".

7.2   The parties held bilateral consultations in Geneva on 19 April 1995, and
in Washington D.C. on 14-16 June 1995. The consultations did not result in a
mutually agreed solution and on 14 July 1995, the United States implemented a
restraint on imports of woven wool shirts and blouses (category 440) from India,
with the restraint being effective as of 18 April 1995 for one year. At the same
time, the United States referred the matter to the TMB in accordance with Article
6.10 of the ATC. The US restraint was later extended through 17 April 1997.

7.3   As required under Article 6.10 of the ATC, the TMB examined the matter
at its third and fourth meetings on 28 August 1 September 1995 and 12-
15 September 1995 and concluded that, regarding the safeguard action taken by
the United States against imports of category 440 from India, "... the actual threat
of serious damage had been demonstrated, and that, pursuant to paragraph 4 of
Article 6, this actual threat could be attributed to the sharp and substantial increase in imports from India".[26] Pursuant to Article 8.10 of the ATC, India requested the TMB to review its decision concerning the US safeguard action
against imports of category 440 from India. The TMB reviewed this matter on
13-17 November 1995 and concluded that it "could not make any recommendation in addition to the conclusions it had reached at its meeting on 12-15 September 1995 .... The TMB therefore considered its review of the matter completed".[27] On 14 March 1996, pursuant to Article 8.10 of the ATC and Article 6
of the DSU, India requested the DSB to establish a panel on the matter in dispute.
The present Panel was established on 17 April 1996.

B.   Claims of the Parties

7.4   India's main claim is that the US safeguard action against imports of
woven wool shirts and blouses was imposed in violation of the requirements of
Articles 6, 8 and 2 of the ATC. India requests that the Panel suggest that the
United States withdraw the measure in question.

7.5   The United States claims that it respected its obligations under the ATC
when applying and maintaining the restraint on imports of woven wool shirts and
blouses from India. Consequently, the United States requests that the Panel dismiss India's claim.

7.6   In particular, India's claim is that the United States did not comply with
the procedural and substantive requirements of Article 6 of the ATC when it imposed the safeguard measure. India argued that the conditions for application of
Article 6.2, 6.3, 6.7 and 6.10 are three-fold: first, there is a substantive requirement that the importing Member demonstrate that an increase of imports of a

---

[26]   G/TMB/R/3 paragraph 26.
[27]   G/TMB/R/6 paragraph 14.

particular product is causing serious damage or actual threat thereof to the domestic industry producing like or directly competitive products. According to India, the United States failed to demonstrate this in its Market Statement since, on its face, the data contained in the US Market Statement were flawed. Second, India asserted that there were also procedural requirements regarding the nature, quality and extent of the consultations. India argued that the United States failed to consult on the specific proposed safeguard action for which the request for consultations was made and that in the consultations with India, the United States failed to demonstrate, with relevant and specific information, that imports of woven wool shirts and blouses were causing serious damage to the domestic industry producing like or directly competitive products. Third, India argued that in order to impose and maintain a safeguard action, the United States had to obtain the endorsement of the TMB. India labelled these last two procedural requirements as a "two-tier obligation".

7.7   In addition, India claims that the application of the safeguard action by the United States, from the date of the request for consultations, is inconsistent with Article 2 of the ATC and Article XIII of GATT 1994.

7.8   The United States claims that it did comply with the requirements of Article 6 of the ATC in that CITA did demonstrate that the particular product was being imported into the United States in such increased quantities as to cause serious damage or actual threat thereof to the domestic US industry producing like and/or directly competitive products. Although not in agreement with the two-tier approach of India, the United States argued that the TMB's conclusions confirmed that the United States was faced with an actual threat of serious damage. The United States also argued that the date of application of the restraint is consistent with the ATC and that India's claim under Article XIII of GATT 1994 does not fall within the terms of reference of this Panel. The United States, in any case, claims that Article XIII is only relevant for non-discriminatory measures whereas Article 6 restraints must be applied on a Member-by-Member basis.

C.   General Interpretative Issues

7.9   Before turning to India's main claim that the US determination of serious damage or actual threat thereof is flawed and does not comply with the substantive and procedural requirements of Article 6 of the ATC, we examine the issues of the burden of proof of the parties, the standard of review of this Panel and the respective roles of the TMB process and the dispute settlement mechanism of the DSU.

1.   Burden of Proof

7.10   India's main claim is that the United States failed to demonstrate the existence of serious damage to the US industry, as required by Article 6.2 and 6.3 of the ATC. India argued that the United States bore the burden of proving that it had complied with the requirements of Article 6 of the ATC. For India, since safeguard actions are exceptional, they are to be interpreted narrowly and it was for the United States to prove that it had respected all the conditions of application mentioned in Article 6 of the ATC.

7.11   On the issue of burden of proof, the United States responded that, traditionally, in GATT practice, it was for the complaining party to present a *prima facie* case of violation before a panel. Thus, the United States argued, it was for India to advance facts which provided convincing evidence that it was unreasonable for CITA, on the basis of the available evidence, to determine that the adverse effects on the US domestic industry of increased woven wool shirt and blouse imports amounted to "serious damage or actual threat thereof".[28]

7.12   The parties seem to have addressed two different aspects of what one might call the "burden of proof" issue. We believe that a distinction should be made. First, we consider the question of which party bears the burden of proof before the Panel. Since India is the party that initiated the dispute settlement proceedings, we consider that it is for India to put forward factual and legal arguments in order to establish that the US restriction was inconsistent with Article 2 of the ATC and that the US determination for a safeguard action was inconsistent with the provisions of Article 6 of the ATC. Second, we consider the question of what the importing Member must demonstrate at the time of its determination. Concerning the substantive obligations under Article 6 of the ATC, it is clear from the wording of Article 6.2 and 6.3 of the ATC that, in its determination of the need for the proposed restraint, the United States had the obligation to demonstrate that it had complied with the relevant conditions of application of Article 6.2 and 6.3 of the ATC.

2.   Standard of Review

7.13   India argued that the task of this Panel, established pursuant to Article 8.10 of the ATC and Article 6 of the DSU, is to determine whether the United States had observed the requirements of Article 6 in good faith, not whether it had acted reasonably. India referred the Panel to the *Transformers*[29] and *Canadian Corn*[30] cases, an anti-dumping case and a countervailing duty case, respectively, where, according to India, the panels reviewed the importing countries' actions and imposed on them the duty to establish all facts on which they had based their actions. In response, the United States argued that the task of the

---

[28]   We note that, for instance, Article 6.2 of the ATC refers to the expression "serious damage, or actual threat thereof" with a comma, as well as to the expression "serious damage or actual threat thereof" without a comma. We decide to use the expression "serious damage or actual threat thereof" without seeking to be dispositive of the issue raised by India and further discussed hereinafter in paragraphs 7.31 and 7.53.

[29]   Panel Report on "*New Zealand - Imports of Electrical Transformers from Finland*", adopted on 18 July 1985, BISD 32S/55.

[30]   Panel Report on "*Canada - Countervailing Duties on Imports of Grain Corn*", adopted on 26 March 1992, BISD 39S/411.

Panel is to consider whether the US authorities could reasonably and in good faith have determined that serious damage or actual threat thereof existed, not whether serious damage or actual threat thereof existed, as such. The United States referred the Panel to the *Fur Felt Hat* Working Party report[31] which, according to the United States, provides authoritative guidance from GATT 1947 practice and procedures concerning the standard of review to be applied in the present case. In the *Fur Felt Hat* case, the Working Party concluded that, in reviewing a US safeguard measure applied against Czechoslovak imports pursuant to Article XIX of GATT 1947, the United States "were entitled to the benefit of reasonable doubt" and the Working Party rejected the Czechoslovak claim.

7.14   In response to India's arguments, the United States argued that the standard of review used in anti-dumping and countervailing duty cases as well as the relevant provision contained in the Agreement on Implementation of Article VI of GATT 1994 (Article 17.6) were not applicable to the present dispute. India rejected the relevance of the *Fur Felt Hat* case which set out criteria for the review of safeguard measures under Article XIX of GATT 1947, since the mechanism under Article XIX was legally different from that under Article 6 of the ATC where, for instance, there was no compensation provided to the exporting Member.

7.15   We do not consider that the reports cited by the parties are relevant to the present dispute. First, we note that the Appellate Body has made clear in the *Japan Taxes* report that past GATT panel reports do not constitute binding "subsequent practice" referred to in Article 31 of the Vienna Convention on the Law of Treaties (Vienna Convention). The Appellate Body also concluded that " ... adopted panel reports in themselves [do not] constitute 'other decisions of the CONTRACTING PARTIES to GATT 1947' for the purpose of paragraph 1(b)(iv) of the language of Annex 1A incorporating the GATT 1994 into the WTO Agreement".[32] We are, therefore, not bound by past GATT reports, although we may follow their reasoning to the extent relevant. Secondly, the reports cited by the parties were adopted many years ago (more than 40 in one case) and they interpreted different agreements in different contexts. Thirdly, the ATC has instituted a new regime for textile products and the DSU has instituted new rules for panels.

7.16   We note that the ATC does not establish a standard of review for panels.[33] However, although the DSU does not contain any specific reference to standards

---

[31]   Working Party Report on *"The Withdrawal by the United States of a Tariff Concession under Article XIX of the GATT"* GATT Document CP/106, adopted on 22 October 1951, (C.P.6/SR.19), version published by the Secretariat in November 1951, preface by Mr. E. Wyndham-White.

[32]   Report on *"Japan - Taxes on Alcoholic Beverages"*; Appellate Body Report adopted on 29 October 1996, (WT/DS8/AB/R, WT/10/AB/R, WT/DS11/AB/R), DSR 1996:I, 97 at 108.

[33]   We note that both parties agreed that the provision on standard of review for anti-dumping cases was not applicable to the present case.

of review, we consider that Article 11 of the DSU which describes the parameters of the function of panels, is relevant here:

> "The function of panels is to assist the DSB in discharging its responsibilities under this Understanding and the covered agreements. Accordingly, a panel should make an *objective assessment of the matter before it*, including an *objective assessment of the facts* of the case and the *applicability of and conformity with the relevant covered agreements*, and make such other findings as will assist the DSB in making the recommendations or in giving the rulings provided for in the covered agreements. Panels should consult regularly with the parties to the dispute and give them adequate opportunity to develop a mutually satisfactory solution." (emphasis added)

7.17   Pursuant to Article 11 of the DSU, we must determine what is "the matter before [the Panel]". This Panel was established pursuant to Article 8.10 of the ATC and Article 6 of the DSU. Article 8.10 of the ATC provides that a Member may bring an unresolved matter before the DSB:

> " ... Following thorough consideration of the reasons given, the TMB shall issue any further recommendations it considers appropriate forthwith. If, after such further recommendations, the *matter remains unresolved*, either Member *may bring the matter* before the Dispute Settlement Body and invoke paragraph 2 of Article XXIII of GATT 1994 and the relevant provisions of the Dispute Settlement Understanding." (emphasis added)

The "unresolved matter" would appear to be the contested right of the importing Member to apply the proposed restraint, as provided for in Article 6.10 of the ATC:

> "If, however, after the expiry of the period of 60 days from the date on which the request for consultations was received, there has been no agreement between the Members, *the Member which proposed to take safeguard action may apply the restraint* by date of import or date of export, in accordance with the provisions of this Article, *within 30 days* following the 60-day period for consultations, *and at the same time refer the matter to the TMB. ...*". (emphasis added)

The only restraint discussed under Article 6 of the ATC is the proposed restraint by the importing Member. Therefore, pursuant to Article 11 of the DSU, the function of this Panel, established pursuant to Article 8.10 of the ATC and Article 6 of the DSU, is limited to making an objective assessment of the facts surrounding the application of the specific restraint by the United States (and contested by India) and of the conformity of such restraint with the relevant WTO agreements.

3. The Role of the TMB Process Versus the Role of the Dispute Settlement Mechanism of the DSU

7.18   In this context, we think it is useful to draw an important distinction between the role of panels under the DSU and the role of the TMB under the ATC as regards safeguard actions. We note that the preamble of the ATC refers to the process of progressive integration of textiles and clothing products into GATT 1994 disciplines over a period of ten years. The role of the TMB, in light of the object and purpose of the ATC, may be understood better if the application of the ATC is described as providing two tracks: a TMB track and a DSU track.

7.19   The wording of the ATC and the DSU confirms that the role and function of DSU panels differ substantially from that of the TMB. For instance, the TMB is not limited to any specific terms of reference as DSU panels are (Article 7 of the DSU). The function of the TMB is to supervise the implementation of the ATC generally and to examine measures taken, agreements reached and any other matters referred to it. The nature of these broad functions confirms the special and multifaceted role of the TMB. This is also reflected in the TMB's rules of procedure, its decision-making rule and its composition. The TMB members are appointed by WTO Members designated by the Council for Trade in Goods but discharge their function on an *ad personam* basis. Pursuant to a General Council Decision, the TMB's membership is composed of constituencies, in most cases of several Members, where most members also appoint alternates. Furthermore, a TMB member appointed by a WTO Member involved in a dispute before the TMB, participates in the TMB's deliberations, although such TMB member cannot block a consensus (Article 8.2 of the ATC). On the contrary, panelists under the DSU are not selected on the basis of constituencies and the citizens of any party to a dispute under the DSU cannot participate as panelists, absent agreement of the parties (Article 8.3 of the DSU). In addition, a panelist may issue a dissenting opinion under the DSU, while the TMB can only act by consensus. Moreover, Article 8.3 of the ATC is clear as to the wide investigative authority of the TMB:

> "3.   The TMB shall be considered as a standing body and shall meet as necessary to carry out the functions required of it under this Agreement. It shall rely on notifications and information supplied by the Members under the relevant Articles of this Agreement, *supplemented by any additional information or necessary details they may submit or it may decide to seek from them.* It may also rely on *notifications to and reports from other WTO bodies and from such other sources as it may deem appropriate.*" (emphasis added)

We note also that, according to Article 8.10 of the ATC, when the TMB process has been completed, a Member which remains unsatisfied with the TMB recommendations can request the establishment of a panel without having to request consultations under Article 4 of the DSU. This is to say that the TMB process can replace the consultation phase in the dispute settlement process under the DSU and is distinct from the formal adjudication process by panels.[34]

7.20   Therefore when differences arise, the ATC requires parties first to seek consultations with a view to reaching a mutually satisfactory solution to the problem, within the specific parameters or considerations set out in the relevant provision(s) of the ATC. If a mutually satisfactory solution is not reached in the consultations, the matter may be or shall be, depending on the applicable provision, referred to the TMB for review and recommendations. In the case of recourse to Article 6 of the ATC, the object of the consultations is to see whether there is a mutual understanding that the situation calls for restraint on the exports of the particular product or not. If there is such a mutual understanding, details of the agreed restraint measure shall be communicated to the TMB which has to determine whether the agreement is justified in accordance with the provisions of Article 6 of the ATC. If there is no agreement between the parties concerned and the safeguard action is taken, the matter also has to be referred to the TMB. According to Article 6.10 of the ATC, in order to conduct such an examination, " ... the TMB shall have available to it the factual data provided to the Chairman of the TMB, referred to in paragraph 7 [of Article 6], as well as any other relevant information provided by the Members concerned". During the review process, the TMB is not limited to the initial information submitted by the importing Member as parties may submit additional and other information in support of their positions, which, we understand, may relate to subsequent events. Moreover, the TMB may hear witnesses on these facts and perform a genuine fact finding and evidence-building exercise on the continuing situation of the parties concerned with the safeguard action, in order to settle the dispute. TMB members deliberate on the basis of all the information presented to decide whether the safeguard action taken by the importing Member is justified and whether serious damage or actual threat thereof to the domestic industry of the importing Member and causation exist.

7.21   The second track is the DSU. If, after recourse to Articles 6.10 and 8.10 of the ATC, the exporting Member is not satisfied with the recommendation of the TMB, such exporting Member can challenge the safeguard action and bring it to the formal dispute settlement process under the DSU. Unlike the TMB, a DSU panel is not called upon, under its terms of reference, to reinvestigate the market

---

[34]   Article 8.10 of the ATC: "If a Member considers itself unable to conform with the recommendations of the TMB, it shall provide the TMB with the reasons therefor not later than one month after receipt of such recommendations. Following thorough consideration of the reasons given, the TMB shall issue any further recommendations it considers appropriate forthwith. If, after such further recommendations, the matter remains unresolved, either Member may bring the matter before the Dispute Settlement Body and invoke paragraph 2 of Article XXIII of GATT 1994 and the relevant provisions of the Dispute Settlement Understanding."

situation. When assessing the WTO compatibility of the decision to impose national trade remedies, DSU panels do not reinvestigate the market situation but rather limit themselves to the evidence used by the importing Member in making its determination to impose the measure. In addition, such DSU panels, contrary to the TMB, do not consider developments subsequent to the initial determination. In respect of the US determination at issue in the present case, we consider, therefore, that this Panel is requested to make an objective assessment as to whether the United States respected the requirements of Article 6.2 and 6.3 of the ATC at the time of the determination.

D.   Review of the US Determination

1.   Article 6 of the ATC

7.22   Before reviewing the US Market Statement, we must determine what are the conditions for application of a safeguard action pursuant to Article 6 of the ATC. In the *Gasoline*[35] and *Japan Taxes*[36] cases, the Appellate Body stressed that pursuant to Article 3.2 of the DSU, interpretation and clarification of the WTO Agreement needed to be achieved by reference to the fundamental rule of treaty interpretation set out in Article 31 of the Vienna Convention. Article 31 of the Vienna Convention provides that a treaty shall be interpreted "in good faith in accordance with the ordinary meaning to be given to the terms of the treaty in their context and in the light of its object and purpose". We must, therefore, when called upon to interpret and apply the provisions of the WTO Agreement, including those of the ATC, endeavour to give effect to them in their natural and ordinary meaning and in the context in which they occur.[37]

7.23   Article 6.2 and 6.3 of the ATC provides as follows:

---

[35]   Report on "United States - Standards for Reformulated and Conventional Gasoline"; Panel Report circulated on 29 January 1996 (WT/DS2/R), Appellate Body report circulated on 20 May 1996 (WT/DS2/AB/R); both reports were adopted by the DSB on 6 June 1996.

[36]   Report on "Japan - Taxes on Alcoholic Beverages"; Panel Report circulated on 11 July 1996 (WT/DS8/R, WT/10/R, WT/DS11/R), Appellate Body Report circulated on 4 October 1996 (WT/DS8/AB/R, WT/10/AB/R, WT/DS11/AB/R); both reports were adopted by the DSB on 29 October 1996.

[37]   See the Appellate Body Report on "Japan - Taxes on Alcoholic Beverages", op.cit., 105-106: "The provisions of the treaty are to be given their ordinary meaning in their context. The object and purpose of the treaty are also to be taken into account in determining the meaning of its provisions. In footnote 19, at page 12, the Appellate Body cited *Competence of the General Assembly for the Admission of a State to the United Nations (Second Admissions Case)* (1950), *I.C.J. Reports*, p. 4 at 8, in which the International Court of Justice stated: "The Court considers it necessary to say that the first duty of a tribunal which is called upon to interpret and apply the provisions of a treaty, is to endeavour to give effect to them in their natural and ordinary meaning and in the context in which they occur". The Appellate Body also stated, in footnote 20, that " .. the treaty's 'object and purpose' is to be referred to in determining the meaning of the 'terms of the treaty' and not as an independent basis for interpretation" and cited further references.

>"2.   Safeguard action may be taken under this Article when, on the basis of a determination by a Member, it is demonstrated that a particular product is being imported into its territory in such increased quantities as to cause serious damage, or actual threat thereof, to the domestic industry producing like and/or directly competitive products. Serious damage or actual threat thereof *must demonstrably be caused* by such increased quantities in total imports of that product *and not by such other factors as technological changes or changes in consumer preference.*" (emphasis added)

>"3.   In making a determination of serious damage, or actual threat thereof, as referred to in paragraph 2, the Member shall examine the effect of those imports on the state of the particular industry, as reflected in changes *in such relevant economic variables as output, productivity, utilization of capacity, inventories, market share, exports, wages, employment, domestic prices, profits* and *investment*; none of which, either alone or combined with other factors, can necessarily give decisive guidance." (emphasis added)

7.24   The wording of Article 6.2 of the ATC confirms two propositions. First, WTO Members have a right to take safeguard actions; second, the decision to impose a safeguard action must be based on a demonstration by the importing Member, before the safeguard action is taken, that the increased quantities of imports are causing serious damage or actual threat thereof.

7.25   In our view, the wording of Article 6.2 and 6.3 of the ATC makes it clear that all relevant economic factors, namely, all those factors listed in Article 6.3 of the ATC, had to be addressed by CITA, whether subsequently discarded or not, with an appropriate explanation. The wording of paragraph 3, which reads

>" ... the Member shall examine the effect of those imports on the state of the particular industry, as reflected in changes in such relevant economic variables as output, productivity, utilization of capacity, inventories, market share, exports, wages, employment, domestic prices, profits and investment.", (emphasis added)

implies two requirements. First, the relevant economic variables must be examined. Second, output, productivity, utilization of capacity, etc. ... are relevant economic variables. The wording of Article 6.3 of the ATC "... the Member *shall examine* the effects ... on the state of the particular industry, as reflected in changes in *such relevant economic variables as output, productivity, etc. ...*" makes clear that each of the listed factors is not only relevant but must be examined. Effectively, the listed economic variables are examples of relevant economic variables, they are presumed to be "relevant economic variables" and must be examined by the importing country in its determination.

7.26   The wording of the first sentence of Article 6.3 of the ATC imposes on the importing Member the obligation to examine, at the time of its determination, at least all of the factors listed in that paragraph. The importing Member may decide - in its assessment of whether or not serious damage or actual threat thereof has been caused to the domestic industry - that some of these factors carry more or less weight. At a minimum, the importing Member must be able to demonstrate that it has considered the relevance or otherwise of each of the factors listed in Article 6.3 of the ATC.[38]

7.27   The last part of Article 6.3 of the ATC, which states that "none of which, either alone or combined with other factors, can necessarily give decisive guidance", confirms that some consideration and a relevant and adequate explanation have to be provided *of how the facts as a whole support the conclusion* that the determination is consistent with the requirements of the ATC.

7.28   Article 6.2 of the ATC requires that serious damage or actual threat thereof to the domestic industry must *not* have been caused by such other factors as technological changes or changes in consumer preferences. The explicit reference to specific factors imposes an additional requirement on the importing Member to address the question of whether the serious damage or actual threat thereof was not caused by such other factors as technological changes or changes in consumer preference.

7.29   We will now proceed to the review of the US Market Statement in respect of which India claims that the US determination is not consistent with the provisions of Article 6 of the ATC.

2.   *India's Claim Regarding the Substantive Requirements of Article 6 of the ATC*

7.30   India claims that the ATC requires a demonstration that the increase in imports is causing serious damage or actual threat thereof and that, in the present case, the actual data and the method of collecting and analysing the data on the state of industry were so seriously flawed that they could not possibly form the basis of a demonstration on the state of industry. India also claims that the United States failed and, in fact, did not even attempt, to demonstrate any causal link between rising imports and declining production. The United States argued that the ATC does not prescribe any specific methodology for collecting data and that the demonstration by CITA was reasonable both with respect to causation and serious damage or actual threat thereof.

7.31   India also requests a supplementary finding by the Panel that:

> "According to the ATC, notably Article 6, the onus of demonstrating serious damage or its actual threat is on the

---

[38]   There may be cases where a lack of information on one or more factors would not preclude a finding of serious damage or actual threat thereof.

> United States, as the importing country. It has to choose at the beginning of the process whether it will claim the existence of "serious damage" or "actual threat". These are not interchangeable because the data requirement would vary with the chosen situation. It would not be valid to transfer a transitional safeguard to a situation of actual threat when the claim of serious damage has failed to gain acceptance."

We are of the view that this claim would normally be considered as a preliminary issue which could have a bearing on our analysis of this section of the panel report. However, in view of our conclusion on the US determination, we address this claim of India in paragraph 7.53.

7.32   We will proceed in the following way: we will first make general comments on the US Market Statement. Then, we will comment on some of the factors mentioned by the United States in the Market Statement; we will also deal with the fact that certain factors were not addressed by CITA. Subsequently, we will address the issue of causation. Thereafter, we will make an overall assessment of the US determination, taking into account the specific requirements mentioned in Article 6.2 and 6.3 of the ATC.

7.33   We commence with two general remarks. First, the US Market Statement, which according to the United States constitutes the totality of the information used by CITA in making its determination, defines specially the product category on which the safeguard action was to be applied: woven wool shirts and blouses, category 440. However, much of the data are not related to that "particular industry" or to that specific segment of production, as required by Article 6.3 of the ATC. The following Section, entitled "Industry Profile", states that the entire woven shirt and blouse sector includes approximately 748 establishments. In a later statement which it submitted to this Panel in an annex to its first submission as relevant evidence for this case, the United States informed the Panel that the specific woven wool shirt and blouse industry was composed of some 15 firms and that the production of two of these firms represented at least 60 percent of the total domestic production of that industry. Nonetheless, in its discussion of serious damage to the US industry, in Section III:A of its Market Statement, the United States provided employment, man-hour and wage information for the woven shirt and blouse industry but not for the woven *wool* shirt and blouse industry. Similarly, all of the information in Section III:B of the Market Statement was based on statements provided by firms making woven shirts and blouses generally. While it was asserted that "[i]n general, this information applies" to the woven wool shirt and blouse industry, it is not clear to what extent the references to "several", "some", "most", etc. companies in the woven shirt and blouse industry would apply to the woven wool shirt and blouse industry which represents such a small portion of the larger industry. These vague industry statements could have been made more precise since the United States did so a few months after, as evidenced in a later statement which it submitted to this Panel in an annex to its first submission as relevant evidence for this case. For instance, it should have been possible to provide information on sales and profits for 1994 or 1993. Second, in its Market Statement, the United States did not make any reference to several factors listed in Article 6.3 of the ATC. The United States did not mention anything about the factor of "productivity" or "inventories" or "exports", all of which could have had some bearing on the overall determination by the United States.

7.34   We now turn to an examination of the specific elements of the US Market Statement. The Market Statement contains six headings under Section III:A "Serious Damage to the Domestic Industry": (1) US Production, (2) Market Share Loss, (3) Import Penetration, (4) Employment, (5) Man-Hours, (6) Total Annual Wages. Then, there are also six headings under Section III:B, "Industry Statements": (1) Employment, (2) Sales, (3) Profits, (4) Investment, (5) Capacity and (6) Prices. We note in this regard that of the eleven economic variables mentioned in Article 6.3 of the ATC no information or comment is provided in respect of productivity, inventories and exports.

7.35   *"A.   Serious Damage to the Domestic Industry"*

   "1.   US Production"

> *"US production of woven wool shirts and blouses, Category 440, declined during the first nine months of 1994, falling to 61, 000 dozen, 8 percent below the 66, 000 dozen produced during January-September 1993. (Table II)"*

Although the accuracy of the US production statistics was questioned by India in general, India did not raise any specific questions about these statistics.

7.36   *"2.   Market Share Loss"*

> *"The share of the US woven wool shirt and blouse market held by domestic manufacturers fell from 53 percent in 1993 to 40 percent during the first nine months of 1994. (Table II)"*

India submitted US statistics showing that in 1993 and 1994 most of the production was exported.[39] When requested by the Panel to provide pertinent data, the United States stated that US export data were not reliable because exporters did not have an incentive to report such exports. In its rebuttal submission, the United States estimated that possibly some 10 percent of the US production was being exported but due to the non-reliability of export data, CITA did not provide any export data in its Market Statement.

---

[39]   India stated that in 1993 the US production was 82000 dozen and exports were 85000 dozen and in 1994 production and exports were 76000 dozen and referred to a publication by the US Department of Commerce, *US Imports, Production, Markets, Imports Production ratios and Domestic Market Shares for Textile and Apparel Product Categories*, various Editions.

7.37   The absence of export data means that the US statistics do not provide reliable indications of changes in market share, i.e. share of apparent domestic consumption. The unavailability or questionable accuracy of government-compiled data cannot constitute a valid reason for not making some assessment of the impact of exports. In a later statement which it submitted to this Panel in an annex to its first submission as relevant evidence for this case, the United States declared that "The assessment is based on discussion with and information provided by trade associations, labour unions, and direct surveys of individual companies". The United States should have been able to obtain more accurate data for its Market Statement from these sources or even directly from the fifteen or so producers in this sector.

7.38   *"3.   Import Penetration"*

> *"The ratio of imports to domestic production increased from 88 percent in 1993 to 151 percent during January-September 1994. (Table II)"*

These data were not challenged by India.

7.39   *"4.   Employment"*

> *"Employment in the industry producing woven shirts and blouses including shirts and blouses made from wool declined to 31, 929 production workers in 1994, six percent below the 1993 level and a loss of 2, 125 jobs. (Table III)"*

This information is not the information required by Article 6.3 of the ATC as it is not specific to the particular industry producing products of category 440, i.e. woven *wool* shirts and blouses. In a later statement which it submitted to this Panel in an annex to its first submission as relevant evidence for this case, the United States was more specific and put forward the number of jobs lost as 15 between 1993 and 1994 (and 12 between June 1994 and June 1995 and nine for the first half of 1995) in the specific sector under examination. The text of the Industry Statement on employment was not related specifically to the particular industry for which the restraint was imposed: "Several companies reported declines in their employment, *some of which* were specifically attributed to the impact of competitive imported goods ...".

7.40   *"5.   Man-Hours"*

> *"The average annual man-hours worked dropped from 62.5 million man-hours in 1993 to 58.9 million man-hours in 1994, a six percent decline. (Table III)"*

As Table III makes clear, these statistics were for the entire woven shirt and blouse industry and no data whatsoever were submitted for the woven *wool* shirt and blouse industry. In a later statement which it submitted to this Panel in an annex to its first submission as relevant evidence for this case, the United States was more specific and stated that there was a drop from 433,000 man-hours in 1992 to 382,000 man-hours in 1994, an 11.8 percent decline in the specific sector under examination.

7.41   "6.   *Total Annual Wages"*

> *"The total annual production worker wages fell from $423.1 million in 1993 to $411.2 million in 1994, a three percent decline. (Table III)"*

These statistics did not relate to the woven *wool* shirt and blouse industry but covered the entire woven shirt and blouse industry. In a later statement which it submitted to this Panel in an annex to its first submission as relevant evidence for this case, the United States was able to submit relevant data for the specific segment of the industry from 1992 to June 1995.

7.42   "B.   *Industry Statements"*

Under Section III:B of the Market Statement, the United States provided statements on the industry which, it pointed out, were "based on information supplied by individual US firms domestically producing shirts and blouses ... In general, this information applies to companies producing men's and women's woven wool shirts and blouses".[40] This reference made by the United States that "In general, this information applies to the [relevant industry] ..." does not meet the requirements of Article 6.3 of the ATC that the information must relate to the particular industry object of the safeguard action, i.e. the industry producing woven wool shirts and blouses.

7.43   "1.   *Employment"*

> *"Several companies reported declines in their employment, some of which were specifically attributed to the impact of competitive imported goods. Some employment declines were in the range of 25-30 percent"*

We refer to our comments made in paragraph 7.39. There is no information specific to the particular industry in the Market Statement.

---

[40]   We note that for Part A of the Market Statement the information relates often to woven shirts and blouses while for Part B of the Market Statement, the information is provided for the even wider sector of "shirts and blouses". The United States adds that "In general, this information applies to companies producing men's and women's woven wool shirts and blouses".

7.44   *"2.   Sales"*

> *"Most companies reported sales declines as they lost mar-*
> *ket share to lower priced imports. Some companies experi-*
> *enced <u>sales declines</u> of 20 percent or more." (emphasis*
> *added)*

No details or factual evidence was submitted. In addition, there is no information specific to the particular industry in the Market Statement. We note that in a later statement which it submitted to this Panel in an annex to its first submission as relevant evidence for this case, the United States said:

> "The two largest US manufacturers of woven wool shirts
> and blouses, representing over 50% of domestic production,
> have reported stagnant sales during the last half of 1994 and
> the first half of 1995."

There appears to be a contradiction between the two statements.

7.45   *"3.   Profits"*

> *"Profit margins have been eroded across the board in the*
> *wool shirt industry as raw material cost increased while*
> *companies were unable to raise prices because of low-price*
> *import competition."*

This statement is vague and imprecise. It is unclear what "erosion" of profit mar-gin means in concrete terms, as it has not been quantified.

7.46   *"4.   Investment"*

> *"Investment levels are <u>stagnant</u> across much of the indus-*
> *try." (emphasis added)*

However, in the chapeau of Section III:A, the United States stated that "... surg-ing imports, ... have resulted in *loss of ... investment*". Both statements are vague and imprecise and appear to be inconsistent.

7.47   *"5.   Capacity"*

> *"Several companies reported a decline in capacity. One*
> *company reported ending all outside contracting produc-*
> *tion (formerly about 25 percent of its manufacturing), rep-*
> *resenting the equivalent of closing four plants. The com-*
> *pany's own manufacturing plants are now running at only*
> *70 percent of capacity. Furthermore, this company also op-*
> *erates several woolen fabric mills which supply the apparel*
> *manufacturing plants, and these apparel manufacturing*
> *plants, and these mills are now running at about 65 percent*
> *of capacity."*

It is unclear to what extent these statements are applicable to the specific woven *wool* shirt and blouse industry. It is said that one company was "running at only 70 percent of capacity", but no further explanation is given. The question thus arises whether this capacity utilization is lower or greater than the preceding year. The reference to the fabric mills is to a different industry.

7.48   *"6.   Prices"*

> *"Prices of domestic products, manufactured mainly from US-made fabric, are substantially higher than import competition."*

Based on Table IV, submitted under Part IV of the Market Statement on "Attribution", it appears that the world average price was $187.23, the US average price was $525-550 and India's average price was $133.85. This difference in prices in itself indicates nothing about the state of the particular US industry.

Causation

7.49   We note that the United States referred explicitly to the "causation" issue in its industry statement concerning employment, sales and profits. The United States also stated in the chapeau of Section III:A of its Market Statement: "The combination of high imports levels, surging imports, and low priced goods from these countries have resulted in loss of domestic output, market share, investment, employment, man-hours worked, and total annual wages." However, we note that, as far as the alleged effects of imports are concerned, the United States referred to a series of factors (in Section III A and B of its Market Statement) which do not contain any specific data concerning the industry producing woven wool shirts and blouses alleged to have suffered serious damage or actual threat thereof. Moreover, while the chapeau of Section III:A mentions a loss in investment, paragraph 4 of the Industry Statement section states that investment levels were stagnant. We also note that concerning the loss of profits (Industry Statement), the United States' allegation concerning un-quantified cost increases weakens the causation analysis because the United States states that factors other than increased imports, such as increases in prices of raw material, were contributing to damaging the wool shirt industry. Concerning the causation referred to in the sub-section on lost sales (Industry Statement), the United States stated that some companies lost sales as they lost market share to lower priced imports; however, without any export data, market shares would not have been adequately determined. The alleged declines in employment (Industry Statement) were said to be specifically attributed to the impact of competitive imported goods, but the declines were not specific to the particular industry of woven wool shirts and blouses. Concerning the alleged decline in the utilization of capacity, the absence of export data affects the information on utilization of capacity, and brings doubts as to whether the reduction of utilization was due to a reduction in exports. In addition to the above specific deficiencies, the United States did not explain how imports may have increased by some 80,000 dozen in the first nine months of 1993, while domestic production decreased by only 5000 dozen.

7.50   Finally, but not the least, the clear wording of Article 6.2 of the ATC " ... Serious damage or actual threat thereof must demonstrably be caused by ... and not by such other factors as technological changes or changes in consumer preference" imposes on the importing Member at least an explicit obligation to address the question whether serious damage or actual threat thereof to the particular domestic industry was caused by changes in consumer preferences or technological changes. The importing Member remains free to choose the method of assessing whether the state of its particular domestic industry was caused by such other factors as technological changes or changes in consumer preferences, but it must demonstrate that it has addressed the issue. The United States made no mention of this issue in its Market Statement.

3.   Overall Assessment of the US Determination

7.51   In assessing the US determination in relation to the provisions of Article 6.2 and 6.3 of the ATC, we reach the following conclusion. As discussed in paragraphs 7.25 to 7.28 including footnote 38, Article 6.3 of the ATC lists eleven economic factors which must be "considered" or "examined" by the importing Member in making its determination, for the particular industry for which the measure is imposed, which in the present case is the woven wool shirts and blouses, category 440. Those factors are: output, productivity, utilization of capacity, inventories, market share, exports, wages, employment, domestic prices, profits and investment. We find that the United States did not examine eight of these factors, i.e. productivity, utilization of capacity, inventories, exports, wages, employment, profits and investment, in the context of the particular industry, i.e. the woven wool shirt and blouse industry, and the United States gave no explanation for not doing so. For five of these factors (utilization of capacity, wages, employment, profits and investment) some information was provided only for the broader shirt and blouse or woven shirt and blouse sectors without being adequately related to the particular US industry. The absence of any data on exports also vitiates the statements on market shares, sales and utilization of capacity for the purpose of demonstrating serious damage or actual threat thereof as well as causation. In addition, the information provided is often vague and imprecise both in the Section III:A and B. Since the United States did not include any specific information for the particular industry concerned, it, therefore, could not make any convincing analysis as to the causation of serious damage or actual threat thereof to that particular industry of woven wool shirts and blouses. The United States did assert in the chapeau of Section III:A of the Market Statement that imports had resulted in various losses (domestic output, market share, investment, employment, man-hours worked, and total annual wages) for US industry, but the United States failed to tie the effects of imports on those economic variables to the particular industry alleged to have been damaged by such imports. Moreover, the United States did not address the issue of whether the alleged state of the particular industry was caused by technological changes or changes in consumer preferences. Finally, the United States did not include any explanation as to why it was not able to collect specific or more precise information for the particular industry when making its determination, while it was able to develop such data a few months after (as evidenced in a later statement which the United states submitted to this Panel in an annex to its first submission as relevant evidence for this case).

7.52   For all these reasons, and recognizing that the right of importing Members to take safeguard restraints must be exercised within the parameters laid down in Article 6 of the ATC, we reach the conclusion that, on its face, the US determination did not respect the requirements of Article 6 of the ATC. This is not to say that the Panel interprets the ATC as imposing on the importing Member any specific method either for collecting data or for considering and weighing all the relevant economic factors upon which the importing Member will decide whether there is need for a safeguard restraint. The relative importance of particular factors including those listed in Article 6.3 of the ATC is for each Member to assess in the light of the circumstances of each case. The importing Member must, however, comply in its determination with the requirements that (i) at least all economic factors listed in Article 6.3 of the ATC are "considered", as indicated in paragraphs 7.25 and 7.26 above, and (ii) the importing Member meet the explicit requirement to confirm that the increase in imports is the cause of the serious damage or actual threat thereof to the particular domestic industry and that the state of that industry is not caused by such other factors as technological changes or changes in consumer preferences.

4.   Serious Damage or Actual Threat Thereof

7.53   As discussed in paragraph 7.31, India requested a supplementary finding on the issue of serious damage or actual threat thereof. We note that the Diplomatic Note did refer to serious damage or actual threat thereof, while the US Market Statement and the notification on 23 May 1995 in the Federal Register were limited to an allegation of serious damage. We do not consider, however, that we need to decide whether serious damage or actual threat thereof is a single concept; whether serious damage is a shorthand for the expression "serious damage or actual threat thereof"; whether actual threat of serious damage is but a lower level of serious damage; whether the two expressions refer to different types of market situation in the importing market; or even whether the Diplomatic Note and the Market Statement together form a single request for consultation with serious damage being used as a shorthand expression for serious damage or actual threat thereof. Whether the United States wanted to demonstrate "serious damage" or, assuming they are distinct standards, "actual threat thereof" or "serious damage or actual threat thereof", it would have had to demonstrate the effects of imports on the particular domestic industry with reference to at least the eleven factors listed in Article 6.3 of the ATC. Therefore, in view of our conclusions in the previous paragraphs concerning these factors, we consider that the US demonstration, contained in the Market Statement which is the totality of the information used by CITA for its determination, does not support a determination of serious damage or actual threat thereof, as a single or as two separate concepts. Similarly, the deficiencies we found in the analysis of causation in the US Market Statement would apply whether the increased quantities of imports were alleged to have caused serious damage or actual threat thereof as a single or as two separate concepts.

5.   *The Obligation to Consult and the Alleged Need for TMB Endorsement*

7.54   India also claims that, on its face, the US measure is inconsistent with the procedural requirements of Article 6 of the ATC. India argued that the procedural requirements of Article 6 of the ATC are the following: a) the Member proposing to take safeguard action shall seek consultations; b) the request shall be accompanied by specific factual information; c) if consultations fail and an action is taken, the TMB shall promptly conduct an examination; d) following that examination, the TMB shall make the appropriate recommendations. For India, the reference to the word "shall" means that all these procedural requirements must be fulfilled for a safeguard action to be consistent with the ATC. India, therefore, claims that the United States could not justify its restraint as a response to an actual threat of serious damage because the US Market Statement dealt only with the existence of serious damage.

7.55   India also claims that the US measure is inconsistent with Article 6 because the mandatory prior consultations were not held on the measure for which the United States obtained TMB "endorsement". According to India, the US measure was never endorsed by the TMB because the TMB endorsed a measure different from the one which formed the basis of the US decision to impose a safeguard action and different from the one on which India and the United States had consulted. India claims that the TMB endorsed a measure to compensate for an increase of imports which were causing a threat of serious damage, while the United States imposed, and India and the United States consulted on, a safeguard action to compensate for an increase of imports which was causing serious damage to the domestic industry.

7.56   With respect to India's claim that the United States consulted on, and referred to the TMB, a measure to compensate for serious damage and not a measure to compensate for actual threat of serious damage,[41] we consider that since

---

[41]   We recall that the US Diplomatic Note requested consultations in respect of sharp and substantial increase in imports from India of the products in category 440 which were causing "serious damage or actual threat thereof" to the domestic industry, the US Market Statement was entitled "Statement of Serious Damage: Category 440" and the notification on 23 May 1995 in the US Federal Register stated that "the sharp and substantial increase in imports of woven wool shirts and blouses,

we have concluded that the US determination did not respect the requirements of Article 6 of the ATC, irrespective of whether serious damage or actual threat thereof is a single or two separate concepts, it is not necessary for us to rule on the issue of whether the consultations were properly held, or on the issue of whether the TMB made a recommendation in respect of the measure on which the United States had consulted with India.

7.57   Concerning India's claim that the US restraint is invalid because the TMB did not endorse the measure which the United States attempted to justify in the Market Statement and on which consultations were held, we note that under Article 6.10 of the ATC, the United States, should it be entitled to impose a restraint, could do so without TMB authorization, although it would be required to refer the matter to the TMB for appropriate recommendations. Article 8.9 of the ATC confirms that the recommendations of the TMB are not binding:

> "The Members shall *endeavour* to accept in full the recommendations of the TMB, which shall exercise proper surveillance of the implementation of such recommendations." (emphasis added)

We, therefore, reject India's claim that under the ATC a safeguard action can be maintained only if adequately endorsed by the TMB.

E.   Alleged Retroactive Application of the Safeguard

7.58   India also claims that the decision of the United States to set the period of application of the safeguard action starting from the date of the request for consultations violates the provisions of the ATC, in particular Articles 1.6 and 2, as well as Article XIII of GATT 1994 because the safeguard action should be applied and made effective only after the expiry of the 60-day consultation period. The United States objected to the right of India to invoke a violation of Article XIII of GATT 1994 in support of its claim and urges the rejection of this claim. In view of our conclusion that the US determination did not respect the requirements of Article 6.2 and 6.3 of the ATC and that, therefore, the US measure violated the ATC, we need not consider whether the date of application of that measure was consistent with WTO rules.

F.   India's Claim that Article 2 of the ATC was Violated

7.59   Since we conclude that the safeguard action taken by the United States violated the provisions of Article 6 of the ATC, it is our view that the United States applied a restraint not authorized under the ATC, which, therefore, constitutes also a violation of Article 2.4 of the ATC.

Category 440, is causing serious damage to the US industry producing woven wool shirts and blouses".

$* * * * *$

VIII. CONCLUSIONS

8.1　We conclude that the US restraint applied as of 18 April 1995 on imports of woven wool shirts and blouses, category 440, from India and its extensions violated the provisions of Articles 2 and 6 of the ATC. Since Article 3.8 of the DSU provides that "In cases where there is an infringement of the obligations assumed under a covered agreement, the action is considered *prima facie* to constitute a case of nullification and impairment", we conclude that the said US measure nullified and impaired the benefits of India under the WTO Agreement, in particular under the ATC. The Panel recommends that the Dispute Settlement Body make such a ruling.

CANADA - CERTAIN MEASURES CONCERNING PERIODICALS

Report of the Appellate Body
WT/DS31/AB/R

Adopted by the Dispute Settlement Body on 30 July 1997

Canada, Appellant/Appellee	Present:
United States, Appellant/Appellee	Matsushita, Presiding Member
	Ehlermann, Member
	Lacarte-Muró, Member

I.   INTRODUCTION

Canada and the United States appeal from certain issues of law and legal interpretations in the Panel Report, *Canada - Certain Measures Concerning Periodicals*[1] (the "Panel Report"). The Panel was established to consider a complaint by the United States against Canada concerning three measures: Tariff Code 9958,[2] which prohibits the importation into Canada of certain periodicals, including split-run editions; Part V.1 of the Excise Tax Act,[3] which imposes an excise tax on split-run editions of periodicals; and the application by Canada Post Corporation ("Canada Post") of commercial "Canadian", commercial "international" and "funded" publications mail postal rates, the latter through the Publications Assistance Program (the "PAP") maintained by the Department of Canadian Heritage ("Canadian Heritage") and Canada Post.[4]

The Panel Report was circulated to the Members of the World Trade Organization (the "WTO") on 14 March 1997. It contains the following conclusions:

(a) Tariff Code 9958 is inconsistent with Article XI:1 of GATT 1994 and cannot be justified under Article XX(d) of GATT 1994; *(b)* Part V.1 of

---

[1]   WT/DS31/R, 14 March 1997.

[2]   Customs Tariff, R.S.C. 1985, c. 41 (3rd Supp.), s. 114, Schedule VII, Item 9958.

[3]   An Act to Amend the Excise Tax Act and the Income Tax Act, S.C. 1995, c. 46.

[4]   Canada Post Corporation Act, R.S.C. 1985, c. C-10; Publications Mail Postal Rates, Canada Post Corporation, effective 4 March 1996; Canadian Publication Mail Products Sales Agreement, 1 March 1995; International Publications Mail Product (Canadian Distribution) Sales Agreement, 1 March 1994; Memorandum of Agreement concerning the Publications Assistance Program between the Department of Communications and Canada Post Corporation (the "MOA").

the Excise Tax Act is inconsistent with Article III:2, first sentence, of GATT 1994; *(c)* the application by Canada Post of lower "commercial Canadian" postal rates to domestically-produced periodicals than to imported periodicals, including additional discount options available only to domestic periodicals, is inconsistent with Article III:4 of GATT 1994; but *(d)* the maintenance of the "funded" rate scheme is justified under Article III:8(b) of GATT 1994.[5]

The Panel made the following recommendation:

The Panel recommends that the Dispute Settlement Body request Canada to bring the measures that are found to be inconsistent with GATT 1994 into conformity with its obligations thereunder.[6]

On 29 April 1997, Canada notified the Dispute Settlement Body[7] (the "DSB") of its intention to appeal certain issues of law covered in the Panel Report and legal interpretations developed by the Panel, pursuant to paragraph 4 of Article 16 of the *Understanding on Rules and Procedures Governing the Settlement of Disputes* (the "*DSU*"), and filed a Notice of Appeal with the Appellate Body, pursuant to Rule 20 of the *Working Procedures for Appellate Review* (the "*Working Procedures*"). On 12 May 1997, Canada filed an appellant's submission.[8] On 14 May 1997, the United States filed an appellant's submission pursuant to Rule 23(1) of the *Working Procedures.* On 26 May 1997, Canada filed an appellee's submission pursuant to Rule 23(3) of the *Working Procedures* and the United States filed an appellee's submission pursuant to Rule 22 of the *Working Procedures.* The oral hearing provided for in Rule 27 of the *Working Procedures* was held on 2 June 1997, at which the participants presented their arguments and answered questions from the Division of the Appellate Body hearing the appeal.

II. ARGUMENTS OF THE PARTICIPANTS

A. Canada

Canada submits that the Panel erred in law by characterizing Part V.1 of the Excise Tax Act as a measure regulating trade in goods subject to the GATT 1994. In the alternative, Canada argues that, even on the assumption that the GATT 1994 applies, the Panel erred in law when it found Part V.1 of the Excise Tax Act to be inconsistent with Article III:2, first sentence, of the GATT 1994. In particular, Canada submits that the Panel erred in law in finding that imported United States' split-run periodicals[9] and Canadian non-split-run periodicals are like products; and in failing to apply the principle of non-discrimination that is

---

[5] Panel Report, para. 6.1.
[6] Panel Report, para. 6.2.
[7] WT/DS31/5, 2 May 1997.
[8] Pursuant to Rule 21(1) of the *Working Procedures.*
[9] We use the terms "periodical" and "magazine" interchangeably in this Report.

embodied in Article III:2, first sentence, of the GATT 1994. Canada agrees with the Panel's conclusion that the "funded" postal rate scheme is a permissible subsidy in accordance with the terms and conditions of Article III:8(b) of the GATT 1994.

1. Applicability of the GATT 1994 to Part V.1 of the Excise Tax Act

Canada submits that the Panel erred in law when it applied Article III:2, first sentence, of the GATT 1994 to a measure affecting advertising services. Canada asserts that the GATT 1994 applies, as the GATT 1947 had always applied previously, to measures affecting trade in goods, but it has never been a regime for dealing with services in their own right. In Canada's view, if the GATT 1994 applied to all aspects of services measures on the basis of incidental, secondary or indirect effects on goods, the GATT 1994 would effectively be converted into a services agreement. More precisely, the GATT 1994 should not apply merely on the ground that a service makes use of a good as a tangible medium of communication. Assuming that the measure at issue is designed essentially to restrict access to the services market, the mere fact that a service makes use of a good as a vehicle or a medium is an insufficient ground on which to base a challenge under the GATT 1994.

Canada asserts that the Panel's decision to consider Part V.1 of the Excise Tax Act as a measure subject to Article III of the GATT 1994 was based largely upon an unwarranted generalization of the terms of Article III:4, as well as a misconstruction of the word "indirectly" in Article III:2, first sentence. Canada argues that it is evident from its text that Article III:4 of the GATT 1994 governs only services measures that affect the ability of foreign goods to compete on an equal footing with domestic goods. Canada submits that advertising services are only subject to Article III:4 to the extent that they affect the "internal sale or offering for sale, purchase, transportation, distribution or use" of a product that is entitled to national treatment under Article III of the GATT 1994. The inference that advertising services in general are covered by Article III:2 of the GATT 1994 is without foundation.

Canada stresses that the concept of "indirectly" in Article III:2 of the GATT 1994 is intended to capture taxes which apply to "inputs" that contribute to the production or distribution of a good, such as raw materials, services inputs and intermediate inputs. It is important to distinguish services inputs that are directly involved in the production or marketing of a good from services that are "end-products" in their own right. In Canada's view, the advertising services of a publisher are not, like labour in the production of a car, an input into the production of a good. Canada asserts that services are often delivered by means of a good, and that the taxation of services that are associated with goods in this way does not "subject" those goods "indirectly" to the tax, because the tax does not affect the costs of the production, distribution and marketing of the goods. Canada argues that, although magazines serve as a tangible medium in which advertising is incorporated, this association, however close, does not meet the tests appropriate to the interpretation of Article III:2 of the GATT 1994. Canada maintains that advertising is not an input or a cost in the production, distribution or use of magazines as physical products. Therefore, the taxation of magazine advertising services is not indirect taxation of magazines as goods within the meaning of Article III:2.

Canada asserts that the Panel mischaracterized Part V.1 of the Excise Tax Act as a measure affecting trade in goods. It is a measure regulating access to the magazine advertising market. Most magazines represent two distinct economic outputs, that of a good and an advertising medium for providing a service, depending on the perspective of the purchaser. According to Canada, the tax is not applied to the consumer good because it is not based on, nor applied to, the price of a magazine. Instead, the tax is calculated using the value of advertising carried in a split-run edition of a magazine and is assessed against the publisher of each split-run magazine as the seller of the advertising service.

In Canada's view, since the provision of magazine advertising services falls within the scope of the General Agreement on Trade in Services (the "GATS"), and Canada has not undertaken any commitments in respect of the provision of advertising services in its Schedule of Specific Commitments, Canada is not bound to provide national treatment to Members of the WTO with respect to the provision of advertising services in the Canadian market.

2. Consistency of Part V.1 of the Excise Tax Act with Article III:2 of the GATT 1994

Should the Appellate Body conclude that Part V.1 of the Excise Tax Act is properly subject to the jurisdiction of the GATT 1994, Canada submits, as an alternative argument, that such measure is consistent with Article III:2, first sentence, of the GATT 1994. First, Canada asserts that the Panel erred in its finding that imported split-run periodicals and Canadian non-split-run periodicals are "like products" within the meaning of Article III:2, first sentence, of the GATT 1994. The Panel disregarded the evidence before it, and based its finding on a speculative hypothesis, thus failing to make "an objective assessment of the facts of the case" as required by Article 11 of the *DSU*. In Canada's view, the "like product" test under Article III:2, first sentence, requires a comparison of an imported product with a domestic product. While the Panel acknowledged the correctness of this test, the Panel failed to apply it by using a hypothetical example for its comparison rather than actual examples of split-run and non-split-run magazines provided by Canada. Canada notes that the Panel asserted that its hypothetical example was necessary because there were no imported split-run periodicals in Canada due to the import prohibition under Tariff Code 9958. However, Canada argues that there are certain "grandfathered" split-run magazines produced in Canada, and that those magazines provide an accurate representation of the content and properties of a split-run edition based on a non-Canadian parent magazine. The Panel did not consider the evidence which had been filed by

Canada,[10] it did not provide any reason why that evidence was not relevant, and instead based its analysis upon an hypothetical scenario. Therefore, Canada argues, the Panel followed an approach which is inconsistent with the letter and spirit of Article 11 of the *DSU*.

Furthermore, Canada submits that the Panel made two errors in its hypothetical analysis of "like products". First, the Panel failed to compare an imported product with a domestic product, and instead it compared two imported "Canadian" editions. Second, the Panel failed to compare products which could be marketed simultaneously in the Canadian market. Canada also argues that the Panel's decision fails to reflect the narrow construction and case-by-case approach required by the Appellate Body Report in *Japan - Taxes on Alcoholic Beverages* ("*Japan - Alcoholic Beverages*").[11] The case-by-case approach requires an analysis based upon the specific properties of the magazines in a Canadian context.

The chief and, for all practical purposes, the only distinguishing characteristic of a magazine is its content. Although Canada recognizes that the Panel did not, in principle, reject the idea that content can be relevant, Canada argues that the Panel evaded a determination of whether split-run periodicals containing foreign content are substantially identical to magazines developed specifically for a Canadian readership.

Canada submits that content developed for and aimed at the Canadian market cannot be the same as foreign content. Content for the Canadian market will include Canadian events, topics, people and perspectives. The content may not be exclusively Canadian, but the balance will be recognizably and even dramatically different than that which is found in foreign publications which merely reproduce editorial content developed for and aimed at a non-Canadian market.

Canada also submits that, even if United States' split-run periodicals and Canadian non split- run periodicals are "like products", Part V.1 of the Excise Tax Act does not discriminate against imported products. Canada affirms that the tax is non-discriminatory, in form and in fact, and has no greater impact on imported products than on domestic products. Because the legislation does not make any distinction between domestic and imported products, the tax is free from any taint of overt discrimination. Canada asserts that there can be no violation of Article III:2, first sentence, unless imported products, as a class, are taxed in excess of like domestic products. Canada submits that the mere potential that an individual, imported item might be taxed at a higher rate than a like domestic product cannot create an automatic violation, when it results from fiscal classifications that are not themselves discriminatory in form or in fact. Article III:2 was not intended to impose fiscal harmonization in tax rates, methods or classifica-

---

[10] Comparing TIME (a United States' magazine) and TIME Canada (a split-run magazine) with Maclean's (a domestic non-split run magazine).

[11] WT/DS8/AB/R, WT/DS10/AB/R, WT/DS11/AB/R, adopted 1 November 1996.

tions. Canada states that its interpretation does not involve the subjectivity of the now-discredited "aims and effects" test. Canada suggests only that if the fiscal categories of a measure are origin-neutral and exhibit no inherent bias, then the mere existence of such categories, with differential rates of taxation, does not violate Article III:2. In the present case, Canada asserts there is no *de jure* or *de facto* discrimination, and the definitions (or fiscal categories) used in the Excise Tax Act display no inherent bias against imported products.

With respect to the second sentence of Article III:2 of the GATT 1994, Canada argues that imported split-run and domestic non-split-run periodicals are not directly competitive or substitutable products according to the criteria in *Japan - Alcoholic Beverages*. Because content is so specific in magazines and because readers are looking for something fairly specific, magazines are not interchangeable or substitutable. Readers buy multiple magazines. These are complex questions of fact.

Canada argues that, in the case at hand, there are two separate determinations to be made under Article III:2. The first sentence relates to whether or not there is discrimination against like products. Only if there is no violation of the first sentence can the Appellate Body decide whether the measure is consistent with the second sentence of Article III:2. On this point, Canada argues, it is not the actual decision of the Panel that is in question, but the fact that the Panel made no decision at all on the second sentence of Article III:2. An examination of the second sentence would involve an examination of factual elements which have not been dealt with one way or the other by the Panel in the first instance.

Canada's position is that the second sentence of Article III:2 is not an appropriate subject for appellate review in this case. Canada argues that the jurisdiction of the Appellate Body is limited to matters that are specifically appealed as constituting errors of law or interpretation in the Panel Report within the meaning of paragraph 17.6 of the *DSU*. The United States failed to raise the Panel's findings on Article III:2, second sentence, as a point of appeal, and therefore, the Appellate Body has no jurisdiction to look into this issue. If the Appellate Body decides to reverse the Panel's findings on Article III:2, first sentence, that should be the end of the matter.

3. Consistency of the "Funded" Postal Rate Scheme with Article III:8(b) of the GATT 1994

Canada submits that, consistent with the Panel's findings, the payments made by Canadian Heritage to Canada Post to provide Canadian publishers with reduced postal rates are payments of subsidies exclusively to domestic producers within the meaning of Article III:8(b) of the GATT 1994.

Canada asserts that nothing in the expression, "payment of subsidies exclusively to domestic producers" implies any limitations on the manner in which the payment must be made. In this case, the payments made by Canadian Heritage to Canada Post are made for the sole benefit of Canadian publishers. In Canada's view, Canadian Heritage is purchasing a benefit for domestic producers.

Canada argues that the phrase "exclusively to domestic producers" does not support the United States' assertion that a payment must actually be made directly to the publishers. Rather, the word "exclusively" is concerned with the distinction between "domestic" as opposed to "non-domestic" producers. Canada submits that the general thrust of Article III is against discrimination between imported and domestic products. In this context, Canada considers that granting a government subsidy "exclusively" to domestic producers means granting a subsidy only to the producers of domestic products, in the sense that it is paid to them alone and not to foreign producers.

Canada asserts that the United States' position is based on a difference of form, not substance, and that the specific form in which the subsidy is paid is irrelevant to the operation of Article III:8(b) of the GATT 1994. The word "including" in a legal text is illustrative, not exhaustive, and it demonstrates that the Members intended to cover a very broad range of subsidies, regardless of the particular form of the subsidy or the manner of payment. In Canada's view, the 1990 panel report in *European Economic Community - Payments and Subsidies Paid to Processors and Producers of Oilseeds and Related Animal-Feed Proteins ("EEC - Oilseeds")*[12] confirms that the payment of subsidies can be indirect, provided that the condition of exclusivity is met. Canada submits that indirect payment merely creates a presumption that a payment not made directly to producers is not made exclusively to them. However, the panel report in *EEC - Oilseeds* clearly leaves open the possibility that the presumption can be rebutted in the right circumstances. In Canada's view, indirect payment creates at most a presumption, but it is a rebuttable presumption.

Canada submits that the broad meaning of "payment" in Article III:8(b) is confirmed by the fact that the word "payment" in the French text of the GATT 1994 appears as "attribution", and not as "paiement". The expression "payment of subsidies" is translated into French as "attribution de subventions", i.e. granting of subsidies. Canada argues the expression "attribution de subventions" clearly does not require that there must be an actual transfer of government funds to domestic producers.

Canada points out that its interpretation of Article III:8(b) of the GATT 1994 does not diminish the protection offered under Article III generally. Whether the cheques are written to Canada Post or to the publishers will not change the competitive conditions between magazines. Canada submits that it makes no sense to suggest that Article III:8(b) should be interpreted in a manner that can only lead to government inefficiencies in delivering subsidies to producers.

---

[12]   Adopted 25 January 1990, BISD 37S/86.

Canada also argues that the panel reports quoted by the United States in its appellant's submission[13] do not support the conclusion that a subsidy must be paid directly to domestic producers to qualify under the provisions of Article III:8(b). Those panel reports do not apply to the facts in this dispute. The method of subsidy payment is not, in and of itself, conclusive in determining whether Article III:8(b) of the GATT 1994 applies. The essential factor is that the payment must be made by the government for the benefit of domestic producers.

B.   United States

The United States agrees with the Panel's findings and conclusions concerning Tariff Code 9958, Part V.1 of the Excise Tax Act and the lower "commercial Canadian" postal rates, as summarized in paragraph 6.1 of the Panel Report, but the United States submits that the Panel erred in determining that Canada's "funded" postal rate scheme is justified by Article III:8(b) of the GATT 1994.

1.   Applicability of the GATT 1994 to Part V.1 of the Excise Tax Act

The United States submits that Canada's excise tax is not exempt from Article III of the GATT 1994 on the ground that it is a "services measure" subject only to the GATS. Canada has failed to demonstrate any significant conflict between the GATT 1994 and the GATS arising from this case or that, in any event, the GATS should be accorded priority over the GATT 1994. The United States argues that Canada is incorrect in suggesting that the GATT 1994 cannot apply to measures whose application affects both goods and services.

The United States asserts that the question of whether the GATT 1994 and the GATS may overlap to some extent is irrelevant. The fundamental legal question, which the panel addressed, is whether the two agreements impose conflicting obligations with respect to Canada's excise tax, and whether one agreement should be given priority over the other. The United States submits that the Panel was correct in pointing out that nothing in the *Marrakesh Agreement Establishing the World Trade Organization* (the *"WTO Agreement"*)[14] suggests that a measure that comes within the scope of the GATS cannot be equally subject to the GATT 1994.

---

[13]   Panel Report, *Italian Discrimination Against Agricultural Machinery*, (*"Italian Agricultural Machinery"*), adopted 23 October 1958, BISD 7S/60; Panel Report, *United States - Measures Affecting Alcoholic and Malt Beverages*, (*"United States - Malt Beverages"*), adopted 19 June 1992, BISD 39S/206; Panel Report, *United States - Measures Affecting the Importation, Internal Sale and Use of Tobacco*, (*"United States - Tobacco"*), DS44/R, adopted 4 October 1994; Panel Report, *EEC - Oilseeds*, adopted 25 January 1990, BISD 37S/86.
[14]   Done at Marrakesh, Morocco, 15 April 1994.

The United States maintains that because Canada's general argument forbidding any significant overlap between the two agreements is incorrect, so too is Canada's more specific argument that Part V.1 of the Excise Tax Act cannot be subject to the GATT 1994 because it applies to advertising services. Measures affecting imported products are not excluded from the purview of the GATT 1994 simply because they take the form of a tax or other measure applied to "services". According to the United States, Canada's view that measures affecting imported goods are exempt from scrutiny under Article III of the GATT 1994 whenever they take the form of taxation or regulation of services would give WTO Members licence to impose a wide range of discriminatory tax and regulatory measures on imported goods. Should Canada's view prevail, a Member could, consistently with the GATT 1994, impose an exclusive tax on the rental of foreign cars, place a prohibitive surcharge on telephone services carried out using imported telecommunications equipment or tax medical services using foreign diagnostic machinery.

The United States asserts that for the purposes of Article III of the GATT 1994, it is irrelevant whether Canada's excise tax could be characterized as a measure affecting trade in advertising services within the terms of the GATS. The tax measure alters the terms of competition for imported split-run periodicals *vis-à-vis* like domestic magazines for the placement of advertisements - as indeed it is intended to do - and thus falls squarely within the purview of Article III:2, first sentence, of the GATT 1994.

The United States also submits that Canada's excise tax applies "directly or indirectly" to split-run periodicals. The sweeping language of Article III:2, first sentence, ensures coverage of taxes (such as taxes imposed on goods or services) that have the potential to affect the competitive position of imported and domestic goods. Thus, the Panel was correct to find that the terms "directly or indirectly" specifically encompass Canada's excise tax on split-run periodicals. The United States points out that the tax is assessed on a "per issue" basis, which plainly links the tax to the physical good, a particular issue of a magazine. The United States also stresses that Part V.1 of the Excise Tax Act is entitled "Tax on Split-Run Periodicals", and the terms of the Excise Tax Act provide that the tax is imposed "in respect of" split-run editions of periodicals.

The United States submits that advertisements, together with editorial content, constitute fundamental, physical components of many, if not most, magazines. It is inconsistent to argue, as Canada does, that a tax concerning inputs is a tax directly or indirectly on a product, but a tax concerning a major component of that product is not. Furthermore, the United States asserts that advertisements affect a magazine's price, cost and competitive position as much as any input used in the production of a product.

The United States also maintains that, by its terms, the first sentence of Article III:2 applies only when imported products are "subject" to internal taxes. Since the language of that sentence includes both direct and indirect taxes on products, it is plain that the first sentence applies even when the immediate object of the taxation is not an imported product. Even if Canada's assertion that the tax applies to "advertising services" is correct, that would hardly be the end of the inquiry; the question would then be whether the tax nevertheless applies at least "indirectly" to split-run periodicals. The answer to that question is plainly "yes", as the language of the Excise Tax Act makes clear. The notion that restricting a major use of a product - in this case, the carrying of certain types of advertising - cannot affect competitive conditions is untenable. By applying a confiscatory tax based on advertisements placed in split-run periodicals, Canada virtually ensures the elimination of such periodicals from the Canadian marketplace - which indeed is the whole point of the tax.

2. Consistency of Part V.1 of the Excise Tax Act with Article III:2 of the GATT 1994

The United States submits that split-run periodicals are "like" domestic non-split-run periodicals. In the United States' view, none of the three separate claims of legal error raised by Canada with respect to the Panel's findings and conclusions on Article III:2, first sentence, are persuasive.

The United States asserts that Canada's argument that the Panel erred by using a hypothetical example as a basis for comparison is without merit. The Panel correctly determined that the application of the tax turned on factors other than the characteristics of the product sold in Canada and that, as a result, imported split-run periodicals and domestic non-split-run periodicals could be practically identical products. The United States points out that the Excise Tax Act does not draw any distinctions based on type of editorial content and, consequently, under the Excise Tax Act a split-run periodical could theoretically be entirely Canadian-oriented. By the same token, a non-split-run periodical need not have any articles with a particular Canadian focus. Thus, according to the United States, Canada's attempt to demonstrate that TIME Canada and Maclean's reflect a different editorial orientation is simply irrelevant because the application of the Excise Tax Act is not based on any such difference.

The United States also submits that, even if one could credit Canada's argument that it is seeking through the excise tax to ensure "original content" in magazines sold in Canada, this result would be contrary to the object and purpose of Article III. In the United States' view, if the GATT 1994 permitted Members to require that imported goods be designed exclusively or primarily for their markets, they could easily insulate their markets from the comparative economic advantages enjoyed by producers in other countries. By requiring "originality", WTO Members could exclude products that are sold in multiple markets or that enjoy the economies of scale that result from such sales.

The United States stresses that Canada has banned importation of split-run periodicals for over 30 years. For this reason, the Panel was entirely justified to use hypothetical examples in its reasoning on the "like product" issue.

According to the United States, Canada's argument that the Excise Tax Act does not impose a higher tax on imported products than on like domestic products is difficult in the light of the fact that, (1) the Act makes only one class of magazines - split-runs - subject to the special 80 percent excise tax; and (2) the Panel found that, for purposes of GATT Article III:2, imported split-run periodicals are "like" non-split-run domestic Canadian magazines. The United States argues that manifestly imported split-run periodicals are subject to a higher rate of taxation than like domestic non-split-run periodicals. That is the end of the inquiry for purposes of Article III:2, first sentence. The United States also maintains that Canada's 80 percent excise tax alters the competitive environment in the Canadian magazine market against imported split-run magazines and thus favours "like" domestically-produced periodicals. Thus, Canada's proposed "discrimination" test based on "imports as a class" is inconsistent with the recent panel and Appellate Body reports in *Japan - Alcoholic Beverages*,[15] where no additional "discrimination" test based on "classes" of imported products was accepted.

The United States requests the Appellate Body to affirm the Panel's conclusions that Part V.1 of the Excise Tax Act is inconsistent with Article III:2, first sentence, of the GATT 1994.

With respect to whether imported split-run periodicals and domestic non-split-run periodicals are directly competitive or substitutable products within the meaning of the second sentence of Article III:2, the United States asserts that it is clear that if there was no competition for readers, there would be no need for Part V.1 of the Excise Tax Act. In its excise tax, Canada has targeted those magazines that are likely to be the most competitive with Canadian magazines for readers.

Regarding the jurisdictional arguments presented by Canada concerning whether the Appellate Body can examine a claim under the second sentence of Article III:2, the United States responds that there were no grounds for the United States to claim that the Panel had made a legal error in not addressing the alternative argument raised by the United States under Article III:2, second sentence. The Panel had resolved the issue by finding a violation of Article III:2, first sentence, of the GATT 1994 and therefore, had correctly stopped at that point. The United States also refers to the recent Appellate Body Report in *United States - Measure Affecting Imports of Woven Wool Shirts and Blouses from India*[16] which upheld the judicial economy approach taken by panels.

In the United States' view, this situation is analogous to the Appellate Body's reasoning concerning Article XX of the GATT 1994 in *United States - Standards for Reformulated and Conventional Gasoline ("United States - Gaso-*

---

[15] Panel Report, WT/DS8/R, WT/DS10/R, WT/DS11/R, and Appellate Body Report, WT/DS8/AB/R, WT/DS10/AB/R, WT/DS11/AB/R, adopted 1 November 1996.
[16] WT/DS33/AB/R, adopted 23 May 1997, DSR, 1997:I, 323, at 341.

line").[17] The procedure suggested by Canada is not consistent with the goals of Article 3.3 of the *DSU*. The parties to the dispute made a number of arguments before the Panel relating to the second sentence of Article III:2 as well as to Article III:4 of the GATT 1994. The United States asserts that there is a sufficient legal basis for the Appellate Body to apply the law to the facts in the panel record in analyzing a claim under the second sentence of Article III:2 should the Appellate Body decide to reverse the Panel's findings on Article III:2, first sentence, of the GATT 1994.

3. Consistency of the "Funded" Postal Rate Scheme with Article III:8(b) of the GATT 1994

The United States submits that the Panel erred in determining that Canada's "funded" postal rate regime falls within the scope of Article III:8(b) of the GATT 1994. According to the United States, neither the intra-governmental transfers of funds between the Canadian governmental entities nor the application by Canada Post of lower postage rates to domestic periodicals amounts to "the payment of subsidies exclusively to domestic producers" within the meaning of Article III:8(b).

The United States argues that any "payment" under Canada's "funded" postal rate scheme is made from one government entity to another, not from the Canadian government to domestic producers as required by Article III:8(b). Canada Post's favourable postage rates for domestic periodicals do not, in themselves, amount to a payment "exclusively to domestic producers", because whether or not there is any "subsidy" reflected in the "funded" postal rates, they take the form of advantageous transport and delivery rates for domestic periodicals. In making its findings, the Panel ignored both the plain language of Article III:8(b) and a series of adopted panel reports under the GATT 1947 that correctly interpreted Article III:8(b) as applying only to the actual payment of subsidies to domestic producers.[18] The United States also submits that the Panel did not clarify how a postal charge could amount to a subsidy payment, nor why postal fees imposed on domestic periodicals should be viewed as payments to domestic periodical producers.

According to the United States, the text of Article III:8(b) plainly requires: (1) that there be a payment, and (2) that this payment be made exclusively to domestic producers. The United States asserts that the use of the word "payment" in the phrase "payment of subsidies" - instead of more general terms such as "provision", "furnishing" or "granting" - indicates that the scope of Article

---

[17] WT/DS2/AB/R, adopted 20 May 1996.

[18] Panel Report, *Italian Agricultural Machinery,* adopted 23 October 1958, BISD 7S/60; Panel Report, *United States - Malt Beverages,* adopted 19 June 1992, BISD 39S/206; Panel Report, *United States - Tobacco,* DS44/R, adopted 4 October 1994; Panel Report, *EEC - Oilseeds,* adopted 25 January 1990, BISD 37S/86.

III:8(b) is limited to measures involving an actual transfer of government funds to domestic producers. Furthermore, the two specific examples of exempted measures set out in Article III:8(b) - "payments to domestic producers derived from the proceeds of internal taxes or charges applied consistently with the provisions of this Article and subsidies effected through governmental purchases of domestic products" - confirm this interpretation. In the United States' view, both types of subsidies are typically effected through monetary payments made by a government to domestic producers.

In response to Canada's reference to the French translation of the word "payment" in Article III:8(b), the United States points out that in the Spanish version of the *WTO Agreement*, adopted at Marrakesh, the translation of "payment" was changed from "concesión" in the GATT 1947 to "pago" in the GATT 1994. The term "concesión" means "grant", whereas "pago" means "payment".

The United States also maintains that the use of the phrase "exclusively to domestic producers" indicates that the payment must actually be made to the producers, and excludes advantages provided by governments to domestic products that may provide indirect benefits to domestic producers. Article III:8(b) reflects a willingness on the part of the framers of the GATT 1947 to allow governments some ability to subsidize domestic production. On the other hand, the United States considers that the narrow terms of the provision suggests that the drafters wished to restrict such subsidies to a particular form, i.e. direct payments, that would not undermine the basic purpose of Article III.

According to the United States, the distinction between (a) payments to domestic producers and (b) advantages conferred with respect to domestic products is significant in the context of the object and purpose of Article III. First, governmental advantages directed to domestic products, such as lower transportation or delivery rates, directly and immediately undercut Article III's fundamental prohibition of less favourable treatment of imported products. By contrast, payments made to domestic producers do not automatically distort competition between domestic and imported products. Second, measures that are reflected in intra-governmental transfers, rate-setting and the like may more easily escape public attention than direct monetary transfers to producers, and thus may be less open to public scrutiny and debate. Third, governments may find it more costly and administratively complex to establish a system of direct payments to producers than to provide advantages directly tied to the treatment of products. For the preceding reasons, the limitation of Article III:8(b) to direct payments to producers may reduce the incidence and magnitude of government advantages provided solely to domestic interests, thereby reducing the possibility of competitive distortions that could undermine Article III's objective of maintaining equal competitive conditions for domestic and imported products.

The United States asserts that the Panel failed to address the question of whether payment was actually made to domestic producers. Instead, the Panel assumed, without articulating its reasoning, that the payment to Canada Post constituted payment of a subsidy to domestic producers, and that the only issue in dispute with respect to the application of Article III:8(b) was whether that payment was made "exclusively" to domestic producers. Neither Canadian Heritage nor Canada Post makes any "payment" to Canadian producers under Canada's "funded" postal rate programme. Rather, Canadian Heritage periodically transfers funds to Canada Post, and the latter does not pay those funds to Canadian producers. Canada Post uses the funds to underwrite, in part, the cost of providing transportation and delivery services for domestic periodicals at low, "funded" postal rates. The United States argues that whether or not Canada's discriminatory "funded" rate scheme reflects a government "subsidy", any such subsidy is not granted directly in the form of payments to domestic periodical producers. Rather, the subsidy is reflected in the preferential rate charged in connection with the transportation and delivery of Canadian-produced periodicals.

If sustained, the United States submits, the Panel's finding in this case would free WTO Members to use a wide range of reduced-price governmental services and tax measures to confer advantages exclusively on domestically-produced goods. Such a result would not only undermine the equality of competitive opportunities for imported and domestic goods that Article III is meant to ensure, but would also upset the balance of rights and obligations reflected in Articles III:2 and III:4, on the one hand, and Article III:8(b), on the other.

III.   ISSUES RAISED IN THIS APPEAL

The appellant, Canada, raises the following issues in this appeal:

(a)   Whether Part V.1 of the Excise Tax Act is a measure affecting trade in goods to which Article III:2 of the GATT 1994 applies, or whether it is a measure affecting trade in services to which the GATS applies;

(b)   If Article III:2 of the GATT 1994 is applicable to Part V.1 of the Excise Tax Act, whether imported split-run periodicals and domestic non-split-run periodicals are "like products" within the meaning of Article III:2, first sentence, of the GATT 1994; and

(c)   Even if imported split-run periodicals and domestic non-split-run periodicals are "like products" within the meaning of Article III:2, first sentence, of the GATT 1994, is it necessary to demonstrate that Part V.1 of the Excise Tax Act discriminates against imported products.

The appellant, the United States, raises the following issue in this appeal:

(a)   Whether Canada's special "funded" postal rates programme qualifies as "a payment of subsidies exclusively to domestic producers" pursuant to Article III:8(b) of the GATT 1994.

IV.   APPLICABILITY OF THE GATT 1994

Canada's primary argument with respect to Part V.1 of the Excise Tax Act is that it is a measure regulating trade in services "in their own right" and, therefore, is subject to the GATS. Canada argues that the Panel's conclusion that Part V.1 of the Excise Tax Act is a measure affecting trade in goods, and, therefore, is subject to Article III:2 of the GATT 1994, is an error of law.[19]

We are unable to agree with Canada's proposition that the GATT 1994 is not applicable to Part V.1 of the Excise Tax Act. First of all, the measure is an excise tax imposed on split-run editions of periodicals. We note that the title to Part V.1 of the Excise Tax Act reads, "TAX ON SPLIT-RUN PERIODICALS", not "tax on advertising". Furthermore, the "Summary" of An Act to Amend the Excise Tax Act and the Income Tax Act,[20] reads: "The Excise Tax Act is amended to impose an excise tax in respect of split-run editions of periodicals". Secondly, a periodical is a good comprised of two components: editorial content and advertising content.[21] Both components can be viewed as having services attributes, but they combine to form a physical product - the periodical itself.

The measure in this appeal, Part V.1 of the Excise Tax Act, is a companion to Tariff Code 9958, which is a prohibition on imports of special edition periodicals, including split-run or regional editions that contain advertisements primarily directed to a market in Canada and that do not appear in identical form in all editions of an issue distributed in that periodical's country of origin. Canada agrees that Tariff Code 9958 is a measure affecting trade in goods, even though it applies to split-run editions of periodicals as does Part V.1 of the Excise Tax Act. As Canada stated in the oral hearing during this appeal:

> Tariff Code 9958 is basically an import prohibition of a physical good, i.e., the magazine itself. In that sense the entire debate was as to whether or not there was a possible defence against the application of Article XI of the GATT. In that case, therefore, there were direct effects and Canada recognized that there were effects on the physical good - the magazine as it crossed the border.[22]

The Panel found that Tariff Code 9958 is an import prohibition, although it applies to split-run editions of periodicals which are distinguished by their advertising content directed at the Canadian market. Canada did not appeal this finding of the Panel. It is clear that Part V.1 of the Excise Tax Act is intended to complement and render effective the import ban of Tariff Code 9958.[23] As a companion to the import ban, Part V.1 of the Excise Tax Act has the same objec-

---

[19]   Canada's Appellant's Submission, 12 May 1997, pp. 2-3, paras. 6, 9, 13 and 15.
[20]   S.C. 1995, c. 46.
[21]   Panel Report, para. 3.33.
[22]   Canada's Statement at the oral hearing, 2 June 1997.
[23]   Panel Report, paras. 3.25 and 3.26.

tive and purpose as Tariff Code 9958 and, therefore, should be analyzed in the same manner.

An examination of Part V.1 of the Excise Tax Act demonstrates that it is an excise tax which is applied on a good, a split-run edition of a periodical, on a "per issue" basis. By its very structure and design, it is a tax on a periodical. It is the publisher, or in the absence of a publisher resident in Canada, the distributor, the printer or the wholesaler, who is liable to pay the tax, not the advertiser.[24]

Based on the above analysis of the measure, which is essentially an excise tax imposed on split-run editions of periodicals, we cannot agree with Canada's argument that this internal tax does not "indirectly" affect imported products. It is a well-established principle that the trade effects of a difference in tax treatment between imported and domestic products do not have to be demonstrated for a measure to be found to be inconsistent with Article III.[25] The fundamental purpose of Article III of the GATT 1994 is to ensure equality of competitive conditions between imported and like domestic products.[26] We do not find it necessary to look to Article III:1 or Article III:4 of the GATT 1994 to give meaning to Article III:2, first sentence, in this respect. In *Japan - Alcoholic Beverages*, the Appellate Body stated that "Article III:1 articulates a general principle" which "informs the rest of Article III".[27] However, we also said that it informs the different sentences in Article III:2 in different ways. With respect to Article III:2, second sentence, we held that "Article III:1 informs Article III:2, second sentence, through specific reference".[28]

Article III:2, first sentence, uses the words "directly or indirectly" in two different contexts: one in relation to the application of a tax to imported products and the other in relation to the application of a tax to like domestic products. Any measure that indirectly affects the conditions of competition between imported and like domestic products would come within the provisions of Article III:2,

---

[24] An Act to Amend the Excise Tax Act and the Income Tax Act, S.C. 1995, c. 46, s. 35(1).

[25] Appellate Body Report, *Japan - Alcoholic Beverages*, WT/DS8/AB/R, WT/DS10/AB/R, WT/DS11/AB/R, adopted 1 November 1996, DSR 1996:I, 97, at 110.

[26] Panel Report, *United States - Tobacco*, DS44/R, adopted 4 October 1994, para. 99; Panel Report, *United States - Malt Beverages*, adopted 19 June 1992, BISD 39S/206, para. 5.6; Panel Report, *Canada - Import, Distribution and Sale of Certain Alcoholic Drinks by Provincial Marketing Agencies*, adopted 18 February 1992, BISD 39S/27, para. 5.6; Panel Report, *United States - Section 337 of the Tariff Act of 1930*, ("*United States - Section 337*"), adopted 7 November 1989, BISD 36S/345, para. 5.13; Panel Report, *United States - Taxes on Petroleum and Certain Imported Substances*, adopted 17 June 1987, BISD 34S/136, para. 5.1.9; Panel Report, *Brazilian Internal Taxes*, adopted 30 June 1949, BISD IIS/181, para. 15.

[27] WT/DS8/AB/R, WT/DS10/AB/R, WT/DS11/AB/R, adopted 1 November 1996, DSR 1996:I, 97, at 111.

[28] *Ibid.*, 115. In this respect, we draw attention to paragraphs 4.8, 5.37 and 5.38 of the Panel Report, and we note that a Panel finding that has not been specifically appealed in a particular case should not be considered to have been endorsed by the Appellate Body. Such a finding may be examined by the Appellate Body when the issue is raised properly in a subsequent appeal.

first sentence, or by implication, second sentence, given the broader application of the latter.

The entry into force of the GATS, as Annex 1B of the *WTO Agreement*, does not diminish the scope of application of the GATT 1994. Indeed, Canada concedes that its position "with respect to the inapplicability of the GATT would have been exactly the same under the GATT 1947, before the GATS had ever been conceived".[29]

We agree with the Panel's statement:

> The ordinary meaning of the texts of GATT 1994 and GATS as well as Article II:2 of the WTO Agreement, taken together, indicates that obligations under GATT 1994 and GATS can co-exist and that one does not override the other.[30]

We do not find it necessary to pronounce on the issue of whether there can be potential overlaps between the GATT 1994 and the GATS, as both participants agreed that it is not relevant in this appeal.[31] Canada stated that its

> ... principal argument is not based ... on the need to avoid overlaps and potential conflicts. On the contrary it is based on a textual interpretation of the provision, on the plain meaning of the words in Article III:2 - more precisely the word 'indirectly' interpreted in its legal context and in light of the object and purpose of the provision.[32]

We conclude, therefore, that it is not necessary and, indeed, would not be appropriate, in this appeal to consider Canada's rights and obligations under the GATS. The measure at issue in this appeal, Part V.1 of the Excise Tax Act, is a measure which clearly applies to goods - it is an excise tax on split-run editions of periodicals. We will now proceed to analyze this measure in light of Canada's points of appeal under Article III:2 of the GATT 1994.

V.   ARTICLE III:2, FIRST SENTENCE, OF THE GATT 1994

With respect to the application of Article III:2, first sentence, we agree with the Panel that:

> ... the following two questions need to be answered to determine whether there is a violation of Article III:2 of GATT 1994: *(a)* Are imported "split-run" periodicals and

---

[29]   Canada's Appellant's Submission, 12 May 1997, p. 3, para. 14.

[30]   Panel Report, para. 5.17.

[31]   Canada's Appellant's Submission, 12 May 1997, p. 3, para. 14; United States' Appellee's Submission, 26 May 1997, p. 13, para. 29.

[32]   Canada's Statement at the oral hearing, 2 June 1997.

domestic non "split-run" periodicals like products?; and *(b)*
Are imported "split-run" periodicals subject to an internal
tax in excess of that applied to domestic non "split-run" periodicals? If the answers to both questions are affirmative,
there is a violation of Article III:2, first sentence.138 If the
answer to the first question is negative, we need to examine
further whether there is a violation of Article III:2, second
sentence.[33]

---

[138]   In this context, we need not examine the applicability of Article III:1 separately, because, as the Appellate Body noted in its recent report, the first sentence
of Article III:2 *is*, in effect, an application of the general principle embodied in Article III:1. Therefore, if the imported and domestic products are "like products", and
if the taxes applied to the imported products are "in excess of" those applied to the
like domestic products, then the measure is inconsistent with Article III:2, first
sentence. Appellate Body Report on *Japan - Taxes on Alcoholic Bever*ages, *op.
cit.*, pp. 18-9.

A.   Like Products

We agree with the legal findings and conclusions in paragraphs 5.22 -
5.24 of the Panel Report. In particular, the Panel correctly enunciated, in theory,
the legal test for determining "like products" in the context of Article III:2, first
sentence, as established in the Appellate Body Report in *Japan - Alcoholic Beverages*.[34] We also agree with the second point made by the Panel. As Article
III:2, first sentence, normally requires a comparison between imported products
and like domestic products, and as there were no imports of split-run editions of
periodicals because of the import prohibition in Tariff Code 9958, which the
Panel found (and Canada did not contest on appeal) to be inconsistent with the
provisions of Article XI of the GATT 1994, hypothetical imports of split-run
periodicals have to be considered.[35] As the Panel recognized, the proper test is
that a determination of "like products" for the purposes of Article III:2, first sentence, must be construed narrowly, on a case-by-case basis, by examining relevant factors including:

(i)   the product's end-uses in a given market;

(ii)   consumers' tastes and habits; and

(iii)   the product's properties, nature and quality.[36]

However, the Panel failed to analyze these criteria in relation to imported
split-run periodicals and domestic non-split-run periodicals.[37] Firstly, we note

---

[33]   Panel Report, para. 5.21.
[34]   WT/DS8/AB/R, WT/DS10/AB/R, WT/DS11/AB/R, adopted 1 November 1996, pp. 19-20.
[35]   Panel Report, para. 5.23.
[36]   Appellate Body Report, *Japan - Alcoholic Beverages*, WT/DS8/AB/R, WT/DS10/AB/R,
WT/DS11/AB/R, adopted 1 November 1996, DSR 1996:I, 97, at 113.

that the Panel did not base its findings on the exhibits and evidence before it, in particular, the copies of TIME, TIME Canada and Maclean's magazines, presented by Canada, and the magazines, Pulp & Paper and Pulp & Paper Canada, presented by the United States,[38] or the *Report of the Task Force on the Canadian Magazine Industry* (the *"Task Force Report"*).[39]

Secondly, we observe that the Panel based its findings that imported split-run periodicals and domestic non-split-run periodicals "can" be like products, on a single hypothetical example constructed using a Canadian-owned magazine, Harrowsmith Country Life. However, this example involves a comparison between two editions of the same magazine, both imported products, which could not have been in the Canadian market at the same time. Thus, the discussion at paragraph 5.25 of the Panel Report is inapposite, because the example is incorrect.[40]

The Panel leapt from its discussion of an incorrect hypothetical example[41] to

> ... conclude that imported "split-run" periodicals and domestic non "split-run" periodicals *can* be like products within the meaning of Article III:2 of GATT 1994. In our view, this provides sufficient grounds to answer in the affirmative the question as to whether the two products at issue *are* like because, ... the purpose of Article III is to protect expectations of the Members as to the competitive relationship between their products and those of other Members, not to protect actual trade volumes.[42] (Emphasis added)

It is not obvious to us how the Panel came to the conclusion that it had "sufficient grounds" to find the two products at issue *are* like products from an examination of an incorrect example which led to a conclusion that imported split-run periodicals and domestic non-split-run periodicals *can be* "like".

We therefore conclude that, as a result of the lack of proper legal reasoning based on inadequate factual analysis in paragraphs 5.25 and 5.26 of the Panel

---

[37] Panel Report, para. 5.26.

[38] TIME and Pulp & Paper are non-split-run United States' magazines which are imported into Canada. TIME Canada is a United States' split-run magazine produced in Canada. Maclean's and Pulp & Paper Canada are Canadian non-split-run magazines.

[39] "A Question of Balance", *Report of the Task Force on the Canadian Magazine Industry*, Canada 1994, First Submission of the United States to the Panel, 5 September 1996, Exhibit A.

[40] Both the United States and Canada agreed that the example of Harrowsmith Country Life was incorrect: Canada's Appellant's Submission, 12 May 1997, pp. 17-18, paras. 64-71; United States' Appellee's Submission, 26 May 1997, p. 32, para. 80; Canada's Statement at the oral hearing, 2 June 1997; United States' Statement at the oral hearing, 2 June 1997.

[41] Panel Report, para 5.25.

[42] Panel Report, para 5.26.

Report, the Panel could not logically arrive at the conclusion that imported split-run periodicals and domestic non-split-run periodicals are like products.

We are mindful of the limitation of our mandate in Articles 17.6 and 17.13 of the *DSU*. According to Article 17.6, an appeal shall be limited to issues of law covered in the Panel Report and legal interpretations developed by the Panel. The determination of whether imported and domestic products are "like products" is a process by which legal rules have to be applied to facts. In any analysis of Article III:2, first sentence, this process is particularly delicate, since "likeness" must be construed narrowly and on a case-by-case basis. We note that, due to the absence of adequate analysis in the Panel Report in this respect, it is not possible to proceed to a determination of like products.

We feel constrained, therefore, to reverse the legal findings and conclusions of the Panel on "like products". As the Panel itself stated, there are two questions which need to be answered to determine whether there is a violation of Article III:2 of the GATT 1994: (a) whether imported and domestic products are like products; and (b) whether the imported products are taxed in excess of the domestic products. If the answers to both questions are affirmative, there is a violation of Article III:2, first sentence. If the answer to one question is negative, there is a need to examine further whether the measure is consistent with Article III:2, second sentence.[43]

Having reversed the Panel's findings on "like products", we cannot answer both questions in the first sentence of Article III:2 in the affirmative as is required to demonstrate a violation of that sentence. Therefore, we need to examine the consistency of the measure with the second sentence of Article III:2 of the GATT 1994.

B.   Non-Discrimination

In light of our conclusions on the question of "like products" in Article III:2, first sentence, we do not find it necessary to address Canada's claim of "non-discrimination" in relation to that sentence.[44]

VI.   ARTICLE III:2, SECOND SENTENCE, OF THE GATT 1994

We will proceed to examine the consistency of Part V.1 of the Excise Tax Act with the second sentence of Article III:2 of the GATT 1994.

---

[43]   See Panel Report, para. 5.21, cited with approval at page 465 herein.
[44]   See Canada's Appellant's Submission, 12 May 1997, p. 3, para. 12, where Canada makes this argument as an alternative point of appeal.

A. Jurisdiction

Canada asserts that the Appellate Body does not have the jurisdiction to examine a claim under Article III:2, second sentence, as no party has appealed the findings of the Panel on this provision. In the United States' view, the procedure suggested by Canada is not consistent with the fundamental goals stated in Article 3.3 of the *DSU*, according to which the prompt settlement of disputes is essential to the effective functioning of the WTO and the maintenance of a proper balance of rights and obligations of Members. Contrary to Canada, the United States asserts that there is a sufficient basis in the panel record for the Appellate Body to apply the law to these facts.

We believe the Appellate Body can, and should, complete the analysis of Article III:2 of the GATT 1994 in this case by examining the measure with reference to its consistency with the second sentence of Article III:2, provided that there is a sufficient basis in the Panel Report to allow us to do so. The first and second sentences of Article III:2 are closely related. The link between the two sentences is apparent from the wording of the second sentence, which begins with the word "moreover". It is also emphasized in *Ad* Article III, paragraph 2, which provides: "A tax conforming to the requirements of the first sentence of paragraph 2 would be considered to be inconsistent with the provisions of the second sentence only in cases where ...". An examination of the consistency of Part V.1 of the Excise Tax Act with Article III:2, second sentence, is therefore part of a logical continuum.

The Appellate Body found itself in a similar situation in *United States - Gasoline*. Having reversed the Panel's conclusions on the first part of Article XX(g) and having completed the Article XX(g) analysis in that case, the Appellate Body then examined the measure's consistency with the provisions of the chapeau of Article XX, based on the legal findings contained in the Panel Report.[45]

As the legal obligations in the first and second sentences are two closely-linked steps in determining the consistency of an internal tax measure with the national treatment obligations of Article III:2, the Appellate Body would be remiss in not completing the analysis of Article III:2. In the case at hand, the Panel made legal findings and conclusions concerning the first sentence of Article III:2, and because we reverse one of those findings, we need to develop our analysis based on the Panel Report in order to issue legal conclusions with respect to Article III:2, second sentence, of the GATT 1994.

---

[45]   WT/DS2/AB/R, adopted 20 May 1996, DSR 1996:1, 3, at 20-27.

B.   The Issues Under Article III:2, Second Sentence

In our Report in *Japan - Alcoholic Beverages*, we held that:

... three separate issues must be addressed to determine whether an internal tax measure is inconsistent with Article III:2, second sentence. These three issues are whether:

(1)   the imported products and the domestic products are "directly competitive or substitutable products" which are in competition with each other;

(2)   the directly competitive or substitutable imported and domestic products are "not similarly taxed"; and

(3)   the dissimilar taxation of the directly competitive or substitutable imported domestic products is "applied ... so as to afford protection to domestic production".[46]

1.   Directly Competitive or Substitutable Products

In *Japan - Alcoholic Beverages*, the Appellate Body stated that as with "like products" under the first sentence of Article III:2, the determination of the appropriate range of "directly competitive or substitutable products" under the second sentence must be made on a case by case basis.[47] The Appellate Body also found it appropriate to look at competition in the relevant markets as one among a number of means of identifying the broader category of products that might be described as "directly competitive or substitutable", as the GATT is a commercial agreement, and the WTO is concerned, after all, with markets.

According to the Panel Report, Canada considers that split-run periodicals are not "directly competitive or substitutable" for periodicals with editorial content developed for the Canadian market. Although they may be substitutable advertising vehicles, they are not competitive or substitutable information vehicles.[48] Substitution implies interchangeability. Once the content is accepted as relevant, it seems obvious that magazines created for different markets are not interchangeable. They serve different end-uses.[49] Canada draws attention to a study by the economist, Leigh Anderson, on which the *Task Force Report* was at least partially-based, which notes:

> US magazines can probably provide a reasonable substitute for Canadian magazines in their capacity as an advertising medium, although some advertisers may be better served by a Canadian vehicle. In many instances however, they would

---

[46]   WT/DS8/AB/R, WT/DS10/AB/R, WT/DS11/AB/R, DSR 1996:I, 97, at 116.
[47]   *Ibid.*, 117.
[48]   Panel Report, para. 3.113.
[49]   Panel Report, para. 3.115.

provide a very poor substitute as an entertainment and communication medium.[50]

Canada submits that the *Task Force Report* characterizes the relationship as one of "imperfect substitutability" - far from the direct substitutability required by this provision. The market share of imported and domestic magazines in Canada has remained remarkably constant over the last 30-plus years. If competitive forces had been in play to the degree necessary to meet the standard of "directly competitive" goods, one would have expected some variations. All this casts serious doubt on whether the competition or substitutability between imported split-run periodicals and domestic non-split-run periodicals is sufficiently "direct" to meet the standard of *Ad* Article III.[51]

According to the United States, the very existence of the tax is itself proof of competition between split-run periodicals and non-split-run periodicals in the Canadian market. As Canada itself has acknowledged, split-run periodicals compete with wholly domestically-produced periodicals for advertising revenue, which demonstrates that they compete for the same readers. The only reason firms place advertisements in magazines is to reach readers. A firm would consider split-run periodicals to be an acceptable advertising alternative to non-split-run periodicals only if that firm had reason to believe that the split-run periodicals themselves would be an acceptable alternative to non-split-run periodicals in the eyes of consumers. According to the United States, Canada acknowledges that "[r]eaders attract advertisers" and that, "... Canadian publishers are ready to compete with magazines published all over the world in order to keep their readers, but the competition is fierce".[52]

According to the United States, the *Task Force Report* together with statements made by the Minister of Canadian Heritage and Canadian officials, provide further acknowledgment of the substitutability of imported split-run periodicals and domestic non-split-run periodicals in the Canadian market.[53]

We find the United States' position convincing, while Canada's assertions do not seem to us to be compatible with its own description of the Canadian market for periodicals.

According to the Panel:

> Canada explained that there is a direct correlation between circulation, advertising revenue and editorial content. The larger the circulation, the more advertising a magazine can attract. With greater advertising revenue, a publisher can afford more to spend on editorial content. The more a publisher spends, the more attractive the magazine is likely to

---

[50]   Panel Report, para. 3.119.
[51]   Panel Report, para. 3.119.
[52]   Panel Report, para. 3.117.
[53]   Panel Report, para. 3.118.

be to its readers, resulting in circulation growth. Similarly, a loss of advertising revenue will produce a "downward spiral". Less advertising entails less editorial, a reduction in readership and circulation and a diminished ability to attract advertising. Magazines can be sold on newsstands, or through subscriptions, or distributed at no cost to selected consumers ... Canadian English-language publications face tough competition on newsstands; they account for only 18.5 per cent of English-language periodicals distributed on newsstands, where space is dominated by foreign publications ...[54]

...Canadian periodical publishers face a major competitive challenge in their business environment that is not common to their counterparts in countries with a larger population to serve. The pivotal fact is the penetration of the Canadian market by foreign magazines. Canadian readers have unrestricted access to imported magazines. At the same time, Canadian readers have demonstrated that they value magazines that address their distinct interests and perspectives. However, foreign magazines dominate the Canadian market. They account for 81.4 per cent of all newsstand circulation and slightly more than half (50.4 per cent) of the entire circulation of English-language magazines destined for the general public in Canada.[55]

This description of the Canadian market for periodicals corresponds to the following passages of the *Task Force Report*, as quoted in the Panel Report:

"[Canadian publishers'] English-language consumer magazines face significant competition for sales from imported consumer magazines. In large measure, this is because the majority of the magazines are from the United States and *are a close substitute.* ... It is reasonable to expect that the content of American magazines will be of interest to Canadians ...".

This report also observes that "there is considerable price competition" on newsstands between domestic and imported magazines", and that:

"the initial effect of the entry of Canadian regional editions of foreign magazines into the Canadian advertising market would be a loss of advertising pages in Canadian publica-

---

[54] Panel Report, para. 3.28.
[55] Panel Report, para. 3.29.

tions offering advertisers a readership with similar demographics".[56]

This description corresponds also to the statement made by the then Minister of Canadian Heritage, the Honourable Michel Dupuy:

> Canadians are much more interested in American daily life, be it political or sports life or any other kind, than vice versa. Therefore, the reality of the situation is that we must protect ourselves against split-runs coming from foreign countries and, in particular, from the United States.[57]

The statement by the economist, Leigh Anderson, quoted by Canada and the *Task Force Report*'s description of the relationship as one of "imperfect substitutability" does not modify our appreciation. A case of perfect substitutability would fall within Article III:2, first sentence, while we are examining the broader prohibition of the second sentence. We are not impressed either by Canada's argument that the market share of imported and domestic magazines has remained remarkably constant over the last 30-plus years, and that one would have expected some variation if competitive forces had been in play to the degree necessary to meet the standard of "directly competitive" goods. This argument would have weight only if Canada had not protected the domestic market of Canadian periodicals through, among other measures, the import prohibition of Tariff Code 9958 and the excise tax of Part V.1 of the Excise Tax Act.

Our conclusion that imported split-run periodicals and domestic non-split-run periodicals are "directly competitive or substitutable" does not mean that all periodicals belong to the same relevant market, whatever their editorial content. A periodical containing mainly current news is not directly competitive or substitutable with a periodical dedicated to gardening, chess, sports, music or cuisine. But newsmagazines, like TIME, TIME Canada and Maclean's, are directly competitive or substitutable in spite of the "Canadian" content of Maclean's. The competitive relationship is even closer in the case of more specialized magazines, like Pulp & Paper as compared with Pulp & Paper Canada, two trade magazines presented to the Panel by the United States.

The fact that, among these examples, only TIME Canada is a split-run periodical, and that it is not imported but is produced in Canada, does not affect at all our appreciation of the competitive relationship. The competitive relationship of imported split-run periodicals destined for the Canadian market is even closer to domestic non-split-run periodicals than the competitive relationship between imported non-split-run periodicals and domestic non-split-run periodicals. Imported split-run periodicals contain advertisements targeted specifically at the Canadian market, while imported non-split-run periodicals do not carry such advertisements.

---

[56] Panel Report, para. 3.118.
[57] Panel Report, para. 3.118.

We, therefore, conclude that imported split-run periodicals and domestic non-split-run periodicals are directly competitive or substitutable products in so far as they are part of the same segment of the Canadian market for periodicals.

2.   Not Similarly Taxed

Having found that imported split-run and domestic non-split-run periodicals of the same type are directly competitive or substitutable, we must examine whether the imported products and the directly competitive or substitutable domestic products are not similarly taxed. Part V.1 of the Excise Tax Act taxes split-run editions of periodicals in an amount equivalent to 80 per cent of the value of all advertisements in a split-run edition. In contrast, domestic non-split-run periodicals are not subject to Part V.1 of the Excise Tax Act. Following the reasoning of the Appellate Body in *Japan - Alcoholic Beverages*,[58] dissimilar taxation of even some imported products as compared to directly competitive or substitutable domestic products is inconsistent with the provisions of the second sentence of Article III:2. In *United States - Section 337*, the panel found:

> ... that the "no less favourable" treatment requirement of Article III:4 has to be understood as applicable to each individual case of imported products. The Panel rejected any notion of balancing more favourable treatment of some imported products against less favourable treatment of other imported products.[59]

With respect to Part V.1 of the Excise Tax Act, we find that the amount of the taxation is far above the *de minimis* threshold required by the Appellate Body Report in *Japan - Alcoholic Beverages*.[60] The magnitude of this tax is sufficient to prevent the production and sale of split-run periodicals in Canada.[61]

3.   So as to Afford Protection

The Appellate Body established the following approach in *Japan - Alcoholic Beverages* for determining whether dissimilar taxation of directly competitive or substitutable products has been applied so as to afford protection:

> ... we believe that an examination in any case of whether dissimilar taxation has been applied so as to afford protection requires a comprehensive and objective analysis of the

---

[58]   WT/DS8/AB/R, WT/DS10/AB/R, WT/DS11/AB/R, adopted 1 November 1996, DSR 1996:I, 97, at 119.

[59]   Adopted 7 November 1989, BISD 36S/345, para. 5.14.

[60]   WT/DS8/AB/R, WT/DS10/AB/R, WT/DS11/AB/R, adopted 1 November 1996, DSR 1996:I, 97, at 119.

[61]   Indeed, this was the explicit objective of the Canadian policy. See Panel Report, paras. 3.118 and 5.25.

structure and application of the measure in question on domestic as compared to imported products. We believe it is possible to examine objectively the underlying criteria used in a particular tax measure, its structure, and its overall application to ascertain whether it is applied in a way that affords protection to domestic products.

Although it is true that the aim of a measure may not be easily ascertained, nevertheless its protective application can most often be discerned from the design, the architecture, and the revealing structure of a measure. The very magnitude of the dissimilar taxation in a particular case may be evidence of such a protective application, ... Most often, there will be other factors to be considered as well. In conducting this inquiry, panels should give full consideration to all the relevant facts and all the relevant circumstances in any given case.[62]

With respect to Part V.1 of the Excise Tax Act, we note that the magnitude of the dissimilar taxation between imported split-run periodicals and domestic non-split-run periodicals is beyond excessive, indeed, it is prohibitive. There is also ample evidence that the very design and structure of the measure is such as to afford protection to domestic periodicals.

The Canadian policy which led to the enactment of Part V.1 of the Excise Tax Act had its origins in the *Task Force Report*. It is clear from reading the *Task Force Report* that the design and structure of Part V.1 of the Excise Tax Act are to prevent the establishment of split-run periodicals in Canada, thereby ensuring that Canadian advertising revenues flow to Canadian magazines. Madame Monique Landry, Minister Designate of Canadian Heritage at the time the *Task Force Report* was released, issued the following statement summarizing the Government of Canada's policy objectives for the Canadian periodical industry:

> The Government reaffirms its commitment to protect the economic foundations of the Canadian periodical industry, which is a vital element of Canadian cultural expression. To achieve this objective, the Government will continue to use policy instruments that encourage the flow of advertising revenues to Canadian magazines and discourage the establishment of split-run or 'Canadian' regional editions with advertising aimed at the Canadian market. We are committed to ensuring that Canadians have access to Canadian ideas and information through genuinely Canadian maga-

---

[62] WT/DS8/AB/R, WT/DS10/AB/R, WT/DS11/AB/R, adopted 1 November 1996, DSR 1996:I, 97, at 120.

zines, while not restricting the sale of foreign magazines in Canada.[63]

Furthermore, the Government of Canada issued the following response to the *Task Force Report*:

> The Government reaffirms its commitment to the long-standing policy of protecting the economic foundations of the Canadian periodical industry. To achieve this objective, the Government uses policy instruments that encourage the flow of advertising revenues to Canadian periodicals, since a viable Canadian periodical industry must have a secure financial base.[64]

During the debate of Bill C-103, An Act to Amend the Excise Tax Act and the Income Tax Act, the Minister of Canadian Heritage, the Honourable Michel Dupuy, stated the following:

> ... the reality of the situation is that we must protect ourselves against split-runs coming from foreign countries and, in particular, from the United States.[65]

Canada also admitted that the objective and structure of the tax is to insulate Canadian magazines from competition in the advertising sector, thus leaving significant Canadian advertising revenues for the production of editorial material created for the Canadian market. With respect to the actual application of the tax to date, it has resulted in one split-run magazine, Sports Illustrated, to move its production for the Canadian market out of Canada and back to the United States.[66] Also, Harrowsmith Country Life, a Canadian-owned split-run periodical, has ceased production of its United States' edition as a consequence of the imposition of the tax.[67]

We therefore conclude on the basis of the above reasons, including the magnitude of the differential taxation, the several statements of the Government of Canada's explicit policy objectives in introducing the measure and the demonstrated actual protective effect of the measure, that the design and structure of Part V.1 of the Excise Tax Act is clearly to afford protection to the production of Canadian periodicals.

VII.   ARTICLE III:8(B) OF THE GATT 1994

Article III:8(b) of the GATT 1994 reads as follows:

---

[63]   *Task Force Report*, Appendix 5, p. 92.
[64]   *Ibid.*, p. 94.
[65]   Panel Report, para. 3.118.
[66]   Panel Report, para. 3.121.
[67]   Panel Report, paras. 3.99 and 5.25.

(*b*)   The provisions of this Article shall not prevent the payment of subsidies exclusively to domestic producers, including payments to domestic producers derived from the proceeds of internal taxes or charges applied consistently with the provisions of this Article and subsidies effected through governmental purchases of domestic products.

Both participants agree that Canada's "funded" postal rates involve "a payment of subsidies". The appellant, the United States, argues, however, that the "funded" postal rates programme involves a transfer of funds from one government entity to another, i.e. from Canadian Heritage to Canada Post, and not from the Canadian government to domestic producers as required by Article III:8(b).

As we understand it, through the PAP, Canadian Heritage provides Canada Post, a wholly-owned Crown corporation, with financial assistance to support special rates of postage for eligible publications, including certain designated domestic periodicals mailed and distributed in Canada. This programme has been implemented through a series of agreements, the MOA, between Canadian Heritage and Canada Post, which provide that in consideration of the payments made to it by Canadian Heritage, Canada Post will accept for distribution, at special "funded" rates, all publications designated by Canadian Heritage to be eligible under the PAP. The MOA provides that while Canadian Heritage will administer the eligibility requirements for the PAP based on criteria specified in the MOA, Canada Post will accept for distribution all publications that are eligible under the PAP at the "funded" rates.

The appellant, the United States, cited four GATT 1947 panel reports as authorities for its interpretation of Article III:8(b).[68] However, these panel reports are not all directly on point. In *Italian Agricultural Machinery* and *EEC - Oilseeds*, the panels found that subsidies paid to purchasers of agricultural machinery and processors of oilseeds were not made "exclusively to domestic producers" of agricultural machinery and oilseeds, respectively. In *United States - Malt Beverages* and *United States - Tobacco*, the issue was whether a reduction in the federal excise tax on beer or a remission of a product tax on tobacco constituted a "payment of subsidies" within the meaning of Article III:8(b). In *United States - Malt Beverages*, the panel found that a reduction of taxes on a good did not qualify as a "payment of subsidies" for the purposes of Article III:8(b) of the GATT 1994.[69] In *United States - Tobacco*, having found that the measure at issue was not a tax remission, the panel concluded that it was a payment which qualified under Article III:8(b) of the GATT 1994.[70]

---

[68]   Panel Report, *Italian Agricultural Machinery*, adopted 23 October 1958, BISD 7S/60; Panel Report, *United States - Malt Beverages*, adopted 19 June 1992, BISD 39S/206; Panel Report, *United States - Tobacco*, DS44/R, adopted 4 October 1994; and Panel Report, *EEC - Oilseeds*, adopted 25 January 1990, BISD 37S/86.
[69]   Adopted 19 June 1992, BISD 39S/206, para. 5.12.
[70]   DS44/R, adopted 4 October 1994, paras. 109 and 111.

In *EEC - Oilseeds*, the panel stated that "it can reasonably be assumed that a payment not made directly to producers is not made 'exclusively' to them".[71] This statement of the panel is *obiter dicta*, as the panel found in that report that subsidies paid to oilseeds processors were not made "exclusively to domestic producers", and therefore, the EEC payments of subsidies to processors and producers of oilseeds and related animal feed proteins did not qualify under the provisions of Article III:8(b).[72]

A proper interpretation of Article III:8(b) must be made on the basis of a careful examination of the text, context and object and purpose of that provision. In examining the text of Article III:8(b), we believe that the phrase, "including payments to domestic producers derived from the proceeds of internal taxes or charges applied consistently with the provisions of this Article and subsidies effected through governmental purchases of domestic products" helps to elucidate the types of subsidies covered by Article III:8(b) of the GATT 1994. It is not an exhaustive list of the kinds of programmes that would qualify as "the payment of subsidies exclusively to domestic producers", but those words exemplify the kinds of programmes which are exempted from the obligations of Articles III:2 and III:4 of the GATT 1994.

Our textual interpretation is supported by the context of Article III:8(b) examined in relation to Articles III:2 and III:4 of the GATT 1994. Furthermore, the object and purpose of Article III:8(b) is confirmed by the drafting history of Article III. In this context, we refer to the following discussion in the Reports of the Committees and Principal Sub-Committees of the Interim Commission for the International Trade Organization concerning the provision of the Havana Charter for an International Trade Organization that corresponds to Article III:8(b) of the GATT 1994:

> This sub-paragraph was redrafted in order to make it clear that nothing in Article 18 could be construed to sanction the exemption of domestic products from internal taxes imposed on like imported products or the remission of such taxes. At the same time the Sub-Committee recorded its view that nothing in this sub-paragraph or elsewhere in Article 18 would override the provisions of Section C of Chapter IV.[73]

We do not see a reason to distinguish a reduction of tax rates on a product from a reduction in transportation or postal rates. Indeed, an examination of the text, context, and object and purpose of Article III:8(b) suggests that it was in-

---

[71] Adopted 25 January 1990, BISD 37S/86, para. 137.

[72] *Ibid.*

[73] Interim Commission for the International Trade Organization, Reports of the Committees and Principal Sub-Committees: ICITO I/8, Geneva, September 1948, p. 66. Article 18 and Section C of Chapter IV of the Havana Charter for an International Trade Organization correspond, respectively, to Article III and Article XVI of the GATT 1947.

tended to exempt from the obligations of Article III only the payment of subsidies which involves the expenditure of revenue by a government.

We agree with the panel in *United States - Malt Beverages* that:

> Article III:8(b) limits, therefore, the permissible producer subsidies to "payments" after taxes have been collected or payments otherwise consistent with Article III. This separation of tax rules, e.g. on tax exemptions or reductions, and subsidy rules makes sense economically and politically. Even if the proceeds from non-discriminatory product taxes may be used for subsequent subsidies, the domestic producer, like his foreign competitors, must pay the product taxes due. The separation of tax and subsidy rules contributes to greater transparency. It also may render abuses of tax policies for protectionist purposes more difficult, as in the case where producer aids require additional legislative or governmental decisions in which the different interests involved can be balanced.[74]

As a result of our analysis of the text, context, and object and purpose of Article III:8(b), we conclude that the Panel incorrectly interpreted this provision. For these reasons, we reverse the Panel's findings and conclusions that Canada's "funded" postal rates scheme for periodicals is justified under Article III:8(b) of the GATT 1994.

VIII. FINDINGS AND CONCLUSIONS

For the reasons set out in this Report, the Appellate Body:

(a) upholds the Panel's findings and conclusions on the applicability of the GATT 1994 to Part V.1 of the Excise Tax Act;

(b) reverses the Panel's findings and conclusions on Part V.1 of the Excise Tax Act relating to "like products" within the context of Article III:2, first sentence, thereby reversing the Panel's conclusions on Article III:2, first sentence, of the GATT 1994;

(c) modifies the Panel's findings and conclusions on Article III:2 of the GATT 1994, by concluding that Part V.1 of the Excise Tax Act is inconsistent with Canada's obligations under Article III:2, second sentence, of the GATT 1994; and

(d) reverses the Panel's findings and conclusions that the maintenance by Canada Post of the "funded" postal rates scheme is justified by Article III:8(b) of the GATT 1994, and concludes that the

---

[74] Adopted 19 June 1992, BISD 39S/206, para. 5.10.

"funded" postal rates scheme is not justified by Article III:8(b) of the GATT 1994.

The foregoing legal findings and conclusions modify the conclusions of the Panel in Part VI of the Panel Report, but leave intact the findings and conclusions of the Panel that were not the subject of this appeal.

The Appellate Body *recommends* that the Dispute Settlement Body request Canada to bring the measures found in this Report and in the Panel Report, as modified by this Report, to be inconsistent with the GATT 1994 into conformity with Canada's obligations thereunder.

CANADA - CERTAIN MEASURES CONCERNING PERIODICALS

Report of the Panel
WT/DS31/R[*]

*Adopted by the Dispute Settlement Body on 30 July 1997
as modified by the Appellate Body Report*

TABLE OF CONTENTS

---

[*] WT/DS31/R/Corr.1.

I.   INTRODUCTION

1.1   On 11 March 1996, the United States requested Canada to hold consultations pursuant to Article 4 of the Understanding on Rules and Procedures Governing the Settlement of Disputes (DSU) and Article XXIII of the General Agreement on Tariffs and Trade 1994 (GATT 1994) on certain measures maintained by Canada, namely, measures prohibiting or restricting the importation into Canada of certain periodicals; tax treatment of so-called "split-run" periodicals; and the application of favourable postage rates to certain Canadian periodicals (WT/DS31/1). These consultations were held on 10 April 1996. As they did not result in a satisfactory adjustment of the matter, the United States, in a communication dated 24 May 1996, requested the Dispute Settlement Body (DSB) to establish a panel to examine the matter (WT/DS31/2).

1.2   The DSB, at its meeting on 19 June 1996, established a panel on the matter in accordance with Article 6 of the DSU. In document WT/DS31/3, the Secretariat reported that the Panel would have the following standard terms of reference and composition:

> "To examine, in the light of the relevant provisions of the covered agreements cited by the United States in document WT/DS31/2, the matter referred to the DSB by the United States in that document and to make such findings as will assist the DSB in making the recommendations or in giving the rulings provided for in those agreements".

1.3   On 25 July 1996, the Panel was constituted with the following composition:

Chairman: Mr. Lars Anell

Panelists: Mr. Victor Luiz do Prado

Mr. Michael Reiterer

1.4   No Members reserved their rights to participate in the Panel proceedings as a third party.

1.5   The Panel met with the parties to the dispute on 11 October 1996 and 14-15 November 1996. The Panel submitted its report to the parties on 21 February 1997.

II.   FACTUAL ASPECTS

2.1   This Panel concerns three Canadian measures: Tariff Code 9958 which prohibits the importation into Canada of certain periodicals; Part V.I of the Excise Tax Act, as enacted by Bill C-103 of 15 December 1995, which imposes an excise tax on certain "split-run" periodicals; and the application of certain postal rates to certain Canadian periodicals including through actions of Canada Post Corporation and the Department of Canadian Heritage.

A. Tariff Code 9958 - Import Prohibition

2.2   In 1965, the Canadian Government enacted Tariff Code 9958, in Schedule VII of the Customs Tariff. It is put into effect by Article 114 of the Customs Tariff which provides that "the importation into Canada of any goods enumerated or referred to in Schedule VII is prohibited".[1] Tariff Code 9958 applies if an issue of a periodical imported into Canada is a special edition, including a split-run or regional edition, that contains an advertisement that is primarily directed to a market in Canada and that does not appear in identical form in all editions of that issue of the periodical that were distributed in the periodical's country of origin. The Code defines an "issue" to include a special annual issue, and a "periodical" to mean a periodical, the issues of which other than the special annual issue, are published at regular intervals of more than six days and less than fifteen weeks and are distributed as issues of a distinct publication or as a supplement to more than one newspaper, but does not include a catalogue, a newspaper, or a periodical, the principal function of which is the encouragement, promotion or development of the fine arts, letters, scholarship or religion.

2.3   For the purposes of determining whether or not an advertisement is primarily directed at the Canadian market, a number of factors are taken into consideration such as whether there are enticements to the Canadian market, references to the goods and services tax, listing of Canadian addresses as opposed to foreign addresses, and specific invitations to Canadian consumers only.

2.4   The Code also applies where an issue of a periodical imported into Canada is an edition in which more than five per cent of the advertising content consists of advertisements directed to the Canadian market. Advertisements directed to the Canadian market include those that indicate specific sources of product or service availability in Canada or which include specific terms or conditions relating to the sale of goods or services in Canada.[2] The publisher of a periodical is notified by the Department of National Revenue for Customs and Excise when a periodical is found to be in contravention of Tariff Code 9958.[3]

2.5   In 1988, the Canadian Parliament enacted an exception to Tariff Code 9958 which allows Canadian publishers to have their periodicals, which must otherwise be Canadian issues of Canadian periodicals, typeset or printed wholly or partially in the United States.

---

[1]   R.S.C. 1985, c. 41 (3rd Suppl.) as amended to 30 April 1996, s.114, Sch. VII, Item 9958, (1996 Customs Tariff: Departmental Consolidation) Ottawa: Minister of Supply & Services Canada, 1996.
[2]   The Department of National Revenue for Customs and Excise has adopted and published guidelines providing details relating to the application and administration of Code 9958 of the Customs Tariff (Revenue Canada Memorandum D9-1-10, 21 May 1993).
[3]   The Importation of Periodicals Regulations (C.R.C., c. 533 as amended on 30 April 1996) describe the review process as carried out by an officer or the Deputy Minister of the Department of National Revenue for Customs and Excise.

B.   Part V.I of the Excise Tax Act

2.6   In 1995, Bill C-103, which added Part V.I - Tax on Split-run Periodicals to the Excise Tax Act, became law.[4] The amendment calls for the imposition, levy and collection, in respect of each split-run edition of a periodical, a tax equal to 80 per cent of the value of all the advertisements contained in the split-run edition. The tax is levied on a per issue basis. The value of all advertisements in a split-run edition of a periodical is the total of all the gross fees for all the advertisements contained in the edition.[5] The term "periodical" means printed material that is published in a series of issues that appear not less than twice a year and not more than once a week. Where an issue of a periodical is published in several versions, each version is an edition of the issue. Each edition of the issue must be considered separately when determining whether an edition is a split-run edition. The definition of "periodical" explicitly excludes a catalogue which is substantially made up of advertisements.[6]

2.7   The amendment defines a split-run edition as an edition of an issue of a periodical that:

(i)   is distributed in Canada;

(ii)   in which more than 20 per cent of the editorial material is the same or substantially the same as editorial material that appears in one or more excluded editions of one or more issues of one or more periodicals; and

(iii)   contains an advertisement that does not appear in identical form in all the excluded editions.

There are two exclusionary provisions. Under the first, the particular edition is not a split-run edition if it is an edition that is primarily circulated outside Canada. In effect, this is an exemption for editions that are distributed in Canada, but are mainly distributed outside Canada. Under the second, a particular edition of an issue of a periodical that would otherwise be a split-run edition is not a split-run edition if all the advertisements in the particular edition appear in identical form in one or more editions of that issue that are primarily distributed outside Canada and that have a combined circulation outside Canada that is greater than the circulation in Canada of the particular edition. The purpose is to prevent a publisher from qualifying for this exemption by having all the advertisements in its Canadian split-run edition also appear in one of its excluded editions that has a very small circulation.[7]

2.8   Further, a grandfathering provision provides limited "grandfathering" treatment to certain existing periodicals that distributed Canadian split-run edi-

---

[4]   An Act to amend the Excise Tax Act and the Income Tax Act, S.C. 1995, c. 46, s.39.
[5]   *Ibid.*, s. 38.
[6]   *Ibid.*, ss.35(1) and 35(5).
[7]   *Ibid.*, ss.35(5).

tions prior to 26 March 1993. A particular periodical is eligible for "grandfathering" treatment and therefore not subject to the tax on split-runs if the number of split-run editions per year does not exceed the number of split-run editions that were distributed during the 12-month period ending on 26 March 1993, provided that the periodicals continue to be similar in editorial content and direction to the split-run editions distributed before that date. If the number of split-run editions per year is increased, the tax applies to the additional split-run editions.[8]

2.9   Depending on the circumstances, the person responsible for paying the tax is the publisher, a person connected with the publisher, the distributor, the printer or the wholesaler of the split-run edition. (The Excise Tax Act stipulates that a person is considered to be connected to another person if one of them is controlled by the other or if both of them are controlled by the same person.[9] A corporation is controlled by a particular person if 50 per cent or more of its share of capital with voting rights belongs to that person or to persons with whom that person does not deal at arm's length. A partnership is controlled by a particular person if the person or persons with whom that person does not deal at arm's length is or are entitled to 50 per cent or more of the partnership's income.[10]) The responsible person is the first of these persons who resides in Canada.[11] The responsible person can be domestic- or foreign-owned or controlled. In order to ensure enforcement and collection of the tax, the tax is imposed on a person who resides in Canada. The persons connected with the responsible person are jointly and severally liable for payment of the tax.[12] As well, where the responsible person is a distributor, a printer or a wholesaler (and if there is more than one), they are jointly and severally liable for payment of the tax.[13] Where a person other than the publisher pays the excise tax in respect of a split-run edition, the person is deemed to have paid the tax on behalf of the publisher of the periodical. The legislation authorizes the person to recover the amount of the tax from the publisher in a court of competent jurisdiction or to deduct or withhold the amount from any amount payable by the person to the publisher or distributor of the periodical.[14]

C.   Funded and Commercial Postal Rates

2.10   In 1981, the Canada Post Corporation (hereafter called Canada Post) was established by the Parliament of Canada as a Crown corporation pursuant to the Canada Post Corporation Act (CPC Act).[15] Crown corporations are created by

---

[8]   An Act to amend the Excise Tax Act and the Income Tax Act, S.C. 1995, c. 46, s. 39.
[9]   *Ibid.*, ss.35(2).
[10]   *Ibid.*, ss.35(3).
[11]   *Ibid.*, ss.35(1).
[12]   *Ibid.*, s. 41.1.
[13]   *Ibid.*, s. 41.2.
[14]   *Ibid.*, ss.41.3(2).
[15]   R.S.C. 1985, c. C-10.

one of three methods: an Act of Parliament; letters patent under the Canada Business Corporations Act; or Articles of Incorporation under the Canada Business Corporations Act. According to a treatise on Crown law cited by Canada, Crown corporations are created to separate the management of an activity from continuous partisan intervention and to provide independence from the close financial controls within the government departmental structure.[16] The Government of Canada gains control over, and accountability from, Crown corporations primarily through the Financial Administration Act (FA Act) and its Regulations. The FA Act endeavours to strike a balance between the desires for public accountability and for private industry independence. Parliament is required to approve the creation, mandate, and financing of new parent Crown corporations. Government approval is required for annual corporate plans operating and capital budgets, and major corporate acquisitions. The FA Act and the CPC Act define the responsibilities for the direction and daily operation of the corporations.

2.11   The Canada Post publication entitled *Publications Mail Postal Rates*, (effective 4 March 1996), describes the three categories of publications mail postal rates which are the subject of this dispute: the "funded" publications rates and the commercial "Canadian" and commercial "International" publications rates. The first two categories apply to periodicals published and printed in Canada. "Funded" rates are rates that are subsidized by the Canadian Government and commercial rates are for publications ineligible for "funded" rates. "Canadian" rates are commercial rates available to Canadian publications and "International" commercial rates apply to all foreign publications mailed in Canada.

(i)   "Funded" Rates

2.12   Since its incorporation, the Government of Canada has provided funding to Canada Post to support special rates of postage for eligible publications through the Publications Distribution Assistance Program (hereafter called the Program). The Program, which was developed to promote Canadian culture, provided funding through Canada Post to eligible Canadian publications, including periodicals, mailed in Canada for delivery in Canada. "Funded" postal rates are available to Canadian-owned and -controlled paid circulation publications that are published and printed in Canada and meet certain editorial and advertising requirements. In January 1990, the Government announced plans to gradually phase out the Program and replace it with a system of direct funding to eligible publications. Since the announcement, funding available for the Program has been gradually reduced. On 30 April 1996, the current policy and funding agreement concerning the Program between Canada Post and the Department of Canadian Heritage (hereafter called Canadian Heritage) was set to expire. At that time,

---

[16]   P. Lordon, Crown Law (Toronto: Butterworths 1991) at 49, 57 and 58. The next five sentences are also from this source.

available funding would have been directed to eligible publishers through a replacement program.[17]

2.13   The Program and its funding structure was extended for three years through a Memorandum of Agreement (MOA), signed in March 1996 and effective 1 May 1996, between the Department of Communications (now the Department of Canadian Heritage) and Canada Post.[18] This new agreement provides for payments of funds in quarterly instalments by Canadian Heritage to Canada Post "in exchange for providing prescribed postage rates for publications deemed eligible to the Publications Assistance Program", and the transfer of the program administration from Canada Post to Canadian Heritage.[19] Canadian Heritage had requested within the new agreement that Canada Post initiate the complete removal of funded publications mail from the regulations associated with the CPC Act, effective April 1996.[20] On 23 April 1996, Canada Gazette published a repeal of the Newspapers and Periodicals Regulations pursuant to Subsection 19(1) of the CPC Act. The revocation was intended to facilitate the transfer of eligibility assessment from Canada Post to Canadian Heritage, to reduce the Program's administrative costs while expediting and simplifying modifications to its policies,[21] and to allow Canada Post and Canadian Heritage to respond more appropriately and more rapidly to Program and customer needs.

2.14   The amounts authorized by the MOA are CD$58 million for the period commencing 1 May 1996 and ending 31 March 1997; CD$57.9 million for the period 1 April 1997 to 31 March 1998; and CD$47.3 million for the period 1 April 1998 to 31 March 1999.

2.15   Canadian Heritage administers the eligibility requirements for the Program based on the criteria specified in Schedule A to the MOA. Canadian Heritage is responsible for the administration of the eligibility requirements for the Program, and Canada Post must accept for distribution all publications that are eligible under the Program once the publication is approved by Canadian Heritage. For eligible publications to receive funded rates, the publisher must first enter into a sales agreement with Canada Post prior to posting under the Program. Rates of postage for publications eligible under the Program are set out in Schedule C of the MOA and are as follows:

    a)   First 10,000 copies of an issue addressed to *Bona Fide* Subscribers and newsdealers in Canada:

        per kg or fraction thereof: Year 1: $0.390

---

[17]   *Canada Gazette*, Part II, Vol 130, No. 10, Newspapers and Periodicals Regulations, repeal, SOR/96-209, 23 April 1996, Regulatory Impact Analysis Statement.

[18]   Memorandum of Agreement (MOA) Concerning the Publications Assistance Program Between the Department of Communications and Canada Post Corporation.

[19]   *Canada Gazette*, Part II, Vol 130, No. 10.

[20]   *Ibid.*

[21]   *Ibid.*

Year 2: $0.395

Year 3: $0.405

or, per individually addressed copy whichever is the greater:

Year 1: $0.078

Year 2: $0.079

Year 3: $0.081

b)   Copies exceeding the first 10,000 copies of an issue addressed to *Bona Fide* Subscribers and newsdealers in Canada:

per kg or fraction thereof: Year 1: $0.430

Year 2: $0.435

Year 3: $0.445

or, per individually addressed copy, whichever is the greater:

Year 1: $0.086

Year 2: $0.087

Year 3: $0.089

(Year 1: 1 May 1996 to 31 March 1997; Year 2: 1 April 1997 to 31 March 1998; Year 3: 1 April 1998 to 31 March 1999.)

2.16   In order to be eligible for funded rates, Canadian publications must generally meet the following criteria: (i) produced by a person or company whose primary business is publishing;[22] (ii) Canadian ownership and control; (iii) published, printed and mailed in Canada; (iv) edited in Canada;[23] (v) eligible editorial categories;[24] (vi) minimum paid circulation requirement;[25] (vii) maximum advertising allowance;[26] (viii) frequency;[27] and (ix) minimum price.[28]

---

[22] Funded rates cannot be used to promote a specific business, service, fraternal, trade or professional organizations (MOA).

[23] An eligible publication must be edited by persons residing in Canada (editing encompasses the commissioning of editorial material and artwork, supervising writers, illustrators and photographers regarding the final format of the material, as well as laying out, copy editing and proofreading, and otherwise preparing the contents for printing) (MOA).

[24] Eligible publications must be published for the dissemination to the public consisting of either news, comment and analysis of news and articles on topics of current public interest; or articles on religion, the sciences, agriculture, forestry, the fisheries, social or literary criticism, reviews of literature or the arts, or be an academic or scholarly journal; or articles promoting public health and published by a non-profit organization administered on a national or provincial basis (MOA).

[25] No less than 50 per cent of an eligible publication's total circulation must be paid circulation (MOA).

[26] No more than 70 per cent of the space, including advertising inserts, in an eligible publication may be devoted to advertising (MOA).

[27] It must be published not less than twice a year and not more than 56 times a year (MOA).

[28] It must have a stated subscription price of $0.50 or more per copy and $6.00 or more per year.

> ### (ii) Commercial "Canadian" and Commercial "International" Rates

2.17   Canada Post has authority to set its commercial rates outside of regulation, pursuant to subsections 16(1) and 21(a) of the CPC Act, for any person who has entered into an agreement with Canada Post for (a) the variation of rates of postage on the mailable matter of that person in consideration of his mailing in bulk, preparing the mailable matter in a manner that facilitates the processing thereof or receiving additional services in relation thereto;...".[29] In order to take advantage of this provision and receive commercial postal rates and service, a publisher must enter into an agreement with Canada Post. For a Canadian publication, this agreement is the "Publications Mail Product Service Agreement",[30] and for a foreign publication mailed in Canada, this agreement is the "International Publications Mail Product (Canadian Distribution) Sales Agreement".[31] These arrangements are intended to benefit Canadian and foreign publications and their subscribers by reducing mailing costs and improving delivery standards. Appendix A of each "Agreement" contains the commercial "Canadian" and commercial "International" rates. These rates are identical to those found in the *Publications Mail Postal Rates* (referred to in paragraph 2.11) which divides commercial rates into those that apply for (i) mail service for Canadian publications that are ineligible for "funded" rates (Rate Code 5); and (ii) mail service for international publications (Rate Code 6 or what are called "International" rates in this dispute). Further, special agreements may be entered into for both Canadian and non Canadian publications whereby terms and conditions (including rates of postage) may be established on a case-by-case basis.

2.18   Publications must meet the six criteria enumerated below in order for their publishers to enter into either a "Publications Mail Products Sales Agreement" or an "International Publications Mail Product Sales Agreement". Additionally for the former, the publication "must be a newspaper, newsletter or periodical, published, printed and mailed in Canada".[32] Additionally for the latter, the publications "must be a newspaper, newsletter or periodical printed outside of Canada or registered under Rate Code 5 prior to 1 March 1992".[33]

Six criteria:

   (i)   published for the purposes of disseminating to the public news, articles containing comments on or analysis of the news, and articles with respect to other topics currently of interest to the general public;

---

[29]   R.S.C. 1985, c.C-10, s. 21(a).
[30]   Canadian Publications Mail Products Sales Agreement, 1 March 1995.
[31]   International Publications Mail Product (Canadian Distribution) Sales Agreement, 1 March 1994.
[32]   Canadian Publications Mail Products Sales Agreement, para. 5.1.
[33]   International Publications Mail Product (Canadian Distribution) Sales Agreement, para. 4.1.

(ii)   devoted primarily to one or more of religion, the sciences, agriculture, forestry, the fisheries, social or literary criticism or reviews
of literature or the arts, or academic or scholarly writings;

(iii)   published at a frequency of not less than four times a year;

(iv)   addressed to a subscriber, non-subscriber, company or to a newsdealer in Canada;

(v)   containing not more than 70 per cent of the space devoted to advertising in more than 50 per cent of the issues published during
any twelve month period; and

(vi)   published by or at the direction of a person whose principal business is publishing.

2.19   The rates for the commercial "Canadian" and commercial "International"
publications mail service are summarized as follows:

Commercial "Canadian" rates:

Minimum postage per addressed copy	Price per copy
(100g or less)	
Local rural rates	$0.103
Local urban rates	$0.231
Regional rates	$0.184
National rates	$0.378

Commercial "International" rates:

Minimum postage per addressed copy	
(100g or less)	Price per copy
Rates for foreign magazines,	
newspapers or newsletters mailed	
in Canada (inbound)	$0.436

Two sub-categories include discounts for palletization and by-pass. Non-
subsidized Canadian publications can receive discounts of $0.01 to $0.02 per
copy if palletized, and discounts ranging from $150.00 to $200.00 per truck load
for a by-pass or downstream entry. These discounts are not available generally to
foreign publications mailed in Canada. Further, the commercial "Canadian" and
commercial "International" categories have not been subject to regulation since
1994 and 1992, respectively.[34]

---

[34]   SOR/94-210, 24 February 1994 and SOR/91-641, 7 November 1991.

III.   MAIN ARGUMENTS

3.1   The *United States* asked the Panel to find that:

(a)   Tariff Code 9958 is inconsistent with Article XI of GATT 1994;

(b)   Part V.I of the Excise Tax Act is inconsistent with Article III:2 of GATT 1994, or in the alternative, Article III:4 of GATT 1994; and

(c)   The application by Canada Post of lower postal rates to domestically-produced periodicals under the "funded" and "commercial" rate systems is inconsistent with Article III:4 of GATT 1994, and is not a domestic subsidy within the meaning of Article III:8 of GATT 1994.

3.2   *Canada* asked the Panel to find that:

(a)   Tariff Code 9958 is justifiable under Article XX(d) of the GATT 1994;

(b)   Article III of GATT 1994 does not apply to Part V.I of the Excise Tax Act, and if the Panel decides that it does apply, Part V.I is consistent with Article III of GATT 1994;

(c)   Article III:4 of GATT 1994 does not apply to the commercial rates charged by Canada Post, and the funds paid by the Department of Canadian Heritage to Canada Post for the "funded" rates are allowable subsidies pursuant to Article III:8(b) of GATT 1994.

A.   *Tariff Code 9958 - Import Prohibition*

(i)   *Article XI:1*

3.3   The *United States* argued that the Canadian import prohibition on the products listed in Tariff Code 9958 is a violation of Article XI:1 of GATT 1994, which prohibits quantitative restrictions on imports. By its terms, Tariff Code 9958 applies both to special Canadian editions of magazines that are also published in versions targeted at readers in other countries (i.e. split-runs) and to magazines produced solely for the Canadian market. In either case, the import ban applies if the periodical contains even a small amount of advertising directed primarily at Canadian readers - single advertisement in the case of split-runs and five per cent or more of the advertising space in the case of magazines generally. The ban eliminates these magazines from the Canadian magazine market, and ensures that only Canadian magazines can compete for domestically-oriented advertising. Canada did so for the specific purpose of ensuring that Canadian magazines can enjoy a monopoly on the sale of magazines containing such advertisements. Advertising is an important source of revenue for magazine publishers. Thus, granting domestic magazines a monopoly on local advertising provides them a competitive advantage over foreign-produced magazines that are denied the right to carry such advertisements.

3.4   *Canada* argued that the United States claim that the Canadian legislation creates a "monopoly" for Canadian publishers of advertisements directed at the Canadian market is inconceivable in the North American environment. The existence of "spillover" advertising, whereby advertisements for generally-available products in wide-circulation US magazines automatically reach the Canadian public, with very significant consequences for the competitiveness of the Canadian industry, is sufficient by itself to prevent the creation of any true monopoly. The "monopoly" effect complained of by the United States has nothing to do with the first part of the Code, dealing with split-runs, or with the Excise Tax Act. It is true that the second part of the Tariff Code prevents the entry of foreign magazines with substantial amounts of advertising directed specifically at Canadian, as a means of preventing an easy way to get around the split-run prohibition. However, the 5 per cent rule applies only to a limited type of advertising with Canadian addresses and phone numbers, and this aspect of the policy has not been carried forward to the excise tax provisions, which are strictly limited to the split-run phenomenon.

(ii)   Article XX(d)

3.5   Canada added that Tariff Code 9958 is a measure intended to secure the attainment of the objectives of Section 19 of the Income Tax Act. The issue is whether Tariff Code 9958 can be justified as a necessary measure within the meaning of Article XX(d). Because it forms an integral part of a package of measures with a single objective, it can be so justified on a natural and reasonable reading of the treaty language. Canadian public policy for the magazine industry is designed to provide Canadians with a distinctive vehicle for the expression of their own ideas and interests. Such a vehicle faces enormous competition from foreign magazines for both advertising and readership. Public policy measures aim to balance the need to establish and maintain a place for Canadian periodicals in their own domestic market while at the same time ensuring that Canadians have unrestricted access to foreign periodicals. To achieve this long-standing policy objective, government policy has focused on two areas: advertising and distribution. The Government of Canada has introduced a series of measures to ensure that magazines with editorial content developed for the Canadian market can compete for the limited advertising revenues. These measures include Tariff Code 9958, Sections 35-41 of the Excise Tax Act and Section 19 of the Income Tax Act. Section 19 of the Income Tax Act allows a deduction for advertising directed at the Canadian market. Tariff Code 9958 restricts the importation into Canada of periodicals whose advertising has been purchased especially to reach a Canadian audience. The general objective of these measures is to help the Canadian periodical industry raise advertising revenues. Tariff Code 9958 ensures the achievement of this goal, with Section 19 of the Income Tax Act.

"Secure Compliance"

3.6   The *United States* referred to the panel on *United States - Standards for Reformulated and Conventional Gasoline ("US - Standards for Gasoline")* which states that a party invoking an exception under Article XX(d) has to demonstrate the following elements:

"(1)   that the measures for which the exception are being invoked - that is, the particular trade measures inconsistent with the General Agreement - *secure compliance* with laws or regulations themselves not inconsistent with the General Agreement;

(2)   that the inconsistent measures for which the exception is being invoked are *necessary* to secure compliance with those laws or regulations; and

(3)   that the measures are applied in conformity with the requirements of the *introductory clause* of Article XX.

In order to justify the application of Article XX(d), all the above elements have to be satisfied".[35]

3.7   Canada's import prohibition fails to meet *any* of these requirements. With respect to the first requirement, Canada has failed to demonstrate that its import ban secures compliance with Section 19 of the Income Tax Act. Canada has not claimed that the import ban is meant to enforce the income tax provisions, only that the import ban and the income tax measures advance the same objective (through different means), which is to channel all domestic advertising to domestic magazines.

3.8   *Canada* noted that the conformity of the Income Tax Act with GATT 1994 is not being challenged. Tariff Code 9958 and Section 19 of the Income Tax Act are conceived to deal with the problem of split-runs with inserted Canadian advertising. The idea is that the income tax provision would cover magazines printed in Canada and the border measure would cover magazines printed outside the country. The effectiveness of the non-deductibility provision standing by itself would obviously be very limited. The problem is that of foreign companies that sold into the Canadian market but are not subject to Canadian income tax. This would be more than a loophole, given the open nature of the Canadian economy and the degree of import penetration. It would largely destroy the effectiveness of the income tax measures.

3.9   Canada drew the Panel's attention to the panel report on *EEC - Regulations on Parts and Components*[36] (*"EEC - Parts and Components"*) which intro-

---

[35]   Panel Report on *United States - Standards for Reformulated and Conventional Gasoline*, adopted on 20 May 1996, at para. 6.31 (emphasis in original).

duces a very stringent test for the application of Article XX(d), under which the non-conforming measures have to be necessary for the enforcement of another law, and not merely in order to ensure that the objectives of that law be fulfilled. This test is entirely appropriate where the issue is the enforcement of regulatory statutes and ordinary fiscal measures designed to raise revenue, where compliance with the statute is virtually synonymous with the attainment of its objectives. If, for example, an environmental measure is complied with, its objective is *ipso facto* attained.

3.10   The *EEC - Parts and Components* panel interpreted Article XX(d) in terms of enforceability as opposed to measures designed to ensure that the objectives of another measure are not undermined. Canada is not challenging that decision or its reasoning. It makes sense in the context of regulatory statutes with prohibitions or even tax statutes that are designed to raise revenue and prevent tax evasion. It is doubtful, on the other hand, that an enforceability test is meaningful in the case of a fiscal or other economic incentive where formal compliance is not the real object, and *substantial* compliance can not be separated from the underlying social and economic objectives the measure is designed to secure. In the case of a fiscal incentive whose sole purpose is to influence business decisions in a certain direction, compliance has to be judged in terms of effectiveness. Canada suggests, therefore, that the application of the exception in Article XX(d) should take account of the nature of the measures under consideration, and that the test in the *EEC - Parts and Components* panel decision should not be rigidly applied without taking account of these circumstances.

3.11   Further, the US consideration that compliance is always a matter of enforceability, no more no less, may be a valid proposition, as held in *EEC - Parts and Components*, for mandatory legislation based on prohibitions or exactions. Compliance and effectiveness are synonymous in the case of the vast majority of legislative measures. But Section 19 is not an ordinary tax measure, designed to raise revenue for the public purse or prevent tax evasion. In the case of a fiscal or other economic incentive whose sole purpose is to influence business decisions in a certain direction, compliance has to be judged in terms of effectiveness as well as enforceability. The distinction is between formal compliance and real or substantial compliance, which in this case has nothing to do with whether deductions are properly claimed but with the policy behind this entire set of measures.

3.12   The *United States* argued that the panel on *EEC - Parts and Components* dismisses the argument that Article XX(d) permits governments to maintain GATT-inconsistent measures to "ensure the attainment of the *objectives* of [GATT-consistent] laws and regulations" rather than to prevent violations of the GATT-consistent laws or regulations.[37] That panel stated that the interpretation it

---

[36]   Panel Report on *European Economic Community - Regulations on Parts and Components*, adopted on 16 May 1990, BISD 37S/132.
[37]   Panel Report on *European Economic Community – Regulations on Parts and Components*, adopted on 16 May 1990, BISD 37S/132, para. 5.17 (emphasis added).

rejects would make the function of Article XX(d) "substantially broader" and would not be consistent with the fact that Article XX(d) applies only in the specific circumstances set out in that paragraph - namely, to secure compliance with GATT-consistent laws or regulations.

3.13   Canada's claim that the import ban does not seek "formal compliance" with Section 19 of the Income Tax Act, but rather "real or substantial compliance", which Canada admits "has nothing to do with whether deductions are properly claimed", is simply another way of stating that the import ban helps advance the same overall (protectionist) aim as Section 19. However, the import ban does not "secure compliance" with Section 19, and thus does not fall within the purview of Article XX(d). If accepted, Canada's view of Article XX(d) would allow WTO Members to adopt all manner of GATT-inconsistent measures on the ground that they further the same objectives as other protectionist legislation. As the *EEC - Parts and Components* panel makes clear, the phrase "secure compliance" does not reach measures that merely help ensure that domestic policy goals are realized.

"Necessary"

3.14   The *United States* noted that the panel report on *United States - Section 337 of the Tariff Act of 1930* ("*US - Section 337*") observed that :

> "[A] contracting party cannot justify a measure inconsistent with another GATT provision as 'necessary' in terms of Article XX(d) if an alternative measure which it could reasonably be expected to employ and which is not inconsistent with other GATT provisions is available to it".[38]

The normal way for tax authorities to enforce income tax provisions is to audit the relevant tax returns, and to make adjustments to those returns where necessary to secure compliance. Tax, civil, or criminal penalties may be imposed where warranted in individual cases. Such measures would normally be entirely consistent with GATT and in any event would be applied to particular taxpayers, not to imports. It is extraordinary for income tax enforcement measures to take the form of restrictions on trade in goods. Canada has demonstrated no basis for why, of all possible measures, it is necessary to impose a blatantly GATT-inconsistent *import ban* to secure compliance with Section 19 of the Income Tax Act nor why normal tax enforcement procedures were insufficient.

3.15   *Canada* stated that the panel in *US - Section 337*[39] held that the term "necessary" required the use of the least trade-restrictive measure available. Canada submits that there are no other measures, less restrictive or otherwise, that

---

[38]   Panel Report on *United States - Section 337 of the Tariff Act of 1930*, adopted on 7 November 1989, BISD 36S/345, para. 5.26.
[39]   *Ibid.*, 392, paras. 5.25-5.27.

would accomplish the objective. If split-runs could be imported, with Canadian advertisements often placed by businesses for which Canadian tax liability is irrelevant, the program would simply no longer work.

3.16   Canada therefore reiterates its suggestion that the application of the exception in Article XX(d) should take account of the nature of the measures under consideration, and that the test in the *EEC - Parts and Components* and the *US - Section 337* panel decisions should not be rigidly applied without taking account of these circumstances. The Panel should recall that Code 9958 and the income tax provision have always been considered part of a single, indivisible package of complementary, indivisible measures and should be treated as such for the purposes of Article XX(d).

3.17   The *United States* stated that even if one were to credit Canada's argument that Article XX(d) covers measures necessary to secure the attainment of the domestic policy goals embedded in other laws, the import ban would still not be "necessary" for such a purpose. The objective of Section 19 is to support Canada's magazine industry. Canada has not shown why GATT-consistent measures (such as subsidies paid directly to producers) would not reasonably be available to it for advancing this objective.

(iii)   Chapeau to Article XX

3.18   *Canada* noted that each term of Article XX(d), including its Preamble, should be given consideration when examining whether Tariff Code 9958 could be justified as a necessary measure within the meaning of the treaty. Since Tariff Code 9958 is a "measure" directed against imports from all foreign countries and not only the United States, it is "not applied in a manner which would constitute a means of arbitrary or unjustifiable discrimination between countries where the same conditions prevail", as stated in the preamble to Article XX. Similarly, having regard to the application of Tariff Code 9958 since its adoption, it could not be claimed that it has been "applied in a manner which would constitute ... a disguised restriction on international trade". Tariff Code 9958 is not applied in such a way as to constitute a restriction on international trade, as the evidence so strongly demonstrates, nor does it prohibit the importation of foreign periodicals into Canada or threaten their dominant position in the English-Canadian market place.

3.19   The *United States* considered that because the import ban does not satisfy the terms of paragraph (d) of Article XX, the Panel does not need to ascertain whether or not it is in conformity with the introductory clause of Article XX. However, were the Panel to reach this issue, it should find that Canada's import ban does not meet the requirements of the introductory clause, because the import ban constitutes "a means of arbitrary and unjustifiable discrimination between countries where the same conditions prevail," and is also "a disguised restriction on international trade." In the *US - Standards for Gasoline* case, the Appellate Body states that whatever else the term "disguised restriction on international trade" means, it could be read to encompass any " . . . restrictions amounting to arbitrary or unjustifiable discrimination in international trade taken under the guise of a measure formally within the terms of an exception listed in Article XX".[40] The import ban's "arbitrary" and "unjustifiable" nature is apparent from the very structure of Tariff Code 9958. Application of the import ban depends on advertising content and on sales in more than one country - factors that are relevant only for purposes of distinguishing between those categories of foreign-produced magazines that compete with Canadian magazines for Canadian advertising revenues and those that do not. The import ban therefore constitutes a "disguised restriction on international trade".

3.20   Moreover, the expression "between countries" in the chapeau to Article XX includes a comparison between Canada and other countries as well as between countries other than Canada. The import prohibition bars only magazines produced outside Canada, thus discriminating in favour of magazines produced in Canada. There are no relevant conditions prevailing in Canada or elsewhere that would justify the discrimination imposed on foreign-produced split-runs. Thus, for the reasons discussed above, the import ban constitutes "arbitrary or unjustifiable discrimination between countries where the same conditions prevail".

3.21   Canada considered that the United States argued that the prohibition on arbitrary or unjustifiable discrimination requires a comparison between other countries and Canada, and not just between countries other than Canada. This, in effect turns this Article into a national treatment proviso. An import prohibition or restriction could never meet this test. The effect would be to remove Article XI almost completely from the range of measures that can potentially be subject to Article XX derogations. The interpretation suggested here is novel. It does not correspond to the way the chapeau to Article XX has been interpreted in the past, as shown by the 1982 decision on *United States - Prohibition on Imports of Tuna and Tuna Products from Canada*,[41] and the 1983 decision on *United States - Imports of Certain Automotive Spring Assemblies*.[42] In both those decisions, a US import prohibition was held not to be discriminatory within the meaning of the chapeau to Article XX, because it applied equally to all foreign countries exporting to the United States.

B.   Part V.I of the Excise Tax Act

3.22   The *United States* argued that the excise tax was designed specifically to shore up Canada's GATT-inconsistent import prohibition. Canada did not deny that this is so, or that the tax was designed to eliminate the competition between

---

[40]   Appellate Body Report on *United States - Standards for Reformulated and Conventional Gasoline*, adopted on 20 May 1996, WT/DS2/AB/R, DSR 1996:I, 3 at 23.

[41]   Panel Report on *United States - Prohibition on Imports of Tuna and Tuna Products from Canada*, adopted on 22 February 1982, BISD 29S/91 .

[42]   Panel Report on *United States - Imports of Certain Automotive Spring Assemblies*, adopted 26 May 1993, BISD 30S/107.

split-run magazines and domestically produced magazines. The purpose of the tax is protectionist - namely, to ensure that only Canadian magazine producers capture all of the revenues associated with advertisements directed specifically at Canadian readers. The Canadian magazine tax is designed to ensure that foreign-based publishers forego the commercially attractive option of publishing a split-run edition of an existing magazine for the Canadian market. Any such edition will be hit with a prohibitive 80 per cent excise tax. This means that foreign magazine producers contemplating sales in the Canadian market can not make use of the economies of scale that split-run editions provide. Split-run editions drive down per unit production costs by spreading the expense of producing articles and photographs over a greater number of magazines. The Canadian tax ensures that no foreign-based publisher can take advantage of those lower costs to compete in the Canadian market against wholly Canadian-produced magazines.

3.23   Canada's policy of protecting its domestic publishing industry from import competition is long-standing. Since the early 1900s, Canada has provided subsidized, lower postal rates exclusively to Canadian-produced magazines.[43] More recently, Canada sought to protect its industry by targeting imported periodicals sold into Canada as "split-run" or "regional" editions. A publisher produces a "split-run" edition of a single issue of a magazine by separating ("splitting") the editorial content (articles, photographs, artwork, etc.) and the advertising content of the magazine. The publisher then produces two or more separate regional editions of the issue of the magazine. Each edition shares some or all of the editorial content, but the advertising content in each edition may differ, because each edition is distributed in a different geographic market and the advertising is directed at that specific market.

3.24   Concerned that imported split-run editions of magazines would divert advertising revenues from domestic competitors, Canada enacted Tariff Code 9958 in 1965 specifically to prohibit the importation of split-run editions as well as any other magazine containing a more than a *de minimis* amount of advertising directed at the Canadian public, and in 1976 prohibited income tax deductions for advertisements placed in foreign-owned publications. Within a matter of a few decades, however, technological advances made it practical for foreign-based publishers to transmit editorial material electronically across the border into Canada and to publish split-run editions in Canada, thus avoiding the application of Tariff Code 9958. To plug this perceived loophole and ensure that split run editions could not compete in the domestic marketplace - Canada enacted a punitive excise tax on split-run editions in December 1995.

3.25   In an opinion dated 15 August 1990, Investment Canada advised Time Canada Ltd., a company controlled by Time Warner, Inc. of New York, N.Y., that its proposal to publish a Canadian edition of *Sports Illustrated* was not in-

---

[43]   *A Question of Balance, Report of the Task Force on the Canadian Magazine Industry*, 1994 (*"Task Force Report"*) at 72.

consistent with Section 15 of the Investment Canada Act. Based on that opinion, on 11 January 1993, Time-Warner announced plans to publish in Canada a special Canadian edition of *Sports Illustrated* magazine. Recognizing that Tariff Code 9958 could not be relied upon to keep a Canadian-produced version of *Sports Illustrated* or other foreign-based magazines out of the Canadian market, the Canadian Government responded to Time's announcement on 26 March 1993, by establishing a Task Force on the Canadian Magazine Industry whose mandate was "to recommend ways in which the current measures [supporting the Canadian magazine industry] could be brought up-to-date".[44]

3.26   The Task Force concluded that it in the absence of additional legislation it was highly likely that a significant number of US split-runs would be sold in Canada. The Task Force estimated that there were 53 potential US consumer magazine entrants into the Canadian market, and 70 potential US business and trade magazine entrants, and that the majority of these would actually enter the Canadian market.[45] In December 1994, the Canadian Government announced its intention to implement the Task Force's recommendation to implement a new excise tax on all split-run magazines that contain ads directed at Canadians.[46] On 25 September 1995, the Government formally introduced Bill C-103, the excise tax bill, in the Canadian House of Commons. In introducing Bill C-103, Minister of Canadian Heritage Dupuy stated: "*Sports Illustrated Canada* managed to get around custom tariff 9958, because most of its content was sent electronically from the United States. It was simply a loophole in the tariff laws since electronic transmission made it possible to avoid tariff regulations. . . . Task Force members explored several avenues and finally concluded that the proposed excise tax was the best solution. It could be designed and implemented in order to avoid split-run editions".[47] In the Parliamentary debate, one Member described the bill in the following terms:

> "[I]t is important to be very clear about the nature of the bill. In essence it is designed to kill international competition between magazines, more specifically magazines which come into Canada. The killing of that competition kills a lot of good things which flow from competition".[48]

3.27   *Canada* argued that the excise tax measure is designed to prevent the diversion of advertising to low-cost publications reproducing recycled editorial content, at the expense of publications created for Canadians. The Excise Tax Act is carefully designed to deal with a particular combination of circumstances. What it targets is the combination of recycled editorial content plus Canadian advertisements. Magazines derive their revenues predominantly from the sale of

---

[44]   Task Force Report at iii.
[45]   Task Force Report at 50-52.
[46]   News Release, Canadian Heritage, December 22, 1994 at 1.
[47]   *Commons Debates* at 14790-1 (Sept. 25, 1995).
[48]   *Commons Debates* at 14795 (statement of Mr. Monte Solberg).

advertising space and from the circulation of the magazine. Advertising revenue is by far the most important revenue stream for Canadian magazines, accounting for 60 per cent of total revenue. Circulation revenue accounts for 33 per cent of total revenue, or $287 million. Advertising revenue is crucial for the Canadian magazine industry, allowing the publisher to provide the magazine at an affordable cost or, in some cases, free of charge.

3.28   Canada explained that there is a direct correlation between circulation, advertising revenue and editorial content. The larger the circulation, the more advertising a magazine can attract. With greater advertising revenue, a publisher can afford more to spend on editorial content. The more a publisher spends, the more attractive the magazine is likely to be to its readers, resulting in circulation growth. Similarly, a loss of advertising revenue will produce a "downward spiral". Less advertising entails less editorial, a reduction in readership and circulation and a diminished ability to attract advertising. Magazines can be sold on newsstands, or through subscriptions, or distributed at no cost to selected consumers. The Canadian market is not large, particularly when compared to the US market. It is also highly fragmented from a language perspective. There are two official languages in Canada as well as a number of other languages. Canadian English-language publications face tough competition on newsstands; they account for only 18.5 per cent of English-language periodicals distributed on newsstands, where space is dominated by foreign publications. Subscriptions are the main source of circulation revenue for most Canadian magazines.

3.29   The constraints imposed by the demographics of the Canadian market have a significant impact on the ability of a magazine primarily addressed to Canadian interests to obtain the broad base of circulation that is necessary to achieve economic viability. Canadian magazine publishers compete with other media for the same limited amount of advertising dollars in the Canadian market. Magazines have been losing market share to other media forms such as direct mail and television. It is unlikely that the share held by magazines will increase. The amount of money spent by advertisers to reach Canadian consumers is also not likely to grow. In addition, "spillover" advertising (the ability of advertisers of internationally distributed products to reach Canadian consumers through US magazines) is a further limitation on the competitive position of the Canadian industry. Canadian periodical publishers face a major competitive challenge in their business environment that is not common to their counterparts in countries with a larger population to serve. The pivotal fact is the penetration of the Canadian market by foreign magazines. Canadian readers have unrestricted access to imported magazines. At the same time, Canadian readers have demonstrated that they value magazines that address their distinct interests and perspectives. However, foreign magazines dominate the Canadian market. They account for 81.4 per cent of all newsstand circulation and slightly more than half (50.4 per cent) of the entire circulation of English-language magazines destined for the general public in Canada.

3.30   Magazines are a particularly good medium for advertisers wishing to reach a specific market defined by regional location. Both Canadian and foreign magazines currently have regional editions in their respective home markets. Publishers and advertisers recognize the importance of regional editions as an advertising vehicle. The marketing strategy behind regional editions is that they allow publishers to offer very specific advertising vehicles for advertisers interested in targeting a particular audience, hence they maximize advertising revenues. Some foreign publishers view Canada as a separate "region" within their own national market. The "Canadian" regional edition produced by such publishers generally contains the same editorial content as the other editions but different advertising content, reflecting the addition of advertisements from Canadian advertisers. The term "split-run" is used in Canada to refer to such a Canadian regional edition. For a foreign publisher, the incentive to produce a Canadian regional edition of its magazine containing advertising directed at Canadians is, of course, profit. A profit for the foreign publisher only requires that the incremental revenue from advertising in the regional edition exceeds the costs of producing the split-run. Since its fixed costs have already been recovered in the larger home market, this offers an inviting prospect for a foreign magazine.

3.31   The Task Force on the Canadian Magazine Industry was established as a result of the anticipated publication of *Sports Illustrated Canada*. *Sports Illustrated Canada* was a split-run edition that was printed in Canada using text that was electronically transmitted from the United States. The editorial content of *Sports Illustrated Canada* was largely the same as the content in the American editions of *Sports Illustrated* but it contained advertisements that had been specifically purchased to reach a Canadian audience. Tariff Code 9958 was not applicable to *Sports Illustrated Canada* because it was printed in Canada rather than being imported. The emergence of *Sports Illustrated Canada* as a new split-run edition revealed the limitations of Canada's existing policy instruments. Accordingly, the Task Force was created to recommend ways to bring these policy instruments up to date. The Task Force's main recommendation was that an excise tax be imposed on advertising contained in split-run editions of periodicals that are distributed in Canada. The object of the excise tax is not to discourage readership of foreign magazines, but to maintain an environment in which Canadian magazines can exist in Canada alongside with imported magazines. It is also intended to foster conditions in which indigenous magazines can be published, distributed and sold in Canada on a commercial basis. The tax is consistent with the broad principles of the cultural and media policies of successive federal governments.

(i)   Article III:2 Versus Coverage Under the General Agreement on Trade in Services (GATS)

Applicability of Article III of GATT 1994

3.32   The *United States* argued that Canada's 80 per cent excise tax on split-run editions is inconsistent with Article III:2, first sentence, of GATT 1994 because it creates an artificial distinction between "split-run" magazines and all other types of magazines and applies the 80 per cent tax solely to split-runs. It therefore applies a higher tax to certain types of imported magazines than to "like" domestic magazines.

3.33   *Canada* argued that this dispute concerns the provision of advertising services to Canadian advertisers and that Part V.I of the Excise Tax Act was a measure pertaining to advertising services. A magazine publisher derives revenue from both the sale of the magazine to consumers and from the sale of advertising space to advertisers. The sale of the right to advertise to a magazine's audience is an advertising service. As the tax imposed by the Excise Tax Act is imposed on the revenues earned through the provision of advertising services by a magazine publisher, it is a tax in respect of the provision of an advertising service. Multilateral trade disciplines on advertising services fall within GATS and not GATT 1994; Article III of GATT 1994 does not apply to Part V.I of the Excise Tax Act. However, the terms of reference direct the Panel to examine only trade matters within the purview of GATT 1994. Thus, the examination of Part V.I of the Excise Tax Act in light of GATS is not covered by the terms of reference. The first distinctive aspect of a magazine is its character as a public good which is largely defined by its content. The second distinctive feature is the magazine's dual nature in that it is both a consumer good and an advertising service with two distinct revenue streams. The two separate revenue streams are circulation revenue, which is derived from the sale of a good, and advertising revenue, which is derived from the sale of a service. The two consumers are readers and advertisers. All magazines exhibit this essential duality, which represents two distinct economic outputs.

3.34   GATT 1994 establishes the standards that govern international trade in goods. The central obligations of GATT 1994 are the tariff concessions by which WTO Members commit themselves (in Article II and the Schedules) to limit the level of tariffs they will impose on imports from other Members. A second obligation is that of the most-favoured-nation ("MFN") obligation in Article I. Articles III through XVII comprise most of the other substantive obligations of GATT 1994. These obligations apply to goods only. Article III of GATT 1994 sets out the national treatment obligation pertaining to treatment of imported goods. The Uruguay Round has produced a similar framework for trade in services. Specific commitments are recorded in national schedules that are attached to, and form an integral part of, the GATS. Every undertaking contained in a schedule to GATS is a binding commitment to allow the supply of the service in question on the terms and conditions specified and to not impose any new measures that would restrict entry into the market or the operation of the service. In the absence of any scheduled commitments, there are no disciplines on the introduction or the maintenance of measures of any type, even those that may be inconsistent with market access or national treatment commitments. Advertising services appear on the Services Sectoral Classification List of the Secretariat under the business sector.[49] The provision of advertising services is consequently a GATS matter, not a GATT matter.[50] Canada has not undertaken any commitments in respect of the provision of advertising services in its Schedule of Specific Commitments. In the absence of any scheduled commitments, there are *no* restrictions on Canada in respect of the introduction of measures concerning the provision of advertising services. In particular, Canada is not bound, nor in any way obliged, to provide national treatment to Members of the WTO in respect of the provision of advertising services in the Canadian market.

3.35   This challenge in respect of the Excise Tax Act measures is an indirect attempt by the United States to obtain trading benefits that it has been unable to obtain directly. In the guise of a GATT goods argument, the United States now attempts to persuade the Panel to allow it to have access to a service sector to which, in full accordance with the terms of international trade law, it is presently not entitled. Should the Panel agree that a Member can obtain benefits under a covered agreement that have been expressly precluded under another covered agreement, the Panel risks introducing uncertainty into the relationship between GATS and GATT disciplines.

3.36   The *United States* argued that the Canadian argument was baseless because: (1) nothing in GATS purports to reduce or eliminate the obligations that GATT has imposed since 1947; (2) GATS does not have primacy over GATT with respect to measures affecting trade in goods; and (3) Canada can observe its obligations under GATT Article III consistently with the provisions of GATS. There is no indication in the Agreement Establishing the WTO, GATT, or GATS, that adoption of GATS was intended as a limitation on the scope of GATT 1994. Had the negotiators intended to adopt a principle as fundamental as the one Canada now puts forward, they certainly would have provided for it in the text of GATT, GATS or WTO Agreement. In the absence of such an indication, or an irreconcilable conflict - neither of which Canada can point to here - GATT and GATS must be applied according to their terms. (It is theoretically

---

[49]   Canada notes that there are three Articles in Part III of the GATS on Specific Commitments, entitled Market Access, National Treatment, and Additional Commitments (Articles XVI, XVII and XVIII respectively). In general, the classification of sectors in national schedules is based on the Secretariat's Services Sectoral Classification List. This reference list of the Secretariat is based on the Central Product Classification (CPC) of the United Nations. See *Services Sectoral Classification List: Note by the Secretariat,* MTN.GNS/W/120 (10 July 1991). See also *Scheduling of Initial Commitments in Trade in Services: Explanatory Note,* MTN.GNS/W/164 (3 September 1993).

[50]   Canada cites United Nations, Dept. of International Economic and Social Affairs, Statistical Office of the United Nations, *Provisional Central Product Classification,* Statistical Papers, Series M No. 77, U.N. Doc. ST/ESA/STAT/SER.M/77 (New York: United Nations, 1991) at 147-148, 173. Item 8711 states: sale or leasing services of advertising space or time. Services provided in soliciting advertising space or time for newspapers, other periodicals, and television stations. Item 8712 states: planning, creating and placement services of advertising. Planning, creating and placement services of advertisements to be displayed through the advertising media. Item 8719 states: other advertising services. Other advertising services not elsewhere classified, including outdoor and aerial advertising services and delivery services of samples and other advertising material.

possible that the same measure may be covered by, and may even violate, both agreements. Indeed, a measure may violate more than one goods agreement as well, provided the measure is within the scope of each agreement and is inconsistent with the provisions of each.) By contrast, the negotiators of the WTO did establish a rule for addressing conflicts between GATT 1994 and the multilateral agreements on trade in goods in Annex 1A to the WTO Agreement.[51] By their terms, GATT Article III:2 covers taxes applied to products "directly or indirectly", and GATT Article III:4 applies even to measures affecting *services* connected to goods, such as "distribution" and "transportation".

3.37   Canada's decision not to inscribe relevant commitments on advertising services in its GATS schedule of specific commitments means that Canada is not assuming certain GATS obligations as to those services. Canada does not thereby insulate all measures having any connection to advertising from review under any other WTO agreement. Such a result would improperly exalt GATS over GATT and other WTO agreements. Canada's view would open a huge hole in GATT because there is no shortage of "service-related" measures that could be used to discriminate against imported goods. Under Canada's interpretation, a Member could, consistently with GATT: tax the rental of foreign cars, place a prohibitive surcharge on telecommunication services that are carried out using imported equipment, or impose a room tax on persons staying at hotels that were built using imported construction materials. Although each of these measures relates to the provision or consumption of a service, each also obviously imposes a competitive disadvantage on imported products and provides protection to domestic production, and each would be within the scope of GATT Article III. It is irrelevant whether or not the excise tax could be a measure affecting trade in advertising services. The excise tax is a direct or indirect tax on a product, split-run magazine editions, within the meaning of Article III:2.

3.38   *Canada* noted that it does not claim that there is a conflict between GATT 1994 and GATS in this case. The two treaties may very well apply in their own respective jurisdiction. GATS does not have as its object, and does not result in, the carving out of part of the jurisdiction of GATT 1994. The negotiators of GATS have merely developed new rules for a sector of international trade to which the existing rules did not apply. They have not, in doing so, redefined the scope of Article III of GATT 1994. The interpretation suggested by Canada of the area of application of Article III with respect to the provisions relating to services would have been the same in 1993 before the GATS treaty came into force. The interpretation is autonomous and based on specific terms of Article III:2 as well as on its intent and its original scope. The issue of overlapping obligations or conflicts arises because of the existence of two treaties, GATT 1994 and GATS, which contain different sanctions with respect to the provisions relating to services. Because of the existence of these two treaties which may apply

---

[51]   See General interpretive note to Annex 1A.

to a given measure, it is necessary to interpret the scope of application of each such as to avoid any overlap. Such overlaps between the areas of GATT 1994 and GATS could lead to conflicts in the application of the treaties which should be resolved on the basis of the rules of interpretation of public international law.

3.39   The Canadian interpretation of the scope of Article III:2 of GATT 1994 and Article I:1 of GATS avoids such overlaps, respects the autonomy of each treaty and ensures the harmonious application thereof. It is not necessary in the instant case to determine the primacy of one treaty over the other. The Panel does not have to decide this question since there is no conflict. What must be decided is the individual scope of Article III:2 of GATT 1994 and Article I:1 of GATS. Part V.1 of the Excise Tax Act is a measure regarding the provision of services which is dealt with by Article I:1 of GATS. It is on the basis of an interpretation of the specific terms of Article III:2 of GATT 1994 and of Article I:1 of GATS, made in accordance with Article 31 of the Vienna Convention on the Law of Treaties, that the scope of application of each of the two treaties must be determined. The analysis of the measure which is the subject of the dispute leads to the determination of which of the two treaties apply. Canada does not rely on the rules of conflict to resolve the question of the applicability of Article III:2 of GATT to Part V.I of the Act. It is the interpretation of the word "indirectly" in Article III:2 which enables Canada to conclude that the Article does not apply to this measure.

3.40   To determine which disciplines apply to a given measure, one must examine not only the object of the tax and the fiscal mechanism used, but most of all one must examine the effects of the tax, by distinguishing between principal and incidental effects. Some relevant factors for such a determination are: the nature of the economic activity covered by the measure, the structure and effects of the measure and the intention of the measure. A measure may have different aspects and may, as a result, attract different disciplines under different agreements, but no single aspect of a measure should be subject to both disciplines at the same time. In any case at the margins of the two disciplines, Canada suggests that the dominant or essential characteristics of the economic activity at issue should control the determination of whether GATT or GATS is applicable. In the case of the excise tax on split-run periodicals, the principal effect is to restrict the access of foreign publishers to the Canadian advertising market since, in principle the periodical could very well be sold on the Canadian market with advertising not specifically addressed to Canada. This is evidenced by the fact that plans for prospective split-runs for the Canadian market are based on actual sales in Canada of the original version of the magazine which does not contain specific advertising for that market.

3.41   The tax is intended to prevent the penetration of the Canadian advertising market by publishers who sell their advertising services in association with split-run magazines. It is clear that the measure pertains to the supply of a service and as such is a measure that WTO Members intended to be disciplined under GATS. This was recognized by the United States Trade Representative, in the *1995 National Trade Estimate Report on Foreign Trade Barriers* (NTE), where Canada's practices with respect to split-run advertising were listed and described under the heading Services Barriers.[52]

3.42   The *United States* responded that Canada's suggestion that GATT or GATS should apply based on the "dominant or essential characteristics of the economic activity at issue" was simply a test Canada had invented. Like Canada's other assertions relating to the GATS, it found no support in any of the WTO Agreements or their negotiating history. Adoption of such a test would alter the rights and obligations of WTO Members, in violation of Article 3.2 of the DSU. The United States submitted that whereas Canada referred to the need to avoid conflicts between GATT and GATS, it had failed to identify exactly what those conflicts were. A true "conflict" between two agreements arose only where compliance with one agreement necessarily resulted in non-compliance with the other. This simply was not the case with respect to the excise tax. Applying taxes to imported split-run magazines in a GATT-consistent manner (i.e., at a rate no higher for split-run than for non-split-run magazines) in no way requires Canada to breach its GATS obligations with regard to advertising services or any other service sector. Moreover, there is nothing that is even "inconsistent" about the obligations that the two agreements impose on Canada. The United States also asserted that, although USTR's *1995 NTE Report* listed the excise tax and other similar Canadian barriers under the heading of "services barriers", the report noted that these practices "restrict US access to the Canadian market for *publications and* media advertising" (emphasis added). In the *1996 NTE* report, the United States discussed Canadian restriction on US publications under the heading "Import Policies", not "Services Barriers".

"Taxes Applied Directly or Indirectly to Products"

3.43   The *United States* further argued that the tax is covered by Article III because it is imposed on the split-run edition which, like all magazines, are "products" for purposes of GATT. Magazines are physical goods that are manufactured, traded, and in the absence of a ban such as Canada's, imported. While the amount of the tax is *measured* in terms of "the value of all advertising in the edition," the tax is *applied* to each split-run edition. By its terms the tax is applied "in respect of each split-run edition of a periodical". Moreover, the tax is applied on a "per issue" basis. In addition, the obligation to pay the tax is imposed on those who produce or trade in the magazine as a final product, such as the publisher, distributor, printer or wholesaler, *as opposed to those who design or purchase advertising*. Finally, even the method of calculating the tax is based on revenues derived from an integral element of the physical magazine itself - the printed advertisements. Thus, the excise tax is applied directly on split run editions themselves, not on a service offered in connection with such editions.

---

[52]   See *1995 National Trade Estimate Report on Foreign Trade Barriers* (Washington, D.C.: United States Trade Representative, 1995) at 38.

3.44   *Canada* argued that the tax is not applied directly to a split-run magazine and in particular it is not based on, or applied to, the price of a split-run magazine. The tax is applied to the value of advertising carried by each issue of a split-run magazine and is assessed against the publisher of the split-run magazine, as the seller of the advertising service. The expression "in respect of each edition" serves as a basis for determining and calculating liability that relates to advertising revenue as the subject matter of the tax. The significant point, which decisively identifies the subject matter of the tax, is that the tax is measured not in terms of the price of the magazine but in terms of the advertising revenues it generates.

3.45   The tax is imposed on the publisher in the publisher's capacity as a provider of advertising services. The tax is tied to the service provided rather than the good. The publisher is the person responsible for the payment of the tax. The distributor, the printer and the wholesaler have been identified as potentially liable where it would be impossible to collect the tax in Canada from the publisher. In such cases, the Act grants those persons a right of recovery against the publisher.[53] Accordingly, there is no doubt that the ultimate liability falls on the publisher, and because the *ad valorem* basis of the tax is advertising, this liability arises directly out of the services dimension of the publisher's business. The collection mechanism is designed to ensure that there is always a person in Canada from whom the tax can be collected. It is doubtful whether collection machinery should ever be used as a basis for characterizing the nature of a tax, and in the particular circumstances of this case it would be entirely inappropriate.

3.46   The *United States* responded that Canada's allegation that the excise tax is collected from the publisher in connection with its provision of advertising services ignored that the publisher was the producer of the magazine as a product. With regard to imported magazines, Canada admitted that it is the *distributor* "who has to pay the tax". A magazine's distributor had absolutely no connection to the provision of any "advertising services". Moreover, if the foreign publisher of the imported magazine did not have a sufficient business presence in Canada, the magazine's distributor who paid the tax would be unlikely to obtain indemnification from the publisher at all. Indeed, the excise tax on split-run magazines was collected in a fashion similar to other excise taxes on products, such as the excise taxes in the *Japan - Alcoholic Beverages* case, and the federal excise taxes in the *US - Malt Beverages* case. Like the split-run tax, in those cases the excise taxes with respect to domestic products were collected from the producer, and the excise taxes with respect to imported products were collected from the importer, who was essentially a type of distributor.

3.47   Article III:2, first sentence, governs taxes applied directly or indirectly to products. Canada's argument that the tax is actually on advertising services confuses how the tax is *measured* (i.e., in terms of advertising fees) with what the tax

---

[53]   *Excise Tax Act*, R.S.C. 1985, c. E-15 as amended by S.C. 1995, c. 46, s. 41.3(2).

applies to (i.e., split-run editions). There is ample additional evidence that the excise tax is a tax applied to split-run magazines as a product:

- The Task Force's recommendation - which the Canadian Government adopted and which the Canadian Parliament enacted - describes the tax as a tax *"imposed on a magazine or periodical"*.[54]

- In introducing the bill to enact the excise tax, Minister of Canadian Heritage Dupuy stated that the excise tax "would *apply to all periodicals* distributed in Canada and containing more than 20 per cent of reused editorial material as well as one or more advertisements aimed at Canadians", and that "[t]he publisher, the distributor, the printer or the wholesaler of *any magazine subject to the tax* would be responsible for paying the tax".[55]

- Following House of Commons passage of the excise tax bill, Canadian Heritage issued a press release describing the tax as follows: "The amendment to the Excise Tax Act will *place an excise tax on split-run magazines* distributed in Canada that contain more than 20 per cent recycled material . . . and one or more advertisements aimed at Canadians".[56]

Thus, during the time the excise tax was being formulated and enacted, Canadian officials had considered the tax to be a tax imposed on split-run magazines. It is only in the context of this panel proceeding, and in the light of US claims that the tax is inconsistent with Article III of GATT 1994, that Canada has advanced the argument that the tax is really a tax on advertising services and not a tax on split-run magazines. Indeed, given the statements of Canadian Government officials that the excise tax was designed to eliminate split-runs from its market, Canada's argument that split-run magazines are neither directly nor indirectly subject to the excise tax is not credible.

3.48   Even if the tax is not applied *directly* to split-runs, it is at a minimum applied *indirectly* to them because it is based on one of the two key uses to which magazines are put - in this case, the placement of advertisements. Moreover, it is impossible to separate the advertising that goes into a magazine from the magazine itself. Advertising is a significant component of commercial magazines, typically accounting for half or more of total pages. A magazine's advertisements can significantly affect its appeal and usefulness to readers. In addition to virtually eliminating their use as advertising vehicles - thus drastically reducing the revenues available to market such magazines - the tax reduces the appeal of such magazines to Canadian readers by effectively eliminating advertisements of interest to them.

---

[54]   *Task Force Report* at vi, 64 .
[55]   *Commons Debates* at 14790, Sept. 25, 1995 (emphasis added).
[56]   *House of Commons Passes Bill C-103, News Release,* Department of Canadian Heritage, Nov. 3, 1995 at 2 (emphasis added).

3.49   *Canada* argued that the excise tax does not apply "indirectly" to a good within the meaning of Article III:2. In discussions at the London session of the Preparatory Committee, it was suggested that the word "indirectly" covers a tax not on a product as such but on the processing of the product".[57] The panel report in *Japan - Customs Duties, Taxes and Labelling Practices on Imported Wines and Alcoholic Beverages*[58] gave an interpretation of the term "indirectly" that was consistent with this reading:

> "The Panel...found that the wording "directly or indirectly" and "internal taxes... of any kind" implied that, in assessing whether there is tax discrimination, account is to be taken not only of the rate of the applicable internal tax but also of the taxation methods (e.g. different kinds of internal taxes, direct taxation of the finished product or indirect taxation by taxing the raw materials used in the product during the various stages of its production) and of the rules for the tax collection (e.g. basis of assessment)".

The concept of "indirectly" in Article III:2 does not capture measures that are disciplined under GATS. It is intended to capture taxes that apply to "inputs" that contribute to the production of a good - raw materials, service inputs, intermediate inputs, etc. The question of whether the excise tax is covered by Article III:2 of GATT 1994 by reason of the expression "indirectly" must be examined in light of the relationship between GATS and GATT 1994.

3.50   Article III:2, to the extent that it allows a challenge of measures relating to services that "indirectly" impact on trade in goods, covers only measures concerning inputs such as raw material or services inputs that are directly involved in the production of a good. Taxes on such production inputs are properly subject to Article III:2 because they affect the costs and prices, and therefore the competitive position of goods that are subject to Article III:2. It is important, however, for the Panel to distinguish service inputs that are directly involved in the production of a good and services that are "end-products" in their own right. The publishers' advertising services, although closely associated with the magazines, are separate products. They are not involved in the production process of the magazines. The advertising services of the publisher are not, like labour in the production of a car, an input in the production of a good.

3.51   In order for a measure with respect to services to fall "indirectly" under Article III:2 of the GATT 1994, it has to affect the competitive situation of the importer on the market. In other words, the provision of the service has to be ancillary to the provision of the good in that market. The situation is reversed where the good produced by the exporter is used to gain access to a service mar-

---

[57]   EPCT/A/PV/9 at 19; and EPCT/W/181 at 3.

[58]   Panel Report on *Japan - Customs Duties, Taxes and Labelling Practices on Imported Wines and Alcoholic Beverages*, adopted on 10 November 1987, BISD 34S/83 at 118, para. 5.8.

ket. In such an instance, the provision of the good becomes ancillary to the provision of the service which has the effect of transferring jurisdiction from GATT 1994 to GATS. Consequently, the argument on Article III:2 (and Article III:4) does not hold. Otherwise, such a restrictive interpretation could considerably diminish the scope of GATS and could lead to absurd situations such as those provided as examples by the United States. For example, irrespective of a Member's right not to make commitments with respect to foreign legal services, it would be impossible to maintain measures that restrict access when provided in a printed format. If allowed, the US interpretation of the expression "indirectly" would force Canada to accord national treatment to foreign publishers with respect to advertising services when it did not make any commitments in that respect in GATS. Such an interpretation would create an imbalance in carefully negotiated concessions on services sectors made by WTO Members during the last round of Multilateral Trade Negotiations. It would also void GATS of its effectiveness as it concerns Canada's right not to make commitments on advertising services.

3.52   If the United States is successful in persuading the WTO to condemn Canada's measures as inconsistent with GATT, the United States will be able to obtain direct access to a market from which it is otherwise properly precluded under international law. The measures in question are designed to protect access to Canada's advertising services market and they are effective in doing so. If the measures are struck down under the guise of GATT inconsistency, the WTO will have facilitated an unnegotiated concession on the part of Canada. The consequences of such an effect are far reaching. If the WTO is in any doubt about the nature of the dispute, it must simply look at what the United States will gain if successful. The United States will not gain greater access for its magazines. These magazines in exactly the same form as they are distributed in the United States already enter unimpeded. It will gain access to Canada's advertising market and the revenues to be had in that market.

3.53   The periodical publication industry is one which combines two commercial activities which are economically linked, the production of periodicals and the sale of advertising services. It cannot be denied that the autonomous economic activity which is the sale of advertising services significantly contributes to the financial viability of the publishing industry. However, this has nothing to do with the designation of two separate activities of an industry for the purposes of the application of GATT 1994 and GATS. The fact that an integrated industry uses some of its commercial activities and revenues so generated in order to facilitate the marketing of some of its other activities should not influence the characterization of the activities for the purposes of determining which sections of the WTO apply to them. The key element in the application of Article III:2, when considering whether a tax applies indirectly to a good, is whether this tax affects indirectly the global income generated by the industry under consideration. Hence the distinction made by Canada between a service as an input in the production of a good, which is within the scope of Article III:2, and a service which is a product of an independent activity such as the advertising services of a publisher, which are within the scope of Article I:1 of GATS. Canada also raised the further distinction which must be made between the services that are within the scope of GATT 1994 and GATS on the basis of the accessory or principal nature of the service. A service, as an input in the production of a good, is an accessory in the production of a good. However, the advertising services of a publisher are the principal product for which a periodical is the accessory.

3.54   A large number of services result in the production of a good. The fact that the result of the provision of the service is physically incorporated in the production of a good is not in itself a key factor in the characterization of the measure which relates to such a service. It is because of the economic integration of the two activities which form the periodical publication industry that advertising, in its physical form, is incorporated into periodicals. It is because a periodical is the accessory of the advertising service, its vehicle, that advertising in its physical form is incorporated into a periodical. It is not because advertising is physically "necessary" to the material production of a periodical as an editorial vehicle. Unlike printing services (the work of the printers), the advertising services of the publisher have nothing to do with the physical production of periodicals. Those services only relate to the financial viability of the integrated activities of the periodical publishing industry. This has nothing to do with the protection found in Article III:2 of GATT 1994. To extend the scope of Article III:2 and of the phrase "indirectly" would result in en extension beyond natural and reasonable meaning in the circumstances. The level of integration of an industry cannot be a factor in the characterization of a measure which relates to one of its activities for the purposes of determining which WTO treaties applies thereto. The only factors applicable are the nature of the measure and the scope of application of each of the two treaties.

3.55   There are no contradictions in the Canadian approach. Canada provided a general description of the periodical publishing industry and pointed out the integration of advertising and publishing activities. This explains the close relationship of these activities as far as overall income for the industry is concerned as well as the accessory nature of periodicals for the advertising services of publishers. Canada's main position is very clear. There is no doubt that the advertising services of publishers are services that are not accessory services or inputs in the production of periodicals. The fact that these services are part of the integrated activities of a publisher and that the income which results from them contributes to the overall financial viability of the industry does not affect the characterization of the activity for the purposes of the applicability of Article III:2. The latter does not apply to measures relating to the ability of a publisher to market its advertising services. Part V.1 of the Excise Tax Act is beyond the scope of Article III:2 of GATT 1994.

3.56   The *United States* asserted that neither the plain meaning of the term "indirectly" in Article III:2, nor the limited negotiating history concerning it, supports a restrictive meaning of that term. Rather, the negotiating history reveals that a tax with respect to the processing of a product was one example, but not necessarily the only example, of an "indirect" tax on a product. Advertisements are a substantial feature or component of a magazine as a product, accounting for half or more of the pages of a typical magazine sold in Canada. It is not logical to say, as Canada does, that a tax with respect to inputs - that is to say, things that are consumed in making a product - is a tax directly or indirectly on a product, but a tax that concerns a major feature or component of that actual product is not. If anything, the latter is more directly a tax applied to the product itself. Advertisements affect a magazine's price, cost, and competitive position as much as any input consumed in the production of a product. The carrying of advertisements is, moreover, a major use to which magazines are put. A tax with respect to a substantial use of a product can be viewed as a tax, directly or indirectly, applied to the product.

(ii)   Conformity of Part V.I with Article III of GATT 1994

3.57   *Canada* observed that there is an artificial quality to any attempt to assess how Article III applies to a tax that has never been applied to a foreign product. It has been assumed that the tax does not apply to imported products in view of the maintenance of Tariff Code 9958. Article III:2 requires a comparison of an imported and a domestic product, a comparison that has to remain purely hypothetical in this case. Subject to this observation, Canada provides an alternative argument to be considered in the event the Panel is of the view that Part V.I is a taxation measure that applies to magazines as "goods" and that an examination of the application of Article III of GATT 1994 has to be conducted.

3.58   The *United States* remarked that, by Canada's own admission, the excise tax applies to imported (as well as domestically produced) magazines. To the extent that the tax had not actually been *levied* on imported split-runs, it is because those imports had been completely banned by Canada. It is entirely possible that even if there were no import ban the excise tax would still not be levied because the tax is set at such a high level that it would likely discourage producers from marketing imported split-runs in the first place. It is well-settled in GATT that the level of actual imports is not the basis for assessing whether a violation of GATT Article III exists. The 1949 Working Party on *Brazilian Internal Taxes* stated that the obligations of Article III "were equally applicable whether imports from other contracting parties were substantial, small or non-existent".[59] This is because the purpose of Article III is not to protect expectations on trade volumes, but rather "expectations on the competitive relationship between imported and domestic products".[60]

3.59   Thus, the plain fact that the excise tax is mandatory legislation that applies by its terms to imported magazines brings it within the purview of Article III. The

---

[59]   The 1949 Working Party on *Brazilian Internal Taxes,* adopted on 31 June 1949, BISD II/181, 185, para. 16 .

[60]   Panel Report on *United States - Taxes on Petroleum and Certain Imported Substances,* adopted on 17 June 1987, BISD 34S/136, 158, para. 5.1.9.

principle that actual imports are not required is especially appropriate in this case because Canada has banned the relevant imports to which the tax would otherwise apply. A WTO Member cannot use a GATT-inconsistent import prohibition to shield its discriminatory domestic regulations from scrutiny. In the absence of the import prohibition, the excise tax would immediately affect imported split-run magazines. By making imported split-runs prohibitively expensive to sell in Canada, the tax would accomplish what the import ban now does: the absence of imported split-runs in the Canadian market. The effect of this scheme is that dozens of US split-runs would be sold in Canada but for barriers Canada has erected to their sale. This case is not based on Canada's treatment of US publishers' split-run magazines produced *in Canada*. Such magazines are not imported products within the scope of GATT Article III.

(a)   Article III:2, First Sentence

Like Product Issue

3.60   The *United States* argued that the Canadian excise tax created an artificial distinction between otherwise entirely like products - split run and non-split run magazine editions - based on the extent to which the same or a similar version of the product was sold abroad. The excise tax defines a split-run magazine entirely in terms of its relationship to another magazine sold outside Canada. It is, therefore, impossible to determine whether a magazine is a split-run based simply upon an examination of its physical form, its editorial content, or its advertising content. The fact that a similar edition of a magazine is sold in a country other than Canada does not differentiate the magazine from another magazine in terms of physical characteristics, end-uses, content, advertising, or any other attribute. In fact, the defining characteristic of a split-run magazine under the excise tax - the existence of another magazine sold outside Canada - is an extraneous factor having nothing to do with the character of the split-run itself.

3.61   *Canada* argued that periodicals with editorial content developed for the Canadian market and split-runs substantially reproducing foreign editorial content are not "like products" within the meaning of Article III:2 and are distinguishable on the basis of their content, the essential characteristic of any magazine. Magazines are distinct from ordinary articles of trade. Magazines are intended, by their very nature, for intellectual consumption as opposed to physical use (like a bicycle) or physical consumption (like food). It follows that the intellectual content of a cultural good such as a magazine must be considered its prime characteristic. Consequently, the "like product" analysis of whether imported split-run magazines share the same characteristics as domestic magazines with editorial content developed for the Canadian market must be approached in terms of intellectual content as opposed to the traditional approach of examining material or physical characteristics. The periodical industry is keenly aware of the importance of editorial content. It is editorial content and its ability to attract readers that determine the ability of a periodical to attract advertising revenues to securing its financial viability.

3.62   Periodicals with editorial content developed for the Canadian market and split-run periodicals envisaged by the legislation are distinct products on the basis of their editorial content. The definition of "split-run edition" reflects this distinction. Editorial material developed for the Canadian market reflects a Canadian perspective and contains specific information of interest to Canadians. The content is qualitatively different from editorial material copied from foreign publications.

3.63   What has been said of the essential properties of magazines is equally applicable to their end-use. The end-use of a magazine is not simply reading; it is the transmission and acquisition of specific information. The information in, for example, a sports magazine, cannot be considered essentially the same as that in a philosophical journal. Any attempt to characterize the "end-use" of products so broadly that they all end up in the same category would deprive this consideration of any real meaning and would run afoul of the principle that the expression "like" in this context is to be narrowly construed.[61]

3.64   The *United States* argued that a distinction of the type Canada had drawn in its excise tax should be inherently suspect under Article III because it is founded on distinctions other than differences between the products being sold in the importing country. In *US - Standards for Gasoline,* the panel rejected an argument that the US "Gasoline Rule" did not provide less favourable treatment to imported products as compared to like domestic products because it treated similarly situated parties similarly noting that

> "in the *Malt Beverages* case, a tax regulation according less favourable treatment to beer on the basis of the size of the producer was rejected".

and observing that, under the US argument in that case

> "*imported goods would be exposed to a highly subjective and variable treatment according to extraneous factors. This would thereby create great instability and uncertainty in the conditions of competition as between domestic and imported goods in a manner fundamentally inconsistent with the object and purpose of Article III*"[62]

---

[61]   Appellate Body Report on *Japan - Taxes on Alcoholic Beverages*, adopted 11 July 1996, WT/DS8/R, WT/DS10/R and WT/DS11/R, DSR 1996:I, 97, at 123.

[62]   *United States - Standards for Reformulated and Conventional Gasoline, op. cit.*, paras. 6.11-6.12 (emphasis added). The United States added that in *United States - Taxes on Automobiles*, DS31/R (11 Oct. 1994, unadopted), the panel (para. 5.59) found that "Article III:4 does not permit treatment of an imported product less favourable than that accorded to a like domestic product, based on factors *not directly relating to the product as such.* The Panel found therefore that, to the extent that treatment under the CAFE measure was based on factors relating to the control or ownership of producers/importers, it could not in accordance with Article III:4 be applied in a manner that also accorded less favourable treatment to products of foreign origin" (emphasis added).

3.65   The same concerns about "highly subjective and variable treatment according to extraneous factors" that the panel identified also apply in this case. The "extraneous factors" on which application of Canada's excise tax depends are the existence or non-existence of a product sold in a country other than Canada, and the extent of that product's similarities to, and differences from, the product sold in Canada. The United States described examples that it considered showed how Canada's distinction between split-runs and other magazines produced odd and arbitrary results based on sales of products outside Canada.

3.66   *Canada* argued that the point is not whether originality could be perceived as such, but whether there was a difference between the two products at issue - the split-run replicating a foreign magazine, on the one hand, and the domestic magazine with original content, on the other. This had nothing to do with "subjective and variable treatment according to extraneous factors" as identified in the panel on *US - Standards for Gasoline*. It made no difference in terms of product characteristics whether the gasoline was handled by refiners, blenders, or producers. Gasoline was gasoline, but any careful examination would show that content differences between split-runs and original Canadian magazines were characteristics of the products themselves. A recurring theme of the United States argument is that the Canadian legislation is not based upon objective product differences; that it is based on a distinction unrelated to product characteristics. This is said to be the result of a definition that depends entirely on the existence of a foreign companion edition with sales outside Canada. In the words of the United States, this is an extraneous factor that has nothing to do with the character of the split run itself. On the contrary, it has everything to do with the character of the split-run itself. The legislation does not focus on the existence of a so-called companion edition as a factor unrelated to the characteristics of a split-run marketed in Canada. It focuses on the fact that the split-run marketed in Canada is to a substantial degree no more than a reproduction of a foreign edition, with the content characteristics invariably associated with such material. It is not the existence of a foreign companion edition, or sales of that edition outside Canada, that counts. It is the reproduction in the Canadian split-run of content that originated in that foreign edition. Contrary to the United States argument, this is a product characteristic of the split-run magazine. The replication of foreign content is not only an attribute of the split-run - a defining attribute, in fact - it is readily discernible from an examination of the product itself.

3.67   Canada further considered that the United States' approach to like products is *necessarily* over-broad because it ignores the only basis on which one magazine can be distinguished from another - the content. If magazines are treated as ordinary articles of manufacture, defined only by the fact that they are physically made up of printed paper and staples, then it would obviously have to follow that all magazines are exactly the same. The United States submission even implies when it refers to Canada's tariff item 49.02, that newspapers, journals and periodicals are like goods. This leads to the second basic principle Canada referred to in this connection: that "like product" determinations under Article III.2 are to be made on a case-by-case basis. The reason for proceeding case-by-case is obvious: to avoid over-generalization and a mechanical or automatic transfer of criteria that are suitable in one context to another context where they no longer properly apply. A case-by-case approach is one that takes account of the particular circumstances. It cannot be denied that cultural products are different, that they have their own distinguishing characteristics. By treating them as if they were ordinary items of merchandise trade, the United States has ignored the entire rationale of the case-by-case approach.

3.68   The chief and for all practical purposes the *only* distinguishing characteristic of a magazine is its content. Content plays a role in the case of cultural products that is analogous to physical properties in the case of ordinary items of trade. Content is what the reader is looking for - the message and not the medium. The end-use of a magazine is the transmission of specific information. A magazine has a utilitarian function - it may be to keep up on current events; to acquire information about specific topics like computers or investments; in some cases, to provide entertainment - but in every case, the function and value of the magazine to the reader is inseparably linked to its specific content or subject matter. The United States' emphasis on physical properties leads inevitably to a lumping together of all magazines as indistinguishable commodities, contrary to the principle of narrow construction and the case-by-case approach. The approach that Canada advocates, giving content the decisive role, does not lead to the opposite extreme. Magazines can easily be classified by type, either broadly or narrowly, on the basis of content. Exactly where the lines are to be drawn can be a matter of judgment, but no more so than in the case of any other like product determination.

3.69   The legislation uses the concept of original material as the defining element - material that is not, to quote the statute, "the same or materially the same as editorial material" in editions that circulate primarily in foreign markets. This criterion of original versus replicated material might seem abstract at first, but in its practical effect it refers to a dividing line that is very easily recognized. Original material means content developed for and aimed at the Canadian market - this means Canadian content in terms of subject matter as opposed to authorship or production. The idea that Canadian content is the same as foreign content is simply not tenable. The events, topics and people covered will be Canadian. They may not be exclusively Canadian, but the balance will be recognizably and even dramatically different than in a replicated foreign publication, where articles on Canada are close to non-existent. Foreign magazines are almost devoid of content dealing with Canada, and what little there is quite logically fails to reflect a Canadian perspective. Even where the topics covered are the same, the perspective will be different. Some of these qualities like "perspective" are admittedly somewhat intangible; but where cultural products are at issue, these assessments cannot be avoided. And they fall well within the legitimate range of the kind of "discretionary judgment" the Appellate Body has identified as inherent in like products determinations for the purposes of Article III - discretionary but not arbitrary. It is the prevailing characteristics of each category that we should look at in determining whether or not publications created for Canada are the same as publications replicated from foreign editions. There may be individual articles that might conceivably have appeared in either type of magazine. Some issues might be more different or less different than others. But the prevailing pattern is what counts. Canadian content and foreign content are significantly different. Local publications deal with local topics. People are preoccupied with their own affairs and communities. Periodicals are the mirror image of those communities. The content of a periodical created for one community will necessarily differ from what is created for another community.

3.70   Further, the only actual magazines the United States has chosen to exhibit in this case are *Pulp & Paper*,[63] which is not a split-run and has no relevance to the Excise Tax Act, *Paris Match* and *The Economist*. *Paris Match* is an imported non-split-run and *The Economist* is an imported split-run that is exempt from the tax as a North American edition without advertising specifically directed at the Canadian market. *None* of these magazines is relevant to the comparison between domestic and imported products that has to be made under Article III:2, first sentence. But the evidence is readily available, because there are grand-fathered split-runs in Canada that can be compared with other domestic Canadian magazines. This evidence has been filed by Canada, although Canada does not bear the burden of proof. The evidence consists of *Time US*, *Time Canada* and *Maclean's* - what the United States would call a foreign companion magazine, a split-run that would be taxable without the grandfathering provision, and an original domestic magazine. And the issue, in a nutshell, is whether the last two - *Time Canada* and Maclean's - are "like" products, having regard to the narrow construction and the case-by-case approach mandated by the *Japan - Alcoholic Beverage* Appellate ruling.

3.71   Canada's evidence in the form of actual magazines provides typical examples of a split-run in the form of *Time Canada*, the parent edition in the form of *Time US*, and a domestic magazine in the form of *Maclean's*. The proper basis of comparison is of course *Maclean's* and *Time Canada*. Almost every article in *Maclean's* deals with Canada. This is true of the editorial, the letters, the business news, the entertainment coverage, the arts, crime, people, the law, much of the news - everything in fact but the lead international stories covering about 8 out of 88 pages. Next, a comparative look at *Time Canada* shows that it has practically *no* reference to Canada or Canadian subject. There are two out of 21 letters from Canadian sources. There is a travel advisory on Montreal, but it turns out to be about an exhibit dedicated to an American landscape architect. The difference between *Time Canada* and *Maclean's* is striking. It would escape no reader and no consumer. This is about as typical an example as one could find. These are mainstream, mass circulation magazines. Canada suggests that there is a significant, objective, discernible difference between a split-run and a magazine created with original content for the Canadian market.

---

[63]   Referred to in paragraph 3.91.

3.72   The *United States* contested Canada's argument that imported split-runs were not like or directly competitive or substitutable with non-split runs because non-split-runs contain original content that is from a Canadian perspective. An examination of the structure of the tax showed this to be false. Moreover, even if this assertion were true it would not form a legitimate basis for distinguishing between otherwise like products. First, by its terms the tax applied or did not apply, to particular magazines irrespective of their editorial "perspective". For example, a magazine published solely for the Canadian market, or that contained no advertising specifically directed at Canadians, automatically avoided the tax regardless of how "foreign" its contents might be. However, the very same magazine became subject to the tax if it had a somewhat different foreign companion edition. Second, the editorial content need not be "original" at all. Rather, a magazine could avoid the tax, but still be identical to what is sold abroad, as long as the publisher did not advertise to Canadians. This suggested that the real basis for the distinction is simply whether the magazine might compete for advertising revenues with purely domestically produced Canadian magazines. That, indeed, is a purpose that Canada did not hide. Finally, even if one could somehow credit Canada's argument that it is seeking through the excise tax to ensure "original content" in magazines sold in Canada this purpose would be equally illegitimate. If GATT permitted governments to require that imported goods be designed exclusively or primarily for their markets, they could easily insulate their markets from the comparative economic advantages of other WTO Members. Such a result would undermine the foundations of international trade.

3.73   The recent Appellate Body report in *Japan - Alcoholic Beverages* shares the focus of the *US - Standards for Gasoline* panel report on objective *product* differences in judging product likeness. There the Appellate Body observed:

> "The Report of the Working *Party* on *Border Tax Adjustments*, adopted by the CONTRACTING PARTIES in 1970, set out the basic approach for interpreting 'like or similar products' generally in the various provisions of GATT 1947:
>
> > ...The interpretation of the term should be examined on a case-by-case basis. This would allow a fair assessment in each case of the different elements that constitute a "similar" product. Some criteria were suggested for determining, on a case-by-case basis, whether a product is "similar"; the product's end-uses in a given market; consumers' tastes and habits, which change from country-to-country; the product properties, nature and quality.

This approach was followed in almost all adopted panel reports after *Border Tax Adjustments*".[64]

The Appellate Body found that the term "like product" in Article III:2, first sentence must be "construed narrowly" in light of the existence of the second sentence of Article III:2 which covered "directly competitive or substitutable" products, and that distinguishing between "like products" and "directly competitive or substitutable" products "is a discretionary decision that must be made [by panels] in considering the various characteristics of the *products* in individual cases".[65]

3.74   Thus the Appellate Body in *Japan - Alcoholic Beverages*, like the *US - Standards for Gasoline* decision, endorsed a case-by-case approach that focused on differences in *products,* rather than on distinctions based on extraneous factors such as the production method. The illustrative list of like-product factors cited by the Appellate Body - end-uses, the product's properties, and so forth - are identical for a magazine sold only in Canada and a magazine for which a companion edition is sold abroad. While "like product" in Article III:2, first sentence, must be interpreted narrowly, it cannot be interpreted so narrowly as to permit less favourable treatment based on distinctions between literally identical products depending on whether a companion product is sold in another market. This interpretation would be so narrow as to eliminate "like product" altogether from Article III:2, first sentence.

3.75   *Canada* considered that the US arguments on the like product issue failed to present any positive evidence that an imported split-run had enough in common with original-content Canadian magazines to allow them to be considered like products. The absence of such evidence is fatal because the United States had the burden of proof. Canada was not suggesting that a magazine had only one attribute. Nor did it back away from the proposition that the assessment had to take into account all the relevant circumstances. But the circumstances had to be weighed and balanced according to their importance, and editorial content was the most important distinguishing feature and was the chief and for all practical purposes the *only* distinguishing characteristic of a magazine. A magazine is nothing without its content which was what defined the end-use and the value of a magazine to its readers. Treating content as "one attribute among many" as the United States would say, would tend to sweep all or at least very broad classes of magazines into the same category. This would disregard the narrow characterization of like products required by the Appellate Body in *Japan - Alcoholic Beverages*.

3.76   As the complainant, the United States bears the burden of proving that Canada acted inconsistently with its obligations under Article III:2, first sentence. This is a principle of long standing in GATT jurisprudence. To date the United States has made no effort to discharge this burden. Instead, it has relied upon

---

[64]   Appellate Body Report on *Japan - Taxes on Alcoholic Beverages*, op. cit., 113.
[65]   *Ibid.,* op. cit., 114 (emphasis added).

general allegations and assertions such as the following: "there is no identifiable difference between split-run magazines, on the one hand, and magazines without a companion edition, on the other hand, in terms of their physical characteristics, appearance, uses, tariff classifications, or even editorial content". Such statements do not constitute the empirical evidence required to both substantiate the claim made by the United States that all magazines are the same or that magazines based on local content are the same as magazines replicating foreign content; and to fulfil the burden of proof borne by the United States.

3.77   While Canada also recognized the definition of what constitutes a "like product" by the Working Party on Border Tax Adjustments, it considered that the "like products" test requires a much more sophisticated analysis than that suggested by the United States. The Working Party had concluded that the determination of what constitutes "like products" must be made on a case-by-case basis in order to allow for the consideration of the specific circumstances of each case. In that context the Working Party suggested some criteria: "... the product's end-uses in a given market; consumers' tastes and habits, which change from country to country; the product's properties, nature and quality".[66] This line of thinking evolved into an established GATT practice and was recently reaffirmed by the panel in *US - Standards for Gasoline*.

3.78   The *United States* considered that with Canada's argument - that the US like product analysis is incomplete because it relies solely on the physical characteristics of magazines, and ignores their editorial content - Canada appears to concede that there is no other basis to consider split-run magazines and other magazines to be "unlike" based on the specific criteria established by the Appellate Body in *Japan - Alcoholic Beverages*. By focusing solely on "editorial content", Canada ignores the Appellate Body's instruction that the analysis of "like product" must take into account "the *various* characteristics of products in individual cases".[67] Editorial content is only one attribute of a magazine, among many. The type, texture, colour, thickness, and even the perfume, of the paper can be important factors to market appeal. The dimensions of the magazine, the manner in which its pages are bound, the typesetting, and the appearance of the ink, can also be significant. The type, appearance, and frequency of advertisements may be a factor in a consumer's purchasing decision as well. Readers may purchase a magazine in part for the information its advertisements contain about where and how to purchase products or services locally. All of these attributes - including editorial content - combine to form an *overall package* that a consumer may or may not be attracted to. For the Canadian and US magazine industries, editorial content generally represents substantially less than 20 per cent of the cost of producing a consumer magazine.

---

[66]   *Border Tax Adjustments* (Report of the Working Party adopted on 2 December 1970), BISD 18S/97.
[67]   Appellate Body Report on *Japan - Taxes on Alcoholic Beverages, op. cit.*, 114 (emphasis added).

3.79 Even if one were to examine editorial content in isolation, Canada's argument that magazines can be differentiated solely according to the percentage of "original" versus "non-original" editorial content they contain is untenable. There simply is no readily identifiable difference in actual editorial content between what the excise tax deems to be "original" and "non-original" content. That is because the distinction drawn by the excise tax is not based on the specific contents of magazines distributed in Canada but simply on whether those contents are used in magazines distributed abroad. A magazine reader in Canada cannot discern whether a magazine is "original" or not based on an examination of the magazine's contents, and thus could not be expected to consider "non-original" magazines to be any different from "original" magazines. For purposes of consumer use - as well as use by advertisers - magazines are judged by what they themselves offer, not by what a companion edition may contain.

3.80 In fact, Canada's "original content" requirement is not really meant to ensure that magazines sold in Canada have any particular type of content. Rather, it is meant to ensure that one type of production method - regional or split-runs - cannot be employed for magazines sold in the Canadian market. A distinction drawn to favour one type of production method has obvious protectionist implications and is not one that GATT should countenance for distinguishing between otherwise-like products.

3.81 Further, Canada's argument that split-runs usually differ from magazines sold only in Canada with respect to the perspective and orientation of their editorial content is legally irrelevant. A panel must assess the distinction that a measure *actually draws*, not a distinction a measure might have drawn but does not. In this case, to the extent the excise tax concerns content, it differentiates between magazines whose content is contained in a product sold in another country and magazines whose content is sold only in Canada. Thus, the excise tax simply does not differentiate between content based on its Canadian focus or perspective. Application of the excise tax does not turn merely on a magazine's "originality". A magazine distributed both inside and outside Canada becomes subject to the tax based solely on the inclusion of a single advertisement that is not identical in both editions. The very same magazine whose several editions do *not* differ in advertising is not taxed. Canada has advanced no basis for distinguishing between magazines based on the type of advertisements they contain.

3.82 For example, a science magazine escapes from the tax even if it contains absolutely no articles about Canadian scientists or Canadian scientific research so long as it is not sold outside Canada. The very same magazine would be subject to the tax if it is sold both in Canada and abroad and contained an advertisement that differed between the version sold in Canada and the version sold abroad. Yet the same magazine would not be subject to the tax if it is sold both inside and outside Canada but did not contain such an advertisement. Thus, the excise tax does not, in fact, distinguish between magazines based on their editorial content, let alone based on the orientation of the content. Rather, it applies based on factors related to whether a magazine was produced for more than one market, and advertising content. Article III:2 does not permit governments to distinguish between otherwise like products based on such business and trade factors.

3.83   With regard to the Canadian assertion that the US analysis of like product with respect to the excise tax is unacceptably general and would necessarily lead to the conclusion that *all* magazines are the same like product, regardless of content, the Appellate Body made clear in *Japan - Alcoholic Beverages* that product likeness for purposes of Article III must be addressed on a case-by-case basis and in the light of all relevant circumstances. Thus, no sweeping once-and-for-all product likeness determinations are appropriate for magazines or other products. The distinction between "original" and "non-original" content was not based on objective content differences, or any differences at all, based on a comparison of products sold in Canada. Whether or not distinctions may ever properly be drawn between magazines based on their editorial content is not an issue that is before this Panel. The excise tax distinguishes between products based on whether a similar product is sold abroad, not on objective content differences between products being sold in Canada.

3.84   Canada argues that because magazines contain intellectual or cultural content, they should receive unique treatment under GATT. Many products, as diverse as works of art, designer clothing, phonograph records and cinematographic films contain intellectual or cultural content. Like magazines, these products were in widespread use prior to the adoption of GATT 1947. But of these products, only cinematographic films were accorded special treatment in GATT 1947. Had the drafters of GATT 1947 sought to treat other intellectual or cultural products differently from products in general, they would have done so.

3.85   *Canada* argued that the United States insists that it is impossible to determine whether a magazine is a split-run simply upon an examination of its physical form, its editorial content, or its advertising. This simply misses the point. A casual reader might not in fact know whether a magazine is a split-run or simply an imported foreign magazine. There might be practically no difference between the two. *Time US* and *Time Canada* are very close. But that basis of comparison is irrelevant, because the comparison is not between imported magazines and imported magazines. The comparison is between imported split-run with the domestic magazine -*Time Canada* and *MacLean's*. And here the reader would have no difficulty in seeing that the two are very different products, offering completely different benefits to the prospective reader. The point, in sum, is not whether a split-run can be identified as such by the consumer. It is whether it can be identified as a significantly different product when compared to a domestic magazine that is not a split-run.

3.86   The United States makes the same point when it says a magazine reader in Canada cannot discern whether a magazine is original or not, based on an examination of the magazine's contents, and thus could not be expected to consider non-original magazines to be any different from original magazines. This is based on the same misperception. The point is not whether originality can be perceived as such, but whether there is a difference between the two products at issue - the split-run replicating a foreign magazine, on the one hand, and the domestic magazine with original content, on the other. And nothing the United States has said casts any doubt on the proposition that difference would be obvious to any reader. This has nothing to do with subjective and variable treatment according to extraneous factors, as identified in the panel report on *US - Standards for Gasoline*. That situation obviously had nothing to do with objective product differences. It makes no difference in terms of product characteristics whether the gasoline is handled by refiners, blenders, or producers, or what data these various companies are likely to hold. Gasoline is gasoline, but any careful examination will show that content differences between split-runs and original Canadian magazines are characteristics of the products themselves.

3.87   At some points the United States refers to split-runs as a production method. In fact it is not a production method, it is a specific type of magazine. The United States says that a distinction drawn to favour one production method over another has protectionist implications that GATT should not countenance. This reflects a passage of the *United States - Measures Affecting Alcoholic and Malt Beverages* ("*US - Malt Beverages*") decision that was specifically overruled in *Japan - Alcoholic Beverages*.[68] In any event, it mischaracterizes the legislation, which distinguishes not on the basis of production method but of product content. The United States argument on like products is based on a highly abstract reading of the Canadian legislation taken out of its real-world context. It is based in fact on a refusal to take account of the effect of the distinction between original and reproduced content on which the legislation is based. But it is only on the basis of the effect of the distinction that one can determine whether in fact the legislation has the effect of taxing imported products in excess of like domestic products.

3.88   Canada noted the United States' contention that Canadian content or Canadian perspective are legally irrelevant, and that a panel must assess the distinction a measure actually draws, not a distinction it might have drawn but does not. In fact, the point is to assess what the legislation actually does - not simply what it says but what it does. It is obvious that the basis of the legislation - content reproduced from foreign sources - has concrete effects. These are effects that any reader can see - from the stories, the people, the subjects and - indeed - the perspective. They determine the character and the subject matter of the publication. The suggestion that these are not objective, visible product differences makes no sense. When the United States says that the nature of the content is irrelevant because that is not the distinction the legislation actually draws, they are asking the Panel simply to close its eyes to the actual operation and effect of the legislation in a real-world context. The implication is that one should look at the form, not the substance; that the assessment should be in the abstract and that the con-

---

[68]   Panel Report on *United States - Measures Affecting Alcoholic and Malt Beverages*, adopted on 19 June 1992, BISD 39S/274, para. 5.25.

crete effect should be ignored. None of this makes sense in the context of Article III:2, first sentence, which requires a finding of excess taxation in fact. One of the reasons why Canadian magazines do not sell well in the US market is precisely that they have a different content, content designed for Canadians. The American public is not attracted to this content. If American consumers can recognize the difference between an American and a Canadian magazine, surely Canadians can recognize it just as easily.

3.89   The *United States* asserted that the terms of the excise tax itself define the distinction Canada has drawn and this is what is at issue in this case. An analysis of the way the tax is structured shows the two to be like products. Canada's claim that the United States had failed to produce evidence of imported split-runs ignores the fact that Canada has banned imported split-runs. Canada could not, on the one hand, ban the relevant imported product, then argue on the other hand that there are no "real-life" examples of how that (banned) product is actually similar to domestic products, or actually competes. In fact, Canada's own example - *Time Canada* and *Maclean's* - does not involve an imported split-run magazine. Moreover, one simply could not say that the concrete effects of the terms of the excise tax are to separate out imported split-runs (of which there are none) that have no Canadian content from domestic non-split-runs that do.

3.90   In the *US - Section 337* panel report, the panel stated that it "had to assess whether or not Section 337 *may* lead to the application to imported products of treatment less favourable than that accorded to products of the United States [i.e. domestic] origin. It noted that this approach is in accordance with previous practice of the Contracting Parties in applying Article III, which has been to base their decisions on *the distinctions made by the laws, regulations or requirements themselves* and on their potential impact, rather than on the actual consequences for specific imported products" (emphasis added). In this case, the excise tax law *itself* did not distinguish between editorial content that is about Canada and editorial content that is not, but is instead based on the existence or non-existence of a similar product in a foreign country, and on advertising.

3.91   The United States questioned the necessity for specific product examples in light of this analysis of the *US - Section 337* panel report and Canada's longstanding import ban. The United States argued that while there were no specific examples of imported split-runs because none exist; should the Panel find specific examples relevant, a useful comparison to demonstrate the "likeness" of imported and Canadian-produced magazines exists between a US (*non*-split-run) magazine, *Pulp & Paper*, and *Pulp & Paper Canada*, a Canadian magazine unconnected to *Pulp & Paper* (US). The two publications have substantially similar editorial content and subject matter - pulp and paper technology, products, processes and marketing. Both contain a number of technical reports on various paper and pulp subjects that have little, if any, connection with particular paper and pulp operations in either Canada or the United States. Both contain information about paper and pulp operations and statistics in both Canada and the United States. Both contain a wide variety of advertisements from suppliers of products and services directly related to the pulp and paper products. Both contain classified advertising sections, and both contain an advertisers' index. Only a handful of pages out of the 78 pages in *Pulp & Paper Canada* were devoted to exclusively Canadian pulp and paper, and the vast majority of the publication consists of advertisements and feature articles that did not focus specifically on Canadian production or issues. Moreover, a Canadian paper industry publication reader study conducted by an independent advertising agency indicated that the two magazines have comparable readership and that readers use these magazines for the same purposes such as product information and mill news. Based on these and other similarities, the United States argued there can be no doubt that *Pulp & Paper Canada* is "like" *Pulp & Paper* (US). The United States further argued that these examples also show the importance of advertisements to the usefulness and appeal of magazines as products. The ads in the pulp and paper magazines are so obviously highly useful to those in the pulp and paper business. Both the Canadian and the US publications go so far as to contain an advertisement directory so that readers can more readily access pertinent advertisements.

3.92   In response to Canada's reliance on the editorial content of the *Time Canada* and *Maclean's,* the United States argued that this editorial content does not show that split-run and non-split-run magazines are not like products. First, one example out of over 1,000 magazines sold in Canada hardly proves the point. The fact is that, under the terms of the excise tax, a non-split-run magazine need not contain any "Canadian" editorial content, as long as the content is not sold outside Canada, or the advertisements in the Canadian and foreign editions are identical. Second, even as to these two magazines, Canada ignores the similarities between the two products, in terms of all factors other than Canadian focus. Indeed, the similarities are so great - including with respect to subject matter - that the two magazines were recognized to be direct competitors by industry witnesses in testimony before a Canadian Senate committee.[69]

3.93   The United States considered that Canada sought to minimize the significance of the fact that its WTO tariff commitments did not distinguish between split-runs and non-split runs. Canada's relevant tariff binding also includes newspapers, which are obviously not like products. However, the fact that Canada's tariff binding reflects the single Harmonized System (HS) heading for all magazines *does* provide support for a finding that split-runs and non-split-runs are the same like product. The Appellate Body in *Japan - Alcoholic Beverages* stated that, while broad GATT tariff bindings that cut across HS headings may not be useful to determine product likeness, GATT 1947 practice has looked to similar categorization in the *HS itself* in determining like product:

> "Uniform classification in tariff nomenclatures based on the Harmonized System (the 'HS') was recognized in GATT

---

[69]   See, e.g. Senate of Canada, Proceedings of the Standing Senate Committee on Banking, Trade and Commerce, Issue no. 49 (30 November 1995) at 57, 64 (testimony of officials of Canadian Magazine Publishers Association).

1947 practice as providing a useful basis for confirming 'likeness' in products. However, there is a major difference between tariff classification nomenclature and tariff bindings or concessions made by Members of the WTO under Article II of GATT 1994. There are risks in using tariff bindings that are too broad as a measure of product 'likeness'.... Many of [the] least-developed countries, as well as other developing countries, have bindings in their schedules which include broad ranges of products that cut across several different HS tariff headings . . .".[70]

3.94   Thus, the Appellate Body distinguished between the situation in which products fell within common HS categories, and the situation in which a Member made broad tariff bindings that cut across multiple HS categories. In this case, all periodicals, whether split-run or not, and whether or not they contain advertising, are included within the same HS category: HS 49.02. The fact that the distinction Canada is drawing in this case is not one reflected in the HS supports our claim that split-runs and non-split-runs are the same like product.

3.95   With regard to the Canadian argument that implementation of its import ban through a provision in its tariff code is proof that there *are* differences in tariff classification between split-runs and non-split-runs, the Appellate Body in *Japan - Alcoholic Beverages* referred to universally-accepted HS nomenclature, not to one Member's protectionist restrictions that happen to find themselves in that Member's "Customs Tariff". The reason why it was practice under GATT 1947 to look to HS nomenclature is because it generally reflects an objective assessment of the intrinsic similarity of products. As far as the United States knew, Canada is unique in drawing lines (in a "tariff-related" provision or elsewhere) based on an artificial distinction such as "split-run" versus "non-split-run". Thus, the Panel should reject Canada's effort to be rewarded for its import ban, and find that the common HS classification of split-runs and non-split-runs provides additional support for a finding that split-runs and non-split-runs are the same like product.

3.96   *Canada* considered that the US reference to the Canadian tariff classification in heading 49.02 had the effect of sweeping not only all periodicals, but newspapers as well into a single very comprehensive classification. The inappropriateness of this kind of result was pointed out by the Appellate Body in its recent decision on *Japan - Alcoholic Beverages*, when it said that "tariff bindings that include a wide range of products are not a reliable criterion for determining or confirming product "likeness" under Article III:2".[71] The use of tariff classifications in this case is especially inappropriate. The categories of products listed under tariff item 49.02 are as diverse as periodicals and newspapers. Where the

---

[70]   Appellate Body Report on *Japan - Taxes on Alcoholic Beverages*, op. cit., 114-115.
[71]   *Ibid.*, 115.

policy framework relates to periodicals and their intellectual *content*, the argument that the two media are "like" would be difficult to sustain. Tariff Code 9958 has effectively carved split-runs out of the general tariff classification; it has been in effect for over 30 years, through several GATT rounds, including the most recent Uruguay Round. The *de facto* exclusion of split-runs from the general tariff classification means at the very least that the US position can derive no support from tariff classification.

3.97 With respect to the support the United States seeks in the HS category, the fact is that this classification is far too broad to serve as a basis for identifying like products. Surely the fundamental point in the Appellate Body decision is that *any* very broad tariff classification is inappropriate, whether it is based on the HS or on tariff bindings. The short answer to the United States argument based on the common HS classification is that, at least in the case of this category, it is far too broad. It puts all magazines and all newspapers into a single global grouping. It also has the practical effect of making editorial content irrelevant. In the circumstances of this case, the use of tariff classifications is inconsistent with the requirement stipulated by the Appellate Body that "like products" under Article III:2, first sentence, should be narrowly construed.

Discrimination

3.98 *Canada* considered that the first sentence of Article III:2 speaks of products "imported *into the* territory" of a contracting party, and it deals with tax discrimination *against* imported products. There is no such discrimination on the facts of this case. To get around this difficulty, the United States has introduced the notion of "foreign-based" split-runs meaning periodicals produced in Canada but replicating foreign editorial content. This is a concept that simply has no legal meaning in the context of Article III:2. If the product is domestically produced, and is not physically moved across the border, it is not an imported product. And if there is no imported product, then there is nothing to which Article III can apply. But even if there were imported split-runs on the Canadian market, the absence of discrimination would be clear. Some imported magazines might attract the tax, but not to any greater extent than the domestically produced split-runs which were and remain the primary object of the legislation. For this reason, the measure is consistent with Article III:2 on its face and in its operation and practical effect. There is no reason why a measure that is non-discriminatory in both form and effect - *de jure* and *de facto* - should be considered inconsistent with Article III:2.

3.99 As the Appellate Body has observed in *US - Standards for Gasoline* in connection with Article III:4 that where there is "identity of treatment - constituting real, not merely formal, equality of treatment ... it is difficult to see how inconsistency would have arisen in the first place". The same conclusion is equally valid here. That the tax is free from any taint of overt discrimination is clear from the terms of the legislation, which make no distinction between domestic and imported products. Canada provided an example of the Canadian-owned magazine, *Harrowsmith Country Life*. Before the adoption of Part V.1, this magazine had two editions - a Canadian edition and a US edition. The Canadian and the US editions had different advertisements and a certain amount of common editorial content. Because more than 20 per cent of the editorial content in the Canadian edition was the same as that in the US edition, the tax would have applied to the Canadian edition (even if the editorial content was entirely produced in Canada). As a result of the excise tax, *Harrowsmith Country Life* stopped publishing its US edition. It could hardly be suggested that the tax is discriminatory in its practical operation, since it was designed to prevent the production in Canada of split-runs.

3.100 The Appellate Body on *Japan - Alcoholic Beverages*[72] held that where imported products are taxed in excess of "like domestic products", the general principle set out in Article III:1 may be assumed to have been violated. There is consequently no need to apply that principle as a "separate test" in order to find an inconsistency with Article III:2, first sentence. The Appellate Body has thus established a balance in the interpretation of Article III:2. The concept of "like products" is to be very narrowly construed, on a case-by-case basis in a way that requires "discretionary judgment"; but once the determination is made, excess taxation of imported products entails a violation without any need to conduct a further inquiry under paragraph 1. The essential elements of the interpretation of this provision have thus been authoritatively identified.

3.101 One question, however, was not addressed in the recent decision: whether taxation of imported products "in excess of" like products is to be determined in terms of classes of products, or whether any single instance of differential taxation creates an automatic *per se* violation even when it results from fiscal classifications that are not themselves discriminatory in form or in fact. The answer is clear both from the wording of Article III:2, first sentence, and from the object and purpose of Article III as a whole, which is the prevention of discrimination against imported products. The use of the plural in referring to "imported products" and "like domestic products" indicates clearly that the concern is with classes of products, not with the isolated instances of differential taxation that necessarily result when product "A" is taxed at a different rate than product "B" because it happens to fall into a different, but non-discriminatory, fiscal classification.

3.102 This interpretation also seems necessary to create a workable rule. Article III:2 is not intended to impose fiscal harmonization in rates, methods or classifications. It therefore remains not only possible but inevitable that domestic fiscal classifications may in certain instances have the effect of subdividing or straddling "like product" categories, or otherwise crossing "like product" category lines. Since fiscal classifications have no other purpose than to allow differences in tax treatment, any such classifications that failed to correspond precisely to

---

[72] Appellate Body Report on *Japan – Taxes on Alcoholic Beverages*, op. cit., 115.

"like product" categories under Article III:2, first sentence, would automatically lead to a violation. Quite apart from imposing a degree of harmonization that goes beyond the language or the purpose of this provision, such an interpretation would lead to an intolerable unpredictability so long as "like product" determinations are to be made on a case-by-case basis, as the recent decision has reaffirmed.

3.103 It could also lead, paradoxically, to results that would make nonsense of the Appellate Body's assumption that excess taxation under Article III:2 automatically entails a departure from the general principles in Article III:1; and that would in fact make nonsense of the underlying purpose of Article III. It could lead to situations where fiscal classifications decisively *favouring* imported products would be considered inconsistent with the first sentence of Article III:2, so long as the tax classification attracting the higher rate contained at least *some* imported products. It makes no sense to say that Article III is automatically violated in any case where tax differences result from domestic classifications that are "origin-neutral" in form and that might even favour imported products in effect - as might well be true of the tax at issue here. A particular instance of differential taxation in such circumstances should not create a *per se* violation, absent a discriminatory effect or cause to believe such an effect to be probable.

3.104 The *United States* considered that the Canadian argument that under Article III:2, first sentence, a "single" or "particular" instance of higher taxation of a certain subset of a broader category of imported like products "should not create a *per se* violation, absent a discriminatory effect or cause to believe such an effect to be probable", meritless for a number of reasons. First, the United States is not confronted with a mere "single" or "particular" instance of higher taxation of imported products than domestic like products in this case. Rather, a broad group of imported products - split-run magazines - is taxed at higher, not lower, rates than a broad group of like Canadian products - non-split run magazines. Canada has neither defined nor identified what it considers to be a "single instance" of discriminatory treatment in the context of this case.

3.105 In addition, Canada claims that the Appellate Body in the *Japan - Alcoholic Beverages* decision somehow left the door open to allow for discriminatory higher taxes applied to certain imported products within a category of like products. The Appellate Body left no such opening. It made it clear at page 19 that "[i]f the imported and domestic products are 'like products', and if the taxes applied to the imported products are 'in excess of' those applied to the like domestic products, then the measure is inconsistent with Article III:2, first sentence". No further test of "discriminatory effect" or discriminatory aim, is warranted. Canada's proposed "discriminatory effect" test based on "classes" of products if flatly inconsistent with the recent panel and Appellate Body decision in *Japan - Alcoholic Beverages* . In that case, once the panel found vodka and shochu to be like products, the taxation of imported vodka at a higher rate than domestic shochu (even though the tax was facially neutral) was found to be a violation of Article III:2, first sentence. This finding was affirmed by the Appellate Body.

3.106 The United States considered that Canada's argument that, in the absence of such a "discriminatory effect" test, a scheme that, overall, favoured imports over domestic products, might be found to violate Article III:2, first sentence, suggested that less favourable treatment of certain imported products could be counterbalanced by more favourable treatment of others. The *US - Section 337* panel decisively rejected any such "balancing" of less-favourable and more-favourable treatment, observing that "such an interpretation would lead to great uncertainty about the conditions of competition between imported and domestic products and thus defeat the purpose of Article III".[73] Similarly, in the panel report on *US - Malt Beverages* report, the panel observed that "Article III...requires treatment of imported products no less favourable than that accorded to the most-favoured domestic products".[74] Thus, the fact that imported and domestic split-run magazines receive the same tax treatment is irrelevant. Rather, the fact that imported split run magazines are taxed more heavily than like domestic non-split-run magazines establishes the requisite higher taxation under Article III:2, first sentence.

3.107 According to the United States, the fact that Article III:2 is phrased in terms of "products" does not mean that tax discrimination with respect to *one* product is outside the scope of Article III:2, or that such discrimination would be GATT-consistent as long as it is restricted to *one* product. In this case the drafters clearly intended non difference between the treatment of the plural and the treatment of the singular. This fact is confirmed by the drafting of the Note *Ad* Article III (which refers to the "like domestic product" and the "imported product") and Article III:3, a special case of application of Article III:2 which refers to the "taxed product". The 1970 Working Party report on Border Tax Adjustments, which is often referred to in this connection, uses the singular and plural forms in free variation. It is not necessary to demonstrate that all imported magazines are taxed more heavily than all domestic like magazines, or even that the average tax on all imported magazines is higher than the average tax on all like domestic magazines.

3.108 Finally, Canada's proposed "discriminatory effect" test appears to be based on predictions of the level of future trade flows. It is well-established that Article III is not designed to protect expectations of relative trade flows, but rather to ensure equal competitive conditions for imported products. Moreover, in this case, the type of effects analysis Canada suggests would be impossible. There is no basis for judging future levels of split-run magazine imports because Canada has completely eliminated them from its market for the last 30 years. Given its GATT-inconsistent ban, Canada should not be permitted to defend the excise tax on grounds that a small volume of imports would be subject to it.

---

[73] Panel Report on *United States - Section 337 of the Tariff Act of 1930*, op. cit., at para. 5.14.
[74] Panel Report on *United States - Measures Affecting Alcoholic and Malt Beverages*, op. cit., para. 5.17.

3.109 *Canada* responded that its interpretation of discrimination under Article III:2 would not require any overall balancing test as the United States stated. It would not require prediction of trade flows and is not an aim-and-effect test in another guise. It says only that if the fiscal categories of a contracting party are origin-neutral and exhibit no inherent bias against imported products, then the mere existence of such categories, with differential rates of taxation, does not violate Article III:2. A simplified example illustrates this point. Suppose raspberries are taxed higher than strawberries, and that all red berries are determined to be like products. Under the Canadian view, there is no violation if the two categories apply to both imported and domestic products and there is no inherent bias against imported products. The United States would say there is a violation because a box of imported raspberries is taxed higher than a box of domestic strawberries. This is accurate only if a single instance of differential taxation creates a violation. Canada submits that there is no violation because imported products as a class are not being subjected to excess taxation over domestic products. The US interpretation leads to results that are close to absurd and would not reflect the language of Article III:2, first sentence, in particular the use of the plural, nor its object and purpose which is non-discrimination or more specifically to protect expectations of the competitive relationship between imported and domestic products. Further, in the *Japan - Alcoholic Beverages* case, it is clear from paragraph 6.19 of the report that the panel based its findings on the assumption that shochu was largely a domestic product.

3.110 The *United States* responded that Canada's attempt to distinguish this case from the *Japan -Alcoholic Beverages* case based on the fact that most shochu was produced domestically in Japan, while in this case one could not show that split-run magazines have a comparable import focus, is inappropriate. Canada has *banned* the relevant imports. Of course there is no preponderance of imported split-run magazines over domestic split-runs. There is also no basis for judging future levels of split-run magazine imports because Canada has completely eliminated them from its market for the last 30 years. Given its GATT-inconsistent ban, Canada should not be permitted to defend the excise tax on grounds that a small amount of imports would be subject to it, or that a small percentage of split-run magazines would be imported. Moreover, the United States contested Canada's claims that the US argument would prevent differential taxation of strawberries and raspberries, if the two fruits were found to be like products. In fact, the distinction the excise tax draws is not analogous to distinguishing between raspberries and strawberries (which are different fruits), but is instead analogous to distinguishing between raspberries and *raspberries*. Specifically, it is analogous to distinguishing between raspberries produced in fields whose harvest is sold only in one country, and raspberries produced in fields whose harvest is sold in multiple countries.

(b)   Article III:2, Second Sentence

Directly Competitive or Substitutable

3.111 The *United States* argued that in the event the Panel does not find split-runs and non-split-runs to be "like products" for purposes of Article III:2, first sentence, it should find them to be "directly competitive or substitutable" products within the meaning of Article III:2, second sentence, of GATT 1994. The Appellate Body in *Japan - Alcoholic Beverages* provided that, in assessing an allegation of a violation of Article III:2, second sentence, one must examine whether:

> "(1)   the imported products and the domestic products are "directly competitive or substitutable products" which are in competition with each other;
>
> (2)   the directly competitive or substitutable imported and domestic products *are "not similarly taxed";* and
>
> (3)   the dissimilar taxation of the directly competitive or substitutable imported [and] domestic products *is "applied . . . so as to afford protection to domestic production".*[75]

Canada has not challenged the fact that split-runs and non-split runs are "not similarly taxed". The 80 per cent tax applies solely to split-runs. Split-runs and non-split runs are "directly competitive or substitutable", and the excise tax is "applied so as to afford protection to domestic production". Thus, the excise tax violates Article III:2, second sentence.

3.112 The Appellate Body in *Japan - Alcoholic Beverages* indicated that "directly competitive or substitutable" products was a "broader category" of products than "like products" in Article III:2.[76] The Appellate Body observed that it was appropriate to examine such factors as physical characteristics, common end-uses, tariff classifications, and the "market place", but that the "decisive criterion" in determining whether products were directly competitive or substitutable was "common end-uses".[77] Split-runs and non-split runs compete in the Canadian market and have common end-uses. Magazines covering the same general subject matter - e.g., current events magazines, hobby magazines, technical journals - compete with each other whether or not they are split-runs. Whether a magazine is split-run or not cannot be determined simply by examining the magazine, but is based, instead, on how similar the magazine is to a magazine sold outside Canada in another country. Split-runs, as defined by the excise tax, do not differ from other magazines in any way related to their ability to compete with other maga-

---

[75]   Appellate Body Report on *Japan - Taxes on Alcoholic Beverages, op. cit.,* 116 (emphasis in original).

[76]   *Ibid.,* 117.

[77]   *Ibid.* (emphasis added).

zines. Indeed, the excise tax is applied precisely, and solely, because split-runs compete with wholly domestically produced magazines for readers and advertising. As discussed above with respect to the issue of like product, the distinction between split-runs and other magazines is not based on content. Even if one could somehow credit Canada's assertion that the content of non-split-runs has more of a "Canadian perspective" than split-runs, this distinction could not possibly be considered a different "end-use".

3.113 *Canada* argued that split-run edition periodicals are not "directly competitive with or substitutable for" periodicals with editorial content developed for the Canadian market. Although they may be substitutable *advertising* vehicles, they are not competitive or substitutable information vehicles. Moreover, as mentioned above, the excise tax on advertising contained in split-run editions was not introduced so as to protect the Canadian production of periodicals and it does not have this effect. Rather, it was adopted to prevent an unfair practice in the advertising service sector. Under the second sentence of Article III:2 and the *Ad* Article III, Paragraph 2, the complaining party must demonstrate that a tax is being applied to imported products or domestic products that are "directly competitive or substitutable" and that the tax is being applied "in such a way as to protect domestic production". The complainant bears the burden of proof. The United States must therefore demonstrate that split-run edition periodicals and periodicals with editorial content developed for the Canadian market are competitive or substitutable products, and that the Parliament of Canada imposed the 80 per cent tax on split-run edition periodicals in order to protect Canadian production of periodicals which are not split-run editions.

3.114 The interpretation of this phrase shares many characteristics with the interpretation of "like products". A case-by-case approach is required here as well - in other words, an interpretation that takes account of all the relevant circumstances, and in particular the unique characteristics of cultural products. It's also a multi-factorial analysis, as it is for like products as well - no single test is decisive. To a significant extent, one takes account of all the factors that go into a like products determination, including properties and end-uses. Because of this common ground, many of the points Canada has made in the context of like products, and how the concept has to be adapted to reflect the special nature of cultural products, are also relevant here.

3.115 Canada noted the United States' unsubstantiated assertion that split-runs and other magazines clearly compete with each other. They do of course compete for the advertising dollar because a split-run recycling foreign content offers a far cheaper vehicle. But competition for advertising is not the issue and is not subject to GATT 1994 disciplines. The only legitimate focus is competition in the consumer marketplace. And the United States has not demonstrated, as it is required to do, that the products at issue are competitive or substitutable, or that they meet the threshold test implied by the word "directly". Substitution implies interchangeability. Once content is accepted as relevant it seems obvious that magazines created for different markets are not interchangeable. They are not substitutes, and certainly not direct substitutes. They serve different end-uses. Canadian periodical consumers have a demand for periodicals containing information that specifically addresses their interests. Canadian magazines contain information developed for and directed to the interests of Canadian consumers over a broad range of genres. Split-runs and magazines with editorial material developed for the Canadian market cannot be considered direct substitutes as information vehicles; and for the same reason they are not in *direct* competition. Ultimately, of course, there may be some degree of competition for disposable income between all cultural products and all luxury products - for everything beyond the necessities of life - but this is far too remote. It is not *direct* competition and it does not therefore fall within the rule. There would not be 1440 different magazine titles produced in Canada alone if the products were directly substitutable, or directly competitive, in the sense contemplated by the *Ad* Article to Article III:2.

3.116 Without embarking on an exercise in economic analysis, there are important respects in which price and demand comparisons are more complicated in the case of magazines and other cultural products than in the case of ordinary commodities. It is not the same as comparing consumer behaviour in response to price changes on a bottle of shochu and a bottle of vodka. There are too many qualitative differences in the case of magazines. To give one example, if the ratio of editorial content to advertisements decreases this can be the same as a price increase. That is a fairly objective, measurable variation, but other qualitative differences of equal importance can also have an effect tantamount to a price change - the quality of the content, the attractiveness of the graphics, the intrinsic interest of the articles.

3.117 The *United States* considered that the very existence of the tax was itself proof of competition of split-runs and non-split-runs in the market. Canada would not have gone to such extraordinary lengths to keep split-runs out of its market if they did not compete with other magazines in the Canadian market. As Canada itself has acknowledged, split-runs compete with wholly, domestically produced magazines for advertising revenue, which demonstrates that they compete for the same readers. The only reason firms place advertisements in magazines is to reach readers. A firm would consider split-runs to be an acceptable advertising alternative to non-split-runs only if that firm had some reason to believe that the split-run products themselves would be an acceptable alternative to non-split-runs in the eyes of readers. According to the United States, Canada acknowledges that "[r]eaders attract advertisers", and that: "The Canadian publishers are ready to compete with magazines published all over the world in order to keep their readers, but the competition is fierce".

3.118 The Report of the Task Force on the Canadian Magazine Industry provides further acknowledgment of the substitutability of magazines produced for the Canadian market and other magazines:

> "[Canadian publishers'] English-language consumer magazines face significant competition for sales from imported consumer magazines. In large measure, this is because the majority of the magazines are from the United States and

> *are a close substitute.* ...It is reasonable to expect that the content of American magazines will be of interest to Canadians...".

This report also observes that "there is considerable price competition" on newsstands between domestic and imported magazines",[78] and that:

> "the initial effect of the entry of Canadian regional editions of foreign magazines into the Canadian advertising market would be a loss of advertising pages in Canadian publications offering advertisers a readership with similar demographics".[79]

Minister of Canadian Heritage the Honourable Michel Dupuy described the situation as follows:

> "Canadians are much more interested in American daily life, be it political or sports life or any other kind, than vice versa. Therefore, the reality of the situation is that we must protect ourselves against split-runs coming from foreign countries and, in particular, from the United States".[80]

Canadian Government officials have repeatedly acknowledged outside this proceeding the close substitutability and competitiveness of split-run and non-split-run magazines. Canada affirmed this fact where it refers to domestic and imported magazines competing for readers. Furthermore, Canada admits that split-run and non-split-run magazines compete for advertising, this itself demonstrates that the two are directly competitive and substitutable, since carrying advertising is a principal use to which magazines are put.

3.119 *Canada* argued that the US reference to the Task Force in the preceding paragraph does not look into the supporting evidence. The evidence before the Task Force, on which its conclusions were at least partially based, was a study by the economist Leigh Anderson[81] which states:

> "US magazines can probably provide a reasonable substitute for Canadian magazines in their capacity as an advertising medium, although some advertisers may be better served by a Canadian vehicle. In many instances however, they would provide a very poor substitute as an entertainment and communication medium".

---

[78] *Task Force Report* at 40 and 42.

[79] *Task Force Report* at 53.

[80] Statement of Minister of Canadian Heritage Michel Dupuy before Canada's Standing Senate Committee on Banking, Trade and Commerce, 5 December 1995, Issue No. 50 at 14.

[81] Anderson, Leigh, An Analysis of Advertising Revenues to the Canadian Magazine Industry: the effect of foreign split-run magazines (19 January 1994). Prepared by Leigh Anderson for the Task Force on the Canadian Magazine Industry.

The report went on to characterize the relationship as one of "imperfect substitutability" - far from the direct substitutability required by this provision. The market share of imported and domestic magazines in Canada has remained remarkably constant over the 30-plus years between the O'Leary Report and the Task Force. If competitive forces had been in play to the degree necessary to meet the standard of "directly competitive" goods, one would have expected some variations. All this casts serious doubt on whether the competition or substitutability is sufficiently "direct" to meet the standard of Ad Article III.

So as to Afford Protection to Domestic Production

3.120 The *United States* argued that the excise tax is applied so as to afford protection to Canadian magazine publishers. In *Japan - Alcoholic Beverages*, the Appellate Body indicated that proof of protective *intent* is not required in order to establish a violation of the second sentence of Article III:2, and that the issue is "how the measure in question is *applied*":

> "Although it is true that the aim of a measure may not be easily discerned, nevertheless its protective application can most often be discerned from the design, the architecture, and the revealing structure of a measure. The very magnitude of the dissimilar taxation in a particular case may be evidence of such a protective application, as the panel rightly concluded in this case. Most often, there will be other factors to be considered as well ...".[82]

3.121 The Canadian excise tax clearly affords protection to domestic production of magazines directed at the Canadian market. It applies in a manner that effectively eliminates from the Canadian market split-run magazines, which compete directly with and are close substitutes for magazines produced solely for the Canadian market. The "very magnitude of the dissimilar taxation" - an 80 per cent tax on the former and no tax on the latter - is proof of the protective application of the Canadian excise tax, as it applies *only* to split-runs and is set at a prohibitive level. The structure and design of the excise tax are clear: the tax makes it uneconomical to sell any magazines that advertise to Canadians and that are produced for another market or for both Canada and another market. The measure thereby insulates the domestic Canadian magazine industry from competition from imported split-runs. The terms of the tax were crafted deliberately to target *Sports Illustrated* magazine, to direct advertising revenues solely to domestically-produced magazines, and to eliminate the competitive advantages conferred on split-runs by virtue of their economies of scale. *Sports Illustrated* Canada ceased publication in Canada with the issue dated 12 December 1995. Time Warner

---

[82]   Appellate Body Report on *Japan - Taxes on Alcoholic Beverages*, op. cit , at 120.

continues to sell subscriptions of the US national edition of *Sports Illustrated* in Canada and also sells the US edition of *Sports Illustrated* on the newsstands in Canada. These copies are printed in the United States and exported to Canada.

3.122 *Canada* argued that it is not applying the excise tax to imported periodicals so as to afford protection to the Canadian production of periodicals. Part V.I of the Excise Tax Act has no effect on the ability of foreign periodicals to enter Canada and to hold a very large share of the Canadian market. The Excise Tax Act applies to all split-run periodicals - wherever produced - in the same way. Contrary to the US contention, the purpose of Part V.I of the Excise Tax Act is not to protect the production of periodicals in Canada, but to prevent the diversion of advertising revenues to magazines based on content produced for foreign markets, and thus to ensure the production of editorial content for Canadians.

3.123 The purpose of Article III is to protect the competitive relationship between domestic and imported goods. As stated in the report on *United States - Taxes on Petroleum and Certain Imported Substances*:

> "... The general prohibition of quantitative restrictions under Article XI ... and the national treatment obligation of Article III ... have essentially the same rationale, namely to protect expectations of the contracting parties as to the competitive relationship between their products and those of the other contracting parties".[83]

Therefore, when Article III:1 specifies that a contracting party must not adopt measures "so as to afford protection to domestic production", the object is to prevent the adoption or maintenance of measures that protect domestic products to the disadvantage of products imported from the territory of another party.

3.124 Part V.I of the Excise Tax Act is not a protectionist measure adopted "so as to afford protection to domestic production" for the following reasons:

(a)   It does not affect the competitive relationship between imported and domestically-produced periodicals;

(b)   it is not based on the physical origin of periodicals, which is what is contemplated by the reference to "domestic production"; and

(c)   far from having a protectionist aim, it is a legitimate response to an anti-competitive abuse in the advertising field, with the ultimate object of ensuring the survival of a distinct Canadian culture.

3.125 Because GATT 1994, including Article III, applies to trade in goods, the expression "domestic production" must refer to the physical production of the good. This refers to its manufacturing, cultivation, extraction, etc. Article III of GATT 1994 cannot address the competitive relationship between service-providers such as the authors and artists contributing to the intellectual material

---

[83]   Panel Report on *United States - Taxes on Petroleum and Certain Imported Substances*, op. cit., at 160, para. 5.2.2.

contained in periodicals. Nor does it protect the competitive relationship between publishers in their capacity as sellers of advertising space. In terms of physical production, the sole perspective that is relevant to Article III, Part V.I of the Excise Tax Act is entirely neutral. It does not have the effect of protecting the production of periodicals in Canada; indeed its principal target was the production *in Canada* of split-run magazines as defined in the Act.

3.126 The measure has valid policy objectives that fit within what the *US - Malt Beverages* decision called a "public policy purpose" that is consistent with Article III. The immediate objective of Parliament was directed against the aggressive marketing of advertising services in Canada by publishers who were recycling in Canada editorial material whose production costs had already been covered in a larger market. The net result of this practice was to cut into the small share of the advertising market available to Canadian publishers, who were producing editorial content specific to Canadians. Part V.I of the Excise Tax Act was drafted in such a way as to curtail this advertising practice and not so as to prevent the entry into Canada of foreign periodicals or in such a way as to disadvantage foreign periodicals in the Canadian market.

3.127 Canada noted that it had never intended to decrease the level of competition between imported and domestic magazines. On the contrary, the members of the Task Force on the Canadian Magazine Industry wrote: "We are convinced that what is being proposed interferes as little as possible with freedom of expression or choice. Indeed, in the final analysis, we are seeking to expand choice by ensuring the continued availability of magazines with original content".[84] These measures did not prevent and were not intended to prevent foreign periodicals from competing in the Canadian market on an equal footing with Canadian periodicals.

3.128 Further, the United States has completely misrepresented the true trade position. There is an enormous penetration of American magazines in Canada, and nothing in the Canadian tax measure would change this or is designed to change this. Nor are there any significant trade effects to the measure. This tax concerns a very narrow segment of the total number of American periodicals streaming across the border daily. This very narrow segment was affected in the same way that a narrow segment of Canadian periodicals was affected. And this narrow segment of both the Canadian and the US industry was affected because the Parliament of Canada believed that a certain practice, a services practice, had to be discouraged.

3.129 Protectionism means protection against imported products. There is no protectionist application to be found in a measure that is not aimed at imported products as such, and that does not in fact have a disproportionate impact on imported products. The excise tax is not aimed at imported split-runs and - more important - it has (or would have) no greater effect on imported split-runs than it

---

[84] *Task Force Report* at 64.

does on domestically produced magazines of the same kind. There is no doubt that the tax insulates Canadian magazines from a certain form of competition in the advertising sector. It does not, however, insulate Canadian producers from competition resulting specifically from *imported* split-runs. The United States has fundamentally mischaracterized the situation when it says "the measure...insulates the domestic Canadian magazine industry from competition from imported split-runs". This is not the effect of the tax. It affects split-runs in general, not just imported products. It is wrong to think of split-runs as an inherently or a presumptively imported product. The actual effect of the tax in practice has so far been very clear. It caused *Sports Illustrated* to move its production for the Canadian market *out* of Canada and back to the United States. The effect was to substitute imported products for domestic products. This is exactly the opposite of what is understood by protectionism. Even apart from what happened in the case of *Sports Illustrated*, the local production of a split-run - a regional edition - makes eminent business sense.

3.130 The *United States* considered the protectionist nature of the tax is evident from its confiscatory character, the statements of the Canadian Government regarding the tax both before and after its enactment, and from the manner in which it applies. The effective date of the tax was deliberately set to eliminate the split-run edition of *Sports Illustrated* magazine. The tax applies only to those split-runs that began publication after 26 March 1993, a few weeks before *Sports Illustrated* launched its Canadian split-run edition, but more than *two years* prior to enactment of the tax. The excise tax applies in a manner that inherently favours Canadian-based producers, who are much more likely than foreign producers to publish magazines directed solely at Canadian readers. Foreign-based producers who wish to expand operations by entering the Canadian market must create a new magazine for distribution exclusively in Canada (or sell their foreign editions in identical form in Canada). The Canadian magazine tax is designed to ensure that foreign-based publishers forego the commercially attractive option of publishing a split-run edition of an existing magazine for the Canadian market. In introducing the excise tax bill to the House of Commons, Minister of Canadian Heritage Michel Dupuy asked, "Why is this tax necessary?", and answered: "Canadian publishers would be at a grave disadvantage if they were forced to compete for advertising revenues with magazines that have recovered their editorial costs in markets which are much larger than the Canadian market".

3.131 Mr. Dupuy's reference to "markets which are much larger than the Canadian market" was undoubtedly a reference to the United States, whose production of Canadian-edition split-runs was significant prior to the 1965 import ban, and whose potential for re-establishing split-run editions in the Canadian market was the basis for the imposition of the excise tax in 1995. The 1961 O'Leary Report, which preceded the import ban, noted that there were 76 US magazines offering split run or regional editions in Canada.[85] In 1994 the Government-appointed Task Force on the Canadian Magazine Industry concluded that it in the absence of additional legislation it was highly likely that a significant number of US split-runs would be sold in Canada. The Task Force estimated that there were 53 potential US consumer magazine entrants into the Canadian market, and 70 potential US business and trade magazine entrants, and that the majority of these would actually enter the Canadian market.[86] (By contrast, although the Task Force report describes in some detail the structure of the Canadian magazine industry, it makes no mention of the existence of split-run editions of *Canadian* publications.) The effect of the 80 percent excise tax is to keep the potential US entrants out of the Canadian market, whether they choose to transmit their magazines electronically for printing in Canada or - should Canada's GATT-illegal import prohibition be removed - to import them. By its terms, the tax applies to all split-runs, whether imported or domestically-produced. The tax makes it unprofitable for split-runs to be sold in Canada. Indeed, this is the whole - and the stated - purpose of the tax. As Minister Dupuy stated: "[The tax] could be designed and implemented in order to avoid split run editions".[87]

3.132 The Canadian argument that the tax is not applied so as to afford protection because it is reasonable to assume that, in the absence of the import ban, split-runs would be published in Canada as much as in the United States was dubious as a factual matter. More importantly, it is legally irrelevant because the tax protects domestic *non*-split-runs from competition from imported split-runs. The appropriate comparison is between the treatment of imported split-runs and domestic *non*-split-runs, not between domestic and imported split-runs. "Article III...requires treatment of imported products no less favourable than that accorded to the *most*-favoured domestic products"[88] not the *least*-favoured. Further, regardless of what Canada's legislators may have intended, the tax does apply, by its terms, to imported split-run magazines. If the import ban were lifted, it would have an immediate and exclusionary effect on imported split-runs.

3.133 In its argument that its excise tax on split-run magazines is meant to address an "anti-competitive abuse in the advertising field", Canada has completely failed to indicate in what way split-run magazines constitute such an abuse, why it has concluded that all, as opposed to some such magazines represent such an abuse, and why its has chosen to apply a tax measure to address such abuses. It is apparent that the "anti-competitive abuse" Canada is concerned about in connection with split-run magazines is competition itself. Canada's real quarrel with split-runs is that they are produced in a manner that takes advantage of economies of scale, in which costs are spread out over a greater number of units pro-

---

[85] Report, Royal Commission on Publications, May 1961 ("O'Leary Report") at 36.
[86] *Task Force Report* at 50-52.
[87] *Commons Debates* at 14790
[88] Panel Report on *United States - Measures Affecting Alcoholic and Malt Beverages, op. cit.* para. 5.17 (emphasis added).

duced. This means simply that split-run producers may have a lower cost structure than other producers, which may put them at a competitive advantage.

3.134 Competitive advantage is not competitive abuse, however. Canada has well-developed competition laws to address any such abuses. If Canada were truly interested in remedying competitive abuses, it would have employed those laws. Those laws do not permit application of remedies in a vacuum, however. They require a detailed analysis of the conduct of particular actors and their position in the market, and do not have as their goal the removal of entire product categories from the market. Indeed, it would be difficult to imagine a less pro-competitive remedy than one that effectively removes competing products from the marketplace.

3.135 Further, Canada's claim that marketing split-runs in Canada is akin to dumping is equally untenable. Dumping is generally understood to mean pricing products in a foreign market below the sales price in the home market, or selling products below cost. Canada has not alleged either such practice in this case. There are well-developed WTO procedures for conducting anti-dumping investigations and for determining dumping margins. These procedures do not allow for imposition of duties in arbitrary amounts (e.g., 80 per cent) across the entire range of imported products on the basis of legislative fiat.

3.136 *Canada* argued that protection is afforded to domestic production for the purpose of Article III:2, second sentence, if there is a "discriminatory or protective effect against imported products". "Imported products" means products physically transported into the territory of a Member. The United States concedes that the *Sports Illustrated* innovation that led to the legislation involved a domestic product, where the only thing "imported" was the electronically-transmitted foreign content. The United States has thus conceded, in the case of *Sports Illustrated Canada*, that there was no discrimination or protective effect against imported products. It follows that "foreign based" split-runs are not imported products if they are printed and published in Canada.

3.137 The Excise Tax Act thus applies to domestic and imported products without distinction, and it is primarily aimed at a form of domestic product. While the tax secures advertising revenues for Canadian publishers, protection in the sense of Article III:1 as read into III:2 means protection against *imported products*. As the preceding paragraph has shown, split-runs are not intrinsically imported products. Even if there were no import prohibition, given the economies of local production and distribution and the ease of electronic transmission, it is likely that most split-runs would be locally produced. It is highly significant, moreover, that, as the United States noted in response to a question at the hearing, the effect of the tax was to induce *Sports Illustrated* to cease its Canadian production and to resume direct imports from the United States. The substitution of imports for domestic products, as the result of a public policy measure, is the direct opposite of what almost everyone understands by protectionism. It suffices by itself to refute the contention that the Excise Tax Act operates to "afford protection to domestic production".

3.138 The excise tax measure is designed to prevent the diversion of advertising to low-cost publications reproducing recycled editorial content, at the expense of publications created for Canadians. It does not guarantee the survival of Canadian magazines that the public does not want. What it targets, very simply put, is the combination of recycled editorial content plus Canadian advertisements. This combination, because the crucial input of content comes with minimal cost, is destructive of fair competition in the market place and consumer choice. It eliminates any possibility of a "level playing field". It would lead ultimately to a reduction of material dealing with the Canadian scene and in turn to a Canadian public that is less well-informed on Canadian affairs. These are not only legitimate legislative concerns; they are far removed from the idea of protecting domestic production which is referred to in Article III. Ultimately, of course, the concern behind this legislation is with the preservation of Canadian culture in the face of an extraordinary challenge from across the border. It is not Canadian public policy to restrict the importation or circulation of imported magazines. It does, however, reinforce the validity of the distinction Canada makes between original content and domestic production as one that is based upon a public policy purpose that has nothing to do with trade protectionism. Split-run editions of magazines compete unfairly for advertising revenues with regular magazines, since their editorial costs are largely paid for in their original market.

3.139 As to the United States' inquiry why Canada failed to apply the WTO dumping procedures, those procedures, and the Canadian domestic legislation that implements them, have never been applied, and would probably not even be applicable, to advertising as a service sector not covered by GATT. The United States also asks, in effect, why Canada has not used the Canadian Competition Act. There is no reason why specially-tailored measures cannot be adopted for specific sectors of the economy that have their own unique characteristics. Competition issues in Canada have never been reserved exclusively to the Competition Act. They are addressed, in the context of specific sectors, through a variety of regulatory statutes. Split-runs and the magazine advertising market are unique. There is no reason why their problems should not be addressed through special legislation. And there is no reason why that legislation should not take the form of a tax. Fiscal incentives and disincentives that have little or nothing to do with raising revenue - ranging from child tax credits to super-depletion allowances - are familiar techniques in Canadian legislative practice.

3.140 The *United States* asserted that, in addition to characterizations by Canadian officials, Canada's submissions to the Panel themselves confirm that the excise tax was structured to protect domestic production. A statement in Canada's submission is instructive:

> "The object of the excise tax is not to discourage readership of foreign magazines, but to *maintain an environment in which Canadian magazines can exist in Canada alongside with imported magazines. It is also intended to foster conditions in which indigenous magazines can be published,*

distributed and sold in Canada on a commercial basis..."
(emphasis added).

Although couched in the best possible light, this statement does not disguise the fact that the purpose of the excise tax is to protect Canadian magazines from import competition. It appeared to be Canada's position that because it does not *completely* restrict imports of magazines, it should be free to impose *certain* import barriers to benefit its domestic industry. There is absolutely no basis in GATT for this position. Canada's contractual obligations under GATT Article III are not limited to affording a certain amount of national treatment to imports; Canada must provide full national treatment. The GATT restricts the types of measures a Member may impose simply to counteract another Members' comparative trade advantages (i.e. to protect domestic producers from legitimate import competition). Tariffs (within bound rates) and certain types of domestic subsidies are among the permitted measures. Internal taxes imposed at rates higher for imported products than domestic like products are not. Moreover, Canada's submissions consistently imply an import penetration much higher than it actually is. Canada's Task Force Report states that , in reality, "Canadian publications account for 67.6 per cent of the magazines sold in Canada in a year".

3.141 Canada asserts repeatedly that the excise tax is designed to encourage "original content", as though such a purpose would justify imposition of a discriminatory excise tax. In fact, the whole notion of "original content" is protectionist in nature. Permitting a Member to require that a product be sold in its territory be a *different* product than that sold abroad would open up the WTO system to serious abuses. For example, a Member concerned about the ability of a local industry to compete with foreign manufacturers of the same product (automobiles, footwear, jewellery, etc.) could impose a prohibitive tax - on the pretext of ensuring that local consumers can purchase products designed exclusively for them - on "non-original" product designs, in order to keep foreign producers from exporting their best-selling products to the Member's market. In order to sell into such a market, the foreign manufacturer would be required to design products and set up new production lines exclusively for that market. That would erase any scale efficiencies the foreign manufacturer might otherwise have gained from sales in its domestic market and to other countries.

3.142 *Canada* considered that the US reliance on the concept of economies of scale is misplaced. The concept is normally associated with large production runs, typically for an international market. A local production run for a single regional market is by definition a relatively low volume production run that does not fit the definition. What the legislation is against is not economies of scale but the clearly unfair competitive advantage that comes from prepaid costs, providing what amounts to a free ride in the Canadian advertising market. The US industry gets tremendous economies of scale through its ordinary operations of publishing large runs in the United States for the international export market. The US publisher is free to produce and then to promote and sell as many copies of the magazine in Canada as possible. None of this is touched by the legislation. The tax does not insulate the domestic Canadian magazine industry from competition for readers. *Harper's*, *Sports Illustrated*, and *Vanity Fair* can all benefit fully from economies of scale of which a Canadian publisher, and in fact most publishers outside the United States, could never dream.

3.143 The United States submits further that the "whole notion of original content" is protectionist in nature, and that the policy has the same protectionist characteristics as if local product designs were to be required. The argument is revealing, because it amounts to a blanket denial that cultural products have any specificity that distinguishes them from ordinary items of trade. Content distinguishes one magazine from another. Original content created for a specific national community differentiates magazines in a way that product design seldom if ever does. The United States has raised a spectre that is not only far-fetched; it is based on a false analogy, and a failure to recognize the distinctive characteristics of cultural products, and of magazines above all. "Original content" does not have to be domestically-produced. Canadian content, in terms of subject matter, does not have to be content produced by Canadians or in Canada. Most often it will, but the assertion that "original content" is inherently protectionist is incorrect.

(c)   Article III:4

3.144 The *United States* argued that if the Panel decides that the excise tax does not fall within the scope of Article III:2, the tax should then be viewed as a measure affecting the sale or use of split-run magazines within the meaning of GATT Article III:4. The excise tax provides less favourable treatment to imported split-runs than to like domestic non-split-runs and therefore violates Article III:4. The excise tax clearly affects the *sale* of split-run magazines. In fact, it is set at a level so high as to prevent any sales of split-runs in the Canadian market. Indeed, Canadian officials have repeatedly stated that to be the purpose of the tax. An 80 per cent excise tax is obviously not intended to generate tax revenue. The excise tax also affects the *use* of split-run magazines, by applying a prohibitive tax whenever they are used to convey advertising to the Canadian public. Moreover split-run magazines and non-split-run magazines are "like products" for purposes of Article III:2 and should thus be considered "like products" for purposes of Article III:4 as well. The panel in *US - Standards for Gasoline* considered that similar factors were relevant to like product analyses under paragraphs III:2 and III:4.[89]

3.145 Finally, the excise tax accords less favourable treatment to imported split-run magazines than to other domestically-produced magazines. As discussed above, by its terms the tax applies to imported split-runs. The excise tax treats imported split-runs less favourably than other purely domestic magazines because it effectively prevents split-runs from being sold profitably in the Canadian

---

[89]   Panel Report on *United States - Standards for Reformulated and Conventional Gasoline*, op.cit., para. 6.8.

magazine market, and makes it effectively impossible for split-runs to be used to carry domestic advertising. Thus, if the excise tax is not covered by Article III:2, it falls within the scope of, and is inconsistent with, Article III:4.

C. Funded and Commercial Postal Rates

(i) Article III:4

> *"Regulations and Requirements Affecting the Internal Sale, Offering for Sale, Purchase, Transportation, Distribution or Use"*

3.146 The *United States* argued that Canada's postal rates for magazines are openly discriminatory and in contravention of III:4 of GATT 1994. Canada Post is a Canadian Government entity that charges domestic magazines lower rates (either "commercial" or "funded" depending on the magazine) than it charges imported magazines that are mailed in Canada. Canada Post also offers certain discounts (such as for "palletization" and "pre-sort") only to domestic magazines. These measures amount to "regulations" or "requirements" that affect the internal sale, transportation, or distribution of magazines in Canada, and provide less favourable treatment to imported magazines than to like domestic magazines, in violation of GATT Article III:4.

3.147 In the report on *EEC - Parts and Components*, the panel recognized that requirements that an enterprise voluntarily accepts to gain government-provided advantages are nonetheless "requirements":

> "The Panel noted that Article III:4 refers to "all laws, regulations or requirements affecting (the) internal sale, offering for sale, purchase, transportation, distribution or use". The Panel considered that the comprehensive coverage of "*all* laws, regulations or requirements *affecting*" the internal sale, etc. of imported products suggests that not only requirements which an enterprise is legally bound to carry out, . . . but also those which an enterprise voluntarily accepts in order to obtain an advantage from the government constitute "requirements" within the meaning of that provision. . . ."[90]

Magazine publishers that sought to make use of the Canadian mails have to agree to pay the postal fees charged by Canada Post. Those charges are requirements - or regulations - wi0thin the meaning of Article III:4.

---

[90] Panel Report on *European Economic Community - Regulations on Parts and Components, op.cit.,* at 132, 197, para. 5.21, Italics in original. *See also, "Canada - Administration of the Foreign Investment Review Act",* adopted on 7 February 1984, BISD 30S/140, 158 para. 5.4.

3.148 Canada Post's postal rates also clearly "affect" the sale, transportation and distribution of imported magazines, because they specify the cost of using the services of Canada Post to transport or distribute magazines to subscribers in Canada. A publisher seeking to have Canada Post transport and distribute its magazines to subscribers in Canada - and virtually all subscription magazines sold in Canada were distributed in this manner - would have to pay the postal fees prescribed by Canada Post. The postal fees directly affected the competitive conditions under which the product is transported, distributed, and sold to subscribers. These rates therefore "affect" the sale, transportation, and distribution of magazines in Canada.[91]

3.149 Canada's discriminatory postal rates have a particular impact on the transportation of magazines in Canada. The drafters of GATT clearly intended to include the rates charged for government-provided transportation services under the disciplines of Article III. Canada Post's divergent postal rates are not based on neutral economic considerations, but explicitly discriminatory criteria - namely, whether the magazine is Canadian or foreign in origin.[92]

3.150 *Canada* underscored the importance of the distinction between the subsidized rates, those rates available as a result of a subsidy granted exclusively to domestic publishers by Canadian Heritage, and commercial publications rates, those rates available to all publishers (Canadian or otherwise) that do not qualify for the subsidy granted by Canadian Heritage. Whereas the subsidized rates are the result of an expressed intention on the part of the Government to assist domestic publishers (as specifically permitted by GATT Article III:8(b)), the commercial publications rates are the result of generally accepted commercial and marketing practices and are not influenced by government policy. Unfortunately, the United States has failed to make this important distinction.

3.151 Canada Post is a corporation in its own right, with a legal personality distinct from that of the Government, and considerable autonomy in the conduct of its operation; far more than would ever be accorded to a government department. Canada Post is a Crown corporation and its objectives are set out in the CPC Act. In addition, under the FA Act, as a Schedule III, Part II Crown Corporation, Canada Post is expected to: operate in a competitive environment; earn a return on equity; not depend on government appropriation; and finally, provide a reasonable expectation that it would pay dividends. Both the CPC Act and the FA Act essentially establish a commercial mandate for Canada Post comparable to a private sector interest.

---

[91] Panel Report on *Italian Discrimination Against Agricultural Machinery*, adopted on 23 October 1958, BISD 7S/64 para. 12.

[92] The United States recommended the Panel to see also, *U.S. - Malt Beverages* (panel found that restrictions on private delivery of imported, but not domestic beer, was inconsistent with Article III:4).

3.152 This legislative framework provides Canada Post with the legal and operational flexibility to implement its commercially-oriented mandate. With respect to publications, i.e., newspapers and periodicals, Canada Post is not a government monopoly and does not have the exclusive right of delivery. Canada Post does not have the power of a monopoly when it sets commercial rates for the delivery of publications.[93] It competes in an open competitive market for its share of the publications delivery market. Any publisher, foreign or domestic, is free to arrange for the delivery of his newspaper or periodical via Canada Post or with any other distributor. Section 14(2) of the CPC Act states that "[n]othing in this Act shall be construed as requiring any person to transmit by post any newspaper, magazine, book, catalogue or goods". Pursuant to Section 2 of the Act, "post" means to leave in a post office or with a person authorized by the Corporation to receive mailable matter. Foreign publishers have the additional option of mailing their copies addressed to Canadian addresses with their own postal administration at the applicable international printed matter rates.

3.153 The principle of national treatment of Article III:4 of GATT 1994 does not apply to the commercial postal rates charged by Canada Post. The United States contends that commercial rates set by Canada Post are "regulations" or "requirements" affecting the internal sale of imported publications. The term "regulation" in the context of GATT 1994 means the rules or orders having the force of law that are issued by executive or administrative authorities of government. The rates for the delivery of letters in Canada are set by regulations.[94] However, the commercial rates for publications are set by market forces and fluctuate with commercial imperatives - not to mention that in many cases they are the result of negotiations with both domestic and international large volume customers pursuant to specific agreements. The responsibility for setting those rates rests exclusively with senior management of the Corporation who exercise their discretion based on commercial principles without government intervention.

3.154 The term "requirement" in the context of GATT also implies a demand or direction proclaimed by an authority within government. Again, commercial imperatives and market forces dictate the commercial rates for publications charged by the Corporation to its customers. The government has never issued a directive to the Corporation regarding publications mail. The Corporation's prices are set to meet market demands and opportunities (as in the case of any private sector company), and are clearly not the product of "laws, regulations or requirements" of Canada. It is incorrect to suggest, as does the United States, that the differen-

---

[93] Canada added that Canada Post does have a limited exclusive privilege with respect to the collection, transmission and delivery of "letters" in Canada, including addressed advertising mail. This exclusive privilege represents in aggregate approximately 50 per cent of total corporate revenues. Canada Post has no statutory protection for the remainder of its business and must compete with existing or potential competitors, as the case may be. The Corporation's exclusive privilege is defined in Section 14 and 15 of the *Canada Post Corporation Act*.

[94] *Letter Mail Regulations*, SOR/88-430 as amended to April 30, 1996.

tial between the commercial rate provided to Canadian publishers and the commercial rate provided to non-Canadian publishers is calculated to place non-Canadian publishers at a competitive disadvantage. Canada Post has no policy of giving a competitive advantage to one segment of its customers over another, and has no interest in pursuing any such practice. For their part, customers have access to competing delivery channels and, as in all open markets, have the ability to negotiate rates in a manner reflecting their purchasing power.

3.155 The international commercial rates reflect the reality that suppliers in any competitive market would attempt to obtain the best possible price. Pricing is set to maximize contribution while remaining competitive. Factors such as the availability and cost to customers of competing distribution channels, currency exchange rates, service standards, etc., are all taken into consideration by Canada Post (as would any company in a competitive market) when setting its pricing. As a Crown corporation with a commercial mandate, Canada Post operates on the same basis as a private sector interest. The commercial postage rate applicable to non-Canadian publications is set on the basis of the commercial business reality that the next-best option faced by mailers of publications that are printed outside Canada is the much higher international rate charged by the postal administration in the country of publication. In the case of publications from the United States, this means a rate for deposit in Canada with Canada Post that is about half of what they would have to pay the United States Postal Service (USPS) for delivery of the same items to Canada. The commercial mandate given to Canada Post requires it to obtain the best possible rate in order to maximize its returns.

3.156 Almost half the direct-deposit foreign periodicals business Canada Post receives is contracted through specific agreements, negotiated on a case-by-case basis subject to customer- and market-specific needs and opportunities as opposed to generic pricing policies. Canada Post's commercial pricing policies are determined by the demands of the markets in which it operates and not by governmental directives or public policy considerations. In the case of commercial publications, there is no direction, instruction or any other obligation to provide this service or to provide this service at certain rates. This means that the management of Canada Post is free to establish commercial services and rates for publications purely on commercial principles and market realities so as to maximize the financial advantage to Canada Post providing such commercial publication services. The decision to maintain a separate, higher rate for international as opposed to Canadian commercial publications is made purely by Canada Post management for commercial reasons and in no way reflects any explicit or implicit request by government that Canada Post use its rate structure to disadvantage foreign commercial publications relative to Canadian commercial publications. The Canadian Government could express its views on commercial and international rates much in the same way it might choose to comment on pricing of a private sector firm. However, to compel change, the Government would have to instruct Canada Post under the directive power in Section 22 of the CPC Act. Indeed, Canada Post has received no instruction or advice - implicit or explicit - to set international commercial rates in excess of domestic commercial rates for periodicals. This action is of Canada Post's own creation based on its perception of market opportunity.

3.157 The *United States* argued that the Government of Canada is responsible for Canada Post's activities, including its so-called commercial postal rates. Canada's argument implicitly concedes that Canada Post is a governmental entity, and exercises a governmental function, when it applies "funded" (subsidized) postal rates to, and provides for the delivery of, certain domestically produced magazines. Canada seeks to convince the Panel that Canada Post sheds its governmental character when it applies its so-called "commercial" rates and provides for the delivery of magazines subject to those rates.

3.158 Canada Post is a wholly, government-owned, government-created chartered body, subject to the control of a board of directors appointed by the Minister responsible for Canada Post. (The existence of a Government Minister responsible for Canada Post is further proof that Canada Post is an arm of the Canadian Federal Government.) The Chairman of the Board and the President of Canada Post are both appointed by the Governor-in-Council. Section 5(2)(e) of the CPC Act provides explicitly that Canada Post is "an institution of the Government of Canada". The Canadian Parliament created Canada Post and fixed its operating mandate. Moreover, Canada Post's mandate to operate, in part, on a "commercial" basis is itself set by the Government. An important oversight role is played by the Minister responsible for Canada Post. In "The Mandate of Canada Post Corporation and its Development", Canada acknowledged that: "Section 22 of the CPC Act provides that Canada Post is required to comply with directions issued by the Minister responsible for the corporation. This gives the Minister powers analogous to those exercisable by shareholders of other privately held corporations through unanimous shareholders agreements".[95] Thus, Canada Post is entirely a creature of the Canadian Government, subject to its direct supervision and control.

3.159 Recent events confirm that the Canadian Government considers Canada Post to be a government entity fully subject to Canadian Government direction, and a vehicle for the expression of Government policy - including through Canada Post's "commercial" operations. On 8 October 1996, Diane Marleau, the Minister responsible for Canada Post Corporation, presented the Canadian Government's reaction to a report issued by an independent task force chaired by Mr. George Radwanski (the "Radwanski Report"). The report addressed financial and policy issues related to the future of Canada Post.

3.160 The Radwanski Report was highly critical of Canada Post and, *inter alia,* charged Canada Post with engaging in unfair competition with its private sector competitors in the delivery of commercial services, such as courier and advertis-

---

[95] "The Mandate of Canada Post Corporation and its Development".

ing mail services.[96] In her press conference responding to the report, Ms. Marleau stated:

> "I want to emphasize that *the government regards Canada Post as a significant federal institution, and that it sees Canada Post continuing to carry out a public policy role* based on the provision of mail to all Canadians, no matter where they live...The federal government is expected to embody certain values and principles in how it carries out its affairs, in particular: fairness, transparency, openness and accountability. *Canada Post is part of the federal government and must live up to these standards. As Minister Responsible for Canada Post,* I expect immediate corrective action wherever these values and principles have been compromised. To this end, I have asked Mr. Ouellet, as Chair of Canada Post Corporation, to develop an action plan for improving the transparency of Canada Post's activities, and addressing these issues...The government will consider the rest of the recommendations of the report of the Mandate Review, recognizing that there are certain basic principles which must guide our deliberations:...
>
> *   *Canada Post is a valuable federal institution.* Canadians have invested in it, and the government must protect this value.
>
> *   Canada Post will remain a Crown corporation and not be privatized, *as long as it continues to fulfil a public policy role.*"...[97]

3.161 With respect to Canada Post's commercial courier service activities, Minister Marleau stated that:

> "[A]s long as Canada Post remains in this line of business, it must compete on a level playing field. As I noted earlier, Canada Post's operations must be conducted under the tenets of fairness, transparency, openness, and accountability".[98]

These excerpts confirm that the Canadian Government considers Canada Post to be a Canadian federal government institution and that the Government is fully responsible for Canada Post's activities - even those carried out in commercial sectors.

---

[96]   The report did not specifically discuss Canada Post's publications mail activities.

[97]   *Speaking Notes for the Honourable Diane Marleau, Minister Responsible for Canada Post Corporation, Release of the Canada Post Mandate Review Report,* 8 October 1996, at 1-3 (emphasis added).

[98]   *Ibid.,* at 3.

3.162 Canada Post's so-called "commercial" (non-subsidized) postage rates reflect an overlay of Canadian government policy having nothing to do with marketplace considerations. Notwithstanding Canada's statement that commercial publications rates "are available to all publishers (Canadian or otherwise) that do not qualify for the subsidy granted by Canadian Heritage", in fact only certain types of publications qualify for commercial mail rates. Among the eligibility criteria are: the content of the publication (e.g., devoted to religion, the sciences, social or literary criticism), the amount of space it devoted to advertising, and whether the publisher is a person whose principal business is publishing. These criteria are all irrelevant as commercial considerations, but are indicative of types of publications which a government might wish to support as a matter of public policy. This suggests that Canada Post continues to operate as an instrument of the Canadian Government in its commercial mail operations and does not operate according to purely commercial considerations.

3.163 Finally, the United States considered that Canada's claim that the disparity in "commercial" rates between imports and domestic magazines reflects the lack of commercially feasible alternative delivery options for imports as compared to domestic magazines is dubious as a factual matter. Also, Canada's explanation that the disparity in rates does not reflect Government policy is suspect in light of the existence of a whole set of Canadian Government policy measures whose explicit goal is to benefit domestic magazines. Even if true, Canada's explanation would not remove this measure from the scope of Article III.4. Article III.4 is precise - a Member must accord "treatment no less favourable" to imports as compared to domestic products - regardless of whether imports have fewer commercial alternatives as compared with domestic magazines. It is in the nature of imported products that they often are in an inferior economic and political bargaining position. Article III was included in the GATT because imports are vulnerable to discrimination.

3.164 *Canada* argued that government ownership is not in itself sufficient to qualify the practices of an enterprise as regulations for the purposes of Article III:4 of GATT 1994. The independent nature of Canada Post's commercial operations for the distribution of publications and the competitive environment within which it operates and sets its rates removes such rates from the provisions of Article III:4. Although at one time the Post Office was an integral part of the Government of Canada and its rates were set by statute and regulation, that relationship was changed in a fundamental way in 1981. Concerned with issues relating to service, management, labour relations and the financial performance of the Post Office Department, the Government decided to turn over the postal administration to a Crown corporation with a commercial orientation and an independent management charged with attaining financial self-sufficiency. The CPC Act gave the Corporation the powers of a natural person, an attribute more typical of a private sector corporation than of traditional Crown corporations. The FA Act later confirmed the Corporation's status as an entity expected to operate in a competitive environment, not to be dependent on appropriations, earn a return on equity and pay dividends to its shareholder.

3.165 At the time of the creation of Canada Post, there were those who suggested that it should remain under the direct control of the Government. It was proposed that its activities be overseen by the Postmaster General assisted by a Secretariat. However, what had happened was that supervision of the Corporation had been entrusted to a board of directors composed of independent outside directors and officers of the Corporation (none of whom are civil servants). The Board, like traditional private sector boards of directors, is empowered to establish the general policy of the Corporation, including the making of decisions concerning finance, personnel management and commercial orientation, without the restrictions inherent in government departments. The Board has, since incorporation, pursued the goal of financial self-sufficiency by allowing management the latitude, in commercial operations, to generate revenues through rate and product management and to manage the Corporation's expenditures in a manner consistent with any competitive enterprise, essentially free of government intervention.

3.166 Crown corporations are distinct legal entities wholly owned by the Crown with boards of directors that oversee the management of the corporation and hold management accountable for the company's performance. The board of directors, through the chair, is accountable to the responsible minister and the responsible minister functions as the link between the corporation and both the Cabinet and Parliament. It is the duty of the board of directors to oversee the management of their Crown corporation with a view to the best interests of both the corporation and the long-term interests of the shareholder. This concept is similar to that of private sector corporations. Boards of directors of Crown corporations are expected to exercise judgement in the broad areas of: the establishment of a corporation's strategic direction; the safeguarding of the corporation's resources; the monitoring of corporate performance; and reporting to the Crown. Each Crown corporation is accountable to Parliament for the conduct of its affairs through a minister who represents the Crown. It is through the minister that the Crown corporation reports on its plans and its performance to the Government and to Parliament.

3.167 Canadian and international commercial categories of rates had been set by Canada Post outside of the regulations since March 1994 and March 1992, respectively. Non-subsidized publications formerly subjected to the rates set out in the *Newspapers and Periodicals Regulations* are now subject to commercial Canadian Publications Mail and International Publications Mail rates, respectively, which are established and approved by Canada Post senior management. They are not established by Canadian Government regulations.

3.168 Canada Post is a corporation with a distinct legal personality. It can contract separately from the Government. It contracts with the Government for the supply of postal and other services. The Corporation is obligated to pay corporate income tax to the Government on its revenues.[99] Contrary to US assertions, em-

---

[99] *Income Tax Regulations, amendment*, SOR/94-405.

ployees of the Corporation are not employees of the Government. Indeed, Section 12 of the CPC Act authorizes Canada Post to hire employees, fix the terms and conditions of their employment and pay them their remuneration. The statutory regime10[100] applicable to employees of the Government does not apply to employees of Canada Post, whose employment conditions and labour relations are governed by the same provisions of the Canada Labour Code that apply to the federal private sector.[101] Furthermore, if Canada Post employees had government employee status, there would have been no need to include a special "deeming" provision in the Act in order to preserve employees' pension rights at the time of the creation of Canada Post. The above attributes are certainly not those of a corporation over which the Canadian Government maintains a "hands-on level of administrative control" as the United States would like the Panel to believe.

3.169 The degree of control that the Government exercises over Canada Post's commercial operations is one dictated by the Government shareholder's interests. The Government requires sound financial administration of the Corporation's business and a fair return on its equity investments. To achieve this goal, the Corporation must offer satisfactory services to customers at a competitive price that will maximize profits. In a competitive environment, pricing policies of Canada Post must take into account basic economic principles of supply and demand. It must consequently consider the effects that its commercial postal rates will have on current or potential competition.

3.170 Canada Post does not have a monopoly with respect to the delivery of publications (newspapers and periodicals) in Canada. Canada Post, through the CPC Act, does have a limited exclusive privilege with respect to the collection, transmission and delivery of "letters" in Canada including addressed advertising mail, but the Corporation has no statutory protection for the remainder of its business and has to compete with existing or potential competition, as the case may be.

3.171 Almost 50 per cent of foreign publications mailed in Canada are accorded special rates negotiated by major foreign publishers pursuant to long-term agreements with Canada Post. Those rates are substantially less than the commercial International Publications Mail rate and relatively close to the commercial Canadian Publications Mail rate[102] The willingness of the Corporation to enter into such special-rate agreements reflects the reality that large foreign pub-

---

[100] Canada states that employees of the Government are appointed by the Public Service Commission under the unique provisions of the *Public Service Employment Act*. Employment conditions and labour relations are governed by the *Public Service Staff Relations Act and the Public Service Employment Act*.

[101] Canada notes that the federal private sector includes such industries as banks, interprovincial trucking, radio, television, railways, ports and the aeronautics industry.

[102] Canada asserts that contrary to what the United States contends, several large foreign publishers enjoy discounts, pursuant to long-term agreements, similar to the mail preparation discounts offered to Canadian publishers.

lishers have the resources and purchasing power to credibly threaten full or partial delivery in Canada via current and potential private distributors. Smaller foreign publishers have neither the volume nor the density of mailings to warrant their effort to access private distribution (often organised on a city by city basis) in Canada. Canadian commercial publishers have credibly threatened to move to private distribution in the past[103] This motivated the Corporation to develop commercial Publications Mail rates that are financially attractive when compared to that of current or potential private distributors.

3.172 Canada Post currently faces competition for delivery of addressed publications.[104] The principal form of competition for the delivery of addressed subscriber copies of daily and weekly newspapers (those not eligible for subsidized postal rates) is delivery by the publishers themselves. In general, almost all such newspapers choose to deliver their own publications wherever volume densities warrant, with the residual volumes being mailed to subscribers via Canada Post's commercial Publications Mail rates. There is somewhat less competition for the delivery of addressed periodicals, where competition exists mainly in the dense urban areas. Competition for the delivery of addressed periodicals is limited because commercial publications rates are designed to attract the delivery of addressed periodicals not eligible for subsidized rates. It is also limited due to Canada Post's successful bid to Canadian Heritage for the delivery of publications eligible for funded rates. Canada Post's competitors cannot enter into the same arrangement with Canadian Heritage because all available program dollars have been committed to the arrangement signed with Canada Post.

3.173 Canadian Heritage agreed to a fixed price contract with Canada Post, taking into account the fact that this would be an exclusive contract for the delivery of eligible publishers' publications at subsidized rates, and therefore committing all of its funding available for distribution assistance of these publications. Obviously, this precludes any alternative supplier of delivery services from signing a similar agreement with Canadian Heritage during the three-year term of the current agreement. However, Canada Post won the exclusive three-year arrangement in the context of a real possibility of a direct-to-publishers funding program without exclusive suppliers. Such an option or an option of awarding an exclusive supply contract to a supplier or suppliers other than Canada Post is again a possibility at the expiry of the current three-year contract. It should be noted that Canada Post is obliged under the current agreement to provide service without limitation at the agreed funded rates to all existing and new publications that are

---

[103] Canada notes that those threats are substantiated by certain factors such as the proximity of the Canadian publications to their markets, generally greater density of those markets (typically commercial trade publications oriented towards businesses in urban areas) and concentration of ownership in the industry.

[104] Examples of such competitors are Globe and Mail Distribution Services Ltd., A1Tours Ltd. (bundle distribution of magazines to business/professional offices), C.D. Woods Ltd., (Vancouver B.C.), Roltek Ltd., Insurance Courier Services Ltd. and an emerging co-operative delivery venture of Canadian trade publications.

deemed by Canadian Heritage to meet the agreed eligibility conditions. If the publisher of an eligible publication chooses to deliver the publication via another carrier, the publisher would not have access to special rates given that Canadian Heritage has chosen to negotiate an exclusive supplier contract with Canada Post for the term of the contract.

3.174 With respect to the use of the Radwanski Report by the United States, the mandate review was partially a review of the appropriateness of the monopoly that the Government has granted to Canada Post on letter delivery. The Report recommends, among other things: (1) that providing universality of service and uniformity of price for lettermail be regarded as integral elements of the mandate of Canada Post; and (2) that the exclusive privilege of Canada Post with regard to lettermail be maintained in its current form. Secondly, the mandate review was a review by the shareholder of the validity of the strategic, operational and financial direction of Canada Post and in this regard the mandate review is similar in nature to periodic reviews conducted in the private sector by shareholders of both publicly and privately held corporations. The recommendations contained in the Report, in whole or in part, are not government policy but rather recommendations to the government for consideration. The government has rejected certain of the recommendations, adopted others and taken the balance under advisement. The Radwanski Report did not address Canada Post's distribution services for publications.

3.175 The *United States* asserted that the fact that the Government has to date not intervened to put a stop to Canada Post's discriminatory postal rates does not mean that it is not responsible for them. A WTO Member cannot create a government institution, allow it to take actions inconsistent with the Member's WTO obligations, and then claim it has no responsibility for the actions of the institution. The market access concessions that WTO Members have negotiated over the years would not be secure if governments could escape their obligation to provide national treatment to imported products by creating government corporations and then claiming that they are not responsible for the discrimination imposed by the entities they themselves created. Intervention by the Government to ensure that Canada Post complies with Canada's international obligations under the GATT is within the power of the Canadian Government. It is especially important that the Canadian Government take remedial action because publishers of imported magazines have only limited alternatives to using Canada Post's services for delivery and transportation of magazines to Canadian subscribers. Indeed, Canada Post itself boasts that, "*We are the only national distribution service that reaches every single address in Canada. No one does this - no other competitor comes close*".[105] Canada acknowledges that Canada Post faces only limited competition for the delivery of addressed magazines. Magazines seeking

---

[105] Canada Post, Publications Mail, Product Guide at B-1 (bold in original).

to reach destinations other than business addresses in major cities have no practical alternative to using the delivery services of Canada Post.

3.176 Because of Canada Post's status as a Canadian Government institution that delivers and transports magazines and other mail, its actions - including the rates it applies - in respect of these activities are necessarily regulations or requirements affecting the internal sale, distribution or transportation of magazines within the meaning of Article III:4. If the Canadian Government told private Canadian delivery services to charge more for delivering imported goods than for delivering domestic goods, it would be in clear violation of Article III:4. If the Canadian Government accomplishes this same result through rate discrimination in its own delivery services, Article III:4 should apply with equal force. With respect to Canada's arguments concerning the Radwanski report, the United States responded that although that report did not refer to publications mail, it was primarily concerned with advertising mail and courier services, which are both commercial services. Thus, the statements made by Minister Marleau with respect to these services as commercial services are equally applicable to publications mail.

Like Product Issue

3.177 The *United States* argued that imported magazines are "like" domestic magazines for the purposes of Article III:4. Canada Post's rates distinguish between magazines based on whether they are imported or produced in Canada. In particular, Canada established two rate classes for magazines that are printed and published in Canada (the "commercial" and "funded" rates) and a third rate class for imported magazines (the "international" rate). Magazines eligible for "funded" rates are not only printed and published in Canada, but have to meet other requirements, namely: (a) the periodical must be typeset and edited in Canada; (b) the exclusive right to produce and publish the periodical must be held by a Canadian citizen, or a corporation controlled by Canadian citizens; and (c) the issue can not be published under license from a foreign publisher, or contain editorial content substantially the same as an issue printed outside Canada that was not first edited in Canada.[106]

3.178 However, all of these categories of magazines are "like products" for purposes of Article III:4 and the distinction that Canada has drawn between them is solely, indeed openly, intended to favour domestic production. Domestic and imported magazines share the same physical characteristics and commercial uses. Neither the location of production, nor the ownership of the right to publish, nor whether editorial content appeared in an issue printed outside Canada, make imported magazines unlike domestically-produced magazines in terms of physical characteristics or end uses. The rates established by Canada Post for imported

---

[106] *Regulations Respecting Newspapers and Periodicals*, Section 3(2) (definition of "Canadian Periodical"), S.O.R./91-179, 28 February, 1991.

and domestically-produced magazines draw an impermissible distinction based on the origin of the magazine, a distinction that, on its face, is applied "so as to afford protection to domestic production".

Treatment of Imported and Domestic Magazines

3.179 The *United States* stated that the rates established by Canada Post discriminate against imported magazines. Canada Post charges rates for domestically-produced magazines that are either 10 or 80 per cent lower on average than the rates applicable to imported magazines. These rates accord manifestly less favourable treatment to imported magazines by comparison to their domestically-produced counterparts. Moreover, Canada Post routinely makes discounts (such as "palletization" and "bypass" options) available to domestic magazines but not to imported magazines that increase the degree of discrimination still further. The higher postal rates for imported magazines are calculated to place them at a competitive disadvantage by comparison to competing domestically-produced magazines by creating a disparity between the distribution and transportation costs for imported and domestic magazines. Article III:4, second sentence, confirms that discrimination with respect to transportation based on the "nationality of a product" is not consistent with Article III:4. Canada has made no secret of the fact that the explicit purpose for its varying postal rates is to protect the Canadian publishing industry from import competition. Canada's discriminatory magazine postal rates represent precisely the kind of protectionist regulatory measure that GATT Article III:4 condemns.

3.180 It is no answer for Canada to assert that Canada Post enters into special lower-rate arrangements with certain larger foreign magazines. Canada Post's standard commercial rates for imported magazines are higher than for domestic magazines. Smaller foreign publishers, who cannot enter into special arrangements, are subject to the standard discriminatory rates. Moreover, negotiations for special rates between Canada Post and larger publishers (both foreign and domestic) presumably use the standard discriminatory commercial rates as the starting point. Thus, the resulting negotiated rates are in all likelihood discriminatory as well. Indeed, Canada states that the negotiated rates offered to large foreign publishers are only "relatively" close to the *standard* commercial rates are offered to Canadian publishers.

3.181 *Canada* argued that the economic factors applicable to foreign and domestic periodicals are not the same which is why their respective rates are different. Those rates are a reflection of competitive situations, not the result of discriminatory practices as was argued by the United States. Canada Post has no policy of giving a competitive advantage to one segment of its customers over another, and would have no interest in pursuing any such practice. Given appropriate competitive factors, it might very well be that certain foreign periodicals would enjoy better rates than non-subsidized Canadian magazines. This is exactly the type of scenario that Article III of GATT 1994 is intended to preserve. If foreign magazines are in better competitive situations, they should be able to take advantage of it. If on the contrary, they are not in such a position, Article III should not be there to grant them advantages that market forces do not provide. In the commercial and competitive environment in which Canada Post operates, it is under no obligation by virtue of Article III:4 to subsidize US publications by setting a better postal rate then what their specific market conditions require.

(ii)   Article III:8(b)

3.182   The *United States* argued that Canada Post's discriminatory postal rates do not constitute the payment of subsidies exclusively to domestic producers within the meaning of Article III:8(b), because domestic producers receive no subsidy payments. Under their 1 May 1996 Agreement, Canadian Heritage provides Canada Post with fixed annual payments to support Canada Post's below-cost "funded" postal rates for certain magazines produced in Canada. Those payments are not distributed to domestic magazine producers; instead Canada Post uses the funds to underwrite the lower postage rates it charges domestically-produced magazines. Thus, Canada's discriminatory postal rates are not direct payments to Canadian producers; rather, they modify the conditions of competition between domestic and imported products in contravention of Article III:4.

3.183   A series of GATT 1947 panel reports had interpreted Article III:8(b) very narrowly to hold that the only subsidies subject to exclusion from the national treatment provisions of Article III are those subsidies that are paid *directly* to domestic producers. So, for example, credit facilities provided to purchasers, and not producers,[107] and payments whose benefits could be partially retained by processors,[108] have been found not to qualify under Article III:8(b). Nor does the annual payment that Canadian Heritage makes to Canada Post constitute a subsidy to domestic producers under Article III:8(b). Canadian Heritage does not provide its funds to domestic producers. The low-priced "funded" postal rate that Canada applies to certain favoured periodicals produced in Canada do not fall within the terms of Article III:8(b). Rather, these rates, together with the "commercial" rate and various discounts applicable only to Canadian-produced magazines, are part of an overtly discriminatory postal rate scheme designed to create further protection for Canada's domestic magazine industry.

3.184   *Canada* argued that the funds paid by Canadian Heritage to Canada Post to enable it to grant Canadian publishers of publications reduced postal rates are allowable subsidies under GATT Article III:8(b), which explicitly recognizes that subsidies to domestic producers are not subject to the national treatment rules of Article III. Paragraph 8(b) applies with respect to all provisions of Article III,

---

[107] Panel Report on *Italian Discrimination Against Agricultural Machinery*, op. cit., at 60, 64, para. 14.
[108] Panel Report on *European Economic Community - Payments and Subsidies Paid to Processors and Producers of Oilseeds and Related Animal-Feed Proteins*, adopted on 25 January 1990, 37S/86, 124, para 137.

including Article III:4. Public policy has been developed to ensure that Canadians, regardless of where they live, have access on a reasonable basis to periodicals. Subsidized postal rates are provided to maximize the opportunity for distribution, particularly in light of Canada's relatively small and widely dispersed population. This measure is critical, since Canadian magazines have only limited access to newsstands and rely mainly on paid subscriptions for circulation. Subsidized postal rates have enabled Canadian magazines to reach a widely dispersed readership. The provision of reduced postal rates is a way of paying subsidies that is compatible with GATT 1994. These payments are made to Canada Post four times a year in return for its undertaking to deliver eligible publications at the agreed reduced rates. The benefit of the subsidies flows directly to eligible Canadian magazine publishers. The Canadian publication industry is the exclusive beneficiary of these subsidies and has to qualify for these subsidized rates in accordance with criteria set by Canadian Heritage before being found to be eligible.

3.185 The decision of the panel in *US - Malt Beverages* lends no support to the US position. This panel held that the expression "payment of subsidies" applies only to direct subsidies and not to other kinds of subsidies such as tax credits or tax abatements.[109] The panel was concerned solely with the distinction between subsidies, tax remissions and differential taxation rates, because a failure to make that distinction would destroy the effect of Article III:2. The formal distinction between taxation measures - benefits not involving direct expenditures by government - and subsidies is vital to the operation of the Article as a whole. Canada's postal subsidy meets the requirement of directness, in the sense in which that concept is used in the *US - Malt Beverages* decision, because a payment by government for the exclusive benefit of the producers is being made. It is only the mechanics of payment that were indirect.

3.186 The position held by the United States is therefore based on a difference of form, not substance. The specific form in which the subsidy is paid is irrelevant to the operation of Article III:8(b), provided that a payment is made by the government for the exclusive benefit of domestic producers.[110] Before being granted the privilege of posting using funded postal rates, a publisher has to sign a service agreement with Canada Post. This simple fact is evidence that publishers are direct beneficiaries. Canada Post is an intermediary, not the beneficiary. Whether the subsidy is paid to Canada Post or paid directly to the publishers, the economic effect is the same, namely that the eligible publishers are the beneficiaries of the subsidy.

---

[109] Panel Report on *United States - Measures Affecting Alcoholic and Malt Beverages*, op. cit.

[110] Canada noted that the *US-Malt Beverages* panel read subparagraph 8(b) having regard to the context of the whole of Article III but, except in the context of taxation measures, it was never stated that for every subsidy to qualify, the payment must be made directly to domestic producers. The panel simply said that the words "payment of subsidies" refer only to direct subsidies involving a payment, not to other subsidies such as tax credits or tax reductions (*ibid.* at 271, para. 5.8).

3.187 In practical terms, payments to individual publishers would be a cumbersome and ineffective method of delivering this subsidy. The administrative and financial burden of such a process would erode the benefits of the program. If an eligible Canadian publisher of a monthly magazine were to receive the payment, the advantages this publisher enjoys relative to foreign competition would be essentially unchanged. Canadian publishers would find themselves in the same position as they are in now, namely with an advantage over their foreign competitors. Therefore, Canadian Heritage provides Canada Post with an agreed-upon payment on a quarterly basis. The current process is far more efficient in minimizing the administrative overhead related to the program.

3.188 Based on the panel report on the *EEC - Payments and Subsidies Paid to Processors and Producers of Oilseeds and Related Animal-feed Proteins*[111] ("*EEC - Oilseeds*"), the United States argued that subsidies not paid directly to producers are not paid to them "exclusively" within the meaning of Article III:8(b). The word "exclusively" as used in this provision is concerned with the distinction between "domestic" as opposed to "non-domestic" producers, not whether third parties benefit from the subsidies. Whether an incidental benefit might be conferred upon Canada Post from the subsidy payment is irrelevant. Under the interpretation of this clause suggested by the United States, virtually any subsidy payment that would confer a third party benefit, however minimal, would be non-compliant. This is surely not the intended application of the exemption. Subsidies have an economic impact on third parties in almost all circumstances. The definition of the term "exclusive" proposed by the United States would lead, in practical terms, to the nullification of the Article III:8(b) exemption.

3.189 The *United States* argued that were Canada to provide payments directly (and exclusively) to domestic producers of magazines, the United States agreed that such payments would be protected by Article III:8(b). Under Canada's postal rate scheme for periodicals, however, domestic magazine producers receive *no* government payments. The only "payments" are made from one government entity (Canadian Heritage) to another (Canada Post).[112] Thus Canada's postal scheme simply does not comply with the requirement of Article III:8(b) that there be "payment . . . to domestic producers".

3.190 With regard to Canada's argument that its funded-rates system satisfied Article III:8(b) because it includes "payments" (to Canada Post), and because the resulting lower postal rates on domestic magazines have the same "economic effect" on domestic producers as payments made directly to them, the United States stated that the mere existence of "payments" (from one government entity to another, in this case) is not enough. The payments have to go to domestic pro-

---

[111] Panel Report on *European Economic Community - Payments and Subsidies Paid to Processors and Producers of Oilseeds and Related Animal-Feed Proteins, op. cit.,* at 124-125, paras. 137-141.
[112] Memorandum of Agreement.

ducers. Under Canada's postal rate scheme, domestic *periodicals* are provided lower postal rates than imported magazines; domestic periodical *producers* receive no payments. Instead, so-called "funded publications" are charged lower postal rates. Because imported magazines do not qualify for these rates, they are placed at a commercial disadvantage in terms of the transportation and delivery of their magazines in Canada. This is precisely the type of discrimination that Article III:4 is meant to prohibit. Canada Post's discriminatory postal rates clearly confer an economic benefit on domestic *products*, but a benefit of that sort is not within the scope of Article III:8(b). That Article applies only to "the payment of subsidies exclusively to domestic *producers*" (emphasis added).

3.191 GATT panels have consistently applied Article III:8(b) strictly according to its terms. They have rejected appeals to ignore its actual language in favour of what Canada claims to be "an economic perspective". They have uniformly denied the protection of Article III:8(b) to measures that provided no direct payments to domestic producers, including measures that may have conferred economic benefits indirectly on domestic producers by favouring the purchase or use of domestic products. Indeed, the "economic benefits" argument was explicitly rejected by the panel on *United States - Measures Affecting the Importation, Internal Sale and Use of Tobacco* ("*US - Tobacco*").[113]

3.192 If Canada's view - that Article III:8(b) encompasses the indirect provision of economic benefits to domestic producers through government advantages conferred on their goods - is accepted, it would dramatically expand the types of measures exempted from discipline under Article III. That is because virtually *any* form of more-favourable treatment accorded by a government to domestic products could be characterized as providing economic benefits similar to the payment of subsidies to domestic producers. Past panels have uniformly interpreted Article III:8(b) to require actual payments to domestic producers. In the panel on *Italian Discrimination Against Agricultural Machinery*, that panel

> "agreed with the contention of the United Kingdom delegation that in any case the provisions of paragraph 8(b) would not be applicable to this particular case since the credit facilities provided under the Law were granted to the purchasers or agricultural machinery and could not be considered as subsidies accorded to the producers of agricultural machinery".[114]

3.193 In that case it could have been argued that even though a subsidy was granted to purchasers of agricultural machinery, economic benefits also flowed directly or indirectly to the domestic producer of the machinery, since the availability of inexpensive credit limited to the purchase of domestic goods would

---

[113] Panel report on *United States - Measures Affecting the Importation, Internal Sale and Use of Tobacco*, adopted 4 October 1994, DS44/R.
[114] Panel Report on *Italian Discrimination Against Agricultural Machinery*, op. cit. para. 14.

stimulate the sales of such goods. However, the panel had correctly interpreted the words "exclusively to domestic producers" according to their plain meaning and found that the Italian credit scheme did not qualify for the Article III:8(b) exemption.

3.194 The panel report on *US - Malt Beverages*, cited by Canada in its submissions, does not deal with the issue of payments to third parties. The panel rejected a US argument that tax credits for small domestic producers of beer and wine constituted a domestic subsidy permitted under Article III:8(b), and holding that

> "Article III:8(b) . . . clarifies that the *product-related* rules in paragraphs 1 through 7 of Article III 'shall not prevent the payment of subsidies exclusively to domestic *producers*' (emphasis added [in original text]). The words 'payment of subsidies' refer only to direct subsidies involving a payment. . ."[115]

The panel thus continued the practice of past panels of invoking a narrow and literal interpretation of that provision. In this case, the only "payment" goes from Canadian Heritage to Canada Post, not to magazine producers. In fact, this "payment" is more akin to an internal transfer of government funds than a true economic "payment" to an unrelated entity.

3.195 In *US - Tobacco*,[116] the panel found that price support payments made to domestic tobacco farmers out of the proceeds of the No Net Cost Assessment ("NNCA") were within the scope of Article III:8(b). The panel rejected an interpretation of Article III:8(b) based on a measure's economic impact:

> "The Panel was cognizant of the fact that a remission of a tax on a product and the payment of a producer subsidy out of the proceeds of such a tax could have the *same economic effects. However, the panel noted that the distinction in Article III:8(b) is a formal one, not related to the economic impact of a measure.* Thus, in view of the explicit language of Article III:8(b), which recognizes that the product-related rules of Article III "shall not prevent the payment of subsidies exclusively to domestic producers," the Panel did not consider, as argued by the complainants, that the payment of a subsidy to tobacco producers out of the proceeds of the NNCA resulted in a form of tax remission inconsistent with Article III:2".[117]

---

[115] Panel Report on *United States - Measures Affecting Alcoholic and Malt Beverages*, op. cit.

[116] Panel Report on *United States - Measures Affecting the Importation, Internal Sale and Use of Tobacco*, op. cit.

[117] Panel Report on *United States – Measures Affecting the Importation, Internal Sale and Use of Tobacco*, op. cit., para. 109 (emphasis added).

3.196 Finally, the *EEC - Oilseeds*[118] panel examined EEC legislation that, like the payments by the Department of Canadian Heritage to Canada Post, included government payments to a middleman rather than to the domestic producer itself, on the theory that the payments would induce the middleman to provide preferential treatment to the domestic producer. The EEC legislation provided for the payment of subsidies to processors of oilseeds whenever they established by documentary evidence that they had transformed oilseeds of Community origin. In that decision:

> "The Panel noted that Article III:8(b) applies only to payments made *exclusively* to domestic producers and considered that *it can reasonably be assumed that a payment not made directly to producers is not made "exclusively" to them.* It noted moreover that if the economic benefits generated by the payments granted by the Community can at least partly be retained by the processors of Community oilseeds, the payments generate a benefit conditional upon the purchase of oilseeds of domestic origin inconsistently with Article III:4. Under these circumstances Article III:8(b) would not be applicable because in that case *the payments would not be made exclusively to domestic producers but to processors as well*".[119]

3.197 Canada mischaracterizes the *EEC - Oilseeds* decision as standing for the proposition that the phrase "exclusively to domestic producer," as used in Article III:8(b), is intended only to distinguish between "domestic" as opposed to "nondomestic" producers. The emphasized language makes it clear that the distinction is between "direct payments to producers" and "payments to ... processors" (who might in turn provide an indirect benefit to producers). So, too, in this case, the only "payments" are to an entity other than the domestic producers (and this "payment" is an internal transfer of government funds).

3.198 *Canada* considered it paradoxical if not contradictory for the United States to challenge Canada Post's international commercial rates on the grounds that Canada Post and the Government are one and the same, and to object to subsidized rates on the grounds that the same Corporation is obtaining, as a third party, a share of the benefits which the postal subsidy extends to Canadian periodical publishers. The argument that the Corporation is obtaining a benefit presupposes that it is an entirely separate entity from the Government: were it an organ of the Government, it would make little difference if it benefitted in any way from the payments, for in this case it would not be a government subsidy but simply a transfer of funds. The United States cannot maintain that the commercial

---

[118] Panel Report on *European Economic Community - Payments and Subsidies Paid to Processors and Producers of Oilseeds and Related Animal-Feed Proteins*, op. cit., para. 137.
[119] *Ibid.*, para. 137 (emphasis added).

rates and subsidized rates are discriminatory because Canada Post is part of the Government in the first case but not part of the Government in the second case. This is a clear contradiction.

3.199 The United States concedes that the protection provided by Article III:8(b) would extend to direct payments made exclusively to domestic periodical producers. At the same time, the United States takes a highly formalistic approach based on a very narrow interpretation of Article III:8(b). However, the formalism which the United States is asking the Panel to enshrine is supported neither by the text of Article III:8(b) nor by GATT practice. The method of subsidy payment is not in and of itself conclusive in determining whether Article III:8(b) applies. The essential factor is that the payment be made by the government for the benefit of domestic producers.

3.200 The panel reports quoted by the United States do not support the conclusion that the subsidy must always be paid directly and exclusively to domestic producers. For example, it cannot seriously be argued that the panel on *Italian Discrimination against Agricultural Machinery* determined that the subsidy had to be paid to domestic producers through actual payments. The panel found that Article III:8(b) did not apply in that case because the credit facilities provided by the legislation were extended to the purchasers of agricultural machinery and could not be considered to be subsidies paid to the producers of agricultural machinery. In the case of the Italian legislation, government support in the form of credit facilities for the purchase of Italian agricultural machinery was granted to the purchasers of agricultural machinery, and in the view of the panel the provisions of Article III:8(b) do not apply in these circumstances. The postal subsidy program involves no similar circumstances, since the Canadian Government's assistance in the form of reduced postal rates does not go to Canada Post Corporation.

3.201 It would appear that the formalism advocated by the United States stems from the report of the *US - Malt Beverages* panel, which dealt with a lower excise tax levied on domestic beer than on imported beer. The United States argued that the clear purpose of the lower tax was to subsidize small producers, and that reducing the excise tax was a way of granting such a subsidy which was compatible with the GATT. The panel concluded that "the words `payment of subsidies' refer only to direct subsidies involving a payment, not to other subsidies such as tax credits or tax reductions". In the opinion of the panel, the prohibition on discriminatory internal taxes in Article III:2 would be rendered inoperative were it possible to offer a general justification for such taxes on imported goods on the grounds that these were subsidies paid to competing domestic producers in accordance with Article III:8(b).

3.202 The *US - Malt Beverages* report must be read and understood within the full context of Article III:2 and with consideration to tax credits and reductions. In that specific case, the tax reductions and exemptions could not be deemed equivalent to the subsidies provided for by Article III:8(b). The panel did not make a determination on all other forms of subsidies. The Canadian postal subsidy, which has nothing in common with a tax abatement, exemption, credit or reduction, is consistent with the provisions of Article III:8(b) and is in no way incompatible with the *US - Malt Beverages* decision. In the present case, payments are made four times a year for the exclusive benefit of periodical producers. Only the mechanics of payment are indirect.

3.203 This interpretation is supported by the *US - Tobacco* report, which the United States quotes and to which it attributes an unwarranted scope in light of Article III:8(b). Without entering into the details, the issue in this case was whether the net self-financing levy on imported tobacco was higher than the self-financing levy on domestic tobacco, since the latter received a *de facto* tax remission by virtue of the operation of the tobacco price support program. The panel did not consider that the payment of a subsidy to tobacco producers out of the proceeds of the self-financing levy resulted in a form of tax remission inconsistent with Article III:2. The panel noted the formal distinction between a tax remission on the one hand and the payment of a subsidy on the other, even if they could have the same economic effect. The economic impact in the case of tax remission is irrelevant to the application of Article III:8(b). The formal distinction between taxation measures and subsidies is vital to the operation of Article III:2. It cannot be concluded from this panel report, as the United States did, that in the case of a producer subsidy, the examination of the measure's economic impact is irrelevant to determine whether the measure is consistent with the provisions of Article III:8(b).

3.204 Lastly, the United States suggests that Article III:8(b) is inapplicable in light of the *EEC - Oilseeds* report, in which the panel provides an unusual interpretation of the word "exclusively". Contrary to the US contention, Canada has not misinterpreted this report. It simply supports a more common interpretation of the word "exclusively". The general thrust of Article III is against discrimination between imported and domestic products. In this context, granting a government subsidy "exclusively" to domestic producers can only mean granting a subsidy only to the producers of domestic products, in the sense that it is paid to them alone and not to foreign producers.

3.205 In the case under study, the payments to processors were an incentive for them to buy oilseeds of EEC origin instead of imported oilseeds. The incentive derived from the fact that the payments made to processors could be greater than the difference between the price processors actually paid to EEC producers and the price that processors would have had to pay for imported oilseeds. This excess compensation created an incentive to buy products of EEC origin instead of imports. It is for this reason that Article III:8(b) was not applicable, for in this case the payments were not made to domestic EEC producers exclusively, but to processors as well.

3.206 The panel demonstrated that the payments could constitute benefits granted to EEC processors if the latter purchased EEC products. There is no parallel between the postal subsidy and the flaws in the EEC system. The United States has failed to demonstrate such a parallel. Moreover, the United States claim that the panel developed a general principle of interpretation by which Article III:8(b) does not apply if there is an intermediary between the government and the beneficiary is groundless. The panel would not have taken the trouble to perform such a complex analysis of the various prices (in paragraphs 136 through 141) were it only a matter of putting forward a general principle. The United States has not presented any analysis comparable to the one performed by the panel.

3.207 Moreover, there is no parallel with the postal subsidy because Canada Post does not receive "bonus payments" for handling and distributing periodicals from Canadian publishers rather than from foreign publishers. The Corporation receives an amount that is stipulated in a memorandum of understanding or contract in exchange for the provision of reduced postal rates. This amount is based on estimates of expected eligible Canadian periodical volumes at the negotiated reduced rates, which estimates are developed independently by each of Canada Post and Canadian Heritage in the course of negotiating the contract. There is no incentive to handle the periodicals of Canadian publishers rather than those of foreign publishers, since delivering a larger number of Canadian magazines than that originally estimated by Canada Post would not increase the Corporation's net income. The postal subsidy does not grant the Corporation any particular benefit. The EEC system provided incentives favouring EEC processors whereas there are no such measures favouring Canada Post in the memorandum of understanding with Canadian Heritage.

3.208 The agreement between Canadian Heritage and Canada Post expressly stipulates the rates paid by eligible Canadian periodical publishers. The terms of the agreement ensure that the payments to the Corporation secure the price it must charge publishers who mail their periodicals at subsidized rates. The contract for the provision of delivery services for eligible publications is at a fixed rate. Canada Post receives a lump sum in exchange for providing delivery services at the reduced rate. It should be noted that the predetermined annual payment to Canada Post from Canadian Heritage is a negotiated value for service in the spirit of any fixed price contract; that is, Canada Post must provide delivery at the agreed reduced rates to all eligible publications in return for the fixed amount. Both parties are aware that variances up or down in a given year relative to each's view of expected volume are to be expected. However, it is each party's studied view that in spite of these risks, it has an equal chance to gain or lose relative to those expectations of volumes. In view of the fixed price nature of the agreement, there is no relevance to arguments of payments in excess of value of service provided. The value provided is by definition exactly what was contracted to be provided in return for the pre-determined fixed payment.

3.209 The United States has conceded that were the payments made directly and exclusively to Canadian periodical publishers, these payments would qualify for protection under Article III:8(b). The question the Panel must consider is whether such a change in the method of subsidy payment would place foreign periodical publishers in a more favourable competitive position in relation to Canadian publishers in respect of the postal subsidy. There is no reason to believe that this would be the case. The method of payment is merely the subsidy's technical, ad-ministrative aspect. It does not reveal who benefits from the subsidy. If payments were made directly to publishers, Canada Post would increase its rates for the delivery and distribution of the magazines that had previously enjoyed reduced rates, in accordance with its practice for commercial services and its profit maximization objectives. Eligible Canadian publishers would continue to buy periodical delivery services from the Corporation at a cost "lower" than the commercial rate, in view of the compensatory payments they would receive. As for foreign publishers, they would continue to buy periodical delivery and distri-bution services from Canada Post at the same rates as before.

3.210 If the subsidy were paid directly to publishers rather than to Canada Post, the effects would be the same. Eligible publishers would be the beneficiaries of the subsidy. Only administrative costs would increase substantially. There is no valid reason in this case, such as for example a concern that provisions of the 1994 GATT would be rendered inoperative, which demand that the Panel uphold an interpretation which would have the effect of replacing the relatively simple and economical existing system with a costly and complicated system. Lastly, there are no grounds for claiming, as the United States has done, that our inter-pretation of Article III:8(b) would have the effect of encouraging the govern-ments of member states to introduce a host of discriminatory measures in favour of domestic goods for the sole reason that these would economically benefit do-mestic producers. Canada is not proposing the abolition of the disciplines in the 1994 GATT but only a reading of Article III:8(b) that respects its terms.

3.211 The *United States* concluded that over the years GATT panels had been very careful to apply the precise language of Article III:8(b) and to avoid ex-panding the scope of that Article to encompass measures other than the direct payment of subsidies that convey economic benefits on the domestic producers. This caution was completely justified because the liberal reading Canada sug-gests for Article III:8(b) would permit governments to employ a wide variety of discriminatory measures in favour of domestic products that could be justified on the ground of conferring economic benefits on domestic producers. Such a result could dramatically alter the competitive environment in the markets of Members around the world. Canada's "funded" postage rate scheme for domestically-produced periodicals was a very good example of a product transportation and distribution regime that may well confer economic benefits on domestic produc-ers but that plainly altered the competitive relationship between imported and domestic products.[120]

---

[120] The United States argued that even if it were concluded that the payments made by Canadian Heritage to Canada Post to support the "funded" postal rates somehow gave rise to payments to domestic producers within the meaning of Article III:8(b), because domestic producers ultimately received an economic benefit, such a benefit would not be provided "exclusively" to domestic pro-ducers. Canada Post itself might well be a beneficiary. This is because Canada Post's pre-determined annual payment from Canadian Heritage might exceed Canada Post's cost of delivering all eligible

IV.   INTERIM REVIEW

4.1   On 23 January 1997, the United States requested the Panel to review, in accordance with Article 15.2 of the DSU, precise aspects of the interim report that had been issued to the parties on 16 January 1997. Canada did not request a review, but wished to reserve its right to respond to the US comments. The Panel ruled that, given the circumstances in this particular case, Canada could submit its response by 31 January 1997. Canada submitted its response to the US comments on 31 January 1997, urging the Panel to disregard a large part of the US comments. Neither the United States nor Canada requested the Panel to hold a meeting. The Panel reviewed the entire range of arguments presented by the parties in their written submissions, and finalized its findings as in Section V below, taking into account the specific aspects it considered to be relevant.

4.2   Regarding Tariff Code 9958, the interim report had focused on the "split-run" rule, which the Panel found to be the principal issue, and had not mentioned the second part of the Code, namely the five-per-cent rule. The United States requested the inclusion of this part in the findings. Canada did not object to this request. The Panel agreed to the inclusion and introduced some drafting modifications in the final report at paragraphs 5.1 and 5.4.

4.3   The interim report had, in a part corresponding to paragraph 5.24 of the final report, stated that the definition of a "split-run" edition relied *solely* on factors external to the Canadian market. The United States suggested that the Panel change this word to *decisively*. Canada objected to this change. However, the Panel considered the US suggestion to be a useful one to improve the accuracy of the findings, and accordingly modified the expression in the way it now appears in paragraph 5.24.

4.4   Regarding paragraph 5.25 of the final report, the United States suggested that the Panel add that "(1) any number of additional hypothetical examples could be devised that would further show that split-run and non-split-run periodicals need not be any different, and that (2) this is to be expected because the definition of split-run periodicals provides that two virtually identical products can be taxed differently depending on whether or not a similar product is sold outside Canada". While the Panel did not disagree with this observation, it was not persuaded that such an addition would enhance the clarity of the logic in the final report. The Panel therefore decided not to introduce the suggested change.

4.5   Regarding the directness of the taxation (paragraphs 5.28 and 5.29 of the final report), the United States argued that this was a case of direct taxation because the excise tax was focused on a particular type of good. The Panel rejected

---

periodicals in a given year. Moreover, Canada Post could further benefit economically from having a captive set of customers who must use its services in order to obtain the "funded" rates. For these reasons, according to the United States, it cannot be said that the benefits of Canada's Publications Assistance Program are provided "exclusively to domestic producers".

this argument. However, in this connection, the United States pointed out that a certain citation of past cases in the interim report could be somewhat misleading. The Panel accepted this point, and modified the paragraphs accordingly.

4.6   Regarding the differences between "commercial Canadian" and "international" rates applied by Canada Post to periodicals, the United States commented that the interim report failed to mention certain additional discount options which were available only to Canadian periodicals. The Panel accepted this comment and introduced some drafting modifications in the final report at paragraphs 5.1, 5.39 and 6.1. The United States further requested that the final report refer to the long-term discount contracts between Canada Post and large-circulation magazine publishers (see paragraph 3.171). Canada objected to this request on the grounds that these agreements or contracts had "never been one of the objects of this dispute". The Panel considered that this particular issue was not presented by the United States in a coherent manner during the proceedings, and that it was too late for the United States to raise this issue as an additional claim at the interim review stage. Accordingly, the Panel did not accept the US request on this point.

4.7   The United States suggested that the Panel restructure paragraph 5.36 of the final report as an alternative argument because, according to the United States, the fact that Canada Post is an entity of the Canadian Government was a sufficient reason to find a violation of Article III:4 of GATT 1994 in this instance. However, the Panel considered such a change unnecessary. In the Panel's view, it was clear that the *Semi-Conductor* case was cited here as supporting evidence, not as decisive reason for finding the violation.

4.8   The United States questioned the appropriateness of paragraphs 5.37 and 5.38 of the final report, suggesting that the examination of Article III:1 of GATT 1994 was unnecessary in this case. Canada did not object to this comment. However, in the Panel's view, the Appellate Body Report on *Japan - Taxes on Alcoholic Beverages* clearly mandates it to engage in such an examination. The Panel therefore decided to retain these paragraphs unchanged from the way in which they appeared in the interim report.

4.9   Regarding paragraphs 5.42 to 5.44 of the final report, the United States considered that the Panel erroneously concluded that the "funded" rate scheme constituted a payment of subsidies permitted by Article III:8 of GATT 1994. The Panel disagreed for reasons elaborated in its final report. The Panel accordingly did not introduce modifications to the final report in this respect.

4.10   The United States also made other drafting suggestions concerning the descriptive part, some of which the Panel accepted and introduced in its final report.

V. FINDINGS

A. Introduction

5.1   This dispute essentially arises from the following facts: *(a)* Canada prohibits imports of "split-run" periodicals (periodicals with the same or similar editorial content as those published in foreign countries, which contain an advertisement directed to the Canadian market) through Tariff Code 9958. Tariff Code 9958 further prohibits imports of periodicals in which more than five per cent of the advertising content consists of advertisements directed to the Canadian market, whether or not an edition with similar editorial content is sold outside Canada; *(b)* Canada, through Part V.1 of the Excise Tax Act, imposes an excise tax of 80 per cent on the value of advertisements in "split-run" periodicals distributed in Canada on a per issue basis; and *(c)* Canada Post Corporation ("Canada Post") applies reduced ("funded") postal rates, funded by the Department of Canadian Heritage ("Canadian Heritage"), to certain periodicals published in Canada. Postal rates applied to Canadian periodicals not eligible for the "funded" rates ("commercial Canadian" rates) are lower than those applied to imported periodicals ("international" rates). Certain additional discount options (such as for "palletization" and "pre-sort") are available to Canadian periodicals but are not generally available to imported periodicals.

5.2   The United States claims that *(a)* Tariff Code 9958 is inconsistent with Article XI of the General Agreement on Tariffs and Trade 1994 ("GATT 1994"); *(b)* Part V.1 of the Excise Tax Act is inconsistent with Article III:2 of GATT 1994, or in the alternative, is inconsistent with Article III:4 of GATT 1994; and *(c)* the application by Canada Post of lower postal rates to domestically-produced periodicals than to imported periodicals is inconsistent with Article III:4 of GATT 1994, and the "funded" rate scheme is not a domestic subsidy within the meaning of Article III:8 of GATT 1994. The United States requests that the Panel recommend that Canada bring its measures into conformity with its obligations under GATT 1994.

5.3   Canada requests the Panel to dismiss the US claims on the grounds that *(a)* Tariff Code 9958 is justifiable under Article XX(d) of GATT 1994; *(b)* Article III of GATT 1994 does not apply to Part V.1 of the Excise Tax Act; even if the Panel decides that Article III of GATT 1994 applies to these provisions, they do not violate Article III of the GATT 1994; and *(c)* Article III:4 of GATT 1994 does not apply to the "commercial" rates charged by Canada Post because they are the result of a commercial and marketing policy and not influenced by government policy and   the "funded" rate scheme is a payment of subsidies allowable under Article III:8(b) of GATT 1994.

B. Tariff Code 9958

5.4   Tariff Code 9958 prohibits the importation into Canada of the following:

"1.   Issues of a periodical, one of the four immediately preceding issues of which has, under regulations that the Governor in Council may make, been found to be an issue of special edition, including a split-run or a regional edition, that contained an advertisement that was primarily directed to a market in Canada, and that did not appear in identical form in all editions of that issue of that periodical that were distributed in the country of origin.

"2.   Issues of a periodical, one of the four immediately preceding issues of which has, under regulations that the Governor in Council may make, been found to be an issue of more than five per cent of the advertising space in which consisted of space used for advertisements that indicated specific sources of availability in Canada, or specific terms or conditions relating to the sale of provision in Canada, of any goods or services except where the indication of such sources of availability or such terms or conditions was primarily directed at persons outside Canada".[121]

5.5   Since the importation of certain foreign products into Canada is completely denied under Tariff Code 9958, it appears that this provision by its terms is inconsistent with Article XI:1 of GATT 1994. Article XI:1 reads in relevant part as follows:

"No prohibitions or restrictions other than duties, taxes or other charges ... shall be instituted or maintained by any [Member] on the importation of any product of the territory of any other [Member] ...".

5.6   The question presented here is whether the import prohibition under Tariff Code 9958 may be justified under other provisions of the WTO Agreement. Canada claims that the measure is justified under Article XX(d) of GATT 1994. The relevant part of Article XX of GATT 1994 reads as follows:

"Subject to the requirement that such measures are not applied in a manner which would constitute a means of arbitrary or unjustifiable discrimination between countries where the same conditions prevail, or a disguised restriction on international trade, nothing in this Agreement shall be construed to prevent the adoption or enforcement by any [Member] of measures: ... (d) necessary to secure compliance with laws or regulations which are not inconsistent with the provisions of this Agreement, including those relating to customs enforcement, the enforcement of monopo-

---

[121]   Paragraphs 2.2-2.3 *supra*.

lies operated under paragraph 4 of Article II and Article XVII, the protection of patents, trade marks and copyrights, and the prevention of deceptive practices; ...".

5.7   The panel on *United States - Standards for Reformulated and Conventional Gasoline* approached this provision in the following fashion. Having stated that the party invoking an exception under Article XX bore the burden of proving that the inconsistent measures came within its scope, the panel observed that the complainant had to demonstrate the following elements:

> "(1)   that the measures for which the exception were being invoked - that is, the particular trade measures inconsistent with the General Agreement - *secure compliance* with laws or regulations themselves not inconsistent with the General Agreement;

> "(2)   that the inconsistent measures for which the exception was being invoked were *necessary* to secure compliance with those laws or regulations; and

> "(3)   that the measures were applied in conformity with the requirements of the *introductory clause* of Article XX".[122]

In order to justify the application of Article XX(d), according to the panel, all the above elements had to be satisfied. We will follow the same approach in the present case.[123]

5.8   First, as to whether the import prohibition under Tariff Code 9958 secures compliance with a law or regulation not inconsistent with GATT 1994, Canada argues that Tariff Code 9958 is a measure intended to secure the attainment of the objectives of Section 19 of the Income Tax Act, which allows for the deduction of expenses for advertising directed to the Canadian market on condition that the advertisements appear in Canadian editions of Canadian periodicals. Since the United States is not challenging the GATT consistency of Section 19 of the Income Tax Act in this proceeding, the issue of GATT consistency is not before the Panel. However, the United States claims that Tariff Code 9958 is not a measure to "secure compliance" with the Income Tax Act.

5.9   The interpretative issue here is what is meant by "to secure compliance with laws and regulations" in Article XX(d) of GATT 1994. In this connection, the panel on *European Economic Community - Regulations on Imports of Parts*

---

[122]   Panel Report on *United States - Standards for Reformulated and Conventional Gasoline*, adopted on 20 May 1996, WT/DS2/R, para. 6.31 (emphasis in original). The relevant part of the panel report was not modified by the Appellate Body.

[123]   We note that the Appellate Body in a recent report stated as follows: "[Adopted panel reports] create legitimate expectations among WTO Members, and, therefore, should be taken into account where they are relevant to any dispute". Appellate Body Report on *Japan - Taxes on Alcoholic Beverages*, WT/DS8/AB/R, WT/DS10/AB/R and WT/DS11/AB/R, DSR 1996:I, 97 at 108.

and Components found this phrase to mean "to enforce obligations under laws and obligations", not "to ensure the attainment of the objectives of the laws and regulations".[124] Canada suggests that this precedent should not be rigidly followed in the case of fiscal or economic incentives in general, and particularly in the present case, because Tariff Code 9958 and the income tax provision have always been considered part of a single, indivisible package. We are not persuaded by this argument. Canada's view will inherently lead to a situation where "[w]henever the objective of a law consistent with the General Agreement cannot be attained by enforcing the obligations under that law, the imposition of further obligations inconsistent with the General Agreement could then be justified under Article XX(d) on the grounds that this secures compliance with the objectives of that law", as was pointed out by the aforementioned panel.[125] We fail to see any differences that would obviate this problem in the case of fiscal or economic incentives. It should be noted, however, that we are neither examining nor passing judgment on the policy objectives of the Canadian measure regarding periodicals; we are nevertheless called upon to examine the *instruments* chosen by the Canadian Government for the attainment of such policy objectives.

5.10   Tariff Code 9958 cannot be regarded as an enforcement measure for Section 19 of the Income Tax Act. It is true that if a government bans imports of foreign periodicals with advertisements directed at the domestic market, as does Canada in the present case, the possibility of non-compliance with a tax provision granting tax deductions for expenses incurred for advertisements in domestic periodicals will be greatly reduced. It would seem almost impossible for an enterprise to place an advertisement in a foreign periodical because there would be virtually no foreign periodical available in which to place it. Thus, there would be no way for the enterprise legally to claim a tax deduction therefor. However, that is an incidental effect of a separate measure distinct (even though it may share the same policy objective) from the tax provision which is designed to give an incentive for placing advertisements in Canadian, as opposed to foreign, periodicals.[126] We thus find that Tariff Code 9958 does not "secure compliance" with Section 19 of the Income Tax Act.

5.11   In view of the above finding that Tariff Code 9958 does not secure compliance with Section 19 of the Income Tax Act, we need not consider whether the import prohibition under the Code is "necessary" to secure compliance with the tax provision or whether the measure meets the conditions in the introductory clause (or "chapeau") to Article XX. Canada has failed to satisfy at least one of

---

[124]   Panel Report on *European Economic Community - Regulations on Imports of Parts and Components*, adopted on 16 May 1990, BISD 37S/132, paras. 5.14-5.18.
[125]   *Ibid.*, para. 5.17.
[126]   An import ban under these circumstances is rather likely to be an enforcement measure in respect of a ban on possession or sale of a product. An import ban on alcoholic beverages might share the same objective as a criminal statute against drunk driving, but if alcoholic drinks are not banned or their sale prohibited domestically, the import ban could not be considered as an enforcement measure of the criminal statute.

the conditions identified in paragraph 5.7 above. Thus we conclude that Tariff Code 9958 is inconsistent with Article XI:1 of GATT 1994 and cannot be justified under Article XX(d).

C.   The Excise Tax Act

5.12   We now turn to the examination of whether the 80 per cent excise tax on advertisements in split-run periodicals under Part V.1 of the Excise Tax Act is compatible with Canada's obligations under Article III of GATT 1994. The United States claims that Part V.1 of the Excise Tax Act is inconsistent with Article III:2 of GATT 1994, or in the alternative, is inconsistent with Article III:4.

(i)   Applicability of GATT 1994

5.13   Since Canada challenges the applicability of GATT 1994 to this part of the Excise Tax Act, we address this issue first. Canada claims that Article III of GATT 1994 does not apply to Part V.1 of the Excise Tax Act because the latter is a measure pertaining to advertising services, which is within the purview of the General Agreement on Trade in Services ("GATS"). Canada further claims that the examination of Part V.1 of the Excise Tax Act in light of GATS is not covered by the terms of reference of this Panel.

5.14   Canada's argument is essentially that since Canada has made no specific commitments for advertising services under GATS, the United States should not be allowed to "obtain benefits under a covered agreement that have been expressly precluded under another covered agreement".[127] Put another way, Canada seems to argue that if a Member has not undertaken market-access commitments in a specific service sector, that non-commitment should preclude all the obligations or commitments undertaken in the goods sector to the extent that there is an overlap between the non-commitment in services and the obligations or commitments in the goods sector. Canada claims that because of the existence of the two instruments - GATT 1994 and GATS - both of which may apply to a given measure, "it is necessary to interpret the scope of application of each such as to avoid any overlap".[128]

5.15   We are not fully convinced by Canada's characterization of the Excise Tax as a measure intended to regulate trade in advertising services, in view of the fact that there is no comparable regulation on advertisements through other media and the fact that the tax is imposed on a "per issue" basis. However, assuming that Canada intended to carve out Part V.1 of the Excise Tax Act from the coverage of its GATS commitments by not inscribing advertising services in its Sched-

---

[127]   Paragraph 3.35 *supra*.
[128]   Paragraph 3.38 *supra*.

ule,[129] does that exonerate Canada from the Panel's scrutiny regarding the alleged violation of its obligations and commitments under GATT 1994?

5.16   In order to answer this question, we need to examine the structure of the WTO Agreement including its annexes. Article II:2 of the WTO Agreement is the relevant provision, which reads as follows:

> "The agreements and associated legal instruments included in Annexes 1, 2 and 3 ... are integral parts of this Agreement, binding on all Members".[130]

5.17   According to Article 31(1) of the 1969 Vienna Convention on the Law of Treaties ("Vienna Convention"), a treaty must be interpreted in good faith in accordance with the ordinary meaning to be given to the terms of the treaty in their context and in the light of its object and purpose. Furthermore, as the Appellate Body has repeatedly pointed out, "one of the corollaries of the 'general rule of interpretation' in the Vienna Convention is that interpretation must give meaning and effect to all the terms of the treaty. An interpreter is not free to adopt a reading that would result in reducing whole clauses or paragraphs of a treaty to redundancy or inutility".[131] The ordinary meaning of the texts of GATT 1994 and GATS as well as Article II:2 of the WTO Agreement, taken together, indicates that obligations under GATT 1994 and GATS can co-exist and that one does not override the other. If the consequences suggested by Canada were intended, there would have been provisions similar to Article XVI:3 of the WTO Agreement or the General Interpretative Note to Annex 1A in order to establish hierarchical order between GATT 1994 and GATS. The absence of such provisions between the two instruments implies that GATT 1994 and GATS are standing on the same plain in the WTO Agreement, without any hierarchical order between the two.

5.18   In this connection, Canada also argues that overlaps between GATT 1994 and GATS should be avoided.[132] We disagree. Overlaps between the subject matter of disciplines in GATT 1994 and in GATS are inevitable, and will further increase with the progress of technology and the globalization of economic activities. We do not consider that such overlaps will undermine the coherence of the WTO system. In fact, certain types of services such as transportation and distribution are recognized as a subject-matter of disciplines under Article III:4 of GATT 1994. It is also noteworthy in this respect that advertising services have long been associated with the disciplines under GATT Article III. As early as 1970, the Working Party on Border Tax Adjustment made the following observation:

---

[129]   We note in this connection that Part V.1 of the Excise Tax Act was enacted in 1995, after Canada's acceptance of the WTO Agreement.

[130]   GATT 1994 is included in Annex 1A. GATS is included in Annex 1B.

[131]   Appellate Body Report on *United States - Standards for Reformulated and Conventional Gasoline*, adopted on 20 May 1996, WT/DS2/AB/R, DSR 1996:I, 3 at 21. Also cited in the Appellate Body Report on *Japan - Taxes on Alcoholic Beverages, op. cit.*, 106.

[132]   Paragraphs 3.38 and 5.14 *supra*.

> "The Working Party noted that there was a divergence of views with regard to the eligibility for adjustment of certain categories of tax and that these could be sub-divided into
>
> > (a)   "Taxes occultes" which the OECD defined as consumption taxes on capital equipment, auxiliary materials and *services* used in the transportation and production of other taxable goods. Taxes on *advertising*, energy, machinery and transport were among the more important taxes which might be involved. ... ;
> >
> > (b)   Certain other taxes, ...".[133]

We also note that there are several adopted panel reports that examined the issue of services in the context of GATT Article III. For instance, the panel on *Canada - Import, Distribution and Sale of Certain Alcoholic Drinks by Provincial Marketing Agencies* addressed the issues of access to points of sale and restrictions on private delivery of beer.[134] The panel on *United States - Measures Affecting Alcoholic and Malt Beverages* also dealt with the issues of distribution of wine and beer.[135] More to the point, the panel on *Thailand - Restrictions on Importation of and Internal Taxes on Cigarettes* specifically addressed the question of advertising.[136]

5.19   In any event, since Canada admits that in the present case there is no conflict between its obligations under GATS and under GATT 1994,[137] there is no reason why both GATT and GATS obligations should not apply to the Excise Tax Act. Thus, we conclude that Article III of GATT 1994 is applicable to Part V.1 of the Excise Tax Act.

(ii)   GATT Article III:2

5.20   The next issue to be examined is whether there is a violation of Article III. The principal claim of the United States is that Part V.1 of the Excise Tax is inconsistent with Article III:2 of GATT 1994. The relevant parts of Article III read as follows:

> "1.   The [Members] recognize that internal taxes and other internal charges, and laws, regulations and require-

---

[133] "Border Tax Adjustments", Report of the Working Party adopted on 2 December 1970 (L/3464), BISD 18S/97, para. 15 (emphasis added).

[134] Panel Report on *Canada - Import, Distribution and Sale of Certain Alcoholic Drinks by Provincial Marketing Agencies*, adopted on 18 February 1992, BISD 39S/27.

[135] Panel Report on *United States - Measures Affecting Alcoholic and Malt Beverages*, adopted on 19 June 1992, BISD 39S/206.

[136] Panel Report on *Thailand - Restrictions on Importation of and Internal Taxes on Cigarettes*, adopted on 7 November 1990, BISD 37S/200, para. 78.

[137] Paragraph 3.38 *supra.*

ments affecting the internal sale, offering for sale, purchase, transportation, distribution or use of products, and internal quantitative regulations requiring the mixture, processing or use of products in specified amounts or proportions, should not be applied to imported or domestic products so as to afford protection to domestic production.

"2.   The products of the territory of any [Member] imported into the territory of any other [Member] shall not be subject, directly or indirectly, to internal taxes or other internal charges of any kind in excess of those applied, directly or indirectly, to like domestic products. Moreover, no [Member] shall otherwise apply internal taxes or other internal charges to imported or domestic products in a manner contrary to the principles set forth in paragraph 1".

Furthermore, the Interpretative Note *ad* Article III reads in part as follows:

"A tax conforming to the requirements of the first sentence of paragraph 2 would be considered to be inconsistent with the provisions of the second sentence only in cases where competition was involved between, on the one hand, the taxed product and, on the other hand, a directly competitive or substitutable product which was not similarly taxed".

5.21   In the present case, the following two questions need to be answered to determine whether there is a violation of Article III:2 of GATT 1994: *(a)* Are imported "split-run" periodicals and domestic non "split-run" periodicals like products?; and *(b)* Are imported "split-run" periodicals subject to an internal tax in excess of that applied to domestic non "split-run" periodicals? If the answers to both questions are affirmative, there is a violation of Article III:2, first sentence.[138] If the answer to the first question is negative, we need to examine further whether there is a violation of Article III:2, second sentence.

(iii)   Like Product Issue

5.22   As the Appellate Body confirmed in its report on *Japan - Taxes on Alcoholic Beverages*, the definition of "like products" in Article III:2, first sentence, should be construed narrowly, on a case-by-case basis, in light of such factors as

---

[138]   In this context, we need not examine the applicability of Article III:1 separately, because, as the Appellate Body noted in its recent report, the first sentence of Article III:2 *is*, in effect, an application of the general principle embodied in Article III:1. Therefore, if the imported and domestic products are "like products", and if the taxes applied to the imported products are "in excess of" those applied to the like domestic products, then the measure is inconsistent with Article III:2, first sentence. Appellate Body Report on *Japan - Taxes on Alcoholic Bever*ages, *op. cit.*, 111.

the product's end uses in a given market, consumer's tastes and habits, and the product's properties, nature and quality.[139] In applying these criteria to the present case, it should be noted that our mandate under the terms of reference of this Panel is not to discuss the likeness of periodicals in general. The question before us, as presented by the United States in its request for the establishment of a panel (WT/DS31/2) and subsequently elaborated,[140] is a comparison between imported "split-run" periodicals and domestic non "split-run" periodicals.

5.23   This comparison, at first glance, might seem impossible in view of the fact that there are no imported "split-run" periodicals marketed in Canada due to the import prohibition under Tariff Code 9958. However, as the panel on "United States - Taxes on Petroleum and Certain Imported Substances" observed, the rationale for the national treatment obligation of Article III is to protect expectations of the Members as to the competitive relationship between their products and those of other Members.[141] In so far as imported "split-run" periodicals are subject to the relevant provisions of the Excise Tax Act (as Canada admits to be the case),[142] the comparison can be made on the basis of a hypothetical import.

5.24   We note in this regard that the Excise Tax Act defines a "split-run" edition of a periodical in terms of its editorial content (whether more than 20 per cent of the editorial material is the same or substantially the same as editorial material that appears in editions that are primarily distributed outside Canada) and advertising content (whether it contains an advertisement that does not appear in identical form in other editions distributed outside Canada). Despite the Canadian claim that the purpose of the legislation is to promote publications of original Canadian content, this definition essentially relies on factors external to the Canadian market - whether the same editorial content is included in a foreign edition and whether the periodical carries different advertisements in foreign editions.

5.25   Putting these external factors aside, imported "split-run" periodicals and domestic non "split-run" periodicals can be extremely similar. In the course of the Panel process, Canada made the following statement:

> "*Harrowsmith Country Life* is a Canadian-owned magazine. Before the adoption of Part V.1 of the Excise Tax Act, *Harrowsmith Country Life* had two editions - A Canadian edi-

---

[139]   *Japan - Taxes on Alcoholic Beverages, op. cit.*, 112. According to the Appellate Body, the narrow construction of the term was necessary in Article III:2, first sentence, "so as not to condemn measures that its strict terms are not meant to condemn".

[140]   See paragraphs 3.104-3.108 *supra*.

[141]   Panel Report on *United States - Taxes on Petroleum and Certain Imported Substances*, adopted on 17 June 1987, BISD 34S/136, para. 5.2.2. See also the Panel Reports on *Italian Discrimination against Imported Agricultural Machinery*, adopted on 23 October 1958, BISD 7S/60, para. 18, and on *United States - Section 337 of the Tariff Act of 1930*, adopted on 7 November 1989, BISD 36S/345, para. 5.13.

[142]   Paragraphs 3.58 and 3.98 *supra*.

tion and a US edition. The Canadian and the US editions
had different advertisements and a certain amount of common editorial content. Because more than 20 per cent of the
editorial content in the Canadian edition was the same as
that in the US edition, the tax would have applied to the Canadian edition (even if the editorial content was entirely
produced in Canada). As a result of the excise tax, *Harrowsmith Country Life* stopped publishing its US edition".[143]

In the case of this particular periodical, if all the volumes of *Harrowsmith Country Life* had been printed in the United States (including its Canadian edition) and
the Canadian edition had been exported to Canada because they were somehow
exempted from the coverage of Tariff Code 9958, and if the publisher decided to
publish the final issue of the US edition after the introduction of the excise tax,
the publisher would have been subject to the tax for the imported Canadian edition. If this publisher thereafter discontinued the publication of the US edition, it
would no longer be subject to the excise tax. Now, let us compare the two issues
of this hypothetical *Harrowsmith Country Life* (Canadian edition) before and
after the discontinuation of the US edition. These two editions would have common end uses, very similar physical properties, nature and qualities. It is most
likely that the two volumes would have been designed for the same readership
with the same tastes and habits. In all respects, these two volumes are "like", and
yet one is subject to the Excise Tax, while the other is not.

5.26   Thus, we conclude that imported "split-run" periodicals and domestic non
"split-run" periodicals can be like products within the meaning of Article III:2 of
GATT 1994. In our view, this provides sufficient grounds to answer in the affirmative the question as to whether the two products at issue are like because, as
stated earlier, the purpose of Article III is to protect expectations of the Members
as to the competitive relationship between their products and those of other
Members, not to protect actual trade volumes. If Tariff Code 9958 were lifted, a
wide variety of "split-run" periodicals ranging from general news magazines to
specialty journals dedicated to specific areas of business or profession could be
imported into Canada. This situation can hardly be called an "isolated instance of
differential taxation" as Canada describes.[144]

5.27   Having found that imported "split-run" periodicals and domestic non
"split-run" periodicals are like products, we need not consider the second sentence of Article III:2. The only remaining question is whether imported "split-
run" periodicals are subject to an internal tax in excess of that applied to domestic non "split-run" periodicals.

---

[143] See paragraph 3.99 *supra*.
[144] Paragraph 3.101 *supra*.

(iv)   Taxation in Excess: "Directly or Indirectly"

5.28   In light of the fact that the excise tax is applied only with respect to "split-run" periodicals, it would seem evident that imported "split-run" periodicals are subject to an internal tax in excess of one that is applied to domestic non "split-run" periodicals. However, Canada argues that the excise tax does not apply "indirectly" to a good within the meaning of Article III:2. According to Canada, the drafting history of this paragraph suggests that the expression "indirectly" was intended to capture taxes that apply to inputs that contribute to the production of a good, and not to end products in their own right. Canada also claims that the panel on *Japan - Customs Duties, Taxes and Labelling Practices on Imported Wines and Alcoholic Beverages* interpreted the term in a manner consistent with Canada's position.[145]

5.29   We note that the excise tax is not "directly" applied to periodicals in that it is levied on the value of advertisements, not on the value of periodicals *per se*. However, it is clear that the tax is applied in respect of each split-run edition of a periodical on a "per issue" basis. Therefore, the tax is applied "indirectly" to periodicals within the ordinary meaning of the terms of Article III:2. Canada's narrow reading of the term "indirectly" is supported only by Canada's own interpretation of the drafting history, which is contested by the United States.[146] Since, according to Article 32 of the Vienna Convention, the preparatory work of a treaty is merely a supplementary means of interpretation to be relied upon in cases where the terms of the treaty, taken in their context and in light of its object and purpose, are ambiguous or obscure, or lead to a manifestly absurd or unreasonable result, we need not take the drafting history into account on this particular point. Furthermore, the panel report cited by Canada in support of its argument referred to taxation on raw materials by way of example. It did not conclude that the scope of the term "indirectly" is limited to taxation on inputs.[147] We thus conclude that imported "split-run" periodicals are subject to an internal tax in excess of that applied to domestic non "split-run" periodicals.

5.30   Having found that Part V.1 of the Excise Tax Act to be in violation of Article III:2, first sentence, we need not examine whether it is inconsistent with Article III:2, second sentence or with Article III:4.

D.   *Postal Rates*

5.31   Now we proceed to examine whether the postal rates scheme applied by Canada Post discriminates against foreign periodicals in contravention of Article III of GATT 1994, as argued by the United States. There are two separate issues involved here: *(a)* whether the fact that Canada Post applies the "commercial

---

[145]   Paragraph 3.49 *supra*.
[146]   Paragraph 3.56 *supra*.
[147]   Paragraph 3.49 *supra*.

Canadian" rates or the "funded" rates to Canadian periodicals, which are lower than the "international" rates applied to imported periodicals, constitute a violation of Article III:4[148] and *(b)* whether the "funded" rate scheme for certain periodicals is allowed as a subsidy within the meaning of Article III:8(b).

(i) *"International" Versus "Commercial Canadian" and "Funded" Rates*

5.32   The United States claims that Canada Post's practice of charging domestic periodicals lower postal rates than imported periodicals is in violation of Article III:4 of GATT 1994. The relevant part of the Article reads as follows:

> "4.   The products of the territory of any [Member] imported into the territory of any other [Member] shall be accorded treatment no less favourable than that accorded to like products of national origin in respect of all laws, regulations and requirements affecting their internal sale, offering for sale, purchase, transportation, distribution or use. The provisions of this paragraph shall not prevent the application of differential internal transportation charges which are based exclusively on the economic operation of the means of transport and not on the nationality of the product",

In examining the relevance of this provision in the present dispute, we also need take into account the first paragraph of Article III, which reads:

> "1.   The [Members] recognize that internal taxes and other internal charges, and laws, regulations and requirements affecting the internal sale, offering for sale, purchase, transportation, distribution or use of products, and internal quantitative regulations requiring the mixture, processing or use of products in specified amounts or proportions, should not be applied to imported or domestic products so as to afford protection to domestic production".

5.33   There is no disagreement between the parties to the dispute that, in respect of this issue, domestic and imported periodicals are like products. We, too, so find. Nor does Canada contest the fact that Canada Post applies higher postal rates to imported periodicals than to domestic periodicals, which clearly affects

---

[148] We are aware that "international" rates applied to foreign periodicals belong to a subcategory of the "commercial" rate scheme in a broader sense. See paragraphs 2.17-2.19 *supra*. However, in so far as different rates are applied between "international" periodicals and "commercial Canadian" periodicals, it is necessary to draw the distinction. We are also aware, as described in paragraph 5.1, that there are additional discounts for Canadian periodicals which are not generally available to imported periodicals. In our view, these additional discounts constitute part of the "commercial Canadian" rate scheme.

the sale, transportation and distribution of imported periodicals. Canada's argument is essentially that since Canada Post is a privatized agency (a Crown corporation) with a legal personality distinct from the Canadian Government, the "commercial Canadian" or "international" rates it charges for the delivery of periodicals are out of the Government's control and do not qualify as "regulations" or "requirements" within the meaning of Article III:4.

5.34   The United States argues that Canada Post is a government entity fully subject to Canadian Government direction because it is a wholly-government-owned, government-created chartered body, managed by a board of directors appointed by the Canadian Government. Canada argues that the different rates charged by Canada Post are a reflection of competitive situations and that the degree of control the Government exercises over Canada Post's commercial operations (including delivery of periodicals) is one dictated by the Government shareholder's interests. In other words, Canada argues here that Canada Post's pricing policy is not a governmental measure subject to Article III:4. The essential question then is whether Canada Post is implementing Canadian Government policy in such a manner that its postal rates on periodicals may be viewed as governmental regulations or requirements for the purposes of Article III:4.

5.35   First, it is clear that Canada Post generally operates under governmental instructions. Canada Post has a mandate to operate on a "commercial" basis in this particular sector of periodical delivery: a mandate that was set by the Canadian Government.[149] Second, Canada admits that if the Canadian Government considers Canada Post's pricing policy to be inappropriate, it can instruct Canada Post to change the rates under its directive power based on Section 22 of the Canada Post Corporation Act.[150] Thus, the Canadian Government can effectively regulate the rates charged on the delivery of periodicals.

5.36   This analysis is unaffected by the fact that Canada Post has a legal personality distinct from the Canadian Government. The panel on *Japan - Trade in Semi-Conductors* faced a similar question with respect to the interpretation of the status of "administrative guidance" given to private-sector entities in interpreting the term "measures" in Article XI:1. The panel stated as follows:

> "In order to determine [whether the measures taken in this case would be such as to constitute a contravention of Article XI], the Panel considered that it needed to be satisfied on two essential criteria. First, there were reasonable grounds to believe that sufficient incentives or disincentives existed for non-mandatory measures to take effect. Second,

---

[149]   From the entirety of Canada's submissions, we take it that the Canadian Government considers Canada Post's pricing policy on periodicals to be driven by "commercial" considerations, although we fail to understand why any document delivery operation aiming at profit maximization would want to make artificial distinctions based on the origin of documents.

[150]   Paragraph 3.156 *supra*.

the operation of the measures ... was essentially dependent
on Government action or intervention. The Panel considered each of these two criteria in turn. The Panel considered
that if these two criteria were met, the measures would be
operating in a manner equivalent to mandatory requirements
such that the difference between the measures and mandatory requirements was only one of form and not of substance, and that there could be therefore no doubt that they
fell within the range of measures covered by Article XI:1".[151]

Applying this two-pronged test, *mutatis mutandis*, to the present case, we conclude that the pricing policy of Canada Post is a governmental measure. First, in
view of the control exercised by the Canadian Government on "non-commercial"
activities of Canada Post, we can reasonably assume that sufficient incentives
exist for Canada Post to maintain the existing pricing policy on periodicals. Second, as analyzed in the previous paragraph, Canada Post's operation is generally
dependent on Government action. This leads us to the conclusion that Canada
Post's pricing policy on periodicals can be regarded as governmental regulations
or requirements within the meaning of Article III:4 of GATT 1994.

5.37   Given that imported and domestic periodicals are like products and that
Canada Post charges lower rates on domestic periodicals than imported ones, this
conclusion might seem sufficient to determine that a less favourable treatment is
accorded to imported products in violation of Article III:4. However, before
reaching that determination, as the Appellate Body has stated, we need to turn to
Article III:1 as a general principle that informs the rest of Article III.[152] Article
III:1 constitutes part of the context of Article III:4, which is to be taken into account in our interpretation of the latter, under Article 31(1) of the Vienna Convention.

5.38   Article III:1 articulates a general principle that internal measures should
not be applied so as to afford protection to domestic production.[153] The protective application of a measure can most often be discerned from the design, the
architecture, and the revealing structure of the measure.[154] We find that the design, architecture and structure of Canada Post's different pricing policy on domestic and imported periodicals all point to the effect that the measure is applied

---

[151] Panel Report on *Japan - Trade in Semi-Conductors*, adopted on 4 May 1988, BISD 35S/116,
para. 109.
[152] Appellate Body Report on *Japan - Taxes on Alcoholic Beverages, op. cit.,* 111. The Report
states: "The purpose of Article III:1 is to establish this general principle as a guide to understanding
and interpreting the specific obligations contained in Article III:2 and in the other paragraphs of
Article III, while respecting, and not diminishing in any way, the meaning of words actually used in
the texts of those other paragraphs".
[153] *Ibid.,* 111.
[154] *Ibid.,* 120.

so as to afford protection to the domestic production of periodicals. In the case of "funded" rates, the scheme is clearly designed to promote domestic production of periodicals with Canadian content under the supervision of Canadian Heritage. In the case of "commercial Canadian" rates, the very fact that they are lower than "international" rates which are applied to imported products strongly suggests that the scheme is operated so as to afford protection to domestic production.

5.39   In light of the above, we find that Canada Post's application of the "commercial Canadian" and "funded" rates to Canadian periodicals, which are lower than the "international" rates applied to imported periodicals (including the availability of additional discounts only to Canadian periodicals), is inconsistent with Article III:4 of GATT 1994.

> ### (ii)   Applicability of Article III:8(b) to the "Funded" Rate Scheme

5.40   Having found that the "funded" rate scheme violates Article III:4 of GATT 1994, we next examine whether this scheme is justified under Article III:8(b) of GATT 1994, as argued by Canada. The relevant part of Article III:8 reads as follows:

> "(b)   The provisions of this Article shall not prevent the payment of subsidies exclusively to domestic producers, including payments to domestic producers derived from the proceeds of internal taxes or charges applied consistently with the provisions of this Article and subsidies effected through governmental purchases of domestic products".

5.41   The United States claims that this provision is not applicable in the present case because the payment of subsidies by Canadian Heritage is not made directly to Canadian publishers, but rather to Canada Post. The United States argues that past panels have interpreted the term "exclusively" narrowly, to mean only direct payments to domestic producers.[155] To support its argument, the United States quotes the following paragraph from the panel report on *European Economic Community - Payments and Subsidies Paid to Processors and Producers of Oilseeds and Related Animal-Feed Proteins* (the "*Oilseeds*" case):

> "The Panel noted that Article III:8(b) applies only to payments made *exclusively* to domestic producers and considered that it can reasonably be assumed that a payment not made directly to producers is not made "exclusively" to them. It noted moreover that, if the economic benefits generated by the payments granted by the Community can at least partly be retained by the processors of Community oilseeds, the payments generate a benefit conditional upon the

---

[155]   Paragraphs 3.191-3.197 *supra*.

purchase of oilseeds of domestic origin inconsistently with Article III:4. Under these circumstances Article III:8(b) would not be applicable because in that case the payments would not be made exclusively to domestic producers but to processors as well".[156]

5.42   We do not disagree with this panel report. However, the United States has failed to show that the factual situation in the present case is similar to that in the *Oilseeds* case. Particularly, the United States has not submitted any evidence to indicate that the economic benefits are partly retained by Canada Post. Furthermore, this argument by the United States is inconsistent with its position regarding Article III:4, where it maintains that Canada Post is a government agency. If Canada Post is a government agency, the payment of funds from Canadian Heritage to Canada Post is merely an internal transfer of resources, and the payment of the subsidy is made directly to Canadian publishers.

5.43   Canada, on the other hand, explains that the payment of the funds from Canadian Heritage to Canada Post is made based on negotiations between the two agencies, taking into account the fact that Canada Post gets an exclusive contract for the delivery of periodicals at subsidized rates.[157] Following the logic of the *Oilseeds* panel cited above, one could argue that there is a reasonable assumption that the "funded" rate scheme is not an exclusive payment of subsidies because the payment is not made directly to the beneficiary. However, in our view, Canada has presented an effective rebuttal to this assumption.

5.44   Thus, we do not find that Canada Post retains any economic benefits from the "funded" rate scheme it applies to certain Canadian periodicals. The payment of the subsidy is made "exclusively" to Canadian publishers that qualify for the scheme. Since Article III:8(b) explicitly recognizes that subsidies exclusively paid to domestic producers are not subject to the national treatment rules of Article III, including those under Article III:4, we find that Canada's "funded" rate scheme on periodicals can be justified under this provision.

E.   Concluding Remarks

5.45   Before concluding, in order to avoid any misunderstandings as to the scope and implications of the findings above, we would like to stress that the ability of any Member to take measures to protect its cultural identity was not at issue in the present case. The only task entrusted to this Panel was to examine whether the treatment accorded to imported periodicals under specific measures identified in the complainant's claim is compatible with the rules of GATT 1994.

---

[156] Panel Report on *European Economic Community - Payments and Subsidies Paid to Processors and Producers of Oilseeds and Related Animal-Feed Proteins*, adopted on 25 January 1990, BISD 37S/86, para. 137 (emphasis in original).

[157] Paragraph 3.173 *supra*.

VI. CONCLUSIONS

6.1   On the basis of the findings set out in paragraphs 5.1 to 5.44 above, the Panel concludes that *(a)* Tariff Code 9958 is inconsistent with Article XI:1 of GATT 1994 and cannot be justified under Article XX(d) of GATT 1994; *(b)* Part V.1 of the Excise Tax Act is inconsistent with Article III:2, first sentence, of GATT 1994; *(c)* the application by Canada Post of lower "commercial Canadian" postal rates to domestically-produced periodicals than to imported periodicals, including additional discount options available only to domestic periodicals, is inconsistent with Article III:4 of GATT 1994; but *(d)* the maintenance of the "funded" rate scheme is justified under Article III:8(b) of GATT 1994.

6.2   The Panel recommends that the Dispute Settlement Body request Canada to bring the measures that are found to be inconsistent with GATT 1994 into conformity with its obligations thereunder.